Classical
Music
in America

■

Classical Music in America

A HISTORY OF ITS RISE AND FALL

∎

Joseph Horowitz

W · W · Norton & Company   New York   London

SINCE THIS PAGE CANNOT LEGIBLY ACCOMMODATE ALL THE COPYRIGHT NOTICES,
PAGES 569–570 CONSTITUTE AN EXTENSION OF THE COPYRIGHT PAGE.

Copyright © 2005 by Joseph Horowitz

For information about permission to reproduce selections from
this book, write to Permissions, W. W. Norton & Company, Inc.,
500 Fifth Avenue, New York, NY 10110

Manufacturing by Maple-Vail Book Manufacturing Group
Book design by Margaret Wagner
Production manager: Julia Druskin

Library of Congress Cataloging-in-Publication Data

Horowitz, Joseph, 1948–
Classical music in America : a history of its rise and fall /
Joseph Horowitz.—1st ed.
p. cm.
Includes bibliographical references (p.   ) and index.

ISBN 0-393-05717-8 (hardcover)

1. Music—United States—History and criticism. I. Title.
ML200.H797 2005
781.6'8'0973--dc22   2004027754

W. W. Norton & Company, Inc.
500 Fifth Avenue, New York, N.Y. 10110
www.wwnorton.com

W. W. Norton & Company Ltd.
Castle House, 75/76 Wells Street, London W1T 3QT

1 2 3 4 5 6 7 8 9 0

In loving memory of my parents

ACKNOWLEDGMENTS

It began to sink in relatively late, around the time I was in college, that there was something incongruous about being at one and the same time an American and a passionate devotee—as a listener, a writer, and an amateur pianist—of classical music. Most of what I have written over the past two decades, most notably my books *Understanding Toscanini* (1987) and *Wagner Nights* (1994), has addressed this incongruity. I long ago suspected that I might some day attempt to put it all together in a history of American classical music. In that sense, parts of this book have appeared, in one form or another, in the *New York Times*, the *Journal of the Gilded Age and Progressive Era*, *Symphony* magazine, the *Times Literary Supplement*, and a 1999 history of the Philadelphia Orchestra edited by the late John Ardoin. Of the many music festivals I have conceived, "American Transcendentalists," at the Brooklyn Academy of Music, generated an early version of "The Transcendental Ives" in my essay collection *The Post-Classical Predicament* (1995). As few people have ever read this book, I have without compunction borrowed from my Ives essay, and also from "The Teachings of Leonard Bernstein" (adapted from an article in the *New York Review of Books*) and "The World's Greatest Piano Career" (adapted from an article on Vladimir Horowitz in the *Musical Quarterly*) in the same obscure volume.

Fellowships from the Guggenheim Foundation, the National Arts Journalism Program at Columbia University, and the National Endowment of the Humanities supported this project. I cannot possibly acknowledge all the people who lent support of other kinds. Both Richard Crawford and Wayne Shirley read the entire manuscript; their wise and generous feedback was invaluable. Judith Tick read everything I had to say against nineteenth-century Boston and calmed me down.

Among those who were witness to or participants in important twentieth-century musical developments, and who shared their experiences with me, were John Adams, Milton Babbitt, Peter G. Davis, Gary and Naomi Graffman, Speight Jenkins, Lukas Foss, Alex Ross, Gunther Schuller, Michael Steinberg, Mark Swed, and Ronald Wilford. Raoul Camus, Megan Marshall, Nancy

Newman, John Spitzer, and William Weber contributed specialized knowledge in areas where I needed help.

Of the many archivists who assisted me, I must above all thank Bridget Carr of the Boston Symphony, Barbara Haws and Rich Wandel of the New York Philharmonic, Gino Francesconi of Carnegie Hall, Brenda Nelson-Strauss of the Chicago Symphony, and John Pennino of the Metropolitan Opera.

I have of course benefited enormously from my many opportunities to produce and present concerts. I must especially thank, in this regard, Harvey Lichteinstein at BAM, Larry Tamburri in his years as executive director of the New Jersey Symphony, John Forsyte and Carl St. Clair of the Pacific Symphony, Bob Freeman both at the New England Conservatory and the University of Texas at Austin, and Pedro Carboné and Angel Gil-Ordóñez, with whom I have collaborated on many an "IberArtists" concert of important Spanish music.

The production and promotion of this book were ably assisted by Maribeth Payne and Courtney Fitch at Norton, by my agent Elizabeth Kaplan, and by Connie Shuman and Katherine Johnson. I am indebted to Klaus Heymann of Naxos for creating the two remarkable annotated web sites that make available recordings of many of the performances and compositions I describe, and even more indebted to my wife, Agnes, and children Bernie and Maggie for tolerating yet another book.

A note on opera titles: I have opted for those most familiar in the United States, whether in English, Italian, German, or French.

CONTENTS

BOOK TWO   "Great Performances": Decline and Fall

APOLOGIA

It is therefore not true to assert that men living in democratic times are naturally indiffcrent to science, literature, and the arts; only it must be acknowledged that they cultivate them after their own fashion and bring to the task their own peculiar qualifications and deficiencies.

TOCQUEVILLE, *Democracy in America* (1835)

■

Compared to classical music in its European homeland, classical music in the United States is a mutant transplant. Deep roots were not importable, nor in the main were they newly cultivated. The resulting foliage, oftentimes resplendent, was as often "peculiar."

By "roots" I mean what grounded classical music in other lands: a canon of homegrown symphonies and/or operas. Americans, too, once assumed that their musical high culture would evolve from a foundation of native works by native composers. An "American Beethoven," an "American Wagner" were confidently anticipated. Even in places out of the way, nineteenth-century Americans regrew the musical high culture of Europe with an astonishing alacrity. Around the turn of the twentieth century—a peak moment—a balance was struck between the American composer, striving impressively toward prominence, and orchestras and opera companies that already rivaled the best abroad. But no American Beethoven or Wagner appeared. Instead, American classical music after World War I was mainly about the act of performance: not composers, but world-famous symphonic and operatic institutions, and celebrated conductors and instrumentalists, were its validating signatures. These, to be sure, were amazing in their way. But, absent a vital national repertoire, they were irredeemably Eurocentric.

A long and interesting period of decline ran its ineluctable course. As if by default, classical music ceded leadership in American musical life to genres more vernacular. Popular music proved the more significant, more distinctive American contribution. By century's end, the transplant too frequently resembled a potted hothouse product. And yet it was potentially ripe for cross-breeding with the popular strains that had displaced it.

This story, as I tell it, unfolds over a period of two centuries. Its governing patterns reveal themselves only gradually. In fact, its course would have confounded any and all nineteenth-century predictions. Americans were slow to realize, if at all, that the Old World template would not hold.

I begin my narrative not with colonial composers, such as Francis Hopkinson, who might as well have been European, but midway through the 1800s, with the Boston critic John Sullivan Dwight. Dwight more than any other individual first defines what Americans meant by "classical music." In so doing, he furnishes a metaphor for an abiding New World tendency: to overesteem venerable Old World pedigrees. Other nineteenth-century musical pioneers, notably the conductor Theodore Thomas, were as adventurous as Dwight was curatorial. In my account, I frequently circle back to these polar influences. To make sense of the trajectory of American classical music requires an act of memory.

■ ■ ■

I undertook this book for three reasons.

The first is that there existed no history of classical music in the United States. Rather, histories of American music—by such estimable authors as Gilbert Chase, H. Wiley Hitchcock, Charles Hamm, and Richard Crawford—encompass a gamut of musics vernacular, traditional, popular, and classical. In this scheme, classical music correctly figures as a minority phenomenon. Typically, it is chronicled as a history of composers. Actually, composers are a minority within a minority: classical music in the United States is more about the New York Philharmonic than Charles Ives, more about the Metropolitan Opera than Aaron Copland.★ This distortion is also a fascination; it is one of the features that sets American classical music apart.

Moreover, this fundamental aspect of American classical music—the orchestras and opera companies, their artists and operators—has been remarkably little studied: the second reason for my book. American classical music as a culture of performance is a dominant feature of American high culture, yet is ignored by cultural historians of the United States who know, study, and consider American literature, theater, painting, and cinema.† Even among

★ Richard Crawford's *America's Musical Life: A History* (New York, W. W. Norton, 2001) represents a significant step in the direction of acknowledging the performer's importance.
† A conspicuous exception is Lawrence Levine's *Highbrow/Lowbrow: The Emergence of Cultural Hierarchy in America* (Cambridge, Mass., Harvard University Press, 1988), which deals extensively with Theodore Thomas and Henry Higginson—as discussed several times in this book.

historians of American music, this neglect persists: they focus disproportionately on classical composers and on performers of *popular* music. An institution as central to the American cultural experience as the symphony orchestra
lacks proper acknowledgment and scholarly attention; the Boston Symphony
Orchestra—in many respects, America's most historic—still awaits serious
book-length treatment.

My third reason: the history I tell has largely run its course. Beginning with
Dwight, American classical music has been identified as a privileged high culture, spurning the popular arts. By the end of the twentieth century, with
postmodernism and the end of high/low stratification, this identity necessarily grew confused, as did classical music generally.

Tocqueville observed of the United States, "The humblest artisan casts at
times an eager and a furtive glance into the higher regions of the intellect.
People do not read with the same notions or in the same manner as they do
in aristocratic communities, but the circle of readers is increasingly expanded,
until it includes all the people."[1] The story of American classical music is of a
borrowing from lands older and more aristocratic, of audiences less elitist and
less tutored by tradition, of patronage and financing more private and more
commercial. The makers of American classical music include entrepreneurs of
every stripe, of whom the most prominent in my account are Henry Higginson, Oscar Hammerstein, David Sarnoff, and Arthur Judson—creators, respectively, of the Boston Symphony, the Manhattan Opera, the National
Broadcasting Company, and Columbia Artists Management. Not inherent to
democracies, but inherent to the United States, is a further distinctive condition of American classical music: a youthful and polyglot society, complicating
the search for musical roots. Whether classical music's "whiteness" was tainted
or enriched by "black" and "red" Americans was an ongoing debate.

Theodore Thomas said, "A symphony orchestra shows the culture of a
community, not opera." In articulating a New World narrative in contrast to
the composer-based European model, I focus inescapably on the concert
orchestra. Not the state or municipal opera house, but the privately supported
concert ensemble, superintended by a board of wealthy or otherwise influential individuals, has been the primary institutional embodiment of classical
music in the United States. The consequences of this emphasis are an ongoing
motif of my account.

My book is two books. The first—"Queen of the Arts": Birth and
Growth—stops with World War I; I use Boston and New York as contrasting
templates for American classical music in its most dynamic phase. This part of
my story reinterprets the Gilded Age; the United States, I argue, experienced
a fin de siècle most clearly evidenced by what cultural historians of the late

nineteenth century know least: its musical life. Book Two—"Great Performances": Decline and Fall—considers feted "great performers" and sidelined
modernist composers, the new middle classes and midcult, and the confusions
of today. The struggle for American independence—for a productive relationship between culture imported and culture homegrown—is a recurrent theme.

This is not a textbook and makes no attempt to be comprehensive. Rather,
I have found it more meaningful to focus on representative people, institutions, and events. I am partial to individuals who were American-born, or
who were otherwise attuned to the American experience, or to whom Americans were exceptionally attuned, or (most especially) who charted paths
remote from Old World models. That I devote more space to Dvořák than
Stravinsky, to Toscanini than Furtwängler, to Gould than Arrau reflects these
priorities and does not imply that Dvořák was the greater composer, Toscanini
the greater conductor, or Gould the greater pianist.

Though my narrative is long, and though I occasionally linger (as for
George Whitefield Chadwick) to redress neglect, there is hardly a topic I
could not have treated at greater length (Arrau, about whom I have written
an entire book, gets half a paragraph). I concentrate on the historic institutions of performance early established in New York and Boston, Chicago and
Philadelphia. I mainly attend to public manifestations of classical music, rather
than music in the home, or in schools, or in publishing houses and other offstage enterprises. These emphases are not indefensible: classical music in
America is not evenly distributed, north and south, east and west. America has
had no Paris or Moscow Conservatory. The Germanic ideal of *Hausmusik* has
been less cultivated in the United States. Still, such lacunae matter: there is
much I could not include without exceeding a manageable length. And there
is much unfinished business for others to research and illuminate.

My personal experience of classical music in the United States begins with
vivid (and unhappy) memories of Mozart and Wagner at the old Met. I have
availed myself of recordings of music in live performance insofar as possible.
Where I must rely on written accounts of what others saw and heard, I
attempt to be selective. The critics I most cite are Henry Krehbiel and William
J. Henderson; America has produced no daily writers on music more impressive than these two.

I have tried sympathetically to consider what is important and influential
even when, as in the case of the power broker Arthur Judson, I find the influence troubling. There are, I hope, no mustachioed villains in my account,
but there are heroes: Higginson, Theodore Thomas, Anton Seidl, Antonín
Dvořák, and Charles Ives in Book One; Leopold Stokowski, Serge Koussevitzky, and George Gershwin in Book Two. Dwight, Judson, Arturo Toscanini,

Aaron Copland, and Leonard Bernstein also figure with special prominence. This list of five performers, three composers, one performer/composer, one critic, one businessman, and one orchestra inventor/owner seems to me a plausible distribution of American classical musical ingredients.

Though the basic framework of my story is chronological, I frequently circle back, as to leitmotifs, to reconsider or replenish pivotal personalities, events, and ideas. The example of Henry Higginson differently instructs my understanding of Boston, of the Gilded Age, and of the "post-classsical" future.

■ ■ ■

As there is no history without interpretation, as I make no pretext of "objectivity," as my narrative is laden with analysis and criticism, the reader may wish to know something about the writer.

I pursue a double professional life. Beginning with a stint as a music critic for the *New York Times*, I have long written about classical music. I quit the *Times* (in 1980) partly because I discovered that I did not believe in the vast majority of events I was required to attend. This estrangement—a disappointment in what classical music had become—provoked the historical exercise of *Understanding Toscanini: How He Became an American Culture-God and Helped Create a New Audience for Old Music* (1987), in which I proposed the Toscanini cult as a metaphor for classical music's twentieth-century decline. A subsequent book, *Wagner Nights: An American History* (1994), mapped the apex of American classical music in the 1890s.

My second career, as a producer and presenter of concerts, began in the 1980s when I served as artistic advisor to an ambitious annual Schubert festival at New York's Ninety-second Street Y. I cut my teeth in arts administration in the 1990s as executive director of the Brooklyn Philharmonic Orchestra at the intrepid Brooklyn Academy of Music. Harvey Lichtenstein, BAM's executive director, had read *Understanding Toscanini*, or at least that part of it nominating BAM and its inquisitive audience as a likely model for rescuing classical music from itself. As the Brooklyn Philharmonic had been deserted by more than two-thirds of its subscribers, there was nothing left to lose—the orchestra became an experimental laboratory for a different kind of concert experience, stressing contemporary repertoire and regularly embracing related popular and vernacular genres.* The orchestra ultimately fell victim to a

---

* I briefly write about my Brooklyn tenure on pp. 530–531; a more detailed account can be found in my *The Post-Classical Predicament: Essays on Music and Society* (Boston, Northeastern University Press, 1995), pp. 186–204.

phantom infrastructure and a soured relationship to BAM, but not until my faith in the possibility of new templates was more confirmed than denied. As working at BAM meant working for Lichtenstein, my grueling job also brought me into daily contact with a visionary cultural entrepreneur: a species once common in American classical music, but no longer. My memories of those years include attending Rimsky-Korsakov's *The Legend of the Invisible City of Kitezh* conducted by Valery Gergiev (not yet a household name) at St. Petersburg's Mariinsky Theater. Harvey turned to me after the first scene and said, "I've got to bring this to BAM." And he did—the entire cast, chorus, orchestra, and production, for four performances panned by the *Times.*

My double life continues. I serve as an artistic consultant to various American orchestras, most regularly the New Jersey Symphony and Pacific Symphony, both of which annually mount interdisciplinary thematic festivals within their subscription season. And I have cofounded a chamber orchestra, Post-Classical Ensemble, in Washington, D.C. The present book, my seventh, in part synthesizes twenty years of writing and research. As I stand by my judgments in *Understanding Toscanini* and *Wagner Nights,* I perforce must repeat them—which I have attempted to do with a minimum of literal repetition. Elsewhere in these pages are subjects that have not, to my knowledge, been written about before. These range from the minutia of certain extraordinary letters of Henry Higginson, to the four-year American career of Arthur Nikisch (arguably the most eminent symphonic conductor of his generation, and yet American conductors of my acquaintance do not realize he once led the Boston Symphony), to broad points of resonance between late-nineteenth-century American composers and contemporaneous American writers and painters. The latter sections of my book which deal with present-day arts policy obviously draw substantially on personal experience.

To my mind, history, among its many other uses, furnishes a necessary context for understanding. The past may not predict the future, but it exerts a shaping influence. Classical music in the United States has evolved peculiarly and yet coherently, informatively. But this has escaped the notice of many who address today's "classical music crisis." Too often, the work of foundations and consultants, marketing directors and public relations experts does not attempt to apply even a short-term historical base. The same mentality, an American affliction, condoned the 1991 destruction of Dvořák's Manhattan home (the *New York Times,* in a supportive editorial, argued "Dvořák Doesn't Live Here Anymore").[2] When Anton Seidl died suddenly in 1898, grieving Americans wrote of the statues to be erected in his memory, but none were. Arthur Judson, who more than anyone ruled American classical music in the early twentieth century, shunned the public eye. Even for a nation as young as the United States, this is recent history, all of it unremembered.

As I write these lines, many Americans find themselves asking questions about the future of American democracy. They worry about the impact of money and of political machination, and about the power of both to sway an electorate already addicted to fast-food news and talk radio. Considered as an experiment in the democratization of high culture, classical music in America restates these questions. It has done without government guidance and subsidy elsewhere taken for granted. The 1930s defeat of an "American BBC," the sales mentality of "music appreciation," a spiraling culture of personality—among innumerable other topics in my account—resonate with pressing issues in the political arena. And yet American classical music has also produced visionary populists not to be found abroad.

To excavate the saga of American classical music is, finally, an exercise in self-comprehension. It is a tale of audacious enterprise and pallid imitation, of cocky independence and provincial insecurity. It enables us to draw detailed comparisons with our Old World parents—and so to see ourselves.

Please see www.wwnorton.com/catalog/fall04/005717.htm for access to annotated Web sites with relevant recordings of American compositions here discussed (beginning with works by Anthony Philip Heinrich, William Henry Fry, and Louis Moreau Gottschalk).

BOOK ONE

"Queen of the Arts": Birth and Growth

■

This our nineteenth century is commonly esteemed a prosaic, a material, unimaginative age. . . . These strictures . . . have certainly much truth to back them. But . . . there is one great opposing fact of such importance that by itself alone it calls for at least a partial reversal of the verdict. . . . This fact is the place that music . . . has held in nineteenth-century life.

MARIANA VAN RENSSELAER
Harper's Magazine, March 1883

Introduction: A Tale of Two Cities (1893)

■

The great event of the 1893–94 New York concert season was the premiere of Antonín Dvořák's symphony "From the New World" at the imposing Music Hall built by Andrew Carnegie on West Fifty-seventh Street two years before.

After the second movement, the house erupted in applause. The conductor, Anton Seidl, turned around. "Every neck was craned so that it might be discovered to whom he was motioning so energetically," reported the *Herald*.

> Whoever it was, he seemed modestly to wish to remain at the back of the box on the second tier.
>
> At last a broad shouldered individual of medium height, and as straight as one of the pines in the forests of which his music whispered so eloquently, is descried by the eager watchers. A murmur sweeps through the hall. "Dvořák! Dvořák!" is the word that passes from mouth to mouth. . . .
>
> With hands trembling with emotion Dr. Dvořák waves an acknowledgement of his indebtedness to Anton Seidl, to the orchestra, to the audience, and then disappears into the background while the remainder of the work goes on. . . . At its close the composer was loudly called for. Again and again he bowed his acknowledgements, and again and again the applause burst forth.
>
> Even after he had left his box and was walking about in the corridor the applause continued. And finally he returned to the gallery railing, and then what a reception he received! The musicians, led by Mr. Seidl, applauded until the place rang again.[1]

After that (as we know from other reports) Dvořák's box was mobbed by music critics eager to congratulate him. The *Herald* critic, presumably Albert Steinberg, called the new symphony "a great one" and distinctively American in flavor. Henry Krehbiel, in the *Tribune*, declared it "a lovely triumph" and wrote of Dvořák's indebtedness to African-American song. But the most memorable of the many reviews appearing the next day, December 16, 1893, was William J. Henderson's in the *New York Times*. Among the most astonishing feats in the history of American music journalism, this three-thousand-word essay (whose length and subject matter would confound any present-day newspaper reader) remains one of the most informative, vivid, and sympathetic descriptions of Dvořák's symphony ever written. It eloquently characterizes each of the four movements and analyzes points of resonance with Longfellow's *The Song of Hiawatha* and the songs of Stephen Foster, with the character of American landscapes and lives, and, most especially, with the slave music of the plantation. To clinch his assessment, Henderson inquired, "Is the symphony American?" His answer:

> In spite of all assertions to the contrary, the plantation songs of the American negro possess a striking individuality. No matter whence their germs came, they have in their growth been subjected to local influences which have made of them a new species. That species is the direct result of causes climatic and political, but never anything else than American. Our South is ours. Its twin does not exist. Our system of slavery, with all its domestic and racial conditions, was ours, and its twin never existed. Out of the heart of this slavery, environed by this sweet and languorous South, from the canebrake and the cotton field, arose the spontaneous musical utterance of a people. That folk-music struck an answering note in the American heart. . . . If those songs are not national, then there is no such thing as national music.

Dvořák had come to New York in 1892 to direct the National Conservatory of Music on East Seventeenth Street. His arrival represented a triumph of persistence by the conservatory's founder, Jeannette Thurber. She was intent on fostering an "American national school" to ground an American repertoire of symphonies and operas. Dvořák was not only a pedigreed great European composer. A butcher's son, he was an instinctive democrat. And he was a tenacious cultural nationalist who identified with peasant song and dance. In the United States, his attention was quickly drawn to "Go Down, Moses," "Swing Low," and other melodies of the black slave. Like many Europeans, he was fascinated, as well, with America's indigenous peoples: a vanishing race rooted in the soil. He accepted the mandate urged by Thurber and others: that he guide American composers toward an idiom as personal to the United States as his *Slavonic* Dances were to his own Bohemian homeland.

The premiere of the *New World* Symphony climaxed a drumbeat of local anticipation. The preceding May, Dvořák had been quoted in the *Herald* on the "real value of negro melodies." He subsequently hinted at the inspirational influence of the *Song of Hiawatha*. Krehbiel, in the *Tribune*, had offered a twenty-five-hundred-word analysis of the *New World* Symphony, including thirteen musical examples.[2]

In Boston, a different drumbeat greeted Dvořák. His missionary presence was resented or ignored. Addressing his espousal of plantation song, John Knowles Paine, the dean of Boston's composers' community, responded with this dismissal of Dvořák, Smetana, and other Romantic nationalists:

> The time is past when composers are to be classed according to geographical limits. It is not a question of nationality, but individuality, and individuality of style is not the result of imitation—whether of folk songs, negro melodies, the tunes of the heathen Chinese or Digger Indians, but of personal character and inborn originality. . . . It is incomprehensible to me how any thoroughly cultivated musician or musical critic can have such limited and erroneous views of the true functions of American composers.

George Whitefield Chadwick, Boston's most performed composer, was also invited to comment on Dvořák's program. His response, in full, read, "I am not sufficiently familiar with the real negro melodies to be able to offer any opinion of the subject. Such negro melodies as I have heard, however, I should be sorry to see become the basis of an American school of musical composition." A third prominent Boston composer, Amy Beach, had this to say: "Without the slightest desire to question the beauty of the negro melodies of which [Dvořák] speaks so highly, or to disparage them on account of their source, I cannot help feeling justified in the belief that they are not fully typical of our country. The African population of the United States is far too small for its songs to be considered 'American.'"[3]

This closing of the ranks was duplicated by Boston's critics. The influential Philip Hale declared himself "not excited" by the local premiere of Dvořák's symphony by the Boston Symphony Orchestra under Emil Paur on December 29, 1893. But Hale was mightily exasperated by the symphony's New York acclaim. In the *Boston Journal*, he opined (1) that it did not sound any more American than it did Scotch or Scandinavian, or "anything you please"; and (2) that it would "undoubtedly be popular, and deservedly popular." Hale's grudging enthusiasm for the work compelled him to deny the pertinence of its ostensible American sources, of which he disapproved. Other Boston critics followed suit. If they conceded that, as Hale put it, "negro airs" might "tint slightly two or three passages of the symphony without injury to its Czech character," they condemned these and other "primitive" inflections. The Darwinian underpinnings of their opprobrium became explicit in a *Boston Transcript* review by William Apthorp, reading in part:

> The general melodic and rhythmic character of the German, Italian and French songs stamps them as examples of a higher stage in musical evolution. . . .
>
> [T]he great bane of the present Slavic and Scandinavian schools is and has been the attempt to make civilized music by civilized methods out of essentially barbaric material. The result has in general been a mere apotheosis of ugliness, distorted forms, and barbarous expression. . . .
>
> [O]ur American Negro music has every element of barbarism to be found in the Slavic or Scandinavian folk-songs; it is essentially barbarous music. What is more, it sounds terribly like any other barbarous music.[4]

Fully seventeen years later, in a Boston Symphony program note, Hale's resentments remained fresh. Citing the New York view that Dvořák had successfully struck an American chord based in part on Negro melodies, he expostulated:

> It is said by some in answer to these statements that, while the negro is undoubtedly fond of music, he is not inherently musical, that this has been observed by all careful observers of the negro in Africa . . . ; that the American negro, peculiarly mimetic, founded his "folk-songs" on sentimental ballads sung by the white women of the plantation, or on camp-meeting tunes; that he brought no primitive melodies with him from Africa, and that the "originality" of his "folk-songs" was misunderstanding or perversion of the tunes he imitated; that, even if the negro brought tunes from Africa, they could hardly, even after long usage, be called "American folk-songs," any more than the tunes of the aboriginal indians or Creole ditties can be called justly "American folk-songs"; that it would be absurd to characterize a school of music based on such a foundation as an "American school."

Hale proceeded to maintain that Bohemians who had been consulted, including Dvořák's own sons, testified that Dvořák had quoted no "negro airs" (although this was never claimed by Henderson and other New York advocates of the composer), and that Dvořák had never "shown himself [to be] a more genuine Czech" than in his *New World* Symphony. "Yet some will undoubtedly continue to insist that the symphony 'From the New World' is based, for the most part, on negro themes, and that the future of American music rests on the use of Congo, North American Indian, Creole, Greaser and Cowboy ditties, whinings, yawps, and whoopings."⁵

Three topics stand out in this tale of Dvořák and two cities. The first is the sheer vitality of American classical music a century ago. That the first performance of a new symphony by a living composer should generate such a consuming sense of occasion is unthinkable today, as is an audience so uninhibited in its enthusiasm as to interrupt the performance halfway through, or a review of two thousand words in which the act of performance—the trivializing subject matter of concert reviews after World War I—barely registers. Of the *twenty-six* paragraphs of Albert Steinberg's notice, twelve analyzed Dvořák's idiom (the flatted seventh tone of his scale, etc.), his folk sources, rhythms and harmonies, instrumentation and structure. To the performance of the new work, Steinberg allotted a single sentence, calling it "most poetical." He dispatched the remainder of the program with a sentence reading, "The orchestra played the 'Midsummer Night's Dream' music, and Henri Marteau played Brahm's [*sic*] violin concerto with an original cadenza by himself." In W. J. Henderson's *New York Times* review, the Mendelssohn and Brahms works were simply ignored; not even the conductor was mentioned.

The second general topic flavoring this Dvořák vignette, and American classical music generally at the close of the nineteenth century, is the intense search for an American cultural identity. "What is America?" and "Who are Americans?" are questions that once amplified the significance of the concert culture of the United States, and partially account for its bygone urgency.

The third general topic is, of course, the dramatic disparity of the two cities as illuminated by Dvořák's agenda. Criticism of New York, whose immigrant melee was unfavorably contrasted with New England enclaves of mature intellectual repose, was a blatant subtext of the Boston critiques. Assessing Dvořák's Boston debut, the 1892 performance of his Requiem, the *Boston News* opined, "After his visit to Boston Dr. Dvořák will probably find it even harder still to take up his residence permanently in New York." When Hale declared Dvořák "homesick" in America and "stupefied by the din and bustle of a new life," it was New York's din and bustle that he impugned. In fact, Dvořák became the subject matter of a journalistic feud between Hale and Henry Krehbiel. "Mr. Krehbiel is now inclined to believe that at last we really have a great national piece of music," Hale taunted in the *Boston Journal* in an article ridiculing Krehbiel's Dvořák campaign. Krehbiel retorted in the *New York Tribune* that the *New World* Symphony was "not so well played" in Boston as in New York. The Boston Symphony's Emil Paur "had evidently taken ample pains in studying it with his band, but he misconceived the tempo of every movement so completely that the work was robbed of half its charm. It reminded one of the dinner at which everything was cold except the ice-cream."[6]

As it happens, Krehbiel was New York's leading authority on a topic of central significance to late-nineteenth-century culture-bearers: music and race. His attitudes were essentially those of Dvořák, with whom he shared his knowledge of "negro" and "Indian" tunes. Both believed that music reflects national characteristics and an almost intangible message of locale. Both considered African-Americans innately musical. Neither proclaimed a hierarchy of races. New England abolitionism notwithstanding, this was not the Boston view.

The two cities were also physically and demographically distinct. Boston was the American seat of learning, social reform, and public-spirited philanthropy. Its Harvard University, Massachusetts General Hospital, and Boston Atheneum had no New York equivalents. Its Cultural Mile comprised the Museum of Fine Arts (1876), Mechanics Hall (1881), the Boston Public Library (1895), Symphony Hall (1900), Horticultural Hall (1901), Chickering Hall (1901), the New England Conservatory (1902), Jordan Hall (1903), the Isabella Stewart Gardner Museum (1903), the Boston Opera House (1909), and, replacing its outgrown predecessor, a second Museum of Fine Arts (1909)—regal edifices regally spaced. New York was the nation's city of finance, commerce, and show business. It had no cultural hub. Musicians gravitated toward Union Square, a teeming neighborhood in which could be found Steinway Hall, the Academy of Music, the National Conservatory, and an assortment of German theaters, restaurants, and saloons. As of 1890 (eight years before greater New York was created with the addition of Brooklyn, the Bronx, Queens, and Staten Island), Germans were the city's largest foreign-born population, outnumbering the Irish 211,000 to 190,000; according to the country-of-birth-of-mother criterion used by the Census Bureau, *27 percent* of New York's 1,515,301 inhabitants were "Germans." According to Baedecker's 1893 guide, if the children of foreign-born parents were excluded, "probably not more than one-fourth or one-fifth of the inhabitants [of New York City could] be classified as native American." Boston was not a city of immigrants. Its Irish, numbering 149,222 out of a total population of 448,477 as of 1890, were a world apart.[7]

The wasp-tongued Hans von Bülow, touring the United States in 1876, told the *Chicago Times*:

> There are two types of musical cultivation: for want of better terminology, I might call them in-breadth and in-depth. In the latter respect, I would consider Boston the most cultivated; but the people are narrow

and too pretentious for the measure of their knowledge. Puritanism has frozen art in New England; it's a miracle that it hasn't killed it altogether in the last 100 years.

The Bostonians feel their indifference not only to an extreme degree: they even display it openly with pride. Presumably they reckon it as one of the Fine Arts. But that it is not. It is simply a form of paralysis. . . . Nevertheless, for a certain sort of technical facility and depth of musical cultivation, Boston takes first place.

Boston's self-perception, as articulated by George Chadwick, stressed "the refining influences of the arts" and of "broad general culture." Another New England composer, Horatio Parker, observed that "the serious musician" in New York was "treated as a mere entertainer." That in New York musicians enjoyed less prestige, that audiences were less consolidated in education and edification, New Yorkers could only agree. Boston, in New York eyes, was afflicted with a priggish insularity, but also blessed with a wondrous aesthetic sensitivity.[8]

The magnitude and intensity of this cultural rivalry was understandable: issues of national identity were at stake. In the history of American classical music, Boston and New York are twin points of origin.

PART ONE

Boston and the Cult of Beethoven

■

CHAPTER 1

John Sullivan Dwight, Theodore Thomas, and the Slaying of the Monster Concerts

■

Patrick Gilmore's Peace Jubilee of 1869 • John Sullivan Dwight and the framing of a sacred "classical music" • The failings of early Boston orchestras • The triumphs of the Thomas Orchestra

The building, a wooden rectangle in Boston's Back Bay, was alleged to be the largest structure in America. Outside, a vast "Shingle City" had sprung up, a place of booths and tents, peanuts and lemonade, festooned with American flags. Inside, one thousand musicians, instruments at hand, sat surrounded by ten thousand choristers. The former, with players from Chicago and Cincinnati, Quebec and Montreal, Albany and Springfield, accounted for 208 violins, 80 violas, 60 cellos, 81 double basses, 16 flutes, 12 oboes, 12 clarinets, 8 bassoons, 12 trumpets, 16 horns, 12 trombones, 4 tubas, and a bass drum 25 feet in diameter, all finely positioned on a gentle incline so that every member was visible from every part of the hall. The latter, including choral societies from as far away as Ohio and Illinois, comprised three steep slopes of humanity stretching to the eaves. Banners and flags hung in profusion from the rafters and beams; over the stage were huge pictures of Handel and Beethoven and, higher up, an arch adorned with two angels gazing upward at the words, "Glory to God on the Highest: Peace on Earth Good Will Toward Men!" The tread of the entering audience, an orderly flood tide, emitted a deep undertone, a steady ocean sound subduing every other noise. At 3 P.M., twelve thousand listeners regarded eleven thousand performers with feelings of astonishment; the astonishment was returned. The Official Programme read in part:

"Let us Have Peace"
Great National Peace Jubilee!
June 15, 16, 17, 18, and 19, 1869
To
COMMEMORATE THE RESTORATION OF PEACE
THROUGHOUT THE LAND

THIS GLORIOUS EVENT IN OUR NATIONAL HISTORY WILL BE
CELEBRATED BY THE
GRANDEST MUSICAL FESTIVAL
EVER KNOWN IN THE HISTORY OF THE WORLD

The Reverend Edward Everett Hale said a prayer. The mayor of Boston proclaimed, "Let the gladsome music resound." There followed an Address on the Restoration of Peace and Union by the Honorable Alexander H. Rice, a speech lasting some forty-five minutes. Many in the vast Temple of Peace could not possibly have heard a word. And yet the quality of attention was intense and the applause frequent. Rice's oration sealed the occasion with its synthesis of patriotism, religion, and art. It ended as follows:

The imagination aspires to grasp, but fails in the effort to conceive of the possible greatness of a free and united people occupying a territory almost boundless in geographical extent, diversified in climate and pro-ductions, and rich in the nameless treasures of Nature. . . .

Let the multitudinous harmonies of these days of Jubilee symbolize a real unity of friendship and brotherhood which shall be universal and unending. We bid you Godspeed in a new career of honors and useful-ness; and we invoke for our beloved and common country that right-eousness . . . which is able to keep the foundations of the Republic secure, until the final triumph of Peace and Virtue on the earth can be celebrated only in that great Jubilee of the "innumerable company" whose hallelujahs shall roll in seraphic sweetness with the ages through the eternal year.

Two concertmasters—Carl Rosa and Ole Bull, of whom the latter was as famous as any violinist known in the United States—strode from the rear of the orchestra through acres of instruments, chairs, and bodies. Then came the conductor, Patrick Gilmore: the "projector" of the Jubilee, realizing the great effort of his life. He praised God and proclaimed a new era of brotherly love.

The peal of the great organ, specially built for the occasion, signaled the singers to rise. Gilmore's baton descended and all commenced Luther's chorale "A Strong Castle Is Our Lord" (today known as "A Mighty Fortress Is Our God"). This first taste of music in the great space was startlingly soft. The hall had been pronounced good for sound because a single violin could be heard in its farthest corners. But, as all recognized at once, two voices penetrated no farther than one, and ten thousand voices did not magnify in volume what one thousand might have produced. The singers tended to lag behind the orchestra. The farthest voices entered later than the nearest. And yet these imperfections were swallowed up in a sublimely ponderous mass of sound. If not very loud, the chorale was grand, solemn, and full. It was answered by an equivalent ovation—the gentlemen applauding, the ladies waving white handkerchiefs.

Next came Wagner's *Tannhäuser* Overture, performed by a "select orchestra" of six hundred under another baton, then a Mozart "Gloria," then the Bach/Gounod "Ave Maria" with the stately Euphrosyne Parepa-Rosa, whose soprano penetrated the building—albeit in miniature, like a picture seen through the wrong end of someone's opera glasses.

Closing the first half was the national air: the "Star-Spangled Banner," begun by twenty-five hundred basses in unison. An equal number of tenors assayed "And the rocket's red glare." The full chorus of ten thousand sang:

> Oh say does that star-spangled banner yet wave
> O'er the land of the free
> And the home of the brave!

The second verse was begun by sopranos and altos in duet. The third was reinforced by organ, drum corps, bells, and—just outside the hall—cannon. The audience demanded, and received, a repeat performance.

After intermission, the concert continued with an American hymn, Rossini's *William Tell* Overture and the "Inflammatus" from his *Stabat Mater* (for which Madame Parepa-Rosa returned), the Coronation March from Meyerbeer's *Le prophète*, and the afternoon's *pièce de résistance*: the Anvil Chorus from Verdi's *Il trovatore*, with drum corps, bells, cannon, and a hundred anvils. Filing in two by two, one hundred helmeted, red-shirted Boston firemen strode to the stage, each shouldering a blacksmith's hammer. Then, in two rows facing the auditors, they struck on cue: right, left, right, left. The cannon, in two batteries, ignited on the first beat of every measure. Electric signals, sent from a small table on the stage, ensured flawless synchronization. The enthusiasm of the crowd was frantic—fans, hats, parasols, even babies were waved aloft. The firemen marched out—and back in again, to encore the entire number. "My Country, 'Tis of Thee" concluded the program. The audience joined in the singing of the final stanza.

The four remaining concerts of the Jubilee attracted audiences as large as twenty thousand. The visiting dignitaries included President Ulysses S. Grant. The repertoire favored oratorio arias and choruses by Handel, Haydn, and Mendelssohn. There were also two movements apiece from Beethoven's Fifth and Schubert's "Great" C major Symphony. The Anvil Chorus had to be repeated. The final concert, on Saturday, June 19, featured six thousand Boston schoolchildren whose silvery voices none could resist. The following day, an extra "sacred" concert encored some of the most successful numbers of the five days. There followed a benefit concert for Patrick Gilmore, for which two-thirds of the festival's singers and instrumentalists donated their services; twelve thousand attended, for a profit of $32,000. The festival proper netted $7,000: $290,000 minus $283,000 in expenditures. Gilmore pocketed all $39,000—to which, everyone agreed, he was eminently entitled.[1]

The Peace Jubilee was a triumph for the city of Boston—its choral tradition, distinctive to New England; its musical leaders, who rehearsed and conducted the performers; its public schools, which systematically taught singing. And it was a mighty national influence. Taking stock, the *New York Tribune* acknowledged many "comical aspects" attendant to the grandiose plan, yet pronounced the result "a pretty serious affair, a magnificent gathering of enthusiasm" certain to "be felt by a class of persons whom the ordinary concert does not reach, because they never go to it." The *New York Sun* took an even bigger view: "The largest gathering of singers and players ever brought together has just been held in the United States. The enterprise has been conceived and executed on a scale in keeping with the vastness of the country, . . . and with the expedition and fearlessness that characterize all our attempts in untried fields of effort." It offered proof that "our people can think of something beyond mechanical inventions and the almighty dollar." It was a "recognition of American art."[2]

■ ■ ■

The man who conceived the Peace Jubilee of 1869 was America's most popular bandmaster before John Philip Sousa. Born in Ireland in 1829, Patrick Gilmore began his career as a cornetist. In Massachusetts, he led various bands before creating one of his own in 1859. In wartime, it enlisted with the Twenty-Fourth Volunteer Regiment.

A genuine humanitarian zeal underscored the Peace Jubilee. Gilmore had seen war. A different kind of inspiration was furnished by the Frenchman

Louis Jullien. He had made a great name in England with his promenade concerts. He arrived in the United States in 1853 with twenty-seven skilled instrumentalists, to which he added sixty of the best local players. He amazed New York with his "Monster Concerts for the Masses," then toured the country, including Boston.

Jullien's personal props included a gilt music stand, a scarlet armchair, and gloves and boots so tightly fitted that his hands and feet looked varnished. For Beethoven, he used a jeweled baton conveyed on a silver tray. Among his own best-known compositions was *Firemen's Quadrille*, with simulated fire and real firemen. Between numbers, he would collapse upon his throne, exhausted from his labors. He was at the same time a master conductor who was observed rehearsing the Scherzo from Beethoven's *Pastoral* Symphony a dozen times and more to secure perfect balance and ensemble,[3] and a missionary for great music who successfully used polkas and quadrilles, cannon and bells, to lure audiences to overtures and symphonies. In his mammoth symphonic spectacles, showmanship vied with art on an equal footing, dynamically absorbing Old World art in a protean New World milieu. Gilmore took note.

Like P. T. Barnum, like Jullien, Gilmore was no grand naif, but a knowing entrepreneurial genius. His 758-page *History of the National Peace Jubilee* is a paean to unbridled showmanship leavened by shrewd intelligence and savvy self-understanding. As with Barnum's classic autobiography, Gilmore's charm, even on the printed page, is so effortless that his feats of persuasion become instantly persuasive. Barnum had instructed, "The bigger the humbug, the better people like it." Gilmore discovered that the bigger the Jubilee, the more people endorsed it. But there were holdouts, of which the most crucial—and illuminating—was Gilmore's antipode: John Sullivan Dwight, Boston's pontiff of musical taste. Gilmore's solicitation is a tale only he can tell.

> It was deemed advisable [to see] the venerable Mr. John S. Dwight, Boston's high-art critic, who from his deep interest in the cause of music, and from the persecutions he has suffered in endeavoring to bring the rest of mankind up to his lofty standard, has never enjoyed, it is said, an hour's "peace on earth" or, it might be added, "good-will towards man,"—good-will towards the heathenish barbarians whose morbid appetites would not permit them to swallow a symphony for breakfast, a fugue for dinner, and an oratorio for supper; then, without wincing, take down a whole German opera before retiring. . . .
>
> [M]r. Gilmore had very little favor in the eyes, and still less in the pen, of this great Rhadamanthus of Music, who condescended to bow to him

at sight, yet ever descended to bow wow at him when out of sight. But the projector of the Peace Festival now felt it his duty to forget the past, and enlist even enemies in the cause if he could, and to remove the most trifling obstacles to success. With this feeling, he entered the classic chamber of the great expounder of musical art in Boston.

"Good morning, Mr. Dwight."

"Good morning," in a very subdued tone, was the reply.

. . .

"Here is the prospectus of a musical festival," continued the visitor; "if you will take the trouble to read it, and—"

"What is it? What is it?" interrupted Mr. Dwight, hurriedly and peevishly, as his eyes fell upon the printed pages. . . . O, you know, I never like these g-r-e-a-t things!" . . .

Mr. Dwight continued to read the marvelous tale before him, interlarding with painful groans the variety of monster musical features that filed along under his optics. Indigestion was already settling in. . . .

As he finished the alarming sketch of the coming *Sängerfest*, he raised his arms, gave a fearful growl, and stood, for once in his life, bold and defiant as a lion in the path. . . . "Any such movement as this should appear as if it were the spontaneous act of a whole community. . . . I cannot say what I will do until I have had an opportunity of consulting with other parties about it." . . .

"Well, sir, . . . may I ask that, if you should not conclude to indorse [*sic*] or assist the enterprise, you will not take the trouble to oppose it?"

"Oppose, oppose," muttered Mr. Dwight; "it would be of no interest or advantage to me whatever to oppose it." . . .

With this the interview ended; Mr. Gilmore departed, satisfied that he had done his duty in performing this unpleasant task,—unpleasant, because it was humiliating to seek the influence of one who for years had frowned not only upon the musical efforts of himself, . . . but also upon those of most all musicians who attempted anything in public that did not spring from . . . the select circle who constitute the would-be high court of musical criticism in the New England metropolis.

It should be admitted, though, that Mr. Dwight never claimed to be much of a musician; but there is one thing sure, he possesses all the elements of discord, and is thoroughly familiar with any descending minor passage.[4]

Dwight was intimate with Boston's preeminent musicians and musical institutions. His base of power was *Dwight's Journal of Music*, the leading American publication of its kind, founded in 1852. *Dwight's Journal* was—and for scholars remains—an invaluable digest of concerts and opera, copiously covering the Boston scene but also closely following events in New York and other American cities, as well as abroad. Dwight solicited reports from farflung correspondents and reprinted important essays on contemporary trends. Notwithstanding his own parochialism, the range of subject matter and opinion was reasonably catholic. In the years, months, and even weeks leading up to the Peace Jubilee, Dwight kept his word not to write or publish anything damaging to Gilmore's plan. In fact, he completely ignored it—even as singing societies sprang into existence, even as the huge coliseum took form, even as singers and instrumentalists flocked to Boston, even as news and expectation charted a steady crescendo in the daily press. Dwight finally broke his silence on June 19, reporting on the initial concert of four days before. "Much as we disliked the extravagance of the plan originally, and shrank from the boastful style of the arena of this greatest musical feast ever held in any part of the world," he reported, "we cheerfully make haste to own that the result so far has in many respects agreeably disappointed us." He found the great chorus inspiring, the great orchestra splendid but hard to hear. He judged the Anvil Chorus a "childish, trivial thing for any grand occasion, and the poor claptrap of 100 anvils was really a failure in point of effect." He conceded that "the guns were wonderfully well timed, think what you will of them." He still resented the "unscrupulous" advertising and puffery.

Dwight attended three of the remaining four festival concerts, skipping the next to last. The verdict from on high was rendered in two immense installments for the *New York Tribune*, reprinted in tandem in *Dwight's Journal* on July 3 and introduced, in part, as follows:

> The Jubilee has been the all-absorbing topic for the last month. As we have been silent about it during the preparation of the mighty work; and since, with all the extravagances of the plan, it has been pushed forward with such faith and energy that the imagination of the People, the "popular heart," perhaps we should even say the good genius of our People, fired and filled with it, has adopted it and made it its own, transforming it as it were into its own likeness; since it has been crowned with such unique success, we can do no less than gather together what we can of its history, weigh its results from our own point of view, and note the impression it has made on others.

Dwight pronounced the Jubilee "a splendid fact which has to be accepted." The concerts themselves elicited a mixed report. The best program was the fourth—"the one really *musical* occasion," with selections by Handel, Haydn, Mozart, Beethoven, and Weber—even if the Fifth Symphony was needlessly truncated, a failure of "valor and faith" provoked by the anvils' success.

What most impressed Dwight was not the music but the moral fervor of the occasion: the "mutual magnetism, the sense of pride, of progress, of cooperation" was a "great good in itself, almost enough to offset the bray, the claptrap, and the humbug." The spectacle of "perfect order" was the "secret of the *great* impression" exerted by the Jubilee—and music alone, ennobling and faith-inspiring, could secure such order.

> An almost boundless sea of live humanity; and all so cheerful, all so happy, full of kindness, rejoicing in the sense of Country and of Brotherhood! . . .
>
> [I]t has given to tens of thousands of all classes (save, unfortunately, the poorest), who were there to hear, and, through them, to thousands more, to whole communities, a new belief in Music; a new conviction of its social worth; above all, of its importance as a pervading, educational and fusing element in our whole democratic life; a heavenly influence which shall go far to correct the crudities, tone down, subdue and harmonize the loud, self-asserting individualities, relieve the glaring and forthputting egotism of our too boisterous and boastful nationality. Thousands now have faith in Music, who never did have much before; thousands for the first time respect it as a high and holy influence, who very likely looked upon it as at the best an innocent, if not a dissipating, idle pleasure. . . . We begin to see how Music is to teach a people manners, mutual deference, and, without outward cold authority, without appeal to fear, but freely and divinely from within, inspire the instinct of respect, of fond and childlike reverence for something still above us, be we where we may,—and this is real Self-respect. So far as the Jubilee has wrought this conversion among unbelieving or different thousands, it has done incalculable good.

Clouding this report, however, was a catalogue of fears and misgivings rehearsed with undiminished enthusiasm. The project "inflamed the imagination of the ignorant or only sentimentally and vaguely musical." It blasphemed against European practices and precedents that Dwight revered: "say, some festival at Düsseldorf, with seven or eight hundred performers, but with Mendelssohn for a conductor, and such an orchestra as only can be found in Germany and such a programme (not only Handel Oratorios, but *Passion music* or *Magnificat* of Bach, and, as it was at this last Whitsuntide, with a Joachim to play Beethoven's concerto)." Gilmore's plan even insulted Boston:

> Or, not to look so far, compare it with our own best efforts here, with the last Handel and Haydn Festival in Boston Music Hall, where audiences of 3,000 people heard three or four great oratorios entire, with the Choral Symphony of Beethoven, and admirable symphony concerts besides, all in one week, impressively performed by an orchestra of hardly more than 100 instruments and chorus of 800 voices; was not that, musically, greater?

And the means—"unscrupulous advertising, meant innocently in this case, no doubt, though questionable to squeamish folk like you and me, dear *Tribune!*"—had tainted the ends. Gilmore had succumbed to "the whole business world," the "swell mob style," the "loud-mouthed quack" who seduces the "simple masses." He had manipulated the press into conveying a false impression that all Boston supported the project, ignoring sentiment in "cultivated circles." Persons who "set themselves against the tide, rather than give in ignominiously to what they could not see to be good, had much the harder trial of their faith, their courage, and their integrity" than did Gilmore and his followers. Meanwhile, endorsements had been shrewdly procured from influential citizens who "were not musical themselves."

All these imperfections were underscored by an aesthetic imperfection: the combination of "heterogeneous" musical elements. This was the danger of "monster concerts" in which "classical works of genius were pressed into damaging promiscuity with musical *mix pickel* for the million." That at such a "bugle's blast" all should rally to a Jubilee of Peace was "a colossal joke." Musically, the festival had registered its chief triumphs "in precisely those selections which were the least purely musical." Those others addressed to "earnest music lovers" suffered from "the mingling of incongruous, internecine elements in the programmes." The "anvils killed the Symphony," and "abstinence from anvils" was made difficult "when a classical programme was for once allowed its course."

What genuine musical dividends the festival achieved, in Dwight's view, resulted from a sage and inescapable scaling down of the first prospectus: a chorus of ten thousand, rather than twenty thousand; a children's chorus of six thousand, versus twenty thousand; a select orchestra of five hundred for certain numbers; a seating capacity of thirty-seven thousand, versus fifty thousand. With these revisions, the "plan gained in the opinion of really musical persons," whose first misgivings were thereby vindicated. Concomitantly,

Dwight's approbation for Gilmore was notably backhanded, as if he were the charmed beneficiary of local conditions conducive to cultural camaraderie. In the business arrangements alone lay "the 'genius' which has been so freely ascribed to the Projector; for surely the conception, the idea itself, did not require creative imagination, nor invention, until it came to the details of execution." Gilmore himself emerges in Dwight's account as a fast-talking barbarian interloper, an "Irishman by birth," a "clever leader of a local band," an "enthusiast of rather a sentimental type," a "man of common education . . . briefly known as a caterer in music to the popular street taste."

With its overtones and undertones of suspicion, jealousy, and outrage, Dwight's mighty response to the Peace Jubilee is arguably more self-revealing than anything he penned about concerts more kindred to his style and taste. He feels his place usurped by an outsider to the city's priestly caste of tastemakers; a grandiose guerilla action has ambushed the lofty enterprise of Boston culture. His fusillade suggests (and closer acquaintance with its author confirms) unresolved tensions between democratic principles and elitist instincts: a conflicted view of the untutored. Were they candidates for edification or obstacles to progress? Embraceable millions or discomfiting rabble? Ultimately, Dwight is a puritan for whom art is purest religion; a purist intent on sanitizing music; a prude on guard against "promiscuous" alliances with popular, sensuous, or sentimental genres. He is a dogmatist prone to a priori judgments. He feels secure in his Boston bastion, but incipiently embattled by a roisterous immigrant mob, chiefly Irish.

On the other side of the barricades, Gilmore eyed his adversaries more generously. "The citizens of Boston," he wrote in his *History*, "are more like one family, perhaps, than the inhabitants of any other city upon the American continent. They are ready at times to do anything and everything to promote the public welfare; but withal they are exceedingly cautious of trying or encouraging doubtful or dangerous experiments." The most conservative among them, "sober-minded old standbys," had viewed the Jubilee as a "dangerous and delusive experiment" that was "forced upon Boston." But when "the great Band of *Faith* came together as they did upon this day, in the flood of harmony they poured forth every vestige of doubt or fear was swept away, joy was in all hearts, and the citizens of Boston, old and young, grave and gay, fraternized in congratulatory exaltation."[5]

If Dwight joined in, it was not for long. As early as July 17, he was writing in his *Journal* that the Jubilee "has not at all reconciled us to the idea that musical effects, musical edification or enjoyment, may be enhanced by the assembling of a whole *Nation* of performers and listeners under one roof. . . . Musically, we are still convinced (and so we believe is every sane musical person) that twenty festivals in twenty places, each with 500 performers, would be a finer thing." And he cautioned, "The success of the Jubilee was unique; let it remain unique, exceptional. It were a foolish ambition that would attempt to reproduce it. . . . The truth is, the Peace Jubilee was entirely an anomalous occasion, ambiguous in its character and motive."

Gilmore stood warned.

■ ■ ■

Whether or not Tocqueville was correct in surmising that men living in free societies are exceptionally prone, by way of compensation, to anchor their thoughts in religious belief, the power of religion is an enduring motif of the American experience. Its ramifications include the religious experience of art. Historically, Americans have inclined to judge and understand high culture for its positive moral content, its power to ennoble and uplift. And they have been quick to mistrust or reject art that seems decadent or blasphemous.

The moral tenacity of the Puritans, Quakers, and other religious sects of early America engendered an aesthetic of plainness rather than decoration. The embodiment of virtue, plain and unsullied, became a pervasive aesthetic criterion. It comes as no surprise that nudity was rare in American painting before the late nineteenth century. Redemptive landscapes were an American specialty. Frederic Church and Albert Bierstadt, Robert Salmon and Fitz Hugh Lane variously evoked American nature infused by God. The phenomenally popular Church, an iconic figure, was no *artiste*, but a devout Christian husband and father who advised aspirant American artists to avoid the temptation of study in Europe.

Wholesome American nature is also a theme in American literature—in Cooper, Longfellow, Thoreau, Bryant. But it is oddly absent from American music. Notwithstanding the ambitious early efforts of Anthony Philip Heinrich, William Henry Fry, and George Bristow, American composers did not write enduring nature symphonies to parallel Church's *Twilight in the Wilderness* or Bierstadt's *Emigrants Crossing the Plains* (or Liszt's *Vallée d'Obermann* or Wagner's *Good Friday Spell*). Notwithstanding the religious works of such latenineteenth-century New England composers as Amy Beach, John Knowles Paine, and Horatio Parker, there is a relative absence, too, of American masses and oratorios; compared to European nations, the United States has produced no sustained tradition of sacred choral music for the concert hall.

But then America's musical high culture has at all times (alas) been less about music composed by Americans than about American concerts of music composed by Europeans. Preponderantly, peculiarly, it is a culture of performance. And here the theme of sacralization—of the pious content and moral power of art—has rung vividly. More than Europeans, Americans have worshipped musical masterpieces and deified their exponents.

In effect, a more applicable analogy from visual to musical art is not from painters to composers, but from museums to orchestras. In Gilded Age America, museums were a proud New World achievement: an edifying showcase for Old World painting and sculpture. Contemporaneously, America created the "symphony orchestra": a showcase for Old World symphonies. And the chief advocate of this showcase was John Sullivan Dwight.

Dwight's background was in fact religious. He was a Unitarian minister before joining the Transcendentalist Brook Farm community in 1841. Much of his early criticism appeared in the Fourierist *Harbinger*. His devotion to the symphonic masters of the eighteenth and early nineteenth century was absolute. He instinctively mistrusted opera as a variant of the theater.

The intellectual mainspring of Dwight's thought was a redefinition of "sacred" music. Before Dwight, New England hymnodic reformers had instilled an understanding of the positive moral effects of music, of its power to enhance the devotional ambience. With Dwight, influenced by radical Unitarian antipathy to conventional church worship, religious music was in effect transplanted from the church to the concert hall. In weighty, redundant prose fortified with Transcendentalist idealism, he argued that music is most "religious" unfettered by text. "Sacred" music was absolute music: "elevating, purifying, love and faith-inspiring." The instrumental music of the great masters was more religious than any music sung to God. Were not some Beethoven adagios "almost the very essence of prayer?—not formal prayer, I grant, but earnest, deep, unspeakable aspiration? Is not his music pervaded by such prayer?" Real music was religion itself:

> I hazard the assertion, that *music is all sacred*; that music in its essence, in its purity, when it flows from the genuine fount of art in the composer's soul, when it is the inspiration of his genius, and not a manufactured imitation, when it comes unforced, unbidden from the heart, is a divine minister of the wants of the soul. . . . To me music stands for the highest outward symbol of what is most deep and holy, and most remotely to be realized in the soul of man. It is a sort of Holy Writ; a prophecy of what life is to be; the language of our presentiments; the rainbow of promise translated out of seeing into hearing.

For Dwight, music was a necessary source of moral instruction. He cited Bach, Handel, Haydn, Mozart, Beethoven, Schubert, Schumann, and

Mendelssohn as blessed influences. He particularly esteemed Beethoven's symphonies as the embodiment of ethical striving, and considered music as entertainment invalid and corrupt. He inveighed against whatever seemed frivolous, bacchanalian, or exhibitionistic. He espoused "classical music."[6]

By this term, Dwight meant music different from, and better than, "popular music." Though American writers distinguished between classical and popular music as early as the 1830s, Dwight was decisive in crystallizing and promoting this weighted terminology. The first issue of *Dwight's Journal*, dated April 10, 1852, announced an intention to "insist much on the claims of 'classical' music, and put out its beauties and its meanings." This elevated subject matter expressly transcended "styles more simple, popular or modern." The music thus privileged, comprising a Germanic canon stopping with Mendelssohn and Schumann, was judged superior both aesthetically and morally. Concomitantly, listeners to popular music were debased by it. Dwight termed Stephen Foster's "Old Folks at Home," the best-known American music of its time, a "melodic itch."

Though Europeans were sacralizing a wordless classical music at the same moment, Americans like Dwight would prove peculiarly intent on achieving pure pedigrees. This zeal reflected insecurities inherent to a borrowed high culture, as well as New England codes of moral/aesthetic sanctity—codes that had prohibited Sunday concerts in Boston until, around midcentury, classical music was discovered to have transcended the realm of mere entertainment. Gilmore's 1869 coliseum threatened an even grander symphonic edifice Dwight was intent on constructing. Three years later, Gilmore undertook a second Jubilee in another great space. This time, Dwight was ready.

The prospectus for the 1872 World Peace Jubilee proclaimed "the greatest series of concerts ever given in the world" on a scale exceeding the 1869 Jubilee and far surpassing such feeble contemporary European efforts as the forty-ninth Lower-Rhine Festival, with 673 singers and 132 instrumentalists. There were three weeks of concerts, beginning June 17, in a new Coliseum seating twenty-one thousand. But greater means did not necessarily produce greater ends. The chorus, numbering up to eighteen hundred (gigantic figures on the conductor's stand gave the pages to be sung), proved unwieldy. The organ was judged "a miracle of noise." There were proportionately fewer "classical" works than in 1869. A blatant travesty were the piano solos, flung into a room five hundred feet long. Sometimes less than half the house was full; attendance picked up after ticket prices were lowered. The chief triumphs were the French, English, and Prussian bands sent by the French, English, and Prussian governments—a revelation for their polish and suavity—and Johann Strauss Jr., Vienna's waltz king, in his first American appearances.

The spirit of the festival again impressed. Boston's *Daily Advertiser* concluded that "the good decidedly preponderated in its concerts over the bad. It brought together a company of foreign artists which could never have been gathered in this country upon any other occasion; and it stimulated the love of music." But Dwight judged the 1872 Peace Jubilee "vain glorious, uncalled for, forced upon us, and fallacious." Of Strauss he wrote, "Great he is in his kind; but the kind is not a great one." He liked best the choruses from Handel's *Israel in Egypt*, "though this was only for the few appreciative ones who were well seated; upon five sixths of the audience it was thrown away, the noise of restless feet all over the great board palace sadly interfering with any calm and fruitful attention on the part of the rest." Absent an adequate patriotic premise (there was no American "peace" to celebrate), Dwight blamed the festival on supportive business interests—a "new Boston," rivaling New York, defacing and confuting "historical, refined, quiet Boston." He resented allegations that the first Jubilee had "converted" him to monster concerts, and reprinted swaths of his own opprobrium from 1869 to prove it was not so—and to demonstrate, specifically, that Gilmore, "in the wonderful 'History' of his," whose "maudlin, rancid sentimental rhetoric" even "his best admirer could hardly have the stomach to wade through," had quoted favorable remarks from *Dwight's Journal* out of context. Once it became clear that the 1872 Jubilee had not succeeded financially, claimed Dwight, "it was marvelous with what a freedom and alacrity so many even of the newspapers began to put out all the errors and short-comings and absurdities of the whole thing, and admit that the 'unprecedented and gigantic musical success' was after all a failure." He concluded, on July 13, "The great, usurping, tyrannizing, noisy, and pretentious thing is over, and there is a general feeling of relief, as if a heavy, brooding nightmare had been lifted from us all."[7]

Never again would Patrick Gilmore, or anyone else, attempt a concert series so heterogeneously varied and gargantuan in scale. The road to classical music beckoned straight and sure.

■ ■ ■

But Boston lacked orchestras of quality to play the classical symphonies. The city's signature musical institution before the Civil War was neither an orchestra nor an opera house, but a choral group specializing in sacred music: the Handel and Haydn Society, founded in 1815. Two years later, the society performed the two compositions with which it would forever be identified: Handel's *Messiah* and Haydn's *Creation*. These were not polished renditions. Rather, the society (then as now) was an amateur organization; its original members included dry-goods merchants, tailors, and bank cashiers for whom rehearsals were sociable occasions much lubricated by "tuning" thirsty throats with wines and spirits.[8]

An early landmark in the society's history was the publication in 1822 of *The Boston Handel and Haydn Society's Collection of Church Music.* Though his name did not appear on the cover, it was the work of Lowell Mason, a merchant turned choirmaster and organist. By skillfully and pragmatically setting hymns to tunes not only of his own, but also by Mozart, Haydn, and other European masters, Mason became the dominant compiler of American hymnals. His quick success in Boston induced him to move there in 1827. That same year he became president and music director of the Handel and Haydn Society. But Mason was at heart an educator. He resigned from the society in 1832 and founded the Boston Academy of Music, dedicated to promoting higher standards of church music as well as music education generally. Eventually, Mason's mission took him to the Boston public schools, which pioneered in the inclusion of music in the curriculum (the six thousand singing Boston schoolchildren at Gilmore's 1869 Peace Jubilee being one legacy of Mason's achievement).

Though Mason disdained the secular, his Boston Academy formed an orchestra in 1833 under his associate George James Webb. Its only notable predecessor, Gottlieb Graupner's Philo-Harmonic Society, had resembled a club as much as a performing ensemble. Webb introduced Boston to seven Beethoven symphonies as well as symphonies by Mozart and Mendelssohn. The Academy orchestra was succeeded in 1839 by a musicians' cooperative, the Boston Musical Fund Society. The prevailing caliber of performance may be gleaned from an anecdote told by Thomas Ryan, an expert and versatile instrumentalist (he later founded the influential Mendelssohn Quintette Club). As a youngster in Dublin, Ryan had played second clarinet in Mendelssohn's Overture to *A Midsummer Night's Dream*, which he now recommended to Webb's orchestra. The parts arrived in Boston with no conductor's score.

> Our orchestra was made up half of amateurs and half of professionals. We could have no lightning-express trains in *tempo*; most music was played *tempo commodo*. All trains were accommodation trains. . . . Therefore, when I say that the *Midsummer Night's Dream* was taken up for the first time by our orchestra, all cultured persons who are familiar with that delicate, fairy-like composition may smile to think that any but experts should attempt the difficult feat of playing it.
>
> [Webb] began by telling us that he had no score; so he stood up

alongside of the first-violin desk and prepared to conduct. Rapping on the desk he gave the signal to begin; out piped two flutes,—nothing else. He rapped again, implying that the players had not been ready to begin, then he said, "We will try again." He gave the signal—and out piped the two flutes. That caused a little titter of surprise, and we all looked quizzically at each other. Mr. Webb, however, dutifully gave the signal for the next "hold" or chord, when two clarinets joined the two flutes! More surprise. At the third hold (chord) the fagotti [bassoons] and horns were added, and at the fourth hold (chord) the entire wood and wind instruments, all sounding most distressingly out of tune. This dissonant and unlooked-for result was followed by a dead pause; then every one of the players broke out with a hearty laugh of derision.

I was on pins and needles and muttered, "Go on, go on!" After a while the people sobered down, and we tried to commence with the string part. The first and second violins . . . began at an "accommodation-train" tempo. At the end of the violin passage, the wood and wind again held a very dissonant chord for two measures, which this time sounded so abominably out of tune that it really was as bad as if each man played any note he pleased; and it was so irresistibly funny that again everybody burst out laughing. . . .

That last dissonant chord ended the first rehearsal of the *Midsummer Night's Dream* overture. We never tried it again.[9]

In 1848, the Germania Musical Society came to town. This was a group of twenty-five idealistic young Germans in flight from the failed revolutions of 1848. Their *pièce de résistance* was the *Midsummer Night's Dream* Overture. In Boston, as in New York, Philadelphia, Baltimore, and points west, the Germania Society set new standards for symphonic performance. Unlike other European "private orchestras," with their entrepreneurial conductors, the Germania was a self-governing community of equals, espousing Communism as "the most perfect principle of society" and seeking in America to instill "love for the fine art of music in the hearts of . . . politically free people." To John Sullivan Dwight, steeped in Germanic idealism and social utopianism, the success of the Germanians seemed "a moral triumph" due in part to "the cordial unanimity, the spirit of devotion, the *merging of the individual in the common interest*, the superiority to petty jealousies, of which their united little band has been so refreshingly an example." This was in April 1853, by which time the Germania had made Boston its hub for two seasons. The group's hectic 1851–52 schedule had included twenty subscription concerts in Boston plus eight-concert subscription series in Providence and Worcester each and additional dates as far away as Baltimore to the south and Montreal to the north. In 1853 the Germania's Boston premiere of Beethoven's Ninth drew over three thousand listeners. Overflowing audiences, with others turned away, were excitedly reported in *Dwight's Journal*. Dwight also (as with Gilmore and others in years to come) sought to encourage "classical" versus "anti-'classical' (anti-serious, anti-ideal, anti-excellent)" programs. A "light" Germania program for Boston might include (of a dozen numbers) the *Pickpocket Quadrille* and *Battle Galop* [sic] alongside the Scherzo from Beethoven's *Pastoral* Symphony, an operatic cavatina, and Mendelssohn's *Rondo brillant* for piano and orchestra. A "serious" program might list (of fewer than half a dozen numbers) concertos by Beethoven and Mendelssohn, overtures by Mendelssohn and Cherubini, and Beethoven's Seventh Symphony.[10] When the Germania orchestra disbanded in 1854, individual members became local musical bulwarks. In New York, Carl Bergmann, an incipient Wagnerite, was made conductor of the Philharmonic. In Boston, Carl Zerrahn—a more conservative musician, but constructive and inspirational, disciplined and unflappable—became the conductor of choice.

A post-Germania landmark was the demicentennial of the Handel and Haydn Society in 1865, for which an orchestra including former Germanians was assembled under Zerrahn. William Apthorp, born in 1848, later recalled:

> I doubt if any of my generation, certainly of those whose experience did not extend to New York or the other side of the Atlantic, had ever [before] heard a well-balanced orchestra. Our notions of orchestral effect were derived from what we heard. I remember distinctly how impossible it was for me, at the time I speak of, to understand what older musicians meant by calling the strings the "main power" in an orchestra. In all orchestras I had heard, the wood-wind—let alone the brass and percussion—was more powerful dynamically than the often ridiculously small mass of strings; especially as the then wind-players seldom cultivated the art of playing *piano*. But, for this demi-centennial of the Handel & Haydn, our local orchestra was increased to nearly a hundred by the addition of players engaged from New York and elsewhere. . . . This was the beginning, not of large, but of what might be called normal orchestras in Boston.[11]

The following year, the Harvard Musical Association created for Zerrahn a band about half as large. The program committee was dominated by Dwight and Otto Dresel, a crusty yet cultivated musician of comparably traditional tastes. The resulting organization, however indispensable, was old-fashioned the day it was born—and as ripe for upstaging as Webb's orchestras of yore. Three years later (the same year as Gilmore's Peace Jubilee) the Theodore Thomas Orchestra began appearing on a regular basis—visits remembered by Apthorp for inflicting "humiliating lessons in the matter of orchestral technique." Even Dwight had to concede that "Boston had not heard such orchestral performances before." Reviewing the Thomas Orchestra's Boston debut—three concerts from October 29 to 31, 1869—he wrote, "With all our pride in our own orchestra, we are very far this side of perfection, and must take a lesson from what is better done elsewhere." Dwight insisted, however, that while Thomas's orchestra played "vastly better than our own, still ours remain the better Concerts." He choked on Thomas's programs, with their "loud and ponderous *effect* pieces of the Liszt, Wagner, Meyerbeer school."* And he decried the absence of unity. Thomas's first program mixed serious and popular, as follows:

> Wagner: *Tannhäuser* Overture
> Beethoven: Adagio, from *The Creatures of Prometheus*
> Weber/Berlioz: *The Invitation to the Dance*
> Liszt: *Les préludes*

> Rossini: *William Tell* Overture
> Schumann: *Träumerei* (arranged by Thomas)
> Johann Strauss Jr.: *The Blue Danube*
> Stigelli: *The Tear* (with trombone solo)
> Strauss Jr.: Two polkas
> Meyerbeer: *Torch Dance*

"Plainly," commented Dwight, "the object was to show what a modern orchestra can do, and how well this particular orchestra can do it, rather than to convey any poetic unity of impression; to startle and delight for the moment, rather than to lift into a pure, ideal atmosphere." *Les préludes* "failed

---

* Dwight's resistance to Wagner was swept aside in the 1880s and 1890s, when American Wagnerism was at its height. Compared to those of the suave, secular Eduard Hanslick, Wagner's great European critical nemesis, Dwight's objections to the Music of the Future were fuzzy, provincial, and religious. For Hanslick, textless music was purer not because it reached closer to God, but because musical meaning resided in formal relations rather than expression of feeling. But music as an end in itself held no discernible appeal to Gilded Age Americans. Half a century later, American critics resisted the neoclassical Stravinsky as an effete, eviscerated formalist. From this perspective, Dwight was a founding father of American music criticism.

to give us the impression of great music." Wagner's *Rienzi* Overture, on October 31, 1869, was "unmitigated noise."

The following season, Thomas returned with programs better suited to Boston tastes. Of ten concerts in two weeks, one was devoted entirely to Beethoven, including the Eighth Symphony and the *Emperor* Concerto. More typical was concert number two:

> Beethoven: Symphony No. 6
> Liszt: Piano Concerto No. 2
> Wagner: *Faust* Overture
> Berlioz: Pilgrims' March from *Harold in Italy*
> Glinka: *Kamarinskaya*
> Schumann: *Genoveva* Overture

Dwight acknowledged that Thomas's 1870 programs were better than before. But he decried "the large admixture of the strange and questionable element of modern 'programme-music.'" His discomfort peaked with Wagner's *Faust* Overture:

> We cannot but regard that as false Art, which seeks new field for originality in giving unredeemed and cheerless, fruitless utterance to those gloomy moods, which, however they may enter into the experience of all, even the noblest, richest, deepest souls, and however essential perhaps to the spiritual economy of life in the long run, have really no right to public expression, but belong, by every modest instinct of propriety, to strictest privacy, at least until the discord is resolved.

And he now carped that the Thomas Orchestra was *too* perfect:

> [I]n the very finish and perfection of such playing, where all works together smoothly like an admirable machine in perfect order,—and in the very sweetness of such blended sounds, one feels at last a something cloying, a certain drowsy, dreamy, lotus-like sensation; so that the music, with all its beauty, seems to lack life and reality.

This self-justifying ambivalence, typical of Dwight under siege, could not disguise the potency of irresistible future developments. "Our concerts"—the Harvard Musical Association performances, with their redeeming roughness of execution and purity of concept—were doomed.[12]

■ ■ ■

A national force, Theodore Thomas towered over every Boston musician.

Born in Germany in 1835, he arrived in New York a decade later. By the age of fourteen he was touring the South as Master Theodore Thomas, the prodigy violinist; he traveled on horseback and packed a pistol. He first led an orchestra of his own in 1862; he was his own business manager and fund-raiser. Beginning in 1864, his concerts were a regular, often nightly, New York attraction. Busy though it was, the Thomas Orchestra could not offer steady employment unless it toured, and so it did. Thomas's core itinerary of twenty-eight cities in twelve states became known as the "Thomas Highway." Performing in sundry auditoriums, railroad stations, and churches, Thomas offered overtures and dances as an enticement for symphonic masterworks, doled out one movement at a time. One specialty was his arrangement of Schumann's *Träumerei.* "Only the strings were used without the basses," an eloquent witness later recalled:

At the end, the beautiful melody grew softer and softer, slowly fading until it seemed to be drifting in the air, first into Shelley's shadow of all sounds, then the daintiest gossamer and filament of elusive and fairy music. . . . Then it grew fainter, and still slowly fainter. . . . With all inten-sion, rapt, leaning forward, the listeners were following it. Of a sudden they awoke to the fact that Mr. Thomas had laid down his baton and there was no sound. For the last minute there had been none. The vio-linists had continued to move their bows without touching the strings, but so strong was the spell, these thralls had believed they still heard that marvelous elfin melody. A strange gasping noise arose as two thousand people suddenly recovered their breath and consciousness, and then looked at one another to see if all this were real.[13]

Even in New York, Thomas's outdoor concerts tolerated such "little extrav-agances" as piccolo players in the trees (for the *Linnet Polka*) and a tuba in the shrubbery (for the *Carnival of Venice*). The showman in Theodore Thomas owed something to the examples of Jullien and Gilmore. Thomas had been one of Jullien's first violins. And, like Gilmore, he capitalized on a Victorian choral tradition stressing the grandeur of sheer numbers. But Thomas, who in later life recalled Jullien as "a musical charlatan,"[14] was a different species of musician. It is enough to know that the high point of his 1882 New York May Festival was a performance of the Immolation Scene from Wagner's *Götter-dämmerung* with the stellar Wagnerian soprano Amalie Materna, or that for his

New York Wagner festival of 1884 audiences were offered lengthy program notes, libretto translations, and a Wagner handbook prepared by Wagner's first American biographer: Henry Finck.

Essentially, these were lessons in the proselytizing of German music and its ennobling spiritual properties. Beethoven and Wagner were the "pillars" of Thomas's programs—the first because he represented "the highest pinnacle in instrumental music," the second because "he represents the modern spirit" and was the master of musical climax. In language as purposeful and severely unadorned as Thomas the man and musician, he wrote, "The man who does not know Shakespeare is to be pitied; and the man who does not understand Beethoven and has not been under his spell has not half lived his life. The master works of instrumental music are the language of the soul and express more than those of any other art."

Thomas himself came to Shakespeare—and to Goethe and Schiller—incidentally, through his youthful stints as a theater musician. His self-reliance, self-education, and self-definition were American traits; he treasured high culture as one who had not acquired it by birthright or pedigree, who expected others similarly unprivileged to acquire it with similar gratitude and alacrity. "Throughout my life," he wrote in 1874, "my aim has been to make good music popular, and it now appears that I have only done the public justice in believing, and acting constantly on the belief, that the people would enjoy and support the best in art when continually set before them in a clear and intelligent manner."[15]

So it was at New York's Central Park Garden where, beginning in 1868 with programs of light music, 1,127 outdoor Theodore Thomas concerts rapidly evolved into a showcase for symphonies by Beethoven, Schubert, Mendelssohn, and Schumann. And Thomas's orchestra was a model of Germanic discipline and polish. It amazed such visiting Europeans as Anton Rubinstein, who declared, "When he accompanies me with his orchestra, it is as though he could divine my thoughts, and then as though his orchestra could divine his. . . . I know of but one orchestra that can compare with that of Theodore Thomas, and that is the orchestra of the national conservatory of Paris." The Wagner soprano Lilli Lehmann reported of Thomas's orchestra that she had never before encountered such unified bowings, smooth blends, and perfect intonation: he was, she summarized, "a man, take him all in all, to whom I would like to erect a monument, for he was a sound kernel in a rough shell, and music, that is his ideal art, was as exalted to him as mine is to me."[16]

Big-boned, formal, flawlessly erect, he was, testified the critic George Upton, "born to command." With few exceptions, he addressed even close friends as "Mr." To stress a point, he would pound tables with his fist. Once, in rehearsal, he threatened to "thrash" a negligent musician; according to the critic Richard Aldrich, "He could take up almost any of his subordinates and lay him upon the table without apparent effort." In later life, he refused an invitation to conduct at the 1900 Paris Exposition—with or without his Chicago Orchestra—because the Dreyfus affair offended his democratic convictions. The following year, a telegram informing him of the death of his oldest son did not prevent him from mounting the podium; he even elected to miss the funeral in New York because, as he later explained, "I have no right to make the public mourn with me. . . . My duty is to stay here." Equally revealing is the story of his wig: when in Chicago he acquired a bald spot at the back of his head and blamed it for aggravating his catarrh; he had a toupee made with a matching bald spot and gravely displayed it to his orchestra saying, "Now, gentlemen, have your laugh and get it over with."[17]

In sum, Thomas was a supreme Gilded Age icon. His meliorist fervor appealed to Dwight and other genteel moralists. To others less genteel, his pronounced masculinity usefully counteracted Gilded Age stereotypes of effete high art. A pioneer type, Thomas was sturdy, pragmatic, dominating, self-made. The embodiment of Theodore Roosevelt's "strenuous life," he hardened his body with icy baths and morning gymnastics. A musical captain of industry, he was a forceful and self-possessed administrator who fiercely resisted would-be rivals; his enemies called him "brutal." Upton testified that he was "not given to the emotional or sentimental," and "disapproved of the eccentricities of dress and manner affected by some musicians." The *Chicago Evening Post* observed that the "high condition of discipline of [his orchestra] is the result not only of Thomas' organizing faculty, but of his own strict subordination of the artistic element in his temperament to the practical. . . . [When he conducts] you will find it difficult to detect the least outward symptom of an inward change even in the most sharply contrasted music."

Thomas the cultural frontiersman and patriarchal *Kultur*-bearer was twice the democrat John Sullivan Dwight was at his Boston desk. But he spoke with Dwight's voice when he called "master works" a "character-building force" and "uplifting influence," termed his concerts "sermons in tones," and condemned popular music as "having more or less the devil in it." He was a moral scourge. Beginning in the closing decades of the nineteenth century, communities across the United States aquired fully professional concert orchestras of their own—a proliferation distinct from the pit orchestras of Europe.[18] Thomas's credo, that "a symphony orchestra shows the culture of a community, not opera," was both visionary and pragmatic.

■ ■ ■

Thomas's influence differed according to venue. His hinterlands impact was that of an unpredicted epiphany: the orchestra itself was all. In New York in the sixties, seventies, and eighties, Thomas was caught up in the cult of Wagner. His debut program as a symphonic conductor, in 1862, included the American premiere of *The Flying Dutchman* Overture; in subsequent New York seasons he gave the first American performances of the *Tristan* Prelude and Liebestod, the *Meistersinger* Overture, and Wotan's Farewell.

Boston was not immune to New York's opera madness or to its Wagner movement. Max Maretzek, Maurice Strakosch, and Colonel James Henry Mapleson, all leading impresarios, brought French and Italian vocal luminaries to Boston in such repertoire staples as *Don Giovanni, La sonnambula, I puritani*, and *Faust*. There was a smattering of German opera beginning in 1864. Wagner was first staged in Boston in 1877, after which it was mainly imported from New York via the Metropolitan Opera or the company of Walter Damrosch. Locally, Benjamin Lang, who studied with Liszt, was a fervent Wagnerite. But Puritan traditions slowed the acceptance of opera in New England (and also of specific operas; *Rigoletto*, whose licentious Duke goes unpunished, was at one time banned). The two reigning institutions of performance, the Handel and Haydn Society and the Harvard Musical Association, were conservative bastions.

Thomas's Boston significance, therefore, transcended "humiliating lessons in performance." As a precocious chamber musician in the 1850s, he insisted on playing the late Beethoven quartets; as a conductor, he endorsed "prompt acquaintance with the latest works of the schools that produce it [*sic*]."[19] He eagerly championed Berlioz, Raff, Rubinstein, Dvořák, Elgar, Richard Strauss. Dwight sought stylistic unity in individual concert programs. In Thomas, the conductor, catholic program-maker, and educator were a unity.

Further acquaintance with the concerts of the Harvard Musical Association dramatizes Thomas's contribution. His first Boston concerts, with their dosage of Wagner, Liszt, and Johann Strauss Jr., played opposite this Harvard Musical Association program of November 4, 1869:

> Mozart: *The Marriage of Figaro* Overture and aria
> Spohr: *The Consecration of Tones*
> Beethoven: Overture, Op. 115 [*Namensfeier*]
> Handel: Selected arias
> Cherubini: *Anacreon* Overture

The association's programming philosophy, summarized by Dwight, was to be "above all need of catering to low tastes," to promote "only composers of unquestioned excellence, and . . . nothing vulgar, coarse, 'sensational,' but only such as outlives fashion." By Dwight's own reckoning, the association permitted itself a "judicious" selection of "modern works," including Berlioz's *Symphonie fantastique*, the first two Brahms symphonies, Wagner's *Siegfried Idyll*, Grieg's Piano Concerto, and Saint-Saëns's *Phaeton*, Symphony No. 2, and Second and Fourth Piano Concertos. Recalling meetings of the Harvard Musical Association program committee dominated by Dwight and Otto Dresel, the composer Arthur Foote wrote, "Two or three of us used to fight like cats to get a performance of, say, a new symphony by Raff or Rubinstein." Apthorp, looking back in 1898, summarized that the Harvard Musical Association concerts had begun "flourishingly," with crowded houses, but that in the 1870s attendance fell and "little by little the stigmata of unpopularity began to show themselves." Resisting "the party of progress," Dwight would not yield. "No committee-man could, in the end, make headway against his triumphant 'system of inertia;' the spirit of the concerts remained conservative to the end." When Johann Strauss Jr. visited Boston for Gilmore's 1872 Jubilee, he proceeded to New York, where the *New York Sun* asked him, "How do you like Boston?" His reply (translated from the German) read, "I did not like it. Boston is Puritanical, stupid, dull. There is no life in the street. There is no display of elegance or luxury. The women are homely, and do not dress nicely. I do not like Boston. But with New York I am perfectly charmed." (He added, "There is one thing that is very poor here, the beer. Oh! In that respect this country is very deficient, very.")[20]

Dwight's Journal of Music ceased publication on September 3, 1881. The Boston Symphony was born in the same year. The orchestra of the Harvard Musical Association folded in 1882.

■ ■ ■

By the time of his death in 1893, John Sullivan Dwight was a marginalized participant in the cultural community he once guided. His subtlest eulogist was William Apthorp, whose obituary may be the most nuanced assessment of Dwight ever penned. Its first paragraphs must be digested in full:

> The remarkable man who has just passed away was one of the most unique figures Boston has ever claimed as her own. Men of naturally fine and sensitive artistic nature, yet without productive promptings, are not very uncommon; neither is it very seldom that we find a man of this

sort who has been content to develop his aesthetic bent in a wholly general way, without giving much heed to the minutiae of special, quasi-technical cultivation in any particular direction. But it is exceedingly seldom that one finds such a man pass a long life in intimate, almost daily, communion with literature and the fine arts, and preserve intact all the native spontaneity and naivete of his feelings, so that he remains quite free from any taint of self-conscious dilettantism, and wholly uninfluenced by merely artificial standards.

What most made Dwight remarkable was his inveterate instinct for culture—as distinguished from mere learning. Perhaps it may have been in a large measure a certain unconquerable mental indolence that prompted him always to take the royal road in everything, to skip lightly over the dry rudiments of every study,—or what to men otherwise disposed would have been study,—and absorb immediately what he could of its final essence. Mentally indolent he certainly was to a high degree; he abominated work; the necessity for work seemed to him, upon the whole, a sad mistake in the scheme of the universe. And, though he did a good deal of it, first and last, in the course of his life, it was never otherwise than irksome to him; he worked, as it were, under protest. Yet, making all due allowance for this mental indolence of his, one must recognize also that his inveterate longing for complete intellectual digestion and assimilation led him, as by an inborn instinct, to bring his mind to bear only upon what was really digestible and assimilable by it. He felt that mere knowledge, or half-knowledge, was of no genuine use to a man, that only that knowledge which has become so thoroughly part and parcel of the man's own self as to be convertible into feeling and instinct is really valuable. So he threw upon his mental receptivity only in the directions whence intellectual or artistic experiences would come of themselves to meet it, and leave their indelible trace on the retina of his mind of their own accord and without effort on his part. What he got in this way he did completely and thoroughly digest; it was absorbed into his very being and became a functional part of himself.

None but the most absolutely genuine, true, and indestructible artistic nature could have gone through life on such a plan without inevitable ruin; but Dwight got no harm from it, the pure gold of his aesthetic sense was only the more refined by the ordeal. His naivete of perception, his ever youthful enthusiasm, his ineradicable power of enjoyment, held out unimpaired to the end. What he was, he was genuinely and thoroughly; fashion had no hold on him, and his refinement never had a touch of dandyism nor finical affectation.

Dwight, Apthorp wrote, possessed scant technical knowledge of music. He could work his way through a piano score, but never attempted to become any kind of pianist. He even found it difficult to follow an orchestral score, especially at a rapid tempo. But his musical instincts "were, in a certain high respect, of the finest." He felt and cherished what was pure, noble, and beautiful, and abhorred the merely grandiose. "He was an optimist, through and through, and wished all art to be as optimistic as himself."

Apthorp remembered Dwight the man as "the most genial of companions" whose "sunny nature and unspoilable power of enjoyment were contagious." A characteristic anecdote: when the building in which he lived at Brook Farm burned to the ground, Dwight ran up a neighboring hill "and was lost in ecstasy at the beauty of the flames against the dark sky." Equally generous is Apthorp's assessment of Dwight's *Journal* as "the highest-toned musical periodical of its day, all the world over." He called Dwight's prose style "at once brilliant, solid, and impeccable"—a judgment difficult to support today. (Apthorp himself was far the better writer and shrewder, more professional critic.) And he sympathetically understood Dwight's "utter disdain for music of the modern schools": all the "high-strung nervous energy, restless striving, and lack of serenity and repose, the way their music reflects the characteristic strenuousness and turmoil of modern life, were totally antipathetic to his nature."[21]

But Dwight's resistance to new music was also a function of his dilettantism, which rendered him susceptible to Dresel's dinosaur opinions and to the last bad performance of Wagner or Liszt he happened to encounter. He loathed Wagner before he had heard a note. He could not assess music in score. In this regard, a fairer assessment of Dwight than Apthorp's is that of Thomas Ryan of the Mendelssohn Quintette Club, whose memoirs are as level as Dwight is tendentious. Dwight, Ryan wrote in 1899, was "very conservative . . . one can honestly say he was more than that,—he was prejudiced" (and this from a musician who idolized Mendelssohn).[22]

A stranger to the modern world, Dwight was nonetheless a timely presence; his sacralization project rhymed with impulses and needs larger than his own. Even Patrick Gilmore's monstrous jubilees emphasized the piety of musical enrichment. In subsequent decades the movement toward "purified" concerts—a pretentious anachronism half a century later—was actually progressive. Rowdy and distracted Gilded Age audiences, accustomed to "mixed" entertainments only, needed to be educated and disciplined if the symphonic canon were to take hold. Programs mixing Beethoven symphonies with Lanner waltzes outlived their purpose, as four decades of Theodore Thomas programs confirmed. In this regard, the spontaneity, intensity of purpose, and sincere enthusiasm Apthorp admired in Dwight served him well. With an effort of empathy, we can still read Dwight—especially the early Dwight— and comprehend the passionate sense that later hardened into dogma. If his 1870 call, in the *Atlantic Monthly*, to "cultivate the instinct of reverence" rings hollow today, five years after the Civil War the impulse to urge Americans toward higher forms of music was magnanimous and intelligible.

> We need some ever-present, ever-welcome influence that shall insensi-bly tone down our self-asserting and aggressive manners, round off the sharp, offensive angularity of character, subdue and harmonize the free and ceaseless conflict of opinions, warm out the genial individual humanity of each and every unit of society. . . . The governments of the Old World do much to make the people cheerful and contented; here it is all *laissez-faire*, each for himself, in an ever keener strife of competi-tion. We must look very much to music to do this good work for us.

And more than rhetoric or dogma fortifies this personal reflection on the music lover's condition: "somehow the minutest fibres, the infinitesimal atoms of his being, have got magnetized as it were into a loyal, positive direction towards the pole-star of unity."[23]

But Dwight is small set beside Theodore Thomas. Even in his prose—in his fewer, better-chosen words—Thomas conveys a broader vision, and a more practical understanding, of cultural uplift. Dwight's tirades against Stephen Fos-ter convey the complexity of threatened authority. Thomas wrote simply, "I have never wished to pose as an educator or a philanthropist, except in so far as I might help the public to get beyond certain so-called 'popular music'— which represents nothing more than sweet sentimentalism and rhythm, on the level of the dime novel." Dwight campaigned against encores with righteous superiority. Thomas explained, "The effect of repetition is never so good as that of the first performance. In the case of master works it creates an anti-climax." Dwight expostulated endlessly, sometimes in the course of a single sentence, on the sublimity of abstract music. Thomas observed:

> To listen to music is restful to the human being, because faculties are called into action and appealed to other than those he ordinarily uses, and also because it absorbs all his attention and frees him from his worldly cares. Instrumental music is especially restful, because it appeals to his imagination and intellect, and permits his own interpretation to the extent of his experience, whereas in vocal music the interpretation is bound by the text.

Dwight's vices—his principled inflexibility of sentiment and opinion—here become virtues: Thomas dignified mores drawn small by Dwight. Van Wyck Brooks, in a famous 1915 formulation, remarked that only the American mind fused "saintliness" and "shrewdness" so that each became "the sanction of the other." Lofty and shrewd in equal measure, Thomas magnified the times.[24]

John Sullivan Dwight and Theodore Thomas were twin lodestars of classical music in the United States: its founding fathers—the first parochial and holding back, the second pressing forward with energies enormous and resilient. Both legacies endured.

CHAPTER 2

Henry Higginson
and the Birth of the
Boston Symphony Orchestra

■

George Henschel's enthusiasm ▪ *Wilhelm Gericke's discipline* ▪
Arthur Nikisch's scandalous Beethoven ▪ *Philip Hale and Henry
Krehbiel assess Dvořák in Boston*

THE BOSTON SYMPHONY ORCHESTRA
IN THE INTEREST OF GOOD MUSIC

Notwithstanding the development of musical taste in Boston, we have never yet possessed a full and permanent orchestra, offering the best music at low prices, such as may be found in all the large European cities, or even in the smaller musical centers of Germany. The essential condition of such orchestras is their stability, whereas ours are necessarily shifting and uncertain, because we are dependent upon musicians whose work and time are largely pledged elsewhere.

To obviate this difficulty the following plan is offered. It is an effort made simply in the interest of good music, and though individual inasmuch as it is independent of societies or clubs, it is in no way antagonistic to any previously existing musical organization. Indeed, the first step as well as the natural impulse in announcing a new musical project, is to thank those who have brought us where we now stand. Whatever may be done in the future, to the Handel and Haydn Society and to the Harvard Musical Association, we all owe the greater part of our home education in music of a high character. Can we forget either how admirably their work has been supplemented by the taste and critical judgment of Mr. John S. Dwight, or by the artists who have identified themselves with the same cause in Boston? These have been our teachers. We build on foundations they have laid. Such details of this scheme as concern the public are stated below.

The orchestra is to number sixty selected musicians; their time, so far as required for careful training and for a given number of concerts, to be engaged in advance.

Mr. Georg Henschel will be the conductor for the coming season.

The concerts will be twenty in number, given in the Music hall on Saturday evenings, from the middle of October to the middle of March.

The price of season tickets, with reserved seats, for the whole series of evening concerts will be either $10 or $5, according to position.

Single tickets, with reserved seats, will be seventy-five cents or twenty-five cents, according to position.

Besides the concerts, there will be a public rehearsal on one after-noon of every week, with single tickets at twenty-five cents, and no reserved seats.

The intention is that this orchestra shall be made permanent here, and shall be called "The Boston Symphony Orchestra."

Both as the condition and result of success the sympathy of the public is asked.

H. L. HIGGINSON

Henry Lee Higginson was a partner in a leading Boston brokerage house and a member of a Boston family connected to the Lees, Cabots, Lowells, Channings, Putnams, Storrows, and other Brahmin clans. As "Major" Higgin-son, he was a veteran of the Civil War, though the saber scar on his right cheek was acquired in a private scuffle over a horse. He had also studied music in his youth—in Vienna, where he acquired the dream of creating a world-class Boston symphony.

Higginson's notice "In the Interest of Good Music," appearing in the Boston press on March 30, 1881, was a characteristically crisp utterance whose boldness, also characteristic, was belied by its simplicity. In fact, no such orchestra as the envisioned Boston Symphony could be heard "in all the large European cities." Europe's were predominantly opera and theater orchestras whose musicians assembled for an occasional concert, not "symphony orches-tras" after the Theodore Thomas model Americans would embrace. And nowhere, at any time, was there an orchestra so single-handedly shaped and supported as Higginson's would be. He intended to make good all deficits as well as to pay all salaries, including that of the conductor, whom he would choose. The conductor, in turn, would exercise artistic control. And yet Higginson was not shy about expressing his own artistic predilections; as he put it in an earlier, more detailed announcement: "I do not like Wagner's music, and take little interest in much of the newer composers, but I should not like to bar them out of our programmes." The same announcement foresaw swift growth in the number of concerts given by the new orchestra—in the summer months, at Harvard University's Sanders Theater, in neighboring towns and cities "as far as is practicable."[1]

Higginson's choice of Georg Henschel (who soon Anglicized his first name to "George") sent a message. Henschel was young, only thirty-one. And he was an outsider to Boston's compact musical community. Born in Germany, celebrated in England, he was not even a conductor, but a composer and concert singer who conducted on the side. Higginson heard him lead a single work, an overture of his own, for the Harvard Musical Association on March 3 and proceeded to hire him ahead of Carl Zerrahn and other local luminaries. Higginson was a worldly man, intimate with Europe. He was intent on curing parochial habits at home.

The Boston reaction was a mixture of gratitude, stupefaction, and trepidation. Orchestral players who banded together as the Harvard Musical Association or the Boston Philharmonic Society would now undertake a third, somewhat larger configuration, but featuring significantly more concerts, more rehearsal time, cheaper tickets, and bigger subsidies. Dwight called Higginson's plan a "coup d'etat, with no pretense of any plebiscite." He also wrote that it "places the best of music within frequent and easy reach of all who love it and cannot afford to pay the prices usual heretofore." He wished the Boston Symphony "God-speed and a long continuance," yet acknowledged that "Mr. Higginson's decided movement . . . may take the wind out of the sails" of existing efforts.[2]

Tickets for the first Boston Symphony season went on sale in early September. At 6 A.M. seventy-five people were already in line at the box office; some had been there since the night before. William Apthorp wrote in the *Boston Transcript*, "Some people, aghast at the rush for tickets, ask, in astonishment, where all this audience comes from." Apthorp speculated that the low prices were a factor, and so was Henschel: "With all his rare talents, with all his inexperience, he occupies the position of musical dictator. . . . The choice of players and the choice of programs both lie in his hands. . . . Never has a man in this city submitted to so exhaustive a test."[3]

The inaugural concert took place on October 22. This was in the twenty-five-hundred-seat Music Hall, then Boston's chief concert house, a plain rectangular space distinguished by its impressive organ and gigantic bronze bust of Beethoven enthroned, both of which adorned the back of the stage. Dwight would have approved the program had his *Journal* still existed; it read:

> Beethoven: *Consecration of the House* Overture
> Gluck: Aria from *Orpheus and Euridice* (with Annie
>   Louise Cary)
> Haydn: Symphony in B-flat
> Schubert: Ballet music from *Rosamunde*
> Bruch: Scena from *Odysseus* (Miss Cary)
> Weber: *Jubel* Overture

The audience filled every seat except some in the second balcony, and everybody who mattered was present. The orchestra, too, was full of familiar faces, but in odd places: Henschel had seated first violins, second violins, and violas in concentric circles around the podium; cellos and basses were split to either side; winds and brass were in back.

Henschel tapped his stand, waved his baton, and the processional chords of Beethoven's overture resounded, one writer reported, "with a crispness and unity of attack and an intensity and resonance of tone that were at once a performance and a promise."[4] Though the novel seating arrangement was found to disfavor the woodwinds, the orchestra had been smartly drilled. And Henschel emanated the vigor that had commended him to Higginson in the first place—as well as a nervous energy, reflecting inexperience, that overdrove his tempos and did violence to his gestures. The audience rose and sang along upon recognizing "God Save the Queen" (not yet well known as "My Country, 'Tis of Thee") in the Weber overture—signaling "a universal sentiment of respect to her Majesty and the mother country," according to the *Traveller*, but merely perplexing Louis Elson of the *Courier*: "An English audience would scarcely do as much for the Star-Spangled Banner, if one of our composers should introduce it into a symphony or opera."

At subsequent concerts, crowded houses remained the rule. The season closed with Beethoven's Ninth Symphony. At the Friday-afternoon public rehearsal, the demand for twenty-five-cent tickets far exceeded the supply. Henschel had to elbow his way into the hall and even up to the stage, onto which the audience overflowed. When season tickets went on sale for 1882–83, the long line was packed with ticket speculators. For 1883–84 Higginson adopted a different strategy, selling tickets for many choice locations by auction and offering subscriptions to the public rehearsals for the first time. Meanwhile, the season expanded: from twenty subscription concerts and the same number of public rehearsals, with an average attendance of

2,084, to twenty-six concerts and rehearsals with an average audience of 2,150 a season later.[5]

Henschel's repertoire was anchored by Beethoven; such "moderns" as Berlioz, Liszt, Wagner, and Dvořák were far less represented than by Theodore Thomas. Brahms, a personal friend of the conductor, was performed but resisted. Higginson advised leavening heavy programs with lighter fare, and this Henschel did. A typical Boston Symphony concert consisted of an overture, a concerto, and a symphony for the longer first part; and shorter, more "popular" numbers—a Lachner march, a Chopin scherzo for solo piano—after intermission. Henschel added risers for the woodwinds and brass, improving the balances within his novel seating plan. He shared these experiments via letter with Brahms, who wrote back that "by far the best feature in all your arrangements of the orchestra is the fact that no committee will be sitting in front of it. There is not a Kapellmeister on the whole of our continent who would not envy you that!" As for Henschel's conducting, it was admired for its warmth and energy, and deplored for "extravagant batonisms . . . hideous to the eye," absence of repose, and roughness of tone. That he conducted his own works, and played the piano, and featured both himself and his wife as vocal soloists, was resented by some, including the anonymous parodist who placed in the *Boston Home Journal* the following announcement:

EGGSCHEL MUSIC HALL.

EGGSCHEL CONCERTS.

Conductor . . . . Henor Eggschel.
November 31, 1881

PROGRAMME:
Overture, "Zum Andenken" . . . . Eggschel
Song, "Vergiss-mein-nicht" . . . . Eggschel
    Mr. Eggschel
Chorus, "And don't you forget it" . . . . Eggschel
    Eggschel Choral Society
Piano fantasia, "Souviens-toi" . . . . Eggschel
    Mr. Eggschel
Duet, "Non ti scordar di me" . . . . Eggschel
    Mr. and Mrs. Eggschel
Organ concerto, "Ne oblivis-caris" . . . . Eggschel
    Mr. Eggschel

Symphony . . . . Eggschel
Presto e non moderato. Andante Prestissimo. Scherzo, sempre
    accelerando. Fuga
("Then you'll remember me")

The Eggschel piano used at these concerts.
All of Mr. Eggschel's compositions on sale at Mr. Eggschel's music
    store.
Tickets on sale at Mr. Eggschel's office.
HENOR EGGSCHEL, Manager.[6]

  The orchestra itself was unanimously praised as the best drilled, most spirited Boston had ever claimed its own. For this Higginson deserved part of the credit. On February 25, 1882, he offered the men contracts for the season to come. Each letter began, "Dear Sir—I wish to engage you for the next season ... under the following conditions." Condition number two read, "Your services will be required on each week, between October 1 and April 1, on the following days: Wednesday morning, afternoon and evening; Thursday morning, afternoon and evening: Friday morning and afternoon; Saturday morning and evening." Condition number four read, "On the days specified you will neither play in any other orchestra nor under any other conductor than Mr. Henschel, except if wanted in your leisure hours by the Handel and Haydn Society, nor will you play for dancing." The letter closed, "I wish to offer my sincere thanks for your labor and zeal during the present season, and hope for your services in the next. In order to facilitate the needed arrangements, your answer is expected by March 2."[*] This private communication quickly made its way into the newspapers, which accused Higginson of making "a direct stab at the older organizations and rival conductors of Boston," of "cornering" and "monopolizing" the city's orchestral talent, of formulating "an idea that could scarcely have emanated from any association except that of deluded wealth with arrant charlatanism." "It is," opined the *Transcript*, "as if a man should make a poor friend a present of several baskets of champagne, and, at the same time, cut off his whole water supply."[7]

  The orchestra appointed one of its members to meet with Higginson, who later recalled:

* In later years, Boston Symphony contracts contained a clause reading, "If said musician fails to play to the satisfaction of said Higginson, said Higginson may dismiss said musician from the Orchestra, paying his salary to the time of dismissal, and shall not be liable to pay him any compensation or damages for such dismissal." See Bliss Perry, *The Life and Letters of Henry Lee Higginson* (Boston, Atlantic Monthly, 1921), p. 308.

The delegate was pleasant and clever and laughed at my statements that the concerts would go on and that it was only a question of who would play. Therefore, on the next public rehearsal day I went to the green-room of the Music Hall and asked the men to come in after the rehearsal, which they did. I then said to them: "I made a proposition to you which you have rejected. I withdraw my proposition. The concerts will go on as they have this year, and in this hall. If any of you have anything to say to me in the way of a proposition you will make it"— and that meeting was over. During the next few days almost every man came to me and asked to be engaged. The delegate from the Orchestra was not one of them.

Meanwhile, the furor in the press subsided. "Mr. Higginson has established a permanent orchestra," explained the *Advertiser*.

His plan is not for next year or a few years only. . . . To assert that this is because of a desire to autocratic control, and that Mr. Higginson is disposed to improve the occasion to gratify a fondness for arbitrary dictation, is a reckless charge so particularly wide of the truth that all who know Mr. Higginson must have read such intimations with almost as much amusement as indignation. . . .

No musician can do his best in the midst of a highly trained orchestra, who has played all the night before at a ball, or who plays every alternate night under a different leader and with different associates.[8]

Higginson had succeeded in impressing on everyone concerned that he meant business, and that his business was to create an institution of a new stamp. He responded to criticism with forbearance. His rejoinder to the press took the form of this announcement, published March 21, 1882:

When last spring the general scheme for the concerts of the Boston Symphony Orchestra was put forth, the grave doubt in my mind was whether they were wanted. This doubt has been dispelled by a most kindly and courteous public, and therefore the scheme will stand. The concerts and public rehearsals, with Mr. George Henschel as conductor, will go on under the same conditions in the main as to time, place, programmes and prices. Any changes will be duly made public when the tickets are advertised for sale.

HENRY LEE HIGGINSON[9]

In January 1882, the Boston Philharmonic Society offered its baton to Theodore Thomas,[10] but Thomas elected to relinquish Boston to Higginson: he would no longer tour New England. The Philharmonic Society folded. The Harvard Musical Association terminated its concerts. Henschel elected to resign after his third Boston season. Higginson, who understood that the orchestra was not all it could be, set off for Europe—partly for pleasure, partly with the intention of finding a more seasoned conductor. At his final concert, on March 22, 1884, Henschel gave the downbeat for Schumann's *Manfred* Overture only to see the entire orchestra rise and begin playing "Auld Lang Syne." At this, the audience stood and proceeded to sing along. He was too much moved to speak.

■ ■ ■

If Henry Higginson hired his first music director in a matter of weeks, he hired his second in a matter of days. Upon arriving in Vienna, he attended a performance of *Aida*. Observing the conductor, he whispered to his wife, "This is just the man to take Henschel's place." That was on October 20, 1883. The following day, he consulted his Viennese friend Julius Epstein, who told him that the leader in question, Wilhelm Gericke, had been on the staff of the Court Opera (today the State Opera) since 1874, that he also led the choral *Singverein*, and that he was as experienced and conscientious a musician as Higginson had already gleaned. Higginson asked if Gericke might take over in Boston. Epstein replied that this was unthinkable, but arranged a meeting on October 21. As it happened, Gericke was feuding over repertoire with Wilhelm Jahn, the director of the opera. He accepted Higginson's offer. A five-year contract was drawn up on October 22. He would become the Boston Symphony's music director as of the fall of 1884 at an annual salary of $7,500.

Gericke was interviewed by American reporters in Vienna and again in Boston in October. They wrote that he was born in Styria (southwest of Vienna) and was thirty-nine years old. He was a bachelor, short and stocky, with a dark beard and handlebar mustache, both neatly trimmed. He was a vivacious conversationalist. He looked more like a shoe dealer or bank cashier than a musician.

The articles[11] also disclosed how little Gericke knew about Boston and America. He expressed concern that his primitive English would hamper him in rehearsal, and was assured that all the members of the orchestra spoke German. He opined that the Boston Symphony gave too many concerts (more, by far, than any Vienna orchestra) and that the orchestra was too small for so vast a space as the Music Hall, with its twenty-six-hundred seats. Upon being shown the programs of the Harvard Musical Association, he remarked, "I am completely dumbfounded. I do not see what is left for me to do here. You seem to have heard everything already; more, much more, than we ever heard in Vienna!"[12]

The program for Gericke's first Boston concert, on October 18, 1884, nevertheless featured a premiere: the Symphony in D minor by Robert Volkmann. This came last. The opening number was Beethoven's *Leonore* Overture No. 3, followed by a violin concerto by Vieuxtemps. The Volkmann was preceded, in the second half, by a string transcription of a Bach "Prelude, Andante and Gavotte."

Gericke reseated the orchestra's strings according to standard contemporary practice: first violins to the left, seconds to the right, violas and cellos toward the center, double basses at the rear. The Music Hall organ had been removed, creating a more resonant acoustic. These changes were noted in the press. But most of the attention was of course focused on Gericke himself. "His manner at the conductor's desk is admirably dignified, self-contained, free from all over-dramatic demonstrativeness, yet sufficiently animated to indicate the enthusiasm with which he burns," wrote Apthorp in the *Evening Transcript*. "His bearing is quiet, unassuming and refined, and his conducting is firm and decisive, and shows in every essential a thorough knowledge of his art. It is without a trace of affectation, and is free from all that can be construed into a desire for display," reported the *Gazette*. The subtext was that Higginson had found a conductor who remedied Henschel's defects, an embodiment of personal and aesthetic composure after the fashion of Theodore Thomas.[13]

But Gericke was less satisfied with Boston than Boston was with Gericke. To Higginson, he confided that the orchestra was no orchestra. He then went to work. Both Higginson and Henschel had favored hiring local musicians in order to minimize hurt feelings. Gericke, for his second Boston season, imported from Vienna a new, twenty-year-old concertmaster, Franz Kneisel, and numerous other new members to replace "old" and "overworked" musicians "no longer fit for the demands of modern and more difficult orchestral playing." He subdued the brass in order to perfect the balance and tone of the ensemble. He insisted on rehearsal conditions never imposed by Henschel or Carl Zerrahn. He disciplined musicians who took the stage intoxicated, in some cases repeatedly. He later wrote:

Before I came to Boston, the members of the orchestra had been used to a great deal of freedom; for instance, members living out of town were allowed to leave the rehearsal at twelve in order to be home for lunch;

or, to reach a train for another out-of-town engagement of their own—
whether the rehearsal was finished or not. It was not easy to make them
understand that their engagement for the Boston Symphony Concerts
had to be considered first and foremost, and that the rehearsal had to be
finished before everything else. It took Mr. Higginson's whole energy to
make them understand that they had to consider me in this way and
rehearse and play as satisfactorily as I thought it necessary.

The dismissed musicians, their families, and their advocates, Gericke recalled,
"were like millstones around my neck." The violinist Sam Franko quit of his
own accord to become Theodore Thomas's concertmaster: he found the
Boston rehearsals "insufferably dull," the performances "full of subtle nuances,
finely balanced," but without "spirit and life." The press reported "more discord than harmony in the relations of the musicians with the director." There
were predictions that the orchestra would not survive. In fact, Gericke
attempted to resign. Higginson would not let him.[14]

Meanwhile, programming was purified. Gericke's inaugural concert
already propagated a new template, contradicting Henschel's practice of ending with popular waltzes, marches, and overtures. Gericke told the *Transcript*,
"In the first part of a programme, near the overture, or other work of short or
medium length, a light work is sometimes fitting; but after a great masterpiece, very, very seldom. I shall end the programme with the symphony, generally. The public are more elevated if they carry home the impression of a
great masterwork, than if a musical trifle follows it." His repertoire, stressing
Beethoven, was less adventurous than Thomas's in New York, less conservative
than had been Dwight's and the Harvard Musical Association's. Notwithstanding his long experience with Wagner in the opera house, he (unlike
Thomas) disliked presenting Wagner chunks in concert. The subscribers
balked at his efforts on behalf of Brahms (whose Third Symphony was
demonstrably unpopular), Bruckner (whose Seventh, according to Gericke,
was at its close played to an audience smaller than the orchestra onstage), and
Richard Strauss (whose *Aus Italien* was deserted "by platoons," according to
Elson in the *Courier*). He was the first local conductor to sometimes dispense
with a soloist.[15]

As he had disciplined his orchestra, Gericke disciplined his audience, and
not merely by insisting on more "serious" programs. Latecomers were not
admitted except during pauses. Encores were discouraged. Elson, for one,
remarked favorably on the increased spontaneity of Music Hall audiences
during Gericke's regime as a further measure of maturity.

Boston auditors are beginning to recognize a good performance when they hear it. . . . How different it used to be in Boston! I can remember concerts in the city where the critic felt very lonely, where musical autocrats fell asleep, and where the small audience was so cold that the conductor's teeth chattered and the Orchestra had to put on ulsters. Of course in those pre-Higginson days applause was unknown, and if once an enthusiastic youth *did* clap his hands, it was discovered that he came from New York, and he was requested by a committee . . . to discontinue such indecorous proceedings. *Nous avons changé tout cela.* We are getting as excitable as a La Scala audience, and when we once establish the good old custom of hissing bad work we shall be all right.

And Gericke himself called his Boston listeners "one of the most cultivated and best understanding musical publics I know."[16]

In Vienna, Higginson had acquired a taste for the waltzes of Johann Strauss Jr. His original Boston Symphony blueprint included the following:

I do not know whether a first-rate orchestra will choose to play light music, or whether it can do so well. I do not believe that the great opera orchestra in Vienna can play waltzes as Strauss's men play them, although they know them by heart and feel them all through their toes and fingers—simply because they are not used to such work—and I know also that such work is in a degree stultifying. My judgment would be that a good orchestra would need, during the winter season, to keep its hand in by playing only the better music, and could relax in summer, playing a different kind of thing. But I should always wish to eschew vulgar music, i.e., such trash as is heard in the theatres, sentimental or sensational nonsense; and so on the other side I should wish to lighten the heavier programmes by good music, of a gayer nature. . . . For instance, in operas the best old French musicians gave us gems—like Mehul, Boieldieu, Auber, Gretry, etc.—and their overtures are delightful.[17]

Henschel had adopted the formula of "lightening heavier programmes"; Gericke had not. But Gericke supported the notion of a summer season modeled after the garden concerts of Germany and Austria. As it happened, the initial summer "Promenade" season materialized in 1885, near the beginning of Gericke's tenure. The conductor was Adolf Neuendorff, a New York fixture more admired for energy than finesse. Neuendorff's first program was representative:

Gounod: March from *La Reine de Saba*
Auber: Overture to *La Muette de Portici*
Waldteufel: *Amour et Printemps* Waltz
Chassaigne: Selections from *Falka*
Wagner: Prelude to Act III of *Lohengrin*
Rossini: Overture to *William Tell*
Mascagni: Intermezzo from *Cavalleria rusticana*
Bizet: *L'Arlésienne* Suite No. 2
Suppé: *Light Cavalry* Overture
Zeller: *Grubenlichter* Waltz
Sudessi: *La coquette*★

For the Promenade concerts the Music Hall's downstairs seats were removed and replaced with tables and shrubs. Light alcoholic beverages were served (a breach of public morals requiring a special annual permit). On opening night Boston's highest social circles turned out in force and there were not enough tables and waiters to meet the demand. The *Boston Globe*, in a front-page review, called the event "more than a 'sea-change' " in concert fare. The *Transcript* reported, "The assembly was as orderly as it should have been, and those who wished to concentrate on the music evidently found that they could hear all they wanted, judging from the frequent applause and calls for repetitions."[18]

If Promenade concerts enabled the men of the orchestra to perform together more often, they did not add to the number of performances of substantial symphonic fare. To this end, the Boston Symphony began to tour ambitiously under its music director, beginning with postseason visits undertaken by Gericke in 1886. At Gericke's urging, the orchestra toured the Midwest extensively in 1887. The following season, Gericke felt ready to venture to New York. The acclaim that everywhere greeted the orchestra validated Gericke's insistence on drill and discipline. He himself recalled, "There is no doubt that this first success in New York affected greatly the Boston audience; from that moment, the Boston Symphony Orchestra began to stand on solid ground. The members of the orchestra began to feel that they belonged to an artistic corporation of the first rank—and in the same measure as the success increased, they took more pride and satisfaction in their work."[19]

Their letters and memoirs document how tenaciously Higginson and Ger-

---

★ According to the small print, "The Programmes for these Concerts will be made up largely of light music of the best class, and will be of the same character as those given at the famous 'Bilse Concerts' in Berlin." In fact, Neuendorff's programs were somewhat less ambitious, musically, than Thomas's Central Park Gardens programs in New York.

icke supported one another. Higginson was losing at least twenty thousand dollars annually on the orchestra and sometimes feared he would have to give it up. And the tours represented a considerable additional expense. "I am sure had the creator of the Boston Symphony Orchestra been another man than Henry L. Higginson," Gericke wrote, "the orchestra would not have reached the age of ten years." Higginson wrote of Gericke, "He has done all that he could do. . . . He never spares himself one moment." At the same time, Gericke in Vienna could not possibly have envisioned the arduous commitment that awaited him in Boston. After five years he discovered himself "thoroughly overworked" and resigned. (Higginson, accustomed to overwork, once observed that Gericke, for all his diligence, lacked the heroic capacity of Theodore Thomas.) At Gericke's farewell concert, on May 23, 1889, the audience rose and shouted, waving hats and handkerchiefs. Gericke managed a little speech in broken English and departed for Europe. The orchestra now numbered seventy-nine men. Its season had grown to seventy-five concerts, plus a summer schedule.[20]

To an astonishing degree, the Boston Symphony thus established by Wilhelm Gericke—a name today unremembered, even in Boston—set the mold for the future, and not only in Boston. The frequency of the concerts; the rituals of applause and respect observed by the audience; the functions of the music director (though not yet reduced by the introduction of "guest conductors"); the length, shape, and core repertoire of the programs (though still sometimes incorporating vocal or keyboard solos)—in all these features, the Boston Symphony of 1889 resembled America's orchestras of fifty or a hundred years later, a resemblance suggesting both resilience and stagnation in the century to come.

■ ■ ■

Richard Wagner's pamphlet "On Conducting," published in 1869, is a landmark in the evolution of the orchestral conductor we know today. Rejecting "time-beating" and mere "elegance" (of which he accused Mendelssohn), Wagner called for conductors of charismatic authority, of new "energy, self-confidence, and personal power," whose signatures of personal prerogative included expressive tempo modifications aligned with modifications of tone, articulation, and phrasing. Addressing the fermata (or hold) at the tail of the four-note motto beginning Beethoven's Fifth Symphony, he wrote:

Our conductors hardly make use of this fermata for anything. . . . Now, suppose the voice of Beethoven were heard from the grave admonishing a conductor: "Hold my fermata firmly, terribly! I did not write fermatas in jest, or because I was at a loss how to proceed; I indulge in the fullest, the most sustained tone to express emotions . . . and I use this full and firm tone when I want it in a passionate Allegro as a rapturous or terrible spasm. Then the very life blood of the tone shall be extracted to the last drop. I arrest the waves of the sea, and the depths shall be visible; or, I stem the clouds, disperse the mist, and show the pure blue ether and the glorious eye of the sun. For this I put fermatas, sudden long-sustained notes in my Allegro."

Of the finale of Beethoven's Seventh he wrote that it was "impossible to take [such] movements too quickly." Of the slow movement of Beethoven's Ninth he wrote, "I am, perhaps, the only conductor who has ventured to take the Adagio section . . . at the proper pace," meaning slowly enough that "the languor of feeling grows to ecstasy." In fact, the exemplar of the new conductor was, of course, Wagner himself. And Wagner's music dramas exemplified the new music that invited and even demanded a galvanizing podium mastermind.[21]

Wagner spawned a group of conductors who revolutionized orchestral performance. At least five—Hans von Bülow, Felix Mottl, Hans Richter, Hermann Levi, and Anton Seidl—may be regarded as direct progeny of Wagner himself. Of this group, Seidl presided in New York. A Romantic *artiste* with chiseled features and long glossy hair, he was, in the words of James Gibbons Huneker, "a baton incarnate"; he "riveted his men with a glance of steel."[22] Seidl arrived in New York in 1885 and never left. In Boston the new breed was introduced in the person of Wilhelm Gericke's successor, Germany's rising star, procured by Henry Higginson from the Leipzig Opera: thirty-three-year-old Arthur Nikisch.

Nikisch was hypnotic, a poised Svengali with fathomless eyes. "He does not really conduct," Tchaikovsky later testified. "He resigns himself to a magical enchantment." During the decades that Theodore Thomas played in New York theater bands and toured the hinterlands, Nikisch, also a violinist, performed under Wagner and Richter in Vienna. He was later Seidl's assistant in Leipzig. As a symphonic conductor, he imperturbably upset tradition. Rehearsing Schumann's Fourth Symphony in Leipzig, he dismantled the orchestra's accustomed reading. After the performance, a small white-haired lady approached him with tears in her eyes and said, "If only my husband had lived to enjoy this happiness, to hear his work played as he felt it and so often explained it to me!" The white-haired lady was Clara Schumann.[23]

In America, Nikisch's significance was instantly appreciated. W. J. Henderson of the *New York Times* traveled to Boston to attend his American debut, on October 11, 1889. Henderson's first impressions conform precisely with the great reputation Nikisch would later establish in Berlin:

> He is a man of short stature and slight figure. . . . His head is rounded well and covered with wavy dark hair, which lies in "admired disorder." His face is pale, and is adorned by a rich brown beard. His eyes are deep set, thoughtful, and expressive. His hands are marvelously white and graceful.
>
> His manner on the platform is self-contained and concentrated. . . . His use of the baton is unique in its simplicity and pictorial in its significance to the eye. . . . The man is full of magnetism. . . .
>
> Mr. Nikisch unquestionably possesses, in addition to his command as a disciplinarian, a rich and generous warmth of temperament. He has a sympathetic appreciation of the composer's feeling that reaches backward across the years and becomes instinct with a vitality that seems contemporaneous with the birth of the work in the composer's mind.
>
> This is the highest tribute that can be paid to a conductor. It is a quality which he shares with a master actor who reveals to us the soul of a dramatic poem. This is what Mr. Nikisch does for a composition. He finds its soul.

In New York, where Nikisch's Boston Symphony played every season, Henderson and his New York colleagues embraced Nikisch with enthusiasm—as they had already embraced Seidl. In Boston, Nikisch split opinion. His heat and spontaneity were favorably contrasted with Gericke's restraint. John Knowles Paine, the dean of Boston composers, told the press, "I find that Mr. Nikisch conducts with great freedom and fire and great expression, and with a fine conception of the works as well as with marked sympathy. Above all, he gives the orchestral instruments full freedom, especially the brass. They are not restrained, as with the previous conductor, but the orchestra can appear in its full glory." Nikisch's "rubato effects" and other liberties were, however, called "theatrical." And the military discipline Gericke had instilled began to slacken.[24]

Nikisch's rendition of Beethoven's Fifth, on November 8, ignited a firestorm of debate. Philip Hale, new to the *Home Journal*, was a Francophile who resisted Wagner. He wrote of Nikisch's Beethoven:

> Mr. Nikisch's performance of the symphony has brought out much adverse criticism; it certainly was remarkable, at times curious and almost

perplexing; it was radically different from others which have been heard and applauded. Was it therefore wrong? Were all the others right? . . .

There were passages which under Mr. Nikisch's direction assumed new and unpleasing forms. . . . And there were portions of the work which were grandly worked up by the conductor and superbly played by the men. How full of beauty was the opening of the scherzo! How exciting was the approach to the finale, and how imposing was the declamation of the first pages of that finale!

William Apthorp of the *Evening Transcript* was Boston's leading Wagnerite critic. He considered Nikisch's concert a "great experience." Of the Beethoven performance, he wrote:

In the Andante con moto, Mr. Nikisch allowed himself to make some quite new, and, as the French say, "unpublished" effects. The most curious of these, perhaps, as the throwing into strong prominence of the second violin part, during the second variation of the principal theme, to the almost complete extinction of the theme itself. . . . But the splendid manner in which Mr. Nikisch made the trumpets and horns bring out the martial second theme went far to console one for such little vagaries. . . . The Finale was glorious throughout, and carried everything before it. Anything more grandly exhilarating were hard to imagine. The audience clapped, stamped and shouted like mad.

Here, however, was Warren Davenport in the *Boston Herald*, in a single blistering paragraph of some two thousand words:

How Mr. Nikisch became possessed of his peculiar ideas regarding the rendition of the classics I am at a loss to conceive, unless they are creations of his own brain. . . . Had Wagner witnessed the almost brutal treatment that his beloved Beethoven's immortal symphony received at the hands of Mr. Nikisch, he would have administered a rebuke that would have startled the obsequious followers of his own theories who are striving to find excuses for the idiosyncrasies of Mr. Nikisch, whose new broom has swept them, with their whims and notions, into the rubbish heap of his own caprice. . . . Never once did [Mr. Nikisch] reach a point of repose. . . . The general effect was one fiendish rasp and blow, with an occasional lull. . . . It is the greatest satire upon the boasted musical culture of a Boston audience that . . . I saw musicians of standing who were as excited and enthusiastic as were the general listeners. I cannot but think that they must feel ashamed of themselves when they stop and calmly think how this boisterous, vulgar display of noise had for the time being paralyzed their better judgment.

Apthorp now responded to Davenport with an equally prodigious fulmination titled, "WHO MR. NIKISCH IS, AND HIS PROBABLE KNOWLEDGE OF THE TRADITIONS FOR THE RENDERING OF THE BEETHOVEN SYMPHONIES." His twenty-five-hundred words began:

> Under the title "That Fifth Symphony," the Boston Herald of Nov. 18, 1889, printed a long article, "sounding an alarm" to rouse the good Bostonians from their careless tranquility, and warning them of a dreadful danger, namely, the imminent decadence of genuine style and consecrated tradition in the domain of classical music, brought about by the pernicious influence of Arthur Nikisch, the new conductor of the Boston symphony concerts. . . .
>
> Before proceeding further, it seems to us of importance to get at a clear idea of the following preliminary questions:
> a. What is tradition?
> b. Does such a thing as tradition exist?
> c. On whom does it devolve to vindicate the integrity of this criterion?
>
> Regarding the first and second points, the greatest of and wisest men of all climes and regions have cudgelled their brains in vain. . . . But granting that a well-defined tradition did exist, then it remains for us, coming to the third preliminary question, to determine who is to be considered the Paladin of such a treasure?
>
> We need not seek far, the Paladin is found—it is the author of the Herald essay.
>
> Who is he?
>
> We do not know. No compendium, no lesson yields light concerning him. . . . He is surely an honorable man, and probably not celebrated, simply because, like the violet, he prefers to bloom in secret.

Apthorp proceeded to observe that Nikisch, in Europe, had excited the admiration of Bülow, Anton Rubinstein, Joseph Joachim, Brahms, and Liszt, among others. He next chronicled, in some detail, instances in which such composers as Beethoven, Weber, and Schumann had condoned interpretive license superseding literal adherence to their own scores. His final sally, to instruct "the Herald's essayist" concerning "to whom the right of criticism pertains," began with a quotation from Gluck: "The mania of wanting to speak about things they do not understand is but a too common failing of people."

Apthorp continued in a similar vein at least until December 2, *twenty-four days* after Nikisch had first led Beethoven's Fifth in Boston. At season's end, he commended the new conductor. Hale's summation was mixed, as was Elson's in the *Advertiser*. Arthur Weld of the *Post*, who was himself a composer, spoke out against Nikisch's "embittered opponents." In New York the consensus was more supportive; as Henry Krehbiel put it in the *Tribune*, "The technical finish of the orchestra's playing is not brought so constantly and impressively to the attention of the listeners as formerly, but in its place we have something infinitely better—a robust tone and a vitality of proclamation which sacrifices nothing of the composer's intended eloquence to the love of placidity and undisturbed euphony."[25]

In subsequent seasons Nikisch continued to split Boston opinion. Many an Apthorp review conveyed the thrill of new experience, as in this account of Wagner's *Tannhäuser* Overture (describing the effect of a countermelody that today is always stressed, but was in 1889 new to Boston):

At the last return of [the pilgrims'] theme, on the three trombones and three trumpets in unison, Mr. Nikisch introduced an effect which we had never heard before, and which, whether legitimate or not, was immensely impressive; he egged on the four horns to play in such an almost superhuman *fortissimo* that the middle parts stood out nearly as distinctly as the melody, and one heard this passage, for the first time, in *full harmony*.

But Nikisch's special enthusiasms—for Liszt, Wagner, Tchaikovsky—were not those of Philip Hale. And when Nikisch assayed works earlier than Schumann, Hale would cavil:

He seems unhappy unless he "rides in the whirlwind and directs the storm." Repose, the quiet beauty of insinuation, delicacy of touch and treatment, these qualities seem abhorrent to his nature. By birth and education his is a theatrical nature; and when he has to deal with the theatrical in music he is admirable, most admirable; but the hot and feverish air of the playhouse soon becomes insupportable.[26]

Nikisch departed Boston after four years—one season before the expiration of his contract—having conducted 388 of the Boston Symphony's 398 nonsummer concerts, including 196 on tour in thirty-two cities. As leader of both the Berlin Philharmonic and the Leipzig Gewandhaus Orchestra, he would soon become Europe's most famous and influential symphonic conductor. A 1913 Nikisch recording of Beethoven's Fifth illuminates his Boston experience. Even making allowances for the primitive reproduction and cramped studio setup (which required reduced strings), Nikisch's Berlin Philharmonic is all about spontaneity and flexibility. The reading, with its constant play of tempo, actually remains radically different from received tradition. But a sympathetic listener can glean its possible impact in live performance. In no other Beethoven's Fifth does the first-movement oboe cadenza make a more mesmerizing impression. The reason is not the oboist, but the conductor, who (contradicting Beethoven) slows and softens—poetically blurs—the preceding passage, and only gradually gathers speed in its dazed aftermath.

Why did Nikisch leave Boston? According to the press, he had been offered the directorship of the Budapest Opera and was advised by Higginson to accept. Nikisch thereupon declined to conduct the orchestra on a three-week western tour at season's end, pleading "complete exhaustion." Higginson collected a $5,000 forfeit for breach of contract, and Nikisch was gone. Higginson's private correspondence reveals that he considered Nikisch a "genius," but was never comfortable with either Nikisch the musician (too many liberties with the text) or Nikisch the man (unfathomable and possibly untrustworthy). The letters confirm that Higginson advised Nikisch to take the Budapest position as his Boston position would not be "renewed." They confirm that Nikisch was to forfeit $5,000 in the event he did not fulfill his obligations in full. Higginson, however, agreed to waive this penalty, but only if Nikisch led the postseason tour. Nikisch was only willing to do so if he received his customary $2,000 annual "bonus." Higginson refused these terms and resorted to legal counsel. Nikisch agreed to pay the $5,000.[27]

Nikisch told reporters that his losses depleted all the savings he had realized from his Boston position (reportedly salaried at $9,000). In New York, the *Musical Courier* sympathetically observed that Nikisch's workload had been "incessant." Higginson's side of the argument may be inferred from a letter dated April 25, 1893. He had stated his terms. He had agreed to forgive the $5,000. Yet Nikisch, by pulling out of the tour, had waited "until I am in a box and without a conductor and with a lot of concerts before me, for which engagements have been made and tickets sold. If I give them up, it will probably cost me $20,000." Higginson also wrote that he had received from Nikisch "several of the most remarkable letters that I have ever received, so far as insolence goes," and that the conductor, though he pled ill health, looked "as well as usual."[28] (In fact, the tour proceeded under the baton of Kneisel, the concertmaster, with several concerts canceled.)

Nikisch's American career marks a defining moment for musical Boston. Never again would the Boston Symphony be entrusted to so confirmed a "Wagnerian." When New York's Henry Krehbiel relished "Mr. Nikisch's successful efforts in troubling the musical waters of Boston" and favorably compared Nikisch's "robust" and "vital" readings to "the love of placidity and undisturbed euphony," he was chiding Boston itself.[29] (Boston's response to Nikisch's interpretive flamboyance resonates with the fate, half a century later, of Serge Koussevitzky's flamboyant Massachusetts-born protégé Leonard Bernstein, whom Koussevitzky groomed to succeed him at the head of the Boston Symphony, but who wound up in New York instead.)

At the same time, that the interpretation of Beethoven's Fifth should have become a matter of urgent civic importance, bearing on a city's cultural pedigree, could only have occurred in Boston. This even New York was quick to concede. Krehbiel, visiting Boston for Nikisch's debut, observed "the gentleness of the city's taste in music, the genuineness of her appreciation, the thoroughness of her understanding and earnestness of her devotion. . . . She is blessed beyond measure in the disposition of her people toward an art which makes for the civic virtues in a degree scarcely equalled by any other agent of civilization." In New York's *Musical Courier*, Otto Florsheim wrote in 1890:

> Boston is more musical than any other city in the United States, New York not excluded. . . . It is not in the number of its concerts, nor in the quality of them that New York is musically inferior to Boston; it is in the quality of the audiences, their unflagging interest in everything musical and their true and unaffected enthusiasm that the latter city shows its musical superiority. Take a concert like last Saturday's twentieth Symphony concert and its preceding public rehearsal. It rained all Friday and it snowed all Saturday. In New York on such unpropitious occasions all concert attendance, even that at our six Philharmonic concerts, decreases in number most materially and the atmosphere puts a damper on all musical enthusiasm in listeners and performers alike. Not so in Boston. Music Hall last Friday afternoon was crowded to overflowing and the ladies had to sit even on the steps of the orchestral platform.[30]

In fact, listeners on the steps of the stage and in the aisles were a commonplace at Boston Symphony concerts. These were the purchasers of the twenty-five-cent "rush tickets." An hour before concert time, they would race into the second balcony, whose 466 seats would fill within minutes. The remaining rush-ticket holders would sit or stand where they could. The waiting line, where they had patiently queued, was a local phenomenon. "There you see people from all over this vast country, young and old, many music students, making the sacrifice of the whole day and studying while they wait," a "graduate of the rush-line" once wrote to Higginson. "Then the excitement of not knowing whether you'll get in and the joy of a seat if you do; and the brilliancy of the music from the second balcony. Oh! It's Paradise! . . . and the neighborliness of dividing your bread and butter and apple with the fellow next, if he hasn't any, and the profitable and pleasant chats it often leads to." Higginson himself gratefully observed that his audience "is not from the Back Bay or from any particular set of people. They are town folks and country folks."[31]

Boston Symphony audiences grew more demonstrative during the Nikisch years, prone to shouting, to the thumping of canes and umbrellas, to "wild" applause. They embodied a distinct community of culture, New England bred, at once brittle and fervent.

■ ■ ■

America, too, had its community of culture in the late Gilded Age—one necessarily less specific than that of Boston and New England, yet nonetheless tangible in its broad attributes. The elite reputation of music as queen of the arts assured an elite place for music critics. The leading critics, accordingly, were leading embodiments of taste and opinion. In fact, more than today, they were leaders.

In New York, the leader was Henry Krehbiel of the *Tribune*. In a cultural community dominated by Wagnerism, he was a dominant Wagnerite. In a polyglot city of immigrants, he was the son of German-born parents. He grew up in a bilingual home in Cincinnati. His formal education was scant. He was self-made, a prodigious autodidact.

In Boston, Philip Hale, beginning with his employment at the *Home Journal* in 1889, swiftly emerged as the most influential music critic. He was (unthinkable in New York) a Francophile. He was eighth in line of descent from Thomas Hale, who settled in Massachusetts in or about 1638. He attended Phillips Exeter Academy, where he also had a private tutor, and Yale College, where he distinguished himself as a writer and musician. He studied organ, piano, and composition with important teachers in Europe, including Alexandre Guilmant in Paris.

Hale early acquired a formidable breadth of learning, lightly worn. The breezy aplomb of his worldly prose set him apart from other Boston writers. No less than Krehbiel, a stylist of ponderous eloquence, he resonated with his milieu; he would even ascribe his personal judgments to "Boston."[32]

Krehbiel cut a figure of formidable girth (he closely resembled William Howard Taft). Hale was tall and elegantly trim; his sartorial signature was a loose black silk tie; for the opera, he always wore white tie and tails. His courtly manner was also caustic. Nothing more inflamed his pen than the influence of German music, language, and mores. A specimen:

> The lady in question is an excellent example of a school of German singers. Possibly nature gives them a good, strong voice; they go upon the stage before they have acquired the art of correctly producing a tone; they are unable to sustain, swell or diminish a tone; they struggle with coloratura; they subordinate singing to action; in order to make a strong impression they force the voice, they shout, so that they soon lose all sense of pitch. . . .
>
> Has not the diet, the cooking of the Germans, much to do with the peculiarities of their composers and singers? . . .
>
> Now the German composers and the German singer subsist mainly upon pork, veal, cabbage and beer. Occasionally some bold musician makes experiments, as did Anton Filz, a celebrated violinist at the court of Mannheim, who died, as Pohl tells us in the Life of Haydn, from immoderate indulgence in raw spiders which he imagined tasted remarkably like fresh strawberries. Wagner, it is true, preached vegetarianism to his disciples,—but he condemned the eating of flesh only in theory, for he heartily enjoyed roast meat. The diet of your average German is indigestible; it puffs out logy men. Could a sparkling operetta in the French style be written after a year's stay at a German boardinghouse?[33]

Hale once described Bach as "counterpoint by the yard—you can begin anywhere and end anywhere; a sausage factory." Naturally, he inveighed against "acute Wagneritis" in all its forms. As with Dwight, this prejudice was not buttressed by informed understanding, as evidenced by gaffes (there is, *pace* Hale, no "overture" to *Götterdämmerung*) and cheap shots (sensibly considered, the love potion in *Tristan und Isolde* is a metaphor, not a literal agent of puppet passions). Of such composers as Brahms, Hale knew no more than he had to in order to invent this choice putdown of the First Symphony:

> In this symphony of Brahms the players seem to wander in a forest imagined by Maeterlinck. The forest is dark, although it is nigh noon, and the sky is clear. No birds sing in this forest. There are no wildflowers in this forest; nor in this forest are there any trees of beauty. The trees,

indeed, seem dream trees, seen in restless sleep. The players wander blindly. Alarmed, they call to each other; they sound their alarm together. They try to weep, but terror forbids tears. They try to be gay; their jests fail without laughter. They suspect the presence of winged things. The air grows dull. . . . Suddenly they come into clear ground, and they see a canal with green water. Beyond is a hospital with the sick people poking out of the windows. A boat is dragged along, and queerly dressed men and women sing a tune that sounds like unto a travesty of the hymn in Beethoven's 9th symphony. Then all is dark. The dreamer wakes. There is darkness. There is the remembrance of a dark dream.[34]

In New York, the influence of Germanic idealism, and the German equation of art with uplift, rhymed with moralizing intellectual norms. Thus absorbed, Wagnerism (as a later chapter will elaborate) acquired a distinctly American cast, spurning the decadence and proto-modernism of European Wagnerites. This manifestation of genteel uplift, embracing the progressive Music of the Future and its heterogeneous New York following, gauged the scope and resilience of the genteel tradition as practiced outside New England. Inside New England, Germans dominated the ranks of the Boston Symphony, yet did not infiltrate the Brahmin elite. A purer, more inbred gentility was practiced. On its fringes, the cultural vanguard was not Wagnerite but aestheticist—an art-for-art's-sake movement associated not with Berlin, but with Paris.

Hale, to be sure, was not Wilde or Beardsley; Boston, to be sure, was not Europe. Wincing at Salome's lust, or the incest of Siegmund and Sieglinde, he was a puritan. But neither was he a meliorist. His preference for absolute music—his rejection of descriptive programs and other extramusical props, his mistrust of the "theatrical"—recalled Dwight and Thomas (who were meliorists and puritans both). It also derived from the aesthetic of Vienna's arch anti-Wagnerite, Eduard Hanslick, who insisted that music, as such, expressed only itself. Hale's decisive affinity, finally, was for Debussy. He was uncomfortable with the sea imagery of *La mer*. He cherished, as antidotes to preaching and prescription, the *Prelude to the Afternoon of a Faun* and *Pelléas et Mélisande*.

Krehbiel, the Wagnerite, was a cultural nationalist: a student of folk music, an admirer of national "schools," a devotee of the soil. For Hale, soil was dirt. He shared the French enthusiasm for musical Russia—the exoticism of Rimsky-Korsakov and Borodin, not the realism of Mussorgsky. He pondered the possibility of an American school and (correctly) applauded George Chadwick for fashioning an incipient American style. But Krehbiel's advocacy of plantation song and "Indian" chant as sources for an American idiom exasperated Hale. His sarcastic putdowns of Congo and Creole "ditties" convey more than a whiff of Social Darwinism. They also suggest a formidable capacity for snobbery. Hale's linked antipathies for the theater, for roots-in-the-soil nationalism, and for the susceptible *vox populi* flavor this characteristic assessment of the Suite No. 1 from Grieg's *Peer Gynt* music, as performed by the Boston Symphony under Nikisch:

> The dance of Anitra is not so original, and the last movement is vulgar and noisy. As a whole the music of this suite is like unto the gracefully rounded sentences of a speaker who has nothing to say. It is fair theatre-music, and while it may be appropriate and effective in the theater, where it accompanies the play, it is out of place when included in the program of a symphony concert.
>
> And the cymbal and the drum delighted the people, and at the end of the fourth number they shouted for joy. At last they were really pleased; at last they heard that which they could understand.[35]

All this forms the backdrop to the major premiere undertaken by Arthur Nikisch's Boston successor, Emil Paur: the first Boston performance of Dvořák's *New World* Symphony, in turn the occasion for formidable jousting between Hale and Krehbiel, Boston and New York. An earlier chapter has already described in outline this defining "tale of two cities," freighted with issues of national identity. Let us revisit Hale's discomfort with Dvořák and his agenda. Consider, for instance, this fusillade, from the *Musical Courier*:

> According to the New York "Herald" the said Mr. Dvořák began to study native music after his arrival in New York. Unfortunately for the future historian we are not told how he studied it, or whether he disguised himself in his exploration so that the music would not become suspicious, frightened, and then escape. It would be a pleasure to read of his wanderings in the jungles of the Bowery and in the deserts of Central Park. It would be interesting to know precisely his first thought on seeing the Harlem goat, an animal now rare. The composer is a modest man, and he has not even hinted at his perilous trips on the Elevated Railway of the Belt Line.
>
> After I read of these adventures and of the intrepidity of the trip to Spillville, Ia., I was curious to hear the symphony, this symphony founded on "negro and Indian tunes," *i.e.*, American tunes.
>
> Then I read in other newspapers statements about Dvořák and this symphony, which convinced me that the work could only be appreci-

ated properly by an audience composed exclusively of intelligent negroes and combed and washed Indians.[36]

Hale patronized Dvořák as a nationalist innocent, buoyed by "the simple faith of a healthy child," imbued with "the spirit of Nature," with "simple and pleasing thoughts." "There is no touch of pessimism. There is no struggle with the Infinite." A primitive of genius, his notion of American music was equally primitive and therefore insidious. The Boston notion that Dvořák was a danger intensified with the premiere of his String Quartet in F, Op. 96, by the Kneisel Quartet at Chickering Hall in January 1, 1893, and the first local performance of the String Quintet in E-flat, Op. 97, on March 19, 1894. Hale found the former (today, as the *American* Quartet, Dvořák's best-known chamber work) "delightful" and "refreshing." He dismissed other writers' impressions that the themes were, as Elson put it in the *Advertiser*, "redolent of the plantation": "the negros evoked by Mr. Dvořák have a singular habit of whistling Scotch and Bohemian tunes." But Hale worried that "a too frequent use of the pentatonic scale might weary after several hearings." Of greater concern was that Dvořák would prove a baneful model. Reviewing the first performance of Chadwick's Fourth String Quartet in E minor (the same key as the *New World* Symphony), Hale detected the "negrophile" influence of Dvořák:

There is the thought of the peculiar Scottish-Negro-Dvořákian thematic construction, with the suggestion of the plain-song cadences that are so often found in folk-songs. There is the thought of the heel-irritating jig, that is known from the Hebrides to Congo-land. I do not mean to say for a moment that there is any deliberate imitation of Dvořák's later music; but Mr. Chadwick has undoubtedly been influenced in spirit, and I regret this, for he is a big enough man to stand on his own legs and work out his own musical salvation.[37]

Certain other Boston voices were more mellow, or more strident: "One can see how monotonous this material might become in the hands of a less talented composer. It is to be hoped that mediocrity will not deluge our programmes in consequence of this innovation." "We are getting heartily tired of the uncivilized in chamber and symphonic music. . . . When the man who belongs to what the geographies used to call the 'civilized and enlightened' part of humankind voluntarily returns to barbarism, one cannot help a suspicion that effeteness of some sort has had a good deal to do with it." Even Dvořák's Requiem, conducted in Boston by the composer himself on

November 28, 1892, was found to possess, in reviews by different writers, "barbaric modulations" and "barbaric musical means."[38]

Krehbiel made fun of these attitudes. He traveled to Boston to hear the Boston Symphony and the Kneisel Quartet assay Dvořák. As we have already seen, he chided Emil Paur for taking every movement of the *New World* Symphony too moderately except the Larghetto (subsequently retitled Largo), which was too fast. Addressing Hale, Krehbiel filed this characteristic exegesis (whose thorough argumentation must be quoted at length):

The [Boston] newspaper critics in their reviews are unanimous in praising the beauty of the music and denying its right to be called American. The sarcastic and scintillant Mr. Philip Hale of "The Boston Journal," in particular makes merry of the term and thinks it wondrously amusing that anything should be called American which has attributes or elements that are also found among the peoples of the Old World. Much of this kind of talk is mere quibbling. Mr. Hale does not deny that Dr. Dvořák's melodies reflect the characteristics of the songs of the negroes in the South, and that the symphony is beautifully and consistently made. If so, why should it not be called American? Those songs, though they contain intervallic and rhythmic peculiarities of African origin, are the product of American institutions. . . . The crude material may be foreign; the product is native. . . .

It has not occurred to The Tribune to claim that with his symphony Dr. Dvořák has founded a national school of composition. The only thing that has been urged in the matter is that he has showed that there are the same possibilities latent in the folk-songs which have grown up in America as in the folk-songs of other peoples. Those folk-songs are accomplished facts. . . . Musicians have never been so conscious as now of the value of folk-song elements. Music is seeking new vehicles of expression, and is seeking them where they are most sure to be found—in the field of the folk-song. We have such a field and it is rich. Why not cultivate it? Why these sneers at the only material which lies to our hand? What matters if the man who points out the way be a Bohemian scarcely two years in the country? The peripatetic gypsy is the universal musician, and he makes Hungarian music in Hungary, Spanish music in Spain, Russian music in Russia, and English music in England. . . . It is characteristic of the vagueness which haunts the musical mind, let us say of Boston, in this matter that the fact that the stamp of Dvořák's individuality is upon this score is cited as proof that it is not American. It would be pity if so pronounced a personality as Dvořák should conceal himself in a composition, but it would be a greater pity if the idea should prevail that in order to be American a composer must forswear himself, and follow a model which is, as yet, non-existent. There are in music schools of materials, schools of manner and schools of models. The new symphony is a highly successful experiment in the first of these.[39]

Boston was not indifferent to the project of cultivating an American idiom. But Dvořák the primitive nationalist sat too low on the evolutionary scale, as did the "negro melodies" and "Indian" chants he adored. Hale (who was no Dwight) wrote more appreciatively of the songs of Stephen Foster or the theater songs and dances of David Braham as distinctly "American" in flavor. In later years, he similarly endorsed jazz. He compared the scherzo of the *New World* Symphony with Chadwick's "symphonic scherzo" (presumably, the antic Scherzo in F later incorporated into the Second Symphony) and found the Chadwick the more American for its "dash, 'smartness,' lack of reverence and general devil-me-care."[40]

In certain respects, Hale was correct. Chadwick's style sublimates the Yankee vernacular and embodies a recognizable Yankee type; it is in fact a purer example of American symphonic nationalism than the *New World* Symphony, which views the United States through a foreigner's admiring ears and eyes. And yet Dvořák's larger insight, his compassionate understanding that in plantation song lay a catalyst protean with significance for all Americans, was confirmed by the twentieth-century burgeoning of an American popular music—ragtime, blues, and jazz—he could not foresee.*

In sum, while New York embraced a Romantic cultural nationalism rooted in the soil, Boston clung to elite cultural forms purged of folk art. As Patrick Gilmore's Peace Jubilee had posed a threat to John Sullivan Dwight, Philip Hale felt threatened by the *New World* Symphony. Behind his easy aplomb, behind ideals of lofty repose, lay New England traditions still young— traditions whose air of ripeness was premature. This was the problem of Boston that estranged Henry James, that drove William Dean Howells to Manhattan, that crippled Amy Beach. At the same time, Boston traditions could refine cultural tasks and furnish the tools of authority to get things done. Now is the moment to return to Henry Higginson and the early history of the Boston Symphony Orchestra.

* For more on Chadwick and on the *New World* Symphony, see pp. 104–110 and 222–231.

CHAPTER 3

Building a Hall,
Choosing a
Conductor

■

Henry Higginson's high character ▪ *He builds*
Symphony Hall ▪ *He hires Karl Muck* ▪ *Henry Russell's*
Boston Opera ▪ *Muck's arrest* ▪ *Higginson,*
Charles Eliot Norton, and the uses of Boston culture

Compared to John Sullivan Dwight and Philip Hale, Henry Lee Higginson was less a pure product of New England. He was actually born in New York, in 1834, but moved to Boston four years later. Though his family, on both sides, was of distinguished Boston stock, his father was far from wealthy. George Higginson, Henry recalled, "never owned a house or a horse of his own until within a few years of his own death." Moreover, "when he was earning very little money, he passed much of his time and any spare pennies possible in charitable work."[1]

Henry attended the Boston Latin School in the company of Boston's elite and proceeded to Harvard University in similar company, but his poor eyesight forced him to abandon college after a few months. The following years were mainly spent abroad: a series of *Wanderjahre* that eventually landed him in Vienna. Higginson now aspired to a modest career in music, a rare calling for a young man of his lineage. An 1857 letter to his father reveals an uncommon twenty-three-year-old:

> As every one has some particular object of supreme interest to himself, so I have music. It is almost my inner world; without it, I miss much, and with it I am happier and better. . . .
> . . . You will ask, 'What is to come of it all if successful?' I do not know.

But this is clear. I have then improved my own powers, which is every man's duty. I have a resource to which I can always turn with delight, however the world may go with me. I am so much the stronger, the wider, the wiser, the better for my duties in life. I can then go with satisfaction to my business, knowing my resource at the end of the day. It is already made, and has only to be used and it will grow. Finally it is my province in education, and having cultivated myself in it, I am fully prepared to teach others in it. *Education* is the object of man, and it seems to me the duty of us all to help in it, each according to his means and in his sphere. I have often wondered how people could teach this and that, but I understand it now. I could teach people to sing, as far as I know, with delight to myself. Thus I have a means of living if other things should fail. But the pleasure, pure and free from all disagreeable consequences or after-thoughts, of playing and still more of singing myself, is indescribable. . . . and this I wish to be most clearly expressed and understood, should any one ask about me. *I am studying for my own good and pleasure.* And now, old daddy, I hope you will be able to make something out of this long letter. You should not have been troubled with it, but I thought you would prefer to know all about it. It is only carrying out your own darling idea of making an imperishable capital in education. My money may fly away; my knowledge cannot. One belongs to the world, the other to me.[2]

In Vienna, Higginson pursued a spartan curriculum for more than two years, arising every morning at 6:30. His weekly educational intake was nine music lessons and two lectures. His dietary intake, usually omitting supper, was limited by his financial resources; he confessed to his father, "A large portion of my yearly expenses are not for myself. . . . I sometimes curse myself for trying to help others when I've not enough money for my own real wants, but again think that money well used is not wasted."[3]

One result of Higginson's Vienna regimen was the discovery that he had no special talent for music. He returned to Boston in 1861 and was swallowed up in the Civil War. From his father, he had inherited a passionate dedication to Abolitionism. "We've been told of our degeneracy for years and years," he wrote excitedly to his brother. "I tell you, Jim, no more heartfelt enthusiasm or devotion was to be found in '76 than now. *Everyone* is dying to go." To his friend Alexander Thayer, later an important Beethoven authority, he wrote, "Tell me there is no American people, is no nationality, is no distinct and strong love of country! It is a lie, and those who have said so to me in Europe simply were ignorant! . . . I, for one, have felt merely delight from the beginning of the war, that the day had come, which was to make me a soldier fighting for freedom for man, for the right and the good, for God." In June 1863, Major Henry Higginson fell in hand-to-hand combat, left to die with a bullet at the base of his spine. He stumbled toward his men until he was discovered and evacuated.[4]

Among Higginson's fallen comrades in arms were Robert Gould Shaw, who famously commanded an African-American Massachusetts regiment, and James Lowell, whom he revered as a paragon of social responsibility. These and other Civil War deaths (which he unforgettably eulogized upon donating Harvard's Soldier's Field in 1890) redoubled Higginson's fervor for community service. He emerged from his Viennese "second home" and from the crucible of war a thirty-one-year-old of wide and varied experience who spoke French and German fluently, who had soldiered with Americans from every walk of life, and who had married the daughter of Louis Agassiz, the eminent Harvard anthropologist. After a series of failed business projects, including an oil venture in Ohio and a cotton plantation with freedmen in Georgia, he joined the stalwart banking firm of Lee, Higginson and Company, cofounded by his father—taken in, he once recalled, "as a matter of charity, to keep me out of the poorhouse." Though Higginson claimed that he never walked into 44 State Street without wanting to sit down on the doorstep and cry, he proceeded to amass a sufficient fortune to undertake his true lifework. The Boston Symphony, on which he expended nearly one million dollars in deficit relief alone, was the most generous of his many philanthropies. His own business sometimes hovered on the brink of bankruptcy. He found money useful to the degree that he could usefully give it away.[5]

What kind of man was Henry Higginson? His talent was less for banking than for friendship. His letters confirm the simplicity of manner for which he was admired. Music, plainly, remained his "inner world" and Beethoven his moral bedrock. Even in later life, consumed by professional duties, he would write of the *Eroica* Symphony (presumably the finale's slow variations), "The gates of Heaven open, and we see the angels singing and reaching their hands to us with perfect welcome. No words are of any avail, and never does that passage of entire relief and joy come to me without tears—and I wait for it, through life, and hear it, and wonder." The most famous portrait of Higginson, by John Singer Sargent, suggests aloofness or arrogance. Though Higginson disliked this picture, he rendered his idealism decisively and bluntly. His relationship to his musicians was paternalistic: he scrutinized them, individually, in performance; he promoted or dismissed them; he supported them in illness or misfortune; he censured those who drank or gambled; he advised them on investments. He attested, "If the world consisted only of musicians, it would go to pieces at once."[6]

As an orchestra owner, he (as we have seen) singularly prohibited his players from undertaking casual work on symphony days. Spurning the union movement, he supported the addition of new members from abroad. Spurning Boston's own conductors, he hired George Henschel, Wilhelm Gericke, and Arthur Nikisch—a twelve-year sequence of music directors plotting a crescendo of artistic growth. But Nikisch's successor, Emil Paur, programmed too much Richard Strauss for Higginson's liking, and was not in a class with Gericke and Nikisch in any case. Higginson deposed him after five seasons and in 1898 got Gericke back. As future events would illuminate, he was now at the very peak of his form.

■ ■ ■

The most notable physical feature of the new hall that the Boston Symphony occupied in 1900, and that still serves as the orchestra's home, is plainness. It is less a "concert hall" than a large rectangular room. The floor is exposed wood. The downstairs seats, with their hard, thin upholstery, are removable. The gilt proscenium is topped by a medallion reading "Beethoven"; eight flanking medallions are blank. This is a functional space in which to hear music—or, at most, a spare church in which to worship it. At first, it did not even have a name; the one it eventually acquired was, simply, Symphony Hall.

It acquired as well a reputation as one of the world's supreme concert spaces. The coffered ceiling, the open grillwork of the two balconies, the niches and statuary—all of which shun the flat surfaces faulted by acousticians—partly account for the warmth, clarity, and presence of its charmed sonic properties.

Not least among the hall's virtues is its exquisite sense of place. No such auditorium could exist in New York or Vienna or Leipzig, even though the old Leipzig Gewandhaus was one of its models. It honors Boston's puritan legacy, and also the sense of history that Boston so early acquired: it looked old the day it opened.

If the hall had a human face, it would be that of the individual who built it and who modestly refused to bequeath his name. Henry Higginson decided that the Boston Symphony needed a new place of residence. The existing Music Hall was called a "fire trap" and "the breeziest and draftiest hall in the universe";[7] what is more, the city wanted to build an elevated railroad line on the property. Higginson disliked New York's new Music Hall built by Andrew Carnegie, with its twenty-eight-hundred seats disposed in a tiered operatic horseshoe. He wanted something much simpler and somewhat smaller, with a capacity of twenty-five or twenty-six hundred.

In Leipzig, the Gewandhaus had chosen an architect by competition from seventy-five applicants. Higginson's method was to choose Charles Follen McKim, of the celebrated New York firm McKim, Mead, and White. Old World royalty would have declared cost irrelevant; Higginson wrote McKim, "As I must bear the burden of the new hall, perhaps quite alone, and as I keep my purse fairly depleted all the time, I must not—cannot—spend too much money." Actually, these instructions were aesthetic: Higginson also wrote to McKim, "I always like the severe in architecture, music, men and women, books." McKim accepted the commission and proposed a novel and elegant design based on a Greek amphitheater, to which Higginson responded, "We feel afraid to try any experiments. While we hanker for the Greek theatre plan, we think the risk too great as regards results, so we have definitely abandoned that idea. We shall therefore turn to the general plan of our Music Hall and of the halls in Vienna and Leipsic [sic], the latter being the best of all."[8]

And so McKim copied the rectangular plan of the Leipzig Gewandhaus, shorn of its elaborate Germanic decoration. Also, with a capacity of 1,560, the Gewandhaus was too little. It was assumed that the Boston hall should be enlarged proportionately in all its dimensions. But Higginson's crowning inspiration was to engage a young Harvard acoustician, Wallace Sabine. Sabine advised him of the superiority of angles to curves. He cautioned against a stage too high or deep (hence the modest capacity of the Symphony Hall stage, to this day requiring a forward extension for oratorios and the like). And, crucially, Sabine told Higginson that to simply increase the linear dimensions of the hall by 30 percent would result in a space far too large for optimum projection. Symphony Hall became the first such structure to be planned with the laws of acoustical science consciously in play.

It was Higginson, too, who proceeded to mastermind fund-raising supplementary to his own contribution. The hall was actually ready on time. But it was not finished according to McKim's expectations. Tellingly, Higginson failed to provide the intended external statuary. Many smaller external details were sacrificed. McKim saw his building being "denuded" and wrote to Higginson that he feared it would seem "more like a deaf, dumb and blind institution, than a Music Hall." New York's *Musical Courier* had this to say: "The building has been described, but must be visited to learn of its cheerlessness and to feel the stern effect of architectural angularity. It has all the aspect and atmosphere of a religious establishment, and no matter if Beethoven's name is carved on the proscenium arch and a copy of the Apollo Belvedere is fixed in one of the cold niches at the end of the hall, it still feels like an armory or a prayer house, where ritual is considered paganism."[9]

The inaugural concert took place on October 15, 1900. Gericke led Beethoven's *Missa solemnis* to dedicate the hall. But first there was a Bach chorale, after which Higginson stepped on stage to a standing ovation. He praised McKim, who was notably absent, for graciously abandoning his original plan in support of another "not entirely to his liking." He also said that the creators of the hall had shown their care "for the happiness, the convenience, the education of the inhabitants for twenty miles around this spot; and it is fitting in a republic that the citizens and not the government in any form should do such work and bear such burdens. To the more fortunate people of our land belongs the privilege of providing the higher branches of education and art. . . . [The orchestra and its leaders have] done our city and our country signal and intelligent service, such as ennobles and educates a nation."[10]

In the end, what the Boston Symphony's new home most resembled was its old home. In size and feel, if not in proportionate dimensions, it was the Music Hall, not the Gewandhaus, that proved Higginson's inescapable model. Like the Boston Music Hall, Symphony Hall was a simple rectangle whose shallow balconies had no bad seats. Like the Music Hall, it secured a special bonding of music, auditors, and venue, a feeling of cultural community sealed by its town-meeting plainness. A larger, more opulent, more stratified space—a Boston Carnegie, in which lesser patrons would have sat hidden beneath the eaves in the topmost balcony—would have made a different statement altogether. Henry Higginson had built a house as bold and obdurate, severe and warm as the gentleman himself.

■ ■ ■

If the Boston Symphony and Symphony Hall were supreme embodiments of purposeful artistic policy, Emil Paur was a misstep Higginson would not repeat. Gericke's return was a corrective; it was his Boston Symphony that Richard Strauss, in 1902, called the "most marvelous in the world."[11] In 1906 Gericke announced he would not come back the following fall. Higginson was now determined, once and for all, to procure the right conductor for Boston. The result was another remarkable illustration of his capacity to know exactly what he wanted and exactly how to get it, a window on Higginson's modus operandi and on Higginson the man.

The window takes the form of a series of letters written to the orchestra's manager, Charles Ellis, and to the composer George Chadwick. These were Higginson's agents abroad during the spring months in which he conducted his eleventh-hour search. He also conferred frequently with his Viennese friend Julius Epstein, whose judgment he trusted implicitly; with the soprano Milka Ternina; and with two key members of his orchestra who knew the European scene: the concertmaster, Franz Kneisel, and the second concert-master, Charles Martin Loeffler, who also happened to be one of America's most important composers. In all, Higginson considered twenty-five candidates, a list including virtually every important name compatible with Germanic repertoire: Hermann Abendroth, Leo Blech, Max Fiedler, Gustav Mahler, Willem Mengelberg, Felix Mottl, Karl Muck, Arthur Nikisch, Hans Richter, Franz Schalk, Ernst von Schuch, Richard Strauss, Felix Weingartner, Henry Wood.[12]

In the letters, Higginson is quick to weed out Peter Raabe ("distinctly second rate"), George Schneevoigt ("the same"), and Fritz Steinbach ("not a conductor of genius"). Kneisel had highly recommended Mahler; Higginson is surely correct in surmising, "I . . . should not expect to have any peace with him." About Mengelberg, Kneisel's advice, as recounted by Higginson, is that he is "rather coarse and much given to fireworks, that he likes the new music and doesn't like the old." This is all Higginson needs to know. The letters reveal, surprisingly, that the young Bruno Walter, only thirty years old, expressed interest in the Boston post and was considered for a one-season trial if no suitable older man were found in time.* Higginson had heard good things about him, but cautions Ellis, "I should have to tell him that I do not like too much modern music, and that I do not want the extreme modern style of conducting, and if he doesn't care to come under these conditions, I do not want him." And again:

> If you see Walther [*sic*] or Mengelberg, you will have to say to them . . . that I do know something about music, and that I have very distinct ideas as to how music should be played; that I shall not meddle with modern music, but that I shall certainly ask them to play the classics as they were played. I was brought up in the Vienna school (as you know)

---

* Walter's candidacy reveals that Higginson considered Boston ready for a Jewish music director. From a letter to his father, we learn that he had never encountered a Jew before arriving in Vienna, "but those whom I have known in Vienna are very talented, true, liberal in views of life and religion, and free-handed to a marvelous extent." To which his father, though a liberal-minded Abolitionist, responded, "You are favored, for I have rarely met individuals of that race that seemed fitted in solid essentials for an intimacy of such a character. I am thankful that really worthy ones have fallen your way." It would be hard to think of a purer example of how considerably Higginson escaped the confines of Boston gentility. See Bliss Perry, *The Life and Letters of Henry Lee Higginson* (Boston, Atlantic Monthly, 1921), p. 125.

and there were plenty of men living then who had heard Beethoven conduct, as well as Mendelssohn, and knew how he wished his music given. I have known Brahms, myself, and heard his music. You know well enough what I wish, and I shall not interfere unduly with any of these men, but I don't want crazy work (such as sometimes even Nikish [*sic*] gave us, and Paur gave us too often), and perhaps you had better tell them that I hate noise.

In short, Higginson's first criterion was not a great name. This was not even his second criterion. He was looking for a major conductor whose tastes in repertoire and in interpretation were compatible with his own (and, incidentally or not, with Boston's). Ultimately, there were four contenders: Richter, Mottl, Nikisch, and Muck. Richter, the most venerable of this quartet, was offered the post in early February but proved unobtainable. On March 30, Higginson declared himself "at wit's end." In early May, writing to Ellis, he expressed mistrust in all three remaining candidates: "Somehow or other, I feel no great confidence in Nikisch's sincerity, although I may be in the wrong; nor do I in Mottl's, either; and Muck is weaker than an 11-year-old child, be it boy or girl. Muck doesn't know anything about resolution or plans." We also find him opining to Chadwick, "There are few musicians and artists whom I have found, in whom I can trust; the most of them seem to me a very shifty lot." It should be understood that Higginson dealt with his conductors directly—there were no artists' agents, as today. And he was accustomed to conducting business with businessmen.

In any event, Mottl, who was offered the Boston podium in November 1905, and whom Higginson considered "a cleverer man than Muck and not so reliable," was not released from his German obligations. Nikisch was thereupon offered a contract for five years, renewable for another five. Higginson had of course had Nikisch before, and had distanced himself from Nikisch's "theatricality." But in private Higginson conceded Nikisch's genius and it speaks volumes for this concession that he was willing to take him back. He wrote to Ellis, "I have rather the impression that Nikisch's heat is more external than internal. He is just as clever as man can be, and knows all the tricks of the trade." He closes, "If Chadwick is with you, my kindest regards to him, and kindest regards to anybody I know who wants them. I do not know whether Nikisch would care for a pleasant message from me." And to Chadwick himself, "I am afraid to pay [Nikisch] any considerable sum of money down, and I think it a very bad business, too. He is a considerable gambler, and he might get rid of his money and then do nothing for us, and be glad of the chance to strike. I don't know."

Higginson was surprised when Nikisch proved uninterested. He had made an offer generous enough, by his reckoning, that Nikisch could pocket ten thousand dollars a year. That left Muck, who could not make up his mind, and whom Higginson privately judged "a powerful jackass." And yet, personal considerations aside, Muck fit the bill. At forty-seven, he was principal conductor of the Berlin Opera. He was a leading interpreter of Wagner at Bayreuth and at London's Covent Garden. He had a reputation for strictness and discipline, the qualities Higginson admired in Gericke. "He is a good musician and would conduct admirably—though not very impressively, perhaps," Higginson wrote Ellis in May. "I fancy he is a broader and stronger man, as well as a warmer man, than Nikisch, and I think he would keep the orchestra in better order." A month later he summarized, again to Ellis, "My own belief is that we are better with Muck than with anyone of the whole crew."

Though Muck had turned him down at least once, Higginson somehow prevailed; and his employer, Kaiser Wilhelm II (who admired Harvard), agreed to release him. The new conductor arrived on schedule in October 1906. He proved everything Higginson had hoped for and more. Stiffly erect and nervously alert, smooth shaven, lean cheeked, and bespectacled, he radiated authority and intensity. He possessed an acute ear and (it was said) a keener knowledge of the instruments of the orchestra than any of his Boston predecessors. So thorough was his preparation, and so economical were his gestures, that he enjoyed putting down his baton and letting the men play by themselves. Though he insisted on proper rhythm and fidelity to the score, he managed to maintain discipline without straitjacketing the musicians as Gericke had sometimes done. His programs were notably unified in concept: sometimes all Classical, sometimes all Romantic—a novelty for Boston. His affinities stopped with early Richard Strauss; he did not believe *Salome* would endure, claimed *Thus Spake Zarathustra* misunderstood Nietzsche, and found *Ein Heldenleben* "a curious instance of the evils of a technique one might almost call too great." But he programmed a decent amount of later music, including Sibelius and Debussy, and also Mahler's Fifth Symphony (of which he made a cause) and Schoenberg's Five Pieces for Orchestra (which he introduced from a sense of duty). Higginson (as we will see) came to regard him as, quite literally, indispensable.[13]

Muck's Boston Symphony regime was not continuous. After two seasons, he was called back to Berlin. His successor for four seasons was Max Fiedler (no relation to Arthur Fiedler, later of the Boston Pops, who joined the Boston Symphony as a violist). Once Muck returned with a five-year contract in 1912, the orchestra was seen to have attained its highest plateau.

Philip Hale now shared his local critical eminence with Henry Taylor Parker, a bit of a cult figure himself. As principal music and drama critic of the *Transcript* beginning in 1905, Parker quickly established a reputation for decisive judgment and eccentric prose. His signatures included a fedora, a huge bamboo walking stick, a German cavalry overcoat, and the byline "H.T.P.," which was said to mean "Hell To Pay." A learned Harvard dropout, he could not read music but keenly adored it. One object of his adoration was Muck and his "incomparable orchestra of the world," at "the apogee of its attainment."[14] In New York, W. J. Henderson wrote in plain English ahead of its time. Parker's English, set down in a nearly indecipherable hand (he would not use a typewriter), was untraceable yet compatible with that part of Boston's cultural milieu that echoed, however faintly, the mannerists and aestheticists of England and France. The tortured and prolix elegance of Toscanini's future hagiographer, the New England–born Lawrence Gilman, was prefigured in such Parker effusions as the following, from a 1922 essay collection:

It is perilous to bear the measuring rule to the orchestral Olympus. But surely it is safe to say that no living conductor has assembled in himself more of the attributes of a great conductor or held them in juster balance than Dr. Muck. *Servans servorum Dei*—the servant of the servants of God—the early Popes used to proudly call themselves. So Dr. Muck might have called himself the servant of the composers whose music he played. He transmitted music to us in the living image of its form and substance, in the voice and in the emotion, as it seemed, in which it was created. Divining, he imparted. Imparting, he enhanced and intensified. For in him is that faculty of divination and that quality of impartment which differentiates the great conductor from the merely able practitioner of his art. The composer writes in emotion, sometimes in an emotion that the music hardly embodies and releases. Divining, penetrating, Dr. Muck enters into this emotion, transmits it, and sometimes releases and heightens it as though he were freeing that, which from sheer intensity of feeling, holds the composer almost tongue-tied. As widely as these composers range, so ranges Dr. Muck's divination. And to do and to be these things is to be a very great conductor.[15]

Among the landmarks of Muck's second Boston tenure were the orchestra's first transcontinental tour and its first recordings. The latter, made in New Jersey in October 1917 for the Victor Talking Machine Company (later RCA Victor), represent a technical landmark; probably for the first time, an entire hundred-piece orchestra was fit into a recording studio (an experiment repeated days later with Leopold Stokowski and the Philadelphia Orchestra).* The Victor engineers had constructed a pair of igloo-like structures into which the players were crammed tightly together in order to maximize proximity to the main recording horn. The first-desk men sat on high stools outside the two structures and played directly into horns of their own; other soloists had to run out of the igloo, play into a horn, and run back.[16] The results are informative. Beethoven's Fifth and other of Nikisch's mercurial prewar Berlin Philharmonic recordings, with a reduced orchestra, are about spontaneity. Muck's recordings are about precision. Though the orchestra's configuration obviously created ensemble problems, and though crudities of reproduction canceled the dynamic contrasts, fine details, and smooth blends for which Muck was noted, the excellence of the orchestra—in particular, the security of the brass and winds—remains apparent.

Of the eight selections, the finest is the Prelude to act three of Wagner's *Lohengrin*. Unlike many conductors, Muck chooses a tempo moderate enough so as not to blur the palpitating triplets. The wedding music of the middle section is slowed down and lyrically shaped. The music-box exactitude of Tchaikovsky's *Marche militaire* is perfectly rendered. The finale to Tchaikovsky's Fourth Symphony is quick and dashing, but the eruption of the "fate" motto in the brass is more military than existential. (Of a 1906 Muck performance of another "fate" symphony, Beethoven's Fifth, Henderson wrote in the *New York Sun*, "We have all heard more tragedy in the first movement and more mystery in the scherzo.")[17] In the remaining numbers (none of which were released until 1995), Muck's tendency to stiffness is more pronounced. Tchaikovsky's Waltz of the Flowers—repertoire chosen by Victor, not Muck—is comically rigid and ponderous, with beer-hall oompahs in the bass. More than unsympathetic, this interpretation sounds contemptuous. At such severe evidence of his Boston legacy, John Sullivan Dwight was surely grinning in his grave.

■ ■ ■

Throughout the early decades of the Boston Symphony Orchestra, opera was the dominant "serious" musical genre in New York. Boston did not ignore opera. Both the Metropolitan and Walter Damrosch's German company visited frequently and influentially. The core Italian, French, and German reper-

---

* It is not known whether Frederick Stock's Chicago Symphony was recorded at full force on May 1, 1916.

toire was implanted, as was the allure of countless vocal luminaries. But the bias of Lowell Mason and John Sullivan Dwight held sway. New England plainness mistrusted display and glamour. And Boston lacked New York's concentration of Germans and Italians hungering for Wagner and Verdi. When at last it acquired an opera company of its own in 1909, a frontal assault on local preferences resulted. The Boston Opera was in every respect a formidable undertaking—which made its failure all the more significant.

The prime movers were Henry Russell, a grandiloquent London impresario fired by the dream of "permanent—I might almost say an eternal—opera in the city of Boston," and Eben D. Jordan, a Boston department-store magnate who, à la Higginson, built an opera house distinguished by its simplicity of design and materials—"in admirable taste and reticent beauty, rather than prodigal sumptuousness," according to Lawrence Gilman in *Harper's Magazine*. As at Symphony Hall, the seats were simply upholstered. As at Symphony Hall, the excellent acoustics, a priority, were overseen by Harvard's Wallace Sabine. "The First Unitarian Opera House," the composer Arthur Whiting dubbed it.[18]

Russell was a notably high-minded entrepreneur. "Every stockholder who signed the parchment buried in the Opera House cornerstone," he proclaimed, "may also be said to have signed the death warrant for the star system in America." Boston would pursue a vision of integrated musical theater. Russell was as good as his word. His seasons of fifteen weeks were impressively punctuated with novelties. His designer, Joseph Urban, was a master of atmospheric lighting who would move on to Broadway and the Met. His conductors included Felix Weingartner and André Caplet, the latter a distinguished French composer and close friend of Debussy. And, at the same time, there were vocal stars aplenty.

Would there be an audience? Over time, Boston's aversion to the public conduct of social life had diminished. By 1900, wealthy Bostonians owned horses and yachts. The Thayers kept stately English homes. The Searses, Dexters, and Curtises commuted regularly to Europe. Eben Jordan rented a Scottish castle every fall; he was an ardent hunter. The opening night audience, for *La Gioconda* with Lillian Nordica on November 8, 1909, was considered sufficiently distinguished, but less ostentatious than its New York equivalent. "They sat," wrote H. T. Parker, "as though to do so on opening nights had been the habit of their lives, while perhaps within they wondered how X across the way or Y around the turn seemed so used to it as well. After all, we are not quite habitual boxholders or subscribers yet." Parker himself was partial to a red-lined opera cloak. Philip Hale wrote, "There is at last an opportunity for the display of fair women in gala costumes which an opera house adds so much to the brilliance of the scene and performances." Hale's preferred opera garb was white tie and tails. Algernon St. John Brenon, of the *New York Telegraph*, visited the Boston Opera and observed, "New York is disturbed by a certain restlessness and indocility, a waiting for points and purple patches and loud unmeasured outbursts. . . . Boston listens seriously, equably, giving the artist the same courteous, careful hearing it would extend to a Huxley speaking on a problem in biology. . . . Above all, Boston listens, not languorously as we do in England, but earnestly, seasoning its admiration with a concentration of intellectual curiosity."[19]

And Boston's tastes were distinctive. Caruso, a cult figure at the Met, was prone to stage mischief: an egg pressed into a colleague's hand, a top hat filled with water, a superfluous pistol blast. Russell was not amused. Caruso returned his distaste; as of 1918, he refused to perform at the Boston Opera. Richard Strauss's *Salome*, a New York success at Oscar Hammerstein's Opera House but banned at the Met after a single performance, was off limits to Boston. Other operas of questionable moral pedigree—*Tristan und Isolde*, Flotow's *Martha*—did well enough. But when Vanni Marcoux, as Scarpia, threw himself upon Mary Garden, as Tosca, their compromising entanglement on a sofa drew audible gasps as well as this protest from Mayor John F. Fitzgerald: "Boston is known throughout the country as the home, during a good many months of the year, of hundreds of students at our schools, colleges, and universities, and parents of these students have the right to expect there shall be no performances at the Opera House which would be demoralizing. I think artists who appear at the Opera House can be effective without offending public taste!"[20] The mayor's lawyer, Francis M. Carroll, was at the next *Tosca* performance, as was a representative of the police commissioner—and the singers were better behaved.

The most distinctive artistic achievement of the Boston Opera was a devotion to French repertoire, peaking in the 1911–12 season, when eleven operas by French composers were offered. In January, following forty-seven rehearsals, *Pelléas et Mélisande* was given. The Mélisande was Georgette Leblanc, who was believed to be the wife (but was actually the mistress) of Maurice Maeterlinck, the Symbolist master whose play was the basis of Debussy's poetically elusive opera. Leblanc arrived in Boston wearing a leopard coat, a brown beaver hat trimmed with parrots' wings, and a long veil of golden chiffon. Her forehead was emblazoned with a huge diamond held by an invisible gold fillet. Russell also presented Leblanc in a spoken version of *Pelléas*, with music by Fauré, and in Maeterlinck's *Monna Vanna*.

Leblanc proved an overdose, but *Pelléas* was an aesthete's delight. A program book, circulated in advance, advised ticket holders that there would be no late seating and that talking or applause would be unwelcome during the orchestral interludes. Urban's designs set new standards: the intimate scenes were played on a stage masked down to a boxlike space; the lighting details included a beam of sunshine on Arkel's white brow and a finger of probing moonlight on the glittering blue grotto that Pelléas and Mélisande explore. In New York, Henry Krehbiel had found *Pelléas* insufferably precious, with dissonant, disjointed music. In Boston, both Parker and Hale were *Pelléas* connoisseurs; "lonely and incomparable," Hale called it, "a strange manifestation of poetic individuality in a grossly material and commercial age."[21]

In short, Russell's Boston Opera, which in 1913 visited Paris itself, flirted with the aestheticist subculture we have already glimpsed in contextualizing Hale's preferences and aversions—a distinctive Boston exoticism that was distinctly marginal. At the twenty-seven-hundred-seat opera house, Debussy's masterpiece was played to swaths of empty seats. In fact, with the novelty of the Boston Opera wearing thin, Boston was found to have a limited appetite for opera after all, and Russell's company folded after six adventurous seasons.

The failure of the Boston Opera, with its predominantly Italian repertoire and predominantly French specialties, affirmed the primacy of the Germanic Boston Symphony. And yet, paradoxically, Karl Muck's German pedigree proved his undoing.

■ ■ ■

The cultural impact of World War I and its attendant Germanophobia, which tarnished thriving German symphonies and operas, German-born conductors, and German-trained composers, would change the course of the Boston Symphony.★

The looming conflict paralyzed Henry Higginson. A determined patriot, he floated war loans to the Allies and accurately foresaw America being drawn into direct conflict with Germany. And yet of his orchestra of a hundred men, only fifty-one were citizens of the United States, and of these thirty-four were foreign-born. Twenty-two were German citizens, of whom nine had applied for American citizenship. There were also eight Austrians. And Muck, with his Swiss passport, was a loyal German serving by permission of the Kaiser. As Higginson well knew, Muck had attempted to enlist in the German army but was turned down (presumably because he was considered too old or insufficiently fit). In deference to the morale of the musicians, Higginson declined

★ A later section of this book, "The Great Schism (1914)," considers the war's effects in detail.

to speak out against the Axis powers. He had also, in 1915, suffered such financial reverses that for a period his brother, Francis, had to help pay off the
orchestra's deficits. Lee, Higginson, and Company had gradually rebounded,
but Higginson remained a man in a quandary. On March 22, 1917, he wrote
to Harvard President Charles Eliot:

> Dear old friend
> [W]e have come to a strange pass. . . . We have a dozen nationalities in
> the Orchestra, and the men have behaved perfectly well toward each
> other since the war began. Dr. Muck . . . has behaved well, and has been
> cordial to me since the war began, as before; and he has been most
> kindly received by audiences here and in other cities. . . . I trust him
> entirely as an artist and as a man, and he has worked as no other conduc-
> tor has worked.
>   Query: Shall I go on with him and the Orchestra? He is the only man
> I know who can conduct for us. The Orchestra is fine, and has set the
> pace for the country. . . . Turn it over, and advise me, for you are a sober,
> hearty patriot and a great figure in education and civilization.

On July 9, in another letter to Eliot, Higginson wrote, "I could not keep the
Orchestra going without Dr. Muck, and should not try. In the first place, conductors who like old and new music are very rare; next, Dr. Muck is the most
industrious, painstaking and the ablest conductor whom we have ever had."[22]

Though Eliot advised Higginson to stand his ground, others, including former President Theodore Roosevelt, wanted Muck to go. Muck became the
subject of wild rumors; he was said to be operating a clandestine radio for
espionage from his summer home in Bar Harbor, Maine. And, following
America's declaration of war in April 1917, Muck was blamed for the Boston
Symphony's failure to play the "Star-Spangled Banner" on tour in Providence, Rhode Island. As it happened, that decision came from Higginson, for
whom the national anthem was aesthetically incompatible with serious music.
The scholar Bliss Perry, who knew Higginson well, wrote in his *Life and Letters of Henry Lee Higginson*, "If Henry Higginson had possessed the political
instinct of the average ward politician, he could have saved the situation; he
had only to dismiss Dr. Muck, to wave the American flag, order the national
anthem played, and make one of his inimitable little speeches to a pleased
audience. But he had no political cunning whatever. He was a weary and perplexed old man of eighty-three, who was simply trying, as always, to discover
his duty and to do it."

Higginson's reminiscences record that:

On Friday, November 2, I asked Dr. Muck to come to my office, which he did. I then said to him: "Will you play the Star-Spangled Banner at the beginning of our concert to-day and always?" His reply was: "What will they say to me at home?" I said: "I do not know, but let me say this: when I am in a Catholic country and the host is carried by, or a procession of churchmen comes along, I take off my hat out of consideration—not to the Host, but respect for the customs of the nation. It seems to me only friendly and reasonable." He said: "Very well, I will play the Star-Spangled Banner."[23]

It was also agreed that Muck would resign upon completing the season. But, with the rumor mills churning and patriotic sentiment at its peak, this was too little too late. On March 25 U.S. marshals appeared at Symphony Hall; only the intervention of Higginson and Charles Ellis prevented Muck's arrest from taking place on stage as he rehearsed Bach's *Saint Matthew* Passion. At the rehearsal's end, the conductor was removed and jailed, then interned for the duration of the war at Fort Oglethorpe, Georgia, as an enemy alien. Though no charges were lodged, it was disclosed by the *Boston Post* in 1919 that he had been carrying on an affair with a twenty-two-year-old girl in the Back Bay; among the letters intercepted by federal agents was one reading:

I am on my way to the concert hall to entertain the crowds of dogs and swine who think that because they pay the entrance fee they have the right to dictate to me my selections. I hate to play for this rabble. . . . [In] a very short time our gracious Kaiser will smile on my request and recall me to Berlin. . . . Our Kaiser will be prevailed upon to see the benefit to the Fatherland of my obtaining a divorce and making you my own.[24]

Even before Muck's arrest, Higginson had told friends that his travails had "destroyed for me all pleasure in the orchestra," that "very much of the joy of the concerts and the joy of music is gone for me." His health declined. In March he was informed of Muck's "base behavior." On May 4, in the course of a concert in his honor, he announced without bitterness that he was retiring from orchestra work; his remarks concluded, "Our Orchestra has always been heartily supported by you and by the public throughout our country, else it could not have lived. It must lie in all its strength and beauty, and now will be carried on by some friends who have taken it up; and for them I ask the same support which you have given me through all these years."

A committee of directors was put in charge of the Boston Symphony (and has presided ever since). Of hundreds of letters of gratitude delivered to Higginson during this year of troubles, one from William Howard Taft read, "If I were to name a man of the highest type of loyalty and patriotism, I would name him to whom this letter is addressed." Theodore Roosevelt wrote, "You have always been an inspiration, not only to those who knew you, but to all your countrymen."[25] Henry Higginson died four days short of his eighty-fifth birthday, on November 5, 1919.

■ ■ ■

If the Boston Symphony fulfilled Theodore Thomas's dictum that a symphony orchestra "shows the culture of a community," it was not the only such local embodiment. The Cultural Mile along Huntington Avenue also included the Museum of Fine Arts; to the east, on Copley Square, was the Boston Public Library. These institutions conveyed a powerful statement about the role of culture in a democratic society, a statement made explicit in the writings of Charles Eliot Norton.

In a Boston community of intellect that was one and the same with practitioners and connoisseurs of music and the fine arts, Norton's was the closest to a focal voice. Oswald Garrison Villard, the liberal publisher of the *New York Evening Post*, attested, "We knew that, outside the college, he was regarded as the outstanding celebrity on Harvard's faculty. He . . . wore the mantle of the last of the Cambridge Immortals. We knew that . . . [influential] English writers regarded him as the leading American thinker, the greatest American scholar, the most cultured figure in American life." Norton's friends included Emerson, Holmes, Lowell, Longfellow, Howells, and Henry and William James. His overseas acquaintances included Darwin, Dickens, Kipling, Matthew Arnold, William Morris, and John Ruskin.[26]

And these relationships mattered doubly to Norton: an ethos of friendship and sociability girded his every notion of civilized behavior. The good man, he wrote, must "keep himself simple, pure, tenderhearted, and sympathetic in relations with those nearest him." Such deportment fostered "open-mindedness, independence of judgment, generosity, elevation of purpose."

In a well-known 1896 essay, "Some Aspects of Civilization in America," Norton depicted a late-nineteenth-century state of siege: an "increase of vulgarity, by which I mean a predominance of taste and standards of judgment of the uneducated and unrefined masses, over those of the more enlightened and better instructed few." Literature, the church, and politics were succumbing to "the crowd . . . to popular demands," rather than deferring to those who "by superior character, intelligence, and education, are more competent to deal with [public interests]." America's elite was not doing its share to raise standards of character and conduct. Nowhere in the civilized world, he wrote, "are the practical concerns of life more engrossing; nowhere are the conditions of life more prosaic; nowhere is the poetic spirit less evident, and the love of beauty less diffused."[27]

The remedy of choice, an antidote to materialism and coarse individualism, was culture. In alliance with an array of Boston tastemakers, Norton advocated museums, orchestras, libraries, and parks as a means of securing harmony and humane decorum. This prescription, reliant on a "more enlightened and better instructed few," resonated with the agenda of England's bellwether of moral betterment: Matthew Arnold. A major influence in the United States (which he visited), Arnold campaigned for the dissemination of "right reason" and "sweetness and light," of "the best that is known and thought in the world." His most famous treatise, *Culture and Anarchy*, assigned responsibility for leadership to an edified, edifying "remnant" fortified with taste and moral intelligence. Like the Boston thinkers to whom he mattered, he complexly balanced ideals of democratized intellectual and spiritual uplift with elitist agencies of instruction.

Ralph Waldo Emerson, a sometime progenitor of genteel ideals, wrote in 1860, "The word of ambition at the present day is Culture." Emerson also wrote, "The foundation of culture, as of character, is at last the moral sentiment."[28] However elusively, these precepts connected with the cultivated gentlemen envisioned in "Some Aspects of Civilization" and *Culture and Anarchy*: temperate, discriminating, decent; immune to carnal "lubricity." Such individuals were prepared for lives of service. As "apostles of equality"—another of Arnold's terms—they would ease class antagonisms. More concretely, if wealthy, they would graciously undertake to fund institutions of culture to which multitudes would prove susceptible.

For present-day observers, Norton and other fastidious tastemakers are easy targets of ridicule as prudes or snobs. A further objection, arguably more fundamental than manners, is political. The Irish tidal wave that had captured City Hall pushed Boston's Yankee leadership into more exclusively cultural endeavors, as well as into a posture of wary defense. The vulgarian hordes Norton decried were partly Irish hordes. And so it fell to the Yankees to edify the Irish. But, as the literary historian Martin Green writes:

> The Irish refused to become fellow-citizens, culturally. They formed a society within a society. They were opposed to the Bostonian enthusiasms—for reason, for education, for reform. They opposed, for instance, the abolition of slavery; out of fear of economic competition with negroes, out of fear of offending Catholic Louisiana and Maryland, out

of a generally reactionary temper. They opposed compulsory education and temperance movements (which they thought ignored, contradicted, the doctrine of original sin), prison reform and women's rights, and so on. They hated even English literature. . . .

All this presented Yankee Boston with a serious problem. She felt entrusted with the destiny of an alien people—socially and educationally underprivileged and so a sacred responsibility—who refused to find that destiny in Boston's version of liberal democracy. If she granted them full political and economic rights, if she allowed them the control of the city, they would move it towards reaction and ignorance and prejudice.[29]

From this perspective, the enterprise of Boston culture becomes in part an exercise in "social control." Such scholars as Paul DiMaggio, Helen Horowitz, and Lawrence Levine, examining Boston and Chicago, have emphasized the role of "native-born elites"—of WASP wealth—in the creation of orchestras and art museums. They depict philanthropists shackled by conservative taste and psychological need, or citizens whose notions of uplift revealed anxious disapproval of immigrant masses. In Boston, writes DiMaggio, the Symphony and Museum of Fine Arts were creations of "cultural Capitalists" for whom high culture represented a haven from societal turmoil. In a similar vein, Charles Hamm, surveying America's late-nineteenth-century musical high culture, writes of "mystifying rituals of dress, behavior and repertory" prized by an elite determined to maintain class privilege.[30]

This vision of an imposed, class-based high culture implicates Henry Higginson as a musical plutocrat. Even so subtle an observor as Green calls Higginson a "cultural policeman," emblematic of "stiff-backed autocracy and social frigidity." Levine's influential *Highbrow/Lowbrow: The Emergence of Cultural Hierarchy in America*, in a remarkably unsympathetic account, deplores Higginson's "paternalistic rule." In Levine's view, Higginson's policy that his musicians not "play for dancing" Wednesdays through Saturdays,★ and his refusal to countenance unionization, signified a power play to "establish his sovereignty" over the players, an ensnaring "web of authority." The same hunger for control, Levine contends, drove Higginson to monopolize symphonic music in Boston and to interfere with programming lest "unworthy" pieces be scheduled. It was Higginson's insistence on expunging casual

---

★ Levine, among other writers, mistakenly states that Higginson demanded that his musicians "devote themselves exclusively to the orchestra." See Lawrence Levine, *Highbrow/Lowbrow: The Emergence of Cultural Hierarchy in America* (Cambridge, Mass., Harvard University Press, 1988), p. 127.

repertoire, Levine continues, that induced the orchestra to create a separate Promenade series "segregating the musical fare so that 'light' music was increasingly relegated to summer performances." The same prejudice against popular taste allegedly informed Higginson's attitude toward the populace at large; Higginson believed that "great music, indeed, great culture, had a limited audience and could be spread to large numbers only by diluting it, a tendency Higginson battled against all of his life." In sum, the Boston Symphony was Higginson's orchestra, his personal instrument, "to a much greater extent than he ever was willing to admit."[31]

A continuing theme of the present study is that Boston culture of the late Gilded Age is at once refined by traditions early acquired and confined by those same traditions. Its elitist currents, spurning the rabble, are balanced by a democratic urge to edify. In pondering Boston's errors of judgment—John Sullivan Dwight's repudiation of Wagner, Philip Hale's condescension toward Dvořák—the historian of culture is challenged to understand what others thought in the context of their own time and place. There is also the challenge to assess the caliber of past thinking. Dwight on Wagner is not merely conservative but shallow. Hale on Dvořák is, more than critical, bigoted. Norton and Higginson are bigger, more complex presences, arguably the two most formidable individual influences on cultural Boston in their day. To dismiss either risks dismissing—patronizing, simplifying, caricaturing—a Boston epoch.

Though neither man is much remembered today (and those who remember the one know little or nothing of the other), a few sympathetic writers have undertaken to reclaim Norton from obscurity. Rochelle Gurstein, in *The Repeal of Reticence*, warmly upholds the sensibility of politeness and sociability that Norton embodied, his linked insistence on good manners and public causes; she defends the "reticence" that safeguarded both marital intimacy and civility of discourse. Green, in a tour de force of intellectual empathy, examines the range of Norton's distinguished friends and finds a rare depth and stability of rooted principles, as well as a range of erudition so real that "Marcus Aurelius, Horace Walpole, Dante, Milton, St. Francis, Gray, are quoted with an exactness, a fullness, an apparent ease, that dazzles." Norton could function as an "Arbiter Elegantiarum of American high culture" because "the main design of his personality, his interests, and his relationships was so large and steady," because "his different talents, energies, feelings of responsibility, and powers of self-discipline all worked into that design so well." More than that, Norton was "the last great organizer and engineer of the arts as general education, the last great statesman of cultural responsibility." He ran a night school for the poor. He was instrumental in building model multiple-family housing for the incoming Irish. As an editor and teacher, he "endlessly put off his own career to promote the careers of others," and served as a "supreme inspiration" to put "high-cultural values above all others."[32]

As in all Green's Boston writings, his appreciation gains power and credibility from a balanced awareness of Boston's ultimate shortcomings. Norton, he concludes, "was so completely and so hopelessly on the losing side in the battle for American culture that his larger professions of faith became rhetorical and empty." But "his idealism, if it lacked contagious vitality, did not lack tenacity or nobility." If Norton deplored modern democracy, he "still believed in 'democratic society,' and even in 'American' ideals, though he must have found it difficult to identify any manifestations of the latter he could delight in." Finally, Norton illustrates "the power of the Boston tradition as a vocation: the quantity of energy and dedication it could evoke in the right temperament, even in its decadence. What he stood for we cannot be enthusiastic about, but that he did stand for something is splendidly manifest, and the massiveness with which he did so compels admiration."[33]

Whether so plausibly subtle an assessment rescues Norton from the grips of "social control" theorists for whom the high culture of the late Gilded Age is ultimately precious or meretricious, the case of the Boston Symphony Orchestra and Higginson plainly occupies a different milieu. It is true that the "cultured generation" fixed on music as a peculiarly potent agent of edification. In its way, Higginson's orchestra joined a lineage including Lowell Mason's hymnbooks, Dwight's *Journal of Music*, and Theodore Thomas's "sermons in tones." As for Higginson himself, he corresponded with Norton on a first-name basis; he upheld (and powerfully) the same ideals of education and uplift, friendship and civility. In the Civil War, he punished his fellow soldiers for profane language. And yet a moment's reflection redirects this simplistic picture.

For many present-day historians, late Gilded Age museums and orchestras mutually embody an escape from social strife, insulated by rituals of decorous behavior. Allegedly, they intimidated and co-opted neophytes; they neutralized class unrest. But however restrained, private, and self-conscious an 1890 visit to the Museum of Fine Arts might have been, attending a Symphony Hall concert was a public experience. The rush tickets, the cheering and applause, the town-hall plainness of democratic décor supported an exercise communal, articulate, and demonstrative. Isabella Stewart Gardner's Red Sox hatband, however startling, was less out of place at a Boston Symphony concert than in any gallery of books or fine art.

If this, and not the university, was Higginson's house of worship, it was partly because compared to Norton he was, for all his breeding and aspiration, relatively self-made and earthbound. It was not merely his limited formal education, but his telling simplicity of speech and manner that distinguished him from the author of "Certain Aspects of Civilization in America." Nor was Higginson remotely the cultural captain of industry Levine portrays. The most obvious explanation for his high-handedness was the one he himself furnished: he was determined to create a world-class orchestra for Boston. If he showed no mercy toward the Harvard Musical Association (from which he resigned) and Boston Philharmonic, they represented the casual conditions—lax rehearsals, changing membership, provincial leadership—that Higginson recognized as a retarding influence. He supported initiatives like the Boston Opera, and Jeannette Thurber's National Conservatory of Music and National Opera Company, which he (correctly) judged farsighted. He rebuffed unionization not as a coal or steel baron might have, resisting higher wages and better working conditions, but because local musicians so empowered would have prevented him from hiring better players from abroad (in an 1884 letter to Higginson, Leopold Damrosch, the conductor of the New York Symphony, decried the "absurd tyranny" of the Musicians' Protective Union in New York).[34]

While Higginson unquestionably influenced artistic policy, Levine's account exaggerates this influence and ignores its constructive aspects. If Higginson supported a Promenade season "segregating the musical fare so that 'light' music was . . . relegated to summer performances," it was partly because in Vienna he had acquired an enthusiasm for the waltzes of Johann Strauss Jr. and other "garden" repertoire. If he supported Gericke's unpopular selections of Brahms and Bruckner, it was because he was a more progressive and cosmopolitan tastemaker than Dwight and the Harvard Musical Association. That he believed great music had a "limited audience" was, one supposes, literally true, yet conceals Higginson's insistence on inexpensive tickets and his delight in their popularity. When in 1889 he had occasion to bid a public farewell to Gericke from the stage of the Music Hall, he did not praise the ennobling rectitude of music, after the fashion of Charles Eliot Norton, but said:

> . . . Why is the hall so crowded? Why do so many listeners of all ages sit on the steps and stand in the aisles each week and each year? They do not come there to please Mr. Gericke or me; they do not come twenty miles to show their good clothes; they come to hear the music, and they listen attentively and quietly, and go away with only a whisper of approval, perhaps, but they are happy. You and I know that very well. That audience is not from the Back Bay or from any particular set of people. They are town folks and country folks, and they come to hear the music at the hands of Mr. Gericke and his Orchestra.[35]

The music historian Steven Ledbetter, in a brief revisionist assessment, has written that "there was no element in [Higginson] of *noblesse oblige*"—a pardonable overstatement. Such well-placed friends as Charles Lowell supported Higginson's lifelong commitment to become a "useful citizen." His father's similar orientation—his admonitions to give away money rather than accumulate it—was partly, one imagines, a class inheritance, even if Higginson, as Ledbetter stresses, "did not grow up in an atmosphere of privilege." In later life, when Higginson strove to imbue others with his philanthropic ideals, he would use such language as:

> Democracy has got fast hold of the world, and *will* rule. Let us see that she does it more wisely and more humanly than the kings and nobles have done! Our chance is now—before the country is full and the struggle for bread becomes intense and bitter.
>
> Educate, and save ourselves and our families and our money from mobs!
>
> I would have the gentlemen of this country lead the new men, who are trying to become gentlemen, in their gifts and in their efforts to promote education.

and:

> Everywhere we see the signs of ferment—questions social, moral, mental, physical, economical. The pot is boiling hard and you must tend it, or it will run over and scald the world. For us came the great questions of slavery and of national integrity, and they were not hard to answer. Your task is more difficult, and yet you must fulfil it. Do not hope that things will take care of themselves, or that the old state of affairs will come back. The world on all sides is moving fast, and you have only to accept this fact, making the best of everything—helping, sympathizing, and of guiding and restraining others, who have less education, perhaps, than you. Do not hold off from them; but go straight on with them, side by side, learning from them and teaching them.

But Ledbetter is surely correct to emphasize that Higginson "was caught in the grip of a powerful enthusiasm for music—the kind that makes one a proselytizer, eager to spread as widely as possible the pleasures that he himself felt in the art. Power for its own sake, even such as comes to a leader in cultural circles, was less important to him than making available the wherewithal for the kind of musical experiences that had so delighted him in his youth."[36]

A more illuminating analogy here than industrial magnates or genteel culture-bearers is Theodore Thomas, whose severe passion for Beethoven Higginson experienced to the hilt. The Higginson who frequented the twenty-cent upper-gallery seats of Boston theaters to hear Italian opera, and who went without meals as a music student in Vienna, was no candidate for *noblesse oblige*. And it is notable that the language of the "boiling pot," characteristic of his appeals to gentlemen of means, is—as was notably not the case with Dwight—not to be found in his speeches and letters about the purposes of music.

Higginson, in short, occupied multiple worlds: of edifying Brahmin culture; of "barbarian" business, at which cultured Brahmins winced; of music-making—his pure, primary passion. Even in relation to his Boston Symphony, he was at once business manager, artistic advisor, and benefactor. If he is to be faulted, it is not on grounds moral or political, but aesthetic. Like Boston, he was losing touch with the times. In old age, he succumbed to the illusion that Karl Muck, who resisted the newer music and styles of interpretation, was "indispensable." He was, finally, a part—the best part—of Boston culture in its late-nineteenth-century decadence: an epoch of great mentors, private and public, but no great writers; of a great orchestra, but no composers of even incipient greatness. The single dominant force of Boston music, of Boston's institutional cultural life, of the institutionalization of America's symphonic culture to come, he was a colossus, an American hero.

CHAPTER 4

Composers and the
Brahmin Confinement

■

The problem of gentility ▪ *The Second New England School* ▪ *Amy
Beach and salon culture* ▪ *George Chadwick and
American realism* ▪ *Isabella Stewart Gardner,
Charles Martin Loeffler, and Boston aestheticism*

In his exceptional 1966 study *The Problem of Boston*, Martin Green attempts
to explain how a city that so humanistically valued and supported its writers
could have failed to produce more memorable writing. The problem, he
decides, was that late-nineteenth-century Boston treated its writers *too* well,
that they were crippled by an absence of critical distance, that Oliver Wendell
Holmes, William Dean Howells, James Russell Lowell, Henry Wadsworth
Longfellow, and John Greenleaf Whittier fatally spurned impolite Romantic
self-scrutiny: "Boston excluded from its literature the telling of deeply personal truths; those truths that reveal the non-social self. . . . Personal truths
Boston decorum forbade, and thereby it forbade significant writing."[1]

In New York, writers were Bohemians: they were not taken seriously by
the city as a whole; they did not court or enjoy respectability; for better or
worse, they were free agents. In Boston, writers were valued members of elite
society. Artists and intellectuals were socially empowered, socially committed.
They earnestly, even religiously pursued a vision of communal culture in
which literature would elevate taste and morality and ward off encroaching
vulgarity and ignorance.

No less than his specific appraisal of Charles Eliot Norton, Green's broader
indictment of cultivated Boston is the more powerful for steering clear of
Gilded Age stereotypes: he compassionately scans the exquisite urbanity, vigorous camaraderie, and farsighted democratic philanthropies of what E. L.

Godkin, the reformist New York editor, called "the one place in America where wealth and knowledge of how to use it are apt to coincide." But Green insists that by 1871, when Godkin wrote those words, Boston culture was irreversibly in decline. It was during the first half of the nineteenth century that what Edward Everett Hale called the "March of Intellect" was in full stride, that "there was the real impression that the kingdom of heaven was to be brought in by teaching people what were the relations of acid to alkalis, and what was the derivation of the word cordwainer." In 1837–38, Hale records, twenty-six lecture courses of eight talks or more were attended by 13,000 Bostonians, out of a population of 80,000. This was a whole evening's commitment: the public habitually arrived early to congregate and chat, and suppered afterward to chat some more. The sponsoring organizations included the Society for Diffusing Useful Knowledge, the Boston Lyceum, the Mercantile Library Association, the Mechanics' Association, and the Historical Society.[2]

As of 1850, the average annual per capita circulation of periodicals was 404 for Boston versus 157 for New York. Four years later, the Boston Public Library opened its doors. The collection, including "new" and "popular" titles, was intended less to serve scholars than the general population. It became the largest free circulating library in the world. Like Boston's landmark public schools and Board of Health, it embodied ideals both humanist and pragmatic, aristocratic and democratic. George Ticknor, whose dream the library was, thus reported an 1836 conversation with the grand duke of Tuscany:

> He asked me where I thought it the greatest fortune for a man to be born. I told him in America. He asked why. And when I replied, that the mass of the community there, by being occupied about the affairs of the state, instead of being confined, as they are elsewhere, to the mere drudgery of earning their own subsistence, are more truly men, and that it is more agreeable and elevating to live among them, he blushed a little but made no answer.

To Richard Henry Dana, a Europeanized Bostonian, Ticknor wrote from Europe, "We have men in the less favored portions of society, who have so much more intellect, will, and knowledge, that, compared with similar classes, here, those I am among seem of an inferior order in creation. Indeed, taken as a general remark, a man is much more truly a *man* with us than he is elsewhere."[3]

But during the second half of the nineteenth century this sanguine Boston vision was ruptured by societal decay: slums and smallpox, prostitution and crime. Concurrently, Boston's high culture, once galvanized by Emerson,

Thoreau, and the Transcendentalists, grew timid and aloof. The central factor was immigration. In 1847 alone, Boston, which had been receiving immigrants at the rate of 4,000 to 5,000 a year, absorbed 37,000 new arrivals; by 1900, 35 percent of the population was foreign-born; more than 70 percent was of foreign parentage. The immigrants, mainly half-starved and unskilled Irish, stoked new Boston industries. As of 1860, factory wages were $4.50 to $5.50 a week; in New York, where production was not yet mechanized, wages ranged from $8 to $10. Impoverished, debased, brutalized, the Boston Irish would not become cultural citizens.[4]

The Brahmins bravely set to work, attempting to assimilate this alien species. But Irish interest in elite culture was limited, and the Brahmins lost heart—and with it, a portion of their idealism. Meanwhile, the new millionaires of the Gilded Age undermined the status of the old aristocracy. The Boston of the March of the Intellect and the Society for Diffusing Useful Knowledge did not suffer a collapse. The closing decades of the century marked the founding of the Museum of Fine Arts in 1876 and (as we have seen) the Boston Symphony Orchestra five years later. In 1895 the Public Library opened its magnificent new Copley Square home, designed by Charles McKim with decorations by Daniel Chester French, John Singer Sargent, Augustus Saint-Gaudens, and James McNeill Whistler. Isabella Stewart Gardner built Fenway Court and opened its art collection to the public in 1903. Symphony Hall was built for the Boston Symphony in 1900, Jordan Hall for the New England Conservatory in 1903, the Boston Opera House for the Boston Opera in 1909. But even Charles Eliot Norton, who notably retained aspirations for the "model and ideal city" earlier culture-bearers had intended to create, suffered bouts of disillusionment; his was a worried holding action, not a cheerful frontal charge. And those around him were more despondent or more evasive in the face of change.

Green identifies James T. Fields, editor of the *Atlantic Monthly* from 1861 to 1909, as bellwether for the debased literary culture of Gilded Age Boston, made safe and tame by chronic habits of affability, by chatty writers whose more serious moods were grandly serene rather than probing.[5] This propensity to remain on dinner-table terms was reinforced by innumerable actual dinners, breakfasts, and club meetings, bubbling with speeches, anecdotes, poems, and jokes. This was a period, too, in which the antislavery fire of New England abolitionism gave way to Social Darwinist mutterings about Africans lagging behind Europeans and Americans; and when Louis Agassiz, Boston's scientist of choice, declared against Darwin in favor of God.

In sum, Green writes, Boston's Gilded Age marked the institutionalization of high culture in forms—museums, orchestras, opera houses—that would adorn the arts by honoring past achievement. As for the present, none of Boston's resident writers left enduring major works. Longfellow's *Christus* is forgotten; his *Song of Hiawatha* survives as a curiosity. Holmes was a club poet. Howells, in Green's view, was incapable of honestly recording his own feelings. Lowell himself confessed, "I feel that my life has been mainly wasted, that I have thrown away more than most men ever had." Norton, discussing Lowell after his death, would write, "I cannot take my readers, however worthy of confidence they may be, within the inner circle of intimacy, of which the charm would suffer, were its sanctity violated and its seclusion disturbed." Green comments, "It is easy to sympathize with, and even to admire, this shutting of the door against all mere gossip; but in point of fact one *must* trust one's readers; to exclude them from that intimacy is to subordinate literary values to social ones, and to stifle literature."[6] Even if four decades after the publication of Green's book some of these reputations—notably Howells's and Longfellow's—are somewhat resurgent, it can be agreed that there are no Whitmans or Melvilles in this group, that in England novelists and critics tackled the great issues of the day, that Boston produced no Dickens or Hardy, Arnold or Ruskin.

Though one would never know it from *The Problem of Boston*, the literary circle Green diagnoses mirrored a composers' circle whose comparable privileges and failures invite cross-diagnosis. Was literature really Boston's paramount cultural adornment, as Green asserts? Music was honored as queen of the arts, said to range higher and probe deeper than mere words, to grasp truths more essential, sublime, or otherwise ineffable. Beethoven was enthroned as no writer could be. More than any museum or university, the Boston Symphony Orchestra showed "the culture of the community." This was the milieu that sympathetically fostered America's first pedigreed generation of homegrown composers (slower to evolve than American writers or visual artists)—composers entrusted with prestigious pedagogical responsibilities and regularly performed by the Boston Symphony to enthusiastic public and critical response. Boston even boasted a pioneering music publisher, Arthur P. Schmidt, who favored Boston composers. Did the hothouse of Brahmin literary culture—its vicarious relationship to grittier realities—translate as tamed symphonies and sonatas? Were Boston's composers both beneficiaries and victims of exceptional local esteem and support?

■ ■ ■

Homegrown composers had appeared in New England long before the Gilded Age. In 1770, the Boston-born tanner William Billings published *The New-England Psalm-Singer* for singing school and meetinghouse choirs.

Billings is the best remembered of the late-eighteenth-century psalm- and hymn-tune composers retrospectively dubbed the First New England School. With other Yankee tunesmiths, he inherited the Puritan passion for psalm singing. But his rugged and untutored "fuging music," in which individual voices imitate one another in discord with New and Old World rules both, was new and exciting. Subsequent composers and compilers of hymn tunes, notably Lowell Mason, tamed Billings's idiosyncrasies. Mason revered Mozart, Haydn, and other European masters—and so did the next notable generation of American composers, a full century after the First New England School. This was the *Second* New England School, whose father, John Knowles Paine, espoused "adherence to the historical forms as developed by Bach, Handel, Mozart, and Beethoven."[7]

Born in Portland, Maine, in 1839, Paine studied at Berlin's Hochschule für Musik, met and played for Clara Schumann, and toured Germany and England as an organist and pianist. He settled in Boston in 1861, and at Harvard held the first chair of music at any American university. He won the friendship and allegiance of the literary elite, including Emerson, Holmes, Howells, Longfellow, and Norton. He advised Henry Higginson. He taught composers of consequence: Arthur Foote, John Alden Carpenter, Edward Burlingame Hill, Frederick Converse, and Daniel Gregory Mason.

Paine's Mass in D (1865) was the first large-scale American work to be performed in Europe. His two symphonies (1875 and 1879) are sizable works, thirsty with ambition, stylistically pliable and acquisitive. The C minor First Symphony keys on Beethoven's Fifth and its famous four-note motto. The fifty-minute Second Symphony, "Im Frühling," admits Schumann's influence. In later life, as Wagnerism permeated north from New York, Paine recanted his earlier rejection of the Music of the Future. In the opera *Azara* (1883–1898), the great undertaking of his later years, the Prelude to act two, with offstage horns, is *Tristan*-esque.

In the first stage of "the process of throwing off a foreign musical domination," writes the musicologist Nicholas Temperley, "the primary goal is to establish that a native product can be as good as a foreign import. This cannot be done by writing nationalistic music because such would be rejected by most of the public as primitive or irrelevant." Paine's cloned Germanic styles and forms signify an American rite of passage. To John Sullivan Dwight, who at the premiere of Paine's Second Symphony was observed "frantically opening and shutting his umbrella as an expression of uncontrollable enthusiasm," Paine was a beacon to the future. To George Chadwick, upon hearing Theodore Thomas conduct the wildly applauded premiere of Paine's First, Paine "proved we could have a great musician, and that he could get a hearing."[8]

Chadwick was the leader among equals of the New England composers of the next generation—more than any such composers' aggregation before or since, a genuine American school of shared interests, enthusiasms, and accomplishments. He studied in Leipzig and Munich. Arthur Foote studied at Harvard with the Berlin-educated Paine. Horatio Parker studied with Chadwick in Boston, then with Joseph Rheinberger in Munich. Amy Beach was the youngest of the "Boston boys," in whose company she was explicitly accepted by Chadwick even though her gender prevented her from attending the boys' frequent gatherings at the St. Botolph Club and Tavern Club. In congenial alignment with Boston performers, scribes, and scholars, this quartet of Boston composers habituated the same clubs, attended the same concerts, and applauded one another with civility and warmth. They also critiqued one another. "The talk was honest and frank to a degree," Foote later recalled. "I learned a lot from it."[9]

Of the four composers, Foote, born in Salem in 1853, favored smaller forms and produced no symphonies or operas. His success was such that his major orchestral works were regularly introduced by the Boston Symphony and his major chamber works by the Kneisel Quartet, often with the composer as pianist. The music itself, much of which remains durable, is in equal parts skilled, amiable, and mild. It easily assimilates a range of stronger voices, German and French. Though he lived to 1937, Foote absorbed no twentieth-century styles. He was not a bigot, like Dwight. Rather, he acknowledged his timidity with typical equanimity: "My influence from the beginning, as well as my predilection, were ultra-conservative." Late in life he could calmly marvel, "How little we . . . realized that Wagner was the strongest musical influence of [the] years 1850–1900."[10] His slender autobiography is the very embodiment of the discreet aversion to intimacy Martin Green faults in Howells, Longfellow, and Lowell. Foote's failure to grow was typical of Boston: like the writers he knew and admired, he was both supported and stifled by a benign cultural environment.

Horatio Parker is today mainly remembered as the composition teacher who provoked Charles Ives's bitter complaints to his father. Ives also said of Parker, "His choral works have dignity and depth that many contemporaries, especially in religious and choral compositions, do not have. Parker had ideals that carried him higher than the popular, but he was governed by the 'German rule.' . . . Parker was a bright man, a good technician, but perfectly willing to be limited by what Rheinberger has taught him."[11]

Parker was fundamentally a church composer; he mainly wrote for chorus. A predominant New Englander rather than a Bostonian, he lived in New York from 1886 to 1893, then settled in New Haven, where he became dean of Yale's School of Music and organized the New Haven Symphony Orchestra. His signature work, the oratorio *Hora Novissima*, was performed frequently in the years following its premiere in 1893. Setting a twelfth-century Latin text evoking heavenly pleasures, Parker conveys a religious fervor freshly experienced. By turns fragrant and gentle, sonorous and grand, ennobled by the broad stride of its harmony and structure, enlivened by good tunes and unexpected touches of orchestral color, *Hora Novissima* is no Victorian corpse; a potent present-day performance would startle even nonbelievers. But Parker remains a stretch for twenty-first-century tastes.

Beach and Chadwick are the Second New England School composers who most matter today—the former because she most vividly gauges the costs of the Brahmin confinement, the latter because in the history of American classical music he is the first symphonic composer to fashion a recognizably American style. They deserve more detailed consideration.

■ ■ ■

Amy Beach and Teresa Carreño, among the most potent musical women of their day, admired one another. Both composed and played the piano. Beach (known as "Mrs. H. H. A. Beach") dedicated her Piano Concerto to Carreño; Carreño (never known as "Madame d'Albert") gave the German premiere of Beach's Sonata for Violin and Piano. Their very different lives document differences between Berlin, where Carreño's husband Eugen d'Albert was a towering artistic presence, and Boston, where Henry Beach kept company with Longfellow and Holmes.

Carreño, born in Venezuela in 1853, was a musical prodigy who gave her New York debut recital at the age of nine and proceeded to support her family. By the age of twenty-three, she was divorced and remarried; she eventually married four times. Amy Marcy Cheney, born in New Hampshire in 1867, was a musical prodigy initially forbidden by her Calvinist mother to touch the piano. Expected to be pious, humble, and modest, she was not encouraged to perform in public. She married once, at the age of eighteen; her husband was old enough to be her father; there were no offspring. Carreño, who also sang, conducted, and ran an opera company, complained that her children made it difficult to practice and purported to keep a loaded gun on her piano with which to shoot trespassers.[12] Beach took her husband's name and agreed not to teach or tour; properly, Dr. Henry Beach was sole provider.

Boston embraced Amy Cheney. Her Boston Symphony Orchestra debut, playing Chopin's F minor Piano Concerto at the age of seventeen, was a triumph. When, as the twenty-seven-year-old Mrs. Beach, she completed her

Gaelic Symphony, the Boston Symphony premiered it to demonstrative public and journalistic acclaim; Philip Hale wrote that she had "brought honor to
herself and the city which is her dwelling place."[13] But if Beach was celebrated and supported by Boston, she was also pampered and patronized in
ways foreign to Carreño and Berlin.

From these circumstances, Amy Beach emerges as a figure of special
interest—because she was a widely esteemed woman in a field dominated by
men, because her natural gift was prodigious, because her artistic development
was shaped or misshapen by conditions she helps us to assess. Conventional in
her outward habits and tastes, she was earnestly religious, invariably polite. But
the artist within her conveyed a Lisztian libidinal charge. Her impassioned
Romanticism set her apart from Paine, Foote, Parker, Chadwick, and other
New England colleagues.

What was the outcome? Her mother fitfully capitulated to Amy's musical
vocation, only to seek advice from a staunch conservative: Wilhelm Gericke,
then the Boston Symphony's music director. Gericke advised that Amy not
enroll in a distinguished German conservatory, as had Paine, Chadwick, and
Parker. Rather she should teach herself to compose by assiduously studying
the great masters. And so Amy became a sort of marital trophy—not a pupil,
teacher, or touring pianist, but a full-time composer. This, Dr. Beach reckoned, was her great gift. He backed her to the hilt, both financially and personally. Returning from his medical office he would daily inquire, "What did
you compose today, dear?" If it was a song, he would sing it, and tell her what
he thought. Amy would spend her days in the music room, studying, composing, and practicing. Pursuant to Gericke's advice, she established a grueling
regimen of self-education, beginning with counterpoint and fugue. Her self-
discipline was tenacious.

John Sullivan Dwight believed that without Handel, Mozart, and
Beethoven "no man can be quite a man." He touted the virility of the big
forms. These were the forms Henry Beach urged on Amy. Three months after
her marriage, she undertook what became a seventy-minute Mass, completed
in 1890. The forty-minute *Gaelic* Symphony came next, followed in 1899 by a
thirty-five-minute, four-movement Piano Concerto. She also produced a Violin Sonata and Piano Quintet, both of them big boned and expansive. Duly
acclaimed as heroic, virile, dignified, and soulful, these works made Beach's
reputation as America's foremost female composer. Arthur P. Schmidt
promptly published everything she produced. Paine, Foote, and other leading
Boston musicians were among her loyalest admirers. Upon hearing the *Gaelic*
Symphony, Chadwick wrote to her, "I always feel a thrill of pride myself
whenever I hear a fine work by any one of us."[14]

The recent revival of this music, so generously acclaimed a century ago, confirms Beach's formidable talent. But much of it sounds overblown or overwrought. For all its authentic intensity, its splendid tunes and incandescent chromatic harmonies, it cannot fully escape the stodginess of the salon. The training, the travel, the worldliness Beach was denied all could have channeled her passion more deeply and acutely.

The proof came in 1910, when Henry Beach died. Amy, at age forty-two, remained a Victorian but was liberated from Boston. She traveled to Europe—for the first time!—in 1911. She hired a European manager and gave recitals. She arranged performances of her *Gaelic* Symphony, and of her Piano Concerto with herself as soloist. She sometimes triumphed; otherwise, the reviews were mixed, harsher and franker than the feedback Boston's critics had offered. She returned to the United States fully three years later, and only because of the war. Revitalized, she left Boston for New York and subsequently lived in California and, mainly, New Hampshire. She returned to Europe frequently.

During her long widowhood, Beach was one of the most admired women in America, a model of female accomplishment among amateur performers and musical clubs, all dominated by women. Her music was often heard, but marginalized: it lacked the mainstream exponents it had once enjoyed in Boston, New York, and Chicago. By cognoscenti, she was dismissed as old-fashioned. This act of repudiation concealed her continued artistic growth. Though Beach had no appetite for jazz—she called it "vulgar" and "debasing"[15]—or for Copland or Prokofiev, her tastes expanded notably. And her own music—more than three hundred works by the time she died in 1944—evolved toward a style more tempered and distilled. A composition such as the Variations for Flute and String Quartet (1916) is music at peace with itself and its place, a New England idyll. More impressive, and much less known, is the one-movement, fifteen-minute String Quartet Beach completed in 1929. It lay unpublished until 1994. Based on three Eskimo tunes, it achieves an idiom leaner and more linear, but also more densely chromatic, than Beach's big Boston pieces. To the ruminative nostalgia of her post-Victorian voice, it adds moments of piercing dissonance. Judged by its "progressive" style, Beach's haunting, elegiac String Quartet might have been composed around 1900, a starting point rather than a swan song.

Green, in *The Problem of Boston*, diagnoses a condition that discouraged critical distance and forbade deeply personal truths. Beach fits this diagnosis and does not. Her deficient training was a dilemma particular to her. Its symptoms included patches of thick orchestration, of unpruned excess and prolixity. A deeper dilemma was particular to Boston. Temperamentally, Beach suited the grand forms that were urged upon her. But she was, accordingly, ill-suited to a Foote-like existence of decorous camaraderie and amiable conversation. The strenuous compositional exertions of her *Gaelic* Symphony were inspired by "the rough, primitive character of the Celtic people."[16] But genteel Boston protected Beach from the primitive; her Celts signify a rough-hewn reality she strives to compass but cannot.

The C-sharp minor Piano Concerto reveals a different kind of shallowness. Green diagnoses a withdrawal from impolite self-scrutiny, from inhabitation of the solitary Romantic ego. Beach called musical composition "veritable autobiography" and spoke of giving expression to "all that is deepest in life." In the long and tempestuous Piano Concerto, the soloist—Beach herself—is hero, by turns contemplative and explosive. Her confrontational posture and savvy capacity for display are qualities utterly uncharacteristic of a Foote, Parker, or Chadwick. Boston invaded Beach's creative recesses. Her mother liked to sit in the music room while Amy composed. Her husband inflicted sentimental poetry, a mountain of clichés, which Amy dutifully set to music. The song "Twilight" supplies melodies for the Largo of the concerto, characterized by Beach as "a dark, tragic lament." The relevant verses by Dr. Beach begin:

> No sun to warm
> The darkening cloud of mist,
> But everywhere
> The steamy earth sends up
> A veil of gray and damp
> To kiss the green and tender leaves
> And leave its cool imprint
> In limpid pearls of dew.

No wonder Beach could write in 1909 about the challenges facing married women who compose at home: "The constant interruptions that beset one who needs repose and time for reflection in such a career require much patience and considerable diplomacy to prevent their distracting influence from devitalizing and unnecessarily wearying the spirits that are so essential to commanding work."[17]

For all its somber drama and symphonic weight, the Piano Concerto is not, on the one hand, a dialectic in which an imploring or imperative protagonist interacts with surrounding forces (as in Mozart's D minor Concerto and Beethoven's C minor, both of which Beach played). Nor, on the other hand, is it an essentially sociable or decorative vehicle (after the fashion of the

Chopin and Saint-Saëns concertos she also performed). The D-flat major dance finale is neither a ritual of victory nor a cumulative celebration. The trajectory is muddled. It is music in conflict with itself by a composer conflicted by her immediate (and only) environment.

These shortcomings are made the more significant by the concerto's superb chiaroscuro and panache. Notwithstanding an abundance of borrowed gestures, it is not lacking in originality—the second movement is a distinctive moto perpetuo whose chattering piano overlays long orchestral tunes—or roof-rattling impact. It deserves a caliber of advocacy—a famous pianist to disclose and champion its highest possibilities—it has yet to enjoy. It underlines the absurdity of Beach's inability to study abroad, the urgency of her discovering—outside Boston, outside the United States—a mentor of genius.

Adrienne Fried Block, in her biography of Beach, finds in the concerto's tempests an encoded representation of "struggles [Beach] encountered from opposing forces at home." But if there is defiance here, it is so much sublimated as to suggest a larger failure of nerve. To all appearances, Beach was happy in her marriage and happily ensconced in a circle of significant friends. She was fairly extolled, in the *Musical Courier*, for her "beautiful womanly nature." In an article on women and motherhood, Beach herself wrote, "A woman must be a *woman* first, then a *musician.*" She joined the Daughters of the American Revolution. She had misgivings about Jews.[18]

As Block stresses, Beach chose the life she led, "a product of her time, her region, her class, her white Anglo-Saxon heritage."[19] As a pioneering woman in a field more than dominated by men, her achievement is astonishing; she cannot be blamed for becoming a vicarious practitioner of the big Romantic genres.

■ ■ ■

From Foote, Parker, and Beach, George Whitefield Chadwick stands apart. Chadwick excepted, Boston's composers did not concern themselves with "What is American music?" or "Should it sound American?" Paine explicitly eschewed a "national" style; music, he believed, was universal, unconfined by geography. Questions of American identity were more likely to occur to outsiders like Dvořák, or first-generation Americans like George Gershwin and Aaron Copland, for whom jazz, folk songs, and popular music became vital points of reference. And yet Chadwick possesses an American voice steeped in the vernacular of cracker-barrel humor, fiddle tunes, and minstrel songs. This affinity—often incidental, sometimes suppressed—was at least occasionally conscious; in his memoirs, Chadwick wrote that he was "determined to make" his *Symphonic Sketches* "American in style—as [he] understood the term."[20]

Even more than Henry Higginson's, Chadwick's background contradicts the imagery of Brahmin privilege and ease. In a memoir, he traced eight previous generations of New England Chadwicks and approvingly quoted John Adams: "Had I ever supposed that family pride were in any way excusable, I should think a descent from a line of virtuous, independent New England farmers for 160 years was a better foundation for it than a descent through royal or noble scoundrels ever since the flood."[21] Chadwick was born in industrial Lowell. The family soon moved to Lawrence: a small-town commercial environment in which his father opened an insurance business. Alonzo Chadwick made his son leave high school to help with the little firm; he also discouraged music, the theater, and dancing. George studied and composed on the sly. A Theodore Thomas concert, with the *Eroica*, was a great boyhood inspiration; he also enjoyed (clandestinely) minstrel and pantomime shows, and opera. His enthusiasms, always eclectic, included Wagner and Johann Strauss Jr. A camping trip in the White Mountains introduced him to lumberjack songs, one of which, with more than seventy verses, he liked so much he arranged it for piano. His first full-time job, at the age of twenty-one, was teaching music—piano, organ, theory, history, and singing—at Olivet College in Michigan. This enabled him to save barely enough money for passage and tuition to the Leipzig Conservatory, where, without a high school diploma, he outshone his German peers. He next studied in Munich, then resettled in Boston in 1880. As director of the New England Conservatory from 1897 to 1930, Chadwick was crusty, blunt, occasionally mischievous, never the aristocrat. He kept his hair short, was clean shaven save for a modest mustache, and wore wool flannel suits. A colleague once remembered that his most vivid impression of Chadwick was of the eminent composer and pedagogue eating a plate of beans on a tray at the local Hayes-Bickford cafeteria.[22]

From the start, Chadwick's music was marked by informality. His first success, in Leipzig, was the *Rip Van Winkle* Overture, an anomaly among more earnest student efforts. His First String Quartet, another Leipzig composition, already features a theme resembling a Stephen Foster tune. It was Chadwick's opinion that he fully found his compositional voice with a Scherzo in F. At its premiere in 1884, it had to be encored by the Boston Symphony Orchestra. Its breeziness—its slurping grace notes make the orchestra giggle and guffaw—is a Chadwick trademark. So is the pentatonic flavor of the scampering main tune, steeped in Anglo-American song. The methodology of this polished miniature may be Germanic, but the composer is an American who thumbs his nose at German teachers. *Jubilee* (1895), from the *Symphonic Sketches*, deserves to be Chadwick's signature. Its Yankee exuberance and heartwarming nostalgia are iconic of Mark Twain's America. A horn flourish nearly quotes Foster's "Camptown Races." The gorgeous second subject, coming next, begs for an Oscar Hammerstein lyric. The materials are vividly colored and recolored throughout.

Chadwick swiftly became the most performed Boston composer (prior to the arrival of Serge Koussevitzky in 1924, his music was played by the Boston Symphony seventy-eight times). Local critics were not slow to recognize that his chipper métier and vernacular inflections signified something new under the sun. William Apthorp, in the *Transcript*, called the Scherzo in F a "gem": "the first theme, with its quasi-Irish humorousness (it positively winks at you), is peculiarly happy. . . . The piquant charm of the whole is irresistible." Reviewing a 1908 performance of the *Symphonic Sketches*, H. T. Parker called Chadwick the most American of American composers. In *Jubilee*, he heard "the echo of negro tunes; but the American quality of the music lies little in that. Rather, it is in the high and volatile spirits of the music, the sheer rough-and-tumble of it at its fullest moments." More recently, Chadwick's 1990 biographer Victor Fell Yellin has shrewdly observed of the Anglo-Celtic second subject that its juxtaposition with a rocking Afro-Caribbean rhythm "magically transforms these two seemingly disparate musical elements into a sonority that has come to be accepted as a metaphor for the wide open spaces of the West: horse and rider cantering into the setting sun,"[23] an effect irresistible when lit by the coda's poetic glow. Yellin's Chadwick annotations also tellingly allude to Currier & Ives and Stephen Crane. In fact, it is a measure of Chadwick's stature that, far more than other turn-of-the-century New England composers, he interfaces with major figures outside music, most notably with William Dean Howells and the literary realists.

In fact, comparison to Howells, himself a bellwether for contrasting tastes in Boston and New York, sharply clarifies what Chadwick was and was not. Howells famously (or infamously) observed that "our novelists . . . concern themselves with the more smiling aspects of life, which are the more American." In context, he was arguing that Americans, empirically, were more cheerful, innocent, and decently maintained than they were miserable, deceitful, and oppressed. He did not deny America its share of "purely mortal troubles," of "sin and suffering and shame." In fact, influenced by contemporary European fiction, he spearheaded a movement toward novels less elitist in style and content, transcending social and class division, speaking to and for all America. He urged writers to exit the drawing room and record all around them, without Romantic varnish. The realists were attacked as vulgar and obscene by those who sought to preserve a more completely ennobling high culture. And yet the movement seemed old-fashioned almost the day it was born, outflanked by writers like Crane, Theodore Dreiser, and Frank Norris whose personal lives rejected Victorian rectitude and whose fictions more realistically visited ordinary lives than the realists did. H. L. Mencken, a savage champion of Dreiser, satirized, "The action of all the novels of the Howells school goes on within four walls of painted canvas; they begin to shock once they describe an attack of asthma or a steak burning below stairs; they never penetrate beneath the flow of social concealments and urbanities to the passions that actually move men and women to their acts, and the great forces that circumscribe and condition personality."[24]

That Howells was an easy target does not invalidate such cunning target practice. In Boston, he puritanically rejected Offenbach as coarse and immodest.[25] He increasingly shifted his focus to New York in search of reality and produced such novels as *A Hazard of New Fortunes* (1891), in which, agog at the Manhattan melee, he adumbrates new empathy for urban laborers and radicals to whom he remains an outsider. His friend Mark Twain, with Missouri and California behind him, drew on a varied world of direct experience; he assumes the voice of Huck or Tom; he makes Howells seem as vicarious as Amy Beach.

In Boston, Howells was for a time president of the Tavern Club, one of Chadwick's principal haunts. Whether or not they had occasion to discuss new aesthetic currents, Chadwick became a singular proponent of what Yellin accurately terms "populist realism." Even as a young man, at Olivet College, he had espoused "making classical music popular." No less than Howells, he steered toward the quotidian. This agenda is laid bare in the two-act opera *The Padrone* (1912), a rare example of American *verismo*, paralleling what Leoncavallo and Mascagni had earlier achieved with *Pagliacci* and *Cavalleria rusticana*.[26]

For *Azara*, John Knowles Paine had set a medieval fable about Rainulf, king of Provence, and his son Guntran, both in romantic pursuit of the same heroine. Horatio Parker's *Mona*, mounted by the Metropolitan Opera in 1912, centers on a sanguinary British princess in revolt against Roman rule, circa 100 A.D. *The Padrone*, singularly, is set in contemporary Boston, amid the rough and tumble of Italian immigrants. Catani, who as "padrone" brutally rules the neighborhood, forces himself upon Marietta, who loves another; she kills him with a knife to the heart. Cheerful American tourists, returning from abroad, and cheerless immigration officials, patrolling the port, complete this picture of "real life." Chadwick eschews the artifice of detachable arias and duets. As in his songs, the word-setting is notably idiomatic, following the stresses of colloquial speech.

But Chadwick's realism, no less than Howells's, paradoxically charts his limitations. Never mind that the libretto is impossibly genteel (it reads like a translation from another tongue); Chadwick, too, is an outsider to this bloody melodrama. His inhibiting urbanity produces stock characters: Catani is a cartoon Scarpia, a mustache-twirling villain whose jealous rages are stilted and square. Dreiser's achievement in *Sister Carrie*—finished in 1900, a dozen years *before* Chadwick completed *The Padrone*—is clarifying. Here is a writer too uncouth for any Boston club, a former reporter whose unfinished prose and charmless eye, doggedly cataloguing the symptoms of social dislocation and urban anomie, barely qualify as "literary," yet who achieves effects of pity and awe that bare the emptiness of hidden lives. Mencken, fastening on Dreiser's gloomy independence, his stubborn and surprising distance from every available aesthetic or stylistic influence, articulates his "essential isolation"[27]—precisely what Boston did not promote.

An inscription by Chadwick for *A Vagrom Ballad*, the fourth *Symphonic Sketch*, composed in 1896, reads:

> A tale of tramps and railway ties,
> And old clay pipes and rum,
> Of broken heads and blackened eyes,
> And the "thirty days" to come

Chadwick attributed the visual inspiration to an encampment of hoboes he would pass by train commuting to Worcester. But this unlikely little tone poem is also obviously indebted to the vaudeville clown with big shoes, tattered derby, and ragged evening clothes. Its mock seriousness is conveyed by a bass-clarinet recitative, a soft-shoe tune for bassoon, and a snatch of a Bach fugue—on the xylophone. A swooning, lachrymose reprise of the dance tune—music reeling in a drunken stupor—weeps tears of self-pity, abruptly dispelled by a finale that chases the clown offstage to laughter and applause. Yellin likens *A Vagrom Ballad* to the style and subject matter of the Ashcan School painter John Sloan. But Chadwick, unlike Sloan, deals with mere appearances, not the pathos of actual lives. A surer analogy would be to Norman Rockwell, or—closer to Chadwick's time and place—the early genre paintings of Winslow Homer.

Homer's canvases of sanguine, wholesome boys' lives, for that matter, fit Chadwick's *Jubilee*. And Chadwick was a composer who, in both Munich and Boston, kept company with paintings and painters. He knew William Merritt Chase and purchased the first canvas ever sold by Childe Hassam. Both Chase and Hassam were important American apostles of French Impressionism— and this is yet another extramusical point of reference, correlating with that side of Chadwick that predisposed him to consider studies with César Franck (in 1879); to conduct new French music with his conservatory orchestra; to limn the seascape opening of his *Aphrodite* (1912) with *plein air* dabs and pulsations (and of course correlating, as well, with that side of Boston we have glimpsed in the writings of Philip Hale and the success of *Pelléas et Mélisande*).

At best, these varied ingredients—Yankee, German, and French; realist and Impressionist writers and painters—achieve a characterful blend. Otherwise, Chadwick's music does not escape being self-conflicted, as with Beach. Chadwick's Second Symphony (1885)—arguably the best American symphony before Ives, and well worth knowing—appropriates the happy-go-lucky Scherzo in F of 1884. It sets the tone but the other three movements lack weight and variety enough to sustain a forty-minute design. Chadwick's Third (1894) tries harder. The first movement is a bustling but labored experiment in Brahmsian subtleties of rhythmic and motivic play. The scherzo is a tarantella, marvelously piquant. The rhapsodic slow movement* is compromised by a stiff fugato, redeemed by a luminous reprise. The finale begins with a terrific horn proclamation; learned motivic interplay dulls energies with which the Presto coda reconnects. Chadwick's high spirits somehow survive: the symphony is as winning or incongruous as Brahms might seem grinning ear to ear.

It is both understandable and disappointing that Chadwick abandoned this particular challenge. He opted afterward for surrogate symphonies: the four-movement *Symphonic Sketches*, the four-movement Sinfonietta, the four-movement *Suite Symphonique*. The *Melpomene* Overture, Chadwick's most performed composition during his lifetime, bravely salutes the muse of tragedy. It begins by imitating the *Tristan* Prelude—but this is a vein of high feeling Chadwick cannot sustain.† More durable is the big Fourth String Quartet, once the most performed of Chadwick's chamber works, echoing with New England hymns and fiddle tunes yet incorporating, in its finale, elements of passacaglia and fugue.

Even though Dvořák is here a tangible influence, to call such music derivative is knee-jerk listening: it explores a veritable lexicon of Americana; it sounds like Chadwick. If Chadwick falls short of our expectations, it is for a

---

* It is considered by the Estonian-born conductor and Chadwick specialist Neeme Järvi the most beautiful in any American symphony (in conversation with the author).

† Douglas Bomberger, in "Chadwick's *Melpomene* and the Anxiety of Influence," argues that Chadwick here quotes the *Tristan* Prelude as a compositional rite of passage, taking it to a different destination: "The composer . . . 'misreads' the Wagner quotation in order to assert his own artistic individuality and come to terms with his debt to his European predecessor." See *American Music*, vol. 21, no. 3 (Fall 2003), pp. 319–348.

different reason: he is ultimately a happy captive of his equable Boston milieu. Yellin, in his biography, sees Chadwick the composer as overburdened with the time-consuming responsibilities of Chadwick the music school director. It is a point well taken that Americans like Chadwick, Paine, Parker, and Foote could not avail themselves of the state and princely stipends enjoyed by a Wagner, Tchaikovsky, or Dvořák. But Chadwick, ideally, needed to get away from more than the New England Conservatory. In his memoirs he regrets "imported Viennese Jews" displacing American-born orchestral musicians, "polyglot populations" displacing "real American life." Not without bitterness, he complained, as well, that Higginson preferred foreign-born conductors to Americans such as himself.[28] But Higginson (as usual) knew what he was doing when he declined to consider local candidates to lead his orchestra. Chadwick could have used a dose of Higginson's worldliness.

In the long view, Chadwick's early music qualifies him as the first American symphonic nationalist. His later symphonic output sometimes steers toward operetta and the movies. To listen to the brassy "title music" and song tunes igniting the *Suite Symphonique* (1909) is to hear the sound of Hollywood to come. The crooning Romanza of the same work, with its divine saxophone solos, inhabits something like Victor Herbert land.

It is arguable that Chadwick never surpassed the Scherzo in F with which he found his way. Unlike Winslow Homer, also Boston-born, who secluded himself in Maine, unlike Mark Twain, an eager and chronic traveler, he did not become a heroic portraitist of physical and psychic American landscapes. But more than any other previous or contemporaneous composer, he partakes in their American vision. *Jubilee* should long ago have become a staple of American "pops" programming. In the American canon, it deserves a higher place than such second-tier Howells "classics" as *The Rise of Silas Lapham*. No mere footnote—no Foote-note—George Chadwick seasoned the genteel tradition with a necessary grain of salt.

■ ■ ■

If Boston's gentility—its mildness, its insularity—provoked literary naturalists in New York and Chicago, in Boston itself the genteel tradition goaded into existence a dissident subculture of letters and music at the opposite extreme from Crane, Dreiser, and Norris: aestheticism.

Henry Adams, Henry James, George Santayana were, to a greater or lesser degree, aesthetes. That is, they disdained the moral criterion for culture: whether or not it was spiritually ennobling or socially sound, great art was aesthetically pleasing. This posture produced habits of irony, of disparagement and self-disparagement, of worldly skepticism or despair at odds with "the more smiling aspects of life." A typically diffident self-observation from *The Education of Henry Adams* reads:

> The boy Henry wanted to go to Europe; he seemed well-behaved, when anyone was looking at him; he observed conventions, when he could not escape them; he was never quarrelsome, towards a superior; his morals were apparently good, and his moral principles, if he had any, were not known to be bad. Above all, he was timid and showed a certain sense of self-respect, when in public view. What he was at heart, no-one could say; least of all himself; but he was probably human, and no worse than some others.

Adams adduced (in himself) "New England" qualities atypical of a Howells or Longfellow: "The habit of doubt; of distrusting his own judgment and of totally rejecting the judgment of the world; the tendency to regard every question as open; the hesitation to act except as a choice of evils; the shirking of responsibility; the love of line, form, quality; the horror of ennui, the passion for companionship and the antipathy to society."[29]

Adams's ambivalence applied to Boston: he often resided elsewhere. James was an expatriate; in *The Bostonians* (1886), he fashioned a withering satire of high-minded propriety and social agitation, of an organizing "city of culture" rigid with prescribed habits and tastes, of humorless "Yankee females"—"spare, dry, hard, without a curve, an inflection or a grace"—who "asked no odds in the battle of life," of a "society in which the casual expression of strong opinion generally produced waves of silence" absent European aplomb. Into the mouth of Basil Ransom, James poured his contempt for "feminized" New England reformers, products of "a nervous, hysterical, chattering, canting age, an age of hollow phrases and false delicacy and exaggerated solicitudes and coddled sensibilities" within which Verena Tarrant, whom Ransom wants to rescue, is entrapped: "With her light, bright texture, her complacent responsiveness, her genial, graceful, ornamental cast, her desire to keep on pleasing others at the time when a force she had never felt before was pushing her to please herself, poor Verena lived in these days in a state of moral tension—with a sense of being strained and aching—which she didn't betray more only because it was absolutely not in her power to look desperate."[30] Boston has turned Verena into a sideshow: the star attraction at feminist seances. A creature of stunted and misdirected potential—young, vulnerable, creatively gifted—she is a veritable Amy Beach.

The Bostonians, quite obviously, is the work of an escapee. Aesthetes who did not, like James, physically escape Boston, escaped into a Boston enclave oblivious or contemptuous of Boston aspirations. In its furthest recesses, the enclave broached a higher, more exotic, more sensual aestheticism: decadence. What Oscar Wilde or James McNeill Whistler were to London, the "Visionists"—encircling the bibliophile/photographer Fred Holland Day, who favored Turkish robes and Chinese silk shirts, cabalistic rituals, and handsome young men—were to Boston.[31] Aesthetes and decadents also surrounded a Back Bay queen bee: Isabella Stewart Gardner. She kept the city, as a society magazine put it, in "a state of social excitement." She was seen in a carriage with a pair of lion cubs. She attended parties swathed in gauze as an Egyptian "nautch girl" or wearing diamonds attached to gold antennas bobbing overhead. She was born in New York; her husband, John Lowell Gardner, inherited a Boston fortune made in the East India trade. The Gardner mansion, at 152 Beacon Street, was an aesthetes' delight whose treasures were purchased under the fastidious supervision of Bernard Berenson. After Jack Gardner died in 1898, Isabella realized their joint dream of a house-*cum*-museum: the four-story palazzo known to this day as Fenway Court. Its glass-roofed central courtyard was framed by carved stone balconies imported from Venice. Its every room was an orchestrated medley of paintings, drawings, tapestries, and *objets d'art*. At night, its galleries might be illuminated by fireplaces, candles, and Chinese lanterns. The Gardner collection famously includes Titian's *The Rape of Lucretia*; Vermeer's *The Concert*; Whistler's *Harmony, Nocturne*, and *Symphony in White*; and the eight-by-eleven-foot *El Jaleo* by John Singer Sargent, a frequent guest who portrayed Gardner, in another famous painting, in *décolleté*. In the view of one recent historian, the house quartered, as well, a male homosexual coterie whose handsome and sensuously refined members, notably including Sargent, were inordinately compatible with the idiosyncratic Gardner as she was with them.

Gardner was also a passionate music lover, and some of the handsome young men she collected were pianists, violinists, and composers. Music was part of the Fenway Court agenda of aesthetic refreshment. In fact, the musical events—some private, some public—she presented in her spacious, high-ceilinged Music Room were a notable contribution to Boston culture, dovetailing with the aestheticist and Francophile tendencies of Philip Hale and the Boston Opera. These were not parlor musicales but formal concerts (no food or drink was served until afterward), the printed tickets for which pointedly omitted the performers' names even when the performer was Paderewski, Busoni, Melba, or Lilli Lehmann. As in painting, Gardner's tastes were eclectic and moderately progressive. She attended the Wagner festival at Bayreuth four times—and the *Siegfried Idyll*, with members of the Boston Symphony, was performed at Fenway Court. Her affinity for modern French music was pronounced. She was of course a devoted subscriber to the Francophile Boston Opera; she befriended Joseph Urban and once hosted a Maeterlinck "lecture" by Georgette Leblanc.

But Gardner's paramount musical loyalty, both in public and behind the scenes, was to the Boston Symphony. She outbid everyone at the annual auctions for choice subscription seats. When she broke her ankle, she had herself carried to her seat on a hammock. The Higginsons were close friends.* Wilhelm Gericke was a constant visitor and sometime performer at Fenway Court. When Karl Muck was jailed and ostracized, in 1918, Gardner tried unsuccessfully to visit him; she left a basket of food. Her core entourage included Timoteusz Adamowski, who played in both the Symphony and the Kneisel String Quartet. And her virtual court musician was the Symphony's associate concertmaster—who also happened to be America's most accomplished aestheticist composer, and the one fin de siècle Boston composer whose national reputation survived World War I.[32]

■ ■ ■

The violinist/composer in question was the wondrously deracinated Charles Martin Loeffler. Though he claimed to have been born in Alsace in 1861, recent scholarship suggests that his actual birthplace was Berlin. He attributed the death of his father, a Berliner, to unjust imprisonment, and afterward acquired a repugnance for German architecture, poetry, and physiognomy, and for "bigmouthed" and "conceited" German music. As a child he also lived in Hungary and Russia. He moved to the United States in 1881 and stayed there, an American citizen, until his death in 1935. But Americans perceived Loeffler

---

* I cannot resist quoting two letters to Gardner from Henry Higginson for their further evidence of Higginson's disinterested philanthropy (the Boston Opera was thought to compete with the Symphony) and range of taste and acquaintance. Higginson also supervised Gardner's investments. On January 9, 1910 [?]: "You've been to the opera this week, & have been more or less edified. You know the value to us of an opera on a solid & healthy basis. . . . Give these folks a chance and some timely help, & we may get an *excellent* article. . . . Pray go to that meeting tomorrow at 3 o'ck & *help in your own way*. There are more ways than one, & no quick-witted party (woman) needs hints from a dull-witted party (man) as to the methods. Bear a hand, Lady." On June 1, 1905: "If you think that you are to have a peaceful life, die at once! So soon as a person has shown his capacity to help his fellow creatures and his will to do so, he will be asked again and again—It is a price and a joy of life—I am glad that you . . . have fallen into that class—You chose the path and are a blessing to many men & women." Quoted in Ralph P. Locke, "Living with Music: Isabella Stewart Gardner," in Ralph Locke and Cyrilla Barr (eds.), *Cultivating Music in America: Women Patrons and Activists since 1860* (Berkeley, University of California Press, 1997), pp. 109–110.

as French, and French were his favorite poets, artists, and composers. His German-accented English was sweetened with French felicities.[33]

Loeffler joined the Boston Symphony as second concertmaster in 1882 and was an esteemed member of the orchestra for twenty-one years. In 1910 he moved to an ample farmstead in Medfield, five miles from Boston, and married after an engagement lasting more than two decades. He continued to advise Henry Higginson, who cherished his musicianship, and also served on the board of the Boston Opera. His success as a composer was such that the Boston Symphony performed his music 117 times during his lifetime; his friend Heinrich Gebhard appeared as piano soloist in Loeffler's *A Pagan Poem* sixty-six times in twenty years with the orchestras of Boston, Chicago, Cleveland, New York, Philadelphia, Pittsburgh, and St. Louis, among others.[34]

Loeffler was a singular personality. His erect bearing, slender carriage, fine features, blond hair, and clear blue eyes impressed as regal or aristocratic. He was impressively well read in three languages. He was variously perceived as modest or aloof, daunting or charming. Reticence, austerity, melancholia, hypersensitivity, even misanthropy were Loeffler motifs. His biographer, Ellen Knight, detects anti-Semitism in certain of his aversions. And it is not amazing that homosexuality has been inferred from the details of his personal life. (A not atypical letter to his future wife read in part, "We love each other without loving and yet we love each other.")[35]

If the general direction of these attributes evokes Henry Adams, so does his proclivity for ambivalence. In 1894, Loeffler went abroad and discovered that he found Boston preferable to "smoky, cloudy, black, rainy" London, even to Paris ("it has appeared to me more vulgar, less original"). Ten years later, a Boston cult figure, he wrote to Isabella Stewart Gardner, "I should like to call your attention to the fact that Bostonians on the whole do not care to hear me play or to acknowledge my musicianship. Several have been singularly rude and independent about telling me all about it." Months later he confided to Rudolf Schirmer, the New York music publisher, "Boston grates on my nerves. . . . I should like [to move to] New York very much." In 1923 he told the musicologist/composer Carl Engel that Boston had become a "stagnant old pool full of old, blind fish and frogs." The same year he told the New York critic Richard Aldrich, "I always lived in the hope, that I might someday change my domicile to New York but alas, it never came. I always disliked Boston."[36]

Loeffler was by then a quasi-recluse in Medfield, devoted, one assumes, to composing. Even in Boston, he was scarcely one of "the boys," alongside Chadwick and Foote. He did not habituate the St. Botolph or Tavern Club. His friends or acquaintances included John Singer Sargent, a credible pianist whose passion for Fauré he shared. But it was Fenway Court that must have kept Loeffler more or less at peace with himself and his surroundings.

Gardner's concerts often featured Loeffler as violinist or composer—including *two* premiere performances of *A Pagan Poem*, the first in a version for two pianos and three trumpets, the second with the Boston Symphony. Gardner also served as an unpaid agent for his music. In 1898 she loaned him a Stradivarius for an indefinite period. The same year, Loeffler wrote to her, "I know you often wish me different on many points, dear Mrs. Gardner, but as to you, I would not have you changed an atom." Some time later he began to express resentment about playing for her guests; he even offered to return the violin. In 1918 she told him the instrument was his to keep; Loeffler wrote, "I hardly know now, how to express to you how deeply I am moved."[37]

Loeffler encouraged Gardner's interest in Verlaine, the Goncourt brothers, and Jules Laforgue. But he also gave her a copy of *Moby-Dick*. His elusive musical tastes may be gleaned from his solo repertoire and playing style. With the Boston Symphony, he performed Bach, Bruch, Godard, Lalo, Mendelssohn, and Saint-Saëns as well as his own *Divertissement* and *Les veillées de l'Ukraine*. Gebhard, among others, categorized Loeffler the violinist as an exemplar of the French school, with "a tone like fine-spun silk yet rich, impeccable technic and intonation, and a style so elegant and polished that it could only be called aristocratic." Scouting abroad for Higginson, he was crucial in recommending Muck for possessing "routine" and "virtuosity," "nerve and life" if not "fire and warmth." He disliked Nikisch. He greatly admired Stokowski and his sumptuous Philadelphia sound.[38]

Loeffler's own music reflects his French bias; Russian and Slavic influences are also strongly audible, as is plainsong; and his late works register enthusiasm for jazz. He delights in sound for its own sake, and expresses a sybarite's pleasure in the exoticism of strange timbres. *La Mort de Tintagiles* (1897, revised 1900) is engendered by a lurid marionette drama by Maeterlinck. In *A Pagan Poem* (1902, revised 1906), the siren call of three offstage trumphets, speaking in chords, signifies a sorceress's spell; it literally draws ever closer—a sonic coup clinched by the final measure, in which six onstage trumpets speak as one. The morbid delicacy of these scores, prescient of *Pelléas et Mélisande*, is fully as decadent, as Symbolist, as their programmatic sources. But their appassionato rhetoric is often fustian; Loeffler's more restrained music of reminiscence, of pasts imagined, wears better. The *Music for Four Stringed Instruments* (1917–19), infused with Gregorian chant, composed in memory of a friend's son killed in combat, is an elegy and hymn whose languorous vicissitudes also convey worldly disillusionment and ennui. His songs, mainly setting Verlaine, benefit from the concision imposed by words. The *Five Irish Fantasies* for tenor and orchestra (1920), mainly setting Yeats, are a potent cycle; John McCormack introduced three of them, with the Boston Symphony, to high acclaim.

Loeffler the composer was extravagantly praised by his aesthetic soul mate Philip Hale. If other critics were less effusive, sentiments of admiration and gratitude were widespread. For James Gibbons Huneker, New York's prophet of modernism, Loeffler was America's leading composer. Both Henry Krehbiel and W. J. Henderson, Germanophile Wagnerites, assessed him warmly, and both knew Loeffler the man; Henderson's obituary in the *New York Sun* said, "Mr. Loeffler was not only the leading American writer of music, but one of the most distinguished in the world."[39]

As late as 1939, Carl Engel, in the *International Cyclopedia of Music and Musicians*, could write that Loeffler was "by many esteemed the foremost 'American composer' of his generation" for his originality, polish, and sensitivity. Engel's entry totaled seven pages, versus five for Edward MacDowell, three-quarters of a page for Chadwick, and one-quarter page for Copland; of contemporaneous Europeans, Richard Strauss received four pages, and Mahler three. But Copland himself, writing in 1953, considered Loeffler an escapist from realities captured by Sandburg, Dreiser, and Norris; Copland's champion Paul Rosenfeld dispatched Loeffler as "one of those exquisites whose refinement is unfortunately accompanied by sterility, perhaps even results from it."[40]

In fact, Loeffler's small output and chronic penchant for revision suggest a lack of fluency. The refulgent climaxes of *A Pagan Poem*, or of the iridescent *La bonne chanson* (1901, revised 1915), an exultant orchestral nature poem, are unforgettable—or, more precisely, addictive. If elsewhere the material is undeniably stretched thin, it remains equally true that Loeffler's present-day obscurity ignorantly dismisses what many once experienced as a Boston golden age.

■ ■ ■

"What the aesthetes achieved," writes Martin Green in *The Problem of Boston*, "was a kind of apotheosis or Transfiguration and Assumption of the Boston tradition, in which it left the earth where it had dwelt so long and for which it had been designed, and mounted aloft, to Rome, Settignano, London, Paris. In so doing it became of course etherialized [*sic*], lost contact with all its more mundane functions, like social service; in some respects . . . it was continued into something logically its opposite (amoralism and world-weariness). But it achieved thereby as it departed a glorious effulgence it had never had before." Though Charles Martin Loeffler does not figure in Green's Boston purview, the description fits. Green also writes, more generally, of failure of nerve afflicting Boston writers, notwithstanding exceptional local esteem and support. In the case of Amy Beach, the failure was cushioned and disguised by friendly Brahmin salons. In the case of George Chadwick, the failure was more relative: his preferred safe and easy road was the one toward which his temperament in any case disposed him. In Loeffler's case, there is the same withdrawal from direct experience, but the cause is different. Unlike Beach or Chadwick, he resonates with an essential Boston despair belonging not only to Henry Adams but also, less persistently, to Norton and others disillusioned by decaying ideals, by defortification of the "model and ideal city." Common to all three composers—to all late-nineteenth-century Boston composers—is the evasion of deeply personal truths and impolite self-scrutiny Green discerns.

Charting the decline of Boston culture, Green finds in the late Gilded Age not creative genius but the "organization and engineering of a high culture whose major forms or achievements belonged to the past"[41]—thus the Fine Arts Museum, the Public Library, the Symphony Orchestra. Truly, the lone iconic hero in musical Boston a century ago is not a composer, but Henry Higginson. For iconic creativity, one must look elsewhere—toward New York.

PART TWO

New York and Beyond

■

CHAPTER 5

Anton Seidl
and the Sacralization
of Opera

■

American opera madness ▪ *English-language opera* ▪
Opera and uplift ▪ *The Metropolitan Opera, Wagnerism,*
and the genteel tradition reinterpreted

The story of opera in Europe supports the story of evolving national cultural identities, of Italian, German, French, and Russian "schools" dictating the style of both music and performance. The foundation of each national school was a national repertoire of works by native composers. And these operas, in turn, were stylistically molded by the native languages in which they were composed. In fact, in the late nineteenth century, Italians heard opera—all opera—in Italian: *Les pêcheurs de perles* was *I pescatori di perle*, *Die Meistersinger* was *I maestri cantori di Norimberga*. Germans heard opera in German. The French heard opera in French. Russians heard opera in Russian.

The story of opera in the United States is, in part, the story of failed efforts: to inculcate a tradition of opera in English, to create a viable repertoire of native works, to foster an American school. And yet, like the American orchestral tradition founded by Theodore Thomas and Henry Higginson even in the absence of a viable native repertoire, opera in America remains a distinctive achievement.

Opera in nineteenth-century America was as polyglot as the languages Americans spoke. It was not, as often in Europe, a fundamentally aristocratic diversion. But it was not fundamentally egalitarian either. It was exclusive and it was democratic. It was elevated art and it was cheap popular entertainment merging with musical comedy and farce. In the 1830s, a Baltimore theater manager, William Woods, refused to sell private boxes "hankered for by a small class"; "every wise manager in America will set his face like a flint against it," he predicted. There were also American opera houses without any boxes, in which all tickets cost the same. Other opera managers catered eagerly to the rich.[1]

Henry James called a box at the opera "the only approach to the implication of the tiara known in American law," the "great vessel of social salvation." As early as 1850, opera is said to have helped solidify New York's patriciate. In some American theaters, however, the opera goers were women of different classes sitting side by side as they did not in Europe. Walt Whitman, at New York's Bowery Theater, approvingly observed opera audiences "packed from ceiling to pit with full-blooded young and middle-aged men, the best average of American-born mechanics . . . bursting forth in one of those long-kept-up tempests of hand-clapping . . . no dainty kid-glove business, but electric force and muscle from perhaps two thousand full-sinewed men." Around the same time, George Templeton Strong grumbled that "everybody goes, and hob and snob, Fifth Avenue and Chatham Street, sit side by side on the hard benches." In Wisconsin, Jenny Lind sang Bellini in a pork butcher's shed. In San Francisco, the Tivoli Opera House had seats with shelves for glasses of beer and wine.[2]

Early on, opera in America mainly meant "ballad operas," composed and sung in English, in which songs alternated with dialogue. John Gay's rambunctious topical satire *The Beggar's Opera* (1728), which arrived in New York from England in 1750, was the best known. Subsequent generations of English opera were better mannered, the most popular being Michael Balfe's *The Bohemian Girl* (1843), a New York triumph in 1844. By that time, English-language opera, still predominant in the United States, more often meant English versions of Italian operas.

Bellini, Donizetti, and Rossini in English, frequently abridged and otherwise altered, spurred interest in the genuine article. The landmark event, in 1825, was a nine-month New York season of Italian opera given by Manuel García and a small but distinguished company. García had created the role of Almaviva in Rossini's *The Barber of Seville*. His wife and son were also competent vocalists. His elder daughter, Maria, was on the cusp of celebrity. His younger daughter, Pauline, was an infant; as Pauline Viardot, she would amaze Europe. The Garcías recruited a local chorus and orchestra. They brought some costumes and made others upon arrival. They helped to build and paint the necessary scenery. They opened on November 29 with *The Barber*. Prices in the two-thousand-seat Park Theatre ranged from twenty-five cents in the gallery to a steep two dollars for a box seat. New Yorkers inquired, in letters to the press, how to dress in the "European manner." Many women came elegantly attired, "decked in native curls, and embellished with wreaths of flowers, or tasteful turbans." The repertoire included more Rossini, two of García's own works, and *Don Giovanni* by Mozart.[3]

The entire enterprise was formidably strange. Some New Yorkers doubted that sung theater in an unfamiliar language could succeed. As it happened, many others actually preferred the exotic pedigree of foreign tongues, especially in combination with an opulent setting. Yet others discovered purely musical pleasures. Maria García married in New York, and as Maria Malibran blossomed as the first local diva. When her father's troupe departed for Mexico, she stayed behind to sing English opera at the Bowery Theater alongside singers who scarcely knew a word of their parts.[4] She gamely prompted her colleagues, and cleverly interpolated "Home Sweet Home" into Rosina's lesson scene in *The Barber of Seville*. As Zerlina, she played opposite a Don Giovanni who did not even attempt to sing. Her farewell appearances, in 1827, were as New York's most enchanting, most beloved singing actress. In Europe, she consolidated her fame. She died there of injuries from a riding accident in 1836, not yet thirty years old.

Meanwhile, a second foreign operatic genre was being domesticated. French opera was implanted in North America where there were French people to sing and understand it: New Orleans. In the years preceding the War of 1812, as many as 150 operas were played to variegated audiences, including slaves (restricted to a section of the gallery). The impresarios John Davis, born in Paris, and James Henry Caldwell, an Englishman, took charge after 1820. Caldwell presented opera in English at the Camp Street Theater, whose patrons included rivermen in buckskins; when he mounted Weber's *The Freeshooter* (*Der Freischütz*), the special effects for the haunted Wolf's Glen excited hurrahs "which made the walls tremble."[5] Davis presented opera in French—since-forgotten works by Auber and Boieldieu—at the Orleans Theater with a polished company that toured the Northeast five times beginning in 1827. In 1868, when New Orleans was still suffering the aftershock of the Civil War, a local observer of the French Opera reported to northern readers, "We can promise you no very grand spectacle, no very costly costuming and decorations; we are too poor for such things now-a-days; but we will insure you a well-bred, musical audience to sit among, an efficient and well-trained orchestra, and a rendering of the masters in operatic art, which will inspire you with a determination to do what you can toward the establishment of as genuine an Opera at home."[6]

Another formidable operatic outpost was San Francisco, where the impresario of choice, Tom Maguire, was an illiterate saloon keeper from New York who fancied diamond rings and diamond-studded scarves. Maguire's New

Opera House, opened in 1856, presented the Lyster English Opera Company, among others. But Maguire dreamt of foreign-language opera with all the trimmings. His Academy of Music, built in 1864, had three tiers of boxes, a grand chandelier, and *Il trovatore* with Euphrosyne Parepa-Rosa. But Maguire's appetite for opera overreached his means; by 1880 he was bankrupt.

Parepa-Rosa (whom we have also encountered at Patrick Gilmore's 1869 Boston Peace Jubilee) was principal soprano of the Carl Rosa Company, which influentially toured the United States and England. By the end of the Civil War, touring opera was pervasive in both English and Italian. The English-language companies were mainly rough-and-ready outfits playing to mixed crowds. The Italian companies were more lavish and fashionable. Among the latter, Max Maretzek's New York–based Astor Place Opera Company mainly traveled to Philadelphia, Baltimore, and Boston with a repertoire including early Verdi. Among the former, the Pyne and Harrison English Opera Company trekked west to St. Louis and Cairo, south to New Orleans, Mobile, and Natchez; the chief attractions included *The Beggar's Opera* and *The Bohemian Girl* alongside *The Barber of Seville*, *The Daughter of the Regiment* (Donizetti), and *La sonnambula* (Bellini). The company's immensely popular *Cinderella* was a version of Rossini's *La cenerentola*, with a much-altered plot and interpolated numbers from three other Rossini operas. Americans kept pace with early and middle Verdi. Gounod's *Faust* arrived, in Philadelphia, in 1863. German opera, for the most part, remained in the wings, poised to enter momentously.[7]

■ ■ ■

By midcentury, New York City was America's primary marketplace for music. Boston's oratorio tradition had no equivalent in New York, and neither city had far progressed toward a resident orchestra of quality. But it was opera that captivated Americans, and New York was opera mad.

From William Steinway's diary, it may be ascertained that he or members of his family attended opera in New York 117 times between 1861 and 1871, encountering sixty different works—more than any New Yorker could sample in a decade one hundred years later.[8]

Walt Whitman, an enraptured opera-thrall, steered readers of his *Brooklyn Eagle* column toward favorite works and singers. On February 24, 1847, he advised that the Olympic Theatre was "giving a run" of popular operas "very neatly got up in a small scale; Miss Taylor appears tonight as Zorlina in 'Fra Diavolo.'" A series of Italian operas was offered on Chambers Street— "tonight 'Lucrezia Borgia.' On Wednesday night it will be pleasanter to go, for then they give 'Lombardi.'"⁹ And a troupe from Havana was playing opera two nights a week at the Park Theatre.

Another snapshot, on December 21, 1854: Giulia Grisi and Giovanni Mario—great names—in *Lucia di Lammermoor* and the first act of *Norma* at the new Academy of Music. A second *Lucia*, in English, was given at Niblo's Garden. Flotow's *Martha* was performed at the Stadttheater. And, at 663 Broadway, Perham's Troupe offered "The Laughable Operatic Extravaganza of DON GIOVANNI; or, The Spectre on Horseback," plus "AN UNEQUALED PROGRAMME OF ETHIOPIAN SONGS, CHORUSES, SOLOS, DUETS, JIGS, FANCY DANCES, &C."¹⁰

The variety of venues here recorded is worth pondering. The forty-six-hundred-seat Academy, on Fourteenth Street, was the closest thing to a grand "opera house" in the European mold. The twenty-five-hundred-seat Stadttheater, on the Bowery, was the city's major German-language theater, presenting Goethe and Schiller alongside melodrama and farce; visitors from other neighborhoods marveled at its dirtiness and informality, and at the quantities of beer sold by venders strolling the aisles. At Niblo's Garden, also home to minstrel shows and military bands, tubs of orange and lemon trees adorned outdoor walks hung with Chinese lanterns; all seats cost fifty cents.

Equally unfashionable was Palmo's Opera House on Chambers Street, an eight-hundred-seat auditorium whose gallery, above the main floor, seated opera lovers on benches with wooden shoulder-high slats for support. Like William Niblo, Ferdinand Palmo was an opera-for-everyone populist who kept prices low; he also arranged for horse-drawn cars, heated in winter, to serve the theater. Castle Garden, a converted fort on the harbor, was home to fairs, balloon ascents, Beethoven's Ninth Symphony in its first American performance, and—as Whitman recalled—feats of "unsurpassed vocalism." The Temple of Muses was actually on the water: a converted steamship, it held nine musicians in its tiny pit and even featured a tier of boxes.

None of these institutions presented opera as the Metropolitan does today. Typically, the premises were rented to an impresario whose job it was to book singers, plan a season, and endeavor to turn a profit. Many failed. Those who succeeded were adroit salesmen whose merchandise might also include pianists and violinists. In significant respects the model merchandiser was Phineas T. Barnum, who also dealt in midgets and mermaids, and whose masterminding of Jenny Lind's first American tour, in 1850, was a legend in its own time. Barely modulating his initial promotional premise—that the Swedish Nightingale was an actual angel descended from on high—he prepared biographies bypassing her more esoteric qualifications in favor of evidence of piety, philanthropy, and eagerness to visit the United States. He manufactured a welcoming pageant, in New York Harbor, so tumultuous that the gates to the pier gave way and at least one man was swept into the river (and rescued). Riding beside Barnum in a decorated carriage, Jenny passed under two triumphal arches of evergreen reading "Welcome Jenny Lind" and "Welcome to America." A throng of ten thousand was waiting at the Irving Hotel. Two hundred musicians, escorted by twenty brigades of firemen, serenaded her with "Yankee Doodle" and "Hail, Columbia."[11]

With receipts totaling $712,000 and ticket prices of up to $650, Jenny's tour was the signature triumph of Barnum's career, a goad and inspiration for entrepreneurs to come. One such was Le Grand Smith, who promoted Germany's Henriette Sontag as the "singing countess"; a "public serenade" outside her hotel, modeled on Barnum's precedent, decomposed when a screaming mob refused to relinquish space to the parading instrumentalists.

But Sontag triumphed in America under a different manager: Bernard Ullman. Ullman, Max Maretzek, and the brothers Maurice and Max Strakosch were cunning rivals and sometime allies, vying for the best singers and biggest audiences at the Academy of Music, "kidnapping" one another's stars and waging "price wars" over fees and tickets. Starting with Lind and Sontag, and with Grisi, Mario, and the contralto Marietta Alboni, New Yorkers feasted on a dazzling array of voices, including one belonging to a virtual New Yorker: Adelina Patti, who in 1844 arrived from Italy at the age of one. She sang in public at seven, and toured—with Ole Bull and Maurice Strakosch—as a child prodigy. Her stage debut, at sixteen, was as Lucia. She entranced with her purity of voice and person, with "singing as beautiful as ever fell from mortal lips." Two years later, she sailed to Europe and a fabled international career.

Complementing this unruly picture of opera in New York were New York's unruly audiences. At the Astor Place Opera House in 1849—the same year Maretzek took charge of opera there—a fight broke out between partisans of the English actor William Charles Macready and the American actor Edwin Forrest. Macready was aristocratic. Forrest was a patriotic populist. When a crowd of ten thousand armed with paving stones attempted to storm the entrances during Macready's *Macbeth*, militiamen fired into the crowd, killing at least twenty-two. Though nothing like the "Astor Place riot" ever erupted over opera, New York's opera mobs remained combustible; the mixture of classes and types was as unrestrained as were the applicable standards of behavior. George Templeton Strong's diary is thick with complaints such as "the music is drowned—or at least one's capacity for enjoying it is paralyzed with vexation by excessive, ill-bred, obstreperous gabblings." And "spent half an hour last night at the Philharmonic concerts—crowded and garrulous— like a square mile of tropical forest with its floods of squalling paroquets and troops of chattering monkeys." And (reporting on a *Norma*) "the house was

crowded and enthusiastic; the louder this lady screamed, the more uproari-
ously they applauded."[12]

New York audiences were marvelously demonstrative. When no encore
was granted "The Trumpet Shall Sound" at an 1858 *Messiah*, reported the
Evening Post, "the Academy was filled with a horrible din of violent instrumentation, frenzied vocalization, shouts, stamping, catcalls, brass trumpets, and
German gutturals." "Shattered by passion," the conductor, the estimable Carl
Anschütz, gave a speech: "Zhentleman and ladeez, it is nevair customary to
repeat ze sacred music." But when he attempted to continue the performance,
the uproar resumed, abetted by listeners who had leaped onto the stage.
Anschütz threw down his baton and stormed off. A backstage conference
resulted in an announcement that the trumpet obligato was too difficult to
repeat, whereupon Anschütz returned, "injured and irate," and the performance proceeded without further incident.[13]

As reported by Edward Wilkins, the American premiere of Verdi's *A
Masked Ball*, in 1861, thronged the Academy of Music with "the high and the
low [and] the middle strata of metropolitan society. . . . Snuffy professors, wild
looking pianists, inchoate prime donne, magnificent artists without engagements, sapient critics, and blasé dilettanti were all mixed up in one grand olla
podrida, talking in as many tongues as the celebrated artificers of Babel." Nine
days later, Abraham Lincoln, en route to Washington for his inauguration,
showed up to hear the new work (about an assassinated American ruler!). The
second-act curtain rose on a performance of "The Star-Spangled Banner."
Isabella Hinkley, the soprano playing Oscar, sang the first stanza half-turned
toward Lincoln's second-tier stage box. Then the entire company joined in,
while a huge American flag, all thirty-three stars blazing, dropped from the
proscenium. Verse number two was taken by Adelaide Phillips, the evening's
Ulrica, to deafening applause. Then came "Hail Columbia," more cheering,
and the resumption of *Masked Ball*.

The opera itself—introduced on February 11, nine days before Lincoln's
visit—enjoyed spectacular success. The conductor was Emanuele Muzio, a
close associate of the composer. And the production featured a grand ballet
and a ballroom scene including several lucky audience members who had
secured the privilege of mounting the stage as extras. The enthusiasm of the
audiences was matched in the press. Observed the *Albion*, "The melodies are
full of ideas, not mere pretty platitudes but themes with brains in them."

A Masked Ball was withdrawn after its ninth performance to make way for
the New York debut of Muzio's nineteen-year-old American protégé, Clara
Louise Kellogg. This was in *Rigoletto*, on February 27. A March 2 gala comprised *Rigoletto*, complete, plus the last act of *A Masked Ball*. Two nights later,

and again on March 9 and 13, *A Masked Ball* was repeated, for a total of twelve and one-third performances. By then, tunes from the opera were being heard on the street organs of New York. In the course of four weeks, Verdi's twenty-third opera, just two years old, had become a local staple.[14]

■ ■ ■

The clamor and novelty of New York opera obscured its artistic deficiencies. Over time, a new clamor arose, determined to elevate standards and taste. When in 1848 Max Maretzek arrived from London, he attended *The Barber of Seville* at the Astor Place Opera House and discovered:

> The orchestra consisted of about thirty-six performers on their individual instruments. They had a leader, Signor Lietti, who did not apparently consider it necessary to indicate the movement by beating the time. On the contrary, he was occupied in playing the first violin part, fully unconscious of the other instruments in the orchestra. But I wrong him. In order to guide them, he was possessed with the monomania of playing more loudly and vigorously upon his fiddle than any of his subordinates. He trampled on the floor as though he had been determined to work a path through the deal planking, and made a series of the most grotesque faces with his nose, mouth and eyes. . . . In the mean time, the other fiddlers not being willing to allow Signor Lietti's violin a greater preponderance of sound, exerted themselves with a purely musical ferocity. . . . At last, straggling and worn out, one after the other, some few completely distanced, and Signor Lietti by no means first in, they terminated the overture. The audience bestowed upon them a round of applause, and the leader demonstrated by three low bows, his intense satisfaction both with himself and the public.[15]

A few years later, young Theodore Thomas was already a fixture in New York's theater and opera bands. Thomas was duly impressed by the singing. "I doubt if there were ever brought together in any part of the world a larger number of talented vocalists than were gathered in New York between 1850 and the early sixties," he recalled. Of Jenny Lind, Thomas wrote, "She was truly a great singer. She had an exceptional voice, compass, technique, and warmth, and impressed one with a sense of grandeur." Of Henriette Sontag, "I do not remember another singer in whom art and experience were combined with such freshness and quality of voice."

But Thomas's reminiscences skewer the orchestras and conductors he first knew as a violinist. The conductors were "time-beaters." The orchestras numbered thirty-five or forty ill-rehearsed players, "generally engaged and formed by some man who was an inferior musician himself, but who was supposed to know the better musicians, and had some business capacity. This man would receive, besides his salary from the manager, a percentage from every man in the orchestra, and whoever was unwilling to submit to this exaction could not get an engagement." In 1857, as conductor for Ullman's company he for the first time encountered excellent singers supported by enlarged choral and orchestral forces. "Ullman used to say that I was ruining him by engaging so large an orchestra. My answer was, 'Then discharge me!' whereupon he would reply, '*Seien Sie doch nicht so hitzig*' ['Don't be so hot-headed']." But even this enterprise was hampered by manuscript parts full of mistakes, missing pages of music, and uncoordinated cuts. Thomas quit conducting opera almost as soon as he had started. His credo, "A symphony orchestra shows the culture of a community, not opera," documents not only a purist's reservations, but a performer's early memories.[16]

The moral gravitas of the symphonic concert, instilled by Thomas, by John Sullivan Dwight and Henry Higginson, condemned the "star system" as practiced by cunning impresarios. The high examples of the Thomas Orchestra and Boston Symphony exerted pressure to reformulate the operatic experience as a musical-dramatic whole. This crusade has been depicted as essentially (and parochially) pious.[17] In fact, as with the orchestras, professionalization and sacralization were mutually at work. When Thomas complained about performances ill-prepared and ill-conducted; when Maretzek declared that opera in America demanded "a complete and thorough reformation"; when James Gibbons Huneker recalled that "in opera the cheap spectacular ruled," that "singers were advertised like freaks," that managers were "always half a step from ruin," inescapable artistic failings were on trial.[18]

But Thomas, unlike Maretzek or Huneker, also harbored misgivings about the opera beast itself and whether it was tamable. The relevant backdrop included a prohibition on all theatrical performances in colonial Massachusetts. Dwight, a century later, found opera impure. It moved the feelings, not the mind. It catered to virtuosity, celebrity, display. It appealed "to easy sympathies which demanded not great culture, powers of thought, or depth of character." Dwight extolled Mozart's *Don Giovanni*. In Italian opera he liked Rossini best, but found him melodramatic. Bellini's "sweet and sickly" melodies softened rather than strengthened the listener. Donizetti was "sugary and feeble." Verdi was stronger, but crude. Wagner was a rebel hedonist.[19]

A portion of the American opera-going public was similarly disposed. In the 1830s *La sonnambula*, sung in English, meshed with a repertoire including

William Michael Rooke's *Amilie* and such "Englished" operas as Rophino Lacy's *Maid of Judah*, a Rossini pastiche interpolating spoken dialogue. As rendered by American and British singers, these operas were simple, direct, and edifying. The virtuousness of the stories, and of the featured sopranos, helped to secure their New York appeal.[20] But the subsequent "new Italian opera" challenged notions of civilizing culture: the Duke in *Rigoletto*, first staged in New York in 1855, is a lecherous murderer who escapes punishment; his guileless victim expires in a waterfront slum.

A traveling company was advised that Boston would not have *Rigoletto*. In New York, an unsuccessful suit was brought against Maretzek to prevent its performance. But Verdi's partisans were just as vehement, and by 1861—when (as we have seen) *A Masked Ball* triumphed at the Academy of Music—*Rigoletto*, *Il trovatore*, and *La traviata* had achieved a controversial popularity. "An exquisite vein of sentiment pervades the music, and colors it with sadness and feeling," wrote a connoisseur of *La traviata*. "It was the true Italian model, brimful of passion, crime, intrigue, and murder," commented a detractor of *Il trovatore*. Other writers were revolted by the courtesan Violetta, living with a younger man, in the former opera; and by the "idiotic" story of the latter, whose Anvil Chorus was unforgettably compared to "a scene of mending a sewer set to music."[21]

Striving toward a more wholesome world of opera, certain Americans extolled opera in English as an antidote to snob appeal, to vulgar glamour, to Old World decadence. The major English-language troupes, retaining favor through the closing decades of the nineteenth century, were distinctly populist. In the large Eastern cities, they played to working- and middle-class audiences, elsewhere to a gamut of working to upper classes. In 1873, Clara Louise Kellogg (whom we have briefly encountered as a protégé of Emanuele Muzio) became the first American to establish a prominent English-language touring troupe, proclaiming "opera for the people"; she herself sang in as many as 125 performances a season. Emma Abbott, the "populist prima donna," founded a comparable company in 1879. It toured extensively in the far West, playing six and seven times a week. Abbott inaugurated thirty-five new opera houses in places like Waterloo, Iowa, and Ogden, Utah.

In an age when many professions were closed to women, and the theater was not, these manager/sopranos paralleled the phenomenon of manager/actresses. In comparison with a Barnum or Ullman, they challenged the taint of the "cheap spectacular." Self-reliant, indefatigable, savvy, they were actually exemplars of American virtue. Abbott even refused to sing Violetta, whom she considered "a wanton who was wicked simply because she loved sin." In Milan (!) she interpolated "Nearer My God to Thee" in *La sonnambula*.[22]

And yet assertive egalitarianism and truculent provincialism minimized the reformist potential of the English-language troupes. They did not even try to signify high art—with a single remarkable exception. This was the work of a fourth woman manager, not a professional singer but a visionary pedagogue: Jeannette Thurber. Like the New York conductor Anton Seidl, like the New York critic Henry Krehbiel, she believed in the inevitability of opera in English as a foundation for opera in America. In 1885, the same year she founded the National Conservatory of Music of which Dvořák would become director, Thurber created the American Opera Company. Like Kellogg's company, or Abbott's, it would tour opera in English. But—subsidized by her husband, a prosperous food merchant, and sparing no expense—Thurber also engaged Theodore Thomas and his world-class Thomas Orchestra. Nor did she skimp on chorus or ballet, sets or costumes or stage effects. Determined to sever the cultural umbilical cord to Europe, she mainly engaged American singers and kept prices low. Her prospectus boasted she would engage "the largest regularly trained chorus ever employed in grand opera in America . . . the largest ballet corps ever presented and as far as possible, American in its composition . . . four thousand new and correct costumes . . . scenery . . . painted by the most eminent scenic artists . . . the front rank of American singers . . . supported by an ensemble which has never been equalled in this country."

Thurber opened her first season not with *Rigoletto* or *Faust*, but with Hermann Goetz's *The Taming of the Shrew*, an American premiere. The fourteen other operas in repertoire sampled Gluck, Mozart, Nicolai, Gounod, Meyerbeer, Delibes, Flotow, Anton Rubinstein, Wagner, Verdi, Victor Massé, and Karl Goldmark. Performances were given as far west as St. Louis. A second season, as the renamed National Opera Company, ventured all the way to San Francisco. The company's orchestra, chorus, and production values were widely praised. The singers were not.

In Boston, where the star system was especially deplored, Thurber's company triumphed. *Lohengrin* "was performed as never before in Boston." All the artists "entered thoroughly into the spirit of the work." The chorus was fresh voiced and well rehearsed, as well as "handsomely and picturesquely dressed and disposed in judicious masses and cleverly scattered groups." One feature "without precedent at a performance of *Lohengrin* in our local experience" was "the close and sympathetic interest manifested by the audience . . . due to the fact that the listeners understood what was sung." The crowning contribution came from Thomas's "unrivalled" orchestra, compared to which "the great Bayreuth festival orchestra can show immense perfection of drill, but not such uniformly fine executive material. . . . There was scarcely a flaw in the instrumental work from beginning to end." A second Wagner production, of

The Flying Dutchman, amazed with its "terrifying" lightning and skillful representation of the closing wreckage and apotheosis. "Never before has grand opera been presented in this city in so complete a manner as by this troupe. We have usually had a few good singers, a poor chorus of ancient singers, a meagre orchestra of musicians who had but little enthusiasm for their work, and a poverty of scenic illustration that was often laughable. None of these faults could be laid at the door of the American Company."

In cities less sophisticated, the company's lack of famous or foreign names was crippling. Its visits also uncovered continued pockets of religious opprobrium. In St. Louis, a prominent socialist condemned Delibes' ballet *Sylvia* as "lewd." In Chicago, clerical complaints caused the company to modify ballet costumes in the same composer's *Lakmé*. The *New York Times* reported (on page one!), "The clergymen had come to sit in judgement upon the ballet and the audience upon the conduct of the clergymen."

By mid-1887, the National Opera was penniless and its members, Thomas included, were suing for wages. The company's aspirations proved extravagant—it spent too much and took in too little. The management splintered. The backers defected. As an alternative to the cheap spectacular, the National Opera Company was too expensive. It was insufficiently exotic. Its trappings were more opulent than its voices. Finally, it was in one sense superfluous: an alternative had already been found.[23]

■ ■ ■

> *Heia, mein Blut! Lustig nun fliesse!*
> *Die mir die Wunde auf ewig schliesse,*
> *sie naht wie ein Held, sie naht mir zum Heil!*★

When composing *Tristan und Isolde*, Richard Wagner confided in a letter, "This Tristan is turning into something *dreadful!*"; he feared it might "drive people mad."[24] The opera's interior trajectory peaks in the third act. Having passed through a hallucinatory delirium, anticipating Isolde's arrival, Tristan jubilantly rips off the bandages that cover a deep sword wound and bleeds to death. The first Tristan, Ludwig Schnorr von Carolsfeld, himself succumbed to delirium and died, at the age of twenty-nine, days following the 1865 premiere.

For the American premiere of *Tristan und Isolde*, at the Metropolitan Opera on December 1, 1886, the Tristan was Albert Niemann, considered in New

---

★ "Flow joyfully, my blood!" sings Tristan in act three, scene two of *Tristan und Isolde*.

York the greatest singing actor of his generation. A decade before, coached by Wagner, Niemann sang Siegmund in the first *Ring of the Nibelung*, at Wagner's Bayreuth theater. Siegmund was his debut role at the Met in 1886. Henry Krehbiel wrote in the *Tribune*, "There is scarcely one of the theatrical conventions which the public have been accustomed to accept that he employs. He takes possession of the stage like an elemental force. . . . The fate for which [Siegmund] has been marked out has set its seal in the heroic melancholy which is never absent even in his finest frenzies."[25]

Niemann's New York Tristan came three weeks later. Photographs of Niemann as Tristan corroborate Krehbiel's description: "The figure is colossal, the head, like 'the front of Jove himself,' the eyes large and full of luminous light, that seems to dart from the tangle of matted [red] hair that conceals the greater part of his face." The emotional veracity of Niemann's performance—of his descent from chivalric reserve to frenzied dissolution—transfixed and terrified the first-night audience.[26]

Niemann's Isolde was Lilli Lehmann, who wrote in her memoirs, "In the whole world there was nothing that could free greater emotions in me than [my] *Tristan* performances in New York with Niemann." Lehmann was herself a regal artist. Like Niemann, she had worked under Wagner at Bayreuth in 1876. She prepared for her first Isolde, at Covent Garden in 1884, by singing every phrase hundreds of times, then each act from beginning to end three and four times consecutively. She eventually amassed a repertoire of 170 roles. In rehearsal, she always sang full voice; in free moments, she might busy herself rummaging in the property room or rearranging the scenery.

Lehmann's magisterial temperament buttressed her limitless self-esteem. Her bearing was queenly, her figure statuesque. When in *Tristan* she sang the Liebestod and the curtain fell, an audience of more than thirty-five hundred, filling every seat and every inch of standing room, sat still for minutes—"silent and motionless," Lehmann remembered, "as though drunk or in a transport, without being conscious that the opera was over." The ensuing applause was described in the *Musical Courier* as "frantic." A writer for the *Musical Courier* later testified that when Wagner was first performed at the Met, "middle-aged women in their enthusiasm stood up in the chairs and screamed their delight for what seemed hours."[27]

The conductor of the first American *Tristan* was Anton Seidl. According to the *Musical Courier*, "No conductor that we have ever heard could build up such massive climaxes, such overpowering, such thrilling altitudes of tone. His breadth . . . was no less wonderful. . . . He was a master of the whirlwind and rode it with a repose that was almost appalling." Krehbiel confirmed, "He attained his climaxes . . . by the most patient and reposeful accumulation of material, its proper adjustment, and its firm maintenance. . . . None of his confreres of Bayreuthean antecedents can work so directly, so elementally, upon an audience as did he." The most orgasmic climax in all Wagner—in all music—crowns the death song of Isolde.

Both the Liebestod and the *Tristan* Prelude were already well known in New York. In fact, New Yorkers were assiduously prepared for the shock of *Tristan*. Krehbiel, Henderson, the *Post's* Henry Finck, and other Wagnerite writers anticipated the premiere of Wagner's already legendary "chef d'ouevre" as the foreordained main event of the New York season. This, too, accounted for "an attention and a genuine enthusiasm which had thus far not been equalled in the musical history of the land." And in the opera's aftermath, critics hungrily tackled a topic little noticed a century later: they inquired what *Tristan und Isolde* was about. That is, they struggled to reconcile the appeal of Wagner's adulterous lovers, who brazenly submit to carnal instinct, with prevailing canons of taste and aesthetics.[28]

Clearly, Gilded Age New Yorkers could no more resist *Tristan und Isolde* than Tristan and Isolde could resist one another. If Tristan and Isolde were therefore victims, not puppets or criminals, it was necessary to understand why. Finck's answer was glib; he argued, for instance, that the potion the lovers drink was nobly intended to "end their life and suffering." That it was Isolde's servant who substituted a love potion freed them from responsibility. Krehbiel more deeply probed the thrill and alarm of emotional surrender yet ultimately—tortuously—found the drama more uplifting than appalling.[29]

This was the American way. *The Ring of the Nibelung*, first presented in full by Seidl at the Met in 1889, was read as a saga of religious or quasi-religious redemption; the culminating end of the gods was "a vast and righteous necessity," "a stupendous deed of morality." *Parsifal*, given in concert by Seidl at the Brooklyn Academy of Music in 1890, was a Christian parable preaching "deep ethical laws." Lilli Lehmann pertinently marveled, "Whence comes the peculiar sense of freedom that is at once felt by everyone in America? . . . There is a moral element in the natural manner of life of the American people, even the poorest feels himself a gentleman, desires to be treated as such, and thereby deems it worth his while to treat others so." In a speech he laboriously composed in English, Seidl called for "great music" to enrich "the great mass of poor people." "The man, who asks for not playing some classical works at the popular concerts," he exhorted, is "not a democrat, is not a republican, not an—American."[30]

■ ■ ■

What had redeemed opera in America, effacing the star system and cheap spectacular, eclipsing Verdi's unrepentant Duke and wanton courtesan, was the arrival of German opera at the unlikeliest of destinations: the new Metropolitan Opera House, created by *arriviste* socialites whose great wealth dictated great occasions at which to parade it. "The world of fashion was still content to reassemble every winter in the shabby red and gold boxes of the sociable old Academy," Edith Wharton later recalled. "Conservatives cherished it for . . . keeping out the 'new people.'" And the eighteen boxes of the Academy of Music were of course fully subscribed. The "new people"—industrialists and bankers accustomed to building yachts, mansions, country clubs—now built an opera house unprecedented in dimension, bigger than any envisioned by Verdi or Wagner. Its breathtaking five-tiered horseshoe auditorium contained 3,615 seats, including 122 boxes.[*][31]

The object was "grand opera": vast spaces; huge, stellar voices; lavish costumes and sets. Henry Abbey, to whom the premises were first leased by the stockholders (who were also boxholders), complied, creating a season of "first class opera" in Italian crammed with singers both famous and expensive. On opening night, October 22, 1883, Christine Nilsson's rendition of the Jewel Song from Gounod's *Faust*—as the "Aria dei gioielli"—was rewarded with a sash of hammered gold leaves and berries, with medallions in the form of Tragedy and Comedy as clasps. Crowning the brilliant audiences thus enticed was Mrs. Caroline Astor, whose annual ball defined high society. Decked in diamonds and pearl moonbursts—she was said to resemble a walking chandelier—Mrs. Astor appeared at precisely nine o'clock each Monday, there to adorn her box to receive guests in the adjoining anteroom or to promenade during intermissions, and to exit ceremoniously before the last act of whatever opera happened to be on. James Henry Mapleson's concurrent Academy of Music season, with the same October 22 opening night, was jealously observed. Reported the *New York Times* of the rival boxholders of New York's two houses of grand opera, "Something more than a hundred of our best families are . . . irretrievably committed to a social war of extermination."[32]

The early Metropolitan has been called "a semi-circle of boxes with an opera house build around them, a private club to which the general public was somewhat grudgingly admitted." And yet there were seats to fill besides the boxes, and purposes to serve beside Mrs. Astor's. If these considerations were not obvious at first, they obtruded when it became known that Abbey,

---

[*] After the fire of 1892, there were seventy-four boxes plus an "omnibus box" of four rows, two sections.

in his efforts to earn back what he had spent, had overpriced the house and lost a considerable sum of money. Faced with the prospect of bailing him out and trying again, the stockholders elected to opt for something much more practical, if much less glamorous. Compared to French or Italian singers, Germans were inexpensive. For reasonable fees, they could be borrowed from the court operas of their homeland; any two cost less than Nilsson alone.[33] New York's German population, estimated at 250,000, clamored for Wagner. And a German conductor, Leopold Damrosch of the New York Symphony, had proposed a plausible cost-cutting scheme. For non-German operas (all of which would be sung in German), he would use Abbey's sets and costumes. For the *Ring* operas, he would copy Bayreuth's sets and costumes. His salary would be ten thousand dollars. Abbey's six-dollar top ticket would be scaled down to three dollars for the 562 downstairs "parquet" seats; in the Himalayan Family Circle, seats would cost fifty cents. The stockholders would pick up the deficit, if any.

The 1884–85 season of twenty-one weeks (November 17 to April 18, including tours to Chicago, Cincinnati, and Boston) totaled 101 performances, of which 44 were of Wagner's *Tannhäuser, Lohengrin,* and—the season's centerpiece—*Die Walküre,* only once previously mounted in New York, and not well. Damrosch's Brünnhilde was Amalie Materna, who had learned the role from Wagner. Marianne Brandt, also an outstanding Bayreuth artist, sang Fricka. The demand for tickets, and not just from Germans, was such that speculators doubled what their messenger boys had paid. Though the performances, liberally cut, ran for more than four hours, though there were no arias, choruses, or ballets, audiences listened with "almost painful attention." Mapleson, who disdained German works and artists at the Academy of Music, was swiftly routed. But Damrosch, who undertook to conduct every Met performance as well as his New York Symphony and New York Oratorio Society concerts, paid dearly for his triumph: two weeks after the first *Walküre,* he expired of pneumonia. His twenty-three-year-old son, Walter, finished the season. The following summer, Walter and Edmund Stanton, the company's manager, went to Germany. The new music director whom they engaged would become the most eminent European musician ever to have settled in the United States. He would impact on opera in America more profoundly than any conductor before or since. Over the course of six seasons, confounding every reasonable hope or expectation, he would turn the fledgling Metropolitan into the world's leading German opera house.

■ ■ ■

Anton Seidl, born in Budapest in 1850, was a student conductor in Leipzig when in 1872 he attended the laying of the cornerstone of the Bayreuth Festspielhaus and heard Richard Wagner conduct Beethoven's Ninth Symphony. The experience was transformative. As he later told Henry Krehbiel, Seidl resolved "at any cost to get near to Wagner." In fact, he became Wagner's surrogate older son through the 1870s, while Siegfried Wagner, born in 1869, was far too young to partake in his father's regimen of composing and music-making, of voracious cultural intake and intellectual repartee. As Wagner's amanuensis— his companion at the piano, at meals, on walks—Seidl lived at Wahnfried as a member of the family. When *Götterdämmerung* and *Parsifal* were new, it was Seidl who made clean copies, who first heard the composer play and sing Siegfried's Funeral Music and Brünnhilde's Immolation. Whist with Wagner and Liszt, readings from Shakespeare's tragedies, disquisitions on the correct tempos in Beethoven's symphonies were representative daily fare. For the first *Ring*, in 1876, Seidl was the de facto assistant conductor.

Six years later, Seidl conducted the historic Wagner troupe that introduced the *Ring* in Holland, Belgium, Switzerland, Germany, Austria, Hungary, Italy, and England. His arrival in the United States in 1885 was an outgrowth of this missionary work; Wagner himself had urged it. He made his New York debut in *Lohengrin*. In rehearsal, he had discovered 180 errors in the parts used by Leopold and Walter Damrosch. "He gave us a new Wagner—the real Wagner," Huneker reported. The impact of so authoritative a reading, in the absence of broadcasts and recordings of performances abroad, is ponderable.

Like the Boston Symphony's Arthur Nikisch, Seidl was poised and mysterious, undemonstrative yet impassioned. Like Nikisch (but more explicitly), he was a disciple of Wagner the conductor, whose landmark manual "On Conducting" prescribed "omnipresent tempo modification" and unprecedented extremes of tempo and dynamics, a recipe for Lisztian license and charisma transferred to the podium. Like Nikisch, Seidl was more mercurial, more prone to pervasive rubato than any conductor we are likely to encounter today. His trademark was the calibrated climax, a cataclysm of tone and feeling. For the audience, watching his back, his spare gestures projected an Olympian composure. For the orchestra, reading his face, the bond to Wagner stripped him bare. "His was the eye omniscient," wrote Huneker; he "riveted his men with a glance of steel." Victor Herbert, his frequent principal cellist and assistant conductor, testified, "Certain passages in *Siegfried* and the wonderful closing scene of *Tristan* always made him cry like a child, so that by the time the curtain had dropped he would be in a state of emotional collapse." Henry Finck called him "the most emotional conductor that ever lived." Krehbiel wrote, "With [Seidl] in the chair, it was only the most case-hardened critic who could think of comparative tempo and discriminate between means and effect. As for the rest, professional and layman, dilettante and ignorant, their souls were his to play with."

Off the podium, Seidl was remote yet accessible. His sculpted features were Gothic. His eyes, behind spectacles, were contemplative or piercing. His raven hair was flowing and glossy. He dressed simply, in black or white suits. He shunned society and seldom spoke or smiled. "When Seidl was silent you could almost hear him thinking. He had the sort of personality that overpowered through sheer existing," wrote Huneker. "His manners had a touch of the churchly, and involuntarily your eye looked for the Episcopal purple ring on his finger." Krehbiel observed, "His face shows a singular combination of youth, perspicacity, calm and inflexible determination, and strength of character . . . a countenance which has behind it a huge reserve force." This was when Seidl was thirty-six years old.

Seidl's devotion to Wagner was absolute. Also remarkable, and remarked upon, was his devotion to the United States. After Wagner's death in 1883, he broke with Bayreuth, whose Wagner coterie he found suffocating. He took American citizenship and bought a summer home in the Catskills. He learned English, if imperfectly. He was "Tony" to his wife and "Mr." Seidl—never "Herr"—to others. The critic Albert Steinberg—like Krehbiel, a close friend—called Seidl "afflicted with 'Americamania' in its acutest form. Everything appealed to him—our democratic ways, our enthusiasm for the works of Wagner, our mixed drinks . . . our American clubs, our American scenery." He was better known by sight than any other New York musician, recognized and greeted on streets and streetcars. The *Morning Journal* called him "preeminently a man of the people, whose life is spent in educating the public to know what music is." The *Sun* remarked, in 1898, "No conductor was ever so popular with a mass of people in this city as Mr. Seidl was."[34]

Seidl's advent doomed Theodore Thomas's nascent career as a theater conductor with the National Opera. He also would supplant Thomas as New York's premier symphonic conductor—with consequences we will soon discover.

■ ■ ■

The first American *Tristan und Isolde*, in 1886, and the first American *Ring* three years later, consummated the belated assimilation of German opera in the United States.

In the decades following the midcentury tours of the Germania Orchestra, of the appropriation of German symphonic music via Dwight and Thomas,

Germans had themselves continued to arrive in great numbers, and nowhere more than in New York. In Manhattan's Kleindeutschland—with Vienna and Berlin, one of three capitals of the German-speaking world—more than one hundred thousand German speakers were also German-born as of 1880. Germans had spearheaded the canonization of Bach, Haydn, Mozart, Beethoven, Schubert, Mendelssohn, and Schumann in the concert hall. The concert hall, too, became home to the new German opera after 1850. Thomas tirelessly and influentially championed Wagnerian Music of the Future. He led the American premiere of the *Tristan* Prelude in 1866, when it had barely been played abroad. His first "Wagner Night" at Central Park Gardens, in 1872, included the American premiere of The Ride of the Valkyries; the public responded by leaping onto chairs and shouting. He programmed swaths of excerpts from the *Ring*. In 1882, he led the *Parsifal* Prelude less than four months after the first *Parsifal* in Bayreuth.

Meanwhile, staged Wagner made slower headway. Its point of origin in New York was the German-language Stadttheater and numerous singing societies whose balls, picnics, and supper parties supplemented rehearsals and concerts. *Tannhäuser*, at the Stadttheater under Carl Bergmann in 1859, was the first Wagner opera to be mounted in America. The first *Lohengrin*, also at the Stadttheater, was led by a lesser conductor, Adolf Neuendorff, in 1871. When Neuendorff led the first American *Die Walküre*, in 1877, the venue was the Academy of Music—Wagner was moving uptown, from benches to cushioned seats. In this ascent, a stellar *Lohengrin*, presented by Maurice Strakosch in Italian at the Academy with Italo Campanini and Christine Nilsson, was a landmark. Though a Cincinnati critic had memorably likened the *Rienzi* Overture to "a brigade of bedlamites in a rolling mill with a nail factory attachment,"[35] though William Henry Fry of the *New York Tribune* had excoriated Wagner as unmelodious, though Dwight had earnestly railed against Wagner in theory and practice, no sustained resistance to the Wagner juggernaut materialized, as in Europe. By the time Wagner arrived at the Met, Americans were ready converts. Seidl's impassioned advocacy, the erotic maelstrom of *Tristan*, the mythic grandeur of the *Ring* were finishing touches.

Literal because remote—he never met Wagner or conducted in Germany—Thomas had dignified the preludes and scenes he extracted; he had conferred respectability. Personal because intimate—he had served the master—Seidl intoxicated a community of acolytes. Wagner now became a cult, a drug, a sublime addiction. At the Met, Seidl conducted three and four times a week. The peerless Wagner ensemble he commanded was compact—the roster of sopranos and mezzos was sometimes as small as eleven singers—and devout—during one stretch, Lilli Lehmann sang all three Brünnhildes in the space of six days, plus Rachel in Halévy's *La Juive* (a feat of stamina unknown today). The operas of the *Ring* tetralogy—*Das Rheingold, Die Walküre, Siegfried,* and *Götterdämmerung*—were staged sixteen, ten, thirteen, and eleven times, respectively, in 1888–89.

The Met's rapt, enraptured audiences completed Seidl's shrine. "One could hardly listen to 'Götterdämmerung' among throngs of intensely young enthusiasts, without paroxysms of nervous excitement," reported Henry Adams. "A new world burst forth!" exclaimed the composer Sidney Homer. "Life would never be the same again, the commonplace was banished from our . . . lives forever!"[36] Twenty-five years after New York's opera mobs had provoked the derision of George Templeton Strong, Wagnerites militantly silenced every disturbance from the boxes; implausibly, they took control of the house.

New York's critics grappled formidably with the operas, their myths and metaphors. The meliorist *Tristan,* the ethical readings of the *Ring* and *Parsifal* (to all of which I have alluded) were supplemented by other commentaries equally wholesome. Howells had called the "more smiling aspects of life" the more "American." So, too, did Siegfried seem American: his high spirits, his physical strength, his instinctive intelligence—he understands the Forest Bird and befriends a bear—evoked the frontier. Echoed Henry Krehbiel of *Siegfried*:

> There is something peculiarly sympathetic to our people in the character of the chief personages of the drama. In their rude forcefulness and freedom from restrictive conventions they might be said to be representative of the American people. They are so full of that vital energy which made us a nation. . . . Siegfried is a prototype, too, of the American people in being an unspoiled nature. He looks at the world through glowing eyes that have not grown accustomed to the false and meretricious.

He was Davy Crockett, who refused education and roamed the wilderness. He was the pioneer of Frederick Jackson Turner's popular "frontier thesis," exuding "coarseness and strength combined with acuteness and inquisitiveness," "restless, nervous energy," "dominant individualism," and "withal that buoyancy and exuberance which comes from freedom."[37]

These vignettes do scant justice to the subtlety and depth of the special pleadings of a Krehbiel or W. J. Henderson, in which investigations of Nordic myth, Greek tragedy, or the philosophy of Schopenhauer contributed to siding Wagner with the angels. The detergent action of the meliorist Wagner scrubbed clean every taint of decadence or racism, sanitized incestuous lovers and unrepentant sinners. And Wagner himself, an unlikelier candidate for redemption than any Tristan, was reportrayed as self-made, democratic, and entrepreneurial in the American mold.

Inevitably, the Met's boxholders rebelled. They had suffered the house being plunged into darkness (a novelty), endured rebuke and derision for arriving late and leaving early. They had foolishly defended their prerogative to talk during performances ("You can no more hinder a man from conversing in his own opera box than you can hinder him from snoring in his own pew").[38] The management tried a clumsy appeasement policy, offering two Italian premieres (sung in German) in 1890. But these works, by Alberto Franchetti and Anton Smareglia, pleased no one. In fact, the directors had already secretly decided, the previous summer, to terminate German opera; on January 14, 1891, they announced that beginning in 1891–92 the house would give performances in Italian and French only.

For the remainder of the season, Seidl's every appearance ignited demonstrations in favor of the departing regime. The final performance, of *Die Meistersinger*, was followed by half an hour of applauding, cheering, and stamping. The popular bass-baritone Emil Fischer—as Hans Sachs making his farewell appearance in his most famous role—spoke briefly in English: "Ladies and gentlemen, it is impossible for me to express what I feel for your kindness and love; and I hope it is not the last time that I shall sing for you here, on this stage, in German." Seidl was presented with flowers by *every* member of the chorus. He motioned for quiet and stammered, "Believe me, ladies and gentlemen, I understand the meaning of this great demonstration. For myself, the orchestra, and the other members of the company, I thank you."[39] Only the appearance of workmen breaking down the sets persuaded the public to go home. In seven German seasons, the Met had given 599 staged performances, including 155 on tour, of which 320 were of works by Wagner. In the larger scheme of things operatic, the years 1884–91 represented a false start, a sublime mutation. Wagner, controversial and obscure not three decades before, was entrenched. But the Met would never again seem a church.

■ ■ ■

So protean is Wagner that he holds up a mirror to any given time and place. It follows that, more than any other New World appropriation of Old World opera, the Wagner movement illuminates the American experience.

As in Germany, France, Italy, and Britain, the influence of Wagner peaked in the late nineteenth century. Wagner not only dominated America's musical high culture for a generation; his world of music and ideas—Wagnerism— inflected general intellectual discourse as no musician's had before. George W.

Curtis and Richard Watson Gilder, the influential editors of *Harper's Weekly* and *Century* magazine, were Wagnerites. Albert Pinkham Ryder, among America's important turn-of-the-century painters, attended *Götterdämmerung* at the Met in 1888, then worked for two days without sleep or food on his turbid, hallucinatory evocation of *Siegfried and the Rhine Maidens*.

The extent to which Wagnerism reached beyond New York has been little studied. Seidl toured widely, both with orchestra and with the Met. In the spring of 1889 alone, he led *Ring* cycles in Philadelphia, Boston, Milwaukee, Chicago, and St. Louis with a company of 164. The perceptive Philadelphia, Boston, and Milwaukee critics had all attended the 1876 Bayreuth *Ring*. In St. Louis, where the *Ring* was advertised as "THE GREATEST OPERATIC ATTRACTION IN THE WORLD," four thousand crammed the thirty-five-hundred-seat Music Hall.[40] Walter Damrosch's company toured Wagner more widely still.

If the sweep and intensity of American Wagnerism correlated with Wagnerism abroad, its uplifting agenda was distinctive. Throughout Europe, Wagnerism attracted aesthetes, decadents, and Symbolists who withdrew into troubled realms of the illogical and unconscious, of disease and psychic disturbance. Baudelaire, Huysmans, D'Annunzio, and Nietzsche were Wagnerites. In England, where a milder Wagnerism prevailed, George Bernard Shaw was a socialist Wagnerite for whom the *Ring* was a Fabian rebuke to rapacious capitalists. European Wagnerism, in its many varieties, supported the avant-garde and challenged the political status quo. Wagnerism in the United States was never decadent and rarely socialist. It stood for the therapeutic uses of art.

Most exceptionally, more than abroad, American Wagnerites were women. To a degree, the feminization of postbellum culture—the equation of the arts with ladies of breeding—is pertinent. But Wagner also offered something new in response to new needs. In the midst of fin de siècle transition and malaise, of class and industrial strife, orthodox religion lost potency. Christians adrift in a spiritual void succumbed to what Nietzsche called "weightlessness." For women, the sensibility of limbo was acute. Professionally shackled, sexually corseted, they were expected to shun the male contagion of money-making. Henry Adams called them "still a study."[41]

As genteel inhibitions fell away, new possibilities of emotional and aesthetic transport arose. In the visual arts, an American Renaissance, challenging mistrust of immoral Europe, relished the sensuous and exotic. John La Farge, with his brilliantly tinted stained-glass creations; Louis Tiffany's unprecedented experiments in glass, metal, and stone; John Singer Sargent's sun-drenched, quasi-Impressionistic watercolors of Asia delighted in art for art's sake. But this aestheticism (which we observed among Boston Francophiles) was a caviar taste. A more prevalent, more complete antidote to anomie and "neurosthenia" was at once a surrogate religion and a carnal escape: for untold Americans, Wagnerism was the therapy of choice. Its eclectic social vision yielded a classless utopia founded in love, shunning the curse of gold. Its healing ecstasies commanded a new urgency of musical experience.

One 1890 New York review called the *Tannhäuser* Bacchanale, with its phallic lunges and dense perfumes, "beyond comparison the most intoxicating piece . . . ever composed. . . . If an abstainer wants to realize the voluptuous dreams of an oriental opium-smoker, he may have the experience without bad after-effects by simply listening to this ballet music." This was one variety of the Wagner cure. The *Tannhäuser* story, of pilgrims and intoxicants locked in mortal combat, ends with Tannhäuser rescued and redeemed. Wagner was here titillating yet reassuring; he stirred powerful and neglected sensitivities yet left no "bad after-effects." Another Wagner cure, more subversive, changed the lives of certain Gilded Age women, including the novelist Willa Cather. In Cather's 1908 short story "A Wagner Matinee," Aunt Georgiana, who once taught music at the Boston Conservatory, returns to Boston a withered Westerner, having settled a Nebraska farm. She attends a Wagner concert (presumably by the Boston Symphony) at which the *Tannhäuser* Overture and *Tristan* Prelude jar awake dormant feeling. The narrator is her nephew, Clark:

> The first number was the *Tannhäuser* overture. When the horns drew out the first strain of the Pilgrim's chorus, my Aunt Georgiana clutched my coat sleeve. Then it was I first realized that for her this broke a silence of thirty years; the inconceivable silence of the plains. . . .
>
> I watched her closely through the prelude to *Tristan und Isolde*, trying vainly to conjecture what that seething turmoil of strings and winds might mean to her; but she sat mutely staring. . . .
>
> Soon after the tenor began the "Prize Song" [from *Die Meistersinger*], I heard a quick drawn breath and turned to my aunt. Her eyes were closed, but the tears were glistening on her cheeks, and I think, in a moment more, they were in my eyes as well. It never really died, then—the soul that can suffer so excruciatingly and so interminably; it withers to the outward eye only; like that strange moss which can lie on a dusty shelf half a century and yet, if placed in water, grows green again. . . .
>
> The second half of the programme consisted of four numbers from the *Ring*, and closed with Siegfried's funeral march. My aunt wept quietly, but almost continuously, as a shallow vessel overflows in a rain-storm.

Cather was herself an exquisite Wagnerite (a dimension of her creative identity yet to be explored). No writer has more brilliantly evoked the interpretive genius of the soprano Olive Fremstad in Wagner at the Met, or more compassionately understood—via Fremstad—Kundry in *Parsifal*, whom she called "a summary of the history of womankind," "an instrument of temptation, of salvation, and of service; but always an instrument, a thing driven and employed."[42]

Wagner's gallery of powerfully and empathetically drawn women—muses and helpmates, scourges and heroines, victims and saviors—conflates aspects of Romantic sentimentality with intimations of the new modernism. Wagner spoke to a gamut of new women. M. Carey Thomas, the founding dean and, in 1894, second president of Bryn Mawr College, throttled her heterosexuality in favor of passionate alliances with other women—such as her intimate friend Mary Garrett, with whom she shared *Tristan und Isolde* as conducted by Seidl at the Met in 1891:

> During the bridal night of Tristram and Iseult as she lies in his arms while this glorious chant rises & falls one thinks passion has said its last word, but when the dying Tristram hears of Iseult's approach & tears open his wound in the wildest excitement it rises higher & over his dead body in the death song of Iseult so high that one fairly breaks down under its weight of splendour. I never in a public place came so near to losing my self control and I never cared so much for an opera.

Later the same year, when Mary Garrett attended *Parsifal*, Thomas wrote, "I am so delighted you were carried away.... I think I should be capable of any thing mad and impulsive after a week of Tristram—& there wd be the rest of one's life unlit with Wagner to repent in." Two years later, Thomas wrote that a performance of *Lohengrin* had made her "feel a little like my real self."★[43]

And yet Thomas's public professional demeanor was impeccably conventional. No less was the American Wagner absorbed within genteel conventions of wholesome aesthetic uplift. In the story of American intellectual life, Wagnerism reinterprets the genteel tradition; it reveals visceral potentialities unglimpsed by George Santayana and such latter-day historians of Gilded Age culture as Alan Trachtenberg and Lawrence Levine. In the story of nineteenth-century American opera, Wagnerism furnishes a final chapter in answer to Verdi, a connection to the canonized German concert composers—

★ In Henry James's *The Bostonians* (1886), Verena Tarrant attends *Lohengrin* in New York. "The girl, on the way to Tenth Street, had spoken only of Wagner's music, of the singers, the orchestra, the immensity of the house, her tremendous pleasure." Verena's prim Boston mentor, Olive Chancellor, is made anxious: "Olive could see how fond she might become of New York, where that kind of pleasure was so much more in the air" (book 2, chapter 31).

and also reconnection to a fledgling, prebellum operatic meliorism. Brünnhilde's redemption echoed (of all things) the triumphant wholesomeness of Bellini's Amina. Of *La sonnambula* and William Michael Rooke's *Amilie* in the 1830s, the music historian Karen Alquist writes, "They taught New Yorkers a new musical style, enabling them to enjoy a broad new repertoire in which elaborate musical structures were no longer reduced to simple ballad forms but could be understood on their own terms. They idealized music, the emotions it could elicit, and the moral lesson it could be used to teach."[44] Alquist could equally have been describing Wagner in New York half a century later. Brünnhilde redeemed was opera redeemed. As Boston had sacralized Beethoven and the symphony, New York sacralized opera and Wagner.

■ ■ ■

Of the opening of a new Italian opera house in 1833, Philip Hone reported in his now-famous diary, "The performance occupied four hours—much too long, according to my notion, to listen to a language which one does not understand. . . . Will this splendid and refined amusement be supported in New York? I am doubtful." Hone also wrote, "To entertain an audience without reducing it to the necessity of thinking is doubtless a first-rate merit, and it is easier to produce music without sense than with it; but the real charm of opera is this—it is an exclusive and extravagant recreation, and above all, it is the fashion."

In his 1908 history *Chapters of Opera*, Henry Krehbiel commented of Hone, "The people of New York were not quite so sophisticated as they are to-day, and possibly were dowered with a larger degree of sincerity." Krehbiel reckoned that opera in America would remain "experimental" until "the vernacular becomes the language of the performances and native talent provides both works and interpreters. The day is far distant, but it will come."[45]

It never did. In retrospect, the American Opera Company was a turning point. Never again would so formidable an attempt be made to establish English as "the language of the performances." Instead, the American aversion to opera in the vernacular would harden.

As Krehbiel well appreciated, French, German, Italian, and Russian sophisticates accepted opera translated into their native tongues. National schools of performance and repertoire emerged. Nations with more limited national schools of opera—Hungary, Bohemia, Finland—even more insisted on opera in the vernacular. In the United States, exceptionally, there evolved no native style of performance and composition; no native canon; no tradition of opera as theater, sung in the language of the audience. Instead, twentieth-century opera in the United States would be a curatorial enterprise, incurably Euro-centric. Krehbiel, in 1908, warned that unless Americans grew accustomed to opera in the language they best understood, there would be no such thing as "American opera." And there is not. Hence, as a postscript to our considera-tion of nineteenth-century opera in America, there follows a brief requiem for opera in English.

We have glimpsed its mainly buried history: the popular ballad operas of John Gay and Michael Balfe, the traveling American and British companies of Clara Louise Kellogg and Emma Abbott, of Pyne and Harrison—of which there were as many as sixty in the 1850s. A fact little known and less pondered is that in 1885, when Leopold Damrosch died and the Metropolitan Opera had offered one season in Italian and a second in German, Anton Schott, one of the company's tenors, proposed restructuring the Met as an English-language house specializing in German opera. "We are to look forward to the time when German opera will be as sacred here as in its own home," Schott told the *New York Times*—an aspiration dictating Wagner in English. German singers, Schott promised, would be "quick to learn your own language."[46] But his plan was rejected and six more seasons of opera in German ensued. The logic of this decision was sound: given the multitude of German speakers in attendance, opera in German *was* opera in the vernacular. Even so, Seidl favored giving Wagner in English. And Krehbiel theorized that modern Ger-man opera, in which language shaped song (rather than the other way around), would focus attention on the uses of sung English and prove a step-ping stone to American opera.

To Krehbiel, nothing could have seemed more obvious than the centrality of language to vocal style. Of the singers he most admired, Jean de Reszke, trained in Paris, was a paragon of French suavity and refinement. Albert Nie-mann, coached by Wagner, placed diction and interiority of feeling (*Innigkeit*) before smoothness of emission and plasticity of line. American singers, by comparison, were as yet eclectics. Jeannette Thurber's American Opera arose at precisely this moment of flux, the same year as Schott's proposal for the Met. Her insistence on Americans in the ballet and chorus was not chauvinis-tic but pragmatic—she earnestly strategized a national school.

Her failure, and that of the larger effort of which she was part, had many causes. She insisted that unless the government supported art, as abroad, American talent—especially when not accompanied by privilege or wealth—would go unrecognized and uncultivated. Seidl and Antonín Dvořák likewise lamented the absence of subsidies and schools for young Americans. If these defects worked in favor of imposed European styles, so did America's polyglot population, which blurred the pursuit of American identity. In the opera marketplace, moreover, many buyers—connoisseurs—had acquired an informed appreciation for great singers, the vast majority of whom were European. Others—snobs and social climbers—preferred European goods simply because they were not American—a psychology of insecurity that would distort American classical music in the century to come. The more glamorous and costly opera became, the more would opera in English become marginalized, relegated to secondary houses and to touring troupes for which the aspirations of Thurber and Thomas were not even a memory. As for the fate of operas by American composers, Oscar Sonneck, the pioneer historian of American music, summarized in 1905:

> To-day we are as far from American opera of artistic importance as we ever have been. Not that our composers lack the power to write dramatic music, but our operatic life has been trimmed into a hot-house product. The one Metropolitan Opera House in New York supplies the whole country with opera. . . . Under these circumstances there is neither place nor time for the production of American operas, and our composers have almost stopped trying their hands at this sadly neglected branch of our art. The struggle against the apathy of the public, . . . against the commercial cowardice and avarice of the managers, seems hopeless.[47]

American operatic creativity would necessarily be pushed to the fringes of classical music: toward Broadway.

If nineteenth-century American opera specialized in the cheap spectacular, twentieth-century American opera would furnish the expensive spectacular. The latter—with its busy celebrities singing the same words in New York, London, Paris, Berlin, and Vienna—would foster a homogenized opera product. The former—with its New World mobs and scheming impresarios, frontier outposts and populist prima donnas—was the more dynamic and distinctive. The Americanized Wagner and Anton Seidl, also Americanized, charted the closest approach to a nascent American school.

CHAPTER 6

Symphonic Rivalry
and Growth

■

The early New York Philharmonic ▪ Tchaikovsky and Carnegie Hall ▪
Wagner at Coney Island ▪ The Chicago Orchestra and class warfare ▪
Theodore Thomas dies

The violinist Ureli Corelli Hill* was in his thirties when in 1835 he left New York to study in Kassel with Ludwig Spohr. He also played in London's Drury Lane Theater orchestra and under Mendelssohn in Germany. The diary of his two years abroad compares musical conditions in four countries. Hill found much to criticize in London. British orchestras did not necessarily surpass their American counterparts. British musicians were "cold, selfish, jealous, mercenary." They feared foreign artists. Their self-esteem was as inflated as their influence in America, where they incompetently trimmed such imported operas as *Der Freischütz*, which Hill now heard unabridged. "The English always cut everything to pieces and the poor Americans copy their abominable lacerations."

But François-Antoine Habeneck's famous orchestra of the Société des Concerts du Conservatoire, which Hill heard performing Beethoven's Seventh Symphony in 1837, was a model of precision, and "they gave such an expression by this means that the music deployed the greatest soul." As for Germany, it was "by far the most musical country in the world." The Frankfurt orchestra played "in perfect tune—a machine could not be more perfect." In Düsseldorf, for the premiere of his *St. Paul*, Mendelssohn commanded a festival orchestra of 174 and a chorus of more than 350. Both this performance

---

* Hill's father reportedly concocted his son's name by combining his own, Uri, with that of a friend named Eli. The second name was taken from the famous Italian composer. No wonder Ureli Corelli preferred to call himself "U. C. Hill."

and a Beethoven's Ninth were thronged, as was a public rehearsal. Such occasions were "altogether unknown in America. . . . It seems astonishing where all the musicians come from."[1]

Hill returned to the United States in 1837 to become New York's primary violin teacher and orchestra leader, and founding president of the New York Philharmonic. This was in 1842, making the Philharmonic as old as Vienna's Philharmonic and forty years older than Berlin's. Its inaugural concert began with a well-drilled rendition of Beethoven's Fifth Symphony, with Hill conducting. The second half included Weber's Overture to *Oberon*.

Though the Philharmonic is the most venerable symphonic organization in America with a history continuous to the present day, Hill's orchestra was in many respects a remote ancestor. It gave only three concerts in 1842. It had no single music director. Its home was the Apollo Rooms, seating seven hundred persons on wooden benches. It was organized as a self-governing musicians' cooperative. Its audience comprised subscribers, their families, and a limited number of their friends. Not until 1851 were "strangers" declared admissible.

Initially, about 40 percent of the member-musicians were of German extraction, a representation that steadily increased to 80 percent by 1875. The prospectus intoned:

> The chief object will be, to elevate the Art, improve musical taste, and gratify those already acquainted with classic musical compositions, by performing the Great Symphonies and Overtures of Beethoven, Mozart, Haydn, Spohr, Mendelssohn, and other great Masters, with a strength and precision hitherto unknown in this country.[2]

The Philharmonic musicians tuned offstage and entered with dignity. All but the cellists performed standing. Of the nine programs constituting the first three seasons, two began with Beethoven's Fifth, two with Beethoven's Third, and two with Beethoven's Seventh. The remaining opening works were Beethoven's Second and Eighth Symphonies, and symphonies by Haydn, Mozart, and Spohr. The hunger for this music was great. Henry Krehbiel recorded in 1892, "It is not surprising to hear that impressions were made by the concerts of the first decade which were never equaled afterward in spite of the continual improvement from a technical and purely artistic point of view."[3]

In many respects, the early Philharmonic developed in parallel with Boston's early orchestras. It somewhat resembled a musicians' club. The concerts instilled a spirit of reverence, counteracting native ballyhoo tendencies.

The level of performance was sufficiently modest that, as in Boston, the concerts of the itinerant Germania Musical Society, beginning in 1848, were revelatory. And, as in Boston, the Germanians deposited an idealistic young German to take over. Compared to Boston's Carl Zerrahn, Carl Bergmann was a notably progressive musician. As conductor of the Germania beginning in 1850 (when he was not yet thirty years old), Bergmann instilled a braver repertoire and a more dynamic approach to interpretation. When the Germania society disbanded in 1854, Bergmann settled in New York and scored the pivotal success of his career leading Wagner's *Tannhäuser* Overture with the Philharmonic at Niblo's Garden. He became co-conductor of the Philharmonic, with Theodore Eisfeld, the following fall. After Eisfeld retired in 1865, Bergmann was the orchestra's sole conductor for more than a decade.

In the course of Bergmann's tenure, the Philharmonic season moderately expanded to six concerts, preceded by public rehearsals. But this represented only a fraction of the city's symphonic activity. Like Zerrahn in Boston, Bergmann was widely active. We have already encountered him leading the city's first staged Wagner performance, of *Tannhäuser* in 1859. Three years earlier, he led a pick-up ensemble in eleven pathbreaking concerts including first American performances of three major Schumann works and two Berlioz overtures, of which Schumann's Fourth Symphony and Berlioz's *Roman Carnival* had to be given twice. Two Wagner selections—the Entrance of the Guests from *Tannhäuser* and the Bridal Procession from *Lohengrin*—were encored and twice reprogrammed. The hall was packed. Symphonic New York was already remote from Boston, already en route to the Wagner decades.

Bergmann's popularity diminished after 1870. His indolence and drinking were topics of complaint. In 1876, the Philharmonic requested his resignation. He died the same year. His detractors included Theodore Thomas, who had played under his baton and partnered Bergmann's cello in the city's most important chamber music series. Eventually, Thomas and his Thomas Orchestra rivaled Bergmann and his Philharmonic, and Thomas took rivalries seriously. In his memoirs, he recalled Bergmann as "a talented musician and a fair 'cello player" who "lacked most of the qualities of a first-rank conductor." Certainly Bergmann lacked Thomas's indomitable energy, to say nothing of his competitive fire. When another German conductor of consequence, Leopold Damrosch, appeared on the scene in 1871, Thomas is said to have greeted him at Schuberth's music store by vowing to "crush whoever crosses my path"—an anecdote which, if apocryphal, deserves to be true.

Damrosch, at age fifty-two, had been Liszt's concertmaster at Weimar and later chief conductor in Breslau. No less than Bergmann or Thomas, he was a dedicated explorer of the newest music, especially if by Wagner or Liszt. A small, garrulous musician whose rabbinical beard emphasized his Semitic features, he traded Thomas's stoic aplomb for fire and spontaneity. A violinist who played under both later reported, "Dr. Damrosch was not so popular with his orchestra as Theodore Thomas was with his. He simply was not one of them. He talked over their heads. The musicians were easily disposed to criticize him, while they stood in awe of Thomas. At rehearsals Damrosch was hypercritical, making the orchestra nervous. When the time came for the actual performance, he was often the first to change his own previous instructions."[4]

Damrosch came to New York, whose cosmopolitan "hustle and bustle . . . with no room for narrowmindedness" impressed him instantly, to take over the Arion Society's fifty-member male chorus. The Arion was one of countless *Männerchöre* that seeded the concert life of American cities, and at the same time furnished a cultural community center. Its activities included carnivals and festivals, an occasional operetta production, and participation in an annual Sängerfest in competition with choral groups from afar. Though such singing clubs, as the *New York Staats-Zeitung* had occasion to observe in 1860, united "the worker, the businessman and the politician," erasing "the social distinctions which divided the German element," elite groups—the Arion among them—began to separate from the pack during the last third of the nineteenth century.[5] Even so, for Damrosch this first New York job was obviously too small. He accepted Thomas's rivalry as an invitation. Acting on a suggestion from Anton Rubinstein, visiting from Russia, he resolved to found a chorus that would break out of the German musical ghetto. Enlisting the support of such great names and names-to-be as the banker Elkan Naumburg, the music dealer Gustave Schirmer, and Frederick A. P. Barnard, the president of Columbia University, Damrosch in 1873 created the New York Oratorio Society. The following season, the group's concerts included a complete performance of Handel's *Messiah*; as with Boston's Handel and Haydn Society, it would become an annual ritual.

Two years later, with Carl Bergmann in failing health, the New York Philharmonic elected Damrosch its conductor. But Damrosch as yet lacked a large following. His ambitious programs, featuring the entire first act of Wagner's *Die Walküre* and generous excerpts from *Götterdämmerung*, would have been unthinkable from Boston's Harvard Musical Association, but cannot be blamed for the plummeting attendance that dictated his departure after a single season. In fact, Bergmann's programs were as progressive—and so would be Theodore Thomas's once Thomas was elected to take over the Philharmonic in 1877. As Thomas continued to maintain his own orchestra, with its own New York season, his pledge to bury Damrosch seemed momentarily credible.

Damrosch fought back with a new Damrosch Orchestra, christened the New York Symphony in 1878, by which time it had already preempted Thomas's scheduled premiere of Brahms's First Symphony when Damrosch had copyists, working day and night, create a complete set of orchestral parts. A year later, Damrosch led Berlioz's *Damnation of Faust*, billed as "the first time in America," though Thomas had managed to present the work in Boston two weeks earlier. Damrosch now created a May festival of seven concerts in five days at the Seventh Regiment Armory; he conducted the American premiere of Berlioz's Requiem with a chorus of twelve hundred. Thomas responded with *his* May festival, also at the Seventh Regiment Armory, fielding a chorus of three thousand. In 1884, Thomas mounted a Wagner festival and took it on tour. By this time, Damrosch was touring too, to the very midwestern cities Thomas considered his own.

The Metropolitan Opera's decision to entrust its 1885–86 season to Damrosch, the consequences of which we have already observed, climaxed this feverish rivalry. Snubbed by the Met, Thomas wound up with Jeannette Thurber's ill-fated American Opera Company. Damrosch's untimely death undid his triumph, yet yielded, in Anton Seidl, a newcomer more formidable still. Meanwhile, young Walter Damrosch, barely twenty-three years old, harbored great ambitions of his own. The new balance of power, ever shifting, pitted against one another Walter's New York Symphony and Oratorio Society, both inherited from his father; Seidl's orchestra at the Met, seizing the burgeoning Wagner movement; and three Theodore Thomas orchestras—the Philharmonic, the Brooklyn Philharmonic, and the Thomas Orchestra, all with overlapping memberships and dovetailing schedules.

Seidl, so blatantly different from Thomas in every respect save repertoire, forced a choice, and New York chose Seidl. Henry Finck happened upon Thomas one evening and inquired, "Hello! Are you still alive?" Thomas bristled, "Yes, and more than ever!" Finck later remarked, "I had simply meant by my question that I had not seen him for a long time, whereas he, with his abnormal sensitiveness, twisted it into an indication that I had thought him musically dead and buried."[6] And Thomas, now in his fifties, was tiring of his prodigious travels. He disbanded the itinerant Thomas Orchestra in 1888. His New York Philharmonic was still a musicians' cooperative, and still gave only six pairs of concerts per season. He envied Boston its Henry Higginson and Boston Symphony.

Walter Damrosch, a lesser conductor than Thomas or Seidl, possessed compensatory assets unknown to either. Thomas, notoriously, was truculent. Seidl was called *Die grosse Schweiger* ("the Great Silent One"). Both stood aloof from a prepotent world of Gilded Age commerce and politics. In this sense Damrosch was the worldliest of musicians. His chronic geniality, an artistic liability, helped him to win friends in high places. He met Andrew Carnegie on a steamship to Europe in 1887 and wound up Carnegie's houseguest in Scotland. The other guests included Senator James G. Blaine, who had almost become president three years before. Damrosch entertained the Carnegies and Blaines with evening lectures explicating Beethoven's symphonies at the piano. In New York the following season, he dissuaded Carnegie from backing a proposed tour to England by Thomas and the New York Philharmonic. "I've nipped it in the bud," he reported to his brother. "Carnegie will be all right if he is worked carefully by some of our directors."[7] Damrosch was again Carnegie's guest in the Scottish Highlands the following summer. The Blaines were there too. Cultural philanthropy was a topic of intense conversation. By 1890, Carnegie had accepted the presidency of the New York Symphony and the New York Oratorio Society; other board members included J. P. Morgan, John D. Rockefeller, Collis P. Huntington, and three Vanderbilts. Damrosch married the Blaines' daughter Margaret the same year, a wedding attended by Supreme Court justices, cabinet members, and the president of the United States.

The year 1891 was pivotal for New York's symphonic rivalries. Thomas found the permanent orchestra he craved—in Chicago. Seidl took over Thomas's New York Philharmonic. And the Damrosch-Carnegie alliance created the most famous concert hall in the United States.

■ ■ ■

Astonishing people, these Americans! Unlike the common impression of Paris, where at each favor, at each grace from a stranger, one senses an attempt at exploitation, American straightforwardness, sincerity, generosity, cordiality without any ulterior motive, readiness to serve you and coddle—it is all simply astounding and touching.[8]

Pyotr Il'yich Tchaikovsky, Walter Damrosch's guest of honor at the opening ceremonies for Andrew Carnegie's new Music Hall, was a candid and copious recorder of his own experience. At fifty-one, he had never before been to America. He marveled repeatedly, with excitement or fatigue, at the extent to which his fame had preceded him. Reporters competed for his attention. At concerts, women gathered in knots to gape; others sprang forward to express delight. "It turns out that I am far better-known in America

than in Europe." "Works of mine that are still unknown in Moscow are performed here several times a season, and whole reviews and commentaries are
written on them. . . . I am far more a big shot here than in Russia. Is it not
curious!!!" "Two societies here played the Fifth Symphony two seasons in a
row." And, to Alexander Siloti, "Nowhere but in America can a person (especially one of your fraternity—pianists) perform so often and earn so much
money. In the first place, piano manufacturers are at sword's edge between
themselves and pay pianists handsomely to woo them to their firms. Secondly,
the need for talented virtuosos is tremendous, for there is a huge number of
cities; concerts are held everywhere, and everyone is well-paid."9

Like many a previous visitor, Tchaikovsky was amazed by the vigor and
optimism of New York and of New Yorkers. "Nowhere outside of Russia have
I seen such a hearty attitude toward foreigners, such a readiness to oblige and
serve you in every way. . . . Life is in full swing here. Although their main
interest is profit, the Americans are still very attentive to art. . . . I must confess
that the scope and grandiosity of all American undertakings are tremendously
appealing to me." "This is a vast city, more strange and original than handsome. There are long one-story houses, 11-story buildings, and one building
(a grand-new hotel) that is 17 stories high. . . . Every little apartment, every
hotel accommodation has a lavatory with a basin, bath, and a washstand
installed with hot and cold running water. . . . Lighting is by electricity and
gas. Candles are not used at all. . . . The elevator runs constantly, going up and
down at an incredible speed."

The New York Symphony and New York Oratorio Society presented six
concerts in celebration of the new hall. For the first, on May 5, the line of car-
riages on West Fifty-seventh Street stretched a quarter of a mile. "The walls of
the new building," reported the *Morning Journal*, "almost shook when that
grand old chorale, 'Old Hundredth,' was sung"; the audience spontaneously
rose and joined the Oratorio Society's four hundred voices. The Rt. Reverend
Henry Potter delivered an address all considered too long, after which Damrosch led his orchestra in Beethoven's *Leonore* Overture No. 3. Then came
Tchaikovsky's turn—leading his *Marche Solenelle*★—followed by Berlioz's *Te
Deum* in its American premiere. At the remaining concerts, Tchaikovsky conducted two unaccompanied choral works, his Second Suite, and his First
Piano Concerto. He reported that the concerto, with Adele Aus der Ohe,
elicited enthusiasm "of a kind that never arises even in Russia." The press
responded in kind. Krehbiel, in the *Tribune*, detected a "trace of barbarism" in

★ So identified in the New York press—presumably the *Festival Coronation* March, according to
Carnegie Hall archivist Gino Francesconi.

the "directness, truthfulness, and forcefulness" of Tchaikovsky's style—which, as a connoisseur of folk music, he applauded (as no Boston critic would).[10]

As for the twenty-eight hundred-seat hall, which would only become known as "Carnegie" a few seasons hence, it was admired for its size (larger than any Russian concert hall, according to Tchaikovsky) and utility (Irving Hall, Chickering Hall, and Steinway Hall, all of which regularly hosted symphonic concerts, were less adequately grand). Though it spurned the New England plainness and Beethoven icons of Boston's halls, by European standards it was democratic and restrained all the same. Morris Reno, president of the Music Hall Company, claimed that every seat commanded a full view of the stage. Even the sixty-two boxes were relatively simple affairs. New York critics tellingly admired the hall's "architectural purity" and "chaste" coloring and lines. And everyone agreed that the acoustics were splendid.

Carnegie, who had put up most of the money for both the land and the building, was no informed devotee of concerts and opera. But his wife, an avid amateur singer, was a member of the Oratorio Society. He himself adored Scottish folk songs and would sing them to Damrosch's piano accompaniments. He could recite Burns and Shakespeare by heart. His passions— Walter observed that he clenched his fists when talking about them—were education and peace. He wrote:

> [Spending] is held to be the duty of the man of wealth: To set an example of modest, unostentatious living, shunning display or extravagance; to provide moderately for the legitimate wants of those dependent upon him; and, after doing so, to consider all surplus revenues which come to him simply as trust funds, which he is called upon to administer . . . in the manner which, in his judgment, is best calculated to produce the most beneficial results for the community—the man of wealth thus becoming the mere trustee and agent for his poorer brethren, bringing to their service his superior wisdom, experience and ability to administer, doing for them better than they would or could do for themselves.[11]

Carnegie and Tchaikovsky, conversing in French, charmed one another. Tchaikovsky told his diary:

> Carnegie, this remarkable original who rose from telegraph boy to become in the course of years one of America's foremost men of wealth, but remained a modest and simple man, never one to turn his nose up— inspires in me unusual warm feelings, probably because he is also filled with kindly feelings for me. During the whole evening, he showed his

love to me in an extraordinarily peculiar way. He clasped my hands, shouting that I am the uncrowned but still genuine king of music; embraced me (without kissing—men never kiss here); he stood on tiptoe and raised his hands up high to express my greatness; and finally threw all the company in delight by imitating my conducting. He did this so seriously, so well, and so accurately, that I myself was enraptured. His wife, an extremely simple and pretty young lady, also showed her sympathy for me in every way.[12]

Carnegie was evidently drawn, as well, to Walter—to his entrepreneurial aplomb, his earnest strivings toward cultural uplift, his gift for proselytization. The many reviews that deplored his inexperience and ineptitude as a conductor could not have escaped Carnegie's notice. Did Walter's travails in the press redouble an attitude of fatherly support? In any event, Carnegie, in addition to his service to the New York Symphony and Oratorio Society (and to Jeannette Thurber's National Conservatory), eventually gave Walter an annual five-thousand-dollar birthday gift. With such abundant backing, Walter was formidably resilient—rebuffed by the Met, he had formed his own Damrosch Opera. In 1903, rebuffed by the Philharmonic, he would recommit to his New York Symphony. His easy manner, good looks, and dreamy German accent undeniably contributed to his popularity—and to a six-decade American career unimaginable had he remained in German-speaking lands, where public support of music and music education leveled the playing field and diminished the impact of private wealth.*

But Carnegie was not disposed to furnish permanent support for Carnegie Hall. Insisting that a good business pay for itself, he covered the annual operating deficit with increasing reluctance. Nor was his loyalty to the New York Symphony permanent: in 1909, as outgoing president of the New York Philharmonic, he supported a Sunday-afternoon Carnegie Hall series of popular classics in competition with a similar Symphony series conceived by Walter. Unlike Henry Higginson, Carnegie did not institutionalize a central, controlling cultural role for himself. In New York, no one did—or could. And Carnegie Hall, commensurately, was home to the New York Philharmonic as well as the Symphony. It was rented, additionally, by the Boston Symphony, the New York Liederkranz, and John Philip Sousa; by the Orphans' Asylum and Workingman's School; for illustrated lectures on Shakespeare and the

---

* Damrosch's one substantial recording—a fits-and-starts rendition of Brahms's Second Symphony, with the New York Symphony—sounds rudderless.

Wonders of America; for graduation ceremonies by the City College of New York and Packard Business School.[13]

The general significance of Carnegie Hall resembled that of the Metropolitan Opera. Like the Met, it moved music uptown from the Deutschtum. Like the Met's, its impressive scale and trappings were a sacralizing influence. In the opinion of the *Herald*, the opening ceremonies were "most interesting as a study of music lovers not under the pressure of the mandates of fashion. . . . There was no idea of chatter. . . . There was no coming and going of dandies and mouthpieces. . . . All was dignified, soft, slow and noiseless, as became the dedication of a great temple."[14] Monster concerts were unthinkable at such temples as Carnegie or Boston's Symphony Hall. Within a generation, times had changed completely. Rather than their own confections, pianists like Anton Rubinstein gave programs of Bach, Beethoven, Chopin, and Schumann—an emerging keyboard canon—for audiences learning attitudes of reverence. And orchestras like the New York Symphony and New York Philharmonic now served Siegfried's Death and Brünnhilde's Immolation to devout acolytes. In fact, in New York Wagner became the dominant *concert* composer. And his high priest, as in the opera house, was Anton Seidl.

■ ■ ■

The most exotic concert of the 1889–90 season took place on Palm Sunday, March 31, at the Brooklyn Academy of Music. Outside the Montague Street entrance (this was the old Academy in Brooklyn Heights, not the present one on Lafayette Avenue), carpets were laid between banks of flowers and plants. A series of drawing rooms hung with watercolors and engravings embellished the foyer. The stage was set as a cathedral. An eighty-four-piece orchestra was partly concealed by fan palms, geraniums, and lilies. A banner on the proscenium showed a medieval "S" alongside the word "PARSIFAL" in flowered green letters. The packed house—including ex-President and Mrs. Grover Cleveland, Brooklyn Mayor and Mrs. Alfred C. Chapin, Dr. and Mrs. Lymon Abbott, and Mr. and Mrs. J. Pierpont Morgan—was considered the most distinguished in the building's twenty-nine-year history.

The "S" acknowledged the Seidl Society, which conceived and presented this "*Parsifal* Entertainment," beginning at 5 P.M. with an abridged concert performance of *Parsifal* act one and part of act two. A ninety-minute dinner break followed. The performance resumed at eight o'clock and lasted until ten. About three-quarters of the score was heard. Anton Seidl conducted.[15]

This was not the first American *Parsifal*. In 1886, four years following the premiere in Bayreuth, Walter Damrosch had led two concert performances at the Metropolitan Opera House, of which Henry Finck commented, "It was a task that [Damrosch] should never have undertaken." Seidl doubtless agreed. The Wagner family, which only learned about Damrosch's performances in 1903, had intended a close watch on *Parsifal*, including a ban on staged performances outside Bayreuth. For Seidl—who felt closer to this Wagner score than any other, and who would conduct it in Bayreuth in 1897, and who did not esteem Damrosch in any event—Damrosch's "unauthorized" *Parsifal*, with orchestral parts copied from a miniature conductor's score he had purchased in London, trespassed on holy ground. Of Seidl's *Parsifal* Entertainment, Lilli Lehmann, who sang Kundry, reported, "There was a Good Friday atmosphere. The place was transformed into a temple." Beyond launching Wagner's last opera with suitable tokens of reverence, the *Parsifal* Entertainment launched as a presenting organization a singular sponsor of Seidl's concert career.

The Seidl Society was a Brooklyn woman's club. Its leader, Laura Langford, was a prominent socialite and author, of whom the Brooklyn *Daily Eagle* (for which she had served as associate editor) testified, "What she does is done with all her might." According to its constitution, the society was "organized for the purpose of securing to its members and to the public increased musical culture and of promoting musical interest among women particularly. It aims to reach all classes of women and children and by its efforts in their behalf to prove the potent influence of harmony over individual life and character."[16] Seidl Society activities included excursions to Brighton Beach, the site of Seidl's summer concerts, with special railroad cars for unescorted women, working girls, and poor or orphaned children. The success of these outings, and of the Entertainment, and of lectures by Henry Krehbiel with musical illustrations furnished at the piano by Seidl himself, led to a series of ten Seidl Society concerts at the Brooklyn Academy of Music in 1890–91.

Eight years prior to its annexation to New York City in 1898, Brooklyn was a city of churches and bucolic parks. Though Brooklyn's 800,000 residents included 260,000 foreign-born, the Plymouth Congregational Church, led by Henry Ward Beecher until 1887, set the cultural tone, not *Singvereine* and *Bierstuben*. The city had long enjoyed music of a higher sort. A philharmonic society was established in 1857 and proceeded to offer seasons comparable in length to those of the New York Philharmonic across the river. As of 1862, the same year the 2,250-seat Brooklyn Academy of Music opened, Theodore Thomas became the sole conductor, with responsibility for hiring the players. The Boston Symphony performed annually at the Academy of Music beginning in 1887. As of 1891, upon Thomas's departure, the Brooklyn Philharmonic Society became sponsor of the Boston Symphony's Brooklyn season of six concerts and public rehearsals, in competition with the Seidl Society's new series.[17]

Seidl's leadership was not the only distinguishing feature of the Seidl Society concerts. In Boston and the hinterlands, Mendelssohn—a genteel cult figure, admired as greatly for the divine equanimity and devout religiosity of his person as for the sublime civility and tempered passions of his music*—was still ascendant decades after his death in 1847. His *Songs Without Words* were essential parlor repertoire. Every choral society sang *Elijah*. According to one 1885–90 survey of classical music concerts, in cities other than Boston and New York Mendelssohn was the most performed composer. During its first decade, the Boston Symphony programmed Mendelssohn more frequently than any composer except Beethoven and Wagner. The New York Philharmonic under Thomas and Seidl, however, registered no comparable Mendelssohn affinity. And in Brooklyn, unconstrained by Philharmonic tastes, the Seidl Society mainly offered contemporary and near-contemporary fare. The opening program was all Wagner. The season also included a Liszt program, a second Wagner night, and a "Grand *Parsifal* Concert." Otherwise, Seidl played two Beethoven symphonies and a smattering of Bach, Mozart, Schubert, and Schumann. These concerts were praised in the *Daily Eagle* for "loftiness of aim and fullness of fulfillment."[18]

But it was at elegant Brighton Beach, on Coney Island, where the elevating impact of Langford's society was most startlingly affirmed. In 1894, the society took over the summer concerts and made Seidl's Wagner nights, once lampooned in the press, an astonishing success. Within promenading distance of the shooting galleries and sideshows of Coney's "Sodom by the Sea," in a pavilion open to stars and sea breezes, patrolled by earnest ushers wearing "S" pins on their dresses, crowds of three thousand would listen with rapt attention to favorite numbers from *The Flying Dutchman, Lohengrin, Tannhäuser, Tristan, Die Meistersinger*, the *Ring*, and *Parsifal*. Seidl conducted fourteen times a week—twice a day—for two months. In 1895, statistics kept by the *Daily Eagle* showed 156 performances of works by Wagner, 50 by Liszt, 46 by Saint-Saëns, versus 33 by Mendelssohn and 20 by Beethoven. The balance of the list read:

---

* Of the *Midsummer Night's Dream* Overture, the *New York Tribune* wrote in 1848 that it "was one of those creations which fill the soul to overflow with a glorious sense of their fullness and completeness—which leave no after-sensation of pain, but a halo of deep and abiding joy, as if we had been blessed with the visible presence of some spirit of Truth and Beauty." Quoted in Nancy Newman, "Good Music for a Free People: The Germania Musical Society and Transatlantic Musical Culture of the Mid-Nineteenth Century" (dissertation, Brown University, 2002), p. 102.

Grieg 37
Dvořák 27
Tchaikovsky 21
Johann Strauss 21
Berlioz 19
Weber 17
Schumann 15
Haydn 15
Schubert 14
Bach 10
Mozart 6
Handel 3
Brahms [the anti-Wagner] 2

Possibly nowhere else—nowhere in Berlin or Vienna or London—was the contemporary "Music of the Future" so assiduously purveyed.* The Seidl Society's Sunday-morning religious services blended seamlessly with this missionary work, of which Seidl himself declared, in a handwritten speech in fractured English:

Those, who like only the airs as "Jonny get your gun" find places on this shore very many. We will play only good music; we know, the people need it, and this is the cause, that the noble ladies of the Seidl Society don't spare the large expenses and the terrible difficult and heavy work to give the good people, what he needs, and what he must have....The people not understand it first, but later he will whistle it with more dash and vigor, as the rich, who sits in his box and—chatter, because—he does not understand it. But the low kind of music demoralizes the people. One of the many good works of the Seidl Society is to give good music for the less rich, for the poor, and in the same time enjoys and

---

* Seidl's Manhattan concerts with his own Seidl Orchestra were scarcely more conservative. As with Carl Bergmann and Theodore Thomas, his New York Philharmonic programs were less his own than when he engaged a freelance ensemble of his choosing. In Seidl's case, especially, the preponderance of contemporary works at non-Philharmonic concerts is remarkable. The Seidl concert of December 1, 1888, at Steinway Hall, for instance, included first performances of D'Indy's *Wallenstein* Trilogy, Cornelius's *Barber of Baghdad* Overture, and (conducted by the composer) Victor Herbert's Serenade for Strings. The balance of the evening was devoted to songs and arias by Gluck, Schumann, and Wagner. To Henry Krehbiel's delight, the Herbert Serenade won "the heartiest applause of the evening." See Krehbiel, *Review of the New York Musical Season 1888–1889* (New York, Novello, Ewer, and Co., 1889), p. 35.

educates himself. This is a grand and glorious mission! And a point to which of must direct the eyes of the whole world, is, that this society works not for money, as the socalled managers of nearly all the musical organizations do, but the noble ladies of this society brings many thousands and thousands dollars together, to enable themselves to give good music for 25 cents to the poor and music needing people. This only women can do. The men must stand still and be astonished before such a grand work![19]

Seidl was now primarily a symphonic conductor. Utilizing New York's pool of experienced orchestral musicians—a group he considered superior to any such in Europe—he led orchestras variously called the Seidl Society Orchestra, the Seidl Orchestra, and the Metropolitan Orchestra fifty and more times a season. The leitmotif of these concerts, far eclipsing Beethoven, was Wagner: a plethora of extracts from the music dramas far exceeding, in length and number, what Wagner excerpts are heard today. With the New York Philharmonic, which had its traditions, Seidl necessarily pursued a more conservative agenda. But even his readings of Bach, Mozart, and Beethoven were formidably Wagnerized with regard to weight, tempo, and rubato. His Philharmonic programs were notable, too, for performances of three important American works: Edward MacDowell's *Indian* Suite and Second Piano Concerto (with MacDowell as soloist), and the premiere of the Second Cello Concerto of Victor Herbert (with Herbert as soloist). Dvořák's music was a special cause; in addition to the premiere of the *New World* Symphony (the impact of which we have already observed), Seidl led the Philharmonic in four Dvořák tone poems, the cello and violin concertos, and two earlier symphonies.

Meanwhile, in Manhattan, the 1891 abandonment of German opera by the Metropolitan Opera's boxholders proved predictably futile. Under the management of Henry Abbey, Maurice Grau, and John Schoeffel, the Met now embarked on its "Golden Years" of astounding French and Italian vocal splendor. Wagner was given in Italian, mainly conducted by Luigi Mancinelli, until November 27, 1895, when Abbey, Grau, and Schoeffel presented *Tristan* in German, led by Seidl, with two of the company's biggest stars: Lillian Nordica and Jean de Reszke. Seidl had become their mentor in Wagner roles. Behind the scenes, de Reszke (who would next undertake Siegfried) joined the public clamor for Seidl and Wagner; according to Finck, he made Grau and Seidl sign a contract ensuring Seidl's return to the pit, whereupon Mancinelli quit the company.[20]

Walter Damrosch had already plunged into the Wagner vacuum, staging

Die Walküre at Carnegie Hall in 1894, then renting the Met for *Die Walküre* and *Götterdämmerung*, then forming a Wagner company of his own. He offered to share conducting with Seidl; Seidl of course said no. With an army of subscribers, the Damrosch Opera Company next rented the Met for eight weeks in 1895. "To re-enter the Metropolitan on such a Wagnerian wave after German opera had been so ignominiously snuffed out five years before," Damrosch later wrote, "was a great triumph and satisfaction for me, especially because my father had laid the foundation."[21] This, in fact, was the impetus for Seidl's 1895 reengagement at the Met, at which point Grau refused to again relinquish the house to Damrosch. The Damrosch Opera maintained an influential but nomadic existence through 1898. By then, both it and the Met were rapidly evolving toward the twentieth-century status quo: French opera in French, Italian opera in Italian, German opera in German. The Met even had a separate Wagner orchestra, brought in by Seidl.[22] To a degree, two companies, German and non-German, were now inhabiting the same opera house. New York's rival conductors and orchestras and opera companies had produced rival audiences influentially agitating for favorite works and performers.

Clearly, though they paid the piper, the Met's bejeweled boxholders could not call the tune or stem the Wagner tide. With the evidence of Wagner's dual presence in the opera house and concert hall now before us, the full force and variety of the Wagner constituency may be gleaned. The Wagner audience was the Prussians and Franconians, Saxons and Bavarians of Kleindeutschland, whose singing societies erased social distinctions. The *Singvereine* took part in *Tannhäuser* at the Stadttheater, and also (without fee) in *Die Meistersinger* at the Met. The Wagner audience was, equally, the fashionable Brooklyn ladies of the Seidl Society, whose Brighton Beach concerts, in a circular structure unfitted with boxes and other signatures of status, joined the best Brooklyn and New York families with earnest intellectuals, music-loving Germans, and incidental patrons who had come to Coney mainly to swim or stroll the boardwalk. Seidl himself inhabited several Wagner worlds. He was a member of the gentlemanly Metropolitan Club and of the Liederkranz, an upscale uptown *Singverein* on Fifty-eighth Street equipped with a substantial concert hall, a billiard room, and bowling alleys, all elegantly appointed. His friends included the reform leader Carl Schurz, a Liederkranz stalwart; Richard Watson Gilder of *Century* magazine; and Robert Ingersoll the "Great Agnostic," the best-known American orator of his time.[23]

But Seidl was not assertively gregarious. He and his wife Auguste, a retired soprano, did not cultivate Carnegies and Blaines. "He lacked the quality of Yankee 'push,' so necessary in this country," observed Finck. Reliant on people like Laura Langford and Henry Krehbiel to push for him, he moved far. But his eventual heart's desire was what Henry Higginson gave Boston and Theodore Thomas was given in Chicago, what even Cincinnati and Pittsburgh now enjoyed: a permanent orchestra. Returning from Covent Garden and Bayreuth in 1897, he was pursued by offers from London, Bremen, Berlin, Munich, Pest, Warsaw, St. Petersburg, and Moscow. Fearing the possibility of his departure, Gilder, among others, quickly mobilized backing for a Seidl Permanent Orchestra. Grau pledged to engage the Seidl Orchestra for the full Met season beginning in 1898–99; he also offered the Metropolitan Opera House gratis for all rehearsals and concerts. Eugène Ysaÿe, one of Europe's ranking violinists, was engaged as concertmaster. Seidl, Finck reported, was "wonderfully elated."[24]

Months later, on March 28, 1898, he was dead. An autopsy revealed gallstone and liver ailments. For the funeral, at the Metropolitan Opera House, the pit was floored over and blanketed with flowers. The coffin was positioned at the conductor's place. A music stand in white roses and violets bore an open score on which appeared portraits of Wagner and Seidl with the inscription "Vereint auf Ewig"—"forever united." Fifteen thousand persons had applied for tickets. Four thousand—seven hundred in excess of the auditorium's proper capacity—streamed through the doors; in the downstairs seats, women outnumbered men twenty to one. Schurz, the designated eulogist, could not bring himself to speak; Krehbiel took his place. The New York Philharmonic played Siegfried's Funeral Music and the Adagio lamentoso from Tchaikovsky's *Pathétique* Symphony. Finck, in the *Post*, called Seidl's career in the United States "the most important 12 years in the history of music in America." The *Staats-Zeitung*, in a page-one obituary, called Seidl "almost irreplaceable." Ysaÿe was offered the New York Philharmonic but said no.[25]

Had Seidl not died at the age of forty-seven, his new orchestra would have become the New York equivalent of Vienna's Philharmonic, anchoring the city's musical life in both concert and opera, transcending (if not healing) the musical rivalries that had frustrated and entertained New Yorkers for more than three decades. Once a jousting ground for Carl Bergmann and Theodore Thomas, for Thomas and Leopold Damrosch, for Thomas, Walter Damrosch, and Anton Seidl, for Seidl and Boston's Arthur Nikisch and Emil Paur at the Brooklyn Academy, New York was now musically leaderless.

■ ■ ■

Thomas had outlived his rivals Leopold Damrosch and Anton Seidl. But he had also outlived his New York appeal and his barnstorming energies. Now settled in Chicago, he felt duty-bound to reject offers to return to New York and, from Henry Higginson, to take over the Boston Symphony. The coveted Boston appointment would have crowned his career; Thomas's abstinence was a remarkable instance of principled behavior.

City of stockyards and railroads, of McCormick and Pullman, Armour and Swift, Chicago[26] was as new and raw as Thomas was old and burnished. It was founded in 1833 and rebuilt after the fire of 1871. Between 1880 and 1890 its population doubled to one million, of which nearly eight of ten were foreign-born or of non-American parentage. There was a saloon for every two hundred people. Thick grease polluted the Chicago River. An overgrown boomtown, a city of laborers, it also spawned an exceptional business elite whose aspirations would prove cultural as well as commercial.

As elsewhere in America, the first cultural stirrings, with regard to music, were instigated by Germans, representing one-third of the foreign population. As elsewhere, there were singing societies and a philharmonic society, organized by Hans Balatka in 1860. As elsewhere, Ole Bull visited. As elsewhere, the Theodore Thomas Orchestra effaced all local efforts. Thomas came regularly beginning in 1869. In 1877, he initiated an annual outdoor summer season at popular prices, a series that would run for thirteen years and total 360 programs. In 1882 and 1884 he led a pair of ambitious May festivals.

By the 1880s, Chicago's Captains of Industry were impressively committed to sponsoring a civic cultural pedigree. Charles Hutchinson—grain trader, meatpacker, banker—was their leader in this enterprise; it is estimated that he gave away over half his income annually. Hutchinson was president of the Art Institute of Chicago from 1881 until his death forty-three years later. He was also a trustee of the University of Chicago from 1890, and of the Chicago Symphony from 1914. As a group, Chicago's cultural leaders were, like Hutchinson, white Protestants of predominantly British descent; like Hutchinson, they combined business acumen with *noblesse oblige* and intense local pride. Many, like Hutchinson (born in Lynn, Massachusetts), either came from New England, with its high-cultural traditions, or kept homes there. In addition to the Art Institute, the University, and the Orchestra, their overlapping trusteeships included the Field Columbian Museum and the Newberry and Crerar Libraries.[27]

A pivotal year for music, for its accreditation as a prestigious civic signature, was 1885. The Metropolitan Opera visited for three weeks under Walter Damrosch; among its twenty-one performances were the Chicago premieres of *Tannhäuser* and *Die Walküre*—a heady Wagner experience. Then came the Grand Opera Festival, featuring a company from New York's Academy of Music performing such favorites as *Semiramide*, *Lucia*, *I puritani*, and *La son-*

nambula. Adelina Patti, on opening night, drew a crowd of six thousand to the barnlike Interstate Exposition Building in Grant Park. Advertised as "Music for the People!," the festival was also an unprecedented social occasion. Four years later, Chicago had a proper opera house: the forty-two hundred-seat Chicago Auditorium Theater, whose architects were Louis Sullivan and Dankmar Adler, and whose supporters included the WASP business elite.

All this forms the backdrop to the Chicago Orchestra. Charles Norman Fay was a minister's son, born in Cambridge, Massachusetts. In Chicago he was, successively, vice president and general manager of the Chicago Telephone Company, president of the Chicago Gas Company, and president of the Chicago Arc Light and Power Company. He supported the Arts Institute, Field Columbian Museum, and American Historical Society. But music was the Fay family's special object of devotion. As early as 1879, Fay wrote to Thomas proposing a Chicago orchestra, with assurance that "as far as money goes, I can form a strong and satisfactory society, with little delay." Thomas was busy with other things. Fay waited: he was not interested in starting an orchestra for anyone else. Fay's sister, Amy, made her American debut under Thomas's baton; she acquired a national reputation as a pianist and pedagogue. Another sister, Rose, became—a rare thing—a confidante of the conductor. Charles's own friendship with Thomas ripened. In 1889, Thomas and Fay met at Delmonico's in New York. Thomas's wife was dying. His savings had been wiped out along with the National Opera Company. He had given up his Thomas Orchestra. New York seemed not to want him. Fay asked if he would consider moving to Chicago. In words to become famous, Thomas replied, "I would go to hell if they gave me a permanent orchestra." And the Chicago Orchestra was born.

In May 1890 Thomas, now a widower, married Rose Fay. The significance of this alliance was social as well as personal. Long itinerant, Thomas entered a world of privilege and wealth. (Remarkably, Walter Damrosch married Margaret Blaine the same year.) With regard to the new orchestra, Fay was as good as his word. He assembled guarantees enough to insure a fifty-thousand-dollar subsidy for each of three seasons. If most of the backers had no special affection for music, their affection for Chicago was special enough. Thomas would enjoy complete artistic freedom. "All my life," he reflected, "I have been told that my standard was too high, and urged to make it more popular. But now, I am not only to be given every facility to create the highest standard, but am even told that I will be *held responsible* for keeping it so! I have to shake myself to believe it."[28]

And Thomas had every intention of doing things his way. He decided to bring sixty musicians from New York, including key members of the old

Thomas Orchestra, to create a core ensemble that could tour from its Chicago base. Only twenty-six additional musicians were hired locally. The Chicago musicians' union objected to no avail. The contracts specified a maximum of 108 concerts. Rehearsals would be called at the conductor's discretion and were unpaid. During the twenty-eight-week season (including eight weeks on the road), members would "play at no balls, and at no performances of any kind in which the orchestra does not take part, without permission of the director."[29]

The inaugural concert, on October 17, 1891, in the cavernous Auditorium Theater, swelled Chicagoans with pride and enthusiasm. The program read:

> Wagner: *Faust* Overture
> Beethoven: Symphony No. 5
> Tchaikovsky: Piano Concerto No. 1 (with Rafael
>   Joseffy)
> Dvořák: *Hussite* Overture

In the next three weeks, Thomas conducted symphonies by Schubert (Nos. 8 and 9), Schumann (No. 3), and Saint-Saëns (No. 3), Bach's Third Orchestral Suite, Dvořák's Violin Concerto (with concertmaster Max Bendix), Tchaikovsky's *Hamlet* Fantasy Overture, and vocal selections by Gluck, Schubert, and Wagner. An all-American program was pitifully attended. The season, overall, included ten additional concerts of comparably "serious" fare, four "popular" programs, and a "request" program of subscriber favorites.

Thomas had purposely pitched the repertoire higher than anything Chicago had known before: it was his mission. But what many in Chicago expected more resembled the summer garden concerts that had made Thomas a local favorite. The orchestra was called "this monster that nobody wants" and "the greatest curse to the musicians of Chicago." Though George Upton of the *Tribune* was a staunch supporter, the city's other leading critic, W. S. B. Mathews, wrote in his *Music* magazine that the orchestra had committed mistakes "of such gravity that any one of them might well have endangered the successful issue of the undertaking." Ticket prices were too high. There were too many "long works." Of Thomas, Mathews wrote that he "no doubt has his own ideas, and, for that matter, will stick to them." Mathews, too, had his ideas. A self-made organist and pianist, a fearless freethinker who early espoused the Music of the Future and admired Arthur Nikisch, he called Thomas's interpretations "conventional and safe, rather than sensational. His work is characterized by great repose, but also by great reserve."[30]

Thomas was taxed by such critiques. The orchestra's annual postseason tours to St. Paul, Omaha, Kansas City, St. Louis, Nashville, Cincinnati, Cleveland, and Milwaukee—Chicago and its environs could not support twenty-eight weeks—proved arduous. The deficits were $53,613 for 1891–92 and $51,381 for 1892–93. Fay and the guarantors loyally made up the difference, but it was clear to all that false expectations had distorted the enterprise. The Thomas Orchestra's lakeside summer concerts had turned a profit; hot July evenings were soothed by overtures and dances, beer and cigars. The winter concerts Thomas now inflicted seemed a penance.

Tensions were brought to a head by Chicago's signature Gilded Age event: the World's Columbian Exposition. This was the fair famous for its amazing "White City" of waterways, lagoons, and monumental Greco-Roman structures and statuary, an urban epiphany bearing witness to (among other things) a degree of civic zeal unimaginable in any city a century later. H. N. Higginbotham, president of the board of directors, called it "the apotheosis of civilization, in which all that is beautiful, useful, wonderful, or for any reason attractive must play its part." The music bureau was lavishly provided with two new halls and an orchestra—Chicago's, expanded to 130 players—for the entire six months. Thomas was named music director for the fair. He scheduled "a perfect and complete exhibition of the Musical Art in all its branches."[31] There would be a noontime concert every day and two evening concerts of lighter music with a split orchestra—all free of charge—plus ticketed concerts of a more serious nature. Singing societies and bands galore would also take part. It would be the capstone of Thomas's career.

Though the fair would not begin until the spring of 1893, an inaugural concert took place the previous fall in the Hall of Manufacturers and Liberal Arts. Reputedly the largest structure in the world, it covered twenty-four acres and spanned four city blocks. Its stage was said to equal in size the entire Metropolitan Opera House. A 190-piece orchestra and fifty-seven hundred choristers were engaged. Thomas had to communicate with the speaker's platform by telephone. He cued his forces with drum rolls. Nothing like it had been attempted since Gilmore's Boston jubilees. The music was mainly inaudible—a fiasco. And worse was to come.

Among the exhibitions at the fair was a copious display of musical instruments, historic and contemporary. For western manufacturers, including Chicago's Kimball Piano Company, the opportunity to vie with better-known brands was irresistible, and prizes for the best instruments would be awarded. But eastern firms complained that the plan, including the allotment of space and the choice of a Chicagoan as sole judge, was prejudicial. Eighteen withdrew, including the two piano makers—Steinway and Chickering—whose success at the Paris Universal Exposition of 1867 had catapulted the

American piano industry to European prominence.* The fair's director-general, Colonel George Davis, was nonetheless persuaded that only pianos made by exhibiting companies should be played at the concerts.

Thomas's soloist for the opening day, on May 2, 1893, was the already legendary Ignacy Jan Paderewski, and Paderewski played Steinways. In front-page stories, two Chicago dailies accused Thomas of supporting Paderewski's Steinway affiliation because William Steinway was a Thomas friend and benefactor. James Healey, of Chicago's Lyon & Healy piano company, called Thomas a Steinway "pensioner."[32] A special investigating committee threatened to remove any unauthorized instrument "at the point of a bayonet if necessary." But Paderewski's Steinway, smuggled onto the fairgrounds in the dead of night, was onstage when he appeared to perform his Concerto in A minor and the Schumann concerto a night later. Lyon & Healy, which also made harps, now accused Thomas of favoring Erard harps, whose North American agent was also the Chicago agent for Steinway. Another investigation was launched, in which Thomas was compelled to take part. He cleared his name but many, offended by his manner, seemed not to care. According to the *Record Herald*, his "lips curled ironically" when he consented to testify about "alleged abuses." The same newspaper called him "a small despot by nature; a dull and self opinionated man."

More troubles followed. The two-thousand-seat Music Hall proved acoustically unacceptable. Thomas moved to the four-thousand-seat Festival Hall May 22 with an all-Wagner program, at which the audience was outnumbered by the orchestra and chorus. As with the Chicago Orchestra at the Auditorium, concert supply far outstripped demand and the serious concerts interested the fewest customers. The financial panic of 1893 weighed in. Aroused by Thomas's insubordination and by the enormous cost of the music program, the fair's National Commission, meeting in mid-May, demanded his resignation by a vote of thirty-nine to twenty. Quipped President Higginbotham, "They will have a sweet time getting it." By the end of July Thomas grudgingly agreed to cut expenses. He resigned in early August, recommending that "for the remainder of the Fair music shall not figure as an art at all, but be treated merely on the basis of an amusement. More of this class of music is undoubtedly needed . . . , and the cheapest way . . . is to divide our two fine

---

* "An industry which had its beginning 70 years ago is now so large that in it this country has now only one rival—Germany; and that country is a rival largely because it made haste to adapt the improvements in manufacture which American makers invented and applied." Henry Krehbiel, *Review of the New York Musical Season 1888–1889*, p. 131.

bands into four . . . for open-air concerts, and our Exposition orchestra into two . . . , which can play such light selections as will please the shifting crowds . . . and amuse them."[33]

Having conducted thirty-eight times at the Music Hall and twenty-eight times at the Festival Hall in little more than three months, Thomas withdrew with his wife to their Fairhaven, Massachusetts, home. When business picked up at the fair in August, he was invited to return and said no. "I cannot tell you what pain these attacks have given me," he wrote to George Upton. "My age and my record should have protected me from them. But let it pass. Art is long." Rose Thomas later reflected, "He was growing old now, and the many hardships and disappointments of life had left their mark and taken away from him the buoyant, indomitable spirit with which he had hitherto faced the world. . . . He was never afterwards the man he had been before. His courage was gone, and for the rest of his life he would drop into despondency and be ready to give up at any little untoward happening."[34]

Thomas had absorbed battle scars enough for two lifetimes. He had endured being bypassed for Leopold Damrosch and eclipsed by Anton Seidl. He had terminated his Thomas Orchestra because, as he bitterly remarked in his memoirs, New York "was now absorbed in its new operatic venture."[35] Jeannette Thurber's National Opera Company had abandoned him and the money he was owed. And there were earlier debacles. In Cincinnati, he had in 1878 accepted the directorship of the College of Music, only to quit in a dispute over the limits of his authority. In Philadelphia, as music director of the 1876 Centennial Exhibition, he went bankrupt after meeting expenses; his library was seized by the sheriff and auctioned for a pittance—to a supporter who gave everything back. The humiliations of the Chicago exposition were cumulative: the combative optimist in Thomas was damaged forever. A fighter by nature, obstinate and proud, he lacked recourse to cynicism or serenity. He battled his new melancholy.

The coming 1893–94 season was the last covered by Fay's three-year guarantee; Thomas fully believed that, at season's end, the orchestra would die. Still, he went doggedly to work. The audiences grew. The guarantees were renewed. The press came around. The deficits shrank. The repertoire maintained its rigor. Thomas was perceived to have become a more amiable autocrat. The appreciation of the trustees was an unaccustomed balm.

In 1896 Thomas was at last able to abandon the "popular" programs that had leavened all previous seasons. He took the orchestra east the same year. The New York Times called it "a well-trained organization of mediocrities." He returned in 1898 with better critical success in New York and triumphant acclaim in Boston, where Philip Hale wrote:

If the phrase is piano, it is played piano without unmeaning expression. The beauty of the phrase makes its way without the aid of rhetorical extravagance. And with what finish and subtlety is the phrase ended! How carefully are crescendos and diminuendos made, and yet with what apparent spontaneity! How clear is the dialogue between instruments! ... The repose of this orchestra is never soporific; nor is it ever feverish; it is the repose of intelligence and confidence.[36]

Back in New York, Thomas was newly encountered by the *New York Press* as "a grim grizzled Teuton warrior, [an] unusually self-contained and reserved man with sensitive spots, which cause him to withdraw into his shell whenever they are touched. Yet, underneath all, there is a kindly tolerance, a comprehensive sympathy, a reasonable way of looking at things." He told the *Press* that he had no plans to leave Chicago or to alter his method there: "I do not adapt my work to audiences, they must adapt themselves to the music."

In fact, the adaptation had at last taken hold sufficiently to ensure the likelihood of permanence. Bravely emulating Boston, the Chicago Orchestra had suffered a premature birth. The infant struggled, gasped for breath, and was firmly supported until conditions for survival—experienced audiences long before established in Boston and New York—were attained. The effort was improbable, the outcome heroic.

■ ■ ■

In 1855, the impresario Max Maretzek, born in Moravia, had marveled, "The artistic thought of the United States is at the present moment engaged in developing itself through the female half of the population. . . . The ladies in this country are the real amateurs and patrons of our own Art. . . . Indeed, beyond the principal cities, it is the ladies alone that patronize and love the Arts. These, alone, know anything about them."[37] Midwestern advances in musical understanding, Theodore Thomas once wrote, were due "almost wholly to women. They have more time to study and perfect themselves in all the arts. They come together in their great clubs and gain ideas."[38] In Gilded Age America, women were far more likely than men to read music, sing, play the piano, and attend musical events. Women's clubs formed choirs and sponsored concerts. In New York, Thomas had collaborated with Jeannette Thurber and witnessed the work of Laura Langford. He would have observed the significant influence of Andrew Carnegie's wife on her husband's musical philanthropy. In Chicago, Anna Millar, the orchestra's manager from 1895 to 1899, played an outstanding role in increasing subscription sales.

But it was doubtless Rose Fay Thomas, at his side, who most directly inspired and instructed Thomas about women's roles in art. She was his emotional bulwark and aide-de-camp. For the 1893 exposition (where the Board of Lady Managers, in charge of the Women's Building, was headed by Mrs. Potter Palmer, queen of Chicago society), she chaired a three-day national convention of women's amateur music clubs. She was no Midwesterner, but a transplanted New Englander who returned to Cambridge, Massachusetts, after her husband's death. Her influence may be inferred from her correspondence and from her valuable *Memoirs of Theodore Thomas*.

It was Mrs. Thomas's observation that "a little experience taught [Thomas] that neither children nor what are called 'wage-earners' were sufficiently advanced intellectually to be able to appreciate the class of music which was his specialty." Writing to a friend in 1892, she said:

> Mr. Thomas is here to establish a great art work, and to make Chicago one of the first musical centers of the world—and not to provide a series of cheap musical entertainments for the riff-raff of the public. The highest forms of art—whether it be in painting, sculpture, architecture, literature, music or any other branch—are not within the comprehension of the masses, they are the delicate blossoms which make the crown and glory of the shrub called humanity, but which roots and branches and stems can only catch vague glimpses of through parted leaves, and never wholly see. So it is a useless task to attempt to produce the highest form in any art, in such a way that it can be appreciated by the ignorant. All that can be done is to *produce* it, and let it stand till the ignorant acquire a little education and begin to understand it.[39]

In short, Mrs. Thomas was of her class: a new milieu for her crusty spouse. Chicago here introduces a different tone to the symphonic enterprise, one not to be heard in New York from the likes of Bergmann, the Damrosches, Dvořák, Thurber, or Seidl, or from Higginson in Boston. This pronounced us-and-them sensibility, whether welcoming or patronizing or condemnatory, was in Chicago made inescapable by manifestations of social unrest central to the civic imagination. One watershed event was the Haymarket Riot of 1886, triggered when a bomb exploded during a labor protest, killing a policeman. In the ensuing panic, six more officers were fatally shot (perhaps by friendly fire), as were a comparable number of protesters. Eight men, six of German extraction, were tried and convicted on scant evidence; four were hanged. Eight years later, employees at the Pullman Car Works walked off their jobs, triggering a nationwide work stoppage, the intervention of federal troops, and the imprisonment of American Railway Union President Eugene Debs.

More than in Boston or New York, the specter of class warfare terrified Chicago's business elite. While the threat of lawless workers was unquestionably exaggerated, Chicago was known as the center of anarchism in the United States for a reason. In the buildup to Haymarket, the anarchist leader Albert Parsons had warned, "Every man must lay by a part of his wages, buy a Colt's navy revolver, . . . a Winchester rifle, and learn how to make and use dynamite." The anarchist editor August Spies boasted that he planned to blow up the Board of Trade Building. Many prominent anarchists were German. Just after Haymarket, "all good citizens" were called upon for vigilante duty by Mayor Monroe Heath. A Law and Order League was formed. The Commercial Club furnished land for an army base outside the city. But a kinder response was equally attempted. Ferdinand Peck addressed the Commercial Club on "The Late Civil Disorder; its Causes and Lessons." A prominent philanthropist, Peck had presided over the Grand Opera Festival of 1885 and there promoted "Music for the People" at prices "within the reach of all" as an antidote to "crime and socialism." Peck's Commercial Club speech pushed for a gigantic opera house for all Chicago: what became the $3.2 million Auditorium Theater four years later. Chicago's commercial leaders played little role in city government, with its Irish and German ward politicians. Their emerging civic responsibilities were cultural. Social engineering was one rationale.[40]

The opening ceremonies for the Auditorium Theater, on December 9, 1889, are informative. Peck hailed the huge hall as an "enduring temple where the rich and the poor and all classes could meet together upon common ground and be elevated and enlightened by the power of music." After thanking the architects, he added, "We must not forget the army of workingmen who have labored with their hands day and night, and have shown a zeal which is without precedent. They knew that they were erecting an edifice for themselves and their associates as much as for any class. They knew that the Auditorium stood for all."

Composed for the occasion was an Auditorium Festival Ode by Frederick Grant Gleason with words by Harriet Monroe. Gleason's cantata traced a history of Chicago "plagues" beginning with the Civil War and the fire of 1871. Next:

> Anarchy appeared,
> A visage, haggard, bleared,
> That screeched. "Your flag
> Is a brilliant rag.

Will it shine so fair
When its stripes I tear
And its stars in the mire I drag?"

War, Fire, and Anarchy are vanquished. A final plague remains, the sole imped-iment to utopian fruition. It is "Greed." If the cantata villainized dissident workers, it also admonished complacent capitalists that there could be no social peace without philanthropy.[41]

The Chicago Orchestra, in this context, complexly embodied the elitist or democratic aspirations of a Rose Fay Thomas, Ferdinand Peck, or Charles Norman Fay. No consistent picture of the orchestra's social role emerges. Though its subscription ticket prices, which some thought too high, were comparable to the New York Philharmonic's, subscriptions to the Boston Symphony (in so many respects Chicago's model) were substantially less expensive.* The orchestra also gave "workingmen's concerts" with tickets for as little as ten cents. Similarly, Chicago's Apollo Club—its most prominent singing society, and a WASP preserve—offered inexpensive workers' concerts from which its regular subscribers were excluded. This initiative, pursued with exemplary zeal, bore fruit; at an 1889 Apollo Club *Messiah*, as reviewed by the *Chicago InterOcean*, many audience members "were musicians, Danes or Ger-mans, following the score from the copies they had brought with them."[42] At the same time, the segregated workers reflected cleavages in the population at large. Unthinkable in New York was the orchestra's refusal to advertise in the German-language press or to supply complimentary tickets to German-language critics. When challenged by the *Freie Presse*, Charles Norman Fay responded, "Germans who have contributed to the support of the orchestra, either in the purchase of tickets or by direct donation . . . are few in number, and their donations have been . . . small in amount."[43] And yet German was the language of the orchestra's rehearsals.

In fact, Chicago's German community was split between professionals,

---

* As of 1891, Chicago Orchestra subscriptions cost $30, $20, and $10 (excluding boxes) for twenty Saturday-night concerts, and $20, $15, and $10 for twenty Friday-afternoon "public rehearsals"—or $0.50 to $1.50 per concert. Higginson's subscription prices, in Boston, were as a matter of policy exceptionally modest: 31¢ or 50¢ per concert (although a considerable number were auctioned at much higher cost, a form of donation). New York Philharmonic subscriptions (for only six concerts) averaged $0.67 to $1.70 per ticket. Higginson (as we have seen) made a point of setting aside 25¢ "rush" tickets for matinees. In Chicago (with a hall double the size of Boston's, too vast to fill), single tickets started at 25¢ and 50¢. Single tickets for the New York Philharmonic began at 75¢. Information furnished by the Chicago Symphony and Boston Symphony Archives. See also Ellis A. Johnson, "The Chicago Symphony Orchestra 1891–1942" (dissertation, University of Chicago, 1955), p. 102.

intersecting with the musical mainstream, and more recently arrived wage earners stigmatized by labor unrest. Notwithstanding its German conductor, membership, and repertoire, the Chicago Orchestra engaged the Apollo Club as its chorus of choice. Nor was there, as in Boston or New York, a prominent aggregation of local composers, mostly German-trained, to fortify the moment. Compared to Higginson's orchestra or Seidl's, Chicago's was emulative, curatorial.

The aging Theodore Thomas—his new marriage, his new susceptibility to melancholy—fits this picture. Thomas's disillusionment was not the product of individual mishaps or failures merely, but of a larger disappointment. The barnstorming populist—plying the Thomas Highway, seducing novice listeners with the vanishing pianissimos of *Träumerei*—seemed not even a memory. His mission of uplift, of educating and elevating audiences toward pure sermons in tones, was in one respect an astonishing success. He laid the foundation for the Boston Symphony, for the Chicago Orchestra, for half a dozen other orchestras. But many listeners fell by the wayside in the process. His credo of 1874, that "the people will enjoy and support the best in art when continually set before them in a clear and intelligent manner," was not sounded in Chicago. Faced with audiences made restless even by Beethoven, with complaints that his programs were too formidable, that too many seats remained empty, he replied, "To those who cannot enjoy the great music, poor fellows, I do not grudge what they can enjoy. . . . I will play for them now and then, but it is not for Tell Overture and Handel Largo that Chicago supports my orchestra. One does not buy a Krupp cannon to shoot sparrows." His hair turned white, his hard features softened. He grew a paunch. He looked, commented the *Chicago Evening Post*, "more like a substantial banker than one of the four most renowned conductors in the world." The Chicago critic George Armstrong wrote in 1905, "When Theodore Thomas first came to Chicago and began playing popular pieces in the old exposition building he was extremely democratic. The sociability of the German abounded in him and he used to sit at the round table with his friends after the concerts were over. But as he gradually educated the public up to an appreciation of classical music Mr. Thomas himself underwent a process of evolution in which he gradually grew more dignified and exclusive."[44]

Thomas's uncompromising repertoire was not only more sober than in the Highway days. He had also grown more conservative. Seidl's irksome success had soured his affinity for Wagner. Though his programs still featured many a *Meistersinger* Prelude and Liebestod, of *Tristan und Isolde* he now said, "I do not believe this music will ever be popular." Asked if he thought Wagner would be "the composer of the future," he opined, "Bach, Handel, Mozart and Beethoven were sons of God! Wagner was an egotist! All sensuousness!" It was possible, he concluded, that Wagner's music "would not live."[45] This 1898 pronouncement was roughly contemporaneous with Debussy's *Pelléas et Mélisande*, Schoenberg's *Verklärte Nacht*, and Mahler's Third Symphony—in all of which Wagner's influence was demonstrably imperishable.

At the forty-two-hundred-seat Auditorium Theater (whose high capacity was partly Ferdinand Peck's way of ensuring the availability of inexpensive nonsubscription tickets), the Chicago Orchestra was envisioned filling twice that number weekly. Thomas quite realistically began insisting that the orchestra needed a smaller home. Like Dvořák, like Seidl, like Thurber, he had doubtless imagined that, as in Germany or Bohemia, American symphonies and concertos would ultimately spring from native soil, would nourish and shape the culture at large. Informing his copious programming for the 1893 exposition was the belief that concert music would become central to the American experience. In retrospect, the failure of music at the fair was prophetic. Surveying the fate of the music bureau's agenda in the wake of Thomas's forced departure, Chicago's *Staats-Zeitung* summarized, "We have good music, but too much of it. . . . Experience teaches that the class which enjoys classical music is a small minority."[46]

■ ■ ■

The Boston Symphony—its paired concerts, its length of season, its tours, its aura of piety—served as a model and inspiration for Chicago. And Chicago served as a model and inspiration for American orchestras soon to come. Its Orchestral Association of Trustees, freeing the orchestra from dependence on any individual conductor or sponsor, laid the basis for broad support and institutional longevity. And it demonstrated that in cities other than Boston an orchestra could "show the culture of the community."

The next city so served was the one with which Thomas had been most associated, after New York: Cincinnati, the Athens of the West, whose 1850 population of 115,000 was the sixth largest in the nation. Its substantial German community had early established a formidable choral tradition. The Thomas Orchestra began visiting annually in 1869. Three years later, a May festival was created under Thomas's leadership, with an orchestra of 108 and eight hundred choristers. This was no Patrick Gilmore extravaganza, but a showcase for serious music; it continued biannually until Thomas's death (and survives to this day). Thomas was also founding music director of the College of Music in 1880, a short-lived appointment.

The Chicago Orchestra catalyzed plans for a Cincinnati Symphony. It originated with the socially prominent members of the Ladies Musical Club. The board of fifteen was exclusively female, with Mrs. William Howard Taft as president. A partial inaugural season, in the spring of 1895, resulted in the appointment as conductor of Frank Van der Stucken. Formerly the director of New York's Arion Society, he was born in Texas but raised and trained abroad. Though Thomas and Walter Damrosch, born abroad, were raised and trained in the United States, Van der Stucken was the first native-born American conductor of a major American orchestra; contemporary accounts describe a musician of formidable force and capacity whose sponsorship of American composers (including himself) was far from negligible.[47] Pittsburgh obtained a consequential orchestra in 1898, under Victor Herbert. The orchestras of Philadelphia and Minneapolis followed in 1900 and 1903. The St. Louis Symphony, after tentative beginnings in 1880, was newly organized in 1907. This remarkable proliferation was unparalleled abroad.

Thomas, meanwhile, was declining physically and growing tired of Chicago's winters. In 1903 he issued an ultimatum to the board: either the orchestra would built its own hall or he would resign and go elsewhere. The trustees duly raised the necessary funds, including $750,000 in the form of more than eight-thousand individual donations from the general public. Orchestra Hall, with twenty-five-hundred seats and a gleaming ivory interior, was inaugurated on December 14, 1904. The program included the *Tannhäuser* Overture, Beethoven's Fifth, and Strauss's *Death and Transfiguration*. Thomas mounted the podium to a storm of applause, which he acknowledged with tears.[48] Twenty-one days later, he was dead, worn out at the age of sixty-nine.

Thomas's death shocked Chicago and the nation. Chicago's telephone operators were instructed to tell callers "Theodore Thomas is dead" before asking, "Number, please." Chicago's newspapers called him "dean of the world of music," the "greatest conductor of his time." Citing Nikisch, Strauss, Mengelberg, Mottl, and Weingartner, Glenn Dillard Gunn plausibly remarked in the *Journal* that "while of sufficient scholarly attainment, [they] lack the great power of organization which distinguished Mr. Thomas." Other tributes read:

The death of no other citizen could have possibly affected so many people, or touched the hearts of so many.

In the course of its history Chicago has not sustained so great a loss as it suffers to-day in the death of Theodore Thomas. For it is the loss not only of a useful citizen, but of an irrecoverable genius, peculiarly fitted to serve the city's higher development at the stage of growth in which he found it.

[T]here has never been another man who has attacked an indifferent, because uneducated, community, with the musical magician's wand, and hammered music into it, year after year, in the face of great discouragements; educating it, teaching it to prefer the complicated to the simple, converting scoffers into enthusiasts, compelling rich men to contribute to the cause, and finally snatching glorious victory from the jaws of defeat.

The trustees of the orchestra, eternally loyal, resolved, "We deplore his death as our own personal bereavement and an unspeakable loss to the higher life of our country; but we rejoice that such a man has lived and labored, and so far as in us lies we resolve that his labors shall not have been in vain."[49]

Richard Strauss wrote from Berlin of Thomas: "What we Germans owe him shall be held in everlasting remembrance." Wilhelm Gericke wrote from Vienna: "His position was unchallenged: the greatest orchestral conductor in the world. He had no equal." George Chadwick wrote from Boston: "I have never had any other teacher or friend in my whole career from whom I absorbed so much in knowledge, in stimulation, or in courage to fight for a high standard and for an ideal." John Knowles Paine and Charles Martin Loeffler—so different from Chadwick, and from one another—also regarded Thomas with reverence and gratitude. In New York, Thomas was recalled from a greater distance. The *Times* described him as an exemplar for "the older generation of music lovers," versus "the 'modern' conductor that has evolved from Wagner's influence." Six years later, the *Musical Courier* would call him "a human metronome, a drill master who never yielded for a moment to a flexible or emotional indiscretion, as he would have called it."[50]

In the wake of Thomas's death, the trustees of the Chicago Orchestra renamed it the Theodore Thomas Orchestra. Though major Europeans were considered, Frederick Stock, Thomas's thirty-two-year-old assistant, was appointed music director. Stock's tenure lasted thirty-seven years. Like his mentor, he was German-born, predisposed to German music and a burnished Germanic sound. He eschewed the flamboyance and glamour of his postwar colleagues in Boston, New York, and Philadelphia. The Thomas-Stock orientation was absorbed by the orchestra as an enduring artistic identity.

At the age of ninety-two, Charles Norman Fay, who knew every president from Grant to Theodore Roosevelt, as well as Generals Sherman and Sheridan, and also Morgan, Rockefeller, and Carnegie, remembered two men as bigger than the rest: Paderewski, who became Poland's prime minister, and Theodore Thomas. They were, he wrote, "the most powerful personalities I have known—MEN AS GREAT AS THEIR WORK."[51] Perennially homeless, Thomas was welcomed by Chicago as a Moses. No other American orchestra began with a music director of such stature, one whose imprint proved as resilient and firm. The Chicago Symphony—so renamed in 1913—was his final legacy.

CHAPTER 7

Leopold Stokowski, Gustav Mahler, Arturo Toscanini, and the Gossip of the Foyer

∎

Leopold Stokowski in Cincinnati and Philadelphia ∎
Gustav Mahler in New York ∎ *Henry Krehbiel and the critics* ∎
Oscar Hammerstein's Manhattan Opera ∎
Arturo Toscanini's Metropolitan Opera

If in the growth of the American orchestra Chicago came to signify something old, the Philadelphia Orchestra came to signify something new. The something new first showed up in Cincinnati, where financial problems had shut down the orchestra in 1907. By 1909 an adequate guarantee fund had been amassed and a new conductor was chosen. In later years he claimed to have been born in 1887. He said Cracow was his birthplace, or that his family was from a town called Stoki or Stokki, near Lublin. Denying reports he was once named "Leopold Stokes," he declared his name at birth "Leopold Antoni Stanislaw Boleslawowicz Stokowski."[1]

In fact, he was born Leopold Anthony Stokowski, in London in 1882. His father, also London-born, was of Polish extraction. His mother was originally named Anne Moore. (His brother Percy plausibly summarized, "Leo was a quarter Polish, English, Scotch, and Irish.") He trained as an organist at the Royal Conservatory of Music and served in that capacity at St. Bartholomew's in New York beginning in 1905. He became music director of the Cincinnati Symphony in 1909.

The pianist Olga Samaroff (born Lucy Hickenlooper in Texas) helped manufacture his pedigree. First, she had to manufacture his debut. Two years prior to marrying Stokowski in 1911, Olga was already a successful virtuoso with shrewd instincts and powerful friends, which she used to interest Cincinnati in her future husband. The only obstacle to Stokowski's Cincinnati appointment was his inexperience: he had never led a symphonic concert. This Olga arranged, with her mother's help, in Paris, where she appeared on May 12, 1909, under Stokowski's baton. Herman Thuman, music critic of the Cincinnati *Enquirer*, and Lucien Wulsin, of the Cincinnati Symphony advisory board, attended. Stokowski was named music director of the Cincinnati Symphony five days later at the age of twenty-seven. He claimed to be twenty-two.

His Cincinnati tenure made Stokowski a name. A 1911 review in *Musical America*, by the composer Arthur Farwell (about whom more later), reported:

> The nature of the attack and accents in the first half dozen bars of [Tchaikovsky's *Marche Slav*] made one realize that the orchestra was under control of a force of very unusual nature. The sense of a high vitalization, of almost superhuman keenness of musical consciousness, increased as the interpretation proceeded. Accents and shadings took on new and intenser values, climaxes became strangely powerful and poignant, and when the conductor came to the close the house was in an uproar and recalled him again and again. . . .
>
> The expectation as to what such a leader would do with the "Pathétique" Symphony was not disappointed. To hear it under the electrical influence of this astonishing conductor were as if one assisted at the creation of the work in the inspired mind of the composer.[2]

When Thuman, in the Cincinnati *Enquirer*, turned lukewarm toward Stokowski, the men of the orchestra drafted a protest, signed by every member. It was published in the rival *Times-Star* and read in part:

> Dear Sir—
>
> We, the seventy-nine men of the Cincinnati Symphony Orchestra, are writing to you personally to protest in a body against the incessant prejudice shown our conductor, Mr. Stokowski, and the orchestra by your musical critic. . . .
>
> Many of us are matured musicians, who have played under the batons of such musical giants as Richard Wagner, Von Bülow, Richard Strauss, Nikisch, Weingartner, Mahler, Toscanini and many others of great renown, and we can with positive knowledge assert that Mr. Stokowski's rendition of the Brahms [first] symphony at our first concert this year was equal to the finest we have ever taken part in. . . .

We who have learned to know the inmost pleasure of association with Mr. Stokowski, who we feel is divinely gifted, who by the turn of a finger sweeps us all before him, must show in this way your error in declining to accede to him the honors already bestowed, both by the masses in Cincinnati and elsewhere, and have hereunder attached our signature.[3]

Thuman resigned two months later. But all was not rosy. Some board members objected to the orchestra's tours and, allegedly, to Stokowski's adventurous repertoire. He quit and was fired, nearly simultaneously, in 1912.

The timing of Stokowski's departure is suggestive. Philadelphia, once the nation's cultural capital, had been home to significant American- and foreign-born musicians, including Benjamin Carr, Francis Hopkinson, Alexander Reinagle, and Rayner Taylor. Its first "Promenade Concerts" were introduced in 1838 by an African-American bandleader and composer, Frank Johnson (who in 1837 became the first American to tour a musical ensemble to Europe). Its Italians and Germans had savored Italian and German opera. Its American Academy of Music (later the Academy of Music merely) was, upon its erection in 1857, America's finest opera house and home to the first American performances of Gounod's *Faust* (in German) and Wagner's *The Flying Dutchman* (in Italian). But Philadelphia had never possessed a Dwight or Higginson, Leopold Damrosch, Thomas, or Seidl to galvanize its classical musical activities. As of 1912, its orchestra and its conductor, Karl Pohlig, were a disappointment to wealthy Main Liners who sought a cultural adornment to rival the orchestras of Boston, Chicago, and New York. As Olga Samaroff was well connected to Philadelphia wealth, by the time Stokowski left Cincinnati Philadelphia's podium was waiting for him. Olga even signed his Philadelphia contract. She also successfully urged him to italicize the Slavic part of his background: this is when his country of origin became Poland, and when the famed accent and syntax of his speech became, if not exactly Polish, foreign to England or America.

Other Stokowski attributes were natural. He was tall and slender. His eyes, in contrast to the romantic pallor of his complexion, were icy blue, his nose was aquiline, his mouth sensuously full. His blond hair, brushed straight back from the forehead, was artistically unkempt. On the podium, he was tense and erect in his embodiment of authority, impetuously fluid in his sudden interpretive inspirations. He was invariably described as "magnetic." (The same adjective was typically applied to Arthur Nikisch, with whom Stokowski had briefly studied in Leipzig, and to Anton Seidl, once Nikisch's senior colleague in Leipzig—a notable lineage of charismatic European-born conductors influential in the United States, even if Seidl and Nikisch were not mutual admirers.)[4]

As in Cincinnati, Stokowski's force of personality was transformative. Certainly the Philadelphia Orchestra as we know it did not exist when Stokowski arrived. "It was no orchestra at all," Stokowski himself once recalled. "It had a stiff rhythm, hard tone, and no flexibility or imagination. Everyone played meaningless notes. Everything was terribly mechanical. There were only four first-class performers, Anton Horner, the first horn, Otto Henneberg, third horn, a remarkable timpanist, Oscar Schwar, and the concertmeister, Thaddeus Rich."

Stokowski showed up for the first rehearsal wearing a light blue shirt open at the neck and gray flannel trousers. He said, "*Guten Tag.* Brahms! First *mooment*"—and the baton descended, catching some of the players unprepared. Stokowski stopped and bent forward, his blue eyes blazing, his stick poised aloft. A second downbeat galvanized the orchestra. "I could hardly recognize the men I had been playing with or the music that we thought we knew so well," recalled Schwar, the timpanist.

> It was as though we had been given some magic potion. Of course, in a way we had, for none of us had ever experienced such authority and vitality before. This man went straight to the heart of the music. . . . With hardly a word of explanation, with no more than the twitch of a wrist or an eyebrow, he extracted the most from every player. Only his facial expressions became more intense and his shoulder muscles more contracted as his burning eyes and curled fingers coaxed us to ever greater expressivity and sonority. At the end of the movement, having played our hearts out in response to the man's irresistible sweep, having been interrupted only a few times by some gentle suggestion or helpful comment, we were all filled with new hope and excitement.
>
> But our joy was short-lived. Before breaking for intermission, Stokowski said, "Gentlemen, we must do better, much better. We are too far from an acceptable performance." Almost the entire rehearsal time was devoted to the four movements of the symphony, the central work of the first program. The reason we had been subjected to comparatively little detailed criticism became painfully clear. Stokowski was not going to waste time or energy or instruction on a group of musicians, most of whom he had already decided would not be members of that orchestra one minute more than necessary. There was no use teaching or scolding, for it was not unwillingness, but sheer inability of all but a few musicians to meet the standards of our new leader.[5]

The Brahms symphony anchored Stokowski's first Philadelphia concert, on October 11, 1912. The other works on the program were Beethoven's *Leonore* Overture No. 3, Ippolitov-Ivanov's *Caucasian Sketches* (an American premiere), and Wagner's *Tannhäuser* Overture. Arthur Judson, reviewing for *Musical America*, wrote, "The reception was not that of an audience merely glad that it had a competent conductor, but wildly enthusiastic because it had discovered a genius." Within two years, Judson would become manager of the Philadelphia Orchestra, embarking on a career scarcely less notable than Stokowski's own.

The orchestra's rehearsal conditions were an immediate bone of contention. With the Academy of Music constantly booked, rehearsals took place in a cramped, low-ceilinged room on North Broad Street. Stokowski's complaints became known to the publisher Edward Bok. Bok not only ensured use of the Academy for all rehearsals, but anonymously pledged to cover any deficits for a period of five years, providing Stokowski remained the conductor. Bok's close friend Alexander Van Rensselaer, president of the Philadelphia Orchestra board, was no less supportive. With this kind of backing, Stokowski fired thirty-two musicians within a year.

And—far beyond Karl Muck in Boston or Frederick Stock in Chicago— Stokowski pressed forward with new music. It is fitting that his first national triumph—the turning point in the Philadelphia Orchestra's reputation, in 1916—was occasioned by a momentous American premiere: of Mahler's Symphony No. 8, the *Symphony of a Thousand*. Stokowski had heard Mahler conduct it in Munich in 1910, an experience he likened to that of "the first white man to behold Niagara Falls." Three Philadelphia performances were scheduled, plus a fourth at the Metropolitan Opera House in New York. Nine hundred fifty choristers were engaged, in addition to an orchestra of 110 and the nine vocal soloists. Rehearsals began in October, nearly four months ahead of the event. In January, workmen began constructing platforms to extend the Academy of Music stage vertically to accommodate twenty-four rows of singers. An apron extension was not undertaken until just before the performances, to keep it a surprise. Six extra performances were scheduled in response to box office demands that drove scalped tickets from ten cents to one hundred dollars. At the March 2 premiere, the audience gasped when a curtain rose to disclose 1,069 bodies massed on the enlarged stage. Samuel Lacier's review in the next day's *Philadelphia Public Ledger* read in part, "Every one of the thousands in the great building was standing, whistling, cheering and applauding, when Leopold Stokowski, his collar wilted, his right arm weary, but smiling his boyish smile, finally turned to the audience in the Academy of Music last night. He had scored, so famous musicians agreed, the greatest triumph of his career, the greatest triumph the Philadelphia Orchestra has known in its sixteen years of life and he had done it on a stupendous scale." Presenting Stokowski with a bronze laurel wreath on behalf of the board, Van Rensselaer stated, "This premiere marks an epoch in Philadelphia's musical history to which no other event is comparable."[6]

The New York performance, on April 9, was attended by Harold Bauer, Pablo Casals, Mischa Elman, Ossip Gabrilowitsch, Percy Grainger, and countless other musical luminaries. The venerable W. J. Henderson, now of the *New York Sun* and a critic not known to gush, wrote, "If Philadelphia believes that Mr. Stokowski is essential to her musical development, let her decline to permit him to conduct great concerts in New York. This is a piece of perfectly disinterested advice. The *Sun*'s musical chronicler would be delighted to see Mr. Stokowski a New York conductor. He has personality, force, temperament, scholarship and imagination. His conducting of the Mahler symphony was masterly. He would be a valuable factor in the musical life in New York."[7]

The same 1915–16 Philadelphia season witnessed two other major American premieres: Schoenberg's Chamber Symphony No. 1 and Scriabin's *Divine Poem*. The following December, Stokowski led the first American performances of Mahler's *Das Lied von der Erde*. In seasons to follow, he never let up.

Stokowski's Mahler Eighth, commended by the Philadelphia Chamber of Commerce, more than made possible Stokowski's repertoire excursions to come; it established the essential civic importance of the Philadelphia Orchestra. It catalyzed two endowment campaigns netting nearly two million dollars. It mobilized one thousand citizens on stage and many more behind the scenes. As one historian of the American orchestra has surmised, "Never before, and probably never since, has a permanent symphony orchestra and its activity been so thoroughly integrated with the life of a city."[8]

■ ■ ■

Nothing comparable to the advent of Stokowski animated the fledgling orchestras of Minneapolis, St. Louis, or Pittsburgh. But in New York the vacuum left by Anton Seidl's death in 1897 was finally, and arrestingly, filled.

The Philharmonic drifted until 1909, by which year the number of performing members had dropped to only thirty-seven, with the remaining seats filled by substitutes. The Metropolitan Opera was being run by Heinrich Conried, of whom it was once quipped that he "knew no more about opera than an ordinary chauffeur knows about airplanes."[9] This set the stage for the nearly simultaneous arrival of two personalities who would seize and shake both institutions as Seidl had a decade before. One, Arturo Toscanini, achieved his greatest renown in the New World. The other, Gustav Mahler, charted an American conducting career tantalizingly brief and enigmatic.

Mahler arrived first—from Vienna, where he had been director of the Opera since 1897. Mahler's Vienna regime was historic: he removed the claque, closed the doors to latecomers, and opened all the cuts in *Tristan und Isolde*. Aligning himself with the Secessionists, he collaborated with Alfred Roller on stagings that overthrew naturalism with symbolic lighting and simplified scenery. In the pit, he was mercurial; according to Bruno Walter, "His every appearance . . . was preceded by the tenseness with which one looks forward to a sensation. . . . Before the opening of the [last] act, he was invariably received with a hurricane of applause."[10]

But ten Viennese seasons left Mahler frustrated and embattled. He warred with the singers and believed the orchestra conspired against him. Though he had converted to Catholicism, his Jewish birth remained a topic of ugly controversy. He sought time to compose and a comfortable income for his family.

It was Heinrich Conried who made Mahler an unrefusable offer: three months' work for seventy-five thousand kronen (fifteen thousand dollars), with all travel and hotel expenses paid. In Vienna, Mahler's salary had been twenty-four thousand kronen plus gratuities and pension. Beginning on January 1, 1908, Mahler conducted fifty-four performances in the course of three New York operatic seasons. His impact was great. But his four-year contract as "chief conductor" was nullified when Conried was replaced by a far more stable and experienced operatic administrator: La Scala's Giulio Gatti-Casazza. And, more important, with Gatti came his imperious conductor, Arturo Toscanini. In 1908–09, Mahler led sixty-seven Met performances to Toscanini's twenty-one. In 1909–10, Mahler appeared at the Met only four times.

The Philharmonic, meanwhile, was in the throes of reorganization. The musicians' cooperative, mired in debts and disarray, had yielded to a group of philanthropic socialites determined to give New York an orchestra comparable to Boston's. They pledged to make good any deficits for three years, to expand the season, and to tour the orchestra for the first time. They needed a conductor. Mahler, displaced at the Met, was the obvious choice. And so it was Mahler who presided over the Philharmonic's transition until illness forced him back to Vienna, where he died in 1911, seven weeks' shy of his fifty-first birthday.

The leader of the guarantors was a dynamo: Mary R. Sheldon. Her husband, George R. Sheldon, treasurer of the Republican National Committee, was a political powerbroker who helped to put Theodore Roosevelt and William Howard Taft in the White House. Unlike the Cincinnati board, New York's was not exclusively female. Unlike the Chicago board, it was not exclusively WASP; Mahler's surest ally would prove to be Minnie Untermyer, daughter of a German political refugee and wife of a prominent attorney. Also, crucially: unlike Cincinnati's or Chicago's, New York's guarantors, eager to succeed, insisted upon something like complete control, with authority even over repertoire and soloists. In fact, Mrs. Sheldon informed the press that though she regarded the orchestra's strings as excellent, "some other parts would have to be reinforced." This situation would have been unthinkable to Thomas or Seidl (witness the latter's impeccable dealings with Laura Langford). And it would lead to trouble with Mahler.

Mahler's three-year American operatic career, coming first, may be summarized as an ephemeral triumph. Two aspects of his Metropolitan Opera performances were instantly distinctive—and characterized, generally, both his style of conducting and the music he composed. First, Mahler was dramatic. He treated opera as theater. Even in Wagner, he did not swamp the singers. He shaped musical structures plastically, according to the action. He was a master of ambience. And he was his own inspired stage director. Second, Mahler demanded clarity. Just as he balanced singers and orchestra, he obtained precise balances within the pit. As in his symphonies, he achieved a mosaic of instrumental voices—think of Klimt's flat, polyphonic canvases—rather than the Romantic cathedral sonority of dominant strings and recessed winds.

Reviews[11] of Mahler's New York debut, in *Tristan*, already registered these trademarks. In later weeks and seasons, Mahler's Wagner was found worthy of comparison to Seidl's. (The cruder Wagner style of Alfred Hertz, who conducted Wagner at the Met from 1902 to 1915, can be sampled on Lionel Mapleson's gritty cylinder recordings, documenting snatches of Met performances between 1901 and 1904.) Mahler's Mozart, by comparison, was something new. Seidl's Wagnerized *Don Giovanni* had been heavy and mirthless. Subsequently, the opera was a showcase for celebrity vocalists. Mahler's *Don Giovanni* retained these celebrities—Antonio Scotti, Emma Eames, Johanna Gadski, Marcella Sembrich, Alessandro Bonci, Feodor Chaliapin—but used them in a new way. As Henderson reported in the *New York Sun* on February 1, 1908:

Mozart's "Don Giovanni" was performed at the Metropolitan Opera House last night in a manner which must have astonished many of the old habitues of the house. For many years this great classic opera has

been offered at the Metropolitan as a bargain counter attraction. . . .
People have been drawn in crowds to hear six stars at prices usually
charged for three. But the mise-en-scene has always been neglected. The
acts have been chopped up [and] Mozart's dramatic unity sent into
outer darkness. And no attempt has been made to unify the styles and
interpretations of the various singers in an organic whole. It has been
every singer for herself. . . . All this has been changed by the artistic influence of one man, and the result was that last night's performance moved
swiftly, steadily, even relentlessly towards its great climaxes.

Henry Krehbiel caviled that Chaliapin, as Leporello, conceived "all his characters as if they had been dug out of the muck of Gorky's stories of Russian low
life." But Mahler's *Marriage of Figaro* the following season, for which he called
twenty rehearsals, seemed to Krehbiel an unqualified triumph: "All the vivacious music foamed and sparkled and flashed like champagne."[12] Mahler's
Fidelio, with Roller's Vienna sets and costumes, again achieved an integrated
musical-theatrical experience unprecedented in New York.

These accomplishments were remarkable but transient. Post-Seidl, post-
Mahler, post-Toscanini, the Met settled into a house more for singers than for
conductors or stage directors. It was with the Philharmonic that Mahler the
conductor more tangibly impacted on the larger sweep of New York's musical
life. His brief regime was a fulcrum between the orchestra's early prime as a
part-time ensemble under Seidl, and its ultimate consolidation as the city's
dominant concert organization.

A heady pace of expansion was dictated by Mrs. Sheldon and the guarantors. Prior to Mahler, in 1908–09, the Philharmonic gave eighteen concerts.
Mahler led forty-six Philharmonic concerts in 1909–10 and forty-eight in
1910–11 before a substitute, concertmaster Theodore Spiering, had to take his
place. Audiences did not, however, grow apace, and many who came arrived
late or left early. The orchestra was considered vastly improved—Mahler
replaced nearly half the players—but without matching the polish and consistency of Boston's. The final ingredient of this mixed report was Mahler's symphonic interpretations, which proved significantly more controversial than his
work in the opera house. In fact, the debate over Mahler's Philharmonic concerts comprises the most interesting part of the story of Mahler in New
York—the most revealing of Mahler as man and musician, and of the American milieu in which he had landed.

Mahler arrived in New York a conductor of opera. As with Seidl and
Toscanini, the New World offered a new opportunity: to conduct an extensive
symphonic repertoire. This opportunity was inherent to America because the

concert orchestra—not, as in Europe, the opera house—was the central institution pursuant to a musical high culture. Thanks to Theodore Thomas, this distinctive orientation was accompanied by a distinctive philosophy of performance. His moralistic fervor, connecting to puritanism and John Sullivan Dwight, produced a style eschewing display, rejecting interpretation. Thomas deferred to the score as holy writ. His sound musicianship, sincerity of purpose, and powers of discipline did the rest. Boston's Wilhelm Gericke and Karl Muck, and Chicago's Frederick Stock, all buttressed this approach, as did countless imported Germans of lesser prominence.

If Seidl represented a new breed, he was at the same time every bit the meliorist Thomas was. Wagner, not Beethoven, was his religion. Thomas was a fundamentalist circuit preacher, Seidl a high priest, hypnotically combining libidinal intensity with sphinxlike composure. His Wagnerized Beethoven challenged conventional wisdom and yet remained comprehensibly aligned with an evolution in performance style paralleling an evolution in music itself: toward romantic extremes of feeling and expression. It was Mahler, conducting Beethoven, who was the non sequitur. High strung, vulnerable, he contradicted earlier American embodiments of podium authority. In fact, he seemed to embody no authority higher than his own. He seemed blasphemous.

What did Mahler's New York concert performances sound like? There are no recordings. But there are reviews, hundreds of them, by writers long familiar with the repertoire as rendered by such eminent conductors—all active in New York before Mahler—as Seidl, Nikisch, Muck, Mengelberg, Steinbach, Strauss, and Weingartner. Here, for instance, is the composer/critic Arthur Farwell, in *Musical America*, on a Mahler performance of Schubert's C major Symphony, D. 944, given November 1, 1910:

> The great Schubert symphony was the feature of the evening. Mahler gave it a big reading, albeit one characterized by many of the personal touches, not a few of them unsympathetic, which mark all his best work. It is a late date at which to praise this symphony, but now, even more than ever before, one realizes that this is music for high Olympus. . . . It is, withal, spontaneous and naïve, and despite the big outlines in which Mahler drew the work, it is with these qualities of spontaneity and naivete that the sophistication of Mahler interfered.
>
> This appeared in the very first bars of the symphony, for the solo horn [*sic*], where an exaggerated effect of dramatic contrast was given to the different phrases of the first melody. The softer phrases seemed to give forth a promise that perhaps Mahler will permit a more beautiful brass tone in his orchestra than he appeared willing to last year.

Again the second theme of the allegro, for the woodwind instruments in thirds, seemed to be accentuated in a degree unbefitting its character. So, also, the lyric beauty of the melody in the andante was somewhat marred by the persistent staccato. However, to many of these little perverse personal elements the great spirit of the symphony shone forth.

The conductor chose a perfect pace for each of the movements, and always gained effective climaxes. He shortened the work by the omission of repeats in the first movement and scherzo, although he wisely granted a repeat of the trio, which is one of the most heavenly moments in all of Schubert. The trio lacked a little of its celestial quality by a reading slightly over-vigorous.

Despite the fact that the imp of the perverse pursued Mahler throughout his interpretation of the work, it was a most memorable event. It must be said that his readings are always alive at every point.

Reading Farwell, one can readily imagine how much Schubert's symphony could sound like one of Mahler's own. Also, Mahler retouched Schubert's orchestration; of the same performance, Krehbiel complained of "brass ornaments" added by the conductor. Henderson wrote, "Surely it never occurred to Schubert to use stopped trumpets when he desired a pianissimo effect. If he wrote 'pianissimo' under his trumpet parts, he probably desired a trumpet pianissimo."[13]

Mahler was by no means the first conductor to retouch symphonies by dead composers. But, at least in New York, no one before had done it so blatantly—whether in pursuit of lucid textures, or in consideration of modern instruments, or for other reasons less scrutable. In the first movement of Beethoven's Fifth, there is a mini-cadenza for solo oboe, inviting a free play of expressive nuance. Mahler's rendering of this passage, in December 1909, astonished Krehbiel:

Mr. Mahler phlebotomized [the cadenza] by giving it to two oboes and beating time for each note—not in the expressive adagio called for by Beethoven, but in a rigid andante. Thus the rhapsodic utterance contemplated by the composer was turned into a mere connecting link between two parts of the movement.... In the finale Mr. Mahler several times doubled voices (bassoons with cellos) and transposed the piccolo part an octave higher. Here he secured sonority which aided him in building up a thrilling climax, but did not materially disturb Beethoven's color scheme. The question of the artistic righteousness of his act may be left to the decision of musicians.

When Mahler added timpani parts to the storm in Beethoven's *Pastoral* Symphony, Krehbiel mused, "We can only wonder that since a 'thunder machine' has been added to the symphonic apparatus it was not enlisted. Very realistic lightning effects are also easily produced on every stage. They might not add to the impressiveness of the symphony from a musical point of view, but they might to its delineation."* To Henderson, Mahler's predilection for kaleidoscopes of sound, which he typically pursued by adding or modifying wind and brass parts, was an egocentric intrusion:

> This business of probing the depths of Beethoven's scores to find things which the master perversely concealed from the native eye grows apace. We used to think that Beethoven's scoring was tolerably simple and that most of it was purely harmonic or constructed on a rational distribution of the component parts of chords.
>
> But we are rapidly learning that it is quite as contrapuntal as Bach's and that what he foolishly supposed were mere thirds or sixths in chord formations are in reality individual melodic voices which must be brought out by exploring conductors.

To Krehbiel, Mahler's editorial hand broached "a question of what might be called moral aesthetics."[14]

All this notwithstanding, Mahler's readings were regularly acclaimed for their freshness, intensity, and acuity. No one found him boring. But there was a "moral aesthetic" gap. The critical reception of Mahler's own symphonies—he performed the First, Second, and Fourth in New York—underlines the issues at hand. That Mahler was himself a composer of stature put him on an easy footing even with a Beethoven or Schubert. He interacted creatively, compositionally, with their scores; he felt no impulse to worship on bended knee. But in the opinion of Henderson or Krehbiel, Mahler the composer was not a candidate for the pantheon. Krehbiel knew exactly what he objected to. The problem, again, was profanation: "It was a singular paradox in Mahler's artistic nature that while his melodic ideas were of the folksong order his treatment of them was of the most extravagant kind, harmonically and orchestrally. He attempted in argument to reconcile the extremes by insisting that folksong was the vital spark of artistic music, but in his treatment of the simple melodies of his symphonies . . . he was utterly inconsiderate of

---

* Half a century before, Jullien's orchestras had "delineated" hail stones by the rattling of a box with dried peas. See Adam Carse, *The Life of Jullien* (Cambridge, UK, Cambridge University Press, 1951), p. 40.

Boston's John Sullivan Dwight, who espoused a pure "classical music," helped to stamp out such "monster concerts" as Patrick Gilmore's World Peace Jubilee of 1872, with its one-thousand-piece orchestra and chorus of eighteen hundred.

Henry Higginson invented, owned, and operated the Boston Symphony Orchestra. He also built Symphony Hall, notable for its New England plainness; even the large rectangle reserved for an inscription, on the Huntington Avenue façade, was left bare.

Of the conductors Higginson hired, George Henschel (top left) was his
founding music director. Wilhelm Gericke (top right) whipped the orchestra
into shape. Arthur Nikisch (bottom left) was a Svengali whose mercurial
interpretations split Boston opinion. Karl Muck (bottom right) embodied
German discipline and authority.

Of Boston's late-nineteenth-century composers, George Chadwick was the first American symphonic nationalist. Amy Beach—then invariably known as "Mrs. H. H. A. Beach"—was accepted by Chadwick as "one of the boys."

Queen bee of the Boston aesthetes was Isabella Stewart Gardner, whose Music Room at Fenway Court hosted many a concert. Her court musician was the deracinated Charles Martin Loeffler.

Leopold Damrosch
founded the New York
Symphony in 1878.
Theodore Thomas, who
vowed to crush all rivals,
is here shown with his
exemplary Thomas
Orchestra at Steinway
Hall in 1890.

MUSIC FESTIVAL

In Celebration of the Opening of

MUSIC HALL

CORNER 57TH STREET & 7TH AVENUE,

MAY 5, 6, 7, 8, and 9, 1891.

The Symphony Society Orchestra,

The Oratorio Society Chorus,

BOYS' CHOIR OF 100, (Wenzel Raboch, Choirmaster.)

WALTER DAMROSCH, CONDUCTOR.

THE MUSIC HALL COMPANY OF NEW YORK, Limited.

Morris Reno, President.

Frederick William Holls, Secretary.   Stephen M. Knevals, Treasurer.

DIRECTORS

John W. Aitkin,   Frederick Wm. Holls,   Stephen W. Clement,
Andrew Carnegie,   Wm. B. Hoyt,   Morris Reno,
Walter Damrosch,   Stephen M. Knevals,   William B. Tuthill.

With a silver trowel, Mrs. Louise Carnegie laid the
cornerstone for the Music Hall that would bear her
husband's name (May 13, 1890); Carnegie is visible
behind the workman in white overalls. The opening
night audience was depicted ascending the main
entrance in *Harper's Weekly* (May 9, 1891). Tchaikovsky,
the guest of honor, inscribed this photograph to
Walter Damrosch "with friendly memories."

Anton Seidl, apostle of Wagner, was New York's most charismatic musician until his early death in 1898. With the Philharmonic, he led the premiere of Dvořák's *New World* Symphony. At Brighton Beach, on Coney Island, he conducted summer symphonic concerts fourteen times a week.

BRIGHTON BEACH

PROGRAMME

SEASON 1889

ANTON SEIDL CONDUCTOR

Week Commencing Saturday, July 6, 1889.

Every Afternoon at 3.30.   **Every Evening at 8.**

The Chicago Orchestra

THEODORE THOMAS, Conductor

Theodore Thomas, who said he would "go to hell if they gave me a permanent orchestra," became founding music director of the Chicago Orchestra in 1891. He is pictured below, ca. 1902.

THE PHILHARMONIC SOCIETY
OF NEW YORK
GUSTAV MAHLER
CONDUCTOR

TO-MORROW EVENING
Wednesday, November 10th, at 8.15
The First of a
Series of Historical Concerts
Arranged in Chronological Order
Beginning with
SEVENTEENTH CENTURY COMPOSERS

At this Concert
MR. MAHLER will play the Bach Klavier in the
Compositions of Bach and Handel
SOLOISTS
MR. THEODORE SPIERING, Violin
MME. RIDER-KELSEY, Soprano
ARTHUR S. HYDE, Organist

Special Announcement
First Concert of the BEETHOVEN CYCLE
Friday Afternoon, November 19th, at 2.30

The SUNDAY AFTERNOON Series
of Concerts
Begins November 21st, at 3

Special Collections Division, Michigan State University Libraries

Henry Krehbiel (opposite, top left), the learned dean of New York music critics, resented Gustav Mahler's strategy to gradually "educate the public," as with his "Historical Concerts" (whose "Bach Klavier" was a modified grand piano). Oscar Hammerstein (opposite, bottom left), founder of the astonishing Hammerstein Opera, presented Mary Garden as Mélisande (opposite, bottom right). Hammerstein's war with Giulio Gatti-Casazza's Met is here depicted in *Puck* (November 11, 1908).

Giulio Gatti-Casazza, David Belasco, Arturo
Toscanini, and Giacomo Puccini (left to
right) at the 1910 premiere of Puccini's *La
fanciulla del west*, setting a Belasco play about
a bandit and a sheriff in love with the same
soprano.

With his dreamy eyes and *beau ideal* profile, New Orleans–born Louis Moreau Gottschalk was the first American pianist/composer of high international reputation; his *The Banjo* remains a dazzling New World entertainment.

A charismatic philosopher who idealized art and spiritualized everyday experience, Charles Ives was equally a vigorous democrat at home with ordinary people and things. His proposed twentieth amendment to the Constitution, which he circulated to leading political figures, would have implemented a national direct democracy.

A SUGGESTION FOR A 20TH AMENDMENT

The following letter was sent to eight leading New York newspapers a few months ago. To date none of them have printed it. Some of the papers returned the copy saying that space prevented their using it. The letter is long, but requires little more space than that which most of the papers give daily to the society columns. It should not be assumed that because these papers did not see fit to publish this letter that they were opposed to it; they may have thought, probably with good reason, that the plan was not well expressed or presented. However, whatever the reason, the fact that it was not printed would indicate that the editors are not especially interested in the idea. Hence this means of presentation by a circular is tried.

If you won't read all of this, read that part in **large print**—at least read **the proposed 20th amendment.** If you do not believe in the idea fundamentally—tear this up; or better, sit down and think out your objections and then present them in any open and fair way you can.

If you believe in the plan show it to others, then **sign your name** on the opposite side as indicated **and mail it to** one of **your representatives** in Congress, **or to the President.**

"The following contains an attempt to suggest a '20TH AMENDMENT' to the Federal Constitution—AN ATTEMPT clumsy and far from adequate, we admit, either in form or in substance, but as its general purpose is TO REDUCE to a minimum or possibly to eliminate, something which all our great political leaders talk about but never eliminate, to wit: THE EFFECT OF TOO MUCH POLITICS IN OUR representative DEMOCRACY—we submit this for what it is worth.

As our political parties today, together with a great chorus of candidates, are by their own declarations out for 'the common good' —that is—'for the people,' and as the people believe that politics are to blame for many of their ills and as political parties generate 'politics,' is it not inevitable and logical that all parties will jump at the chance of embodying in their platforms any plan which will eventually eliminate the cause of these troubles—in other words, all political parties?

We hope the Republican party will not become so over-enthusiastic about this proposed amendment that it will claim a prior right to it—even a monopoly!

But seriously—if it is so and it apparently is, that a dispassionate examination of social phenomena in this and other civilizations indicates that THE INTUITIVE REASONING OF THE MASSES IS MORE SCIENTIFICALLY TRUE AND so OF GREATER VALUE TO the wholesome PROGRESS of social evolution THAN the PERSONAL ADMONITIONS of the intellectual only—that is, in the ever-flowing undercurrent of the man relation, the ethical and religious impulse predominates—the intellect being a stabilizing rather than a primal organic force—if this is so, is it not only natural but essential, that mankind do more towards registering the results of this intuitive reasoning, and its deeper impulses and to formulate more direct means for their expression? And if this mass intuition and deeper consciousness has been valuable, even in the crude way it has had to function, of how much greater value will it be to society if THE VARIOUS PREMISES WHICH IT NEEDS TO ACT UPON more accurately can be more clearly and universally presented. If one will admit that God made man's brain as well as his stomach, one must then admit that the brain (the majority brain) if it has the normal amount of wholesome food —truth (in its outward manifestations, specific knowledge, facts, premises, etc.—which UNIVERSAL EDUCATION IS FAST BRINGING) will digest—and will function, as normally as the stomach, when it has the right kind of food. If one won't admit that, he comes pretty near admitting that God is incapable. The writer believes that THE AMERICAN PEOPLE are willing to make or try to make a greater contribution to social progress; that they have faith in themselves and ARE WILLING TO TAKE RESPONSIBILITY AND if occasion requires willing to take TIME TO THINK ACCURATELY and SERIOUSLY—AND further that they, WITH THE PREMISES BEFORE THEM WILL BE more INSPIRED BY THE SENSE OF JUSTICE, not only social justice, or any relative justice—but justice in the absolute—than are many self or party-appointed leaders. THE NEED OF LEADERS in the old sense IS FAST GOING—BUT THE NEED OF FREER ACCESS TO GREATER TRUTHS AND FREER

EXPRESSION IS WITH US, and with this greater and deeper freedom, the sum of all consciousness—the people are finding their one true leader—they are beginning to lead themselves. Utilizing public opinion in any but a general way may seem hopelessly impractical to the hard-headed business man (so termed) and to the practical politician, altogether too practical. To photograph with good results, the universal mind and heart will be a big job—a tremendous job—but one that was successfully started in 1776—and the bigger the job the more reason why the American people will tackle it with courage and equanimity. TO BE AFRAID TO TRUST THE MIND AND SOUL OF THE PEOPLE IS A COMMON ATTRIBUTE OF THE TIMID. There is every reason to hold with John Bright that the first 500 men who pass in the Strand would make as good a parliament as that which sits at St. Stephen's. Wendell Phillips, a student of history and a close observer of men, as George Williams Curtis says, 'rejected the fear of the multitude which springs from the timid feeling that the many are ignorant and the few are wise; he believed the saying, too profound for Talleyrand, that EVERYBODY KNOWS MORE THAN ANYBODY.' Because a man does not express an opinion, do not assume that he has none. Ask him and find out that mankind is thinking—and thinking seriously and is interested in its thought. And we doubt that the quality of the thinking of the masses will be as inferior as some of the practical voices think. In working out a system of universal expression there will be severe disappointments, disastrous sloughing offs, dark days, trials and discouragements, but no greater problems than we have survived. It is the belief of the writer that THE MAKERS OF OUR FEDERAL CONSTITUTION HAD in mind THE HOPE OF A BROADER DEVELOPMENT OF direct POPULAR EXPRESSION. Obviously, more DIRECT EXPRESSION was as IMPOSSIBLE IN 1780 as it is POSSIBLE IN 1920. The process does not change the form of our government. It tends to protect and perfect it. We respectfully submit the following:

SECTION 1.

Article 20. (20th Amendment.) On a day, nine* months previous to the day on which the people shall meet in their respective states to vote by ballot for electors (Article 12) for President and Vice-President, the said people of the United States shall submit to Congress all and whatever plans, opinions and suggestions which each and all desire to offer in relation to future Federal legislation; and in this connection and upon the same ballot there shall be contained not over twenty questions, the subject matter of which shall relate to whatever Congress considers, does most fundamentally and vitally affect the public welfare. . Such questions shall be presented as clearly as is possible so that the answers may readily indicate the opinion of the public. All citizens of the United States, male and female (and over the age of 21, possibly 18), shall be required to return answers or opinions to these specific matters and questions which shall be returned to the Government in addition to the other suggestions, opinions, etc., that the people may wish to submit (as suggested above). The result of these suggestive ballots shall be made known to Congress who shall analyze, classify and orderly arrange these plans, suggestions and answers into subdivisions and make the complete findings public. Whichever ten of the foregoing plans and suggestions as a result of these ballots shall have been the most numerous, shall then be suitably assimilated, condensed and presented to the people in the form of proposed laws (together with an essential digest of each) five months before

*This was drafted some years ago but revised recently in the hope that it could be put before Congress so that it might be a definite help in the coming election. This is hardly possible now, but the "plan in principle" should be publicly and seriously discussed. The sooner some such amendment is enacted the sooner will the duties of Congress be made more manifest.

There will be no plank in any party platform more important!

their essence, robbing them of their characteristics and elaborating them to death."★15

Mahler's signature juxtaposition of the quotidian and the sublime flew in the face of attitudes fostered by the likes of Dwight and Thomas, who railed against popular music and raised the symphony onto a high and unsullied altar. The American penchant for sacralization—the European tendency was less extreme—may be faulted as a puritanical excess, or a symptom of insecurity. And the concomitant emphasis on textual fidelity—on objectivity, versus subjective interpretation—may be partly understood as a defense against claims that only Germans could understand Beethoven. But these American traditions were also strengths, signifying a musical high culture more distinctive and evolved than Europeans, unless they visited, could possibly imagine. As Henderson was moved to write in 1908 in response to exaggerated Viennese accounts of Mahler's financial terms of engagement at the Met:

> It is always instructive to read European newspapers on American affairs. It gives us the much needed opportunity to see ourselves as others see us—with their eyes shut. . . . Do we not all reek with malodorous lucre? Are we not a nation of tradesmen? . . .
>
> Doubtless the Viennese observer of American barbarism might find a . . . conviction of our benighted condition in the indisputable fact that the artistic cataclysm which separated Mr. Mahler from the Imperial Opera in the Austrian capital and brought him to this city has not been measured here by the yardstick of European pride. The coming of the new interpreter of German operas was awaited with interest and received with pleasure, but there was no public excitement.
>
> The stock market was not affected. This comment is made because it would naturally be expected of us in Europe. It would be quite useless to remark in passing that we do not grow excited over the arrival of new interpreters from Europe, for the sufficient reason that we have already heard many of the best Europe has ever known.16

■ ■ ■

★ The response of New York's leading critics to Mahler the composer, while not prophetic, was by no means undiscerning. The Second Symphony was generally esteemed; the First was not. I cannot resist quoting Henderson on the finale of the latter: "At one place in the movement Mahler sang a cantabile theme of such rare beauty and emotional potency that it did the hearer to wonder that he did not bend his talents oftener in the direction of such art. . . . The conclusion of the movement reverts to the manner of its beginning . . . and suggests that when the weather is bad in Tyrol it is beyond the powers of language to characterize." See New York Sun, Dec. 17, 1909.

Worldly New York music critics like Henderson took a reasonable pride in American achievements. They could be hypersensitive toward those who did not. In Mahler, they encountered a wall of misunderstanding.

Even if it was money that lured him to the United States, Mahler cannot be accused of cynicism or indifference. He diligently learned scores he had never before conducted, even a few—too few—by Americans. In rehearsal, his concertmaster later recalled, he "always worked flat out. Every minute counted. There were no breaks." He complained to Bruno Walter that the Philharmonic was "a real American orchestra. Untalented and phlegmatic." (In fact, the Philharmonic Mahler inherited was an inferior American orchestra, judged by the standards of Boston or Chicago, or by its own prior estate.) But Mahler was also seduced by America. "The people here are tremendously unspoilt—all the crudeness and ignorance are—teething troubles," he wrote to Roller weeks after his Met debut. "Here the dollar does not reign supreme—it's merely easy to earn. Only one thing is respected here: ability and drive!" A day later, in another letter, he advised his father-in-law, Carl Moll, "I am determined that you, too, must one day experience first hand this life which is so extraordinarily exuberant and refreshing for a European. . . . All the stories about America which circulate among us originate with that disgusting type of German you know as well as I do. . . . A truly native American is a high-minded and capable person."

But these impressions, and others like them, were acquired willy-nilly—not from any concentrated effort of exploration or understanding. Compared to Seidl or Dvořák—and this comparison mattered, because it mattered to many who remembered—Mahler exhibited a self-absorption indistinguishable from arrogance. He knew the New World as he encountered it—not, like Dvořák, as an avid student of plantation song and Native American chant, or, like Seidl and Dvořák both, a mentor to the American composer. His offenses were not malicious, merely tactless. In October 1909, by which time he should have known better, he told *Musical America*, "The best orchestra in the world today is, to my mind, that of Vienna. Munich, Dresden, Berlin and Paris have splendid organizations, but that of Vienna attained under Hans Richter a perfection that I know of nowhere else." It would have cost him nothing to have mentioned the Boston Symphony (which he had privately informed Willem Mengelberg was "only equaled" abroad in Vienna).[17] In the same interview, Mahler announced, "It will be my aim to educate the public, and that education will be made gradually and in a manner which will enable those who may not now have a taste for the best later to appreciate it. . . . There will be special cycles, such as the Beethoven, for those who love this lofty symphonic music and for the education of my orchestra, and the historical, in which we shall play the music from the time of Bach down to the modern composer."[18]

When Mahler performed his own First Symphony on December 16 and 17, 1909, Krehbiel, who was the Philharmonic's program annotator, requested permission to reprint a letter in which Mahler described aspects of the work. Mahler responded by prohibiting Krehbiel from writing anything at all about the symphony. Krehbiel responded with a program note reading in part:

> In deference to the wish of Mr Mahler, the annotator of the Philharmonic Society's programmes refrains from even an outline analysis of the symphony which he is performing for the first time in New York on this occasion, as also from an attempt to suggest what might be or has been set forth as its possible poetical, dramatic, or emotional contents. . . . Mr. Mahler's conviction, frequently expressed publicly as well as privately, is that it is a hindrance to appreciation to read an analysis which with the help of musical examples lays bare the contents and structure of a composition while it is playing. . . . All writings about music, even those of musicians themselves, he holds to be injurious to musical enjoyment.[19]

Eventually Mahler found himself in conflict not only with members of the press, but with the Philharmonic guarantors. First there were disagreements over salary. Then, in January 1911, the guarantors formed a subcommittee to supervise what music Mahler would program. In her memoirs, Alma Mahler described the climactic blowout, at which "the ladies had many instances to allege of conduct which in their eyes was mistaken. . . . A document was then drawn up in legal form, strictly defining Mahler's powers. He was so taken aback and so furious that he came back to me trembling in every limb." Days later, Mahler's health took a turn for the worse. In May, by which time he was back in Vienna, Alma told an American interviewer that she held the Philharmonic responsible for her husband's decline: "You cannot imagine what Mr. Mahler has suffered. In Vienna my husband was all powerful. Even the Emperor did not dictate to him, but in New York, to his amazement, he had ten ladies ordering him about like a puppet." The guarantors, the article continued, denied these accusations, "insisting that [their relations with Mahler] were always agreeable, and that the illness of the conductor came about through his extreme nervousness."*[20]

---

* Though Alma is a notoriously unreliable memoirist, the memories of Ferruccio Busoni, who appeared with Mahler as soloist, back her up; in an "Open Letter about America," he accused the Philharmonic Society's "president" of having precipitated Mahler's death. See Marc-Andre Roberge, "Ferruccio Busoni in the United States," *American Music*, vol. 13, no. 3 (Fall 1995), p. 314.

On May 18, Mahler was dead. Vienna gave him a hero's funeral. In New York, Krehbiel's fifty-inch obituary, in the *Tribune*, ignited a firestorm of controversy. It began:

> Gustav Mahler is dead, and his death was made to appear in some newspaper accounts as the tragic conclusion of unhappy experiences in New York. As a matter of fact [he] was a sick man when he came to New York three years ago. His troubles with the administration of the Philharmonic were of his own creation. . . . He was paid a sum of money which ought to have seemed to him fabulous from the day on which he came till the day when his labors ended, and the money was given to him ungrudgingly, though the investment was a poor one for the opera company which brought him to America and the concert organization which kept him here. He was looked upon as a great artist, and possibly he was one, but he failed to convince the people of New York of the fact, and therefore his American career was not a success.[21]

Krehbiel's Mahler obituary has perplexed and offended Mahler's various biographers. He was a pontifical writer, but not normally this intemperate. His exceptional animus toward Mahler cannot be defended, but can be understood. Two grievances permeate his postmortem analysis. The first was that Mahler neglected to appreciate the importance of New York, that "it is a fatuous notion of foreigners that Americans know nothing about music in its highest forms." Krehbiel's second grievance—a subtext—was that Mahler neglected to appreciate the importance of Henry Krehbiel. And Krehbiel was very important, the acknowledged leader of a critical community that, unlike New York music critics of today, meshed seamlessly with the musical community it reported and assessed.

To scan Krehbiel's career is to glean how two relationships conditioned his disappointment in Mahler. Anton Seidl had accepted Krehbiel as one of his few New York intimates. And Seidl was a Mahler antipode: he projected a serene authority; he bonded fraternally with his musicians; he interacted amiably and productively with the ladies of the Seidl Society; he embraced America. Concurrently, Krehbiel was Antonín Dvořák's chief mouthpiece and advocate in the press. Krehbiel was accustomed to his eminence. Mahler sought no advice and cultivated no graces. He was not the man to champion American music, as Seidl had championed Edward MacDowell. He was not the man to compose a *New World* Symphony after the fashion of Dvořák. He was, finally, not really cut out to be music director of an American orchestra, sensitive to the needs of a cultural community, its scribes, audiences, and benefactors.

Mahler's successor at the helm of the Philharmonic, selected by the guarantors, was Josef Stransky, who would ultimately quit music to become an art dealer. Quipped *Musical America*, "After much upheaval, search, and negotiation, the New York Philharmonic Society . . . has engaged Josef Stransky. . . . Without disrespect to Mr. Stransky, there are reasons which cause this circumstance to remind one of Aesop's fable of the mountain in labor which finally brought forth a mouse."[★22] An eclipse descended upon New York's symphonic fortunes. A new round of opera madness had begun.

■ ■ ■

As the New York Philharmonic's program annotator, Henry Krehbiel clashed with Gustav Mahler over the meaning of Mahler's own First Symphony. As critic for the *New York Tribune*, he relentlessly pursued Mahler in the name of aesthetic purity. A decade earlier, he befriended Antonín Dvořák and became his American advocate; he feuded with Boston's Philip Hale, and defended African-Americans, on Dvořák's behalf. A decade before that, he befriended Anton Seidl and tirelessly championed Wagner in books, reviews, and lectures.

Other American music critics have dramatically exerted influence. John Sullivan Dwight set the tone for Boston and helped to run the Harvard Musical Association. Virgil Thomson, in the 1940s *New York Herald-Tribune*, corralled conducting engagements and performances of his own music in exchange for good notices. Claudia Cassidy, in the 1950s *Chicago Tribune*, helped to decide who would conduct the Chicago Symphony. But Krehbiel's role within a city's community of artists and thinkers was exceptional. He is the very bellwether of musical New York in the late Gilded Age: its intellectual center, registering the capacities and limitations of genteel learning and experience.

In a superb critical community also including W. J. Henderson and James Gibbons Huneker—the former a peerless vocal connoisseur, the latter a vir-

---

* *Musical America* mentioned Henry Hadley and Frank Van der Stucken as Americans overlooked by the guarantors. By 1911, complaints that American orchestras favored European conductors over local candidates were already common. The complaining was not necessarily plausible: George Chadwick felt overlooked by Henry Higginson in his capacity as conductor, but was not a conductor to compare with a Gericke, Nikisch, or Muck. As conductor of New York's Arion Society, of the Cincinnati Symphony, and of the Cincinnati May festival, Van der Stucken was, however, a leader of established competence and authority. He was also a substantial composer and an informed advocate of American music. Stransky's undistinguished New York career suggests that Van der Stucken, born in Texas, might indeed have been a more credible 1911 choice, assuming he was interested in a second New York post.

tuoso harbinger of modernism—Krehbiel was the "dean": a sobriquet acknowledging his pontifical tone, long memory, and daunting erudition. He read six languages and wrote a dozen books, including an important study of African-American folk song, a popular musical appreciation text, a scholarly treatise on the Wagner operas, and a two-volume history of opera in New York not superseded by later writers. He completed the first English-language edition of Alexander Wheelock Thayer's monumental *Life of Beethoven*. He translated operas, composed exercises for the violin, and edited collections of songs and arias.

As I have already stressed (in comparing him with Philip Hale), Krehbiel was the self-taught son of German immigrants. Born in Ann Arbor in 1854, he was a reporter for the *Cincinnati Enquirer* before becoming music critic of the *New York Tribune* from 1880 until his death in 1923. This robust background engendered an elusive combination of populist and elitist. Like Theodore Thomas (also self-made) he regarded art as a sanctum within reach of anyone, provided they had the perspicacity and persistence to attain it. Like Thomas—and Seidl and Dvořák (who refused to attend the Metropolitan Opera even when Seidl was conducting)—he was never reconciled to the influence of individual wealth on American institutions of high culture. An apostle of music's ennobling properties, he had no use for *noblesse oblige*.

Equally embodying the larger New York milieu, so distinct from Boston, is Krehbiel's style of argument. He disdains the suavity of Philip Hale and the stylistic vagaries of H. T. Parker. He is singularly long-winded—not, as with Dwight, through dullness and repetition, but because he never runs out of breath. His tortuous sentences and vast paragraphs are leisurely yet intense. He takes time to ponder and respond. His gravitas, sublimating powerful visceral energies,★ attains a charged repose.

Scanning an opera new to New York, he is ever articulate. His verdicts—as preserved in *Chapters of Opera* (1908) and *More Chapters of Opera* (1919)—remain shrewdly provocative. Of Puccini's *La bohème* he reports:

Puccini's music discloses little of that brightness, vivacity, and piquancy which we are naturally led to expect from it by knowledge of Murger's story, on which the opera is based. . . . However, [absence of the light

---

★ In his autobiography, the composer Richard Rodgers writes of his student years at New York's Institute of Musical Arts: "One of my [favorite teachers] was Henry Krehbiel. . . . Whenever he was scheduled to talk, I would leave home a half-hour early in order to make sure of getting a front-row seat. . . . As he spoke he would become so emotional that tears rolled down his long red beard." See Andrea Olmstead, *Juilliard: A History* (Urbana, University of Illinois Press, 1999), p. 55.

touch of humor] is a characteristic not of Puccini alone, but all the composers in the Young Italian School. They know no way to kill a gnat
dancing in the sunlight except to blow it up with a broadside of trombones. Puccini's music in "La Boheme" also seems lacking in the element of characterization, an element which is much more essential in
comedy music than in tragic. Whether they are celebrating the careless
pleasures of a Bohemian carouse or proclaiming the agonies of a consuming passion, it is all one to his singers. So soon as they drop the intervallic palaver which points the way of the new style toward bald
melodrama they soar off in a shrieking cantalena [*sic*], buoyed upon by
the unison strings and imperiled by strident brass until there is no relief
except exhaustion. Happy, careless music, such as Mozart or Rossini
might have written for the comedy scenes in "La Boheme," there is next
to none in Puccini's score.

Of Strauss's *Salome*:

A reviewer ought to be equipped with a dual nature, both intellectually and morally, in order to pronounce fully and fairly upon the qualities of this drama by Oscar Wilde and Richard Strauss. He should be an
embodied conscience stung into righteous fury by the moral stench
exhaled by the decadent and pestiferous work, but, though it make him
retch, he should be sufficiently judicial in his temperament calmly to
look at the drama in all its aspects and determine whether or not as a
whole it is an instructive note on the life and culture of the times and
whether or not this exudation from the diseased and polluted will and
imagination of the authors marks a real advance in artistic expression,
irrespective of its contents or their fitness for dramatic representation.[23]

Krehbiel's exegeses of the Wagner operas—in *Studies in the Wagnerian Drama*
(1891)—are among the most memorable in the English language. He is also, as
when documenting the veracity of Albert Niemann's Siegmund, a peerless
recorder of Wagner in performance. But, more surely than *Salome* (which may
be as meretricious as Krehbiel supposed), Wagner also charts his limits. To
experience *Tristan und Isolde* via Krehbiel is equally to experience the thrill and
alarm of emotional surrender. The "tumultuous lava current," he writes,
assaults "one's emotional part more than the intellect or judgment"; it threatens
a sensuous indulgence; it disarms wary intellect's discriminating check on
unfettered feeling. The Prelude, a picture of unslaked sexual arousal, makes him
squeamish. The ending, he worries, departs from the ethical Wagner trope of

"erring man's salvation through the self-sacrificing love of a woman." His gen-teel discomfort connects to Dwight's mistrust of emotion, a viewpoint simpli-fied to the point of silliness in the Reverend Hugh Reginald Haweis's *Music and Morals*, printed twenty-five times between 1872 and 1934. But Krehbiel's scruples equally warrant comparison with Nietzsche's resistance to Wagnerian narcosis—for both, Wagner threatens an emotional totalitarianism.*

Though Krehbiel finally succumbs to the Liebestod as "purifying and ennobling," he is left nursing a nagging ambivalence. Experiencing *Parsifal*, his moral/aesthetic compass is fatally disturbed. "When one has escaped the sweet thralldom of the representation . . . there arise a multitude of doubts touching the essential merit of the drama." He considers Parsifal's celibacy a relic of "medieval fanatics" and "crazed monks." He calls Parsifal's rejection of wom-anly love, and preference for male company, "a conception of sanctity which grew out of a monstrous perversion of womanhood, and a wicked degrada-tion of womankind." Aesthetes to come might find decadence, Wagnerian or otherwise, titillating or liberating; for Krehbiel it is merely distasteful.[24]

To return to our New York narrative: to better understand Krehbiel and his bellwether genteel sensibility is to better understand Mahler's New World career, undone by perceived personal excesses and errors of taste. Unknow-ingly, he suffered in comparison with Seidl and Dvořák. And by the time of his passing, there was someone else who had achieved things Mahler had not. Krehbiel and New York had glimpsed a newborn musical institution that transcended the fickleness of public taste, the egotism of artists, the rapacity of promoters, and the innocence of guarantors. Its mastermind—following P. T. Barnum, whom he studied and admired—was in equal parts rascal and genius, a cigar-champing David obsessed with the project of slaying Goliath. Though his taste in sopranos was as sophisticated as Barnum's was opportunistic, he was also at least half the cultural democrat Barnum was. Of all the lives docu-mented in this history of classical music in the United States, his is the least plausible, truly stranger than any fiction.

■ ■ ■

Born in Berlin to prosperous German Jewish parents, Oscar Hammerstein (a name today associated with his grandson, the famous lyricist) pursued a var-

---

* In *The Metaphysical Club* (New York, Farrar, Straus and Giroux, 2001), Louis Menand posits that the distinctive absolutist passions of the Civil War contributed to intellectual and emotional circumspec-tion in the Gilded Age. In the case of Krehbiel, as with Oliver Wendell Holmes Jr., in Menand's account, such circumspection deserves to be taken seriously.

ied and demanding regimen of musical studies to the age of fifteen, when a dispute with his father impelled him to pawn his violin and book steerage passage to New York. Though he arrived without means or introductions, he swiftly ascended to the top of the cigar trade—a lucrative preamble to his career in the theater. He also acquired a wife, a family, American citizenship, and a lifelong reputation as an inimitable personality and undefeatable impresario.

The Hammerstein presence was defined by a dangling cigar and a high black top hat worn outdoors and in. He kept no secretary, wrote few letters, and worked buried in papers, music, and unpaid bills. His preferred residence was a pair of rooms above a theater. Launching even his most expansive undertakings, he disdained the support of a board of directors, relying only on himself and his tireless sons, Arthur and Willie. He frequently took to the street penniless but for a bill Arthur or Willie had thrust into his pocket. When all the Hammersteins were broke, as periodically occurred, Oscar would cash in on some new invention (he eventually held about a hundred patents), if not for better cigars then for, say, the better extending and shortening of men's suspenders. So irresistible were the stories told about him, and those he told about himself, that he was more written about in the press than any man of his time save Theodore Roosevelt (whom as police commissioner was once called upon to pass on the decency of a Hammerstein "living picture" touching a degree of nudity previously unseen on any New York stage).

Merely typical was the hundred-dollar bet that he could compose an opera in forty-eight hours. Hammerstein locked himself in a room with a piano and plenty of paper. His opponents in this wager, including James Huneker, engaged organ grinders and a monkey to frustrate the great endeavor. Completed on time, and in three scenes, the opera was anointed *The Kohinoor*. When it was objected that *The Kohinoor* was unfit for production, Hammerstein produced it. It played for six weeks as part of a variety show. Carl Van Vechten judged it of all operas "the worst on record." Huneker recalled, "The opening chorus consumed a third of the first act. . . . Two comic Jews, alternately, for half an hour sang 'Good morning, Mr. Morgenstern, Good morning, Mr. Isaacstein.'" Hammerstein in fact composed prolifically, if insignificantly. As a producer of vaudeville, his significance was prodigious. His international roster of entertainers, unrivaled in the United States, included top attractions from London, Paris, and Berlin as well as the first trained fleas exhibited in a stage show, the first Broadway company of African-American singers and dancers, and the painstakingly inept Cherry Sisters, at whom Arthur and Willie threw vegetables and fish (deflected by a net). Even more prodigious was Hammerstein the builder: in New York, Philadelphia, and London, in locations likely and unlikely, he erected thirteen theaters of his own design, each suitable for the production of his heart's desire: grand opera. This *idée fixe*, pursued impressively but erratically for more than two decades, culminated in 1906 with the creation of the Manhattan Opera, of which he was owner, architect, builder, and producer. With its excellent acoustics and sight lines, the thirty-one-hundred-seat house itself surpassed the Metropolitan Opera House in every respect save fashion: the forty-two boxes faced the stage, rather than one another, and there were no grand entrances. Twenty Saturday nights were set aside at popular prices. "It is society in the broad sense that I hope to attract and to please," Hammerstein said.[25]

Hammerstein detested Heinrich Conried as a fraud. Flinging the gauntlet, the Manhattan Opera gave performances on Mondays, Wednesdays, Fridays, and twice on Saturdays: the same schedule Conried kept at the Met. Hammerstein instantly bested Conried's musical leadership—Mahler's arrival was a year away—by entrusting nearly every performance to Cleofonte Campanini, a conductor of marvelous versatility and inspirational energy. He went shopping for singers and came back with Alessandro Bonci, Maurice Renaud, and Charles Dalmorès—refined artists not to be found on the Conried roster. With relentless aplomb, he subsequently added such great names as Emma Calvé, Luisa Tetrazzini, and John McCormack—not to mention the most legendary of living sopranos, Nellie Melba, who called him "the most American of Americans, and the only man who ever made me change my mind."[26] Hammerstein also personally recruited the Manhattan Opera chorus, instantly acclaimed for its freshness, precision, and good looks—choral qualities unknown at the older house. Hammerstein's audiences shared his passion for opera as a purely aesthetic entertainment exempt from traditional social purposes. They silenced the slightest disturbance. Even downstairs, many women came simply attired.

In Huneker's opinion, Hammerstein's habit of watching every performance from a kitchen chair in the wings, visible to all on stage, exercised a decisive influence on the singing and playing. Of the company's inaugural season, Krehbiel wrote:

> The chief things which fad and fashion had to offer at the Metropolitan Opera house were noticeably absent from the Manhattan. On a score of occasions there were large gatherings representative of wealth and what is called society at the house in Thirty-fourth Street, but generally the audiences were distinct in their composition. . . .
>
> Many things contributed to the measure of success which Mr. Hammerstein won. There was a large fascination in the audacity of the

undertaking, and its freedom from art-cant and affectation. Curiosity was irritated by the manager's daring, and admiration challenged by the manner in which he kept faith with the public. He seemed to be attempting the impossible, but he accomplished all that he said he would do. . . .

[Campanini's] zeal fired all the forces employed at the opera house. A company gathered together from the ends of the earth succeeded in giving one hundred thirteen performances of twenty-two operas, and making many of the performances of really remarkable excellence. The reason was obvious at nearly every presentation; from the principals down to the last person in the chorus and orchestra, every one had his heart in his work. Not only the desire to do their duty, but the pardonable ambition to do better than the rival establishment, inspired singers and players alike.

To which Melba added, in a statement to the press, "I have never enjoyed any season in America so much as the one now closing. . . . What courage Mr. Hammerstein has shown and what wonders he has done! I think there must be something in the conditions of American life to encourage him, for I know of no opera manager in any city of the world who, single-handed and under circumstances of such difficulty and competition, would have risked his fortune in opera."[27]

Though Hammerstein's first-year repertoire was standard, year two revealed a discerning dedication to modern opera in the form of the new French school. The highlights included Offenbach's *Tales of Hoffmann*, then unknown in New York, and three important American premieres, all featuring the electric Mary Garden: Charpentier's *Louise*, Massenet's *Thaïs*, and Debussy's *Pelléas et Mélisande*. Krehbiel cherished *Hoffmann*, with Renaud as the three villains. He appreciated *Thaïs* and *Louise*. As for *Pelléas*, it served to flag his opposition to the modernist experiment emerging in the wake of Wagnerism. Maeterlinck's drama seemed to him "infantile," "on the borderline between the marionette drama and that designed for the consumption of mature minds." Debussy's music sounded monotonous and dissonant, bristling with "combinations of tones that sting and blister and pain and outrage the ear."

If *Pelléas* (so admired by Hale and Parker in Boston in 1912) marked the limits of Krehbiel's endurance, the Manhattan Opera's second season, taken as a whole, marked the limits of endurance for the rival regime. Conried's predominant artistic strategy had been to bundle onstage as frequently as possible his tenor sensation (which he claimed to have discovered but had not), Enrico Caruso. In 1905–06, Caruso appeared sixty-one times, more than one-third of the company's performances. "The fact now to be recorded," quipped Henderson in the *Times*, "is that the public has gone to the opera in the season just ended, almost solely for the purpose of hearing Enrico Caruso. The public has not cared a rap what opera was sung." Conried himself, according to his biographer, declared "that he never thoroughly enjoyed opera unless Caruso sang." Conried also engineered the phenomenally profitable American stage premiere of *Parsifal* in 1903, an initiative shunned by previous managements in deference to the wishes of the composer and his widow, who wanted to reserve the work for Bayreuth. The American premiere of *Salome* in 1907—by which year, as Krehbiel observed, it was "getting difficult to keep the Caruso cult on its old hysterical plane"—was another quick-buck scheme. This backfired when the directors declared the work "objectionable and detrimental to the best interests of the Metropolitan Opera House" and forbade further performances.[28]

Adding to Conried's headaches was the "Monkey House Scandal": on November 16, 1906, Caruso was arrested in the monkey house of the Central Park Zoo for allegedly pinching the buttocks of a Mrs. Graham. He got off with a ten-dollar fine, but cost Conried weeks of nasty headlines. Then there was Billy Guard, Hammerstein's publicity ace, who effectively promoted Bonci as "the new and better Caruso" and spread rumors that Caruso had lost his voice; to some, the Monkey House Scandal suggested a Billy Guard coup. When Conried retaliated by hiring Bonci away from Hammerstein, Hammerstein helped himself to another celebrated tenor, the clarion-voiced Giovanni Zenatello. Ticket sales slumped at the Met. Conried's health went into decline. Mahler's appointment in 1907 furnished some relief, but was too late. Early in 1908, Conried quit. It seems his job was offered to Mahler, who turned it down. Partly through the intervention of Otto Kahn, who had regularly patronized and discerningly admired Hammerstein's house, and who as chairman would become a prime mover at the Met, the new manager would be (as we have seen) Giulio Gatti-Casazza of La Scala. He would come to New York with his own conductor. The resulting Italian juggernaut, a reformation compelled by Hammerstein's success, would sweep aside all rivals, inside the house and out. Thus would the Met, not the Manhattan Opera, become the chief artistic beneficiary of Oscar Hammerstein's one-man revolution.

■ ■ ■

Seidl, Nikisch, Stokowski—the conductorial new breed—exuded an intangible, wizard-like authority. The authority Arturo Toscanini exuded was as tangible as his legendary temper. The son of a tailor and sometime Garibaldi

Redshirt, he cultivated no airs save fanatic dedication—screaming, throwing, pounding were signature Toscanini gestures. At La Scala, of which he became artistic director at the age of thirty-one, he led the first Italian performances of operas by Weber, Tchaikovsky, Wagner, and Debussy. When the tenor mistimed an entrance in *La forza del destino*, Toscanini stopped him and made him begin again. When the audience demanded an encore in *A Masked Ball*, he left the theater and did not return for three years. He resumed his post through 1908.

Fortuitously, Mahler's Vienna regime, 1897–1907, was concurrent with Toscanini's in Milan. Small, excitable men, ruthless idealists, they despised routine. They ruled singers and intimidated audiences. They promoted new works and new ways of understanding works too well known. Mahler, the pariah, was manic or morbid, ungainly, neurotic; Toscanini, the *contadino*, was dapper and indestructible. His dark eyes sat mysteriously in pools of shadow. His obsessive, nearsighted gaze was "fiery," "brilliant," but also—like the gaze of the blind—vacant, unfocused, wistful. It conveyed anxiety or rage, vulnerability or pain. It inspired loyalty and fear.

He made his Met debut in *Aïda* on November 16, 1908. Krehbiel wrote, "Of the new conductor it must be said that he is a boon to Italian opera as great and as welcome as anything that has come out of Italy since Verdi laid down his pen."[29] A few weeks later came *Götterdämmerung*, a reading, if less universally admired in every detail, confirming Toscanini's versatile command of German repertoire. As notable, judging from the press, was his command of certain pampered singers. Often told was the story of how Geraldine Farrar had interrupted a rehearsal of *Madama Butterfly* to put the new conductor in his place only to be informed that "only the sky has stars."

Partly to fortify Toscanini, partly to counteract Hammerstein's insurgency, Gatti put the company into such high gear that something had to give—with Hammerstein being the intended something. The orchestra was expanded to 135 players, the chorus to two hundred singers divided into Italian and German wings. Elaborate new sets and costumes were produced. A smaller house, the New Theater on Sixty-second Street and Central Park West, was opened. In 1909–10, the company gave 359 performances of forty-two operas and twenty-five dance works—an astonishing figure that included 38 presentations at the New Theater; 75 in Brooklyn, Baltimore, Philadelphia, and Boston; and, in the postseason, 68 with a split company in Chicago and ten other cities, plus another 18 in Paris in May. Hammerstein kept pace, opening a new opera house in Philadelphia and touring with herculean abandon; on Christmas Day 1909, his companies played *Tosca* and *Tales of Hoffmann* in New York, *Faust* and *Aïda* in Philadelphia, *Le jongleur de Notre Dame, Cavalleria rusticana*, and *Pagliacci* in Pittsburgh, and *Mignon* and *Le caïd* in Montreal. Hammerstein novelties now included *Salome* in French with Mary Garden, who stripped nearly naked in the Dance of the Seven Veils, a production seen in New York but curtailed in Chicago and Philadelphia and abandoned in Boston; and Strauss's *Elektra*, also in French, prepared with ten weeks of rehearsal and toured to both Philadelphia and Boston. (The Met did not offer *Elektra* until 1932, did not offer *Pelléas* until 1925, did not return to *Salome*, following its scandalous 1907 premiere, until 1934.)

In 1909–10, Gatti and Hammerstein accounted for more than three hundred performances of opera in New York alone. But Hammerstein was self-destructing. His aversion to persons of wealth and status, amounting to a phobia, proved suicidal: the American system, with its absence of state support, linked opera inextricably to fashionable society. Hammerstein notwithstanding, Melba and then Garden (who became a New York cult) filled the Manhattan Opera boxes and orchestra seats with high-paying customers, two of whom—the music-loving telegraph magnate Clarence Mackay and his wife, an accomplished professional singer—became stalwart partisans of the company. Mrs. Mackay sold quantities of subscriptions to her friends. Upon attending Garden's 1907 debut, Mr. Mackay instructed Arthur Hammerstein to tell his father not to worry about money. Oscar told Arthur, "Tell Mackay to go to hell." When the Mackays hosted a musicale with Campanini and the Manhattan Opera Orchestra, Oscar took offense and informed them they were not to enter the Manhattan Opera again. Campanini, Mrs. Mackay's friend for three years, had grievances of his own: he wanted more rehearsal time to compete with Toscanini. The net outcome was that Hammerstein undertook his fourth Manhattan Opera season with neither the services of Campanini nor the support of the Mackays. In April 1910 he cut a deal with Otto Kahn and the Met, selling his Philadelphia Opera House, his scenery and costumes, and the performing rights to the operas of Strauss and Massenet for $1,250,000 on condition that he refrain from producing opera in New York, Boston, Philadelphia, or Chicago for ten years. He died nine years later. The *Times* ran a page-one obituary reading in part:

> His death removes from the public eye one of the most interesting personalities the melting pot of America has produced. Manifestations of his many-sided genius were so varied that had he shunned the spotlight of publicity, a claim even Mr. Hammerstein in his most modest moment would not have made, it would have sought him out. For his was one of those seemingly charmed lives in which the most insignificant episode reflected some ray of unusual interest.

Carl Van Vechten, in an "epitaph," wrote of Oscar Hammerstein:

> He was not, as a matter of fact, what is called a good loser. He groaned
> and moaned over loss, but in a few days the board was erased and with a
> clean piece of chalk he was drawing a new diagram, making a new plan.
> I admired him; more than that, I liked him. He was a figure, he lived his
> own life; he fashioned it sometimes with difficulty but he always carved
> it out. He was an artist; he was a genius. I have met few men who have
> seemed to me as great.[30]

Absent Hammerstein's rivalry, the Met continued to present an unsurpassed international galaxy of singers. Musical preparation and production values sustained the higher standards introduced by Mahler (if without achieving anything as aesthetically refreshed as his *Fidelio* or as revelatory as his *Don Giovanni* and *Marriage of Figaro*). Even for *Il trovatore*, according to the tenor Giovanni Martinelli, Toscanini called "a minimum of 50 rehearsals of two hours or more . . . [and he] staged the opera himself." Along with many lesser works, Toscanini introduced America to Mussorgsky's *Boris Godunov* and Gluck's *Armide*. And he led three world premieres: Giordano's *Madame Sans-Gêne*, Humperdinck's *Königskinder*, and Puccini's *La fanciulla del west* (with *Gianni Schicchi*, new in 1918, marking the first of only two occasions in its history when the Met introduced an opera with an important future).

La fanciulla generated special interest not merely because of its famous composer, who attended, but because of its subject matter. Adapting David Belasco's frontier melodrama *The Girl of the Golden West*, Puccini set his opera in California and populated it with singing miners ("Whiskey per tutti!"), a bandit, a sheriff, a Wells Fargo agent, a "red Indian" (with squaw), a traveling minstrel, and a Pony Express rider. The musical sources, according to the composer, included American folk songs, a cakewalk, and Native American tunes. For the premiere, on December 10, 1910, all ticket prices were doubled. Caruso, Emmy Destinn, and Pasquale Amato were the principal singers. Italian and American flags were draped over the boxes. There were fifty curtain calls, but the eventual response was lukewarm. Puccini was striving for an integrated musical drama less reliant on set pieces and big tunes than *La bohème*, *Madama Butterfly*, or *Tosca*.

And the American setting backfired. In contradictory pronouncements, Puccini claimed that he had not attempted "to assimilate essentially American themes," that he wanted to "reflect the spirit of the American people" and "the strong, vigorous nature of the West," that though he had never been West, he had "read so much about it" that he knew it "thoroughly." Eighteen years before, W. J. Henderson (as we have seen) had asked of the *New World*

Symphony, "Is it American?" and answered yes. Reviewing *La fanciulla*, he wrote, "Is it American? Not in the least. It is an Italian opera on an American story. All that is American in the opera is the work of Belasco. The thematic bases of the musical score belong to the plains of Lombardy, not the Wild West, to the slopes of the maritime Alps, not of the Sierras." Like Henderson, Krehbiel had Dvořák, of beloved memory, on his mind when he echoed, "The absence of anything in the score savoring of American music was a disappointment. . . . When Puccini reached London after the American premiere of 'The Girl' he answered the criticism of want of American color in the opera by saying that the slave songs of our South were barbarous noises."[31]

If Toscanini continued full throttle, with Hammerstein out of the way Gatti began to watch his pocketbook. The expanded chorus and orchestra shrank. Gatti and Toscanini disagreed over rehearsal allotments, and whether there could be a stage band for *A Masked Ball*. Meanwhile, Toscanini wound up in a torrid extracurricular affair with Farrar. These factors contributed to his startling decision to quit New York and return with his wife to Italy. He last appeared at the Met on April 14, 1915, and would never again conduct staged opera in the United States. In seven New York seasons he had led 479 performances.

Toscanini's departure ended eight years of the most frantic and distinguished New York operatic activity, beginning with Mahler and including Hammerstein's comet. The legacies are complex. Hammerstein was a formidable catalyst for modern German and French opera, for Mary Garden, for opera in English, for opera beyond New York. As part of the counterattack against the Manhattan Opera, Otto Kahn, the Met's chairman, had concocted an operatic syndicate with interlocking boards: the genesis of the short-lived Chicago-Philadelphia Opera, which included Garden, Campanini, and Hammerstein's props. The Boston Opera also shared trustees with the Met; it, too, as we have seen, specialized in Hammerstein's French specialties.

Gatti's regime and its illustrious casts would continue until 1935. But never again would the Met be challenged and spurred by a local competitor, let alone an Oscar Hammerstein. And never again would a New York opera house be shaken and transformed by a conductor of genius equipped with the plenipotentiary authority that Seidl assumed was his, and Mahler and Toscanini demanded.

■ ■ ■

Jenny Lind, the great American musical celebrity of the nineteenth century, was perceived and admired as a veritable angel; whether or not she was angelic, sublimity was what Americans wished to worship. She was the more revered for seeming transcendant, ineffable.

The twentieth century worshipped differently. New kinds of newspapers and magazines, then radio, then television fostered a prying intimacy. Private lives and other proofs of mere mortality, previously idealized or shunned, came to matter. The public was eager to succumb, yet exacted a level playing field. The celebrity was worshipped still, but as flesh and blood. The quotidian, even the prosaic reassuringly affirmed the common touch.

In the decade before World War I, three Metropolitan Opera artists were remarkable early embodiments of twentieth-century celebrity. Significantly, none was French—the Gallic ideal being refined, if not effete. None was German—Teutonic greatness was vague, mysterious, *innig*. Two were Italian, one was American, and all three expounded the earthy verismo of *Madama Butterfly* and *Tosca*, antitheses of Jenny's Bellini and Rossini. All three seemed as sexually robust as Jenny had seemed virginally pure. All three arose from humble beginnings. If they were not in every respect exemplars of democracy, its values and attitudes, perception could alter—could create—reality, could maximize popular appeal.

Coming first was Caruso, the biggest, sunniest, most resilient of all opera stars. In Seidl's day, the great tenor was Albert Niemann, a mega-presence of discomfiting intensity. At the turn of the century, Jean de Reszke was the tenor of choice, a paragon of *beau ideal* elegance. Caruso was happy and fat, ate pasta, and smoked smelly Egyptian cigarettes. One of twenty children, born to poverty in Naples and poorly schooled, he was unspoiled by fortune and wealth. His friend Victor Herbert commended his "warm glow of democratic modesty." His amiability took the form of onstage pranks and skilled crayon caricatures of his colleagues. Facing a cheering holiday audience, he might shout, "Mairy Kreesmus!" He regularly lost at poker and lunched publicly at the Knickerbocker Hotel.[32]

Not to be overlooked was his wholesome tenor voice, a ringing instrument well known to all Americans with wind-up Victrolas. On stage, it conveyed Nemorino's bumpkinly good-heartedness and Rodolfo's romantic ardor. In *Pagliacci*, Caruso's plainness and bulk inspired pity. As the high-caste Radames, Caruso was irredeemably, endearingly plebeian. Of his late-career triumph as Eleazar, in Halévy's *La Juive*, Krehbiel wrote that he succeeded "perhaps for the first time . . . in giving perfect verisimilitude to a tragic impersonation."[33] In wartime, he sang at Liberty Bond rallies and memorably recorded George M. Cohan's "Over There!" His fame at no time precluded a disarming familiarity: in costume, on the street, Caruso remained a recognizable human being.

The next biggest Met star was Caruso's sometime partner—in *Tosca*, in *Butterfly*, in *Carmen*, in *La bohème*—Geraldine Farrar, born to a Philadelphia Phillies outfielder. There had been other American vocal celebrities. Adelina Patti was American by accident. Lillian Nordica, the turn-of-the-century "Yankee diva," taught lessons in pluck and hard work. Olive Fremstad and Mary Garden were Callas types; dauntingly absorbed by Isolde and Kundry, Thaïs and Mélisande, they were incomprehensible *artistes*. Even had they not been European-born, these mesmerizing early-twentieth-century sopranos— the one demonic, the other ethereal—would not have seemed "American." Farrar, by comparison, was like Caruso a familiar type writ surpassingly large. With her sapphire blue eyes, gleaming teeth, and lithe physique, she was an exuberant, no-nonsense *femme fatale*, a combination tomboy and minx. As Carmen, she famously slapped Caruso (to his surprise and consternation). As Humperdinck's fairy-tale Goosegirl, in *Königskinder*, she appeared at the city gates trailed by a flock of geese (trained by herself). She was a silent movie star whose films included *The Woman God Forgot* and *The Hell-Cat*. She married (and divorced) a Hollywood actor and had a much-rumored affair with a German prince (her affair with Toscanini was not rumored). She sang Juliette in a nightgown and as Leoncavallo's Zazà lifted her skirt to spray perfume on her lace panties. Her frantic young followers adored her cheekiness and combative independence; W. J. Henderson christened them "Gerryflappers" and wearily explained that he so described "a girl about the flapper age who has created in her own half baked mind a goddess which she names Geraldine Farrar."[34] Ultimately, Farrar was as American as apple pie, as worldly as Fremstad and Garden were exotic.

The third incandescent Met star just before World War I was at first glance an unlikely candidate for maximum appeal: he was ferocious and aloof, and spoke little English. But compared to a Nikisch or Seidl, conductors whose sphinxlike composure could be read as arrogance, Arturo Toscanini was a reassuringly scrutable genius: temperamental because hypersensitive, tyrannical because high-principled. "You can't make out here what people do know," Henry James's Strether says of Europe in *The Ambassadors*; Americans "fall to denying what they cannot comprehend," wrote Alexis de Tocqueville. Americans comprehended Toscanini's masculinity, objectivity, and efficiency. He spurned interpretation in deference to the written score. He was, as a Chicago paper put it, "the man who knows his business." The *Musical Courier* said he conducted "not only artistically but scientifically." He was every bit the fundamentalist Theodore Thomas was, but with the libido of a matinee idol.[35]

Toscanini's chief advocate in the New York press was Max Smith: a new critical type, a pugilistic populist who considered Nikisch "pretentious" and "pompous." Eager for converts, Smith trumpeted Toscanini's singularity and denounced as "small fry" colleagues who questioned his preeminence. To Krehbiel, Toscanini's musical memory—he never used a score—was barely worth a yawn. To Smith, it warranted a soapbox oration:

> In New York, Toscanini has conducted twenty-two operas. The number of pages in the full scores of those works, as, thanks to Lionel Mapleson, librarian of the Metropolitan Opera Company, I have ascertained, is approximately ten thousand. Yet that does not nearly represent the prodigious amount of material that he has filed away in his mind ready for immediate use. In countries outside of the United States he has conducted by heart not only seventy other operas, thus bringing the number of operatic scores he has committed to memory to the stupendous figure of ninety-two, but has also produced various oratorios, symphonies, and tone-poems.

Toscanini was equally appropriated by Smith as one of us:

> "When Toscanini leaves his house, he knows exactly where he is going," one of his admirers remarked in discussing the conductor's way, "and he proceeds in that direction as eagerly as a hound on a trail. That is something you rarely find among musicians, most of whom wander about with their heads in the clouds."

> Toscanini does not conform to the traditional type of absent-minded musician. Neatness, order, punctiliousness, nicety, are characteristic of the man as well as the artist.

> Toscanini approaches his task objectively rather than subjectively and that explains why he succeeds so well with the music of various schools and epochs.[36]

If less breathlessly, other writers fastened on Toscanini's exciting irritability, his quaint superstitiousness, his meteoric rise from the cello section of a touring Italian opera troupe. Leo Slezak, an important Metropolitan Opera tenor from 1909 to 1913, lamented the American penchant for "press work" and "publicity," machinations devised by hired hands to "keep one's name before the public." But Toscanini, whose threats not to conduct excited return threats not to sing or play, needed no publicist. Taking it all in from a height, Krehbiel read the handwriting on the wall and groaned:

During the period of which I am writing [1908–18], even in journals of
dignity and scholarly repute the gossip of the foyer and the dressing
rooms of the chorus and ballet stood in higher esteem with the news
editors than the comments of conscientious critics. . . . If in this [the
newspapers] reflect the taste of their readers, it is a taste which they have
instilled and cultivated, for it did not exist before the days of photo-
engraving, illustrated supplements and press agents. . . . The phenomenon, inasmuch as it marked the operatic history of the decade of which
I am writing more emphatically than any period within a generation, is
deserving of study.[37]

The groans grew louder in the years preceding Krehbiel's death in 1923. Ever
obeisant to nineteenth-century canons of rectitude, he winced at twentieth-
century glamour, at the circus hoopla surrounding Stokowski and Toscanini,
at the aesthetic blasphemies of Mahler and Strauss. He was spared the ultimate
ascent of music's furthest rising star. More than Lind or Caruso, more than any
singer ever could, Toscanini would symbolize classical music—all of it, uniting
the polarities of Thomas's probity and Seidl's glamour. As no conductor
before or since, he would himself become sacred, even eclipsing the heavenly
deities Beethoven and Wagner, both of whose exalted New World legacies he
would uniquely absorb and promote.

CHAPTER 8

Antonín Dvořák
and Charles Ives
in Search of America

■

William Henry Fry and Louis Moreau Gottschalk ■
Edward MacDowell's arrested development ■ *Dvořák and* Hiawatha ■
Charles Ives and Transcendentalism

"It's for the 'Byronism'—the unrest and unhealthiness of his music—that we generally glorify Beethoven," reflected George Templeton Strong in 1861. "That's his special characteristic in estimate. We value him not for the repose of his strength, nor for the unequaled energy of his healthy action, but for his weird, uncanny intensities and his paroxysms of despairing gloom."[1] The most important American musical diarist of his day, Strong is one signpost of New York opinion—and rings yet another change on the Boston/New York polarization of taste. A more different take on Beethoven than John Sullivan Dwight's cannot be imagined.

Dwight, of course, was a professional critic, not a dilettante diarist. If we seek his opposite number in New York, we enter the orbit of a writer from another planet, the first music critic for a major American daily newspaper. While Dwight was revering the ennobling Beethoven and planning rites of worship for the Harvard Musical Association, William Henry Fry's columns in Horace Greeley's influential *New York Tribune*, beginning in 1852 (the same year Dwight founded his *Journal*) and ending with his early death in 1864, fulminated over the neglect of contemporary and American composers. Two merely typical outbursts:

It is the chief business of Philharmonic Societies to play living pieces or compositions by men alive; by that means Art is advanced. If they are not played Art dies; for Art cannot be sustained by studying the works of the dead almost exclusively. The age must be heroic to itself or it deserves to be covered by ignominy and stricken from human annals.

There is no taste for, or appreciation of true Art in this country. The public, as a public know nothing about Art. . . . It is time we had a Declaration of Independence in Art, and laid the foundation of an American School of Painting, Sculpture, and Music. . . . The American composer should not allow the name of Beethoven, or Handel or Mozart to prove an eternal bugbear to him, nor should he pay them reverence; he should only reverence his Art, and strike out manfully and independently into untrodden realms.

Assessing *Fidelio* for the *Philadelphia National Gazette* in 1839, Fry no less than Strong repudiated in advance the genteel Beethoven of postbellum Boston: "The cast of Beethoven's mind was essentially sentimental and sombre, and his playfulness, with rare exception, is allied to eccentric wildness, and a quality kindred in its way with its expression of sadness and misanthropy." This is plausible criticism. Just as often, Fry attacked with scattershot: that the *Magic Flute* Overture was "for the head, not the heart," that Wagner ignored "most of the established laws of musical beauty . . . and set up in their place sheer ugliness and melodies so-called which even the most acute and attentive ear finds nearly impossible to apprehend or retain."[2]

What essentially separates Fry from Dwight—what accounts for his cocky refusal to mystify greatness, for his ferocious advocacy of American works—is that Fry was himself (as he never tired of stressing) a composer of consequence, the first native-born American to write for large orchestra and the first to write a grand opera. In fact, he wrote three of them, of which the second, *Leonora*, was produced in Philadelphia (where it received twenty-two performances) and New York, and the third, *Notre Dame de Paris*, was conducted by Theodore Thomas. Thomas also led Fry's symphonies. Fry the composer did not lack popularity and acclaim. But his taste of success, and travels abroad, heightened his infuriated awareness that the United States lacked the means to school, present, and promote its own creative musical talent. His crowning frustration was that the New York Philharmonic chose to ignore him. The resulting feud was famously brought to a boil by the *Santa Claus* Symphony, a thirty-minute, one-movement fairy tale Fry called "the longest instrumental composition ever written on a single subject, with unbroken continuity."

And so, one supposes, it was. The scenario, published in full in the *Tribune*, includes, "A Snow Storm and Episode of a perishing Traveler," "Santa Claus comes in his sleigh and distributes Christmas Gifts," "Sunrise," and "Joy of Children on discovering their toys." Louis Jullien introduced *Santa Claus* on December 24, 1853. The critical reception was mixed. "The effects produced by the violins, con sordini, and throughout the snow-storm scene are excellent, though perhaps not quite legitimate," wrote Charles Burkhardt in the *Albion*. "With all due deference, we deny their entire originality." Fry testily rebutted such mild complaints in the *Tribune*, beginning, "We have seen it stated that the composer of 'Santa Claus' intended it for an occasional piece—a sketch, etc. This is not so. He intended it—in regard to instrumentation—as the means of exposing the highest qualities in execution and expression of the greatest players in the world."

Days later, a brief *Santa Claus* review by Richard Storrs Willis in the *Musical World and Times* incited a sustained exchange in which the New York Philharmonic also became embroiled. The central topic, framed by Fry, was, "How are Americans to win their way in composition unless their compositions are played?" The music historian Vera Brodsky Lawrence has commented that though Fry's broadsides have been hailed as "the archetypal Declaration of Rights for American Music and Musicians," they rather constituted "an uninhibited display of self-glorification intermingled with an outpouring of personal grievances, frustrations, wounded vanity, boastfulness, bitterness, abusiveness, defensiveness, offensiveness, pretentiousness, idiosyncratic pronouncements, and an apparently unappeasable hunger for adulation." But the Willis-Fry debate retains interest.

"I make common cause with Americans, born or naturalized, who are engaged in the world's Art struggle and against degrading deference to European dictation," Fry trumpeted. He called himself "the apostle of a new lyrical faith, if anything, and not an almsman, receiving thankfully the broken meats from the tables of classic composers and rehashing them, instead of offering fresh, substantial viands." Willis stuck to his guns, retorting that *Santa Claus* was no "symphony" but an unconstrained "fantasia." "My dear Fry," he wrote, "I admire your genius, but it is genius astray. . . . You are a splendid frigate at sea without a helm." And, poking Fry's wounds, Willis defended the New York Philharmonic: "You must come up to their high standard of Art if you, or anyone else, expect to be heard. The Temple of Art is an universal temple, and that you are an American is no reason that you should have free admission there." Another notable New York composer, George Bristow, now joined the fracas in the pages of the *Musical World and Times*, declaring that the Philharmonic was dedicated to a "systematized effort for the extinction of American music." He thereupon publicly resigned from the Philharmonic

Society, of which he happened to be a member. The Philharmonic directors issued a statement of their own, defending their obligations to Art. And they accepted Bristow's resignation. (He was later reinstated.)[3]

What does Fry's music sound like? *Leonora* is a bel canto Italian opera; the New York performance was even given in Italian translation. But neither does Fry disdain German and French influences. In *Santa Claus*, which Jullien proceeded to perform more than forty times in the United States,[4] the amalgamation is *sui generis.* It is also deliciously cinematic. A baby falls asleep to the Lord's Prayer, chanted syllabically by high strings. A soprano saxophone—newly invented—sings "Rock-a-Bye Baby." The Perishing Traveller, accompanied by swirling chromatic storm-scales, is a lachrymose star-turn for Jullien's famous double bass soloist, Giovanni Bottesini. Santa Claus is a high bassoon, chortling a Papageno ditty punctuated by sleigh bells. In the concert overture *Macbeth* (1864), exemplifying Fry's serious side, a recurrent theme in trombones and tuba precisely insinuates "Double, double toil and trouble/Fire burn and cauldron bubble." Elsewhere, the orchestra mimics "All hail Macbeth!" and—at the close—"Long live King Malcolm!" The catchy tunes and narrative fire, however innocent, are contagious.

Judged by the Philharmonic's "high standard of Art," *Santa Claus* is idiotically frivolous. *Macbeth* suffers by comparison with Verdi, an obvious model. But there are other contexts for judgment. As Burkhardt wrote of *Santa Claus* in the *Albion*, this music "demands our attention for more reasons than one. It is American; it is home-made and therefore entitled to fair hearing and to lenient judgment." What is more, Fry was writing for prebellum New York, for a polyglot music crowd that was itching to have fun. His music's outrageous pretentions and incidental charms perfectly suited Jullien's Monster Concerts for the Masses. In fact, he is more profitably contextualized alongside his American brethren than in the shadow of Bellini, Verdi, or Beethoven. That is, he is one of four important American composers for orchestra from 150 years ago, the others being Anthony Philip Heinrich, Bristow, and Louis Moreau Gottschalk.

Heinrich, the "Beethoven from Kentucky," is a Germanic iconoclast, born in Bohemia in 1781 and self-taught. He first visited the United States in 1805 and later wound up settling in Philadelphia, then Pittsburgh (to which he walked, a distance of three hundred miles), then Kentucky, where he lived in a log cabin before relocating (as a permanent guest) on a Louisville estate. In 1820 his *The Dawning of Music in Kentucky; or, The Pleasures of Harmony in the Solitude of Nature* was published; it totaled forty-six compositions and 269 pages. His other Kentucky opuses include *The Yankee Doodleiad*, a "National Divertimento" for piano and strings, and *A Chromatic Ramble of the Peregrine*

Harmonist, in which a solo pianist must also sing while rambling "among the flats and sharps," losing himself "in knots of Chords." Heinrich next moved to Boston and finally, in 1837, to New York, where he died twenty-four years later. In the latter city, alongside Fry, he was a personage: teacher, violinist, conductor, feuding critic, enterprising self-presenter and self-promoter. His Grand Musical Festival of 1842 assembled a local orchestra of unprecedented size to perform the *Grand Overture to the Pilgrim Fathers* and six other Heinrich creations alongside Haydn, Beethoven, and Rossini. A second such concert in 1846, "upon a scale of grandeur seldom equaled in this or any other country," consisted of ten works by Heinrich only. He shared his Grand Valedictory Concert of 1853 with Mozart and Weber. These events were well attended and received, but it may be doubted whether the orchestras thus assembled, including many New York Philharmonic musicians, were adequately prepared. Heinrich's orchestral scores employ up to forty-four individual parts, often moving at exceptional speeds. Eschewing development and formalized structure, they eagerly scramble and recycle seeming scraps of Haydn and Beethoven. They sometimes cite "Hail Columbia" and other national airs. Their means of organization and continuity signify bold invention or bold incompetence. This boldness is at all times impressive. Time has not tamed Father Heinrich.

Though his subject matter was frequently American, Bristow is the competent traditionalist among this quartet of early Americans. A member of the Philharmonic's first violins until 1879, he also led the violins for Jullien's orchestra and for Jenny Lind. His Symphony in F-sharp minor, performed by the Philharmonic in 1859, sounds like Mendelssohn or Schumann. His opera *Rip Van Winkle* ran for four weeks at Niblo's Garden in 1855. With its simple tunes, spoken dialogue, and a romantic subplot featuring Rip's daughter, it is a cheerful diversion steering clear of Fry's grander productions. The *Musical World* exclaimed, "Sebastopol has fallen, and a new American opera has succeeded in New York!"

Gottschalk is of course the most famous and accomplished of the midcentury Americans and the most audibly a product of the New World. Raised on saucy Caribbean musical delicacies, he flouts Europe not primitively and aggressively, like Fry or Heinrich, but with sublime insouciance and practiced finesse. This is because he was in part a cultivated European. He was born in 1829 in New Orleans, a city semi-French, semi-Spanish, semi-American, with (as we have seen) a thriving operatic culture. His father was an English businessman of Jewish extraction, educated in Germany. His mother was a white Creole of upper-class French descent. From the age of thirteen he studied in Paris, where he became a successful pianist/composer whose admirers

included Berlioz and Hugo. His French and Spanish conquests, unprecedented for an American instrumentalist, were avidly followed in New York.
He arrived in that city in 1853. This was three years after Jenny Lind. The
opera craze was in high gear, and with it an appetite for solo pianists and
violinists.

Gottschalk's American acclaim was swift. He charmed sophisticates with
his courtly manner, epicurean palate, and spicy stories. Legions of female
admirers, smitten by his dreamy eyes and *beau ideal* profile, would storm the
stage and clutch for his white gloves. William Henry Fry declared him (in one
and the same review) "a superlatively great artist," a "splendid artistic model of
originality, enthusiasm, devotion, triumph," and "one of the medals placed in
the corner stone" of "the lyrical history of the country." Three seasons later,
he gave eighty concerts in New York alone. He then took off for Havana and
points south. He settled briefly in Puerto Rico, and Martinique, and
Guadalupe, where he retreated to the upper slopes of a volcano. Recalling
these "years foolishly spent, thrown to the wind, as if life were infinite, and
youth eternal," he wrote in his memoirs of "voluptuous languor," of "indo-
lently permitting myself to be carried away by chance, giving a concert wherever I found a piano." His escape from civilization ended with a triumphant
return to New York in 1862.[5]

Around this time, Gottschalk observed:

I am daily astonished at the rapidity with which the taste for music is
developed and is developing in the United States. At the time of my first
return from Europe I was constantly deploring the want of public interest for pieces purely sentimental [i.e., possessing inherent "feeling"]; the
public listened with indifference; in order to interest it, it became necessary to astound it; grand movements, tours de force, and noise had alone
the privilege in piano music, not of pleasing, but of making it patient
with it. . . . From whatever cause the American taste is becoming purer.[6]

But he also met, in St. Louis, "an old German musician with uncombed
hair, bushy beard, in constitution like a bear, in disposition the amenity of a
boar at bay to a pack of hounds. I know this type; it is found everywhere." He
subsequently remarked, "All the musicians in the United States are German."
Germans and purifiers made common cause, and Gottschalk—a creature of
the tropics, an intimate of music black and brown, of black- and brown-
skinned women—was the hedonist enemy. In New York, the Wagnerite critic
Theodor Hagen facetiously counseled that with his "natural capacity for
technics" Gottschalk might, pending a few years' diligent study of Bach and

Clementi, master some of the simpler classics, and that there also existed certain minor compositions by Chopin and Weber "which, we think, Mr. Gottschalk would be able to perform satisfactorily." But Gottschalk's chief American nemesis was (needless to say) Boston's John Sullivan Dwight, who charged the red cape, snorting that this "young Creole," succumbing to popular music and popular taste, neither composed like the masters or performed their masterworks. Gottschalk, in response, boycotted Boston for nearly a decade (after which he decided he liked its polish, intellect, and vanity). Though he had performed the *Pathétique* and played other Beethoven sonatas in private, he had assumed that his natural vocation was to play music that was actually his. In his memoirs, he called *Dwight's Journal* "the reservoir of every little bilious envy, of every irritating impertinence, of all sickly spleen which . . . gives the writer the small comfort of injuring all those who give umbrage to their mediocrity." He also wrote, "Those whose taste is not eclectic have no more right to govern criticism than a man with a jaundice or green spectacles to decide upon the coloring of a picture." According to New York's Willis, who enjoyed Gottschalk's Havana cigars, Gottschalk once offered in rejoinder an impromptu speech:

> Understand then that I am simply Gottschalk, and nobody else. . . . I could not be other, if I would—and I certainly would not be, if I could. I compose just to suit myself, and if my way please you, I am delighted—if not, I cannot help it.
>
> The Germans and their music I don't much like—with exceptions, of course. A sonata of Mozart sounds thinnish to me, of only Homeopathic potency, and very "mildly drawn." Those little bits of melodies in one hand and little bits of accompaniment in the other—don't ask me to like them—I cannot.[7]

Gottschalk was brought down not by Boston moralists but by the California variety: an outing with a student from the Oakland Female Seminary was inflated into a national scandal; fearing vigilantes, Gottschalk escaped to South America. He died, apparently of a ruptured appendix, in 1869 at age forty in a suburb of Rio de Janeiro. He was buried in Brooklyn's Greenwood Cemetery.

According to Willis, Gottschalk said, "The end and aim of art is to please, not to instruct or indoctrinate." Gottschalk's piano works—he wrote more than one hundred, all in short forms—still please, still disdain to edify. They profitably belong to an era when distinctions between art and entertainment remained blurred. Worldly yet unself-conscious, they combine a Chopinesque command of the pearly Romantic keyboard with easy access to the pungent vernacular strains he encountered on New Orleans streets, in South American dance halls and North American music halls. *Bamboula*, composed when Gottschalk was all of sixteen, was a Parisian sensation: the Conservatoire even selected it as a competitive trial piece. The earthy, striding vigor of this Creole *danse des négres* is firsthand, more native than colonialist; its exoticism transcends kitsch. What other American has produced a virtuoso etude as original and enduring as *The Banjo* (1855), whose rapid-fire strumming intimates Stephen Foster's "Camptown Races" in a whirlwind of pulsating, strobe-lit color? In the *Souvenir de Porto Rico* (1855), a "peasant march," the driving syncopations and dizzy filigree prophecy ragtime and jazz. Gottschalk is here a pioneering Pan-American. He was also, notwithstanding his southern origin, a committed Abolitionist and Civil War composer; *Union* (1862) is a stirring patriotic potboiler whose ingredients include "The Star-Spangled Banner," "Hail Columbia," and "Yankee Doodle." (In the opinion of his biographer S. Frederick Starr, Gottschalk consciously embraced democracy in government and culture more than any previous American musician.) The two-movement "Romantic symphony" *Night in the Tropics* (1859), composed for a monster orchestra including the latest valved brass, and Afro-Cuban drums and maracas, testifies to Gottschalk's Gilmore-like flair for gargantuan spectacle, as well as a nascent gift for the larger forms. A languorous sunset, coming first, is sublimely expansive. The climactic, roof-raising *fiesta criolla* is cunningly paced and varied; there is even a comically incongruous fugal episode. This is top-drawer American repertoire, virtually unplayed by American orchestras.

With Gottschalk's death, there was no one effectively to champion his music or to build on his compositional achievement. Due to Dwight, to Theodore Thomas and the touring Anton Rubinstein, to the eradication of monster concerts and the sacralization of Beethoven, the cultural climate had fundamentally changed. Not until the mid-twentieth century would Gottschalk enjoy an overdue revival. Not until 1997 was something like the original score of *Night in the Tropics* reconstructed, by Gunther Schuller. The more ambiguous accomplishments of Gottschalk's American contemporaries have been more modestly revisited. The first (inadequate) recording of Heinrich's daunting orchestral music appeared in 1978, the first sampling of Fry's orchestral output in 2001. Bristow's *Rip Van Winkle* was produced in 1974 after a hundred years' slumber.

Such discontinuities characterize the story of classical music in the United States generally—the sustained lineage of composers French, German, Italian, or Russian is nowhere to be found. And so it was that the composers of the late Gilded Age charted an earnest new beginning. In Boston, the beginners, keying on Handel and Beethoven, Mendelssohn and Schumann, were Paine,

Parker, Chadwick, Foote, and Beach. In New York, rampant Wagnerism dictated a less tempered Romantic style.

■ ■ ■

As of 1900, the most eminent American concert composer was Edward Mac-Dowell. When MacDowell was offered a position at Columbia University in 1896, the nominating committee named him "the greatest musical genius America has produced." Four years later, Rupert Hughes, in *Famous American Composers*, called the MacDowell piano sonatas "far the best since Beethoven." Lawrence Gilman, later chief music critic of the *New York Herald-Tribune*, in 1908 considered MacDowell's music "not unworthy of the golden ages of the world."[8]

MacDowell began his musical studies in New York, where he was born in 1860. At the age of fifteen he was taken to Europe. He eventually settled in Germany, to work with distinguished teachers, to be encouraged by Liszt, and to make his reputation. As with Gottschalk, his fame preceded him upon his return to the United States—to Boston, in 1888. He attracted superior pupils. His music was successfully performed by the Boston Symphony under Gericke, Nikisch, and Paur. But MacDowell did not fit in. He moved to New York in 1896, to become Columbia's first professor of music. He was feted by Anton Seidl, who considered him a greater composer than Brahms (for whom Seidl had poor regard). Krehbiel called his Second Piano Concerto, which Mac-Dowell performed in New York under Thomas and Seidl both, the best work of its kind "produced by either a native or an adopted citizen of America."[*][9] But MacDowell clashed with Columbia President Nicholas Murray Butler and resigned in 1904. After that his mental health deteriorated; he died four years later, having regressed to a condition resembling childhood.

What went wrong for MacDowell in the United States? In Boston, he was perceived as moody and withdrawn. His correspondence with his close friend George Templeton Strong—son of the famous New York diarist, and a gifted expatriate composer—reveals an outsider's perspective on the close-knit

---

* Such was his excitement in anticipation of an American canon that, responding to the American premiere of Tchaikovsky's Fifth Symphony on the same March 5, 1889, Theodore Thomas program, Krehbiel wrote, "It is not to depreciate the symphony, but only because there was a patriotic as well as artistic interest in the composition of Mr. MacDowell, that I confess to having derived keener pleasure from the work of the young American than from the experienced and famous Russian. Tchaikowski I have often had an opportunity of praising; Mr. MacDowell, a New Yorker, has only recently entered the field." See Henry Krehbiel, *Review of the New York Musical Season, 1888–1889* (New York, Novello, Ewer and Co., 1889), pp. 97–98.

Boston scene. Neither MacDowell nor Strong cared for the Boston composers or trusted them, Foote especially. They strategized endlessly over how MacDowell should handle Foote and Chadwick. Perform them? Praise them? Ignore them? MacDowell urged Strong to join him in Boston. Strong replied that he would have "to mix to a certain extent with 'society' . . . and did I meet these men at such houses, I simply should eventually cease going: verdict: crank: result social failure, perhaps leading to the reverse of any vestiges of possible popularity as man and teacher. Epilogue, financial vacuity." But Mac-Dowell prevailed, and Strong arrived. They were now observed to reinforce one another's unsociability. Chadwick's memoirs subsequently revealed his eager anticipation of "the companionship of these two men, as colleagues and sympathetic additions to our circle. . . . In this I was disappointed." Of MacDowell he wrote:

> With me, MacD was very frank & companionable for a time. He and Mrs. often came to our house, and we had many long walks, rides, and talks together. Of others he was suspicious and shy. It was difficult to get him to commit himself on any subject except publishers and royalties. . . . He disliked some of our friends, especially Arthur Whiting, who was a bit too witty for him. . . .
>
> He would not go out among people if he could help it and was very ill at ease when he did so.[10]

MacDowell and Strong mistrusted the chumminess of the Boston boys. There was "talk of forming a 'composer's club'," MacDowell complained in March 1890,

> —and the abuse I heard indulged in about almost everybody was immense—I got kind of mad at all that backbiting and at last when Chadwick said the object of the proposed club ought to be the "exchange of ideas" I saw the chance I had been waiting for and got up and I fear rather drily said "I don't think I care to swap" and cleared out. . . . I know I shouldn't write all this for it is gossip of the <u>wretchedest</u> sort—but still <u>those things do make me mad.</u>

Strong replied, "Your answer . . . to Chadwick and Foote was simply <u>fine</u>. A composers club, under the circumstances, is an impossibility. . . . I only wish they would write better music than they do: if they did, there would be less talk."[11] Strong lasted only months in Boston.

Compared to Chadwick and Foote, MacDowell and Strong were devotees of Romantic solitude. Their aversion to a composers' club fits—in fact, memorably embellishes—Martin Green's picture of "the problem of Boston." But MacDowell's problem, whatever it was, intensified in New York. To Chadwick, MacDowell seemed the victim of descending "shadows" he was powerless to resist.[12] That these shadows are scarcely apparent in MacDowell's music may be a clue to his physical and creative demise.

If the Second Piano Concerto (1889) was MacDowell's signature vehicle as a virtuoso composer/pianist, what kind of composer was he? The concerto begins with an exceptionally beautiful reverie: a dream. The soloist enters with stentorian D minor bravado, a knight astride his snorting steed. He jousts mightily with his enemies. It is all very exciting, but incompletely real; at the movement's close, the dream reverie returns—in the piano. Movement two is a dizzy scherzo, bubbling with high spirits. Only an ephemeral cloud, wafting through the coda, acknowledges what has gone before. The finale, heralded by trumpets, deftly recycles material from the earlier movements (as Liszt might have), but (to a degree unthinkable in Liszt) it is merely cheerful, not heroic.

In short, this is a young man's concerto; it plays at brooding and jousting, then discards its armor. But MacDowell, at age twenty-nine, was no longer a young man. In his once-popular *Woodland Sketches* (including *To a Wild Rose*), *Fireside Tales*, and *New England Idylls*, he continued to explore a Romantic toy chest of elves and fragrant meadows, Indians and log cabins. In 1903, with his creative years behind him, he revealingly confided that the Dirge, from his *Indian* Suite, was what pleased him most "of all my music."[13] An American variant on Siegfried's Funeral Music, from *Götterdämmerung*, it abandons melodrama and nostalgia to seek profundity, and tenuously rises toward the "world-sorrow" MacDowell here aspired to express.

These limitations are set in sharp relief by a contemporaneous American who more fully inhabits the Wagner/Liszt mode, who commands something like their heights and depths of erotic/demonic abandon and mystical/religious ecstasy: MacDowell's friend Templeton Strong. Strong's fifty-minute *Sintram* Symphony (1888), inspired by Dürer's phantasmagoric *Knight, Death and the Devil*, steaming with *Tristan* and *Parsifal* and Bruckner, is formidably and precariously epochal; its breadth of stride cannot be found among MacDowell and his other Boston and New York colleagues. Seidl conducted *Sintram* in Brooklyn and New York in 1892 and 1893. W. J. Henderson, in the *Times*, (correctly) found the work too long, but believed that it placed Strong "in the front rank of the younger living composers." "His themes are his own; his treatment of them is strongly individual; his instrumental colors are bold and characteristic. He is a complete master of the subtleties of modern harmony, and his chromatic modulations move with perfect fluency...."

There is intense force and masterful directness in his style." Krehbiel, in the *Tribune*, wrote of the huge first movement that "it might fairly be questioned whether it has ever been equaled by an American symphonist in strength and fitness of idea and mastery of treatment."[14] In Switzerland, where Strong resettled, the symphony was conducted by Ernest Ansermet in 1912 and 1932. Here is yet another American overdue for revival and exploration.

As for Edward MacDowell, a victim of overexposure, it is impossible to dissent from the verdict of Wilfrid Mellers, in his *Music in a New Found Land*, that MacDowell represents "a boy's view of the American past, looked back to from a premature middle age." Mellers identifies as "probably his finest achievement" the first three of the *Sea Pieces*, of which number three—*A.D. MDCXX*, an evocation of the Mayflower—equates the Puritans with "American heroism." The striding, hymnic grandeur of this piano morsel, less than two minutes long, achieves what is rare in MacDowell: a distinctive New World voice more organic than wigwams or Uncle Remus. MacDowell's own view of musical nationalism was that of a cosmopolitan German: he admitted local color, be it American, "Nordic," or "Keltic," but disavowed conscious efforts to create an American style. "Nationalism must be based on the spirit of the people, not upon the clothes they wear. . . . Out of our idealism, our music will grow." MacDowell also wrote:

> Purely national music has no place in art. What Negro melodies have to do with Americanism still remains a mystery to me. Why cover a beautiful thought with the badge of slavery rather than with the stern but at least manly and free rudeness of the North American Indian? . . . Masquerading in the so-called nationalism of Negro clothes cut in Bohemia will not help us. What we must arrive at is the youthful optimistic vitality and the undaunted tenacity of spirit that characterizes the American Man.[15]

The Bohemian clothes were those of a composer even more famous than MacDowell: Antonín Dvořák, whose American presence from 1892 to 1895 was a lightning rod for debate on the future, and future sources, of American music—a debate in which MacDowell, Chadwick, and Beach all became embroiled.

■ ■ ■

More than Isabella Stewart Gardner in Boston, more than Rose Fay Thomas in Chicago, more than Laura Langford in Brooklyn, more than Mrs. William Howard Taft in Cincinnati, Jeannette Thurber was a visionary activist who helped to steer the course of American music. Her American Opera Company of 1885 was (as we have seen) a noble failure based on a farsighted premise: that only if opera in English were mightily validated and disseminated would an American operatic repertoire of consequence materialize. Her National Conservatory of Music, founded the same year (the projects were linked), was longer-lived. Its premise was that only if gifted young Americans studied in the United States could an American school of composition be properly nurtured.

Thurber had herself studied abroad: at the Paris Conservatory. Others of her generation went to Leipzig or Berlin or Vienna. Concurrently with Chadwick at the New England Conservatory, she created an American music school of unprecedented quality and prestige. Her distinguished faculty included Seidl, Rafael Joseffy, and Victor Herbert—New York's premier conductor, pianist, and cellist. Her curriculum was notably progressive for requiring solfeggio, for offering music history to supplement the usual courses of instruction in performance and composition, and for making available full scholarships to needy students, including students of color. In fact, African-Americans were prominent at every level of study. If this partly signified a philanthropic urge, it was in equal part a practical strategy. As early as 1861, the diary of George Templeton Strong—the father of the composer—includes this prophetic entry: "I wonder that none of our symphony writers has taken up the Nigger-melody. 'Oh Susanna, don't you cry for me'—'Carry me back to old Virginny'—'Rose Rosa Lee'—'Dixie's Land,' etc., etc., have a very special character, an *aroma* as yet unknown in 'classical' music. A composer of respectable ability could make himself a reputation by embodying it in symphony or overture."[16] Like many New Yorkers, Thurber sensed in plantation song the makings of an American music to come.

The arrival of Dvořák in September 1892 as director of the National Conservatory came at a propitious moment. Possibly at no other time did American performers, critics, and audiences so concertedly attend to new works by American composers. "All-American" concerts were a ubiquitous phenomenon, supported by Anton Seidl, Walter Damrosch, Frank Van der Stucken, and Henry Krehbiel, among many others. But the movement was running out of steam. Krehbiel, as of 1890, wrote, "The American composer . . . after long suffering neglect, now seems in imminent danger of being coddled to death." Losing patience with the organic evolution of a distinctive American style, he now began to favor the conscious absorption of indigenous sources: a more overt nationalism. Dvořák in New York, a coup Thurber was not shy to publicize, conferred an indispensable imprimatur on America's fledgling nationalist school. He had hardly set foot in Manhattan before learning, and not only from Thurber, that (as he wrote to friends in Prague) "the Americans expect great things of me and the main thing is, so they say, to show them to the promised land and kingdom of a new and independent art, in short, to create a national music. If the small Czech nation can have such musicians, they say, why could not they, too, when their country and people is so immense." And Dvořák—overwhelmed by new excitement and attention, by the scale and pace of American life, by the caliber of American orchestras—more than took the bait. "It is certainly both a great and a splendid task for me and I hope that with God's help I shall accomplish it. There is more than enough material here and plenty of talent."[17]

By talent, Dvořák meant American composers and instrumentalists, including his own pupils, some of whom he found "very promising." By material, he meant American sights and sounds, American roots: "another spirit, other thoughts, another coloring . . . something Indian." There were no indigenous people in Bohemia; like other Europeans, Dvořák was fascinated by the Native American (and had already read Longfellow's *The Song of Hiawatha* in Czech). And there were no blacks in Hapsburg lands; in New York, he had for the first time heard such "negro melodies" as "Swing Low, Sweet Chariot," in which he detected, as he famously told the *New York Herald* in May 1893, the necessary foundation for "the future music of this country":

> These beautiful and varied themes are the product of the soil. They are American. . . .
>
> In the negro melodies of America I discover all that is needed for a great and noble school of music. They are pathetic, tender, passionate, melancholy, solemn, religious, bold, merry, gay or what you will. It is music that suits itself to any mood or any purpose. There is nothing in the whole range of composition that cannot be supplied with themes from this source.

Days later, in a letter to the *Herald*, Dvořák added, "It is to the poor that I turn for musical greatness. The poor work hard; they study seriously. . . . If in my own career I have achieved a measure of success and reward it is to some extent due to the fact I was the son of poor parents and was reared in an atmosphere of struggle and endeavour."[18]

And so it was that Dvořák stumbled upon two of the defining American sagas: the Indian Wars and the slave trade; and that he would, however fortuitously, challenge and illuminate American notions of race and identity. It bears stressing that even Gilded Age Americans of learning and sophistication, even onetime Abolitionists and fervent Unionists, were prone to subscribe to theories of racial hierarchy, and—in preoccupation with "progress" and "civilization"—to assume the innate inferiority of red- and black-skinned humans.

Louis Agassiz—Boston's most famous scientist, founder in 1854 of Harvard's Museum of Comparative Zoology, ever popular clubman, bosom friend of James Russell Lowell, father-in-law of Henry Higginson—deplored slavery and supported the Union cause. More influentially, he was the prophet of "polygenism": he taught that blacks and whites had evolved at different rates and belonged to different species; that racial differences were deeply ingrained; that blacks were irredeemably inferior; that racial interbreeding would be biologically catastrophic; that all of this, defying Darwin, was "determined by the will of the creator." After 1860, Agassiz had few scientific allies in Cambridge. But his views fed Social Darwinism and anti-immigrant fear in the culture at large. One should not be amazed that Charles Eliot Norton (who despised slavery) did not believe in racial equality, or that Barrett Wendell, a Harvard English professor of influence and reputation, would not sit at table with blacks, even with Booker T. Washington (whom he otherwise respected).[19]

We have seen that the 1893 World's Columbian Exposition in Chicago engaged Theodore Thomas and his orchestra to document a history of musical progress. Thomas's stated intention was to illustrate improvement "in all grades and departments from the lowest to the highest." Thomas, in the fair's concert halls, staked out the supreme forms. The bottom rungs were on view along the Midway, just outside the halcyon White City. Frederic Ward Putnam, of Harvard's Peabody Museum of American Archaeology and Ethnology and a former Agassiz student, and Sol Bloom, a showman, here presented, amid an ostrich farm, an animal show, and other such attractions, living exhibits of Native Americans and other such peoples. In the Algerian Theater, a dancer was accompanied by an oud and a frame drum. In the Egyptian village a belly dancer, made notorious as "Little Egypt," was joined by a traditional takht. In the Dahomeyan exhibit, at the far end of the Midway, scantily clad Africans with swords and spears danced to drums and bells, a presentation described in a souvenir album as "cannibals," including blood-thirsty "female Amazons," illustrating the "extreme of barbarity." Americans, commented the *Chicago Tribune*, were thus afforded "an unequaled opportunity to compare themselves scientifically with others . . . tracing humanity in its highest phases down almost to its animalistic origins." This context of understanding informed Philip Hale's discomfort with Dvořák's *From the New World* later the same year. John Sullivan Dwight had earlier called African-

Americans "simple children," "inferior to the white race in reason and intellect." Hale (as we have seen) believed that the plantation songs Dvořák espoused were as much white as black, and that they contaminated high art in any event. He rejected out of hand that blacks or Indians or Creoles or cowboys could be construed as emblematic "Americans."[20]

This was one New World of music and ideas into which Dvořák plunged in 1892, except that his formative exposure occurred not in Boston or Chicago but in a Manhattan neighborhood flooded with Germans, Irish, Slavs, and Russian Jews. His home at 327 East Seventeenth Street was close to the Academy of Music, Steinway Hall, and, at Seventeenth and Irving Place, the National Conservatory; to the Lower East Side, festering with tenements, anarchists, and bohemians; to the southern tip of the theater district, featuring vaudeville from noon to midnight alongside higher fare; to a plethora of eating and drinking establishments, of which his favorite (and Seidl's) was Fleischmann's at Broadway and Tenth. Though not a garrulous man, he was exploratory. He was also, according to James Gibbons Huneker, one of the great imbibers of all time, "as dangerous to a moderate drinker as a false beacon is to a shipwrecked sailor"; he chased cocktails and beer with Slivavitch. Huneker was the first to share with Dvořák a book of "negro melodies." But Krehbiel was the expert—and Krehbiel was no Agassiz. At the Columbian Exposition Krehbiel did not gawk at the Dahomeyans but, as he recorded in his pathbreaking *Afro-American Folksongs*, admired their war dances with drums and bells:

> The harmony was a tonic major triad broken up rhythmically in a most intricate and amazingly ingenious manner. The instruments were tuned with excellent justness. . . . The players showed the most remarkable rhythmical sense and skill that ever came under my notice. Berlioz in his supremest efforts with his army of drummers produced nothing to compare in artistic interest with the harmonious drumming of these savages. The fundamental effect was a combination of double and triple time, the former kept by the singers, the latter by the drummers, but it is impossible to convey the idea of the wealth of detail achieved by the drummers by means of exchange of the rhythms, syncopation of both simultaneously, and dynamic devices.

The same book chastises "one class of critics" for "their ungenerous and illiberal attitude" toward black Americans. Krehbiel was also an appreciative student of music Jewish, Hungarian, Slavic, Scandinavian, Russian, Oriental, and Native American. These historic writings, in the *Tribune*, do not hierarchize race. That Krehbiel shared Dvořák's "roots in the soil" nationalism, that he handed Dvořák choice specimens of African-American and Native American song, that he served as Dvořák's most copious New York advocate—all this fortified Dvořák's enthusiasm for American folk music.[21]

Agassiz, born in Switzerland, first came into contact with black people in Philadelphia in 1846. "I scarcely dare tell you the painful impression I received," he confided to his sister:

> As much as I try to feel pity at the sight of this degraded and degenerate race, as much as their fate fills me with compassion in thinking of them as really men, it is impossible for me to repress the feeling that they are not of the same blood as us. Seeing their black faces with their fat lips and their grimacing teeth, the wool on their heads, their bent knees, their elongated hands, their large curved fingernails, and above all the livid color of their palms, I could not turn my eyes from their face in order to tell them to keep their distance, and when they advanced that hideous hand toward my plate to serve me, I wished I could leave in order to eat a piece of bread apart rather than dine with such service. What unhappiness for the white race to have tied its existence so closely to that of the negroes in certain countries! God protect us from such contact![22]

Dvořák, born in Bohemia, first came into contact with black people in New York. A pivotal encounter was with a stocky, self-possessed, twenty-five-year-old from Erie, Pennsylvania. Harry Burleigh had learned the sorrow songs from his blind grandfather, a former slave. He became Dvořák's personal assistant and family friend. Dvořák considered "Go Down, Moses" as "great as a Beethoven melody"; he encouraged Burleigh to transcribe this and other slave songs for voice and piano, and to sing them in solo recital. In later years, Burleigh became famous for doing just that, a precursor to Paul Robeson and Marian Anderson. He revered the memory of Dvořák.

Having attended Buffalo Bill's "Wild West" in New York with Thurber, Dvořák also mingled with Native Americans, members of the Kickapoo Medicine Show that encamped for two weeks during his 1893 summer sojourn in Spillville, Iowa. In rural Bohemia, Dvořák kept company with peasants and played the organ in church; belonging to a proud Hapsburg minority, he had resisted pressure to move to Vienna or to Germanize his first name as "Anton." Both the blacks he befriended in New York and the traveling Indians he befriended in Iowa were, significantly, cultural outsiders who cherished a religious music "of the soil." And Dvořák—who spoke English, who once wrote that the composer "must prick his ear," that "nothing must be too low or too insignificant for the musician," that "he should listen to every whistling boy, every street singer or blind organ-grinder"—absorbed other powerful New World impressions: the sanguine energy of the American city, and the emptiness of the vast Western prairie, which he found "sad to despair."[23]

The Largo of the *New World* Symphony, steeped in the sorrow songs, was turned into an ersatz spiritual, "Goin' Home," by Dvořák's student William Arms Fisher. Another student, Harry Rowe Shelley, was privileged to be present when Dvořák auditioned the newly composed tune, singing "with great passion and fervor, his eyes bulging out; his blood purple red in the neck veins . . . his whole body vibrating." The same music, the same movement, while not a narrative, is as Dvořák attested pregnant with *The Song of Hiawatha*, with the death of Minnehaha, with a West of the imagination (Dvořák had yet to journey there) conveyed by smooth textures and spread chords, by uncluttered, unadorned musical space. Willa Cather here heard "the immeasurable yearning of all flat lands." W. J. Henderson, reviewing the premiere, perfectly captured the polyvalence of "an idealized slave song made to fit the impressive quiet of night on the prairie. When the star of empire took its way over those mighty Western plains blood and sweat and agony and bleaching human bones marked its course. Something of this awful buried sorrow of the prairie must have forced itself upon Dr. Dvořák's mind."[24]

With its incessant tom-tom and exotic drone, the "primitive" five-note compass of its skittish tune, its whirling and hopping buildup, the Scherzo of the *New World* Symphony depicts the Dance of Pau-Puk-Keewis at Hiawatha's wedding:

> First he danced a solemn measure
> . . .
> Treading softly like a panther
> Then more swiftly and still swifter,
> Whirling, spinning round in circles,
> Leaping o'er the guests assembled
> Eddying round and round the wigwam,
> Till the leaves went whirling with him,
> . . .
> Stamped upon the sand and tossed it
> Wildly in the air around him;
> Till the wind became a whirlwind
> Till the sand was blown and sifted
> Like the great snowdrifts o'er the landscape.

Elsewhere, a solo flute suggests "Swing Low" in movement one. The stentorian "Indian" theme and fleet, savage chase of the finale arguably parallel Hiawatha's climactic battle with Pau-Puk-Keewis.[25] With its Indian threnody, the coda—a dead march, a cry of pain, a loud last chord fading to silence—seals one of the symphony's meanings: it is, all of it, an elegy for a vanishing race. Embracing the myth of the noble savage, the *New World* is far the best of the many musical evocations of *Hiawatha*. Embracing the myth of the virgin West, it is the most eloquent musical equivalent of the canvases of Catlin, Remington, and Bierstadt.★ Obviously, crucially, Dvořák's sadness of the prairie and sadness of the Indian resonate, as well, with homeward longings (and with who knows what other personal sadnesses). More than a Bohemian symphony with an American accent, *From the New World* is a reading of America drawn taut, emotionally, by the pull of the Czech fatherland.

In Spillville, Iowa, with the symphony mainly behind him, Dvořák refined the plain attire of his American style. The *American* String Quartet, there composed, breathes new contentment (Dvořák's secretary Josef Kovařík called this summer holiday the happiest period of Dvořák's life). For many first listeners, in Boston and New York, the pronounced pentatonic flavor of all four movements contributed to impressions of "southern melodies" and "plantation effects galore." The little-known Suite for piano, Op. 98 (also orchestrated), begun in Iowa and finished in New York, is a New World postcard. In Spillville, Dvořák had listened to interracial Kickapoo Medicine Show musicians, including two "niggers," who intermingled Native American chants with banjo and guitar. In the *American* Suite, prairie vacancy mates with cakewalk, and (in the finale) an A minor "Indian" tune turns into an A major minstrel song. The effortlessly inclusive "American" idiom of this music transcends the exoticism of Rimsky-Korsakov's contemporaneous *Capriccio Espagnol* (1887); it does not even sound like "Dvořák." Not long before leaving New York for good, Dvořák composed his Cello Concerto—not an "American" work, though Victor Herbert's Second Cello Concerto (Dvořák heard and acclaimed the premiere, conducted by Seidl) spurred its composition. The *Humoresques* for solo piano, begun in Spillville and finished in Prague, are a hybrid leave-taking: the popular No. 7 is a skipping plantation dance with striding left hand; the obscure No. 4 begins, incredibly, with a bluesy foretaste of Gershwin, then circles back to Bohemian meadows and forests. Many a composer, foreign- or native-born, had previously concocted

---

★ A visual presentation, created for the Brooklyn Philharmonic (1993) by Peter Bogdanoff of UCLA in collaboration with the author, drives home these correlations with American painters. It has also been presented by the Pacific Symphony Orchestra.

"American" vignettes by simply quoting American songs. Dvořák, who quotes nothing, burrowed into the American musical psyche.

In sum, Dvořák's American catalogue features his best-known symphony, string quartet, and concerto, each the best-known work of its kind ever composed in the United States. Influenced by American spaciousness and innocence, by Seidl and Wagnerism, Dvořák in New York disengaged from the denser motivic and contrapuntal interplay of his earlier, more Brahmsian scores. The *New World* was his last symphony, a turning point; its programmatic complexion led to the tone poems of later years[26] (in a style no longer "American": Dvořák, ears "pricked," was at all times a creature of his environment).

America's influence on Dvořák is richly apparent; Dvořák's influence on America remains permanently controversial. Judging from enrollment figures both Dvořák in New York and Chadwick at the New England Conservatory succeeded in stemming the outflow of Americans to German schools of music.[27] If none of Dvořák's composition students achieved enduring fame, Harvey Loomis, Harry Rowe Shelley, and Rubin Goldmark were notable composers in their day whose output included titles like *A Negro Rhapsody*, *The Call of the Plains*, *Lyrics of the Red Man*, and *Old Black Joe*. Goldmark was also an important teacher whose own students included Aaron Copland. Edwin Franko Goldman, among Dvořák's students, was an important bandmaster; William Arms Fisher, an important music historian and publisher. Of the African-Americans at Dvořák's National Conservatory, Burleigh enjoyed a distinguished career as a recitalist and composer (his *Songs on Poems of Laurence Hope*, art songs divorced from the vernacular, deserve revival). Will Marion Cook, more briefly associated with Dvořák, became a pioneer of black musical theater and a mentor to Duke Ellington; Cook and Burleigh in fact encapsulate alternate trajectories for early-twentieth-century black music—the one toward jazz, the other toward more "dignified" genres.

Though he was not the first significant composer to appropriate African-American and Native American elements—Gottschalk (as Dvořák acknowledged) got there first; Frederick Delius and Edward MacDowell both composed "Indian" and "Appalachian" works before 1900—it was Dvořák's example that spurred hundreds of songs and sonatas, symphonies and operas mining plantation song and Indian chant. And Dvořák's compositional influence was felt in other ways. It was George Chadwick's formidable Fourth String Quartet in which Philip Hale detected Dvořák the "negrophile." Chadwick's *Jubilee*, similarly, is both unmistakably American and unmistakably indebted to Dvořák: his *Carnival* Overture. Amy Beach was productively redirected by Dvořák. She conceived her E minor *Gaelic* Symphony, quoting Gaelic songs toward which she felt an Anglo-Saxon affinity, after hearing the

E minor *New World*; her later, haunting String Quartet (1929) incorporates Eskimo tunes. Of the more "barbaric" Indianists, the best was Arthur Farwell, who called himself the first composer "to take up Dvořák's challenge . . . in a serious and whole-hearted way."[28] The pinnacle of the Indianist movement, however, was attained not in search of an "American school," but by a European: Ferruccio Busoni, in his memorably poetic *Indian Fantasy* for piano and orchestra (1913) and the related *Indian Diary* No. 1 for solo piano (1915). Busoni performed the American premiere of the Fantasy with Stokowski and the Philadelphia Orchestra, to a puzzled reception—after which this and countless lesser efforts, likewise quoting indigenous specimens collected by Alice Fletcher and Natalie Curtis, swiftly disappeared.

Then as now, Dvořák in America was criticized—especially in Boston, where Paine, Chadwick, and Beach all initially distanced themselves—as a naif. He seemingly failed to recognize signal differences from Old World conditions: that, while some Americans might have African and indigenous roots, white-skinned American composers did not; that a distinctive national musical identity need not be based on folk song; that, as he ultimately acknowledged in 1895, America was inherently polyglot, a nation of immigrants. Dvořák romanticized and stereotyped the Indian and slave. He did not anticipate the twentieth-century burgeoning of popular music, which divorced classical music from jazz and "negro melodies." *Porgy and Bess* notwithstanding, the folk-based symphonies and operas he foresaw could and would not anchor America's musical destiny.

All this may be so, but does not shrink Dvořák's legacy. His intuition that black music would gird a future American music was wonderfully prescient. A pedigreed outsider, he influentially validated African-American music. Embracing Gottschalk and Stephen Foster and the corner street singer, he pushed for a broad understanding of music—its sources, its audience, its relationship to culture and society. He provocatively saw music as a necessary means of defining America, an ecumenical vehicle for articulating the New World. If he failed to supply a stylistic model, more than any American composer before, and more than most since, he conveyed the grandeur, pathos, and creative potential of the American experience. He would not have understood the curatorial or Eurocentric attitudes of many American musicians to come. His message remains inspirational.

■ ■ ■

Of the two most impressive American composers before 1920, Charles Ives supported Dvořák's emphasis on conscious American roots; no less than

Dvořák, he insisted that the composer "prick his ear," that "nothing must be too low or too insignificant for the musician." And Charles Tomlinson Griffes produced a spare Indianist string quartet vignette much closer to Farwell (who befriended him in New York) than to the Boston boys. But neither really fits into Dvořák's New World.

Born in Elmira, New York, in 1884, Griffes studied in Berlin and returned to the United States in 1907 a highly competent composer of German-style songs in German. The French Impressionists and Scriabin greatly influenced such subsequent compositions as *The Pleasure-Dome of Kubla Khan* (1912, orchestrated 1917) and *The White Peacock* (1915, orchestrated 1919). Griffes also composed in "Japanese" style, with nondirectional harmonies and delicately tinted instrumental effects including a harp standing in for a koto. This period of exoticism links with Charles Martin Loeffler, who admired *Kubla Khan*. Griffes, however, (correctly) considered Loeffler's style prolix. Late in his brief thirteen-year composing career, he repudiated "the reputation of an oriental-ist and nothing more" and forged a mature idiom combining exotic fragrance and sensuality with primal sinew. In this regard, he may be considered a New York Loeffler: exotic, even decadent, but more than decorative.[29] (It may be worth recording that, presumably like Loeffler, Griffes was gay.) This new side of Griffes—engaged, visceral—is sealed by the *Three Poems of Fiona MacLeod* (1919) for voice and orchestra (or piano) and the taut, fifteen-minute Piano Sonata (1918). The MacLeod songs, setting a once-popular "Celtic" poet whose real name was William Sharp, are a kind of music Mac-Dowell wished he could write and which Loeffler did not attempt. A *Tristan*-esque lushness and chromatic edginess embellish high passions of loss and yearning. The sonata, a taut, tightly organized exercise in New World diable-rie, conveys terror. If its hallucinatory frenzy evokes Scriabin, its savagery is American. Though it belongs in the same top drawer as the piano sonatas of Ives and Copland, though a white-hot 1950s recording by William Masselos should have made it an American staple, it remains little performed. The MacLeod songs—of which "The Rose of the Night," a necromantic Liebestod, is a peak American achievement[30]—are even less known. Griffes's Three Preludes for piano (1919), skirting atonality and a more drastic conci-sion, limn a new direction. He died, age 35, the following year.

From 1907, Griffes taught at the Hackley School in Tarrytown, a short commute from New York City. He struggled for recognition: pre–World War I New York had no Seidls to influentially champion American works. But Pierre Monteux's Boston Symphony performances of *The Pleasure-Dome of Kubla Khan* were a triumph in Boston and New York in 1919. Around the same time, Stokowski conducted four Griffes works on one program in Philadelphia. The dissonant Piano Sonata, by comparison, confounded contemporary opinion; *Musical America* discerned "no disclosure of beauty or tangible invention."[31] Griffes's early death, from empyema, occasioned a spate of performances, and of belated publications, by G. Schirmer. Monteux, Stokowski, Prokofiev, and Percy Grainger were among the signers of a condolence message to Griffes's mother, calling him "one of the most gifted of contemporary American composers." Had he lived, American music would have acquired a post-Romantic master; Copland and other modernists of the postwar decades could not have envisioned themselves starting out in a void.

Compared to Griffes, Charles Ives, born in Danbury in 1874, was unknown during his creative years. But he lived long enough—to 1954—to glimpse his eventual fame as the most formidable of all American concert composers. He was acclaimed by twentieth-century modernists, not excluding Arnold Schoenberg, as a prophet of the new. No less than Griffes, however, he was a product of his own time and place. A maverick within the genteel tradition, espousing Germanic uplift, he combines "Boston"—Ralph Waldo Emerson and Henry David Thoreau—with "New York"—the earthy democratic eclecticism of Walt Whitman. Steeped in the sounds of his Connecticut boyhood, of chapel hymns and corny theater tunes, he is a more advanced example—far more advanced—of Chadwick's American voice.

Whitman wrote, in *Democratic Vistas*, "I say that democracy can never prove itself beyond cavil until it finds and luxuriantly grows its own forms of art, poems, schools, theology, displacing all that exists, or that has been produced in the past under opposite influence." He also once scribbled, "American opera—put three banjos, (or more?) in the orchestra—and let them accompany (at times exclusively,) the songs of the baritone or tenor."[32] Whitman's vision of an egalitarian American language, boldly intermingling the classical and vernacular, finds fruition in the voice of Ives—an American Everyman who cherished the quotidian; a vigorous democrat at home with ordinary people and things; a charismatic philosopher who idealized art and spiritualized everyday experience, whose music is equally prone to plain and extravagant speech.

A cranky outsider, Ives profited from a certain remoteness from European models. At Yale, it is true, he studied composition with Horatio Parker (and also excelled at baseball). Like Chadwick, Parker had studied composition with Joseph Rheinberger in Munich. But Ives, who never sought instruction abroad, called his father—a sometime New England bandmaster—his principal teacher. He also powerfully identified with Emerson, who in 1837 had advised Americans, "Our day of dependence, our long apprenticeship to the learned of other lands, draws to a close. We will walk on our own feet; we will work with our own hands; we will speak our own minds." In the same breath, Emerson wrote, "I embrace the common, I explore and sit at the feet of the familiar, the low." His soulmate Thoreau, in a passage of which Ives was fond, echoed, "Natural objects and phenomena are the original symbols or types which express our thoughts and feelings, and yet American scholars, having little or no root in the soil, commonly strive with all their might to confine themselves to the imported symbols alone."[33]

More than any subsequent writers or musicians—more than any twentieth-century influences—Emerson and Thoreau furnish an Ives template. As Transcendentalists, they stressed the experience of individual inspiration. They disdained the harsh puritan God of other American denominations. They espoused self-reliance, God in nature, and social reform. Most Transcendentalists believed in the possibility of an intuitive identification with God, a Universal Intelligence (Thoreau's term) manifest in nature: a source of goodness. Ives identified with these attitudes, and he identified with Emerson and Thoreau as people, as thinkers, and as stylists. Their unreined individualism captivated him. Though Ives undertook a public vocation in the life insurance business parallel to his private career as a composer, though by middle age he was wealthy and successful, he pursued a lifestyle as reclusive—as ostentatiously simple, in its way—as Thoreau's. No less than Emerson or Thoreau, Ives was intensely democratic. He was too much the loner to seek worldly influence through social experiments like Brook Farm. But he possessed a warm and meddlesome social conscience. His proposed twentieth amendment to the Constitution, which he circulated to leading political figures, would have implemented a national direct democracy. Like Emerson and Thoreau, Ives was religious by temperament. He felt a kinship with the New England come-outers, who removed themselves from institutions that violated their conscience. Ives's Christianity was less heretical, but he was far from an orthodox worshiper. ("Many of the sincerest followers of Christ," he wrote, "never heard of him.") He followed Emerson and Thoreau in his religious regard for nature, in his conviction that the world is a wholesome place, in his insistence that art, like nature, is moral. Ives aspired to the condition—immortalized by Thoreau in *Walden*—where art, religion, philosophy, and daily life become one and the same. Among the advertisements he wrote for the firm of Ives and Myrick was one beginning:

"I appeal from your customs: I must be myself"—says Emerson in his "Self-Reliance."

There is a tendency, today, to minimize the individual and to exaggerate the machinelike custom of business and of life.

Some men fit quite easily into a mechanistic system, while others feel that their individuality will or is being gradually standardized out of them.

Work in the life insurance field certainly doesn't cramp individuality, ingenuity, or initiative. Men of character, who are capable of sustained hard work, who like to overcome obstacles, who are interested in human nature, may well consider the profession of life insurance.[34]

The ecstatic "music" of Emerson's poetry and prose transcends rational exegesis. The music of Ives likewise violates orthodoxies of grammar, of harmony and form. Though its dissonance and "difficulty" parallel the new language of Schoenberg an ocean away, Ives did not know the music of Schoenberg and other turn-of-the-century European innovators. His stubborn self-sufficiency dictated a singular isolation from mainstream "classical music." "Listening to concert music seemed to confuse me in my own work . . . to throw me off somewhat from what I had in mind," he later wrote. Nor did Ives hear his own music; for decades it lay unperformed. He irritably shunned the company and even the approbation of "celebrated musicians."

The interior vision into which Ives withdrew was nourished by George Ives's sound world of hymns, marches, and Civil War songs, a world equally divorced from European high culture and its American parlor parody. But Transcendentalism—its inherent music of the mind and senses—was an equally potent catalyst. Thoreau said of music, "Our minds should echo at least as many times as Mammoth Cave to every musical sound. It should awaken reflections in us." Thoreau also wrote, "I wish to hear the silence of the night, for the silence is something positive and to be heard. . . . A fertile and eloquent silence. . . . Silence alone is worthy to be heard. . . . The silence rings; it is musical and thrills me."[35]

Thoreau played his flute in rural solitude. In the "Thoreau" movement of his *Concord* Sonata (1911–15)—as memorable as any piano music composed by an American—Ives asks that a flute be played. In fact, Ives's essay "Thoreau," from his impressive *Essays Before a Sonata*, sketches a program for his composition "Thoreau." Thoreau sits in his doorway at Walden, "rapt in reverie, amidst goldenrod, sandcherry and sumach." Though "he realized what the oriental meant by Contemplation and forsaking of works," he does not contemplate in this style. Ives, accordingly, does not imitate Eastern music: "Thus it is not the whole tone scale of the Orient but the scale of the Walden morning which inspired many of the polyphonies and harmonies that come to us through his poetry." And Ives's gently rippling music—barless, fragmentary, transparent—does evoke the early morning's fluttering of leaves and wind, and also the fluttering of half-formulated early-morning thoughts. In "The Housatonic at Stockbridge," from *Three Places in New England*—as poetic as any American orchestral music—Ives's trembling and oscillating strings fashion an incorporeal sonic landscape: the "thrilling music" of Thoreau's silence; a transcendental ether, physically and metaphysically aquiver; a half-heard, half-seen aureole crowning mist, water, and floating leaves.

Emerson, in Ives's essay "Emerson," is a "seer," "invader of the unknown," "America's deepest explorer of the spiritual immensities," "a recorder, freely describing the inevitable struggle of the soul's uprise." His strength is his optimism—"a possession which gives the strength of distance to his eyes, and the strength of muscle to his soul." Ives also writes, "To think hard and deeply and to say what is thought, regardless of consequences, may produce a first impression, either of great translucence or of great muddiness, but in the latter there may be hidden possibilities." Here is Emerson himself, in his poem "Music":

> 'Tis not in the high stars alone,
> Nor in the cup of budding flowers,
> Nor in the redbreast's mellow tone,
> Nor in the bow that smiles in showers,
> But in the mud and scum of things
> There alway, alway something sings.

In the *Concord* Sonata, "Emerson" oscillates from shouted excitement to lofty self-assurance, from the "mud and scum" of country tunes to chilly ecstasies. The fate motif of Beethoven's Fifth—here "knocking at the door of Divine mysteries"—infiltrates at will. All is striving and conviction.[36]

Ives (who of course knew the *New World* Symphony, and seemingly alludes to it in his precocious First Symphony of 1898), rejected the appropriation of Indianisms and plantation song; he argued that composers should stick closer to home: to what they know best. He was inspired—partly, no doubt, by Horatio Parker—to meld the music of home, the music of his Connecticut childhood, with art music traditions acquired from Europe:

> The man "born down to Babbitt's Corners" may find a deep appeal in the simple but acute Gospel hymns of the New England "camp meetin'" of a generation or so ago. He finds in them . . . a vigor, a depth

of feeling, a natural-soil rhythm, a sincerity—emphatic but inartistic—which ... carries him nearer the "Christ of the people" than does the Te Deum of the greatest cathedral. ... If the Yankee can reflect the fervency with which "his gospels" were sung—the fervency of "Aunt Sarah," who scrubbed her life away for her brother's ten orphans, the fervency with which this woman, after a fourteen-hour work day on the farm, would hitch up and drive five miles through the mud and rain to "prayer meetin'," her one articulate outlet for the fullness of her unselfish soul—if he can reflect the fervency of such a spirit, he may find there a local color that will do all the world good. If his music can but catch that spirit by being a part of itself, it will come somewhere near his idea—and it will be American, too—perhaps nearer so than that of the devotee of Indian or negro melody. In other words, if local color, national color, any color, is a true pigment of the universal color, it is a divine quality, it is a part of substance in art—not of manner.[37]

Probably the best-loved image of Ives the iconoclast, striding far ahead of his time and place, is of Ives the haranguer, shouting "Sissy!" and "Listen like a man!" at obtuse contemporaries. But, whatever truth adheres to Ives's characterization of effete artists and culture-bearers, he was—again—living less in the future than in the past, remembering the New England parlor of his childhood and shutting out the New York of his mature years. By the decade of the 1910s, when Ives was at his creative peak, New York–based critics such as Carl Van Vechten and Paul Rosenfeld, New York–based composers such as Leo Ornstein and Edgard Varèse were already committed modernists. This was also the period of Frank Lloyd Wright, John Marin, Alfred Stieglitz, Isadora Duncan, Carl Sandburg, and Ezra Pound. Living in Manhattan, Ives made contact with none of these composers, writers, and visual artists. His lifestyle was that of a proper businessman. He was discomfited by sensuality. He denounced homosexuals as "pansies," "lily-pads," "old ladies," "pussy-boys." He disliked the company of bohemians. His veneration for Bach and Beethoven did not extend to Tchaikovsky (too interested in "getting an audience"), Wagner (lacking "wholesomeness" and "manliness"), Debussy ("voluptuous," "slimy"), or Ravel and Stravinsky ("morbidly fascinating," "false beauty").[38] His disdain for the feminized Connecticut culture he recalled was exacerbated by knowledge of his own complicity. He feared his sentimentality. His First Symphony, his peerless songs both incorporate and critique the genteel. He was prone to denounce as "effeminate" sensual and aestheticist tendencies that actually threatened the genteel tradition.

In some ways, the contemporary American musician Ives most revealingly evokes is Theodore Thomas. At first the analogy seems preposterous. Thomas was upright. He repudiated popular music. His repertoire stopped with Bruckner, Sibelius, and Richard Strauss. But Thomas, too, was a prepossessing autodidact, self-made and self-reliant. He was caustic and pugnacious. A pioneer in the wilderness, he exuded moral fervor. No less than Ives—or Emerson, or Thoreau—he was religious by temperament, an optimist, and a democrat. Finally, in compensation for prevailing stereotypes of artists and musicians, he conspicuously embodied an exaggerated masculinity. He was athletic. He disapproved of eccentricities of dress and demeanor. He looked like a banker. Ives demanded music of "wholesomeness, manliness, humility, and deep spiritual, possibly religious feeling."[39] These words, and also Ives's rejection of music dominated by "manner"—a rejection of aestheticism—could equally have been uttered by Thomas.

Thomas attained his peak popularity during Ives's Danbury years. But by the time Ives came to New York in 1898, Thomas was old-fashioned. Like Ives, he was devoted to an earlier world, buoyed by security and optimism, by the fortitude of Beethoven.

■ ■ ■

In an 1895 article for *Harper's Magazine* Dvořák complained that he was unable to teach a highly promising young American; though the National Conservatory had awarded a scholarship, "he sorrowfully confessed that he could not afford to become my pupil because he had to earn his living by keeping books in Brooklyn. Even if he came just two afternoons in the week, or on Saturday afternoon only, he said, he would lose his employment, on which he and others had to depend." Dvořák continued:

> In any other country, the State would have made some provision for such a deserving scholar, so that he could have pursued his natural calling without having to starve. With us in Bohemia, the Diet each year votes a special sum of money for just such purposes, and the imperial government in Vienna on occasion furnishes other funds for talented artists. Had it not been for such support I should not have been able to pursue my studies when I was a young man. Owing to the fact that, upon the kind recommendation of such men as Brahms, Hanslick and Herbeck, the Minister of Public Education in Vienna on [*sic*] five successive years sent me sums ranging from four to six hundred florins, I could pursue my work and get my compositions published, so that at the end of that time I was able to stand on my own feet.

American publishers, he added, were unwilling

> to take anything but light and trashy music. . . . Thus, when one of my
> pupils last year produced a very creditable work, and a thoroughly
> American composition at that, he could not get it published in America,
> but had to send it to Germany, where it was at once accepted. The same
> is true of my own compositions on American subjects, each of which
> had to be published abroad.[40]

The American composer was denied a place, a viable professional niche.

We have observed how William Henry Fry (who was independently
wealthy, and drew a salary as a critic) and George Bristow (who supported
himself as an orchestral violinist and teacher) decried the neglect of the
American composer (except by the visiting Frenchman Jullien), how Edward
MacDowell (who did not fit in Boston, and who in New York quarreled with
Nicholas Murray Butler over the place of music in academia) felt more comfortably situated in Europe, and how Charles Tomlinson Griffes wound up
teaching at a preparatory school. We have observed among the "Boston boys"
a surer social and cultural role for the composer, and a local music publisher—
Arthur Schmidt—who did his part. Even so, George Chadwick made his living teaching and administering a conservatory, Amy Beach was a kept
creature, and both were as stifled as they were supported by the coziness of
musical Boston. Neither they nor any other Boston composer disclosed a
capacity for honest self-scrutiny. Thoreau, writes Martin Green, "withdrew
from the Boston community, and his achievement clearly owes much, in
many ways, to that act of virtue. He did not allow those conditions to work
on him with any concentrated force." Green also writes that when in later life
Emerson, "though a genuinely solitary man," was seduced into joining James
Fields's *Atlantic* circle "in the role of serene sage," his creative powers dissipated
"in a state of bland, benign vagueness."[41]

Rekindling the fires of Thoreau and Emerson decades later, Charles Ives
necessarily withdrew. His split identity, separating public business from reclusive art, solved the dilemma of the placeless American composer. It enabled
him to peer deeply, to "invade the unknown," to hear the music of silence, to
connect with the Beethoven model of the Romantic artist contemptuous of
the marketplace and passionately at one with himself. His lucrative career in
insurance was both a financial necessity—no one would publish or perform
such music as his—and a buffer. Sequestered in retirement, he railed against
the movies, the radio, the telephone, popular music, and the automobile. His
willful ignorance of world events—on one occasion in the 1930s, he was dis-

covered unaware of Roosevelt's reelection[42]—was a form of self-protection. He clung to his faith in progress and human goodness. When, late in life, he revisited Danbury with his nephew, he moaned aloud to see how much had changed. All his life, he kept such mementos as a football, knee pants, baseballs, and spiked shoes.

Obviously, Ives the rebel—who early discovered the expressive shock of massive dissonance, of eclectic sources, of densely layered musical speech—consorts with decades of subsequent American composers. His spirit animates figures as recent as Lou Harrison and Elliott Carter. But he was too much the murky Germanic to direct Aaron Copland and other postwar Francophiles. Though he tangibly influenced Henry Cowell and Carl Ruggles, he was for other "ultra-moderns" more a lodestar than a stylistic guide. In his own time, he glancingly resonated with the new writers and poets—Carl Sandburg, Vachel Lindsay, Sherwood Anderson—espousing spontaneity and free verse, or redrawing small-town vignettes; one of his best-known songs sets Lindsay's "General William Booth Enters into Heaven." But otherwise Ives's poets are differently significant: they are German Romantic, or genteel, or of a sentimental parlor variety that his settings—as of Robert Underwood Johnson's "The Housatonic at Stockbridge"—lovingly transcend. That he is, however paradoxically, of his own fecund time and place is, finally, not so terrible a fate.

If Ives the outsider prefigures the posturing estrangement of Schoenberg, Varèse, and other twentieth-century artistic militants, Ives the insider—the genteel democrat, preaching uplift and "America"—represents the outer limits of a project begun half a century before by Gottschalk, Fry, Bristow, and Heinrich, articulated and accelerated by Dvořák, enlisting composers as different, and as differently disposed, as Paine, Chadwick, MacDowell, Farwell, Griffes, and (most popular of all) John Philip Sousa: that of validating and defining an American musical voice. Though conventional wisdom vaguely dismisses this enterprise (Ives excepted) as dim and obscure, its topography is arrestingly varied: compared to the generation of Copland and Gershwin, American composers before the 1920s—before American political hegemony and global cultural sway—could be closer to Europe or farther away. Their Old World cultural parents were less distant in time—and so was an untrammeled New World, untouched by European worldliness.

Ives complexly embodies it all: proximity to Europe, plus a lingering American innocence. He culls the Transcendentalists; alone among composers, he attains the ranginess of Whitman and Melville. (To Hawthorne, who gauged the greatness of *Moby-Dick*, Melville wrote, "You were archangel enough to despise the imperfect body, and embrace the soul"—a perfect encomium for Ives.) In the world of turn-of-the-century American music, he stands apart, yet in the long view keeps company with Theodore Thomas, Anton Seidl, and Henry Higginson, heroically tilling terrain more virgin than any to be found abroad. If his style of expression—so abandoned and variegated, so invested in mud and scum—is unfinished, so was America. If it ignores swaths of the contemporary American experience, he lived—deeply—in the American past. That is why, in his music, we recognize him not only as American but also as an emblematic American, speaking for all because speaking of origins. It is why he seems at once maverick and familiar.

Coda: Music and
the Gilded Age

■

*"Social control," "sacralization," and the debunking of Gilded Age
culture ▪ The coming of modernism ▪ Arthur Farwell and musical
grassroots ▪ In defense of nostalgia*

Edith Wharton's *The Age of Innocence*, set in Manhattan in the early 1870s,
begins with Christine Nilsson singing at the Academy of Music. The opera is
Gounod's *Faust*. The world of fashion has assembled in the boxes. In their
own eyes the embodiment of New York, the fashionables are prisoners of
convention: Newland Archer arrives late because "it was 'not the thing' to
arrive early at the opera; and what was or was not 'the thing' played a part as
important in Newland Archer's New York as the inscrutable totem terrors that
had ruled the destinies of his forefathers thousands of years ago." Newland
takes his place among "all the carefully-brushed, white-waistcoated,
buttonhole-flowered gentlemen who succeeded each other in the club box,
exchanged friendly greetings with him, and turned their opera glasses criti-
cally on the circle of ladies who were the product of the system." That "the
German text of French operas sung by Swedish artists should be translated
into Italian for the clearer understanding of English-speaking audiences"
seems "as natural to Newland Archer as all the other conventions on which
his life was moulded: such as the duty of using two silver-backed brushes with
his monogram in blue enamel to part his hair, and of never appearing in society without a flower (preferably a gardenia) in his buttonhole." The box
opposite belongs to "old Mrs. Manson Mingott, whose monstrous obesity had
long since made it impossible for her to attend the Opera." It contains a surprise: the Countess Olenska. This finding is assessed by Laurence Lefferts, who
has devoted long hours to such questions as when to wear a black tie with
evening clothes and the matter of pumps versus Oxfords for the feet. The
countess is next appraised by Sillerton Jackson, as great an expert on "family"
as Leffert is on form. Taking it all in, Newland elects to visit the box in question and inspect the countess for himself. Meanwhile, Victor Capoul, as Faust,

is "vainly trying, in a tight purple velvet doublet and plumed cap, to look as pure and true as his artless victim." Madame Nilsson, "in white cashmere slashed with pale blue satin, a reticule dangling from a blue girdle, and large yellow braids carefully disposed on each side of her muslin chemisette," listens "with downcast eyes to M. Capoul's impassioned wooing," and affects "a guileless incomprehension of his designs." Opera, in short, is here depicted as an expensive backdrop to social display and intrigue, a metaphor for artifice and pretension, a pastime as vicarious and silly as the fashionables themselves.

This well-known vignette may be the single most defining image of Gilded Age high culture. And yet Wharton no more purports to describe all of New York culture than her bemused 1921 novel of New York society describes all of New York. The same Academy of Music, as we know from the *Evening Post* of July 26, 1859, contained a basement "lager beer cavern":

> A long room … where, in a cloud of cigar smoke and amid the fumes of lager and liquor, the artists and their friends refresh themselves with copious libations. The conductor has a subterranean communication from the stage to the place, and—with Brignoli, Amodio, the members of the orchestra, and a number of the initiated *habitués* of the opera house—meets there his friends. . . . Between the acts of the opera the cavern is crowded, but as soon as the music commences, the rotund German drops his lager; the Frenchman shrugs his shoulders and says "*Mon Dieu*"; the Italian quotes Count Luna in *Trovatore* and sings "*Andiamo*"; the yellow Cubans and Spaniards give a twirl to their moustaches; the English or New York swell struts toward the stairs, and in a few moments the motley crowd are in the seats or lobbies.[1]

This is a fair reflection of New York opera in its boisterous adolescence.

Again: in countless descriptions, the personification of the early Metropolitan Opera is Caroline Astor, whose annual ball defined high society. It was she who decreed that to appear at the opera every Monday night at nine o'clock was the thing to do. She would enter her box wearing a diamond stomacher that was believed to have belonged to Marie Antoinette. But it was not Mrs. Astor's taste which decreed that for seven seasons all opera be given in German, that Wagner dominate the repertoire, and that a religious silence be enforced while music was being performed. In fact, at no other moment in its history was the Met less a plaything of the rich. Though the boxholders revolted and terminated Anton Seidl and German opera in 1891, renewed Germanic pressure (as we have seen) forced the Met to take Seidl and Wagner back. An uneasy balance of power prevailed, with rival German and non-

German companies coinhabiting the same institution. For the late Gilded Age, as true a picture of the Met as Mrs. Astor's box is the screaming ovation for Isolde's Liebestod. So polyglot was New York that as of 1918 the Met's president, board chairman, and dominant shareholder was an immigrant German banker. So confused were hierarchies of status and wealth that the banker in question, Otto Kahn, was denied a box because his parents were Jewish—and that he seemed not to care.

Lewis Mumford, in a famous 1931 study, called the decades from 1865 to 1895 brown: "The prevailing palette . . . ran most easily through the gamut from yellow brown to dark sienna. In the best work of the period these somber autumnal colours took on a new loveliness: a warm russet brown."[2] Theodore Thomas, who validated Wagner for the Gilded Age, turned him a respectable brown, even russet brown. But Seidl's Wagner unleashed the red lava of erotic turmoil: catalyst for a veritable fin de siècle supported by the aroused intellectual advocacy of Henry Krehbiel, W. J. Henderson, and other formidable apostles of the Music of the Future. If meliorist American Wagnerites were innocent of European decadence and modernism, the visceral thrill and transformative impact of concerts and opera would never again so galvanize classical music in the United States—except briefly, in wartime, when Arturo Toscanini's Beethoven would do battle with Hitler.

The imagery of Newland Archer and Mrs. Astor nevertheless remains. In a 1991 survey of the whole of America's late-nineteenth-century musical high culture, Charles Hamm, a leading music historian, found a "mystifying ritual of dress, behavior, and repertory" prized by an elite determined to maintain class privilege. Outside music, many contemporary scholars remain essentially contemptuous of Gilded Age culture-bearers and intellectuals, depicted as inanely timid, arrogantly elitist, or stupidly racist.[3] More often than not, such portraiture misapplies a twentieth-century template of understanding. The present-day observer of late-nineteenth-century behavior must grapple with a different reality: people of intelligence once believed in superior and inferior races, in religion being threatened by science, in the inevitability of class distinctions sharper than in subsequent decades. They also lived in times of much greater economic and social instability. They were not any more obtuse or self-interested than we are today.

The mantra of social control (which we have observed applied to Gilded Age Boston) bedevils such accounts. Art museums, libraries, universities, orchestras, and opera companies, we are told, were created partly in order to co-opt the restless energies of the less privileged. In Alan Trachtenberg's *The Incorporation of America—Culture and Society in the Gilded Age*, a central 1982 text, high culture is subjected to a political analysis revealing a chimerical "vision of a harmonious body politic under the rule of reason, light, and sweet, cheerful emotion," a "normative ideal of culture which served as protection against other realities." Commensurately, Trachtenberg observes "the wish for a conspicuous display of philanthropy on the part of wealthy donors, and for status on the part of the gentry, for whom the custodianship of culture provided desirable opportunities for *noblesse oblige.*" The aesthetic experience is essentially "feminine"—"receptive, passive, spectatorial."★ Its utility as "an alternative to class hostilities" earned it "a cardinal place among instruments of social control and reform." It embodied an "anti-democratic bias," a "hierarchy of values corresponding to a social hierarchy of stations or classes."

Trachtenberg's analysis, fresh in its day, shrewdly ferrets hidden meanings. But, applied to actual institutions of culture, it is more a hunch than a study. While concert halls are cited in passing, only museums receive any specific attention: "organized by the urban elite, dominated by ladies of high society," their palatial architecture and hushed corridors conveying "an idea of art as public magnificence" supported by private wealth, their holdings celebrating "European and classical masterpieces" as the "highest, purest art."[4] Not mentioned in this seminal study of "culture and society in the Gilded Age" are Theodore Thomas, Henry Higginson, or Anton Seidl; or the religious plainness of Symphony Hall; or the subversive erotic maelstrom of the Wagnerites. In fact, the argument for social control is not supported by close acquaintance with the musical high culture of the period. Though genteel habits of thought and feeling could act as a suppressant, though "civilization" could tame rowdy dissidence, it does not follow that America's pioneer institutions of classical music can be summarized as fundamentally patronizing and antidemocratic.

In Boston, bastion of respectability and tradition, John Sullivan Dwight was an explicit strategist of social control. Philip Hale was a snob. Amy Beach was cut off from the larger urban reality. Charles Martin Loeffler was hyperrefined. Charles Eliot Norton, though he retained belief in a democratic society, deplored "modern democracy." But in Higginson, who mattered most, the urge to uplift was not suppressive. Plainspoken, self-made to a notable degree, he was an impassioned sharer of the music he loved. To reduce him to an agent (however unwitting) of "control" applies a cramped stereotype to behavior astonishing for its generosity. To reduce the Boston Symphony to such an agent—to ignore the spontaneous sung farewell to George Henschel,

---

★ A key text propagating this stereotype is Ann Douglas, *The Feminization of American Culture* (New York, Knopf, 1977), which sees Gilded Age women confined to "a claustrophobic private world of over-responsive sensibility." For a critique, see Joseph Horowitz, *Wagner Nights: An American History* (Berkeley, University of California, 1992), pp. 230–232.

the uproar over Nikisch's Beethoven, the rush-ticket holders racing upstairs or sitting on the steps to the stage, the sheer urgency of mission as communally experienced on a weekly basis—is an exercise in sophistry. One cannot summarize, as an important sociologist has done, that Boston's orchestras and museums were creations of "cultural Capitalists" for whom high culture, which they defined and segregated, represented "refuge from the slings and arrow of the troubled world around them."[5] It is enough to observe that the *noblesse oblige* of countless Brahmin tastemakers preceded the Irish tidal wave; they did not necessarily seek to civilize out of fear.

Chicago is where social control most credibly applies to institutions of music. The psychology of social crisis and class conflict was more acute than elsewhere. It was in Chicago that Rose Fay Thomas distinguished "the highest forms of art" and their elite audience from "cheap musical entertainments" for "riff raff" and "the masses." Chicago was where the Auditorium Theater was built in response to Ferdinand Peck's call for social engineering. A leading historian of Gilded Age Chicago has identified "culture"—meaning top-down high culture—as Chicago's answer to social instability. A study of Chicago's Gilded Age cultural institutions states that Anglo-Saxon benefactors attempted "to use art to alter what disturbed them about American life."[6] And, to be sure, the Chicago Orchestra was not the kind of answer articulated at Hull House, where Jane Addams influentially rejected the ideal of philanthropy as a unilateral act of enlightenment just as she rejected top-down social reform. At the same time, Peck, equally an advocate for opera and for the poor, was not a plutocratic elitist but a utopian pragmatist, not a social controller but a full-blown social reformer for whom the Auditorium Theater would bridge the gap between rich and poor; in his experience, the elevating effects of high culture were an article not of wishful thinking but of earnest conviction.* Had Charles Norman Fay mainly had social engineering in mind, he would not have made his plan for a Chicago orchestra contingent on the availability of a single conductor. And whatever one makes of the orchestra's policy of denying complimentary tickets to German-language

---

* When Auditorium stockholders objected to the sale of box seats (for fifty cents) at the Apollo Club's workingman's concerts, Peck and Apollo director William Tomlins refused to budge. When the stockholders next asked that the velvet appointments of the boxes be protected by canvas from the "tobacco, grease, and other ill-advised concomitants of poorly educated existence," Peck replied via the press, "Protect nothing! If I had my way I would double the velvet hangings for the occasion." Peck himself shunned the box seats of the city's theaters. See Mark Clague, "Chicago Counterpoint: The Auditorium Theater Building and the Civic Imagination" (dissertation, University of Chicago, 2002), pp. 376, 99.

newspapers—a precinct of the local press associated with anarchism and political agitation—this was not the behavior of an agency of social control.

It is of course in New York, finally, where the social control model parts company with the real world of concerts and opera. In Chicago, Thomas mobilized upward through his marriage with Rose Fay; with its harsh depiction of his early colleague Carl Bergmann, its relative denigration of Wagner and Wagnerism, Thomas's late autobiography documents disaffection for New York and Deutschtum. For Seidl, in New York, this scenario of professional advancement was unnecessary. The German community that honored him was powerful. When shortly before his early death a movement was begun to create a permanent Seidl Orchestra, the philanthropists, both Anglo and German, came to him. Many influential New York Germans—think of the impresarios Grau, Conried, and Hammerstein—were Jewish. James Gibbons Huneker, a connoisseur of Russian and German downtown haunts, was also a connoisseur of Jewish contributions to the cultural mix; he once wrote, "In Europe there is room for race prejudice, but not in America. . . . We need the Jewish blood as spiritual leaven; the race is art-loving." William Dean Howells, arriving in New York, wrote to a Boston friend, "There are lots of interesting young painting and writing fellows, and the place is lordly free, with foreign touches of all kinds. . . . Boston seems of another planet." The *Musical Courier* testified, "In New York, where there is no civic pride, . . . the mixture of population prevents a consolidation of any one artistic direction." A 1987 sociological analysis, by Paul DiMaggio, amplifies, "New York elites . . . were less successful than Boston's in reproducing their status intergenerationally and in controlling positions of influence. . . . Although New York's population was larger, wealthier, and included more artists than Boston's, the greater cohesion of Boston's upper class facilitated cultural entrepreneurship, while the size and fragmentation of New York's elite impeded it."[7]

In Boston, the genteel paraphernalia of culture, Charles Eliot Norton presiding, sounded a loud chorus of instruction, approbation, and alarm. New York had Richard Watson Gilder of *The Century*, a voice in the crowd. In Boston and Chicago, the great orchestras ruled musical affairs. In New York, the rivalry between orchestras, and between conductors, seemed never ending; in opera, warring impresarios gave way to warring opera houses until Oscar Hammerstein—a German Jew who as a dominant cultural force loathed the fashionables in whom Trachtenberg's model invests so much power—was paid off in 1910. The lager cavern at the Academy of Music assembled ethnic constituencies that coexisted, sometimes uneasily, in the community of culture. The omnipresent Germans, who migrated uptown to Carnegie Hall and the Met in the closing decades of the century, were themselves a complex amalgam of rich and less rich, traditional and progressive, Catholic, Protestant, and Jew interacting with or displacing the genteel elite. In a concert milieu so cosmopolitan and dynamic, social rites served no predominant purpose. *Noblesse oblige* was a fractional part of the whole, as was a plutocracy of wealth in which strong personalities as different, and differently motivated, as Andrew Carnegie, J. P. Morgan, John D. Rockefeller, William Steinway, and William K. Vanderbilt somehow commingled (or did not). In any case, it was not the plutocrats who set the tone but the rough-hewn democrats Thomas (in his pre-Chicago mode) and Dvořák; and Seidl, who preached democracy—missionary work for "good men and women" versus "the rich"—at Brighton Beach; and Krehbiel, who joined Dvořák and Jeannette Thurber in espousing a polyglot America, a national identity rooted in the soil, to fortify and uplift a common culture. Unimaginable in Boston or Chicago was the charity concert presented by the National Conservatory at Madison Square Garden on January 23, 1894. Dvořák conducted the conservatory orchestra in music by Mendelssohn, Rossini, Liszt, and Volkmann. Maurice Arnold, an African-American composition student whom Dvořák prized, led his own *American Plantation Dances*. The finale was the premiere of Dvořák's new arrangement of Stephen Foster's "Old Folks at Home" for soprano, baritone, and chorus. The soprano soloist was Sissieretta Jones, nationally famous as the "Black Patti." The baritone was Harry Burleigh. The chorus was all black. The capacity audience spilled into every available standing-room space.

Amplifying this picture of intermingling genres, races, and classes was the city's democratic social fabric. Francis Neilson, a young writer and actor closely associated with Seidl, recalled half a century later of the hotel restaurants, where "free-lunch counters" provided hearty meals, for a five-cent tip, to any imbiber who purchased a cocktail, beer, or milk-and-seltzer: "Almost any day of the week, between the hours of eleven and one, a sprinkling of men connected with the drama, literature, journalism, and art might be found in the barrooms of Broadway's big hotels. . . . In those days the man of business, the scientist, the doctor and lawyer would be found in the company of artists, glad to be in close touch with them and to dispense their quips and sallies to an ever-widening circle." Seidl, we have seen, was "popular with a mass of people" in New York, "recognized everywhere in public." In the absence of telephones and radios, face-to-face social relations were the norm. "When a man would stroll down Broadway," Neilson wrote, "people became better acquainted." The café, as in Europe, was—in Huneker's words—"a rendezvous for newspaper men, musicians, artists, Bohemians generally . . . the best stamping-ground for men of talent."[8]

It is difficult to say in what sense this city's musical life was "antidemocratic." Even the cherished notion that the high culture of the late Gilded Age was "elitist" is hard to reconcile with the New York reality. Theodore Thomas, in an 1899 conversation with Theodore Dreiser, criticized the early New York Philharmonic for standing "a little apart from the common crowd," for concerts perceived by "the general public" as "mysterious rites, celebrated behind closed doors, in the presence of a select unchanging company of believers." But, Thomas continued, he had pursued a mission in New York and elsewhere that began "at the bottom instead of the top" and made "the cultivation of symphonic music a popular movement."[9] Furthermore, that the New York Philharmonic once seemed sectarian—as a musicians' cooperative, it termed its subscribers "members"—did not make it notably fashionable. And by the time Seidl became its ever-popular conductor, and the Thomas Orchestra folded, the Philharmonic no longer connoted "closed doors" of any kind; its most acclaimed concert, in 1892, presented a symphony infused with plantation song and Indianist refrains. At the Metropolitan Opera, Wagnerism excited a leveling passion. When Germans took possession of the house, their singing societies even invaded the stage, in *Die Meistersinger*. Their controversial eviction in 1891 evinced ongoing cultural warfare in which class distinctions were neither decisive nor irrelevant.

The historian Thomas Kessner, in a recent study of Gilded Age New York, revisits the city's business magnates—including Carnegie, Morgan, Rockefeller, and Vanderbilt—with fresh appreciation for their audacious aspiration and colossal resolve. "All New York was demanding new men," Henry Adams recalled in his *Education*:

> And all the new forces condensed into corporations, were demanding a new type of man,—a man with ten times the endurance, energy, will and mind of the old type;—for whom they were ready to pay millions at sight . . . for the old one had plainly reached the end of his strength and his failure had become catastrophic. The Trusts and Corporations . . . were revolutionary, troubling all the old conventions and values. The new man could be only a child born of contact between the new and old energies.

Kessner also observes that these new men distrusted one another. "Rather than work together to advance a big-business hegemony, they kept their exchanges to a minimum at a level that was barely civil. . . . New York's circle of businessmen was too large and too diverse for any one group of interest to dominate." In New York's circle of musicians and music businessmen,

Theodore Thomas and Oscar Hammerstein were new men of this type. They, too, secured no hegemony. Thomas mistrusted the Damrosches and Anton Seidl. Hammerstein made war on the Met. Kessner observes of Boston that its "tightly organized commercial elite formed a circle of conservative men who were more concerned with avoiding loss than venturing for gain." New York, in comparison, embodied a "distinctive egalitarianism" rejecting "the past's confining influence." By 1900 it had become the center of world capitalism. "It was also the center for social reform, unions of every stripe, intellectual radicalism, elite philanthropy, the social gospel movement, and a freewheeling municipal politics that empowered the working class." Classical music deserves inclusion on this list.[10]

■ ■ ■

The historical discourse on social control is reinforced by the discourse on "sacralization." We have traced the sacralization of Beethoven in Boston and of Wagner in New York. The concept is useful, even indispensable, in chronicling the long-emerging distinction between "culture" and "entertainment." Its best-known practitioner is Lawrence Levine, whose *Highbrow/Lowbrow: The Emergence of Cultural Hierarchy in America* is a landmark 1988 study. Levine valuably tracks the sacralization movement across the arts—musical, visual, dramatic—in turn-of-the-century America; John Sullivan Dwight, Theodore Thomas, and Henry Higginson figure prominently in his narrative. The account gains urgency from his impatience with restrictive genteel norms. He decries the "bifurcation" of culture into high and low; he deplores the elevation of symphonies and plays that had excited more popular, less reverent acclaim before stratification set in. The agents of change he identifies are upper-class snobs spurning the rabble. The outcome is dessicated art worshipped by an elite, pacified audience preoccupied with status.

Rose Fay Thomas, in Chicago, may plausibly exemplify the new attitudes Levine describes, but Henry Higginson (whose skewed portrayal in *Highbrow/Lowbrow* is addressed in an earlier chapter) does not. New York opera at midcentury truly illustrates the raucous vitality Levine admires, but once Rossini and Donizetti made way for Verdi and Wagner, these same audiences needed disciplining. And it is misleading and confusing to further argue that in subsequent decades the Academy of Music and Metropolitan Opera "were deeply influenced if not controlled by wealthy patrons whose impresarios and conductors strove to keep the opera they presented free from the influence of other genres and other groups."[11]

Cultural historians argue insightfully that late-nineteenth-century institutions of culture abetted the consolidation of class identity, of a durable monied elite combining new wealth with old; this is overtly what happened (as we have seen) with the creation of the Metropolitan Opera. The Boston Symphony, too, was clearly "embedded in a Brahmin community." But it does not follow that the "sacralization of art" was "the work of . . . 'cultural capitalists,'" or that by the 1880s upper-class New Yorkers "had created a set of cultural institutions they clearly dominated and in which they set class-specific aesthetic standards, most prominently at the Metropolitan Museum of Art, the Metropolitan Opera, and the New York Philharmonic," or that these institutions "derived their programmatic ideas" from the upper classes, and "principally catered to the city's economic elite."[12] Only writers innocent of the history of music could make such assertions. A defining vignette for musical sacralization in this period would be the reverent silence imposed by *Parsifal* or *Tristan*. Composers, not monied elites, were here the prime agents. Secondarily, sacralization was instigated by priestly and hypnotic performers like Seidl or Arthur Nikisch, or by performers less "religious" who nonetheless served a holy repertoire distinct from "entertainment." Theodore Thomas exemplifies this latter group, as do the pianists Anton Rubinstein and Hans von Bülow, whose American impact we will eventually consider.

These were artists, too, who incomparably elevated standards of performance for an audience not fashion enslaved but religiously impassioned. Attendant socialites and others desiring to be seen were as likely to resist as to submit.★ For more fervent acolytes, sacralization dictated the insatiable ovation interrupting the first performance of the *New World* Symphony, or the frenzied Wagnerites who screamed delight. This phenomenon may have fortuitously served other purposes, including class consolidation. But it essentially documents aesthetic, not sociological, change.

The trajectory that propelled Wagner from the Stadttheater to the Met excellently demonstrates the lowbrow-to-highbrow scenario Levine adduces, but it does not follow that Wagner was thereby vitiated. More fundamentally, the Wagner cult escapes Levine's condemnations because sacralization was aesthetically intrinsic to Wagnerism. Wagner inhabited a Romantic *Weltan-*

★ In 1872 Horace Greeley, then a presidential candidate, was observed at an Anton Rubinstein recital "transported . . . to the land of dreams. . . . In his ecstatic trance his audible breathing was a comforting assurance to the myriads who look to him to save the country that he still lived." A few months later the *New York Weekly Review* published "Nature's Sweet Restorer," beginning, "At nearly every concert where the better class of music is performed you may see somebody asleep. . . . The oratorio, the Thomas Symphony concerts, the Rubinstein concerts all are attended with great regularity by faithful slumberers." See *Dexter Smith's* (Dec. 1872) and *Dwight's Journal of Music* (Apr. 19, 1873). I am indebted to R. Allen Lott for these references.

schauung binding art and religion, adumbrating themes of worldly travail and spiritual transcendence. He generated an ideology—Wagnerism—streaming with fin de siècle intellectual currents. As a stage in sacralization, Wagnerism struck a balance between spontaneity and ritual. It refined taste and behavior without resorting to cultural taxidermy. It illustrates the sacralizing impulse in American classical music not as inhibitive or intrusive but, in its only intellectually distinguished phase, substantially resonant with its subject matter.

If Levine's book is powered by dismay at the damage wrought by sacralized culture in the course of the twentieth century, there is nothing wrong with that.★ Determined to root out the culprits, he tracks them deep into the nineteenth century, which cannot be gainsaid: merely consider John Sullivan Dwight and his purification project, stamping out the monster concerts. But Levine's heartfelt populism—he prefers democratized cultural expression and reception; he mistrusts wealth; he dislikes ostentation—misleads him into overly equating the "highbrow" mentality of his own times, and its antidemocratic disparagement of the popular arts, with the practices and pronouncements of Thomas and Higginson in another era.

When and how did classical music become parochially "elitist" and restrictively "antidemocratic"? When did reverence degenerate into a species of snobbery? Less in the Gilded Age, less at the turn of the century, than (as the remainder of this book will argue) during the interwar decades. That Thomas, Higginson, or Seidl religiously worshipped music did not make them snobs. Even Oscar Hammerstein, who despised the rich, sacralized grand opera as "the most elevating influence upon modern society, after religion." So uplifted by opera was Hammerstein that he could say, "I leave the house with the same feeling I might have after hearing a great sermon or a great church ceremonial. I sincerely believe that nothing will make better citizenship than familiarity with grand opera. . . . There cannot be the slightest question about its refining effect upon a community."[13] It was after Higginson, Seidl, and Hammerstein—after World War I—that sacralization turned into a popular movement, a midculture, rejecting contemporary culture, enshrining dead European masters and celebrity performers. Compared to New York's late-nineteenth-century audiences, or Boston's—audiences with something to give—the Toscanini audience of the thirties and forties was intellectually stunted. The Wagnerian glow of sacralization yielded to commercial glare: a proprietary spotlight illuminating select brand names and marketing claims to greatness. Juxtaposed with the elitism of this phenomenon—a distinction not

---

★ The same could be said of my own *Understanding Toscanini: How He Became an American Culture-God and Helped Create a New Audience for Old Music* (New York: A. A. Knopf, 1987).

of class, but of kind—Dvořák's 1895 Madison Square Garden concert, with its Stephen Foster tune and black singers, its student composer and musicians, more evokes Hull House than any purported plutocracy of ownership and consumption.

In truth, the picture of late Gilded Age orchestras and opera houses ensnared by machinations of social control and sacralization is an extrapolation, a cultural metaphor for the social inequities and corporate dominion of the period. George M. Pullman, in Chicago, created a model workers' town adjacent to his railroad car works: a supervised environment including an indoor shopping arcade, a library stocked with five thousand volumes, a free school with a playground (a rarity), a park with a miniature lake, an athletic club, a one-thousand-seat theater, a hotel, a bank, a church. The streets were paved. The lawns were maintained. Garbage and sewage were regularly disposed of. All children were vaccinated for smallpox. Adult education classes were offered. The theater booked family entertainments only. A military band gave weekly concerts in the summer. Liquor was prohibited except at the expensive hotel bar. Prostitution was outlawed. Each facility in the model town was expected to yield a 6 percent profit. The church was expensive: no denomination could afford to rent it. The library charged a fee: it had few members. Rents were relatively high. Workers could not own their houses; company ownership of all public space and every home, a spokesman explained, was a necessary part of "a single control of plan and expenditure, which would have failed if a single lot had been sold." "Spotters" were employed as informers; potential troublemakers were evicted. According to an influential 1884 investigative article in *Harper's*, by the economist Richard Ely, the town of Pullman was a "sad spectacle," a "population of eight thousand souls where not one single person dare speak out openly his opinion about the town in which he lives. One feels that one is mingling with a dependent, servile people."[14] This regime cannot be translated into Theodore Thomas's style of leadership, or Henry Higginson's. There were no musical Pullmans.

Not for nothing did Gilded Age culture-bearers decry the new industrial order as dehumanizing and antihumanist. Wagnerism, dominating the musical life of the century's final decades, was in part a compensatory movement, a countervailing initiative against lives overregulated and controlled.

■ ■ ■

The post–Gilded Age period, which we have examined in some detail, is more difficult to compass. Dvořák departed, Seidl died, Thomas aged. In Boston, the controversies of the Nikisch years receded into memory; Muck struck a steady middle course. In New York, Damrosch was dull; with the passing of Mahler, the guarantors entrusted the Philharmonic to a lesser conductor. Of America's two galvanizing musical leaders in the years before World War I, Toscanini, at the Met, was increasingly estranged by contemporary aesthetic currents. Only Stokowski, in Philadelphia, kept abreast.

To apply a wider lens: abroad, Picasso, Joyce, D. H. Lawrence, Kandinsky, Stravinsky, Schoenberg were among the new beacons. At home, the Chicago poets included Carl Sandburg and Vachel Lindsay. T. S. Eliot and Ezra Pound were already writing and being written about. H. L. Mencken championed Nietzsche, Conrad, Dreiser. Huneker espoused Hauptmann, Munch, Strindberg, Wedekind. Dostoyevsky was in vogue, as were Bergson's "life force" and Freud. The Armory Show of 1913 showcased Cubism, Matisse, Toulouse-Lautrec, and stimulated a group of Americans, including Alfred Stieglitz, to organize a show of their own. Diaghilev's Ballets Russes—minus *The Rite of Spring*—triumphed in its American debut tour of 1916. African-American music was in a state of vigorous arousal, activated by the likes of Scott Joplin, Will Marion Cook, and James Reese Europe. Greenwich Village discovered Eugene O'Neill. Randolph Bourne, in a characteristic 1917 manifesto, proclaimed "a spirit freely experimental, skeptical of inherited values."[15]

To what degree did American classical music partake? Its notorious wild man, aligned with the literary rebels, was an ephemeral pianist/composer, Leo Ornstein, whose meteoric tone clusters confounded and amazed. Loeffler and Griffes were offshoots of turn-of-the-century aestheticism—the one mild, the other early arrested. Ives, however incidentally a practitioner of contemporary "free verse" and mysticism, stood alone—uninfluenced, uninfluenceable. There is no American concert composer of the prewar period in parallel with the likes of Eliot, Pound, O'Neill, or Stieglitz. It was the new Europeans who stirred the pot. Between 1908 and 1911, Mahler's First, Second, and Fourth Symphonies were auditioned in New York, under the composer's baton, with a combination of consternation and genuine interest. Debussy's *Pelléas et Mélisande* was more to Boston's liking, in 1912, than it had been to New York's. Boston endured Schoenberg's Five Pieces for Orchestra in 1914. "Richard Strauss" was in 1913 listed by the *Nation* alongside tango, eugenics, the slit skirt, sex hygiene, white slaves, John Masefield, and the double standard of morality as one of "a conglomerate of things important and unimportant" which "involve an abandonment of the old proprieties and the old reticences."[16]

Strauss's *Salome* most excited special fascination and special resistance. At a "public rehearsal," on January 20, 1907, many fled the Met at the beginning of the final scene, in which Salome addresses the severed head of John the Baptist. Those who stayed offered only brief and scattered applause. A "grip of strange horror and disgust" afflicted the ashen silent majority. Following the premiere, two days later, the board of directors—including J. P. Morgan, William K. Vanderbilt, and August Belmont—declared *Salome* "objectionable and detrimental to the best intent of the Metropolitan Opera House."[17] It is important to consider that Otto Kahn, of a more progressive board faction, supported giving *Salome*, and that two seasons later (as we have seen) Oscar Hammerstein's company presented it without incident to a different New York constituency. But the affronted sensibilities at the Met cannot be written off as merely ignorant or inane.

Certainly this smattering of the newest European music was resisted by the mainstream American critics. Philip Hale, in Boston, acknowledged "beautiful suggestions of mood" and "strangely beautiful effects of color" in the Schoenberg Pieces, but was mainly alarmed. When *The Rite of Spring* arrived in Boston in 1924, he found it "irritatingly tiresome" as a concert work. W. J. Henderson, in New York, rejected modernism with certain allowances: in 1925, he conceded that "to deny that [Schoenberg's] *Pierrot Lunaire* has force and delineative quality is futile"; in 1928, he called Stravinsky's *Apollo* "chaste, dignified, restful . . . genuinely beautiful"; in 1931, he declared that "nothing by any modernist" surpassed the absorbing if gruesome impact of Berg's *Wozzeck*. His putdown of Strauss's *Death and Transfiguration* and *Thus Spake Zarathustra* in 1897 was virtuosic:

> I challenge any living man to say honestly that he ever came away from the performance of a symphonic poem by Richard Strauss with any finer impulse of his nature quickened, with any high emotion warmed, or with any sweeter sensibility touched . . . to prod the dying man to more gasps and record them with phonograph and metronome for future reproduction on trombones in syncopated rhythms; to turn the face of the convalescent to the light and read in it wild dreams of the fever-drained mind that they may be hereafter voiced in the stentorous pantings of stopped horns or the sepulchural [*sic*] moanings of the violas; to read the vision of a world-wreck in the mind of a drunken man hearing the tolling of the midnight hour that it may afterward be hurled at an amazed audience in a stunning clangor of tympani, bass drum, cymbals, and gong—these seem to be worthy objects for the art of music, according to the gospel of Richard Strauss, prince royal of tonal decadents.[18]

Predictably, it was Henry Krehbiel who most fully articulated and defended the boundaries of fin de siècle genteel taste. More firmly than Hale or Henderson, he drew the line at Schoenberg and Stravinsky. His impatience with the pretentious "monotony" of *Pelléas*, and with Mahler's eclecticism, has been documented here. We have earlier sampled, as well, the snorting preamble to his investigation of *Salome*'s "pestiferous" odor. Holding his nose, he issues findings that impressively limn a rearguard American aesthetic credo, circa 1900. The complete report—thirteen pages, in *Chapters of Opera*—is worth reading in full, not least for its creative language: no less than Henderson, Krehbiel was challenged by Strauss's musical pyrotechnics to comparable feats of descriptive extravagance. He documents "the stridulous whirring of empty fifths in the violins," the "crepitating volubility" with which Strauss endows Herod. He is a vivid reporter and shrewd analyst: "Dissonance runs riot and frequently carries the imagination away completely captive"; "only the pompous proclamations of the theme which is dominant in Jochanaan's music saves it from being called commonplace." Essentially, however, his critique hinges on aesthetics: even if we concede—a reluctant concession, a sign of the times—that truth is not always beautiful, that "ugliness is entitled to be raised to a valid principle" in opera as an "aid to dramatic expression," *Salome* remains essentially meretricious. Like Henderson, Krehbiel dismisses Strauss as an opportunist; the ending of *Salome*, read by Krehbiel, outrages "every sacred instinct of humanity," and merely for effect: "Strauss, to put it mildly, is a sensationalist despite his genius, and his business sense is large." Subsequently, reviewing *Elektra*, Krehbiel dismissed the Strauss operas in toto:

> Interest burns itself out speedily because it finds no healthy nourishment in them; nothing to warm the emotions, exalt the mind, permanently to charm the senses, awaken the desire for frequent companionship, or foster a taste like that created by a contemplation of the true, the beautiful, and the good. Pathological subjects belong to the field of scientific knowledge—not to that of art. A visit to a madhouse or infirmary may be undertaken once to gratify curiosity; aesthetic pleasure can never come from frequent contemplation of mental and moral abnormalities or physical monstrosities.[19]

Krehbiel somehow stayed the course until his merciful death, in 1923; his swan song was titled "The Curse of Affectation and Modernism in Music."

Henry Krehbiel steadfastly pursued true art in the realm of Arnoldian sweetness and light. Strauss was obviously no seeker of beauty or goodness; neither did he seek truth. If Henderson at least found truth in *Wozzeck*, he mourned the absence of beauty and goodness there. When Richard Aldrich— Henderson's opposite number at the *New York Times* and, like Henderson, a pallbearer at Krehbiel's funeral—died suddenly in 1937, W. J. Henderson, age eighty-one, ended his critical career with a bullet to the head.

Even James Gibbons Huneker, of the Old Guard, was no connoisseur of modernist gloom. Surer harbingers of the new musical fashions were new writers still marginal: Paul Rosenfeld, Carl Van Vechten, Lawrence Gilman. The most prominent prophet was of course Stokowski. It was not only that he had already, in 1915, performed Schoenberg's Chamber Symphony, and Mahler's Eighth and *Das Lied von der Erde* a year later; Stokowski cared nothing for the moral criterion in art (or, as became known, in his personal affairs). He was an epicure, a sensualist, a relativist, an experimentalist for whom the new was virtuous in and of itself. That his early career coincided with the likes of Muck, Stock, Stransky, Toscanini, and Walter Damrosch was an incongruity of musical history. At the same time, he remained a relatively local figure—only in the twenties did he establish a New York base via the League of Composers; only then did he introduce Americans (at last) to *The Rite of Spring*, and to such essential Stravinsky as *Les noces* and Symphonies for Wind Instruments, to such essential Schoenberg as *Pierrot Lunaire*.

In American classical music, the spirit of adventure, pushing into new realms of experience, was actually more tangible during and before the Wagnerian 1880s and 1890s. These were the decades in which Mariana Van Rensselaer, a distinguished critic of art and architecture, held that "the place of music" was the "great opposing fact" contradicting notions of "a prosaic, a material, unimaginative age," the decades in which the Chicago music critic W. S. B. Mathews wrote, "There are few periods in the history of any country, ancient or modern, in which progress in art has been so rapid as in the progress in music in this country since the Civil War."[20] The emptiness that craved *Tristan*, the energies that urged a New World compositional canon, began to diminish after 1900. If Krehbiel is the best guide to the surging fin de siècle trajectory of concerts and opera, no writer furnishes a comparable overview of the more inchoate prewar years. One witness to the period offers an exceptional underview—one that will enable us, by way of summary, to survey American musical developments at the grassroots level, and away from the metropolitan centers of the Northeast.

■ ■ ■

We have already encountered Arthur Farwell as the author of an appreciative description of Gustav Mahler's interpretation of Schubert's Ninth Symphony, pursued by "the imp of the perverse," of vivid first impressions of the young Leopold Stokowski, and, finally, as a significant Indianist composer in the footsteps of Dvořák. A prophet and apostle of a coming American music, an enraptured visionary, a Romantic swept up in the optimism, mysticism, and experimentalism of early-twentieth-century artists and thinkers, Farwell was born in St. Paul in 1872. He acquired galvanizing impressions of Beethoven, Schubert, and Wagner "all in a jumble" from Nikisch and the Boston Symphony while attending the Massachusetts Institute of Technology as a fledgling electrical engineer.[21] He switched to composing and studied seriously with George Chadwick. He was also smitten by Anton Seidl and by Wagnerism, in which he detected "primal forces of man and nature" suited to Americans. He went to Germany and took lessons with Humperdinck and Pfitzner. Back in Massachusetts, he could not find a publisher for his *American Indian Melodies* and so in 1901 founded the Wa-Wan Press, for eleven years a historic outlet for new American works, named after a peace ceremony of the Omahas. His Wa-Wan Society of America, begun in 1907, similarly strove to take up where Dvořák had left off. Farwell's own Indianist music, if a mixed bag, includes at least one keyboard work—the *Navajo War Dance* No. 2 of 1905— whose dissonance and rhythmic bite suggest a New World Bartók. Like Bartók, too, Farwell admired indigenous songs and singers as models of unmediated poetry and wisdom. John Kirkpatrick, the first pianist to champion Ives's *Concord* Sonata, edited and performed the *Navajo War Dance* No. 2. Another Farwell keyboard miniature, the ghostly *Pawnee Horses*, was once called by Charles Martin Loeffler the best composition yet written by an American.[22] An expanded a cappella choral version of *Pawnee Horses* is a tour de force both primal and complex.

Farwell also esteemed cowboy and Hispanic songs as "a vast mine of valuable musical ore, to be wrought into music of new types and colors. In view of the Teutonic domination in America, it presented what . . . might be called 'the margin of the unGerman.'" He traveled the country giving lecture-recitals, meeting and organizing composers, investigating and documenting vernacular strains. In Los Angeles, he thrilled to hear Spanish-American and Native American singers at the home of the pioneering ethnomusicologist Charles F. Lummis, and sampled Lummis's collection of wax cylinder recordings of such music. In the Southwest, he heard an Omaha song "so complex and difficult in its rhythm as to render it virtually impossible . . . to be sung by any known singer except an Indian"—the germ of *Pawnee Horses*. He created a version of the familiar "Dying Cowboy" ("Bury me not on the lone prairie"), striving rhythmically to retain the "free and easy way of singing it" as heard on the plains. In all these pre-1910 endeavors Farwell aimed for the creation of a new musical order, worthy of "poetic and picturesque aspects of our land."[23]

In a subsequent phase of his mercurial career, Farwell created open-air pageants as a catalyst for a distinctively American musical art. A pivotal influence were the annual Grove Plays of San Francisco's Bohemian Club, produced in an eight-hundred-acre Redwood forest seventy-five miles north of the city. David Bispham, a leading American baritone and a Farwell associate, took part in the 1910 production, *The Cave Man*. His memoirs report a natural auditorium "unequal in the world," a proscenium arch framed by two gigantic trees, superb outdoor acoustics, an excellent orchestra hidden from view, elaborate lighting and scenic effects, and an audience seated on felled logs.

> Cave men are dimly seen climbing upward until they are replaced by shepherds climbing still upward in shadow, singing as they go. As the shepherds reach a higher level they are replaced by farmers who climb in turn up the hill in a stronger light, and farmers are replaced in turn by warriors with helmets and shield. The warriors are succeeded upon a higher level still by white-robed philosophers climbing in a light which is growing ever stronger. The hillside is thronged with the processional of the ages, the chorus of voices singing in ever heightening rhapsody, which is increased by the spiritual voices of boys from a distance, singing:
>
> > Man awaketh from the dream of the senses;
> > Time falleth from him like a shadow;
> > Glory clotheth him for evermore![24]

The Grove Plays and similar pageants of the period reinforced Farwell's predilection to seek a different social function for music. As supervisor of Municipal Music for New York City from 1910 to 1913, he presented free orchestral concerts. He next organized a New York Community Chorus open to all without audition. In 1916 he helped to create a Song and Light Festival in Central Park, at which thirty thousand massed to hear and see an orchestra lit by lanterns. In 1925 he undertook a Theater of the Stars in the San Bernardino Mountains of California.

The Indianist movement spearheaded by Farwell is today vaguely remembered (if at all) as naïve and culturally exploitative. But judged by his writings and music Farwell was no naif. He viewed Native American chant as one part of a varied tapestry of Americana. His lifelong reverence for the Native American—which began in childhood, when he lived for a time in a Native American village on Lake Superior, hunted with Native American guides, and heard the speeches of "the old priests"—was an honorable product of his time. As a music publisher, he abhorred sentimentality "like poison,"[25] and if it cannot be said that all Wa-Wan publications transcend kitsch, his own best

Wa-Wan works deserve to be perpetuated as superior early efforts to create an American concert music.

But the chief fascination of Farwell's vision is that, a generation before the interwar "ultra-moderns," he directed Americans away from the concert hall and opera house. No previous writer or composer so powerfully articulated the conviction that the New World required institutions and genres other than concert and opera, that the musical needs of Americans were more opposed than served by "the standards of the centres of conventional and fashionable musical culture." Is America "merely trivially or luxuriously going to amuse herself with the work of the craftsmen of other lands, as a spoiled daughter of wealth might toy with some rare scarab of the Nile or Etruscan bracelet?" he asked rhetorically in *Musical America* in 1909.

America set up and had in operation a great definite machinery for the performance and propagation of European music, when that was all there was to have, and before the American composer, in sufficient numbers and force to count, had come on the scene. . . .

The whole American people for generations has thus been educated and trained to the idea that the only real music is European music. . . .

[T]he idea "American composer," taking it in the broadest sense and in relation to the history of music, is a new idea in the world. A place must be made for this new idea. To make this place something must be displaced a little, moved to one side or readjusted. But even a very slight readjustment of so massive a machine as the national musical life—a readjustment which must be made, too, while the machine is running— is a pretty serious and difficult affair. It throws out of gear the calculations of many people.

In the same breath, Farwell called for adjustments by the artists' managers and publishing houses of the East. Versus "the vice-like grip which European musical tradition has upon the generation still in power in our musical life," he quested—sometimes vaguely, sometimes not—for America's "great unwritten music," an "ascending deflection in the course of music and of humanity" compatible with the Grand Canyon, with Lincoln and Whitman, with democracy.[26]

No less than in the case of William Henry Fry ranting against the New York Philharmonic, the sum total of such plans and polemics reflects excitement and frustration in equal measure. Certainly the influential and nurturing intimacy of such missionaries as Thomas, Seidl, or Dvořák was by 1910 a thing of the past for the American composer. Stokowski, master missionary of the present, was a committed internationalist. Ives, who fashioned an American voice in some ways answering Farwell's call, remained inaudible. Farwell's failure to secure funding for a second Theater of the Stars season, in 1926, was a personal turning point. His dream of a communal American musical experience—a dream arguably resonant with Billings and the New England singing schools, with jazz and the Cotton Club, with Woodstock and the sixties—died a lingering but decisive death. The pageantry movement was supplanted by the radio, the phonograph, and the movies; by New World mores of "greatness" that grew more, not less, Eurocentric.

Farwell's later music, including an intriguing series of *Polytonal Studies* for piano (1940–52), is conceived for the concert hall. After a lifetime of looking forward, he grew nostalgic. For all his experimentalism, he never made peace with modernism. Ever a product of Dvořák and of American Wagnerism, he increasingly considered the music of his time spiritually bankrupt; he called Richard Strauss, even Debussy and Brahms, "Godless" and "soul-less." In 1909, chronicling the "*Wanderjahre* of a Revolutionist" for *Musical America*, he had written of meeting Seidl at Bayreuth in 1897:

> The "Great Silent One" now asked me to take a walk, and we passed along the road until we came to a bridge over a little stream. Here he paused, and . . . spoke most eloquently for some time upon the beauty and nobility of the music of *Parsifal*, upon his memories of the earlier Bayreuth, his homesickness there now, and his desire to go back to his beloved New York. No incident of my wanderings has impressed itself more deeply upon my memory than this privileged moment, when the soul of this silent man so simply, so nobly revealed itself. It was the last time that I was ever to see him.

In 1949—eight years before his death—Farwell again reflected on Seidl and New York, for the *Musical Quarterly*, and wrote:

> For all those in any degree sensitive to the spirit of music and romance, the presence of Anton Seidl, famous alike for the depth of his silence and the height of his art, tinged the atmosphere and the consciousness of the city with a peculiarly individual and glowing quality of feeling such as it has not known before or since. Seidl was among the last of the typical nineteenth-century conductors, immediately preceding the advent of the more dazzling, but, as many hold, less sympathetic virtuoso-conductor. What one felt, in Seidl's evocation of orchestral or operatic masterpieces, was his reverential love for the nobly beautiful in music

and his complete self-effacement, which made it possible for this beauty to go forth to his hearers unaffected by any slightest intrusion of his own personality. And because of this, and of his known love for New York, it was downright affection, rather than admiration or awe, that New York returned to him.[27]

■ ■ ■

In a 1998 essay "In Defense of Nostalgia," the American historian Jackson Lears wrote, "We need to take nostalgia seriously as an energizing impulse, maybe even a form of knowledge. The effort to revalue what has been lost can motivate serious historical inquiry; it can also cast a powerful light on the present." Lears invites reconsideration of Victorian reticence, of "the determination to declare certain realms of experience beyond public discussion or display, the frame of mind dismissed as puritanical by legions of cultural radicals. Reticence . . . is not merely repression; it is a way human cultures map out fundamental categories of meaning."[28]

In the third act of *Tristan und Isolde*, Tristan emerges from a long coma, the result of a wound. He is suicidal and amnesic. Dredging up his past, he succumbs to paroxysms of delirium and clairvoyance. He attains a state of illumination, which paradoxically drives him to tear off his bandages and expire. When Albert Niemann bared his bloody wound at the first New York *Tristan*, in 1886, it was too much. Henry Krehbiel wrote, "An experienced actress who sat . . . at my elbow grew faint and almost swooned. . . . [Niemann] never again ventured to expose the wound in his breast, though the act is justified, if not demanded, by the text."[29] This act of reticence registered not repression, but the visceral immediacy of Tristan's pain as experienced by Niemann and by a virgin audience innocent of the sensory onslaught of our daily media intake a century later.

In different cultures, Wagnerism registered socialism or nationalism, irreverence or piety. Anton Seidl, Henry Krehbiel, and other fin de siècle Wagnerites looked at Wagner with respect and reverence—and saw something of themselves. Today, we look at Wagner and wince at his racism. We identify with his ambivalence about redemption. We are fascinated by his depictions of weakness and evil.

The current popularity of novels and films set in turn-of-the-century America is not just a function of quaint or picturesque costumes and customs. Niemann was the most tortured, most impassioned Tristan of his era. His reticence gauged a shifting equilibrium between intense emotional appetite and intense moral aspiration. It registered a moral compass.

BOOK TWO

"Great Performances": Decline and Fall

■

Very often I get the impression that audiences seem to think that the endless repetition of a small body of entrenched masterworks is all that is required for a ripe musical culture.... Needless to say, I have no quarrel with masterpieces. I think I revere and enjoy them as well as the next fellow. But when they are used, unwittingly perhaps, to stifle contemporary effort in our own country, then I am almost tempted to stake the most extreme view and say that we should be better off without them!

—AARON COPLAND (1941)

Introduction: The Great Schism (1914)

■

The wave of anti-German feeling that swept Karl Muck off his Boston podium infiltrated lives public and private throughout the United States.

Only decades previously, the prestige of German learning and art had peaked in America. Germany was the land of Goethe, Kant, Humboldt, Beethoven. With the coming of the Great War, even the teaching and speaking of German came under attack. German-Americans were suspected of espionage; they were said by the Red Cross to have sabotaged bandages with ground glass. Overnight, the vigorous subculture of German-language newspapers, theaters, singing societies, and schools disappeared. Now there were "Germans" and "Americans" only; no hyphenates remained. The *Saturday Evening Post* urged that the "scum of the melting pot" be cleaned out of schools, the press, and the government.[1]

The peculiar ferocity of the attack on Germans and German-Americans had a peculiar cause. In the case of the Revolution and the Civil War, the reasons Americans fought were obvious and the enemy was self-evident. The same would be true of World War II. But reasonable Americans differed over whether to go to war in Europe in 1917, and over which side to join.

Americans needed convincing that their adopted cause was just. To this end, a Committee on Public Information (CPI), the government's first large-scale attempt to manufacture propaganda, was launched. To stamp out the image of the civilizing German, *Kultur* was linked to "Prussian militarism" and the "wanton murder" of Belgian babies. "In the vicious guttural language of *Kultur*," read one CPI advertisement, "the degree A. B. means Bachelor of Atrocities."[2] This was the climate in which families resisting "flying squads" promoting bond purchases found their homes painted yellow and supposed draft dodgers were forced to kneel and kiss the flag, in which more than fifteen hundred alleged spies and traitors were arrested, and others shot or hanged.

Meanwhile, the first modern mass war cost the lives of eight million soldiers. It introduced gas warfare, barbed wire, and the machine gun. At the battle of the Somme, the largest military engagement in recorded history, eleven British divisions arose along a thirteen-mile front and began walking forward. Out of 110,000 attackers, 60,000 were killed the first day. No previous war had seemed so impersonal or illogical, so meaningless or absurd.

World War I discredited the genteel tradition. The genteel scholars and writers were ardent Germanophiles; many had studied in Germany. It made no difference—or, rather, it made matters worse—that in most cases they became wartime patriots, supporting Woodrow Wilson's dream of a war to end all wars in a sunburst of moral resolve. The moralism of Gilded Age artists and intellectuals, including their insistence on the moral function of art, could not survive the carnage of the war or its destructive diplomatic aftermath. As early as 1915, the *New Republic* pertinently inquired, "Is it not a possibility that what is today taking place marks quite as complete a bankruptcy of ideas, systems, society, as did the French Revolution?" Americans were left pondering why men had died, as Ezra Pound wrote, "for a botched civilization." "The plunge of civilization into this abyss of blood and darkness," wrote Henry James, "is a thing that . . . gives away the whole long age during which we have supposed the world to be, with whatever abatement, gradually bettering."[3] Discredited were the politics of Romantic nationalism and the aesthetics of grandiose sentiment. The concept of civilization as pursuant to truth and beauty was truly shattered.

The rejection of American optimism dictated a rejection of Gilded Age letters—of the "smiling aspects of life" William Dean Howells had adduced in justification of the relative "purity" and "innocence" of the American novel compared with a French "tradition of indecency" less applicable to New World experience.[4] Van Wyck Brooks's landmark prophecy, *America's Coming of Age* (1916), downgraded Henry Wadsworth Longfellow and James Russell Lowell in quest of an American voice less puritanical and moralistic, less impractically closeted and implausibly sanguine.

The bearing of these trends on classical music was as obvious as it was drastic. America's musical high culture was essentially a German import. Artists and repertoire were mainly Germanic, as were the ideals of uplift that music was thought to serve. As of 1900, Wagnerism—the wholesome American variety—reigned supreme. After 1915, German composers, Wagner included, were downplayed or banned. Of the composers listed on Boston Symphony programs, the proportion from German or Hapsburg lands dropped from 62 percent in 1916–17 to 29.7 percent in 1918–19. In New York, the Philharmonic did without all living German composers (of whom Richard Strauss was already a canonized master). Oswald Garrison Villard, the chairman of the Philharmonic board (and editor of the *New York Post* and *The Nation*), was asked to resign because he opposed America's war declaration. The German/Austrian repertoire quotient shrank from 65 to 40 percent. Wagner's Liebestod became "Isolde's Love-Death," *Die Meistersinger* was called *The Mastersingers*.[5]

At the Met, Wagner was banned even in translation, along with the rest of the German repertoire. In the boardroom, Mrs. William Jay, whom we have seen agitating against Karl Muck as a "dangerous alien," argued against Mozart and Beethoven, *The Magic Flute* and *Fidelio*, as follows: "Given in the German language and depicting scenes of violence, German opera cannot but draw our minds back to the spirit of greed and barbarism that has led to so much suffering."[6] (In Europe, as *Musical America* reported, German music continued to be enjoyed by English and French audiences. At Covent Garden, Thomas Beecham performed Wagner in English.)

Meanwhile, individual German musicians were no longer wanted. So prevalent were Germans in American orchestras that German was commonly the language of rehearsals. It was replaced by English, and as were German players by Americans. Twenty-nine German-born members of the Boston Symphony were interned.[7] The conductor of the Cincinnati Symphony, Ernst Kunwald, was made to join Muck at Fort Oglethorpe. The Chicago Symphony's Frederick Stock temporarily resigned. The New York Philharmonic's Josef Stransky, though Bohemian, took steps to become an American citizen. At the Met, Giulio Gatti-Casazza dismissed six German singers and lost others (including the irreplaceable Olive Fremstad) owing to repertoire restrictions. Of the departing vocalists, Johanna Gadski was married to a German reserve officer and had hosted a celebration when the *Lusitania* sank; she did not return to North America until 1929. The violinist Fritz Kreisler, already highly popular in the United States, had actually served in the Austrian army on the Russian front at the war's beginning; he felt compelled to cancel all his American engagements except those for charities to which he had pledged his support. Even Enrico Caruso, though a certain reject for reasons of health and age, was criticized for not enlisting in the Italian army; in compensation, he sang at Liberty Bond rallies at the rate of three a month.[8]

The general disruption may be imagined: canceled tours, even, as in the case of new operatic ventures in Philadelphia and Chicago, canceled seasons. The more profound disruption was long term. Not until 1991 would the New York Philharmonic again acquire a German music director. Shopping to replace Muck, the Boston Symphony was reported to be considering Ernest Bloch, Ossip Gabrilowitsch, Vincent D'Indy, Pierre Monteux, Sergei Rachmaninoff, Leopold Stokowski, and Sir Henry Wood. In 1918, an eighth non-German, France's Henri Rabaud, was named Boston's music director, to be followed by his countryman Monteux in 1919 and the Russian Serge Kousse-vitzky in 1924. Concurrently, the orchestra's proportion of French repertoire ballooned from 12 percent in 1916–17 to 46.5 percent in 1918–19. Nationally, the Austro-German repertoire dipped sharply, and never rebounded: from a high of 80 percent of the total symphonic repertoire in 1875, it leveled off at about 50 percent.[9]

The positive impact of these developments on American musicians was less than might have been predicted. *Musical America* was urging as early as 1918 that a "dark horse" American be appointed to the Boston Symphony podium, and prepared a list of possible candidates, including Henry Hadley, a notable composer who had conducted the orchestras of Seattle and San Francisco. Three decades earlier, George Chadwick had considered himself a plausible Boston Symphony music director and privately decried Henry Higginson's preference for Europeans. In fact, the Boston Symphony would first appoint an American music director in 2001; the day of the American conductor was still distant. As for composers, the Great War duly occasioned a surge in Amer-ican works performed by American orchestras, but this mainly subsided after 1920. One obstacle, ironically, was that American music was so largely Ger-manic in orientation: the new order, with its new enthusiasm for music French and Russian, was as averse to Chadwick and Foote, MacDowell and Strong as it was to Brahms and Wagner. Prior to Koussevitzky's arrival in 1924, the Boston Symphony gave seventy-eight performances of works by Chadwick, aptly acclaimed for their tangy American flavor; Koussevitzky, in twenty-five seasons, gave five. Of the other prominent Boston composers of the late Gilded Age, Koussevitzky led no Paine, no Parker, no Beach, and ten performances of Foote.[10]

Chadwick died, embittered by neglect, in 1931. In 1937 and 1944 Foote and Beach passed quietly from the scene. Even more than foreign-born conduc-tors, a new generation of native-born composers buried them with alacrity. Virgil Thomson, a leading postwar Francophile, called the music of Paine, Chadwick, and Beach "a pale copy" of "continental models" and reckoned their scale of achievement "a sort of adolescence." Leonard Bernstein termed this "the kindergarten period of American music," whose "fine, academic imi-tations" of European masters were actually intended to sound like Brahms and Liszt: "The more they did, the better." The prominent Polish-born musicolo-gist Hugo Leichtentritt, who actually studied with Paine at Harvard in the 1890s, looked back in 1946 and found "an American flavor . . . only rarely and faintly perceptible" in Boston composers of half a century before, composers entitled to be remembered "through only a small selection of their most char-acteristic and accomplished works, performed on special occasions."[11]

This exaggerated disdain—a product of modernism, ignorance, and preju-dice—betokened a fresh start by Thomson and other American composers for whom past American models figured as negative examples merely. But the fresh start was also a late start: one reason (among many) why postwar com-posers were swiftly eclipsed by postwar performers.

■ ■ ■

In 1927, Charles Edward Russell called the symphony orchestra America's "foremost cultural asset," its "sign of honor among the nations," its one "divi-sion of representative art" in which "achievement has gone beyond debate."[12] Russell was both a popular socialist writer and an authority on Theodore Thomas: a conjunction underscoring the degree to which American sym-phonic culture once seemed excitingly egalitarian. His patriotic pride reflected his abiding esteem for Thomas, and also the international prestige undeniably acquired by the Boston Symphony, the Philadelphia Orchestra, and (belatedly) the New York Philharmonic.

Russell was correct to claim the virtuoso concert orchestra as a distinctive American achievement, remarkable in a country born more recently than Bach, Mozart, or Beethoven. But his claim was also curious, the equivalent of Germany calling the Berlin Philharmonic its musical "sign of honor" rather than, say, the symphonies of Beethoven, or Austria calling the Vienna Opera its "foremost" cultural attainment, rather than, for instance, the operas of Mozart. When Dvořák, Jeannette Thurber, and Henry Krehbiel pursued the creation of an "American school," the American voice they sought to foster was a composer's voice, not an orchestra's.

This, then, was a second postwar schism, as formidable as the turn against Germany. Supplanting the creative act, the act of performance became the defining focus of American classical music: the great orchestra, the great opera house, the great conductor, violinist, pianist, or singer. John Sullivan Dwight had made Beethoven an object of reverence. Anton Seidl had sacralized Wag-ner. Now it would be Arturo Toscanini who stirred the most worshipful adherence: a conductor—and one, moreover, narrow in outlook and mission.

And there were further ruptures in the unfolding of America's musical high culture. The Russian Revolution and World War II chased countless potent musicians to American shores. The newcomers included an array of Europe's most important composers, and battalions of individual performers so galva-nizing they instantly dominated the field. Native-born talent, struggling for a place in the sun, was now shadowed by the likes of Stravinsky, Schoenberg, Hindemith, and Bartók, by Rachmaninoff, Heifetz, Horowitz, and Schnabel.

Finally, America itself produced a new world of popular culture so vibrant and pervasive it displaced high culture as a national marker. Jazz defined American music more than symphonies and operas ever did or would. Orchestras were relegated to the status of great white hope: a futile strategy to purify and transcend the wild Harlem nights of Ellington and Armstrong, an exercise in retrenchment.

The Old World, to be sure, was not immune to these pressures. There, too, world war fractured the world of art. Composers lost stature; performers gained. Popular music (an American export) challenged and influenced opera and symphony. But Richard Strauss remained Germany's first musician. Italy (for a time) had Puccini, Scandinavia Sibelius. In Paris, important composers—Stravinsky and Falla among them—were as thick as important writers. And, far from being displaced, they fed on popular culture.

America, with its late start, had yet to acquire a Strauss, Puccini, Sibelius, Falla, or Stravinsky. The postwar schisms were cumulatively momentous because their point of impact was fragile. However vigorous, American classical music was nascent, and especially so with regard to what mattered most: an anchoring native canon. In no European country was the twentieth-century history of classical music subject to such wrenching external pressures, to the colonizing influence of such powerful outsiders.

A backward glance encapsulates the outcome. Dvořák, New York's most famous musician in the 1890s, was a composer (imagine such a thing today); his sights were fixed on the music of the present and on America. Toscanini, New York's most famous classical musician of the interwar decades, was a performer; he was dedicated to the music of the past and of Europe. Dvořák and Toscanini even document two types of musical celebrity. Dvořák was a reluctant celebrity—he had to be coaxed by Seidl to stand up and acknowledge the ovation for his Largo. But he was also a public celebrity—daily, he could be found smoking cigars and sipping beer opposite Seidl at Fleischmann's restaurant. Toscanini was an eager celebrity—he enjoyed his fame. But he was a private celebrity, chauffeured from his Riverdale home to NBC's Studio 8H, there to perform for an invited audience. His glamour was a function of his remoteness. This comparison, in its multiple dimensions, documents a sea change in less than half a century.

PART ONE

The Culture of Performance

■

CHAPTER 1

The Big Three

■

The Toscanini cult ▪ *David Sarnoff and NBC* ▪ *Leopold Stokowski and innovation* ▪ *Serge Koussevitzky and education*

Theodore Thomas's dictum that a symphony orchestra shows the culture of the community had come true in at least two cities before World War I. The Boston Symphony and the Philadelphia Orchestra were the signature cultural institutions for the communities they served. If the Chicago Symphony seemed less august, by the late twentieth century its high prestige was as unquestioned as its high contribution to the civic identity. By then, the same was true of the Cleveland Orchestra. But at no time has a New York City orchestra embodied New York City, unless the New York Philharmonic's very inconsistency may be said to register the city's frantic pace and protean diversity: a metropolis too big and varied to yield any single artistic or intellectual symbol.

Historically, the Philharmonic has had to compete even with other orchestras: the New York Symphony and Brooklyn Philharmonic, both creations of the Gilded Age; the Boston Symphony and Philadelphia Orchestra, both regular visitors by 1920. Such Philharmonic benefactors as Joseph Pulitzer competed with Harry Harkness Flagler and Andrew Carnegie, whose musical loyalties lay elsewhere. And the Philharmonic itself, as we have seen, grew slowly and sporadically. Its home moved from the Apollo Rooms, Niblo's Garden, the Academy of Music, and the Metropolitan Opera House to Carnegie Hall (and later from Carnegie to a Lincoln Center facility repeatedly modified in pursuit of acceptable acoustics). It had no father—no Higginson, Thomas, or Stokowski—to oversee the process of ripening. When maturity was finally thrust upon it, in 1909, the guarantors lacked sound leadership. Only with the arrival in 1922 of Willem Mengelberg, who had already made his Amsterdam Concertgebouw Orchestra matter, did the Philharmonic acquire something like the respectability of more solid symphonic organizations in smaller cities. The next conductor finally galvanized a disciplined "great orchestra" in peak estate. What it took was a reign of terror. How this was imposed is the subject matter of a peerless inside report by Winthrop Sargeant, a Philharmonic violinist before becoming a music critic.

Sargeant was initially a member of Walter Damrosch's New York Symphony, which by the 1920s, thanks to Flagler, was giving forty and more New York concerts a season and touring extensively (in 1920 it became the first American orchestra to travel to Europe). Damrosch imported distinguished first desk players and distinguished guest conductors (Mahler, Bruno Walter, and Otto Klemperer all made their American symphonic debuts on his podium). His repertoire, if increasingly conservative, was famously eclectic. As a barnstorming pioneer, he bears comparison with Theodore Thomas except that, unlike Thomas, he was not a great leader of men. In Sargeant's account, his orchestra was a motley assemblage susceptible to a good-natured resilience and camaraderie. Gripped by an "age-old European sense of paternalism," the players sought a "feudal protector." Damrosch provided jobs and a modicum of dignity; he was treated with "the respect, servility, self-depreciating clownishness and occasional truculence characteristic of the peasant serving his great lord." But in 1927 the Symphony, a relic in its own time, collapsed into a merger with the New York Philharmonic. Twenty Symphony members were to be retained by the "New York Philharmonic-Symphony," chosen by audition by Mengelberg's successor, Arturo Toscanini. "Stories had been leaking out of the Philharmonic rehearsals for some time. . . . They outlined a picture that was too definite not to have some foundation: that of an irascible Italian who combined all the most frightening qualities of the dictatorial temperament with all the most frightening qualities of genius."

Sargeant survived this trial by fire and landed in an orchestra as unlike the New York Symphony as an army is to a circus: "The power that welded it into a unit came from the top, from the absolute and omniscient dictatorship wielded by Toscanini. . . . Individually many of the Philharmonikers would willingly have cut each other's throats. Every man worked for himself, conscious that his survival depended purely on his own efforts." As for Toscanini:

> His aim was not to teach a tradition, but to bend the bowing, fingering, breathing, and the very emotions of the last second fiddler or bass clarinetist to every mercurial shading of his implacable will. . . . He started methodically converting the Philharmonic into a dependent organism, every member of which seemed to become a mere extension of his own agile brain, body and emotions. For Toscanini, the orchestra player had

no will of his own. He became a hypnotized creature reflecting one single will—the will of the maestro. . . .

At his rehearsals it was possible to be harassed, worried and overcome with a sense of one's own inadequacy, but it was impossible to be bored. A galvanic enthusiasm was communicated from maestro to players during every tense moment, and somehow the fear of the whiplash failed to generate the resentment that might have conflicted with it. The maestro induced a continuous psychology of crisis into everything he did. There is a state of mind that occurs to men in war, in the face of natural cataclysms, or in emergencies like fires and shipwrecks, where the individual is suddenly loosened from the petty egotisms of normal existence, and loses himself in the overwhelming necessity for action. In this state of mind he often accomplishes prodigies far beyond his everyday capacities, and he accomplishes them by a sort of automatism, in a condition of complete self-forgetfulness. Toscanini had the curious ability to generate this state of mind continuously in a hundred men faced with problems that were purely musical. Each movement of a symphony became an emergency which demanded every ounce of energy and concentration if it was not to end in overwhelming catastrophe. Each performance was played as though our very lives depended on its perfection.[1]

The psychology of crisis impelled the men to take such emergency measures as practicing at home and calling section rehearsals. And it punished every actual and potential rival. At the Met, Toscanini had made easy work of displacing Mahler. At the Philharmonic, Mengelberg's departure was swift and inexorable: Sargeant observed his rehearsals degenerate "into a state of anarchy." And there was a third casualty of the Toscanini juggernaut. This was Wilhelm Furtwängler, in his thirties already Germany's leading symphonic conductor and Nikisch's successor at the Berlin Philharmonic since 1922. Furtwängler mounted the New York Philharmonic podium before Toscanini did: in 1925. His first Philharmonic concert excited a fifteen-minute standing ovation. But his star waned with Toscanini's arrival in 1926. He seemed too Germanic. Times had changed, and so had the New York critics.

Of the Old Guard, only W. J. Henderson, now of the *New York Sun*, remained. With Henry Krehbiel's death, and the merger of the *New York Herald* and *New York Tribune*, the critic of the *Herald-Tribune* beginning in 1923 was Lawrence Gilman, a writer whose catholic tastes were trapped in a tortured Baroque prose style. Olin Downes, new to the *Times* in 1924, was a blunt and labored stylist. Compared to a Krehbiel, Henderson, Huneker, or Gilman, he did not aspire to literary or intellectual distinction. A populist, he hugged simple truths and enthusiasms. Rather than worldly, he was patriotic, even chauvinistic. His 1918 layman's guide, *The Lure of Music*, omitted all German and Austrian composers, resulting in a canon starting with Rossini.

Henderson and Gilman admired Furtwängler. Downes complained that, like those of other Germans, his readings "dragged" and were "sentimental." When Furtwängler did not defer to the literal dictates of the score, his penchant for subjectivity irked Downes, who intuited (correctly) a Germanic presumption to deeper currents of affinity. When Furtwängler's performances were (like his baton technique) imprecise, Downes was insensitive to the Germanic quest for *Innigkeit*—interiority. The "facts," he wrote, were that Furtwängler's Philharmonic concerts were deficient in "virtuoso finish" and "beauty of tone." He appealed (as no previous critic would have) to "the verdict of the public." He objected to programs "made in Germany." Furtwängler reportedly asked that the *Times* send a different critic to his concerts. Downes, in private, was heard to refer to Furtwängler as "swine." Of "The Return of Arturo Toscanini," Downes wrote:

> In listening to operatic and orchestral interpretations of Toscanini it has often seemed that after all the statement holds true of the quality of the Italian mind, the racial mind that has the finest facture of any in the world; the genius which, at its height, combines marvelously the qualities of analysis and perception, the objectivity of form, and the consuming fire of creative passion. . . .
>
> If ever there was a man who justified the theory of aristocracy built upon the fundamental conception that men are not born free and equal, that some are immeasurably superior to others, and that their superiority is justification for their control of others' acts and destinies, that man is Arturo Toscanini.[2]

Furtwängler last conducted the New York Philharmonic in 1927. His subsequent absence from the United States (he died in 1954) deprived American audiences of one of the century's dominant musical personalities. In America, Toscanini dominated. If the magnitude of his New York achievement was at first not appreciated abroad, something was done about that in 1930. Early in the century, Krehbiel and Henderson had caustically complained of Old World ignorance of New World musical standards. In 1929 Gilman wrote of an unnamed London critic, "We doubt if our British colleague would have believed us if we had told him that . . . America had been listening for twenty years, off and on, to performances of operatic and symphonic music under Arturo Toscanini the like of which most European capitals had never heard."

Now the mountain was going to Mahomet: the New York Philharmonic would tour France, Switzerland, Italy, Germany, Austria, Hungary, Czechoslovakia, Belgium, and England. The trip began in Paris, where Toscanini was called "a master of all conductors" and the orchestra's precision was termed "inexplicable," "wondrous," "absolute." In Berlin, the audience included the admiring conductors Bruno Walter, Otto Klemperer, Erich Kleiber, and George Szell. Szell, who also heard Toscanini and the Philharmonic in Prague, later described his "Toscanini shock": "This was orchestral performance of a kind new to all of us. The clarity of texture; the precision of ensemble; the rightness of balances; the virtuosity of every section, every solo-player of the orchestra—then at its peak—in the service of an interpretative concept of evident, self-effacing integrity, enforced with irresistible will power and unflagging ardor, set new, undreamed-of standards literally overnight." Never before had American classical music so set standards for the world. Significantly, the vehicle was not a composer (and Toscanini's tour repertoire included no American works), but an orchestra under a foreign conductor. Of the Philharmonic's 112 musicians, about 20 were American-born.[3]

Toscanini shock was international, but varied according to local need and disposition. In Italy, the home of opera, what symphonic ensembles existed in Toscanini's youth were notoriously undisciplined. His dictatorial insistence on new executant standards was a practical necessity. In Germany, the interwar years brought a reaction against Romantic subjectivity. However fortuitously, *neue Sachlichkeit*—the "new objectivity"—rhymed with Toscanini's ideal of self-effacing textual fidelity. For American audiences, Toscanini combined the probity and polish of a Thomas with the electric charge of a Seidl. His simplicity of approach, eschewing "tradition" as "the last bad performance," answered Boston's objections to Nikisch and New York's discomfort with the interpretive "arrogance" of Mahler or Furtwängler. Both because he was Italian and because he preached a fundamentalism bypassing the historical record, he relieved American classical music of its no longer welcome dependency on Germanic models and norms. He offered living proof that one did not have to be German to understand Beethoven. As significant, he and his New York Philharmonic fostered a new musical priority: performance as an end in itself.[4]

Older priorities shrank accordingly, beginning with repertoire. Every previous conductor of consequence to Americans—think of Thomas, Seidl, Gericke, Nikisch, Muck, Mahler, Stokowski—was vitally concerned with introducing new and unfamiliar music. To a degree unprecedented in New York or elsewhere, Toscanini recycled canonized masterworks. Forty percent of his Philharmonic repertoire comprised music by Beethoven, Brahms, and

Wagner. He already specialized in works he would repeat for twenty-five years to come, including Beethoven's Third, Fifth, and Ninth Symphonies, the Schubert *Unfinished*, excerpts from Mendelssohn's *Midsummer Night's Dream*, the Prelude and Liebestod from *Tristan und Isolde*, the Funeral Music from *Götterdämmerung*. He frankly disliked contemporary music, of which he offered smatterings of Ravel and Prokofiev—and of Stravinsky, who wrote in his 1936 autobiography, "What a pity it is that his inexhaustible energy and his marvelous talents should almost always be wasted on such eternally repeated works that no general idea can be discerned in the composition of his programs, and that he should be so unexacting in the selection of his modern repertory!" As for American music, in 1922–23, the Philharmonic launched an "Americanization" project stressing native repertoire. This ended with Toscanini, of whose tenure the Philharmonic's most recent historian has written, "As far as its relevance to the musical needs of New York at that moment was concerned, it might just as well have been in Berlin or Vienna or Milan."[5]

Repertoire shrinkage correlated with shrunken functions for both conductor and orchestra. Seidl, Gericke, Nikisch, Muck, Mahler, and (initially) Stokowski were full-time conductors in New York, Boston, and Philadelphia, leading every or practically every concert of the orchestras they commanded. With their rangy programs, they were educators, alert to the music of the moment. They pursued a mission larger than themselves. Toscanini was a new species: a part-time principal conductor.* He at no time led more than fifteen weeks a season. At the age of 60, he relished the opportunity—his first—to regularly lead a world-class concert orchestra. He was, he told the press, "coming nearer to the truth" of the Classical and Romantic masters; younger conductors could seek out new and novel works, as he himself once had done.[6]

This redefinition of the music director's job, and of the orchestra's purpose, was supported by Toscanini's starstruck champions on the Philharmonic board and in the press. Only W. J. Henderson, who had been around the

---

* Josef Stransky, as the Philharmonic conductor from 1911–12 to 1919–20, led every one of the orchestra's concerts. Beginning in 1920–21, the composer Henry Hadley became "associate conductor," entrusted with the "Americanization of the Philharmonic"; his programs invariably included at least one work by a native-born composer. In 1921–22, for the first time, "guest conductors" were added: Willem Mengelberg and Artur Bodanzky. In 1922–23, Stransky and Mengelberg were listed as "conductors," Hadley as associate conductor, and Willem van Hoogstraten was guest conductor. And so it went—with Furtwängler becoming one of the guests in 1924–25—until Toscanini was listed with Mengelberg as "conductor" in 1927–28. Though Toscanini became the orchestra's preponderant conductor as of 1929–30, he was never the only "conductor."

longest, noticed that a Toscanini concert was not about music—was "not a concert at all," but "the return of the hero, a Roman triumph staged in New York and in modern dress." He also wrote of the prevailing "appetite for sensationalism":

> It is our misfortune that we have come to demand that every orchestra reading should ravish or stir us to violent demonstrations. . . .
>
> If the local musical public ever finds out that there is no sound reason for excitement about Mr. Toscanini . . . there will be a depression in the atmosphere of Carnegie Hall. . . . Conditions were infinitely better in those far-off days when Theodore Thomas conducted concert after concert without creating any excitement and yet without lessening the belief that he was a great conductor.

Gilman proclaimed Toscanini "the greatest musical interpreter who ever lived," "the priest of beauty," the "consecrated celebrant," "custodian of holy things," "guardian of spiritual themes." Olin Downes's reviews typically included such necessary observations as, "The entire audience rose when Mr. Toscanini entered. He was obviously in the best of physical health, and his energy and concentration on his task were evident in his quick advance to the podium, his bow, brief and courteous, and the rap of the baton on the stand of the nearest player. These are the Toscanini rites. They betoken the quality of the man and the musician and the things the public has come to expect of him."[7]

Previously composers, not performers, had been sacralized, and less extravagantly; even John Sullivan Dwight, revering Beethoven, had not erected so high a pedestal. When letter writers complained about Toscanini's parochial repertoire, Gilman and Downes defended it. Gilman wrote, "The blunt truth is that only a great conductor is good enough to conduct great music." Both he and Downes equally believed that only great music was good enough for a great conductor. In fact, Toscanini eclipsed the great composers he served. A new type of listening was fostered: not to the symphony, but to its performance. And nothing gave greater pleasure than comparing different performances of a given symphony, especially if rendered by the same illustrious conductor. A purer and more persuasive example of what Theodor Adorno called "regressive listening" would be hard to find.

The New York Philharmonic now became indistinguishable from Arturo Toscanini—nothing less, nothing more. It follows that with Toscanini's announced resignation, to take effect in 1936, the disbanding of the Philharmonic was seriously pondered. Gilman, in a nation radio address, observed:

Toscanini is leaving us; and we who have listened to him discerningly, season after season, are well aware of what we are about to lose. But we must face the fact with all possible fortitude and philosophy. . . .

To minimize his loss would be an act of treachery toward our assumed allegiance to that ideal of lofty and self-effacing service which this great artist has exemplified. It would be an act of gross ingratitude to an interpreter who has re-created the music of the masters with unforgettable beauty and fidelity.

The Philharmonic's dependency on Toscanini was also financial: in the midst of the Depression, he was its only reliable draw. The loftier his star, the lowlier seemed his every colleague. His congregants were loyal to Toscanini first—not to music or to the orchestra. The orchestra's directors—whether or not they curtailed the season or reduced the number of players—were stuck with having to name a successor.

In 1932, in a speech honoring the fiftieth anniversary of his Berlin Philharmonic, Wilhelm Furtwängler had likened American orchestras to *Luxushunden*—"lap dogs." When this analogy was reported in the American press, he told the *Times* that he "intended to convey the idea that orchestras had grown to be more of a necessity to German communities than elsewhere on account of the greater age of German musical culture and national traditions, as compared with which American musical development is young." Furtwängler was wrong: orchestras—and their leaders—were American necessities. It was the music they played, rarely American, that was a lesser necessity than in Berlin or Vienna.[8]

■ ■ ■

For all Toscanini watchers, his departure from the New York Philharmonic followed a familiar pattern. As when Toscanini had quit La Scala (in 1908 and 1929) and the Met (in 1915), a gathering storm of rumors and denials, grievances and reassurances heralded an inevitable rupture. But Mussolini's Italy was too small for two dictators, and, at sixty-nine years of age, Toscanini was not interested in again running an opera house. Anyway, America wanted him back: as events would confirm, the growing Toscanini dependency was nationwide.

In short, a second coming was in order. Its engineer was David Sarnoff, president of the Radio Corporation of America and mastermind of the affiliated National Broadcasting Company. Called by a *Life* film documentary "the incarnation of the American dream," Sarnoff was a Jewish Horatio Alger, born in a Russian shtetl and raised on Manhattan's Lower East Side. He left school at age thirteen and purchased a newsstand. Eight years later, as an American Marconi telegrapher, he transmitted news of the sinking *Titanic* for seventy-two hours without sleep. While others continued to regard the "wireless" or "radio" as a message service, he foresaw a "radio music box." As of 1938, his radio empire totaled 142 broadcasting stations.

In his youth, Sarnoff had sung in a synagogue choir and frequented the upper balconies of the Metropolitan Opera. As a broadcasting scion, he was, beginning in 1934, a member of the Met's board of directors. With mere business associates, he was considered introverted and opaque: he shunned small talk and did not relish NBC's comedians, quiz shows, Westerns, and dance bands. Rather, he sought the company of artists and thinkers—"to share their dreams and disappointments," he said, "and to rejoice in their triumphs." As a point of pride, he wished to create a radio berth for high culture and the life of the mind. At the same time, he pioneered a medium epitomized in America by the likes of Amos 'n' Andy. His higher aspirations (as a later chapter will show) were partly prodded by government pressure. Competition with William Paley's Columbia Broadcasting System was also a factor.

With Toscanini on the podium, the Philharmonic broadcasts, begun by CBS in 1930, were unrivaled for glamour and prestige. With Toscanini gone, Sarnoff trumped CBS and the Philharmonic: he created an NBC Symphony expressly for Toscanini. This Sarnoff operation was typically visionary and astute, naïve and parochial. It so happened that the American Federation of Musicians had recently negotiated a contract requiring NBC to expand its 74-man staff orchestra to 115, of which Toscanini's orchestra (not, as claimed, "the first full-scale, full-time major orchestra to be maintained by an American broadcasting organization," but a part-time elite subgroup) would require 92. That said, Sarnoff agreed to keep only 31 of the pre-Toscanini staff musicians, and he did not stint on paying top salaries for distinguished newcomers.

"Very surprised Maestro's acceptance radio proposal," cabled the Philharmonic to Mrs. Toscanini. "Would like to know if Maestro has considered ill effects that this contract would have on our season." Toscanini cabled back, "Was surprised at your surprise. I will ask nothing of Sarnoff, who will arrange things to suit his own interest just as the Philharmonic has done and will always do." Toscanini's first NBC Symphony broadcast was on Christmas Day 1937: a Vivaldi concerto grosso, Mozart's G minor Symphony (K. 550), and Brahms's First. Leonard Liebling, editor-in-chief of the *Musical Courier*, called the concert the biggest radio event since King Edward's abdication. The *New York Post*, in an editorial, said it "outweighed our last note to Japan in conversation." *Time* commented, "Even those US lowbrows who were listening in to this highbrow stuff could feel the hypnotic power that was welding 92 separate instrumental voices into one voice."9

In fact, the sound of NBC's new orchestra made hypnotically audible the energies of ninety-two musicians in a state of sustained peak arousal. Toscanini had simplified his approach. Earlier nuances and pockets of calm made way for a scourging Savonarola fury, a demonic insistence on throbbing songfulness and febrile excitation even in music where songfulness and excitation would have been thought inappropriate. The urgency and efficiency of this late Toscanini style, an all-purpose formula bypassing considerations of tradition or national idiom, of historic or poetic allusion, suited America. Though still routinely celebrated for projecting a selfless "textual fidelity," the scathing brilliance of such readings screamed "Toscanini!"

The Philharmonic was defeated. To succeed Toscanini, the directors had chosen an underexperienced Englishman of Italian extraction: thirty-six-year-old John Barbirolli, who had first led a Beethoven symphony as recently as 1932. Barbirolli could not possibly eclipse the orchestra, as Toscanini had. And the orchestra, *sans* Toscanini, was not the Boston Symphony after Muck, or Chicago after Thomas, or Philadelphia when Stokowski was away: Toscanini's had been a fragile achievement based on a psychology of crisis that only a Toscanini could activate.

Barbirolli's departure after five seasons solved nothing. Meanwhile, Toscanini's new radio orchestra clinched the shrinkage process. Even more than the Philharmonic, it projected no *raison d'être* beyond serving Toscanini—or, by extension, David Sarnoff. Their interests meshed. Sarnoff's infatuation with high-culture glamour and prestige was defined and delimited by an infatuation with Old World pedigrees. In the Old World itself, radio orchestras, governmentally subsidized, would promote native and contemporary talent by design. NBC's radio orchestra, privately supported, would promote Toscanini and Sarnoff, Beethoven and Brahms. Spurred by world war, Toscanini fought the good fight: for a musician in his seventies, he acquired a significant number of new or recent American and Soviet works by such composers as Barber, Copland, Gershwin, Harris, and Shostakovich. Still, in a period when other American orchestras were more than doubling their quota of contemporary compositions, he was more than ever associated with the symphonies of Beethoven.

As it happened, American classical music was still young enough (there being no American canon) to embrace Beethoven as a wartime patriotic marker, so long as his mouthpiece was Toscanini (or was it vice versa?). Toscanini's antifascist credentials had long been impeccable. At La Scala, defying Mussolini, he had refused to play the party hymn or to display Mussolini's picture. His new position at NBC coincided with his exile from Europe, and with courageous appearances with the Palestine Orchestra; the Nazis denounced "Toscanini and his Jewish boosters."[10] In 1942, temporarily estranged from Sarnoff (about which more later), he led the New York Philharmonic in a Beethoven cycle flung in the teeth of Mussolini and Hitler. With the NBC Symphony, he led ten all-Beethoven concerts. The day after Italy's surrender, in 1943, he conducted a special half-hour broadcast including the first movement of Beethoven's Fifth Symphony, Rossini's *William Tell* Overture, the Garibaldi hymn, and—a Toscanini specialty, delivered with eyes blazing, singing along in his hoarse baritone—the "Star-Spangled Banner." For VE Day, he "completed" the Beethoven's Fifth of the year before as "Victory Symphony Act II." For VJ Day the following fall, the *Eroica* was "Victory Symphony Act III."

In Toscanini's scorching broadcast performances, this music of curled-lip defiance—its imagery of the freedom fighters Egmont and Florestan, of *sic semper tyrannis* (the *Leonore* Overture No. 3), of autocracy undone by arrogance (*Coriolanus*) and hubris (Beethoven shredding his dedication of the *Eroica* to Napoleon)—inspired a singular national catharsis. At no other moment did classical music in the United States acquire such exceptional urgency and purpose. As for Toscanini himself, he was wrapped in the flag. The mass appeal of his all-purpose formula, of his political heroism, of his tempestuous personality made him the central symbol of classical music for all Americans, its cherished validator and guarantor.

There was, however, a cognitive contradiction. At NBC, Toscanini's concerts were not public events, but celebrity turns for an invited audience (a ploy ensuring both prestigious exclusivity and immunity from the tax on entertainments where admission was charged). At Radio City's streamlined, "state of the art" Studio 8H—the "largest broadcasting studio in the world," notorious for its poor acoustics—NBC's special guests listened with tense adoration, a synthetic audience for a synthetic concert. This shrinkage of the concert experience—complementing a shrunken repertoire and the shrunken functions of conductor and orchestra—may have fine-tuned the spotlight on Toscanini the great performer, but America's favorite musician, never heard to speak, never glimpsed on the street, barely seemed mortal. Fortunately, remedies were at hand: his self-made origins, his simple personal habits and tastes. What is more, the prying media machinery of postwar America—a gargantuan version of the "gossip of the corridor and the dressing rooms" once decried by Henry Krehbiel—could be relied on to intimately and confidentially confect a less threatening Toscanini. His very remoteness rendered him malleable.

A Toscanini makeover was unveiled by *Life* on November 27, 1939. Using Toscanini's five-year-old granddaughter as a prop, Herb Gehr photographed the Maestro hugging Sonia, fingering the piano with Sonia in his lap, taking a "conducting lesson" from Sonia, and playing hide-and-seek with Sonia on the lawn—at all times attired in black bow tie, vest, and jacket. The text of this cover story (nothing less than a pun) read:

> Few people know much about the patrician-faced little Italian musician who keeps his private life to himself and, above all, avoids photographers. . . .
>
> The world knows Toscanini as a great conductor with a fearful temper, an unfailing memory and the power to lash orchestras into frenzies of fine playing. But only Toscanini's close friends know him as a simple, affectionate man, who works hard, is unbelievably modest and never understands why people grow tongue-tied when they meet him or why musicians grow pale and falter when he comes to hear them perform. . . .
>
> Toscanini's father was an unmusical tailor. His mother was an unmusical housewife. None of his known ancestors was a musician.

This formulaic "other Toscanini" now partnered the aloof Toscanini deity: a combination equally suiting distant star-gazing and up-close behind-the-scenes peeks. NBC's public relations apparatus, boasting a technological prowess and reach never before associated with classical music, promoted the Maestro accordingly: a skewed barrage of reverence and ballyhoo. One NBC release shouted, "World's Largest Drum Rushed to New York for Toscanini Concert." Equally typical was the hushed tone of such scripted announcements—written to sound spontaneous—as "Ladies and gentlemen, we are speaking from the NBC studios in Radio City. . . . In the studio there is an air of tenseness during these few minutes before the concert begins, a feeling that this is a particularly momentous program—and we feel sure that the members of the radio audience have a similar feeling."[11]

In fact, NBC announcers could create the look and feel of Toscanini's unseen concerts: "Mr. Toscanini returns to the stage to accept the audience's applause in his customary unassuming way." "The enthusiasm of the audience in the studio, I feel sure, is only an echo of what all of us are feeling." John Barbirolli wrote home after attending his first NBC Symphony concert in 1938: "I came away musically exalted and otherwise terribly depressed and disgusted. . . . It is the strangest sensation-mongering audience with all sorts of theatrical stunts and altogether upsetting." Virgil Thomson commented in 1946, "The manners of the staff are in no way encouraging to personal expansiveness. At every turn one is disciplined, guided, scolded, administered. It is almost impossible to get into the place or out of it without being pushed around mentally or physically by somebody in a uniform." The composer Roy Harris called the Studio 8H personnel "watchdogs of capital."[12]

Toscanini's NBC Symphony recordings, on NBC's RCA Victor, furnished an ideal promotional tool. Then, on February 18, 1948, came TV. Sarnoff himself appeared on camera to introduce "a great day for radio, for television, for music, and for the public. . . . Tonight, for the first time in the history of this great science and art of radio, we are televising the great music of Wagner, the great interpretive genius of Toscanini, and the playing of his gifted artists in his orchestra. Never before in the history of the world was this possible." But this was not the first televised symphonic concert—CBS and the Philadelphia Orchestra had beaten NBC by ninety minutes. As ever with Sarnoff, salesmanship and art were locked in a tense stand-off.[13]

In the annals of art-music merchandising, Sarnoff's Toscanini crusade can only be compared with P. T. Barnum's historic Jenny Lind campaign of 1850. Barnum, too, intermingled ballyhoo and reverence, but with different needs. Jenny was sold as a saint; her marriage helped to undo her. Toscanini, already sanctified, was remade as a regular guy; his married life helped to humanize him. Barnum's crusade was a blithe exercise in hucksterism (everyone knew Jenny was no angel from the sky). Sarnoff's was an earnest and deluded exercise in uplift so complete that even Toscanini might have been taken in by it.

Time magazine put the finishing touches on the new portrait in 1948: a profile, "The Perfectionist," whose cover art featured the smiling "other Toscanini." "There are two Toscaninis," *Time* explained. The other Toscanini loved parties, practical jokes, and "good-looking women." Visitors would often find him watching a televised boxing match, "jumping up & down in his chair like an eight-year-old," or the children's show *Small Fry Club*, which (never taking his eyes from the screen) he called "Fry Small."[14]

Toscanini now enjoyed the same forms of celebrity as Sinatra or Garbo. In her food column for the *New York Herald-Tribune*, Clementine Paddleford shared the ingredients for "soup for Toscanini" ("He's not fussy about food— except his soup"). The gossip columnist Earl Wilson reported that Toscanini was as inaccessible as the president, but he managed to check the contents of Toscanini's dressing room refrigerator ("milk and some vino"). The other Toscanini peaked in 1950 when NBC sent its Symphony on a transcontinental tour. The occasion was an implausible "war of the speeds." When in 1948 CBS's Columbia Records unveiled its new, nonbreakable "long playing" disks (LPs), with twenty-three minutes to a side—the equivalent of five breakable 78 rpm disks—RCA countered with nonbreakable, seven-inch, 45 rpm disks with the same playing time as the twelve-inch 78s. (Toscanini loyally endorsed the "remarkably faithful" sonic properties of this short-lived classical music product, which RCA successfully converted into a pop music format.) Two years later, RCA lost the war; amid wholesale staff dismissals, it belatedly began producing LPs of its own, including a barrage of Toscanini releases. It was this repertoire that Toscanini, supported by catch-up LP marketing, now took on the road.

This typically commercial NBC strategy was typically accompanied by an artistic mission. Playing twenty-one concerts in twenty states, Toscanini and his orchestra were the most potent classical music roadshow since the barnstorming days of Theodore Thomas. NBC called the tour "a great and lasting monument to American culture." This it was not: the only American works, alongside music by Haydn, Beethoven, Brahms, Tchaikovsky, Dvořák, Debussy, and Strauss, were encores: "Dixie" and "The Stars and Stripes Forever." But the Toscanini tour was a great and lasting monument to Toscanini generally, and to the other Toscanini in particular. Judging from press accounts, the unprecedented opportunity to glimpse the Maestro in the flesh outweighed every other fascination. The *New Yorker* sent a writer aboard the Toscanini train to inventory the contents of his "concert bag" (four towels, two bamboo fans, Oculav for his eyes, bicarbonate of soda, a family picture, and a silver box containing rock candy). In New Orleans, he was seen tapping his foot while listening to jazz. In Los Angeles, Bob Hope waited ten minutes outside Toscanini's dressing room. In Sun Valley, Toscanini rode the ski lift to the top of Mount Baldy.

His unaffected eagerness to "try everything" endeared him to everyone— and not least to his musicians, who had never before enjoyed his daily company. In fact, the most unexpected beneficiary of the NBC Symphony tour was the NBC Symphony. Liberated from Studio 8H—the glass-faced control booth and rattle-proof programs and invited audiences—it resembled a normal orchestra giving normal concerts for normal people in normal halls. Toscanini had never seemed so happy. The musicians never felt so musically fulfilled.[15]

But this interlude was short-lived. Straddling culture both mass and elite, Toscanini at NBC was loftier and more common than any previous classical music hero. The forces at play were too big to manage, but were overseen: once lord of La Scala and the New York Philharmonic, Toscanini had become corporate property. As "NBC's great conductor"—a telling promotional formulation—his professional itinerary atrophied. He did not conduct a staged opera after 1937. He almost never appeared before orchestras other than the

NBC Symphony. He was contractually bound to record only for RCA. Sarnoff's sincere commitment to high culture extended no further than NBC's marquee. Though he was prepared to placate Toscanini and to delight him, Sarnoff was also prepared to cashier him, which he did in 1954, when Toscanini was eighty-seven. The orchestra was cashiered too (it limped on, autonomously, as the Symphony of the Air before quietly expiring). Toscanini died in 1957. Mourned by America, he was buried in his truer home: Italy.

In Turin and Milan, Toscanini had been a potent early champion of Brahms and Wagner. He had led the premieres of *Pagliacci* and *La bohème*. At La Scala, beginning in 1898, he had created a national house of culture. Pressing forward, he had conducted the first Italian performances of Tchaikovsky's *Eugene Onegin* and Debussy's *Pelléas et Mélisande*, and he gave Strauss's shocking *Salome* in 1906, before it had been seen in New York, Vienna, or London. His second Scala regime, beginning in 1921, anchored postwar national renewal amid poverty, inflation, and political strife. The conductor Gianandrea Gavazzeni testified, "The public with Toscanini, during that era, was educated to consider the theater not as something for amusement, but as something with a moral and aesthetic function, which enters into the life of a society, in the life of a culture."[16]

The American Toscanini entered very differently into the life of culture and society. If, as elsewhere, he elevated performance standards, he more significantly elevated the act of performance as an isolated attainment. He became the first conductor of international consequence fundamentally to divorce himself from the music of his own time. Even as his functions shrank, his reputation and influence grew: no previous conductor, no previous performer, had become the most famous living symbol of classical music. This distinction had appropriately been accorded composers whose lives in music organically embraced performance—the composer/pianist/conductor Beethoven, the composer/pianist/conductor Liszt, the composer/pianist Brahms, the composer/conductor Wagner, the composer/conductor Richard Strauss.

After Toscanini, the great names of classical music would be conductors who did not compose, performance specialists estranged from the creative act. Herbert von Karajan, compared to a Thomas, Seidl, or Nikisch, was a "music director" whose mission was so preponderantly curatorial, so disproportionately dedicated to masterpieces of the past, that it necessarily shrank to an exercise in self-glorification. In the case of Toscanini, exiled in America in old age, this exercise was utterly galvanizing, marvelously self-sufficient. But there was only one Toscanini.

∎ ∎ ∎

Toscanini's glamour and good looks were inherent to the man: like Liszt or Nikisch, he was the consummate showman whose theatricality was knowing yet effortless. Leopold Stokowski's glamour and good looks were both real and plotted. The artful disarray of his long pale hair, the exquisite exoticism of his untraceable foreign accent were too obviously beguiling. Toscanini's orchestral wizardry was inherent to his perfectionism: his espousal of absolute textual fidelity effectively cloaked his personal imprint. Stokowski's wizardry was of the Merlin variety. Had he been able to take his Philadelphia Orchestra to Europe, as Toscanini had toured his New York Philharmonic and so inflicted "Toscanini shock," the resulting "Stokowski shock"—which impressed musicians as un-Stokowskian as Dimitri Mitropoulos and Joseph Szigeti[17]—would have been threefold: for every German or Frenchman astounded by the polish and virtuosity of his orchestra, a second would have been perturbed by the satin finish of its sound, and a third would have been dismayed by the uses to which it was put.

But it was in the area of symphonic shrinkage that Toscanini and Stokowski essentially parted company. Stokowski courageously sustained earlier notions of the larger purposes conductors and orchestras should serve. It was a losing battle, but gloriously fought.

We have so far observed Stokowski's career through World War I: his manufactured Paris debut, his precocious Cincinnati success, his impact in Philadelphia. As of 1916, when he introduced Mahler's *Symphony of a Thousand*, his Philadelphia Orchestra was already widely admired, but only written accounts can today conjure up its actual sound. Beginning in 1917, Stokowski began to make records—and as with Toscanini's Philharmonic, we can hear what the excitement was about. Unlike Toscanini, Stokowski at all times took a keen interest in the mechanical reproduction of music. Toscanini's parched NBC Symphony recordings, with their absurdly close pickups, are from an engineering standpoint among the most inglorious in the history of the phonograph. Stokowski's Philadelphia recordings, also for RCA, were state of the art in the commercial field. He also invited Bell Laboratories to make experimental recordings at the Philadelphia Academy of Music. And the Bell recordings, some in stereo and in live performance, are the truest documentation of what Rachmaninoff described in 1929: "Philadelphia has the finest orchestra I have ever heard at any time or any place in my whole life. I don't know that I would be exaggerating if I said that it is the finest orchestra the world has ever heard." More vividly than Stokowski's studio recordings, with their stitched-together four-minute takes, his Bell disks illustrate the "sense of a high vitalization, of almost super-human keenness of musical consciousness" that Arthur Farwell (as we have noted) observed in Stokowski as early as 1911.

Toscanini's famous reading of Beethoven's Fifth was razor sharp. Stokowki's, captured in concert by the Bell engineers in 1932, is the most feline Beethoven on record. It races or glides on cat's paws, a marvel of rippling musculature, of poised power and energy. In Toscanini's version, the honest fury of the first movement and the blazing affirmation of the finale are indelible. In Stokowski's, the most memorable movement is the least dramatic: the Andante, taken as an Adagio, but with such flexibility of pulse and with long phrases (contradicting Beethoven's markings) so firm and shapely that it never sounds slow. In Romantic repertoire, the Bell recordings convey the painterly abandon with which Stokowski reveled in the responsiveness of his instrument; he rolls out the plushest magic carpet of sound ever to enfold Wotan's Farewell or Brünnhilde's Immolation. Bell also recorded a brief 1932 address to the audience, a Depression-era pep talk asking listeners at the Academy of Music to consider what the Philadelphia Orchestra "means to humanity—to our culture and civilization." But Stokowski is not thinking politically; he continues, "I think it means, first of all, *delight*—delight in *sound*." He was the ultimate sonic sybarite.

Toscanini's Beethoven—his symphonic style generally—derived from Verdi: explosive accents and clipped, clean diction ("Don't eat the notes!" he would bellow), forward pressure and pointed, accelerating climaxes, bright trumpets and crisp timpani. He holds the line taut and favors the short breath span of the human voice. Stokowski's symphonic style is based even further afield from Beethoven. Toscanini played the cello in the opera pit; Stokowski inhabited the organ loft. The soft-edged attacks and majestic swells and recessions, the smooth textures and lavish colors he adored all derive from the Romantic organ of his youth. His way of "rolling" chords, and of violating rests (rewriting note lengths) in order to bind a sound to its neighbor, fabricates a cathedral acoustic.

The tensile strength and flowing cantabile of the "Philadelphia sound" were partly a function of another heterodox Stokowski hallmark: "free bowing." In every other orchestra, the up and down bow strokes were uniform; in Stokowski's, they were not. He reasoned that by having his players bow individually and naturally, he could obtain a warmer, more intense, more continuous sound. "I am completely opposed to standardization, regimentation, uniform bowing, uniform fingering and breathing, and all other conventions which tend to make an orchestra sound mechanical," he wrote in his book *Music for All of Us*. On another occasion, he explained that he instructed his musicians: "Do not crush your real individuality, but express your individuality through the music." Stokowski's own individuality, which his instructions mirrored, was also expressed in various seating experiments unique to Philadelphia. He tried positioning the strings at the rear of the stage, or massed to the left. "I shall keep experimenting," he pledged. "I have no system." He kept his word.[18]

The Stokowski sound was not for everyone. Nor was it for all music. Significantly, the two composers Stokowski most recorded were the two composers he most remade. His transcriptions of such Bach organ works as the Toccata and Fugue in D minor—transcriptions that may or may not have been abetted by his copyist, Lucien Caillet—showcased his orchestra's particular splendor, and so did the symphonic Wagner as extrapolated by Stokowski. A medley of love music from *Tristan und Isolde*, seamlessly combining passages from acts two and three without regard to the opera's narrative sequence, was a Stokowski specialty. The Bell recordings include a live *Tristan* Liebestod from 1931. The deep-toned string choirs, the kaleidoscopic play of timbre, the vast dynamic range and sudden crescendos convey an infinity of possibilities. And these possibilities are exercised. The result is a hedonistic sonic drama an ocean removed from the dire existential drama of Wilhelm Furtwängler's contemporaneous Berlin renditions. Furtwängler is *innig*; Stokowski, overt. For Furtwängler, Isolde's death orgasm is a metaphysical event; for Stokowski, an occasion for sensuous abandon. Postclimax, the fatigued coda of Furtwängler's Liebestod signifies extinction of the will; the robust cadential surge of Stokowski's strings, in the same passage, insists upon postcoital pleasure. If Stokowski's Wagner more evokes Hollywood than Bayreuth, his virtuosity intoxicates the senses and disorients the brain; issues of taste are held at bay. Toscanini, espousing textural fidelity, disavowed "tradition." But Stokowski's Bach and Wagner are more truly liberated from Old World tradition than Toscanini ever was.★

Stokowski's constancy of innovation, his efficiency as a drill master, his gift for publicity, and his audible achievements attracted gifted players. One close observer of the outcome was the composer/pianist Abram Chasins, who began teaching at the neighboring Curtis Institute in 1926. Winthrop

---

★ I am indebted to Mark Obert-Thorn for supplying CD copies of the Stokowski/Bell recordings, of which only the Beethoven's Fifth is currently commercially available (via the Philadelphia Orchestra). Of Stokowski's studio recordings, his Wagner—in particular, the sensuous lyricism of excerpts from *Tannhäuser*, *Lohengrin*, *Tristan und Isolde*, and *Parsifal*, as recorded between 1927 and 1937—best conveys "Stokowski shock." No singer ever surpassed Stokowski's Philadelphia Orchestra in this music.

Sargeant, analyzing Toscanini's hypnotic effect, discovered a "psychology of crisis." Chasins wrote of Stokowski in rehearsal:

> His complete absorption and involvement, more than his grasp of the music, and his imaginative disclosures of its hidden beauties won the awesome respect and slavish cooperation of his musicians. This was the connective bond between him and his orchestra. Each man felt person-ally responsible for producing the sound that Stokowski's piercing eyes and transfigured face compelled him to create. Sometimes, Stokowski made demands that were foolhardy, even infuriating, but the players were always innately flattered that he asked so much of them. Regardless of their personal feelings toward their conductor and of their frequent disagreements with his interpretations, they were immensely proud to be members of an orchestra for which the impossible was deemed possible.[19]

Even before a performance, Stokowski's theatricality was innate. Chasins has documented how he would secrete himself in his dressing room and do deep-breathing exercises. "If someone said 'Good evening,' or merely brushed past him when he was on his way to the stage, he would wheel around and return to his room to restore his former degree of concentration." This could delay a concert by as many as fifteen minutes. In performance, Stokowski told Chasins, he yielded to what seemed an occult power, con-ducting with a maniacal abandon that left him wringing wet.[20] On other occasions, he seemed impassive while actually listening with an intense con-centration that froze his features. All of this contributed to an impression of arrogance and remoteness. And Stokowski was unquestionably aloof. He identified his players by instrument, not by name. He only met with them by appointment. The Stokowski personality was powerfully ineffable.

Stokowski's penchant for the exotic predisposed him to obscure foods and restaurants, as well as to a mixed drink combining heavy cream, pineapple juice, and honey. The record producer Charles O'Connell, who observed him slyly adding pure-grain alcohol to the foregoing concoction, also reported of Stokowski, "He would get as many different items as possible onto his dinner plate and make a kind of pâté of them, and then eat the whole dinner with a spoon."[21] The same spirit of adventure informed his repertoire excursions. In collaboration with New York's League of Composers, he created a series of mega-events beginning in 1929 with a staged version of Stravinsky's *Les noces* (of which he had previously conducted the American premiere). This led, the following year, to Stokowski's first collaboration with the League using the

Philadelphia Orchestra: a double bill of Stravinsky's *The Rite of Spring* (of which he had, again, previously conducted the American premiere) and Schoenberg's *Die glückliche Hand*, both staged in the United States for the first time.

In collaboration with the League of Composers, Stokowski subsequently conducted staged versions of Stravinsky's *Oedipus Rex* and Prokofiev's *Age of Steel* in Philadelphia and New York, and, in New York only, a staged performance of Schoenberg's *Pierrot Lunaire* with Philadelphia Orchestra members. In concert with the Philadelphia Orchestra, he also gave first American performances of Stravinsky's *Song of the Nightingale*, *Mavra*, and *Symphonies of Wind Instruments* and of Schoenberg's Variations for Orchestra and *Gurrelieder*. The *Gurrelieder*, in 1932, was a Stokowski extravaganza, with 532 performers; released on fourteen 12-inch disks, it was in its day the longest symphonic work ever recorded in full. Of the music of Schoenberg's Second Viennese School colleagues, Stokowski and the Philadelphia gave American premieres of Webern's Passacaglia and Berg's *Wozzeck*—the entire opera, staged; it required eighty-eight preparatory rehearsals, sixty stage rehearsals, and a special gift from Mary Louise Curtis Bok.

Stokowski specialized in Russian music. He led the first performances of Rachmaninoff's Rhapsody on a Theme of Paganini and Fourth Piano Concerto (both with the composer at the keyboard), and the Symphony No. 3. He gave the first performance outside Russia of something like Mussorgsky's original *Boris Godunov*, untouched by Rimsky-Korsakov, and also the first American performance of excerpts from Rimsky's own late masterpiece, the *Legend of the Invisible City of Kitezh*. Of Shostakovich, he gave first American performances of the Symphonies 1, 3, and 6, and the First Piano Concerto. He gave the American premiere of Medtner's Piano Concerto No. 1, with the composer as pianist. He gave first American performances of three Miaskowski symphonies. A short list of other notable American premieres featuring Stokowski and the Philadelphia Orchestra would include works by Bruch, Busoni, Chávez, Enescu, Hindemith, Lourie, Malipiero, Poulenc, Ravel, Sibelius (the Fifth, Sixth, and Seventh Symphonies), Szymanowski, Villa-Lobos, and Weill. Stokowski also supported native talent, if far less lavishly than Koussevitzky in Boston. His attentions were typically eclectic and included such wild men as Cowell, Ornstein, and Varèse. Finally, no account of the Stokowski repertoire could fail to mention his transcriptions and adaptations, encompassing works by forty-five composers from Albéniz to Weber. The creativity of these efforts cannot be underestimated. The twenty-five-minute symphonic synthesis of Wagner's *Das Rheingold*, for example, is a masterpiece of its kind, full of cunning subtleties of construction—as well as an unattributed borrowing from the "Entrance of the Gods" as scored by the German conductor/composer Herman Zumpe.

Stokowski was not, as conductors go, an exceptional reader or rehearser of new scores. Nor was he a close acquaintance of certain composers whom he espoused. In fact, his advocacy of contemporary composers was less focused—and, arguably, less effective—than that of Koussevitzky, who consistently championed Copland, Harris, and Piston in Boston; or of Otto Klemperer, who promoted Janáček, Hindemith, Stravinsky, and Weill in Berlin. Stokowski, by comparison, simply sought new sounds and symphonies. He would try something, then try something else. "Stokowski conducted everything, without judging it," Chasins observed. "Judging, he believed, was the public's job. His obligation and goal was to make available to the largest audience as much contemporary music as possible so that it could be evaluated."[22]

And Stokowski—with his self-made success, patchy education, and unassuming parentage—was a populist. "Music is a universal language," he wrote in *Music for All of Us*. Try to imagine a Toscanini or Furtwängler authoring a comparably titled volume, or opining, "Formerly music was chiefly confined to privileged classes in cultural centers, but today, through radio and records, music has come directly into our homes no matter how far we may live from cultural centers. This is as it should be, because music speaks to every man, woman, and child—high or low, rich or poor, happy or despairing—who is sensitive to its deep and powerful message." Stokowski also called for state-subsidized broadcasts and recordings of "the most outstanding new compositions of younger composers, so that all music lovers over the whole country can hear them and have an opportunity to follow these latest developments of their national art."[23]

In Philadelphia, part of the Stokowski show was his way of rebuking listeners who did not take an interest in "latest developments." One impromptu lecture, occasioned by an exodus during Scriabin's *Poem of Ecstasy*, began, "I consider this poem one of the two best musical compositions written in modern times. I notice that whenever we present music of a novel sort to the audiences in this city the people here fail to give us a chance to do any justice to the music. It is impossible for any orchestra to do its best work in such an atmosphere of hostility. . . . You have no right to condemn the music that we present after having heard it but once."[24] In order to discourage coughing, Stokowski had the orchestra cough on cue. To reprimand latecomers, he had members of the orchestra arrive late, in breathless haste. Bidding farewell prior to a foreign excursion, he quipped, "I hope when I come back your colds will be better."

It was Stokowski's considered opinion that "most adults have difficulty absorbing ideas." His preferred audience was of youngsters. In Philadelphia, his Young People's Concerts, begun in 1921, were a labor of love. When he presented *The Carnival of the Animals*, he announced that there was an elephant backstage. "Do you believe me?" he continued. "Or perhaps you do not want to see an elephant?" The children roared. Stokowski walked off and returned leading a young elephant by the ear. He had also assembled three ponies, a donkey, and a camel. In 1933, spurred by the Depression, Stokowski began Saturday-afternoon Youth Concerts for audiences aged thirteen to twenty-five. The top ticket was seventy-five cents, and conductor and orchestra donated their services. Stokowski's Youth League members chose repertoire, wrote program notes, designed brochures and posters, and, as "bouncers," evicted overage listeners. A potent force in his skirmishes with recalcitrant adults, they met regularly at his Rittenhouse Square residence, a former coach house fronted by a garage door, whose chartreuse living room included a Stokowski-designed fireplace and Navajo rugs. Stokowski was accustomed to greeting his many young visitors in red or yellow lounging pajamas. Some young musicians, with whom he slept, were called his "nurses." "Nurses are lifesavers," he once explained to Chasins. "They are angels of mercy who rejuvenate us." To a friend who inquired if he had a "conscience," he replied, "None. Conscience is that which hurts when everything else feels marvelous. The percentage is against it."[25]

After more than two strenuous Philadelphia decades, all this was both too much and not enough. Stokowski craved a regular radio showcase, like Toscanini's with the New York Philharmonic. He wanted to take his orchestra abroad, as Toscanini took his Philharmonic to Europe in 1930. He was celebrated and appreciated in Philadelphia; even in bad weather, the line for non-subscription seats curled around the block of the Academy of Music. But he was also unquestionably embattled. The Depression, and the orchestra's first deficit in many years, exacerbated resistance to new music among the board members. He resigned in a fight with the board, returned in a reduced capacity, then in 1941 departed for good.

In the final analysis, one marvels not that Stokowski should have left Philadelphia, but that he lasted for twenty-eight years. In midcareer, not yet sixty years old, he dreamt of new formats, new audiences, new venues, new technologies. He needed to break out. Foremost in his thinking was Hollywood—its glamour, its mass impact and appeal. In the mid-1930s, Stokowski appeared in two Hollywood films: *The Big Broadcast of 1937* and *One Hundred Men and a Girl*. He met Greta Garbo; their liaison was feasted upon by reporters, columnists, and photographers on two continents. Then, in 1940, Walt Disney released *Fantasia*, a two-hour cartoon with Stokowski conducting the Philadelphia Orchestra (except in Dukas's *The Sorceror's Apprentice*). Stokowski appeared in silhouette, summoning the gothic splendors of the D minor Toccata and Fugue. The remaining repertoire ranged from Beethoven to Stravinsky.

It was Stokowski who had inspired Disney to commit to a full-length classical music showcase. Only *Time* magazine could have offered the following interpretation, in its second cover story featuring Stokowski: "Deciding to go the whole artistic hog, [Disney] picked the highest of high-brow classical music. To do right by this music, the old mouse opera comedy was not enough. The Disney studio went high-brow wholesale, and Disney technicians racked their brains for stuff that would startle and awe rather than tickle the audience."[26] Stokowski anticipated future collaborations with Disney, but Disney took no interest in cultural uplift. The media mogul whose aspirations more matched Stokowski's was David Sarnoff, and Sarnoff was a confirmed Toscanini/Beethoven man. Espousing classical music and contemporary culture, Stokowski wound up without a niche—or a national podium.

His relationship to Sarnoff's NBC Symphony summarizes Stokowski's eclipse. In April 1941, Arturo Toscanini sent Sarnoff a letter beginning, "My old age tells me to be [*sic*] high time to withdraw from the militant scene of Art." Sarnoff, to whom fame seemed the pedigree of art, hired Stokowski to take Toscanini's place with the NBC Symphony. Stokowski's broadcasts unleashed a barrage of American and/or new works, including Schoenberg's Piano Concerto (a premiere, with Eduard Steuermann) and Copland's *Short Symphony* (an American premiere), probably the two most difficult contemporary compositions the NBC Symphony ever tackled, as well as two of the most important. He also conducted a children's concert including works by child composers, and used recorded rehearsal excerpts as part of an on-the-air interview introducing Prokofiev's sixteen-year-old *Love for Three Oranges* Suite. Meanwhile, Toscanini's "state of mind, health, and rest," all factors figuring in his resignation letter, improved sufficiently to permit resumption of his former duties; he and Stokowski shared the NBC Symphony in 1942–43 and 1943–44. In June 1944, NBC announced that Stokowski's contract would not be renewed. Stokowski had this to say:

> If I am an acceptable American conductor who enjoys bringing music
> of American composers to the American public, it would seem fair that
> I should have the same consideration as a conductor who has not made
> himself an American citizen [Stokowski took American citizenship in
> 1915] and who very seldom plays American music. . . . The people of the
> United States have the right to hear the music being composed by

young talented Americans as well as all the great music of all countries composed by great masters. The radio stations are permitted by the Government to use certain wavelengths. This gives the radio stations privileges and also *demands* of them to fulfill their *responsibilities* to the American people.

As far as classical music in America was concerned, the future lay with Toscanini and the European past.[27]

Stokowski looked forward to making a series of Hollywood films. He hoped to become music director of the New York Philharmonic. In fact, his influence and celebrity had peaked. His legacy remained where he had left it: in Philadelphia. Eugene Ormandy, his unremarkable successor, retained something like Stokowski's plush sonic signature and an affinity for the Slavic repertoire that served it, but nothing like Stokowski's iconoclastic genius. A generation of Americans grew up on RCA's Stokowski/Philadelphia recordings (until they were supplanted by RCA's Toscanini/NBC Symphony remakes). Other Stokowski legacies led nowhere. He spawned no school of technique or interpretation. No conductor of prominence supported or followed his far-flung repertoire excursions. A free spirit, an American original whose Philadelphia Orchestra was a distinctive New World creation, Stokowski blazed a trail of might-have-beens.

If at all a charlatan or showman, Stokowski was essentially a principled fantasist. He created his own personal history, his own orchestra, his own style of music-making. If he misjudged his post-Philadelphia opportunities, his impatience with the symphonic norm, its rites and repertoire, was irremediable. His belief in music as a "universal language" was not a belief in Bach and Beethoven merely; he embraced music of Latin America, Africa, and Asia, and of the composers—Chávez, Cowell, Harrison, Messiaen, McPhee, Varèse, Villa-Lobos—to whom such universality mattered. He may yet prove prophetic.

■ ■ ■

In the early 1930s, the New York Philharmonic, the Philadelphia Orchestra, and the Boston Symphony—each a singular instrument serving a singular master and a singular mission—achieved parity as America's "greatest orchestra in the world." Boston's conductor was Serge Koussevitzky.

The eminence of the Boston orchestra had dipped sharply after the deportation of Karl Muck and the loss of many Germanic members. Muck's replacements, necessarily non-German, were Henri Rabaud in 1918 and

Pierre Monteux in 1919. Rabaud, whom Monteux had recommended,[28] was more a composer than a conductor, too French in style and repertoire. Monteux, who had led premiere performances of major works by Debussy, Ravel, and Stravinsky, was by far the more experienced, more versatile leader, but he reconstituted the orchestra only to face a crippling strike.

The Boston Symphony was the only American orchestra to withstand unionization. Henry Higginson (as we have seen) opposed it. His opposition was effective because he paid higher salaries and offered longer seasons than elsewhere, and because of personal relationships he maintained with many of the players. After Higginson, the Boston Symphony no longer paid higher salaries than other orchestras did, and the trustees were a distant and impersonal presence. When the men requested a pay raise of more than 50 percent, and the board said no, seventy-three of them joined the union. One of the new union members was the concertmaster, Frederic Fradkin. On March 5, 1920, a backstage altercation between Fradkin and Monteux provoked a public snub of the conductor: Fradkin refused to rise from his seat during the applause for Berlioz's *Symphonie fantastique*. He was summarily dismissed. Thirty-six musicians sided with him and refused to play for Monteux. It bears mentioning that this was front-page news in Boston:[29]

FRADKIN-MONTEUX CLASH
STIRS SYMPHONY PLAYERS

The trustees prevailed but Fradkin and one-third of the roster needed replacing. Monteux, a portly, undemonstrative *maitre* of enormous technical accomplishment, therefore had to rebuild the Boston Symphony not once but twice. This he achieved, only to discover his contract unrenewed after five difficult years.

The board had decided to opt for a more glamorous and exotic music director. Koussevitzky was—a novelty—Russian. He made his name in Moscow as—a greater novelty—a double bass virtuoso. Having married into wealth, he created his own publishing house; his clients included Scriabin, Stravinsky, Prokofiev, Rachmaninoff. He next created his own orchestra. He left Russia in 1920 and eventually settled in Paris, where his Concerts Koussevitzky, again with an orchestra of his own making, championed new Russian and French composers; notable premieres included Ravel's orchestration of Mussorgsky's *Pictures at an Exhibition* (commissioned by Koussevitzky). (This French connection linked not only with Rabaud and Monteux but, further back, with Boston's own considerable Francophile tradition.) Monteux, in Boston, had raised eyebrows with his adventurous and eclectic pro-

grams. Koussevitzky's first Boston program, on October 10, 1924, was a statement and a challenge: from the eighteenth century, a Vivaldi concerto grosso;
from the nineteenth, Berlioz's *Roman Carnival* Overture and Brahms's Haydn
Variations; from the twentieth, Honegger's cacophonous locomotive imitation, *Pacific 231* and—an orgasmic finale—Scriabin's *Poem of Ecstasy*. Philip
Hale found the new conductor "magnetic." H. T. Parker called him "a master
of line, color, tone and characterization."[30]

Onstage and off, Koussevitzky was a presence. Instantly noted were his personal and sartorial elegance (including his signature capes), his opulent and
aristocratic household, his remote aura, and his magisterial podium manner,
ardent yet prepossessed. (He used a full-length mirror to teach his students
how to bow.) It was also quickly apparent, at least to the musicians, that he
was a self-made conductor; in contrast to the utter professionalism of Muck
and Monteux, he was learning on the job. His stick technique was imprecise.
He had trouble with complex rhythms. He was not an adept score reader and
in fact in his early Boston years employed an assistant, Nicolas Slonimsky, to
play through new pieces on the piano while he learned to lead them.

Though it was Monteux who rebuilt the orchestra, Koussevitzky was not
humble about taking credit and replacing players he did not like. His
rehearsals, if less violent than Toscanini's, were tempestuous. His garbled
English, if less primitive than Toscanini's, was at least as colorful. One of his
violinists, Harry Ellis Dickson, was both a keen admirer, convinced Koussevitzky "was the greatest conductor who ever lived," and a shrewd observer.
Dickson's Koussevitzky transcripts include "Gentleman, you play all the
wrong notes not in time! And please made important, you play like it is
something nothing!" and "Gentlemen, you are awfully not togedder. You play
di notes in time, but vot is between di times you don't care about. Please
made it tremendously your attention! And you are awfully bad in tune today.
Or too high, or too low. Ve cannot permit us di luxus to be not in tune!"
Dickson also testified:

Almost every rehearsal was a nightmare, every concert a thrilling experience. Those were the days when it was expected of conductors to be
tyrannical and temperamental, and Koussevitzky was no exception.
During his reign there were in the B.S.O. one hundred and five players
and one hundred and six ulcers. (One man had two.) In the vicinity of
Symphony Hall in the Back Bay section of Boston there is, within a
half-mile area, the greatest concentration of doctors' offices of any similar area in the world. Most of these doctors got their start during the
Koussevitzky era.[31]

Every great conductor is a great motivator. No less than Toscanini or Stokowski, Koussevitzky inspired his musicians to give all they had and more. A common theme of Koussevitzky watchers was his capacity to instill pride, zeal, and love. Dickson observed an uncanny instinct to awaken in every player "a sense of individuality and self-respect." He also noted, "Few conductors I have ever known, if any, loved music qua music with such fervor. And he approached each work with such immersion, sincerity, and dedication that even an undeserving new work would emerge with force and conviction, and he was able to convey his enthusiasm to us in the orchestra."[32] At concert's end, the musicians would be as soaking wet and emotionally spent as the conductor.

Koussevitzky's high regard for the players was collective: they were his treasured steeds. Before a trip he would admonish them to eat well, to dress warmly, to rest adequately. He made them feel important. For audiences, too, the Koussevitzky influence was bonding. Stokowski, who on one occasion showcased his face and hands with a spotlight, would scold inattentive listeners. Toscanini, whose entrances were brisk and business–like, tolerated his auditors. Koussevitzky's slow bow of greeting was impeccably gracious; he was an apostle of shared experience. To the patrons of Symphony Hall he embodied a principled commitment to the orchestra and its community. Especially in the first decade of his quarter-century tenure, guest conductors were rare; Koussevitzky conducted 115 times and more a season. In his absence he normally entrusted the orchestra to his concertmaster, Richard Burgin, a highly competent conductor with no podium career or aspirations outside the Koussevitzky orbit. If jealous and possessive, Koussevitzky was equally a proud and caring music director. He was parental.

When in 1940 the union issue revived in Boston, it was Koussevitzky, rather than any member of the board, who took the lead in solving it: a fatherly intervention. The catalyst for the new labor militancy was electronic media: recordings (which could substitute for live music), radio (which could broadcast recordings), and movies (for which music could be recorded on the soundtrack) were taking away thousands of musicians' jobs. The instrument for the new militancy was James Caesar Petrillo,[33] who quit school after grade four, ran a saloon, and played the trumpet before becoming president of Chicago's American Federation of Musicians Local 10 at the age of thirty. In the rough–and–tumble of Chicago labor, Petrillo was such a power that he could prevent a mayoral inauguration parade from engaging a high school band instead of unionized professionals. His strategies included "standby music," requiring the engagement of musicians whether or not they were needed when recorded music was played; free band concerts subsidized by the city; and royalties on recordings, motion pictures, and broadcasts applied toward musicians' wages. In 1940 Petrillo became president of the AF of M. Muscling leverage through his control of broadcasting and recording opportunities, he swiftly moved to unionize classical music soloists. This enabled him to force a showdown in Boston. The violinist Joseph Szigeti and the pianist Rudolf Serkin were prevented from appearing with the Boston Symphony, as was the conductor Bruno Walter. RCA ceased recording the orchestra. It could no longer broadcast. It was banned from certain auditoriums in New York and Massachusetts.

Ernest B. Dane, chairman of the trustees, intransigently opposed unionization as a matter of principle; he personally pumped a fortune into the orchestra to compensate for lost revenues. But Dane died in 1942. Around the same time, Koussevitzky invited Petrillo to his Berkshires estate. Petrillo arrived in a bulletproof limousine accompanied by bodyguards. Koussevitzky was amazed by Petrillo's knowledge of the orchestra's finances and impressed by his candor and tact. Petrillo pledged not to jeopardize Koussevitzky's ability to hire the finest musicians. As of December 1942, the Boston Symphony became a union shop. Koussevitzky could no longer call or prolong rehearsals at will. Asserting new prerogatives, the musicians closed all rehearsals: Koussevitzky's outbursts could no longer entertain visitors. One such outburst, reported by Dickson, was "Gentlemen, I do no like your sound. Since you join the union you play like employers!"

Dickson also observed of Koussevitzky, "One of his constant pleadings was for 'more dolce.' Indeed 'dolce' became for him a word signifying perfection in music. . . . If he thought it was too loud, he would admonish the players to play more softly and 'more dolce.' If it was too soft, he would say, 'I cannot hear the dolce.'" Leonard Bernstein, similarly, recalled "long disquisitions on legato. . . . 'it must be *varm*, varm.'" "Velvety" and "aristocratic" were other adjectives commonly applied to Koussevitzky's Boston Symphony. Koussevitzky played a string instrument and the symphonic sound he preferred was string-based: his recordings are beautifully sung. Where there are tricky shifts of meter and tempo, as in Copland, his technical limitations are audible. In Tchaikovsky, a specialty, he allows himself surprising rubatos. But a Koussevitzky recording never sounds eccentric, vulgar, or extreme. Virgil Thomson, in the *Herald-Tribune*, called the Boston Symphony "overtrained": "The music it plays never seems to be about anything, except how beautifully the Boston Symphony Orchestra can play."[34] Koussevitzky's studio recordings may sometimes be vulnerable to this exaggerated accusation. Like most conductors, he is better represented in live performance. In an October 9, 1943, broadcast of the Mussorgsky/Ravel *Pictures*, the sudden breadth of the "Great Gate of

Kiev" conveys the kind of electricity, galvanizing players and listeners, that Koussevitzky's admirers relished; the performance ends on an unforgettably high plateau of elation.[35]

It may be argued that Koussevitzky the interpreter fails to challenge or provoke, an observation that cannot be applied to such famous Koussevitzky contemporaries as Toscanini, Stokowski, Furtwängler, Otto Klemperer, or Evgeny Mravinsky. Abundant challenge and provocation lay elsewhere: in the choice of repertoire, in the larger pedagogic mission. Compared to Stokowski, Koussevitzky mounted the more organized, more traditional challenge to Toscanini-style shrinkage. No one was more appreciative than the American composer. For selected Americans Koussevitzky designated his orchestra a kind of training school: a means of hearing their music, a basis for growth. The first such beneficiary was Aaron Copland. He was introduced to Koussevitzky in Paris by his teacher, Nadia Boulanger. Koussevitzky heard the young man's *Cortège macabre* and was converted. His first Boston season included Copland's Symphony for Organ and Orchestra; his second, Copland's *Music for the Theatre*; his third, Copland's Piano Concerto. In all, he performed eleven Copland works (and Burgin led an additional two), including five first performances. And these performances were in every way a committed act of advocacy. "The program for the week is carefully planned so that the major portion of the rehearsal period may be devoted to the new work," Copland wrote in a 1944 tribute.

> To Dr. Koussevitzky each untried composition is a fresh adventure—the outcome is as unpredictable as the delivery of an unborn babe. The composer is present, of course, for morning rehearsals; these are generally followed by evening discussions with the conductor in preparation for the next day's work. Throughout the week conductor and composer may run the gamut of emotions from liveliest elation to darkest misgivings. But come what may, by Friday afternoon the work is ready for its public test. The conductor walks to the podium with a full sense of his responsibility to the composer and to the work. No wonder other premieres seem perfunctory by comparison.[36]

Koussevitzky, who was childless, treated Copland and Lukas Foss as surrogate sons. Upon appointing Foss the Boston Symphony's pianist in 1944, he explained that very few of the works he scheduled had piano parts—Foss could spend his time composing, supported by the Boston Symphony; he also had a habit of handing Foss his tailored suits after four or five wearings. Other American composers in the Koussevitzky orbit included Samuel Barber,

Howard Hanson, Roy Harris, Edward Burlingame Hill, Walter Piston, and William Schuman. Twice Koussevitzky brought to Carnegie Hall two all-American programs in the course of a single season. He did not disdain Gershwin, compared Paul Robeson to Fyodor Chaliapin, and declared himself captivated by Rodgers and Hammerstein's *Oklahoma!* He listed as "fundamental" American emotions energy, gaiety, and love of freedom.[37] Of contemporary Europeans, he especially championed Sibelius, Prokofiev, Stravinsky, Shostakovich, and Martinů.

There were notable omissions from the Koussevitzky repertoire. He had little use for Chadwick and other turn-of-the-century Bostonians (some of whom were still very much alive), or for Varèse, Ruggles, Antheil, and other "ultra-moderns." He did not touch the nontonal Schoenberg. He only once programmed music by Webern or Berg—the former's Op. 10 Five Pieces, the latter's Violin Concerto and *Lulu* Suite, all first American performances. Compared to Fritz Reiner in Cincinnati and Pittsburgh, he seldom conducted Bartók. But only Koussevitzky could so prominently have brought Bartók's Concerto for Orchestra into the world. Prodded by Reiner and Joseph Szigeti, he visited the composer in a Manhattan hospital to propose a commission. When Bartók declined, Koussevitzky announced that it was too late, and handed him a check for five hundred dollars.[38] The premiere was scheduled for December 1 and 2, 1944. In rehearsal, Koussevitzky (typically) proclaimed the new work "di greatest since Beethoven." Bartók, in the balcony overlooking the stage, found many things too fast, too slow, too loud, too soft. Koussevitzky asked that he write down all his corrections. Bartók wrote furiously for the duration of the rehearsal; he was still writing when it was over. Koussevitzky met with him and reported, "Gentlemen, Bartók say 'Everything is fine!'"[39] Following the two scheduled performances, Koussevitzky decided to program the concerto twice more: on December 29 and 30. The latter performance—wonderfully atmospheric, notably assured—was broadcast nationally. In 1944 Bartók was not the towering twentieth-century master he posthumously became.

Other important Koussevitzky commissions (via the Boston Symphony or the Koussevitzky Music Foundation) included Hindemith's *Konzertmusik* for Strings and Brass, Stravinsky's *Symphony of Psalms*, Britten's *Peter Grimes*, and Copland's Third Symphony. The long, long list of significant American or world premieres during his Boston tenure includes such staples as Falla's *El amor brujo* and Harpsichord Concerto; Harris's Third Symphony; Mahler's Ninth Symphony; the Mussorgsky/Ravel *Pictures at an Exhibition*; Prokofiev's two violin concertos, Fifth Symphony, and *Peter and the Wolf*; Ravel's Piano Concerto for the Left Hand; and Strauss's *Metamorphosen*. The Stravinsky premieres included the Concerto for Piano and Winds, *Oedipus Rex*, and the Violin Concerto. Koussevitzky's programming priorities were such that in some seasons the list of guest soloists was not announced. The unscheduled repetition of a new composition was not unique to Bartók's concerto. "Few conductors have been as finicky in their choice of works," wrote Copland. "Absolutely nothing but Dr. Koussevitzky's private conviction as to the value of a work will result in its performance. . . . He has often told me that the director of an orchestra should be the musical leader of his community. It is not enough that he himself have faith in the work he plays; the orchestra and public he serves must also be convinced of its value."[40]

The capstone of Koussevitzky's educational mission was the Berkshire Music Center at Tanglewood. Beginning in 1936, the Boston Symphony gave summer concerts in the Berkshires. In 1938, a fan-shaped "shed" was built, seating five thousand and open on all sides to an expansive lawn seating another eighteen thousand. Two years later, Koussevitzky added to this Tanglewood Festival of summer concerts a school for more than three hundred young musicians. The composition faculty included Copland and Hindemith. Koussevitzky taught conducting—his first crop of pupils included Bernstein and Foss—and was himself one of the conductors of a zealous student orchestra. Instrumental instruction was offered by members of the Boston Symphony. An opera division was led by Herbert Graf. Opening the center, Koussevitzky proclaimed, "If ever there was a time to speak of music, it is now in the New World. . . . So long as art and culture exist there is hope for humanity." When in 1942 the trustees decided to cancel the festival and its school during wartime, Koussevitzky admonished them for abandoning their "true and patriotic duty," and (shades of Henry Higginson) proceeded to subsidize the festival himself via his foundation. At a press conference, he called the Music Center "the vision of my life." His performances that summer, with the Music Center orchestra, of Shostakovich's new *Leningrad* Symphony and Harris's Third were politically charged occasions of such magnitude and intensity that music indeed bespoke "hope for humanity"—the Koussevitzky equivalent of Toscanini leading Beethoven at Carnegie Hall. After that, the festival limped through the war and the school was suspended. With the full resumption of Tanglewood in 1946, *Time* reported what Koussevitzky had to say when visitors called it "an American Salzburg": "Why a Salzburg? Let's have courage to say it. In early stages Salzburg was ideal place—now it is the most commercialized thing you can imagine. Most people who come to Salzburg are snobs who come to say they have been in Salzburg. They must rehearse too quick, in a week, maybe less. Why not a Tanglewood, U.S.A.? We play here something that is more perfect than ever a performance in Salzburg."[41]

It was true: compared to Tanglewood, U.S.A., with its outdoor mass audiences, Austria's Salzburg Festival was an elitist enclave. In wartime, democratic zeal was a Koussevitzky motif. He became a U.S. citizen. He spoke of America's obligation to the arts as a "historical mission" and argued that "American freedom" was the "best soil" for a civilizing dissemination of high culture, a "spiritual power" that "must be placed at the disposal of the great masses of men and women of America."[42] Echoing the preachings of Dvořák, Jeannette Thurber, and Anton Seidl a half-century before, he called for inexpensive tickets, for government subsidies created through an arts tax, for a U.S. Department of Fine Arts. He decried the plight of gifted composers unable to earn a living. His own Koussevitzky Music Foundation was established in 1942 to "encourage contemporary composers and provide them with opportunities to create new works." He predicted, "The next Beethoven vill from Colorado come." Meanwhile, it was Toscanini, NBC's apostle of Beethoven, whose public image was refashioned in *Life* and *Time* as "American."

Like Toscanini, Koussevitzky fostered a cult—albeit a more localized, less popular one. Like Toscanini, he was too sure of his own greatness. A 1947 biography by the Boston critic Moses Smith acknowledged Koussevitzky's abusive behavior in rehearsal, and reported his musicians resorting to a system of signals to maintain ensemble in complex music—the kind Koussevitzky had difficulty conducting—"out of sheer self-protection." Koussevitzky responded with a ludicrous and futile lawsuit. None of the book's dirty linen compared to Stokowski's young "nurses" or Toscanini's dalliance with Geraldine Farrar. When he died in 1951, his eulogists did not neglect to mention Koussevitzky's "irreproachable private life."[43]

Koussevitzky's career ended oddly, paradoxically. "It is my child, it is my creation," he told a radio interviewer about Tanglewood. "It is my blood and tears. I will never give it up." He designated Bernstein his successor and even outlined a three-year plan that would gradually plant Bernstein on the Boston podium. But the board in 1949 pushed aside Koussevitzky and Bernstein both, and named Charles Munch its new conductor on a year-round basis. Munch had no interest in being a Koussevitzky. While remaining a city with a great orchestra, Foss later wrote, Boston "ceased from one day to the next to be a mecca for young composers, a center of symphonic premieres that made the nation sit up and take notice." As the Boston Symphony went its own way, Tanglewood became Koussevitzky's legacy. And his main protégé was Bernstein, pursuing—not in Boston, but in New York and Tanglewood—a varied agenda for American music and musicians, for America itself.[44]

CHAPTER 2

More Conductors

■

*Frederick Stock and Fritz Reiner in Chicago ▪ Artur Rodzinski
and George Szell in Cleveland ▪ Otto Klemperer in Los Angeles
and New York ▪ Dimitri Mitropoulos in Minneapolis and New York*

Toscanini, Stokowski, and Koussevitzky cast long shadows on the rest of the symphonic field: compared to those of New York, Philadelphia, and Boston, more than a dozen American orchestras of consequence labored in relative obscurity. Of these, the least obscure was the orchestra Theodore Thomas had founded in Chicago, and which upon his death in 1905 had been entrusted to his thirty-three-year-old German-born assistant, Frederick Stock. Stock's Chicago Symphony seldom visited the Northeast. Its broadcasts and recordings were primarily of local interest, meaning the larger Midwest, which the orchestra toured exhaustively. Stock himself, like his mentor, disdained glamour and eschewed flamboyance. His commitment to Chicago was absolute. His popularity was immense. As a full-service conductor and community leader, he was the polar opposite of Toscanini.

If Stock's national reputation was never great, his posthumous reputation is all but invisible. In important reference works, he is dismissed as a colorless routineer.[1] In 1992, the Chicago Symphony issued a two-CD *Tribute to Frederick Stock* intended to restore his name. It does. Reviewing the last of Stock's three New York visits, Virgil Thomson wrote in the *Herald-Tribune* in 1940, "The Brahms third symphony was a dream of loveliness and equilibrium . . . one of those rare and blessed readings in which the music seems to play itself . . . pastoral, poetic and effortlessly convincing."[2] The same could be said of Stock's beautifully played 1941 recording of Schumann's Fourth Symphony in the CD *Tribute*, a performance equally notable for its sustained animation and warm, robust textures. The CD set also discloses the orchestra's virtuosity—as easy as breathing—in Paganini's *Moto perpetuo*: a witty transcription by Stock himself incorporating snatches of Beethoven's *Eroica* Symphony. The music-making throughout, including live broadcast performances of Rimsky-Korsakov, Liszt, and Elgar, is generous and ripe. The Schumann symphony lacks the cosmic chill with which Furtwängler invests the fourth-movement introduction in a famous 1953 recording, or Furtwängler's ecstasy in the final climactic rush. Stock's 1940 version of Sibelius's *Swan of Tuonela* is handsomely atmospheric; Stokowski's with the Philadelphia (1929) is both handsome and harrowing. But there is a dimension of the Stock experience not to be found (or sought) in a Furtwängler or Stokowski, Toscanini or Koussevitzky: the live 1935 performances in this *Tribute* document a special camaraderie. Stock's spoken remarks are casual, welcoming, and funny. He invites the audience to sing along in Elgar's *Pomp and Circumstance*—and it does. He predicts that the "I-will spirit of Chicago" will result in summer concerts—and it did. He signs off, "I'm sorry to say time is up. And as the Irish say, 'Auf wiedersehen'—good night!"[3]

Stock's thirty-seven-year record of achievement as music director also included, in 1913–14, the implementation of inexpensive "popular concerts" as a regular feature of every season, with seats at fifteen to fifty cents. With the cooperation of the Civic Club and the Civic Music Association, the orchestra sold tickets in targeted ethnic neighborhoods. Stock's initial skepticism about this venture was quickly dispelled by the enthusiastic response. Six years later, he initiated children's concerts, which, like the popular concerts, he relished conducting. In 1919 a singular training orchestra for young people, the Civic Music Students Orchestra (today the Civic Orchestra) was begun, with Stock as one of the regular conductors. For Chicago's "Century of Progress" world's fair of 1933, Stock conducted an Exhibition Orchestra (the Chicago Symphony expanded to one hundred players) for a full month of low-priced concerts, including an American program featuring George Gershwin as pianist/composer. The following summer, when the fair was repeated, George F. Swift contracted Stock and the Chicago Symphony for ten weeks of free outdoor concerts, given twice a day. The Detroit Symphony performed concurrently. It was estimated that this "experiment in the democratization of music" attracted something like two million listeners. In 1935, supporting a national trend toward outdoor summer performances, Stock began the Chicago Symphony's concerts at Grant Park. He closed his first summer season leading an orchestra of 225 in Dvořák's *New World* Symphony and shorter works by Rimsky-Korsakov, Johann Strauss Jr., and Tchaikovsky. One hundred thousand attended; another hundred thousand were turned away.[4]

In Theodore Thomas's day (as we have seen), "workingman's concerts" were sporadically undertaken by the Chicago Orchestra. "Popular concerts" were treated as an expendable weaning strategy. Rose Fay Thomas expressed an elitist ambivalence toward "the masses." There were many empty seats. As of 1913, Stock's sixth season, the *Chicago InterOcean* juxtaposed the "struggles and quaint experiences" of earlier times with this present-day reality: "The confirmed Friday afternoon habitues, both those who step out of their limousines in furs and velvets, and those who wait patiently until they can push everybody aside in their three steps-at-a-time scramble to the gallery, consider it a heresy to have an engagement with anybody but Mr. Stock on Friday afternoon. As for the Saturday night regulars they would rather go without their dinner than miss a Brahms symphony or a Debussy tone poem." When in 1921 there was talk of his moving on to the New York Philharmonic, Stock told the press, "I have been devoted to music in Chicago all my life and I love my work here. I feel, in fact, that it would be disloyal for me to leave Chicago, and I do not intend to, no matter how flattering an offer may be made to me." When in 1936 the Philharmonic reportedly checked on his availability to succeed Toscanini, the *Chicago Daily News* reported, "Mr. Stock . . . countered the impending proposal by remarking that the Chicago Symphony was doubtless the only orchestra with no contract between the conductor and board of directors. The negotiator returned to his luggage." More than any other American orchestra, Chicago was a model of stability. Its music directors stayed put and so did its musicians. The Civic Orchestra served as a feeder to replenish the ranks. Longtime principal players often appeared as soloists. Transcending the act of performance, the Chicago Symphony democratically and wholeheartedly embraced Thomas's aspiration that an orchestra shows "the culture of the community."[5]

In the first decades of his long tenure, Stock—himself a prolific and skilled composer—was an eclectic programmer, quick to introduce recent music by Debussy, Ravel, Scriabin, Mahler, Prokofiev, and Stravinsky. An enthusiastic American (he changed the language of rehearsals from German to English during World War I and became an American citizen in 1919), he also played lots of American music. Later in his tenure, his conservatism grew uncomfortably restrictive. The Americans he most favored were local: John Alden Carpenter, Leo Sowerby, Frederick Stock. His subscription programs included no Gershwin and only a single work by Copland—the Symphony No. 1, in 1934. (His repertoire was compared unfavorably with that of the Illinois Symphony; supported by the federal Works Progress Administration, it offered fifty-five world or American premieres in six years.) Stock died suddenly, in 1947 at the age of sixty-nine. *Time* magazine, which two years earlier had compared the Chicago Symphony favorably to the New York Philharmonic, reported, "Conductor Stock loved Chicago. . . . His mission, in which he largely succeeded, was to foster in Midwesterners the belief that symphonic music could be as American as Milwaukee beer, as free of foreign snobbery as Michigan Avenue."[6]

Stock proved hard to replace. Three conductors—Désiré Defauw, Artur Rodzinski, and Rafael Kubelik—tried and failed over a period of nine seasons marked by hostilities with the trustees and the press. Fritz Reiner, who came and stayed, reconnected to the orchestra's German roots, but in certain respects less resembled Thomas or Stock than Toscanini (whose La Scala and NBC orchestras he guest-conducted). Reiner had arrived in the United States from the Dresden Royal Opera in 1922, at age thirty-three, to take over the Cincinnati Symphony. It had run adrift since the days of van der Stucken, Stokowski, and Kunwald. From the first, he established a fearsome American reputation as a thorough musician, a deft technician, and an aloof martinet. He astounded the Cincinnati orchestra with his knowledge and his ear, and terrorized it with his hooded eyes, predatory gaze, and sadistic humor. "Any day on which he failed to lose his temper," one observer remembered, "was a day in which he was actually too sick to conduct." He would ask a player where he had studied and, on being told, would reply (in English, German, or Italian), "You were cheated! You should get your money back!" By 1925–26, only twenty-seven of the musicians he first encountered in Cincinnati were left in an orchestra of ninety-two. In 1928, his friend Béla Bartók was soloist in the American premiere of his First Piano Concerto, and later reported to Reiner that no European performance had "come up to the standard of precision shown in Cincinnati." Entangled in a marital squabble that scandalized the locals, Reiner left the transformed Cincinnati Symphony in 1931. Seven years later, as music director of the Pittsburgh Symphony, he again drove an ensemble in limbo to unsuspected heights of disciplined achievement. In his decade as music director, the seasonal turnover of musicians frequently exceeded 50 percent.[7]

The logic of Reiner's Chicago appointment was obvious: a Germanic orchestra, estranged from itself, sought discipline and direction. But Reiner was not the full-service music director Thomas and Stock had been. He conducted no popular concerts, no children's concerts, no outdoor concerts, no Civic Orchestra concerts. In Cincinnati and Pittsburgh, his repertoire had included Gershwin (with whom he struck up a friendship), Copland, and other younger Americans; in Chicago, he was less exploratory. He continued to make his home in Connecticut. All the same, he superintended the Chicago Symphony diligently. Until a heart attack slowed him down in 1960, Reiner (like Koussevitzky, Stokowski, and Stock) led twenty or more weeks of concerts per season; he relinquished his orchestra to guests relatively infrequently.

Reiner's Chicago decade made the orchestra famous as it had never been before. On his many RCA studio recordings, he can seem tight and remote. Recordings of live performance tell a different story. Such memorable Reiner/Chicago readings as Beethoven's *Leonore* Overture No. 2 (October 24, 1957) or Schumann's Second Symphony (October 31, 1957) are as notable for breadth and heat (but not warmth) as detail and unanimity. His Beethoven Eighth (February 6, 1958) is, like Toscanini's, spectacularly taut and fiery; unlike Toscanini's, it profits, as well, from a wicked sense of humor and an earthy response to folk dance.[8]

Reiner and the Chicagoans toured the Northeast triumphantly in 1958; of a Carnegie performance of Brahms's Third Symphony, Paul Henry Lang wrote in the *Herald-Tribune* that it "grew like a cleansing tide sweeping away the debris left on the stage of Carnegie Hall by the smart, smooth, and sentimental performances so often heard there." Reiner's detractors found his brand of music-making as cold as Reiner the man. To his admirers, Reiner's Chicago orchestra was a paragon of power, clarity, and integrity. That he was not the leader of culture Thomas and Stock had been mattered little at first: Chicago had its traditions. But there were cumulative frustrations—that the Reiners did not live or socialize locally, or support fund-raising and promotional activities, or cultivate confidantes within the organization. At Reiner's seventieth birthday party, in 1959, Fritz and Carlotta were strangers to many of the trustees and their wives. Two months later, at a rehearsal, he announced that he had canceled a long-promised tour—the orchestra's overdue debut in Europe, Russia, and the Near East. He called it "unfeasible" and "awful" and alluded to rainy Russian weather. Some of the players hissed. Later that day an old dress suit was spread on the floor of the musicians' dressing room with a sign reading, according to some reports, "Farewell, European Tour—Thanks, Fritz" or, according to others, "Unfeasible = rain in Moscow." There were footprints on the fabric.[9]

Many in the Chicago Symphony family never forgave Reiner. Meanwhile, his health declined. In 1962–63 he was designated "musical adviser," and yet the trustees named his successor, Jean Martinon, without his advice. Martinon's contract stipulated that he make his home in Chicago. Tour or no tour, the orchestra Martinon inherited was world renowned as a high-performance machine, a reputation it sustained, after Martinon's brief tenure, under Georg Solti. I once attended a Solti/Chicago concert at Carnegie Hall. During the tumult following Brahms's First Symphony, a man in front of me waved his right index finger in the air. He was signaling that the Chicago Symphony was "number one": world's greatest.

Actually, Reiner's Chicago Symphony had competition as America's "world's greatest orchestra," and from an unlikely contender with a late start. Before 1900, Cleveland had been visited by the Thomas Orchestra, by Walter Damrosch's New York Symphony, by Higginson's Boston Symphony under the likes of Nikisch and Gericke. Its Germans had formed their singing societies and sporadic philharmonics. The prime mover of musical affairs, as in Cincinnati, was a woman. Upon graduating Phi Beta Kappa from Vassar in 1890, Adella Prentiss had wintered in Germany, where the Berlin Philharmonic under von Bülow left an indelible impression. An accomplished pianist whose friends already included the Rockefellers, she returned to Cleveland with a mission. By the time she married the baritone Felix Hughes, in 1903, she had begun her Symphony Orchestra Concerts, which from 1901 to 1920 presented 162 performances by eleven orchestras—a list including Muck's Boston Symphony, Stokowski's Philadelphia Orchestra, Mahler's New York Philharmonic, the Pittsburgh Orchestra under Richard Strauss, and Chicago's orchestra with Thomas and then Stock. It was Adella Prentiss Hughes who discovered the conductor Nikolai Sokoloff and decided he was the man to lead a Cleveland Orchestra. She proudly called herself "the mother of 90 musicians." As late as 1942, by which time she was no longer the orchestra's manager but remained a member of the board, the conductor Erich Leinsdorf would observe, "She acted as if she *were* the Cleveland Orchestra. There were some who not only disliked Mrs. Hughes with great passion but who would almost automatically vote against anything and anyone she promoted. She was, like many domineering women, truly formidable, full of vitality, peremptorily decisive, musically knowledgeable—which made her part of a small board minority—and so direct as to be considered by softer and less-outspoken people rather tactless."[10]

The conductor who fine-tuned the Cleveland Orchestra and made it matter outside Cleveland was Sokoloff's successor, Artur Rodzinski. He had previously served as assistant to Stokowski in Philadelphia and as music director of the Los Angeles Philharmonic. Rodzinski was a picturesque and eccentric personality, known for packing a loaded pistol at all performances as a good luck charm. He could be warmly gregarious or impossibly irate. In Cleveland, as later with the New York Philharmonic and the Chicago Symphony, he proved a brilliant trainer and repairman for young or broken orchestras. He also realized an implausible aspiration to regularly mount fully staged operas within the orchestra's subscription season. The fourteen operas he led in Cleveland included major works by Wagner and Strauss, beginning with *Tristan und Isolde* in 1933. Though there were no famous singers, the opening night ovation lasted forty-seven minutes. The peak of Rodzinski's Cleveland decade occurred in 1935 when, taking a page from Stokowski, he led the

American premiere of a major contemporary opera and brought it to Manhattan. This was Shostakovich's *Lady Macbeth of the Mtsensk District*, which Rodzinski deemed "the best opera written in this century." He flew to Moscow to secure the score. Both Cleveland performances were sold out. A third performance at the Metropolitan Opera, also sold out, was attended by Damrosch, Gershwin, Heifetz, Klemperer, Koussevitzky, Reiner, Stokowski, Stravinsky, Toscanini, and Walter. When Rodzinski mounted *Tannhäuser* in Cleveland in 1936, Olin Downes of the *New York Times* was there and wrote, "The performance was exhilarating and it was illuminative of the position that an orchestra and its various agencies can hold in a community of which it is genuinely a part and a musical center."[11] Rodzinski's Cleveland Orchestra recordings crackle with excitement.

Seven years later, Rodzinski became the New York Philharmonic's music director. He was briefly succeeded in Cleveland by Leinsdorf. Then, in 1946, came George Szell and world fame. From the start, Szell exhibited an exceptional capacity to get what he wanted from the board. His Cleveland contract stipulated that the roster, with its eighty-two-member maximum, be increased by eight in his first season, an expansion for which Rodzinski and Leinsdorf had lobbied in vain. Szell was paid forty thousand dollars, compared to thirty thousand dollars for Rodzinski and eighteen thousand dollars for Leinsdorf. He was called not "conductor" but "music director and conductor." He had the Severance Hall stage setting replaced. He masterminded an annual ceremony of firings and hirings, and personally negotiated all salaries above minimum scale. He demanded that hair be cut and beards shaved, that socks extend over the calf, that coats and ties be worn at all times on tour. He specified what brand of toilet paper be installed in the Severance bathrooms. He kept close tabs on staff members. In contrast to Mahler and Furtwängler in New York, or Reiner in Chicago, he embraced the peculiarities of American symphonic management and so regarded the trustees—to most of whom he remained "Mr. Szell"—as necessary colleagues.

Szell had begun his career as a prodigy. By the time he was twenty, he had conducted the Berlin Philharmonic and joined Richard Strauss's staff at the Berlin State Opera. He was director of the German Opera and Philharmonic in Prague before World War II chased him west. In New York, he found the Philharmonic and Metropolitan Opera insufficiently serious; when some years later someone called him "his own worst enemy," Rudolf Bing, the Met's general manager, famously retorted, "Not while I'm alive." In Cleveland, no one dared declare war on George Szell. He vowed—repeatedly, emphatically, publicly—to create a perfect symphonic vehicle, combining European tradition with American precision and discipline. As of 1951 he informed the *Cleveland Press* that "the Cleveland Orchestra is a much, much finer instrument than the New York." A year later he wrote to Artur Rubinstein, "The Orchestra is really TOPS. I mean it and, as you know, I am not in the habit of kidding myself." In 1964, in a letter rebuking his musicians for their latest contract demands, he said:

> Rudi Serkin, the other day, said to me after our concerts, "There never was an orchestra like this." I would like to go one step further and without any exaggeration and megalomania say, I don't think it likely that there ever or very soon will be an orchestra like this because we understand one another musically, deeply and closely, and I don't recall a relationship of a conductor and an orchestra in the 50 or 60 years I can remember that could have competed with this. It is up to you, Ladies and Gentlemen, to make the wise decision continuing this and it is equally up to you to destroy it.[12]

The musicians, in turn, called Szell "Dr. Cyclops" for his thick spectacles and control mania. In rehearsals, he micromanaged every crescendo and diminuendo. According to Daniel Majeske, his concertmaster from 1969, "He spelled out everything in millimeters and micrograms. He certainly could have been a pharmacist." Another Cleveland violinist, Kurt Loebel, reports Szell saying of his drilled nuances, "We calculate the inspiration." Loebel recalls Szell's rehearsals and performances as "a matter of life and death." After half a century of service with the Cleveland Orchestra, he testified, "The difference between playing in the Szell orchestra and all others is that in Szell's orchestra I could not hear any violinist that sat behind me, in front of me, or beside me. We were so precisely together that you couldn't distinguish any differences." Szell's astounding 1968 in-concert recording of Prokofiev's *Classical* Symphony bears witness: the acrobatic strings are phenomenally exact.[13]

In the course of Szell's twenty-four-year Cleveland tenure, ending with his death in 1970, the orchestra secured an international reputation buttressed by its many recordings, by its European debut in 1957, and by annual New York visits beginning in 1958. Michael Steinberg of the *Boston Globe*, reviewing a 1964 Carnegie Hall concert, wrote, "It is because of its unanimity as an orchestra even more than for its surpassing virtuosity in other ways that I would call the Cleveland Orchestra uniquely great, or perhaps even uniquely an orchestra." It was Szell's ideal to achieve complete homogeneity of sound, phrasing, and articulation within each section—strings, winds, and brass— "and then—when the ensemble is perfect—[achieve] the proper balance between sections plus complete flexibility—so that in each moment one or more principal voices can be accompanied by the others. To put it simply: the most sensitive ensemble playing." To legions of Szell admirers, this "chamber music" approach was revelatory. Like Toscanini (whom he acknowledged as an inspiration and admired with reservation) or Reiner (with whom he was inevitably compared), Szell honed an instrument whose clarity and responsiveness conveyed selfless honesty and maximum versatility. Unlike Reiner's or Toscanini's, his music-making seemed cold-blooded to his detractors; more than Reiner's or Toscanini's, it equally seemed denatured. No less than Reiner's Chicago Symphony, Szell's Cleveland Orchestra was about the act of performance; Szell increasingly lost interest in the "temporary music" of the present and recent past. Unlike Toscanini or Reiner, he combined autocracy with paternalism. His patronizing style of supervision was virtually colonialist: no New York or European orchestra would have tolerated such know-it-all hectoring for a quarter century. Szell conceded as much when he quipped that he could "lower his pants" on the New York podium "and nobody would notice," or when he argued that Bülow, in tiny Meiningen, could achieve executant standards unthinkable in cosmopolitan Berlin. As a musical phenomenon, Szell's singular Cleveland Orchestra was as unique to America as had been Stokowski's *sui generis* Philadelphia sound.[14]

■ ■ ■

If with Toscanini, Stokowski, and Koussevitzky, Reiner and Szell were the European conductors who rose highest in the United States during the first half of the twentieth century, the two who fell farthest were Otto Klemperer and Dimitri Mitropoulos. No less than the success of others, their failure helps to define the American cultural environment in which they could not flourish.

A physical giant, a wild yet austere personality, Klemperer embodied Weimar culture—new music, new aesthetics, new thought—as director of Berlin's Kroll Opera from 1917 to 1931. He was consumed by a reformist mission: to present recent operas of quality; to challenge the "star system"; to replace naturalistic stagings with the scenic creations of such artists as László Moholy-Nagy and Oskar Schlemmer; to achieve a new unity of music and drama. He championed Hindemith, Weill, Janáček, and, above all, Stravinsky. At the same time, the latest Schoenberg and Berg were not for him. In fact, his penchant for neoclassicism made him an important advocate for a new kind of Bach, Mozart, and Beethoven, purged of Romantic nuance and rubato. If Klemperer's interpretive principles resonated powerfully with the *neue Sachlichkeit* of the Bauhaus, his temperament was an Expressionist cauldron. To

Lotte Lehmann, rehearsing *Lohengrin* in 1912, he seemed "an evil spirit, thumping [the piano] with long hands like tiger's claws, and dragging my terrified voice into the vortex of his fanatical will."[15]

In salient respects, Klemperer resembled Mahler, whom he assisted as a youth and whose example he revered. Like Klemperer at the Kroll, Mahler in Vienna had dominated and unified every aspect of repertoire, production, and performance; had overturned canons of verisimilitude; had passionately demanded a dispassionate clarity of texture. Mahler's signature achievements at the Vienna Opera had included revisionist stagings of *Fidelio* and *Tristan* designed by Alfred Roller. Klemperer's signature achievements at the Kroll included a famously stark, stylized version of Wagner's *The Flying Dutchman*. "The Dutchman . . . looks like a Bolshevist agitator, Senta like a fanatical Communist harridan, Erick . . . a pimp," reported the *Allgemeine Musikzeitung*, which in the same breath accused the Kroll of "damaging Berlin's reputation as a culture center." Other journals denounced the Kroll as "anti-Christian." Summarizing the reasons the Kroll was closed in 1931, Thomas Mann listed, "because [it] occupies a strong position on the intellectual left, because it stands at the crossroads of social and cultural interests and is a thorn in the eye of . . . obscurantism. If opera today is still or has once again become an intellectual issue and a subject of intellectual discussion, that is in the first place the merit of this institution." *Musical America* got an early taste of Klemperer in 1927. He was one of many musicians surveyed on the topic of the Beethoven centenary. He responded, "If you will ask me the best way to celebrate his centenary, I will tell you it is not to play him for a year. He is played too much. Everyone plays Beethoven, and no one listens to hear the men who write today. . . . I do not know why this insistence on music men who are dead."[16]

Hitler's coming ended Klemperer's prewar German career. Born a Jew, he moved his family to southern California in 1935. Two years before, he had become music director of the Los Angeles Philharmonic. The Los Angeles orchestra was the 1919 creation of William Andrews Clark Jr., inheritor of a mining and railroad fortune. Clark treasured the memory of Anton Seidl, a frequent guest in his father's New York home. He studied the violin in Paris. Like Henry Higginson in Boston, he followed his dream, single-handedly financing an orchestra of his devising. He hired the musicians, hired and advised the conductors, and even took a seat among the violins. He purchased the lease of Cline's Auditorium, with twenty-six-hundred seats. His first music directors were Walter Henry Rothwell, who had conducted in St. Paul; Emil Oberhoffer, who had conducted in Minneapolis; and Georg Schneevoigt, who came directly from Europe. Artur Rodzinski took over from 1929 to 1932—his first American appointment, preceding Cleveland. Then, with suitable fanfare, the forty-seven-year-old Otto Klemperer appeared. "My task here is that of a pioneer," Klemperer wrote to a friend. "But the people are endlessly grateful and ready to love me.... About the life (and everything that goes with it) I still often have doubts."[17]

Some of Klemperer's doubts concerned Will Clark. He drank to excess and once appeared naked at Klemperer's bedside. His fortune depleted, he had for some time been attempting to divest himself of the Philharmonic, but alternative support was not forthcoming. Three weeks after Klemperer's arrival, Clark disappeared for Europe. He died suddenly in 1934. A reorganization resulted in the appointment, as manager, of the stout and exuberant Mrs. Leiland Atherton Irish, a dedicated and effective fund-raiser who urged Klemperer to omit the mournful finale of Tchaikovsky's *Pathétique* Symphony and, on another occasion, insisted that the pianist Eduard Steuermann be photographed in a chef's apron and hat. One of Klemperer's duties was the annual Easter Sunrise Service at Forest Lawn Memorial Park, at which he had to conduct excerpts from *Parsifal* and *Die Meistersinger* for an audience at daybreak. The orchestra's regular Auditorium home, with excellent acoustics, suffered from squeaky seats and a noisy ventilation system. Traffic noise was audible, as were hymns from an adjoining Baptist church.

Klemperer often found Los Angeles "an intellectual desert."[18] But he threw himself into his job, committing up to fifteen weeks per season. He attended parties and board meetings and led student concerts with commentaries composed and delivered in English. He cherished the company of Arnold Schoenberg, whom he helped to obtain a teaching position at UCLA and from whom he took lessons. Schoenberg was frustrated that Klemperer (as in Germany) did not program his most "advanced" music. But Los Angeles heard a gamut of Schoenberg's tonal compositions, including the premiere of his transcription of Brahms's G minor Piano Quartet, a memorable symphonization suggested to Schoenberg by Klemperer himself. Among the orchestra's guest conductors were Schoenberg and Stravinsky. The repertoire included many challenging and impressive works new to Los Angeles—symphonies by Bruckner, Mahler, Sibelius, and Shostakovich, and Berg's Violin Concerto.

Though Klemperer was a success, though the seasons lengthened and audiences grew, though one local critic wrote, "Make no mistake, the man has perhaps one equal and no superiors in this country," he remained restive. He felt isolated and oppressed. He sought a beachhead in New York or Philadelphia, from which Toscanini and Stokowski were departing. But American symphonic culture was in thrall to more glamorous conductors. The Metropolitan Opera was about singers. The leading music critics were out of sympathy with modernism, with *neue Sachlichkeit*, with Stravinsky and

Schoenberg. When Klemperer obtained a tryout with the New York Philharmonic in 1934–35 and 1935–36, he programmed Berg, Bruckner, Hindemith, Janáček, Mahler, Schoenberg, and Shostakovich. W. J. Henderson, who had heard Seidl and Mahler, wrote that Klemperer trailed "clouds of glory behind him." But he was never again invited to lead the orchestra. In 1939, a huge tumor was discovered in his brain. Its removal left the right side of his face and body partly paralyzed. Though the tumor was benign, a period of extreme psychological disturbance ensued. Klemperer left his Los Angeles post. In New York, he took to hiring taxis (for which he could not pay) for entire evenings. His clothes were dirty, he ate irregularly, he walked unsteadily and with a stick. He wore an eyepatch. His mood careened from hilarity to rage. In 1941, he agreed to enter what he did not realize was a mental institution in Rye, New York. He confronted the medical director, Dr. Daniel J. Kelly, with such anger that Kelly reluctantly allowed him to leave—and thereupon informed the police, who issued an eight-state warning that Klemperer was "dangerous." The *New York Times* ran a front-page story headlined, "KLEMPERER GONE: SOUGHT AS INSANE."[19]

Had Klemperer's tumor killed him, his American years would have been recalled as a grotesque pendant to a notable if ephemeral European career. Instead, he reemerged in Europe, psychologically stabilized, as the most esteemed survivor of a generation mainly deceased. His rejuvenation was characteristically tortuous. For Stock, Stokowski, and Koussevitzky, American citizenship proved a valued calling card; Klemperer's American citizenship, obtained in 1940, proved a liability. Though he was able to resume his operatic career in Communist Budapest in 1947, the State Department, taking notice of his leftist sympathies, refused to renew his passport. Compelled to return to New York, he had to forego important European engagements and recordings. A concert and recording contract with London's Philharmonia Orchestra came to the rescue in 1954. A German passport was quickly arranged. Almost as quickly, Klemperer's 1955 recordings of three Beethoven symphonies, with the Philharmonia, consolidated his reputation. In 1958, he nearly died of severe burns when he fell asleep while smoking. Following two operations and eight months of hospitalization, he gradually resumed his new career in London and continental Europe. He returned to the United States to conduct the Philadelphia Orchestra in 1962. With the passing of Toscanini and Furtwängler, he had achieved unsurpassed international fame as a venerated apostle of Beethoven and other old masters.

Klemperer's amazing personal odyssey was accompanied by shifts in musical identity. His manic and depressive moods generated tempos faster or slower than the norm. But, as in Klemperer the man, there was also a missionary constancy: he maintained absolute resistance to the vagaries of Romantic *Innigkeit*, to Furtwängler's subjective probes. At every stage of his career (documented by recordings and broadcasts), his most characteristic performances, rigorously projecting outward design, amassed a magisterial poise and weight. In later life, his extreme age (he retired in 1972 at age eighty-seven), crippled face, dour intellect, and great height complicated his intended simplicity; the affect was epic. As with Toscanini in his late career, Klemperer's signature "objectivity" paradoxically accompanied an overpowering personal imprint.

■ ■ ■

Late in life, Klemperer was asked, "Do you think there is a connection between great gifts and great suffering?" Ever antisentimental, he loathed fussy language (or music-making);* his metaphysics remained private. On this occasion, he responded with banter. Then, abruptly, he reached for his Bible and read from *Ecclesiastes*: "For in much wisdom is much grief; and he that increaseth knowledge increases grief." This rare concession acknowledged what all could glean: Klemperer the survivor, who all his life gravitated to the music of faith, to Bach and to Bruckner, evoked a modern-day Job. Like Mahler, he had converted from Judaism to Catholicism; like Mahler's, his was a religious personality, beyond sect, whose embattled resilience suggested a moral fable.

But no twentieth-century symphonic conductor seemed more strangely or potently religious than Dimitri Mitropoulos.[20] He was born in an obscure Greek village. His grandfather was a priest; two uncles were monks on Mount Athos. His lodestar was St. Francis. He wore a large crucifix next to his heart. With his bald head and big-boned features, he looked like an anchorite and practically lived like one. He gave away most of what he earned—to students, to colleagues, to peddlers on the street. Unmarried, often celibate, he disdained the trappings of wealth, privilege, and domesticity. A student in Berlin from 1921 to 1924, he affixed himself to Ferruccio Busoni and absorbed the influence of Furtwängler and Klemperer, Erich Kleiber, Bruno Walter, and Richard Strauss. He achieved sudden celebrity in 1930 when he led the Berlin Philharmonic in a concert including Prokofiev's Third Piano Concerto, which he both played and conducted. By then he had returned to Athens,

---

* Claudio Arrau once recalled, "When I was playing the five Beethoven piano concertos in London with Klemperer, we came to this little trill in the second movement of the *Emperor* [m. 25]. Klemperer said: 'What are you *doing* there?' 'Just playing a trill the way I think it should be played.' '*A trill is a trill!*'" See Joseph Horowitz, *Conversations with Arrau* (New York, Knopf, 1982), p. 39.

where he taught and conducted for more than a decade. In 1936 Koussevitzky invited him to conduct in Boston, where his impact was sensational. In 1937 he became music director of the Minneapolis Symphony and stayed for a dozen years, a tenure as picturesque and inspirational, in its way, as Koussevitzky's or Stokowski's back East.

The Minneapolis orchestra was formed in 1903 by Emil Oberhoffer (whom we have glimpsed in Los Angeles) in association with a lumber magnate, Elbert L. Carpenter. Oberhoffer was a born educator—his nineteen-year music directorship, fortified with frequent tours, was influential throughout the Midwest. His successors were Henri Verbrugghen in 1923 and Eugene Ormandy in 1931, of whom the latter galvanized the orchestra as an instrument of performance. Mitropoulos inherited a highly competent ensemble and transformed it into a laboratory for a kind of contemporary fare Koussevitzky rarely touched. His concertmaster as of 1944 was Louis Krasner, who had premiered Berg's Violin Concerto and Schoenberg's. In Minnesota, he performed both with Mitropoulos and gave the first performance of the Roger Sessions concerto. Mitropoulos befriended and championed the twelve-tone composer Ernst Krenek, who turned up at Hamline College in St. Paul in exile from Austria. Mahler, Vaughan Williams, Milhaud, and Morton Gould were other composers for whom Mitropoulos raised a flag. This barrage of challenging and unfamiliar music would have merely annoyed had Mitropoulos been a mere conduit. He was instead a powerful advocate. Here is an off-the-cuff speech occasioned by a 1945 performance of Alexander Tansman's Fifth Symphony (in an eighteen-program subscription season including Berg, Hindemith, Kabalevsky, Khachaturian, Mahler, Milhaud, Respighi, Schoenberg, Shostakovich, Szymanowski, Tcherepnin, Vaughan Williams, Walton, and the Americans David Diamond, Morton Gould, and Charles Miller):

> What sense does it make to embrace modern inventions and conveniences, modern films and radio shows, but to utterly reject modern sounds? Could you take a sporting interest in these contemporary works? That is to say, could you not accept the challenge of *listening* first and then deciding, on a piece by piece basis, what to embrace and what to discard? Listening to a new work of music is an *experiment*, and as any scientist can tell you, an experiment can be its own reward, at least in terms of intellectual satisfaction. We don't have to ask that all modern works we hear should be supremely great works of art. Most of them aren't, and we would be naïve to expect them to be, but we are more naïve if we close our ears to them.[21]

Leopold Stokowski as he looked in 1912—the year after he left
Cincinnati to take over the Philadelphia Orchestra; he claimed to be
twenty-five years old but was actually all of twenty-nine.

In 1916 Stokowski led the American premiere of
Mahler's Symphony No. 8 with an orchestra of 110
and 950 choristers. He likened his first experience of
the work, as led by Mahler in Munich, to that of
"the first white man to behold Niagara Falls."

For Arturo Toscanini's 1944 Red Cross benefit at Madison Square Garden, the souvenir booklet produced a Toscanini image suggesting Christ. "On Tour with Toscanini and RCA Victor," a 1950 publicity brochure, depicted Toscanini's democratized Saturday-night radio audience. In 1954, David Sarnoff appeared on screen to introduce the first Toscanini telecast as "a great day for radio, for television, for music, and for the public."

Serge Koussevitzky conducting the Boston
Symphony in the Brahms Requiem in 1933,
and with his protégé Leonard Bernstein.
Bernstein recalled his mentor's "long
disquisitions on legato . . . 'it must
be *varm*.'"

J.B.Sanroma

The resident martinets in Cleveland and Chicago were George Szell (upper left, above) and Fritz Reiner. Dimitri Mitropoulos, not a martinet, was saluted by the *Minneapolis Star* (March 18, 1949) when he left the Minneapolis Symphony for New York; a photo spread included pictures of his "strenuous" conducting style, and his 1943 summer job as a Red Cross volunteer blood custodian. As music director of the New York Philharmonic, he had to contend with Bruno Zirato and Arthur Judson (opposite, lower right, with Judson in the middle).

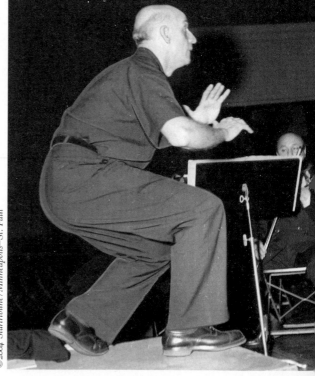

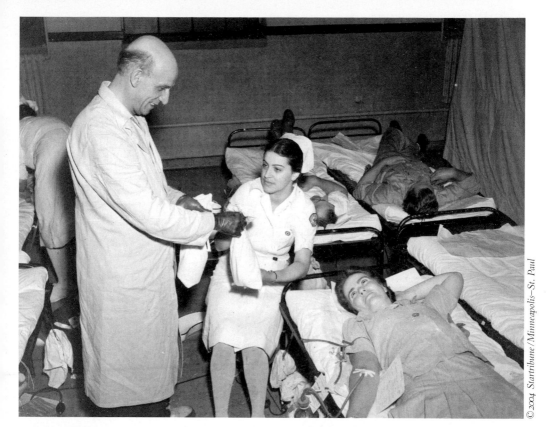

Nadia Boulanger with her onetime pupils (left to right) Aaron Copland, Virgil Thomson, and Walter Piston. George Gershwin with Walter Damrosch, who commissioned Gershwin's Piano Concerto in F.

This *Victor Record Review* story (November 1940) begins, "Rarely has it happened in the history of recorded performances that two such artists as Jascha Heifetz and Arturo Toscanini have combined their respective talents (each pre-eminent in his own field) in the interpretation of such a prodigious masterpiece of Beethoven's Concerto in D major for Violin and Orchestra, Opus 81." Heifetz's antipode Joseph Szigeti joined Benny Goodman for the 1938 premiere of Béla Bartók's *Contrasts*—initially titled Rhapsody for Clarinet, Violin and Piano.

The most famous of Vladimir Horowitz's several comebacks took place at Carnegie Hall on May 9, 1965, after a twelve-year absence; he was mobbed by fans upon leaving the hall. Three years later, his Carnegie Hall recital was recorded for television, with the cameras onstage.

Rudolf Serkin and the brothers Adolf (left) and Hermann Busch were among the founders of the Marlboro Festival in Vermont, a mecca for the cultivation of Germanic chamber music in the United States. Serkin's performance of Beethoven's *Choral* Fantasy for piano, orchestra, and chorus—here in a 1987 public rehearsal with Felix Galimir as concertmaster—was a traditional highlight of the Marlboro season.

Glenn Gould, the most original North American keyboard talent of his day, performed fifteen times with Leonard Bernstein and the New York Philharmonic. The audience crowded the flower-strewn stage when Van Cliburn, who willed himself a Russian, won the first International Tchaikovsky Competition in Moscow in 1958.

Bernstein's "The Drama of *Carmen*," on TV's *Ford Presents* (March 11, 1962), compared the dialogue from the original score with recitatives composed by Ernest Guiraud after Bizet's death; in arguing for the superiority of the former, Bernstein celebrated *Carmen* as a near cousin to American musical comedy. The search for American identity was also a frequent subtext of Bernstein's New York Philharmonic Young People's Concerts.

Reuters/Corbis

The Three Tenors (left to right: Plácido Domingo, José Carreras, Luciano Pavarotti) diluted and vulgarized what they purported to disseminate. A more auspicious audience-expansion vehicle is the Los Angeles Philharmonic's new Disney Hall, which makes listeners part of the main event.

Los Angeles Philharmonic Archives

The sermonette was accompanied by a plea for blood donations. As his listeners appreciated, Mitropoulos himself had dedicated the summer of 1943 to a Red Cross unit, collecting donated blood within a seventy-five-mile radius of Minneapolis. As "blood custodian," he was responsible for setting up cots, washing test tubes, and cleaning up afterward: a twelve- to fourteen-hour regimen maintained for three months. He wrote to David Diamond, "Every time I wash the tubes which have been used to transfer the blood of a human being from his veins to a little jar, I feel more hopeful and more real, and even sometimes I find myself dreaming of quitting my abstract, smug profession . . . although I know that, like an old alcoholic, sooner or later I will come back to my onions."[22]

This vignette was characteristic. Mitropoulos was a familiar everyday figure, walking to the store, waiting for the bus, attending church on Sundays. His favorite pastime was catching movies at odd hours, often sitting through double or triple features by himself or with friends or members of the orchestra. He indiscriminately enjoyed comedies, melodramas, gangster sagas—whatever was playing. His typical public attire included black turtlenecks and tunics that accentuated his monastic aura, as did the spartan furnishings of his home. On tour, he shared buses and railroad coaches with the musicians, and carried his belongings in a rucksack slung on his back. When the orchestra manager protested, he switched to a more dignified suitcase. He was also censured by the board for using the concert hall as a pulpit to urge support of Henry Wallace's third-party presidential candidacy, a 1948 challenge from the left. Such indiscretions were tolerated because Mitropoulos was loved by many and admired by most. Upon performing Berg's *Lyric* Suite in 1939 he wrote to his lifelong Greek confidante Katy Katsoyanis: "Last night, my dear friend, I felt the greatest relief I've ever felt in my life: I managed to make the audience and the musicians understand, love, and warmly applaud the Alban Berg Suite that is so full of problems. It's a victory and a sure measure of my persuasive forcefullness of expression. You must understand that the tragic and passionate element was projected with magnifying lenses, and so they couldn't resist me. I managed to hypnotize them, like a real Yogi."[23]

If Mitropoulos also experienced his share of failures, it was not the fault of his orchestra. His Minneapolis recordings document a condition of hypercommitment. Mitropoulos considered a 1942 recording of Schumann's Symphony No. 2 representative of what he had accomplished. Its slashing accents and jagged outlines, its sinewy musculature and raw energy make for an exhausting and discomfiting listening experience, a revisionist portrait of the composer as a nascent Expressionist. Mitropoulos's Minneapolis discography also includes Mahler's Symphony No. 1, to which the Mitropoulos style organically adheres. One need only recall Arthur Farwell's account of Mahler's own performance of Schubert's Ninth, with its "exaggerated" phrasings and dynamics pursued by "the imp of the perverse," to recognize the truthfulness of this 1940 recording. No less than Mahler—his scoring and conducting— Mitropoulos rejects the Romantic cathedral sonority: the warm blanket of strings, the recessed winds and percussion favored by generic conductors give way to shards of intense melody and tone. No wonder Mitropoulos also excelled in Berg and Webern, and in Strauss's *Elektra*.

Complementing such Mitropoulized renditions was the shock of the conductor's lithe, quivering frame, of his massive hands clawing the air, of his raw features contorted into a demonic gargoyle. He used neither baton nor score. His visual memory was such that, as countless composers discovered to their bewilderment, he knew every note, every measure number, every page number by heart. But, as certain composers also had occasion to observe, his ear was less acute. If the rough textures and ripping intensities of a Mitropoulos performance ultimately constituted an acquired taste, Minneapolis Symphony concerts were never dull. In 1939 *Time* magazine reported that "some of the most brilliant U.S. conducting since the peak days of Stokowski and Toscanini was being done in snow-crusted Minneapolis."[24] Four years later, when the orchestra visited Carnegie Hall, there were complaints about Mitropoulos's too "violently personal" style, but also inescapable acknowledgment that the Minneapolis Symphony was a force to be reckoned with.

Throughout Mitropoulos's Minneapolis tenure, his departure to some higher place was fatalistically anticipated. He led the New York Philharmonic, the Philadelphia Orchestra, and, in a return engagement, the Boston Symphony with powerful results. Finally the call came: from New York. At the close of his final Minneapolis subscription concert, on March 18, 1949, he walked to the lip of the stage and said, in part, "Unfortunately, the inexorable laws of destiny [rule] the chosen people. . . . They have to follow their duties and not their heart's desires. So I'm going someplace where I don't know if I'm going to be happy. But I have to go. I have to climb the mountain that is expected from me to climb more, until I go, like everyone else, and find our common father." To Louis Krasner he confided, "I simply can't resist. I am too weak *not* to go, do you understand. . . . I have to go, even though I know I am probably going to my doom."[25]

Mitropoulos's trepidation was complex. His correspondence[26] reveals a self-flagellating streak of which he was aware, as well as artistic insecurities. He feared the Philharmonic workload, with its four concerts per week. But he surely reflected on other reasons why the orchestra had proved a conductor's graveyard. In Philadelphia, Boston, and Chicago, Stokowski, Koussevitzky, and

Stock stayed put. In New York, no music director after Josef Stransky had lasted more than four seasons in a true leadership capacity. Players and listeners, trustees and administrators were poorly prepared to understand or support the repertoire priorities uppermost on Mitropoulos's agenda.

His New York failure was not unredeemed by memorable patches of success. No other conductor could so plausibly and unaffectedly have shepherded the Philharmonic to the six-thousand-seat Roxy movie palace, where for two weeks in September 1950 it appeared on the same bill with *The Black Rose* (starring Tyrone Power), Milton Berle, and the Roxyettes, offering four 45-minute concerts daily, seven days a week. No other conductor could cheerfully have observed, to a *Herald-Tribune* columnist, that his novice listeners had been so absorbed that when he turned around to have a look, they had stopped chewing their chewing gum. Later in the same season, Mitropoulos conducted Berg's *Wozzeck* in concert, its first New York hearing since Stokowski brought it up from Philadelphia two decades before. The occasion was electric; Olin Downes, in the *Times*, echoed general sentiment in acknowledging "one of the historic achievements in the history of Carnegie Hall,"[27] a recording of which remains perhaps the most galvanizing *Wozzeck* ever documented in sound.

But more legendary than the Roxy gig, or Berg's Expressionist masterpiece, was the orchestra's mounting abuse of its increasingly beleaguered music director. So fractious a collection of Italians, Germans, and Jews was the Philharmonic that actual fistfights were not unknown backstage. This pugnacity could also be visited upon conductors, but never as rudely as upon one who would not fight back. One watershed incident, in 1950, was provoked by the Philharmonic's first performance of Webern's Symphony, Op. 21, music the likes of which the players had never encountered. As was often the case with Mitropoulos, the rehearsals were a magnet for New York's musical intelligentsia, including composers thirsty to encounter (however belatedly) the European vanguard. As Milton Babbitt later recalled, Theodore Cella, the harpist, picked up his part and flung it at Mitropoulos's feet, then bolted offstage. Mitropoulos turned to face the dark auditorium with an expression of bewildered pain. He never again scheduled Webern with the Philharmonic.[28]

Mitropoulos's attitude, expressed on another such occasion, was, "I can afford to forgive." He insisted on treating the players with "obeisance full of love." More than a few members of the Philharmonic loved him in return. To others, a conductor who lived plainly in a nearby hotel of no distinction, bought his own groceries at a Sixth Avenue delicatessen, and held court at a place called Beefburger Hall could not be taken seriously.

Mitropoulos's Philharmonic concerts seemed to many erratic, even unfathomable—not merely for what he programmed, but for how. Juggling musical and box office priorities, he might follow Schoenberg's Violin Concerto with Kodály's *Dances from Galánta*, or Schoenberg's *Pelleas und Melisande* with a dance by Falla. Not atypical was a 1953 concert comprising (in this order) Respighi's orchestration of Bach's C-sharp minor Passacaglia and Fugue, Prokofiev's First Violin Concerto, George Rochberg's *Night Music* (a distinguished premiere), and Beethoven's Fifth Symphony. In Boston, Koussevitzky secured a pact with his adoring audience: they would respect what he chose to conduct. In Philadelphia, Stokowski was aloof and censurious: he disciplined the subscribers. In Minneapolis, Mitropoulos was revered as a superior arbiter of what music mattered, whether or not mere mortals could compass its complexities. In New York, where Mitropoulos gave first performances of core twentieth-century repertoire by Berg, Mahler, Schoenberg, and Shostakovich, his shrinking audience was at sea. Even Mitropoulos's frustrations told. Following a tepidly received rendition of Rachmaninoff's *Symphonic Dances*, Babbitt encountered him backstage in a state of icy rage: "You see?" he exclaimed, "they don't even like *that* shit!" Following a rehearsal of Schoenberg's *Erwartung*, he wrote to Katy Katsoyanis:

> Alone in the midst of so many people, with parts badly written and badly annotated, I came to the point of asking myself, what is the use to struggle when you know that the results can't be of any contribution except to a group of sophisticated people who selfishly come to enjoy my tragic struggle. Believe me, I resent them just as much as those who will not understand anything. The price is too big to pay, and I am wondering sometimes if this kind of distorted and screwy beauty is of any transcendental value. I am wondering sometimes if . . . I am trying to realize the impossible, a pure egotistical occupation which has in itself nothing more than the pleasure of self-destruction.[29]

Weeks later, on December 7, 1952, Mitropoulos suffered a heart attack. He returned to work the following April. He was finished off on April 29, 1956, by Howard Taubman, who had replaced Downes at the *New York Times*. The *Times* that day printed an eight-column article based partly on information fed to Taubman by William Lincer, the Philharmonic's principal violist. Headlined "The Philharmonic—What's Wrong with It and Why," it read in part:

> Because Dimitri Mitropoulos is musical director . . . he bears the heaviest responsibility. He is a serious, dedicated musician, with strong sympathies for the repertory of the late nineteenth century and for certain

areas of twentieth-century music. His flair is for dramatic music, and he can communicate an almost feverish intensity.

Such virtues, applied to classical and early romantic music, become failings, for these works need proportion, delicacy, occasional repose. . . .

Mr. Mitropoulos, moreover, has not established his capacities as an orchestral drillmaster. It may even be asked whether he cares about refinements of execution. It follows that Mr. Mitropoulos may not be the wisest choice for musical director.[30]

The following fall, the Philharmonic announced that Leonard Bernstein would share direction of the orchestra beginning in 1957–58. As of 1958–59, Bernstein was in charge. Mitropoulos suffered a second heart attack in January 1959. Then, on November 2, 1960, an old man at sixty-four, he was felled by a third, massive coronary while rehearsing Mahler's Third Symphony in Milan. His health notwithstanding, he had rapidly achieved new eminence in Germany, Austria, and Italy, with growing ties to La Scala and to the Vienna Philharmonic. If, like Otto Klemperer, he had managed to survive into old age, he might have acquired something like Klemperer's mantle of authority. The different ending of his life story yielded a different fable: not of Job-like perseverance, but of hardships incurred when a religious selflessness is subjected to real-world conditions, even in the realm of art.

■ ■ ■

As musical personalities, Klemperer and Mitropoulos were obviously different, yet shared similarities bearing on their American travails. For both, repertoire was paramount; performance was not an end in itself. In fact, both (if only for a time, in the case of Mitropoulos) were dedicated composers. On the podium, both disdained "technique." "During a concert," Klemperer once explained, "I completely expose myself to the action of the music and do not care about purely technical problems; if one should have to think about the technique of conducting all the time, that would tie down an important part of the concentration"—words Mitropoulos could equally have uttered. Neither cultivated a manicured tonal sheen. Nor was either a manicured personality. At tea with the Philharmonic's lady subscribers, Klemperer would deposit his great bulk on a sofa, then struggle to his feet to address an admirer, perhaps upsetting his cup.[31] He was frequently at a loss for words and his wife was no help. Mitropoulos did not even have a wife: not only was he quietly known to be homosexual; he felt no need for a cosmetic marriage.

In America, especially, Klemperer and Mitropoulos seemed "intellectuals."

The one made his name among the Berlin avant-garde, the other read dog-eared volumes of Mann and Kierkegaard for pleasure. Both projected a beleaguered moral intelligence, scarred by twentieth-century adversities. Though it is tempting to hypothesize what might have happened had Klemperer become music director of the New York Philharmonic or Philadelphia Orchestra, or had Mitropoulos left Minneapolis for Philadelphia or Boston, in fact both were inimical to the United States. Their alien status is clarified once they are aligned with a common object of intense identification and absolute admiration: Gustav Mahler, also a composer, an intellectual, a tea-party risk, a scarred moral scourge. Klemperer's take on Los Angeles audiences—"My task is that of a pioneer. . . . The people are endlessly grateful and ready to love me"—is Mahler in New York revisited. Mahler complained that the New York Philharmonic was "phlegmatic—a typical American orchestra." Klemperer considered the Vienna Philharmonic superior to any American ensemble. Mahler in America was a man without a place; so was Klemperer. Mitropoulos (like Klemperer an American citizen) was—like Mahler, like Klemperer—attracted and repelled by American innocence. "In our country or in Europe, people are suspicious . . . they soil you!" he wrote to Katy Katsoyanis. Again: "Here is why America is better. There is everywhere an encouraging breath—for work, for morality. When they see you as a god, an apostle, a leader, you feel the need to be pure as possible before people who are ready to adore you, to follow you, to respond to you." But in another letter to Katsoyanis, in 1938: "I've explained to you that since I haven't been able, up to now, to relate spiritually with any American being, this means that it will never happen to me. I came to this country at too mature an age, and it is now quite impossible for me to link myself completely with the environment and with the people. Most of all, the absence of romanticism, or warmth, makes me feel far more alone than if I chose to be alone in a warm environment." A week later, disgusted by American isolationism in the face of Hitler: "There's selfishness everywhere; all is well as long as America is not affected. They're intoxicated with *comfort* and nothing else interests them. The ambition of every one of my musicians is to buy a car."[32]

Mahler's understanding of tragedy as endemic to humankind—an understanding that permeates his music even (or especially) when it scales the heights—was Klemperer's understanding and that of Mitropoulos; it underlies the discomfort they experienced in America. Klemperer fled Berlin and the Nazis. For Mitropoulos, Athens seemed (as Vienna seemed to Mahler) corrupt and inbred; even his mother's death in 1941 did not draw him back. A transcendental condition of worldliness and suffering was for Klemperer and Mitropoulos, as for Mahler, a tragic yet indispensable European condition.

They were fatalists at odds with American smiles and "can do" optimism, with the enterprise of perfectability. The technocrats Reiner and Szell, the sensualists Stokowski and Koussevitzky were more compatible with the robust American experience. Toscanini, in his ferocious political mode, remained impervious to the world of existential strife that Mahler, Klemperer, and Mitropoulos endured. Their unknown planet was the more remote from born-and-bred Americans, including the behind-the-scenes operative guiding America's culture of performance: the musical powerbroker Arthur Judson. It was Judson, in the wings, who appraised Klemperer's failings, Judson who supported and influenced the appointment of more malleable conductors: Barbirolli as Toscanini's successor, Eugene Ormandy in place of Stokowski. It was Judson who insisted that Klemperer not program Mahler's Second Symphony in New York, and who took umbrage when he did. When we encounter Judson at length in a later chapter, the full measure of his estrangement from the Mahler world of Klemperer and Mitropoulos will become apparent.

If Judson's influence crippled the fragile Philharmonic and standardized the free-thinking Philadelphia Orchestra, the Boston Symphony, left to its own devices, could not replace Serge Koussevitzky. Charles Munch led wild rides in the French repertoire he cherished, but discipline diminished and the worlds of new music and music education that Koussevitzky had cultivated fell to the side. These conditions set the stage for the ascendance of the orchestras of Chicago and Cleveland—of Reiner and Szell—after 1950.

Elsewhere, there were plenty of seasoned conductors to go around: a musical by-product of World War II. Pierre Monteux, twelve years after his forced departure from the Boston Symphony, returned to the United States in 1936 to become music director of a West Coast orchestra that had fallen on hard times. Monteux more than revived the San Francisco Symphony; sixteen years later he was eager to leave. The United States was not yet a level musical playing field, east to west; Monteux felt far away from the prestigious Northeast, not to mention Europe. Though popular in San Francisco, he would—as one musician complained—arrive "the day before a season started and [depart] the day after it ended. He lived in a hotel or in a hotel/apartment." That San Francisco's hearty remoteness was not unmixed with provincialism was unwittingly confirmed by Monteux's obscure 1954 successor, Enrique Jordá, whom the trustees loyally supported for a decade. It was George Szell who blew the whistle—a famous story. Engaged as a two-week guest in 1962, he left after week one. A local critic, Alfred Frankenstein, wrote to Szell as follows: "We were very much distressed, of course, to learn that you could not conduct here this week, and hope you had a good refreshing rest. . . . There has been a grand crop of rumors all over the country about your withdrawal from the local scene, and this has not been at all good for the San Francisco Symphony. It would, therefore, be a just, proper and pleasant gesture if Mr. Jordá could be invited to serve as guest conductor in Cleveland next season." Szell *publicly* replied:

Dear Mr. Frankenstein:

Up until this moment I have tried to be as polite and discreet as possible about my early departure from San Francisco. Your letter of March 24th, however, contains a tactless provocation which compels me to step out of my reserve.

Since you presume to tell me what would be a "just, proper and pleasant" thing to do, I feel forced to say that your delicate dual position as Music Critic of the Chronicle and Program Annotator for the San Francisco Symphony, which in itself is liable to cast grave doubts upon your objectivity, should have prompted you to exercise particular restraint in this matter. It is entirely out of order for you to suggest my taking a step designed to be interpreted as implicit approval of what I found to be the saddest state of musical affairs I have encountered in any American or European city during the almost fifty years of my active conducting career.

Since you have reopened this question which I thought had closed, and because it is a matter of public interest, I reserve the right to make our correspondence accessible to other persons.[33]

Jordá was hastily replaced by Josef Krips, an important Viennese conductor who had turned up in Buffalo beginning in 1954. His San Francisco tenure lasted from 1963 to 1969.

Ormandy, who reliably maintained the polish of the Philadelphia Orchestra for more than forty seasons, had the longest tenure of any conductor in the United States. The Franco-Russian Vladimir Golschmann raised the St. Louis Symphony from relative obscurity to relative prominence between 1937 and 1956. Golschmann subsequently turned the Denver Symphony into a finer orchestra than what he inherited in 1964. Britain's Eugene Goossens led the Rochester Philharmonic, then in 1931 took over from Fritz Reiner in Cincinnati. Antal Dorati, a Hungarian with extensive experience in Germany and France, in 1945 reorganized the Dallas Symphony by importing most of his musicians.[34] Four years later, he succeeded Mitropoulos in Minneapolis and later served as music director of the Detroit and National Symphonies. William Steinberg was an important conductor in Cologne, Prague, and Frankurt before being restricted to the concerts of the Jewish Culture League. He emigrated to Israel, then to the United States. He was Buffalo's conductor before in 1952 finding a home with the Pittsburgh Symphony, which had lacked a music director since Reiner's departure four years earlier. Though late in life he briefly became conductor of the Boston Symphony, Steinberg led his Pittsburgh orchestra until his health gave out in 1976. Paul Paray, born in Monaco, brought new luster to the Detroit Symphony from 1951 to 1963. Erich Leinsdorf, born in Vienna, briefly (as we have seen) led the Cleveland Orchestra before the arrival of Szell; he later served as music director in Rochester and Boston.

Without exception, these were distinguished and dedicated musicians. But they neither possessed nor aspired to the glamour of Toscanini, Stokowski, or Koussevitzky. They were not gripping perfectionists in the mold of Reiner and Szell. If, in and of themselves, they were mostly found not to offer a complete concert experience, this was a sign of the times. Before the advent of the culture of performance—in the days of Thomas and Seidl, of Higginson's Boston Symphony—new repertoire generated excitement enough. After World War I, new repertoire was found daunting, not enticing (a topic to which we will return). Also, radio and recordings began to replicate the orchestra in the living room: concerts were found inherently less novel, less special (another forthcoming topic). Absent glamorous conductors, absent popular contemporary repertoire, absent the singularity of the concert hall, celebrity soloists increasingly defined the program at hand. Not the resident maestro, but the famous visitor playing the famous concerto was what sold tickets and (however superficially) created a sense of occasion.

Thomas and Seidl, Gericke and Muck had also regularly engaged violinists and pianists, but violinists and pianists did not constitute the main event. Nor were the Big Three reliant on soloists: Koussevitzky was an inept accompanist; the older Toscanini got, the more he bullied his guests; Stokowski's interest in the concerto literature was at best selective (his sumptuous accompaniment for Rachmaninoff in the latter's 1929 recording of his Second Concerto is unsurpassed).

Post-Toscanini, post-Koussevitzky, post-Stokowski, the soloist became the star.

CHAPTER 3

The World's Greatest
Soloists

■

Sergei Rachmaninoff and America ▪ Touring virtuosos ▪ Jascha
Heifetz and Vladimir Horowitz ▪ Artur Schnabel and Rudolf
Serkin ▪ Van Cliburn, Glenn Gould, and the OYAPs

If failed revolutions in German-speaking lands spurred a decisive mid-nineteenth-century exodus of musicians to the New World, the successful Russian Revolution of 1917, its chaotic prelude and aftermath, triggered another dramatic musical migration. The immigrant Germans had been tenacious advocates of communal symphonic and choral undertakings. The arriving Russians were striking individualists: virtuosos.

Crowning this sudden influx was its most complete musician: Sergei Rachmaninoff. A throwback to the nineteenth century, before performance specialists took over, he arrived highly accomplished as a conductor, pianist, and composer. Born in 1873, he had composed prolifically since his teenage years. Political turmoil made him a wanderer. He lived for a time in Dresden and undertook his first American tour in 1909. He left Russia for good in 1917 and eventually settled on Manhattan's Upper West Side.

Though he was offered both the Boston and the Cincinnati Symphony, Rachmaninoff in exile essentially quit conducting (his three recordings conducting the Philadelphia Orchestra in his own music document a latent mastery). His compositional output plummeted. He capitulated to the American hierarchy: performance first. The first solo recital of his career took place in Northampton, Massachusetts, on November 4, 1909. He subsequently transformed himself into a touring solo artist, under contract to RCA Victor. He was still touring when he appeared in Knoxville, Tennessee, sixty-nine years old and ill, in February 1943. He died weeks later at his home in Beverly Hills.

Rachmaninoff's twenty-six-year exile was profound. In the United States and Switzerland, he employed Russian servants and retained Russian customs. His sense of isolation must have been exacerbated by his incurable romanticism; he inhabited a different musical world from his sometime compatriots Stravinsky, Prokofiev, and Shostakovich. Doubtless these were factors in Rachmaninoff's diminished creative output after 1917. (He had already composed three of his concertos, his three sonatas, his three operas, and the bulk of his solo piano music.) And it is notable that subsequent to leaving Russia, he set Russian only once, for the choral Three Russian Songs of 1926. At the same time, there is another, more prosaic explanation for Rachmaninoff's lowered productivity. Once he decided to concentrate on the piano, he had to acquire a repertoire of concertos and recital programs. And he was a perfectionist who practiced and prepared assiduously. If this preempted creative work, his re-creative genius flourished. Liszt and Anton Rubinstein left no recordings. Busoni left only a few. Rachmaninoff left many, and they beggar description.

In his classic study *Schubert's Songs*, Richard Capell writes of Feodor Chaliapin, one of Rachmaninoff's close friends, singing "Ständchen"—outwardly, among the mildest of Schubert Lieder: "How the song revives and flowers in Chaliapin's art! Not to be forgotten is his [rendering] of 'Komm, beglücke mich' ['Come, delight me']—wheedling, anticipative, irresistible."[1] Chopin's evergreen C-sharp minor Waltz, as recorded by Rachmaninoff for RCA in 1927, is an identical act of sorcery. The insinuating inflections, the majestic breadth of texture (Rachmaninoff adds notes in the left hand), the veiled, will-o'-the-wisp velocity of the faster sections create a demonic vignette undreamt of by the composer.

Lamentably, RCA saw fit to record Rachmaninoff in only two of the big solo works in his relatively small recital repertoire: Schumann's *Carnaval* (from 1929) and Chopin's *Funeral March* Sonata (1930). In the Funeral March, he famously rewrites Chopin's dynamics so that the march returns fortissimo, not quietly (as written), after the central Trio. The entire movement is reconceived as an arch. Even more remarkable is a comparable adjustment to movement one. Rachmaninoff fixes on the galloping rhythm of the opening theme (here played with rare clarity and precision). When the galloping theme returns in *sotto voce* left-hand octaves at the beginning of the development section, Rachmaninoff renders them fortissimo: a Cyclopean eruption. Afterward, the theme growls and rumbles, restless and insatiable, in counterpoint with powers more benign. Still later, when Chopin instructs fortissimo, Rachmaninoff is soft; he has relocated the climax. The vicelike grip of this pianist's musical intelligence partners Romanticized freedom and passion. Of a Rachmaninoff performance of another Chopin sonata, the B minor, W. J. Henderson wrote in the *New York Sun* in 1930, "The logic of the thing was impervious; the plan was invulnerable; the proclamation was imperial. There was nothing left for us but to thank our stars that we have lived when Rachmaninoff did and heard him."[2]

Though in gravitating to performance Rachmaninoff gravitated to the American norm, he was not a versatile objectivist after the (ostensible) fashion of a Toscanini, Reiner, or Szell. He specialized in Chopin, Schumann, Liszt, Scriabin—and Rachmaninoff. He hardly played contemporary works other than his own. If his submission to the recital regimen in his later years—the trains and hotels—seems an indignity, he never abandoned composing even when, as in the Third Symphony (1936), he seemingly lost his way. Conventional wisdom notwithstanding, he did not cease to evolve. Such works as the Fourth Piano Concerto (1926, revised 1941) and *Corelli* Variations (1931) abandon his trademark long melodies. The Rhapsody on a Theme of Paganini (1934), a model of compression, relents for a single big tune: the famous eighteenth variation, which Rachmaninoff quipped he wrote "for my manager."

Rachmaninoff was not immune to America and its popular arts. A whiff of Hollywood is discernible in the Third Symphony. The same cannot be said of the *Symphonic Dances* of 1940. This late masterpiece, among the most remarkable symphonic compositions to be conceived on American soil, is a valediction. Summoning his waning creative energies, Rachmaninoff fashioned a musical testament whose keynote is metaphysical intensity. The three movements originally bore titles: "Midday," "Twilight," and "Midnight." These are stations of life. The finale ends in a blaze of glory, effacing strains of *Dies irae*; near the close, the composer inscribes "Alliluya." But the work's most poignant moment comes in the first-movement coda, which pacifies the "vengeance" motto of an earlier metaphysical exercise: the confessional First Symphony, a youthful effusion Rachmaninoff discarded following its disastrous 1897 premiere. This private allusion—the First Symphony was unknown in 1940; only posthumously has it been deservedly revived—is a closing of the circle, the completion of an unlikely creative odyssey, courageously aloof from contemporary fashion and taste, begun in prerevolutionary Russia and ending, Russian still, in southern California.

Stravinsky called Rachmaninoff a "six-foot scowl." His severe crewcut and gimlet eyes disclosed little else. Of Rachmaninoff the man, Alexander and Katherine Swann, who knew him well in his years of exile, reminisced in 1944: "In spite of a deeply affectionate family, in spite of his great success all over the world, and the devotion of his audiences, Rachmaninoff lived shut within himself, alone in spirit, and everlastingly homesick for Russia. The Russian spirit and habits were all-powerful in him." The Swanns also reported they "practically never saw him annoyed, displeased, fussing, or excited."[3] His personal poise was awesome and implacable.

■ ■ ■

Franz Liszt is considered the progenitor of the solo piano recital. He famously said of an 1839 Milan concert without assisting artists, "*Le concert c'est moi.*" He might equally have said, "*L'orchestre c'est moi.*" Three years before, in a joint program, Berlioz conducted the March to the Scaffold from his *Symphonie fantastique*, after which Liszt gave his keyboard transcription of the same music. According to Sir Charles Hallé, an important conductor and pianist of the day, Liszt's playing registered "with an effect even surpassing that of the full orchestra, creating an indescribable furore. The feat had been duly announced in the programme beforehand, a proof of his indomitable courage."[4] Both as pianist and composer, Liszt ingeniously expanded the outer limits of the piano and its player. By contemporary standards, his repertoire also included an unusual amount of music by composers other than himself, notably Beethoven, Chopin, and Schumann.

The most idolized pianist after Liszt was Russia's Anton Rubinstein. No less than Liszt's, his larger-than-life presence—physical and musical—filled great spaces without the benefit of an orchestra or assisting artists. His leonine countenance and disheveled hair evoked Beethoven (Liszt dubbed him "Van II"). Like Liszt, again, he was a significant composer. Unlike Liszt's, his music has faded with time. More than Liszt's, his repertoire featured the masterworks of dead masters. Rubinstein founded the St. Petersburg Conservatory in 1862 and is considered the father of the "Russian school" of pianism—a breed volcanic in sonority and temperament, heroically subjective in style. Meanwhile, the Liszt of the violin was Niccolò Paganini (whom Liszt first heard in 1832, and of whom he wrote, "What sufferings, what misery, what tortures in those four strings!").[5] Paganini played concertos and caprices of his own devising. Post-Paganini, such violinists as Sarasate and Wieniawski were—like Rubinstein on the piano—known equally as practitioners of their own and of others' music.

More than half a century before Rachmaninoff's arrival, the United States notably welcomed eminent foreign virtuosos. Pertinent is Lewis Mumford's formulation that "pioneering may in part be described as the Romantic movement in action." The American psyche adored heroic individualism. Democratized American audiences loved to be amazed by feats of precision, power, and acrobatic display. American fees topped any to be accumulated on tour in Europe. Transatlantic steamships, beginning in the 1840s, and the growing network of railroad lines penetrating the American heartland boosted the frequency and range of mid-nineteenth-century touring artists. Casting an eye on the New World's eager, impressionable listeners, Robert Schumann wrote, "The [European] public has lately begun to weary of virtuosos, and . . . we have too. The virtuosos themselves seem to feel this, if we may judge from a recently awakened fancy among them for emigrating to America; and many of their enemies secretly hope they will remain over there." To which Eduard Hanslick, dean of Vienna's music critics, added, "America was truly the promised land, if not of music, at least of the musician."[6]

Though the United States heard neither Paganini nor Liszt, it did not lack impressive visiting virtuosos. These included the Norwegian violinist Ole Bull, who could bow all four strings at once; Leopold de Meyer, dubbed the "lion pianist" for his mane and the "Lyin' Pianist" for his machinations against certain rivals;[7] Henri Herz, whose piano recitals were prodigiously promoted for sharing the stage with "A Thousand Candles"; and Sigismond Thalberg, whose "matinee musicales" were aimed at "ladies belonging to the first families of the city."[8]

Meanwhile, America produced its own Louis Moreau Gottschalk. But (as we have seen) certain Americans clamored for more than Gottschalk's *Bamboula* or Herz's Thousand Candles; they craved a great pianist playing great music. The way was paved by such estimable artists as Richard Hoffman and William Mason in New York, Otto Dresel and Ernst Perabo in Boston, and Carl Wolfsohn in Philadelphia. Then, in 1872, Anton Rubinstein arrived for a two-hundred-plus concert tour fortified with mighty doses of Bach, Beethoven, Chopin, and Schumann—as well as music by the pianist himself.★ He also appeared frequently with Theodore Thomas's orchestra, which he considered peerless in Europe save for François Habeneck's orchestra in Paris. Rubinstein's repertoire and artistry gravely delighted Thomas and other sacralizing types. Types more populist were cheerfully galvanized by his

---

★ For his farewell recital, Rubinstein composed a set of variations on "Yankee Doodle" about which a New York critic quipped that it was "prepared in accordance with all the canons of art and . . . in opposition to all the canons of taste." See R. Allen Lott, *From Paris to Peoria: How European Piano Virtuosos Brought Classical Music to the American Heartland* (New York, Oxford University Press, 2003), p. 228.

animal magnetism. In Boston(!), women rushed the stage to embrace him, and his clothes were rent by admirers in search of souvenirs. George W. Bagby's "Jud Brownin Hears Ruby Play," a favorite recitation for thirty years, narrated: "By jinks, it was a mixtery! He fetched up his right wing, he fetched up his left wing, he fetched up his center, he fetched up his reserves. . . . The house trembled, the lights danced, the walls shuck, the sky split, the ground rocked. . . . I knowed no more that evening." In 1919, a quarter century after Rubinstein's death, James Gibbon Huneker would write, "No artist of his emotional caliber has appeared on the scene, nor is there likely to be one. . . . The plangency of his tone, fingers of velvet, fingers of bronze, the sweep, audacity and tenderness of his many styles—ah! There was but one Anton Rubinstein."[9]

But there was Hans von Bülow, who gave 140 American concerts, up to six a week, in 1875–76 (we have encountered him in Boston, where he premiered Tchaikovsky's B-flat minor Concerto), and who even more than Rubinstein championed not the living but the dead (his own compositions being a negligible accomplishment). Compared to Rubinstein, Bülow was a more literal, more accurate, less flamboyant player—more "Germanic." And his programs were even more demanding. Of Beethoven, he offered no fewer than twelve sonatas, plus the Fourth and Fifth Concertos; of Chopin, the B minor Sonata and many shorter works; of Schumann, the *Kreisleriana, Faschingsschwank aus Wien*, and Third Sonata. Unlike Rubinstein, whose tastes were conservative, Bülow also specialized in Liszt. His twenty solo recitals—dispensing with the usual assisting violinist or soprano—included one in New York comprising Beethoven's Sonatas Op. 31, No. 3, Op. 101, Op. 106 (*Hammerklavier*), and the *Diabelli* Variations—a program of nearly indigestible bulk.[10]

Both Rubinstein and Bülow found American audiences in many cities in the diaper stage; both were impressed by the eagerness to grow and learn. Bülow in particular—the first eminent pianist to tour the United States exclusively playing the music of others—was a sacralizing influence to set beside Thomas. In fact, the progression from de Meyer to Herz to Thalberg to Rubinstein to Bülow, logging nearly a thousand American concerts between 1845 and 1876, encapsulates the progression from entertainer to "interpreter," itself a gauge to rapidly ripening audience taste and capacity. De Meyer's repertoire of character pieces, fantasias on "airs" from well-known operas, and renderings of "Hail Columbia" and "Yankee Doodle"—all self-composed—admitted no firm distinction between popular and art music. Herz ventured into Beethoven, but only as a chamber musician partnered by violin and cello. Thalberg played movements from Beethoven concertos. Rubinstein played mainly other people's music. Bülow did so exclusively.★[11] In their wake came Leopold Godowski (1884), Moriz Rosenthal (1888),[†] Eugen d'Albert (1889), Vladimir de Pachman (1890), and Ferruccio Busoni (1891), all famous virtuosos solidifying the keyboard canon Rubinstein and Bülow had instilled. A singular phenomenon, in 1887, was the eleven-year-old Polish prodigy Josef Hofmann, of whose American debut Henderson wrote, "The customary standards of criticisms are abolished by this youthful prodigy. . . . Josef Hofmann played, not only like an artist, but like a master."[12] Finally, in 1891, there was Ignacy Jan Paderewski, whose pre–World War I celebrity paralleled the Caruso cult and the Gerryflappers. His chrysanthemum of pale red hair, dreamy countenance, and lordly bearing transfixed female admirers whose "zealous devotion" was likened by the *New York Times* to that of "fanatics [who] listen to a sermon of a prophet of a new religion."[13] He inspired Paderewski candy, soap, toys, and—inevitably—shampoo. His private railroad car seemingly visited every town with a piano, to be greeted by brass bands

★ In Europe, the canonizing pianists included such earlier artists as Carl Czerny, Ignaz Moscheles, and Franz Liszt, all of whom were influentially playing Bach and Beethoven before 1850. As in other realms of classical music, including the parallel canonization of symphonic repertoire, the United States started late and caught up fast.

† Rosenthal's New York debut was so remarkable I cannot resist quoting Henry Krehbiel's *Tribune* review at length:

> In Liszt's fantasia on themes from "Don Giovanni" Herr Rosenthal fairly intoxicated his listeners and carried their judgment and even their decorum captive by a most astounding display of technical skill. As he approached the climax of his technical feat a murmur of delighted surprise went through the hall; in another moment scores of people began swaying from side to side; old concert-goers, who probably never thought that they could be so worked upon, nudged their neighbors and testified their astonishment in audible tones; some of the musicians in the back rows of the orchestra rose to their feet to catch sight of the player; and thus the enthusiasm grew until it broke down all barriers, and more than a score of measures before the conclusion of the music was reached the applause burst forth and overwhelmed the tones of the pianoforte. Herr Rosenthal's American reputation was made.

Though some writers, notably Lawrence Levine in *Highbrow/Lowbrow: The Emergence of Cultural Hierarchy in America* (Cambridge, Mass., Harvard University Press, 1988), have unfavorably contrasted late-nineteenth-century audiences, conditioned by new high-culture canons, with more demonstrative midcentury audiences, such newspaper accounts as Krehbiel's document an admirable balance between discernment, decorum, and spontaneous display of feeling. Later the same season, the New York piano connoisseurs who interrupted the Liszt Fantasy (a Mozart paraphrase of genius, transcending the self-composed operatic paraphrases earlier performed by de Meyer, Herz, and Thalberg) savored Bülow's performance of Beethoven's last and most rarified piano sonata. Krehbiel approvingly reported, as a measure of the "depth and sincerity of the musical culture of the New York public," that the "most spontaneous outburst" of approbation during the pianist's Beethoven recital series came "on April 4th, after the Sonata, op. 111." See Krehbiel, *Review of the New York Musical Season 1888–1889* (New York, Novello, Ewer, and Co., 1889), pp. 10, 181—182.

and mayoral orations. His Barnum, Hugo Gorlitz, would distribute free tickets to students who pledged to stampede "as though overcome with a mad desire." His American earnings were estimated to exceed one thousand dollars per selection, including encores. Paderewski the pianist, in Henderson's opinion, achieved "a perfect preservation of the vocal illusion," a demonstration of "singing tone and perfect control of every variety of tone color."[14] His own Minuet in G and A minor Concerto were among his favored vehicles.

All this forms the backdrop to Rachmaninoff and other Russian refugees. They were beneficiaries of Russian schooling and tradition, of a fabled Romantic lineage traceable via Rubinstein to Liszt. They were vituosos to the manner born, products of a musical culture less susceptible to ensemble expression—to Germanic symphonic and chamber music—than to individualized feeling, a culture in which personalized re-creative flair linked to the creative act: in which performers were composers. Over time, however, performance took over: Rubinstein was a lesser composer than Liszt, Paderewski a lesser composer than Rubinstein, Hofmann a lesser composer than Paderewski. Also, Liszt and Rubinstein were widely esteemed exponents of older, less showy music: of Beethoven. Paderewski and Hofmann were not.

Rachmaninoff, who called Rubinstein "the unequalled pianist of the world" not so much "for his magnificent technique" as for his "profound, spiritually refined musicianship," was therefore a throwback. Changing fashion, which discarded the composers Rubinstein and Paderewski, was powerless to discard Rachmaninoff's more potent yet equally old-fashioned compositions; he was the most important pianist/composer after Liszt. Again unlike Paderewski or Hofmann, he was a Romantic for whom intellect remained paramount, one whose brain was never sidetracked by his own seductive sounds and dazzling fingers. He frequently performed late Beethoven—the Op. III Piano Sonata. (His recordings, alas, include a single, abridged solo Beethoven performance: of the C minor Variations, an interpretation improbably uniting virtuosity, expressive variety, and—a Rachmaninoff signature— sovereign structural design.)[15]

Younger Russians to come—the generation born around 1900—were by comparison performance specialists who at best barely composed. Koussevitzky,* of Rachmaninoff's generation, already fits this generalization. So do

---

* Two earlier Russian conductors deserve a footnote. Vassily Safonov (1852–1918), a sensational Tchaikovsky interpreter, was conductor of the New York Philharmonic and director of Jeannette Thurber's National Conservatory from 1906 to 1909. Modest Altschuler (1873–1963), a pupil of Safonov at the Moscow Conservatory, in 1903 organized a Russian Symphony Society in New

the violinists Mischa Elman and Nathan Milstein—the first a master of sensuous tone and spontaneous feeling, the second a Romantic of exquisite refinement; Elman anchored his career in the United States after 1911 and Milstein after 1929. A fourth Russian émigré, Gregor Piatigorsky, was the most celebrated cellist in the United States during the interwar decades. But by far the two most acclaimed American-based performance specialists after Rachmaninoff were Jascha Heifetz and Vladimir Horowitz—"the world's greatest violinist" and "world's greatest pianist," respectively.

■ ■ ■

When Jeannette Thurber assembled Dvořák, Seidl, Joseffy, and others for her National Conservatory, one object was to bind a city's leading musical personalities to one another and to a central pedagogical mission. Fundamental to her plan—a goal she pursued tenaciously but unsuccessfully—was state support. When her husband's fortune dwindled, so did the National Conservatory.

In Russia, however, two national conservatories flourished. The one in St. Petersburg, as we have seen, was created by Anton Rubinstein in 1862. It was an outgrowth of the Russian Musical Society, whose Moscow branch, begun by Anton's brother Nicholas in 1866, was the Moscow Conservatory. These were not self-supporting music schools in the American fashion, to the side of the major institutions of culture. They *were* major institutions of culture and employed as teachers Rimsky-Korsakov, Tchaikovsky, and other major composers and performers, some of whom (as in America) were eminent foreigners. One such, Leopold Auer, taught violin at the St. Petersburg Conservatory from 1868, when Anton Rubinstein discovered him in London, until 1917, when he quit Russia for the United States. Auer's predecessor in Moscow was Henri Wieniawski. Wieniawski was the more famous violinist, but Auer was the master pedagogue, progenitor of a "Russian school" that would sweep the West. It was he who in Moscow taught Elman and Milstein, and also Efrem Zimbalist, Toscha Seidel, Michel Piastro, and Richard Burgin—all names to reckon with. Finally, it was Auer who disclosed to the world the prodigy Jascha Heifetz.

Born in Vilna in 1901, Heifetz played the Mendelssohn concerto at the age of six and began studies with Auer three or four years later. He performed the Tchaikovsky concerto with Nikisch in Berlin in 1912. Fleeing war and revo-

York, with which he gave the world premiere of Scriabin's *Poem of Ecstasy* (1908) and the American premiere of the same composer's *Prometheus* (1915).

lution, he made his American debut at Carnegie Hall on October 27, 1917, the occasion for the most famous of Heifetz stories: that Elman, in a box, remarked to the pianist Leopold Godowski, "Isn't it hot in here?," and that Godowski replied, "Only for violinists." Heifetz was perceived to have elevated the art of the violin to new and undreamt-of heights. In fact, no vocalist, conductor, or pianist has ever crafted or sustained such preternatural perfection of technique. The Heifetz mechanism seemed both infallible and limitless. Meticulously, scrupulously, he weighed every deft turn of phrase. He could swell his sound to a razored opulence, or trim it to a finespun, flawless thread. His impassive countenance—bow flying, fingers racing—conveyed poise complete and unfathomable.

Superhuman, too, was Heifetz's consistency. Decade after passing decade, he would tour the United States—his career was at all times American-based—with a standardized program of appetizers, entrees, and desserts. At Carnegie Hall, he might give as many as five recitals in a single season. Invariably, he would play to packed and expectant houses. As surely as Toscanini, he was the "world's greatest." No less than Toscanini, he delivered the notes with such speed and precision that (however inadvertently) the ear was drawn to the performer's art, not the composer's. His sister Pauline married Samuel Chotzinoff—once Heifetz's accompanist, later factotum to Toscanini and artistic administrator of the NBC Symphony. Like Toscanini, Heifetz was an RCA recording artist, hyperbolized by Sarnoff's publicists. RCA engineered a single Heifetz/Toscanini collaboration: the Beethoven concerto, in 1940. For the producer Charles O'Connell, in the control booth, "It was rather entertaining to observe these two men, so alike in some ways, yet so disparate in age, disposition, and musical outlook, working together during the recording. Outwardly they observed the most rigid punctilio; actually, they were as wary as two strange cats, each determined to give the other no opening for criticism, each fiercely resolved upon perfection in every mood and tempo." The *Victor Record Review* crowed, "Rarely has it happened in the history of recorded performances that two such artists as Jascha Heifetz and Arturo Toscanini have combined their respective talents (each pre-eminent in his own field) in the interpretation of such a prodigious masterpiece as Beethoven's Concerto in D major for Violin and Orchestra, Opus 61."[16]

Toscanini was the world's most expensive conductor, paid $3,334 (after taxes) per concert by the New York Philharmonic in 1931–32, $40,000 for ten weeks by NBC in 1937–38. Heifetz commanded the highest fees of any soloist. In 1919–20, the New York Philharmonic paid him $2,250, versus $2,000 for Kreisler and $1,500 for Rachmaninoff. In 1949–50, his Philharmonic fee was $9,500, versus $8,000 for Artur Rubinstein and $3,800 for

Milstein. His 1953 RCA contract guaranteed him $495,000 over ten years, at a time when cars could be bought for $2,000. When he joined forces with Rubinstein and Gregor Piatigorsky, the result was known as the "million dollar trio"; it reportedly collapsed when Heifetz sparred with Rubinstein over who would get top billing (Heifetz won). Only Heifetz could have successfully insisted that his concerto come last on every symphonic program in which he was featured. In a formal interview, asked about how he memorized music, only he could have replied, "I'd rather not answer that. That is my trade secret." His Park Avenue home had a concealed bar with a cash register. His privacy, his earning power, his luxurious lifestyle all fed the Heifetz mystique. As with Toscanini, even his foibles fed his image. "HEIFETZ FORGETS" was the front-page news when, in Dallas, the Sibelius concerto temporarily came to a stop.[17]

The most frequent observation about Heifetz the musician, at all times, has been that his playing, appearances notwithstanding, is "not cold." These protests are of course significant. Heifetz was not remotely a bland violinist. But Kreisler, whom Heifetz displaced, projected more tenderness and warmth, Milstein a worldlier elegance. The Heifetz antipode was Joseph Szigeti, whose range of repertoire and expression was unrivaled. Though Szigeti had studied with Jenő Hubay—Budapest's Leopold Auer—he remembered Hubay's class for its atmosphere of "puerile rivalry," for the concentration on "externals," for the absence of chamber music.[18] He went his own way. Next to colleagues of comparable eminence, he lacked technical ease and disdained sweetness of tone. But juxtaposed with the lyric probes of Szigeti's 1943 recording with Bruno Walter, the Heifetz/Toscanini Beethoven concerto is no deeper than its glistening mirrored surface.

That Heifetz seemed a commercial property was not just a function of his high fees and occasional Hollywood film appearances. In every sense precious, his was a jeweler's art, lonely and impeccable. He played Prokofiev and Sibelius,★ and commissioned concertos from Mario Castelnuovo-Tedesco, Louis Gruenberg, Erich Korngold, Miklós Rózsa, and William Walton. But the major twentieth-century composers and concertos were, for the most part, not for him. Szigeti anchored his art in the present. His intimate relationship with his countryman Béla Bartók was formative. From Bartók—his field recordings of peasant song—he acquired a roots-in-the-soil sensibility, and—

★ Heifetz did not authorize for release his most electrifying concerto recording—of the Sibelius, made in 1934 with Leopold Stokowski. Stokowski and the Philadelphia Orchestra challenge him at every turn. Heifetz ordered Victor to destroy the metal masters but retained his own shellac pressings. Using these, the Philadelphia Orchestra issued the recording on CD in 1999.

in his playing—an earthy directness, wedding naked feeling with naked tone. He rendered the Hungarian and Slavonic Dances of Brahms and Dvořák without a trace of irony or a grain of sugar. He memorably partnered the composer in Stravinsky's important Duo Concertante, premiered Bloch's Violin Concerto, and championed Berg, Honegger, Martin, Milhaud, Ravel, Roussel. His Bach made the Russians sound eviscerated. His performances and recordings of the sonatas of Beethoven and Brahms—as bona fide duos, with such pianists as Bartók, Artur Schnabel, and Egon Petri—made ever more pervasive "violinistic" renderings seem sleek and featureless.

The example of Szigeti, whose American debut took place in 1925, and who settled in California during the Second World War, proved that a major American solo career could coexist with important contemporary music; it illustrated how close identification with leading creators could refresh and enrich the performer's art. Heifetz, though unique, spawned legions of would-be Heifetzes, moths to the flame. In this respect, Szigeti was the more singular phenomenon.

■ ■ ■

The culture of performance was powered by a newly democratized audience—the topic of a forthcoming chapter. The new audience worshipped but did not notably change Toscanini or Heifetz. But the world's greatest pianist was more vulnerable.

Vladimir Horowitz studied in his native Kiev with Felix Blumenfeld, a distinguished pianist and composer whose teachers in St. Petersburg had included Anton Rubinstein and Rimsky-Korsakov. He left Russia with Milstein in 1924 with a special passport as a "child of the Soviet Revolution" in pursuit of "artistic refinement and cultural propaganda." Neither returned. He made his American debut in 1928, playing Tchaikovsky with the New York Philharmonic, and settled in the United States in 1939 at the age of thirty-six. With Toscanini and Heifetz, he crowned the RCA pantheon.[19]

Horowitz was from the start a merchandiser's dream. Even his notorious unreliability was turned to his advantage. No film star played such tantalizing games of hide-and-seek. He retired at least three times: 1936–38, 1953–65, and 1969–74. Had these withdrawals seemed ploys, they would have irritated. Rather, they seemed necessities. Horowitz exerted the fascination of a psychological and physical mechanism strung so taut that it had to implode and yet did not—usually. No wonder his disappearances bred rumors of shock therapy and institutionalization. Then, each time he remastered his will to perform, curiosity ran riot. Were the legendary fingers still as accurate and fast? Could the legendary sonorities still shake the stage? And also, more revealingly, had Horowitz the musician ripened with age? Could he silence nagging doubts that he was not a great artist? By way of reassurance, his advocates periodically proclaimed a "new Horowitz."

Was Horowitz a great artist? At first American critics answered "no." "Too uncomfortably brilliant," reported William Spier in *Musical America*. "His fingers allow him no repose. They are still in the puppy stage." In the opinion of the *Nation*, Horowitz reduced "every emotion to black and white, and every intention to technique." There was no question of the breathtaking elan, intensity, and virtuosity of Horowitz the instrumentalist—of his "magnificent muscularity," "heaven-storming octaves," "phenomenal strength and speed." To most New York critics, the twenty-five-year-old Russian expatriate seemed a pianist of fabulous promise. For the New York public, he was already fabulous.

But the critics soon caught up; like Toscanini in America, Horowitz achieved popular acclaim first, consolidated critical acclaim second. Like Heifetz's, his celebrity was fortified by a Toscanini connection: in 1933, Horowitz married Toscanini's younger daughter, Wanda. He placed his father-in-law's photograph on his piano. He began to acquire something like Toscanini's aura of integrity. Then came his first retirement in 1936. According to 1939 press releases heralding his return to the American stage, Horowitz had vastly matured. He collected fine art and read fine books. His collaborations with Toscanini, in concertos by Brahms and Tchaikovsky, were said to measure commensurate artistic gains. "Nothing Mr. Horowitz had done here has indicated more impressively his growth as interpreter as well as virtuoso of his instrument," wrote Olin Downes of a Horowitz/Toscanini Brahms Second Concerto in 1940. When, eight years later, Horowitz and Toscanini played the Brahms B-flat again, *Time* discerned "new maturity and depth." But it was Howard Taubman, in the *Times*, who played the Horowitz-equals-Toscanini equation to the hilt. "The wild, volatile virtuoso of two years ago has become one of the most mature, responsible musicians," he wrote in 1948. Five years later, Taubman proclaimed "The Transformation of Vladimir Horowitz." Away from the piano and the concert hall he seems to have arrived at a great inner relaxation." And there were further Toscanini analogies: like his father-in-law, whom he resembled "in many ways," Horowitz had turned down huge fees for "unworthy" projects; like his father-in-law, he aimed "to make every phrase sing."

In fact, Horowitz and Toscanini were remarkably unlike one another, as musicians and men, and neither was as regular a guy as Americans made him out to be. Two months following his announced "transformation," Horowitz quit the stage, a victim of nervous collapse. And yet, incredibly, the New Horowitz endured. Samuel Chotzinoff wrote in 1964, "Horowitz has, through study and contemplation, come to believe in the absolute supremacy of the composer, the same belief that is the foundation of the art of his great father-in-law." Reviewing Horowitz's 1965 comeback, Harold Schonberg in the *Times* heard "a grander, more spacious line," and interpretations "emotionally more poised, more of a piece, less driven and nervous."

Horowitz's recordings shed perspective on his singular career. He first recorded his trademark concerto, the Rachmaninoff Third, in London in 1930. He made a second recording for RCA in 1951. With its surprise dynamics and convulsive intensity, this reading is tremendous in its way, but reveals a new *coup de théâtre* mentality alien to the composer. A third Horowitz recording of the same concerto, in 1978, is a brutal and labored affair. Meanwhile, it was the young Van Cliburn, in 1958, who most made this music—the concerto itself—sound memorably beautiful.

In fact, Horowitz typically excelled in lesser music: brains-in-the-fingers cameos by minor Romantics. At his famous 1965 comeback recital at Carnegie Hall, the crowd saved its loudest roar for a ninety-second encore. Horowitz's performance of Moszkowski's Etude in A-flat major, Op. 72, No. 11 (preserved on the in-concert recording) is not just an astounding lesson in high-speed articulation; it is equally a lesson in interpretation. The lightning swells and diminuendos, the sudden dabs of color, the vanishing-act coda, whose four floating chords ascend into silence—these and other sleights of hand prove magically self-sufficient. Horowitz sounds happiest, most completely himself, in this type of music. Employing his clairvoyant aural imagination, his prankster's sense of fun, he empties his full bag of tricks. Depth, decorum, fidelity are unnecessary, even out of place; a superior sort of pandering is the very *raison d'être*.

Could the Horowitz career have evolved differently? A 1934 version of the finale of Tchaikovsky's First Concerto, the earliest available recording of Horowitz in concert, is elegant—as deft, as lyrically aromatic and airy as his 1943 performance with Toscanini, also recorded in concert, is brutal and blunt. Boris Asafyev, the preeminent Soviet musicologist of his time, once praised a 1923 Horowitz recital for (among other virtues) its "clarity and simplicity of purpose in combination with refined elegance and grace." One can understand why political turmoil impelled Horowitz to leave Russia; at the same time, his musician's role was healthier there: the child of a cultivated family, connected to the musical elite, he composed, he played chamber music and partnered singers (he once accompanied Schubert's *Winterreise* from memory), his solo repertoire was huge and not unadventurous. It speaks volumes that his 1920s sonata partner was Nathan Milstein.

But Horowitz's move to the United States doomed him to a career of maximum fame, fortune, and virtuosic display. The populist fervor of his American following, intensified by wartime, excited a possessive adulation. RCA's relentless hype, the aggressive salesmanship of Arthur Judson (who at one time had Horowitz playing an average of one concert every two days), the harsh scrutiny of Toscanini—it would have taken a saint to resist these influences. Horowitz was no saint. His playing turned nervous, neurotically intense. According to his pupil Byron Janis, Horowitz advised him to "do things simply for the sake of arresting the audience's attention—a sudden pianissimo, an unexpected accent . . . you must exaggerate." On another occasion, Horowitz was quoted confessing, "If you play Classic music in correct style on a big piano and in a big hall, it will bore most of the audience."

Horowitz's fellow pianists were seduced by his miraculous sound. And they followed his brave lead when he explored Scriabin, or Scarlatti and Clementi, or the lesser-known Chopin and Schumann. To the musical public at large, however, Horowitz did not—could not—exist apart from his hyperbolic reputation. In the final and most legendary phase of his career, as documented by *Time* in a 1986 cover story, he would only perform Sunday afternoons at four o'clock, having dined on Dover or gray sole flown in fresh that day. He traveled with an entourage including his wife, his housekeeper, his manager, his piano technician, and his $40,000 concert grand, which had to be removed by crane from the living room of his fourteen-room Manhattan townhouse. His normal nightly regimen included "watching a triple feature of adventure and horror movies on his videocassette recorder." He commanded "a fee of as much as half a million dollars for a single concert and never less than $100,000."

This cartoon, to which Horowitz had to live up (or down), was one cost of playing the celebrity game. His artistic fate is illuminated by a 1987 film documenting Horowitz recording Mozart's A major Piano Concerto, K. 488, with Carlo Maria Guilini and the La Scala Orchestra. He is mainly attuned to people: players, listeners, technicians, music businessmen. His what-do-you-think-of-me expression is answered with bravos and applause. During a break, he wants to know if certain critics who are present find his playing "too free." His very face, unhappy in repose, craves a response.

The film *Horowitz Plays Mozart* makes visible what the ears detect: Horowitz was less immersed in music than he was aware of himself in relation to his necessary audience. This strange dislocation haunted his strange career. Once he left Russia, his repertoire shrank. Disoriented, he lost touch with new music, with the very world of culture. Obsessed with what others saw, heard, and thought, he canceled concerts, took sabbaticals, spent countless months—more than anyone else would get—worrying over the editing, advertising, and promotion of his infrequent recordings. For three decades, from 1951 to 1982, he did not perform in Europe. His fears, his abilities, his eagerness to please impelled a complex mating ritual—Horowitz eyeing and ignoring, stroking and rebuffing his public—bypassing music.

In America, Horowitz became known as an exemplary descendant of Anton Rubinstein, a final link in a chain of Romantic heroes also including his hero Rachmaninoff. More accurately, Horowitz was an inspired aberration, an intriguingly disfigured transplant. If he serves as a model, it is of the performer circumscribed and overshadowed by his own celebrity.

■ ■ ■

We have seen how waves of German immigrants inculcated German music in the United States; how the orchestras of New York, Chicago, and Philadelphia were founded or first led by Germans; how the Germanophile Henry Higginson set the early course of the Boston Symphony; how before World War I German training directly or indirectly shaped nearly every important American composer. As the 1848 revolutions were a watershed, sending west the Germania Orchestra and such individual musicians as Carl Zerrahn and Carl Bergmann, the Third Reich expelled, willfully or not, countless important conductors, composers, and instrumentalists. But the Great War had poisoned the German well, and the new immigrants did not flourish in the New World as the old ones had.

Of the eminent conductors to arrive from Germany in the 1930s, Otto Klemperer failed to secure a major East Coast podium and Erich Kleiber wound up in Havana and Buenos Aires. Fritz Busch also became a regular at Buenos Aires's Teatro Colon, then after the war returned to Europe to pursue at England's Glyndebourne Festival the kind of ensemble opera he had once practiced in Dresden. Only Bruno Walter, an American resident from 1939, established an enduring presence with the New York Philharmonic and the Metropolitan Opera, but as a pastured *eminence gris*; he never enjoyed the authority of a Toscanini, Stokowski, or Koussevitzky.★

★ Gunther Schuller, who played under Bruno Walter in New York, remembers him as the most patronizing of all the immigrant conductors. "He would *explain* to us that Mozart was a really great composer" (interview with the author).

As non-Germans dominated American podiums, Russians dominated among solo artists. Of the Austro-German pianists and violinists who fled Hitler for the United States, the biggest name belonged to Artur Schnabel. In the tradition of Clara Schumann and Hans von Bülow, he propagated the Germanic master composers. An antivirtuoso, he projected an electrifying or sublime probity. His concerts were passionate rites of homage. His teacher in Vienna, the great Leschetizky, famously said of him, "You will never be a pianist; you are a musician"; he was exempted from the Liszt Hungarian Rhapsodies and directed toward Schubert. He settled in Berlin in 1900. The Schubert piano sonatas and Mozart piano concertos Schnabel there championed were novelties; more than any other artist, he added these works to the standard repertoire. He was also the first to record all thirty-two Beethoven piano sonatas. In Berlin Schnabel was a dominant force: he took part in an important early performance of Schoenberg's atonal *Pierrot Lunaire*; he composed atonal music of his own; he was a leading pedagogue at the State Academy.

In the United States, to which he emigrated in 1939, Schnabel doggedly pursued his Berlin course. For most American audiences, schooled in Heifetz and Horowitz, his repertoire seemed impossibly serious. His erratic technique—his wrong notes and muddy passagework—was bothersome. His compositions were anathema; Mitropoulos gave Schnabel's First Symphony in Minneapolis in 1946: a fiasco. Schnabel gained a cult following in New York via the New Friends of Music, a chamber music organization founded in 1936 by one of his pupils. He played concertos with Mitropoulos, Klemperer, and Stock, sonatas with Szigeti. He was (he said) "intoxicated by the sonorities of the Philadelphia and Boston Symphony Orchestras and their perfection of execution such as I had never heard before—which does not mean that I had not heard interpretations equal to theirs, or even surpassing them, because perfection of execution and interpretation are, it is hardly necessary to say, not identical." He missed Klemperer's Kroll and the other opera houses of Berlin, with their range of new works by Berg, Hindemith, Korngold, Krenek, Pfitzner, Rathaus, Schoenberg, Schreker, Strauss, and Stravinsky. A radio commercial extolling soap left him reflecting, "It is depressing to see how these splendid American people are maltreated and exploited, and how they are deliberately isolated from many of the noble things of which they are capable." As the war dragged on, Schnabel felt "marooned" in the United States. In 1943, he abandoned professional management: "These men had little interest in music, not much of a feeling for it, and no respect for quality. At least, that is what I think. They seemed rather to be salesmen of this kind of merchandise; and apparently their desire was, along the line of least resistance, to sell as much as possible, as quickly as possible, to as many customers as possible." He taught privately and composed. He died in 1951.[20]

The leading violinist in Schnabel's Berlin was Adolf Busch. Busch moved to Switzerland in 1926. After 1933, Hitler, who cared about music, tried to lure him back. Though (unlike Schnabel) Busch was not Jewish, he wanted no part of the Third Reich. Replying to a letter from a German publisher signed "Heil Hitler!" he wrote, "We live in Switzerland, which means that we consider your greeting an insult." He resettled in the United States in 1940. As a violinist, he exemplified the "German school." His performances were fiercely pure, denuded of superfluous detail. Like Schnabel, he was in every sense not a virtuoso. Like Schnabel, he acquired a modest American following of connoisseurs, including many German-Americans, as did his duo partner and son-in-law, the pianist Rudolf Serkin. After Busch died in 1952, Serkin established the most formidable American solo career of any Germanic artist. Born in Bohemia but a product of Viennese schooling, he joined Fritz Reiner and George Szell in reactivating the Germanic influence on American musical life.

Though stylistically Serkin resembled Busch, he was a more secure instrumentalist than either Busch or Schnabel, a tornado of speed, precision, and power in the big sonatas and concertos of Beethoven and Brahms. That his tone was never sensuous, that his physical agitation at the keyboard did not preclude foot-stomping and other extraneous noises, that he wore spectacles and looked professorial all contributed to an impression of hard work and unvarnished integrity. Like Busch and Schnabel, like Thomas and Seidl, he seemed an ethical force.

The intensity, clarity, precision, and frequent high velocity of Serkin's pianism made him more compatible with the Toscanini style than other Germanic instrumentalists, and his 1936 American debut, with Toscanini and the New York Philharmonic, was a decisive success. Uncomfortable with the rituals of fame, Serkin was no celebrity. But he was also—like legions of New World Germans and Austrians before him, with their Philharmonic societies and Singvereine—a prodigious organizer. Toscanini, Horowitz, Heifetz were beneficiaries, not builders, in America. When late in life Heifetz taught at the University of Southern California, he had to advertise for students—and, wary of his ways, they would not come. Horowitz, in all things irregular, sporadically mentored at home. Toscanini, lonely on Olympus, was no teacher. Serkin accumulated a family of students and disciples, and created or commanded institutional structures to support, guide, and inspire them. His operational headquarters were the Curtis Institute, in Philadelphia; the Marlboro Festival, in Vermont; and the Leventritt Foundation, in New York—all of them small, selective, and rarified, as shy of the spotlight as Serkin himself.

Mary Louise Bok, whose father began the Curtis Publishing Company, founded the Curtis Institute of Music in 1924. Located in four turn-of-the-century mansions near Rittenhouse Square, it is in some respects the closest American equivalent to the conservatories of Moscow and St. Petersburg. Generously endowed, it provides free tuition for every student, which means that talent (as in Russia) is the main criterion for admission. No other American conservatory has amassed as many great names on its faculty: in addition to Serkin, Emanuel Feuermann, Wanda Landowska, Gregor Piatigorsky, William Primrose, Fritz Reiner, and Elisabeth Schumann have taught there. The list of distinguished graduates is long. Though pre-teenagers can enroll, it resembles an undergraduate institution with no fixed term of study; only for singers is there a postgraduate curriculum. The student body is tiny: under two hundred. Unlike the major European and Russian conservatories, Curtis cannot claim to transmit a nation's cultural inheritance, nor is it integrated into a national system of education and performance. Its narrow mission stresses purely musical skills, and Philadelphia is not New York. It is, in short, an elitist enclave where young musicians study music.

From 1926 to 1938, Curtis's director was Josef Hofmann (whom we have encountered touring the United States as a fabulous prodigy): an artist of idiosyncratic Romantic refinements, an unlikely model for young Americans. A different early influence was that of Leopold Stokowski, who in 1931 commandeered Curtis to assist in preparing Berg's *Wozzeck* with the Philadelphia Orchestra; twenty-five students supplied stage music, four student vocalists appeared in the cast, others sang in the chorus or helped with scenery and costumes. Curtis students also took part in historic Stokowski performances of Schoenberg's *Gurrelieder* and *Die glückliche Hand*. Afterward, Curtis retained close ties to the Philadelphia Orchestra—many of its players are Curtis teachers or former Curtis students—but without Stokowski both institutions settled into less challenging routines. Hofmann's successor was a composer: Randall Thompson, who for two years attempted to steer the curriculum toward contemporary music and extramusical instruction. Thompson's successor, the violinist Efrem Zimbalist, was a worldly and old-fashioned Russian finely attuned, like Hofmann, to the production of virtuosos. As Zimbalist's successor, in 1968, Serkin was by comparison a major performing artist in midcareer who embodied traditions both highly tangible and highly accessible. He promoted chamber music. He invigorated lapsed conducting and opera programs under the German-born Max Rudolf. As a teacher, he was absolute in his dedication and demands. Leschetizky in Vienna, Auer in St. Petersburg—master pedagogues—had produced artists of all styles and types. If Serkin's Curtis progeny—including Eugene Istomin, Seymour Lipkin,

Richard Goode, and André-Michel Schub—were more homogeneous, so had become the musical world in general.

Marlboro was founded in 1950 by Serkin, Busch and his brother Hermann (a cellist), and the flutist Marcel Moyse. Conceived as a chamber music workshop, it quickly evolved into a summer-long festival bristling with Serkin's energy. Versus the crowds and glamour of the Tanglewood model set by Koussevitzky, it hid from the prying world. Essentially, the festival was (and today remains) an intensive workshop: chamber music as a way of life. Repertoire was prepared for weeks at a time; if a piece was ready (and some never were), it was scheduled for public performance in a wooden theater seating 650 on folding chairs. Other performances took place privately, in the dining hall. Serkin and such senior colleagues as the violinists Alexander Schneider and Felix Galimir and the pianist Mieczyslaw Horszowski would turn up alongside teenage violinists, cellists, and pianists. Even when, from 1960 to 1973, Pablo Casals visited to coach and to conduct a chamber orchestra of indescribable zeal and virtuosity, audiences were secondary; Marlboro was about learning.

It was also, undeniably, about Europe. The one contemporary composer regularly on the premises was Leon Kirchner, who had studied with Schoenberg at UCLA and was the closest American equivalent to a significant contemporary German composer. With Galimir, who had known and worked with Schoenberg, Berg, and Webern in Vienna, Kirchner attuned Marlboro to the advanced music of Berg, Webern, and Schoenberg. And Kirchner also invited to the festival many important contemporary composers, including Elliott Carter, Aaron Copland, Luigi Dallapiccola, and György Kurtág. But there was no one to attune Marlboro to America. (Serkin himself, in a career spanning more than six decades, performed two American works.) Building on the influence of Schnabel, on the German emigrant wave of the 1930s, Marlboro was a linchpin in the formidable upsurge of chamber music activity in the United States after World War II. It is ponderable that after a century of classical music in America, no American musician exerted the influence Serkin did in Vermont. Had the Boston Symphony appointed Bernstein to succeed Koussevitzky, Tanglewood might have served as a balancing mecca, dedicated to a more American cause.*

Edgar Leventritt was a prominent New York attorney of German-Jewish descent. He was also a skilled pianist and violinist whose friends included

---

* Or consider, in contrast to Serkin and Marlboro, the case of George Balanchine, who imported classical ballet to the United States not by worshipfully transplanting Petipa but by improvising an Americanization project whose musical sources ranged from square dance, Gottschalk, Sousa, Gershwin, Ives, and Richard Rodgers to Bach, Mozart, Tchaikovsky, Stravinsky, and Webern.

Serkin and Busch, as well as George Szell, William Steinberg, and Yehudi Menuhin. He died in 1939, survived by his widow Rosalie and a daughter of the same name, a gifted amateur pianist. The Leventritt's Park Avenue apartment was New York's most prestigious private venue for chamber music. The apartment also served as a rehearsal and teaching space. Mrs. Leventritt conferred constantly with Serkin and Szell via telephone. Her Leventritt Foundation quietly subsidized Marlboro, the Casals Festival in Prades, France, and other musical causes. And, in memory of Edgar, it established a Leventritt Competition for pianists and violinists.

The Leventritt did not resemble the famous music competitions of Brussels, Warsaw, and Moscow. It had no rules, no application forms, no scheduled frequency, no required repertoire save a concerto by Mozart, Beethoven, or Brahms. In a given year, if a competition were held, the jury would pick a winner or not; there was no second place. Little or no money was awarded. But a Leventritt winner carried the imprimatur of Serkin and Szell, and of such other frequent jurors as William Steinberg and Isaac Stern. He or she could be expected to play with major American orchestras. Serkin, Szell, or Stern might prove a mentor. The blue-ribbon Leventritt jury and the Leventritt support system resulted in an extraordinary track record—most winners (a list including Eugene Istomin, Alexis Weissenberg, Gary Graffman, Van Cliburn, Pinchas Zukerman, and Itzhak Perlman) enjoyed eminent careers.[21]

Nothing more typified the Leventritt than its audience: there was none. Even at Carnegie Hall, contestants played for the jurors and a few invited guests. When there was a winner, a brief announcement would appear in the *New York Times*. Publicity was never courted. Though the intense privacy of the Leventritt process provoked resentment, Leventritt artists were reasonably eclectic in schooling and style. That for the duration of the competition, from 1940 to 1976, no winner prominently championed American music (John Browning, who premiered the Barber Piano Concerto, is at best a partial exception) is not very surprising. Nobody noticed or cared.

In truth, both Szell and Serkin were engaged in a kind of colonization project. Serkin's version was friendlier and more caring, and the Boks and Leventritts were generous and effective patrons. But to recall the efforts of Dvořák and Thurber, of Thomas and Seidl and Koussevitzky is to understand what Serkin's tutelage was not. The European experience was offered as an end in itself—not, as Henry Krehbiel had once eloquently theorized, as a stepping stone toward a mature classical music culture indigenous to the United States.

■ ■ ■

The story of American concert artists gathers momentum in the mid-twentieth century. In the nineteenth, it was preponderantly a story of singers: the opera-mad decades were peppered with Americans, of whom we have glimpsed the barnstorming divas Clara Louise Kellogg and Emma Abbott. Among the headline singers of the early Metropolitan Opera we have observed Geraldine Farrar's special allure, alongside other pre–World War I American-born vocalists—Lillian Nordica, Emma Eames, Olive Fremstad, Louise Homer, Mary Garden—of great reputation. American instrumentalists were slower off the mark. For a century after Louis Moreau Gottschalk, no American pianist excited world acclaim. Edward MacDowell and Amy Beach were impressive pianists who mainly composed. Among violinists, Maud Powell (1868–1920), a deft artist who introduced the United States to the concertos of Tchaikovsky, Sibelius, and—with the composer in the audience—Dvořák, and Albert Spalding (1888–1953), of the famous ball-manufacturing company (he played tennis assiduously), achieved prominence alongside a daunting procession of visitors, beginning with Wieniawski, Ysaÿe, and Kreisler. The day of the American conductor was delayed by an ongoing influx of important Central Europeans. Thor Johnson, who led the Cincinnati Symphony from 1947 to 1958, and Alfred Wallenstein, music director of the Los Angeles Philharmonic from 1943 to 1956, were among the Americans who ascended highest in the shadow of Toscanini.

The 1950s was the watershed decade. First stranded, then ruptured by World War II, Europe's opera houses and orchestras were busy rebuilding. The steady influx of dazzling Russian and Germanic instrumentalists had suffered interruption. New opportunities arose for American artists both at home and abroad. The American conductor came of age in the person of Leonard Bernstein—the topic of a later chapter. We will shortly survey a new generation of American singers, a dominant presence at the Met. Isaac Stern, born in Odessa in 1920 and raised in San Francisco, became the first American-trained violinist to conquer Europe. (Yehudi Menuhin, born in New York in 1916 and also raised in San Francisco, supplemented his initial American studies with tutelage abroad; he made his home in Europe.) But it was in the realm of the piano that Americans suddenly and most dramatically proliferated.

In 1958, *Time* claimed, "There is more first rate instrumental talent in the United States than in the whole of Europe."[22] Every one of the ten young pianists listed in substantiation had studied exclusively in North America. Jacob Lateiner and Gary Graffman, who dubbed his generation the "OYAPs," for "Outstanding Young American Pianists," studied with Isabelle Vengerova at Curtis; Graffman also worked with Serkin and Vladimir Horowitz. Eugene Istomin and Seymour Lipkin were Curtis graduates as well; both studied with

Serkin and Horszowski. Byron Janis studied privately with Horowitz. Artur Schnabel privately taught Leon Fleisher and Claude Frank. Rosina Lhevinne, at Juilliard, taught Van Cliburn and John Browning. As Americans, some OYAPs aimed for greater versatility in style and repertoire than their European counterparts, even though the influence of Schnabel, Serkin, and Horowitz was variously audible. Fleisher, whose driving energy and big sound served a powerful musical intellect, was a formidable exponent of Beethoven and Brahms; unlike his mentor, he also excelled in Liszt and Rachmaninoff. But the OYAPs did not forge an "American" style, if only because, with their European teachers, they played so little of the American music that might have helped to shape it. An illuminating counterexample was the signature American chamber ensemble: the Juilliard String Quartet, formed in 1946. The Juilliard's aggressive, unmediated approach to Beethoven, Bartók, and Schoenberg was anchored, in part, by its allegiance to Elliott Carter and other Americans. Challenging the comforting traditionalism of Marlboro, it seemingly brandished contemporary New York—impetuous, brash, self-defining—as the measure of all things musical.

Perhaps chamber music, with its elite following, was more conducive to the boldness of the Juilliard statement than were piano concertos and recitals. And the American keyboard repertoire was undeniably thin. But what repertoire existed was not pursued. An exception that proved the rule was William Masselos, an incandescent exponent of top-drawer American piano works by Griffes, Ives, and Copland, who somehow could not land the career he deserved. Two years younger than Masselos—that is, with Masselos marginally of the pre-OYAP era—was William Kapell, who died in a 1953 airplane disaster at the age of thirty-one. On the cusp of international prominence, Kapell had become an impassioned champion of the Copland Piano Variations and Piano Sonata, and stood ready to tackle Ives and Sessions in defiance of timid audiences and managers. Either Masselos or Kapell might have furnished a model for a homebred "American" pianism nourished by, and nourishing, a living American repertoire.

Fleisher called Kapell "without question the greatest piano talent this country ever produced." Pierre Monteux called Fleisher "the pianistic find of the century." But the most unusual piano talents among the OYAPs, and the strangest careers, belonged to a Texan and a Canadian: Cliburn and Glenn Gould. These were not New World pianists of the sort Masselos or Kapell might have fathered. But they were also unlike the pianists anyplace else.

In 1954 the Leventritt winner was a nineteen-year-old for whom Serkin and Szell had no use (it credits their liberality that they supported the verdict). He had blue eyes and frizzy blond hair and stood six feet, four inches tall. At

Juilliard, he was surely the only pianist to sing in Billy Graham's choir at Madison Square Garden. Gary Graffman later wrote:

> At the time Van entered the Leventritt, . . . pianists were Central or Eastern European, or at least of that extraction. It looked so odd to see a *cowboy* play the *piano*. . . . The Leventritt jury—and the audience, of which I was one—were astonished by his relaxed yet seemingly limitless virtuosity, and when he finished an electrifying performance of a Liszt rhapsody, there was a good moment's stunned silence before the judges could gather the temerity to ask him to play a little something else. He was still sitting at the piano, awaiting instructions, and I remember that he turned to them at that moment, before beginning the next piece, and shyly asked, "Would y'all mahnd if Ah went and got a glass of WAW tuh?"[23]

Van Cliburn differed from Graffman and the other OYAPs in countless ways. They earnestly purveyed Beethoven; he preferred Tchaikovsky and Rachmaninoff. Crewcut 1950s musical personalities, they conveyed intensity with coiled rhythms and steely tones. Cliburn sat tall in the saddle, poised and unhurried. His organ sonorities were Romantically lustrous. Though his teacher Rosina Lhevinne was Russian, he did not sound like Rachmaninoff or Horowitz, or the Soviets Richter and Gilels. The warm sheen and spacious architecture of his performances communicated not the glitter of the moment but a soothing remembrance of things past: a clairvoyant dream of the Moscow of his imagination. Four years later, in Moscow itself, Cliburn took part in the first Tchaikovsky International Piano Competition. Upon landing he asked to be driven directly to Red Square so that, fulfilling a childhood wish, he could see the Church of St. Basil. He visited Tchaikovsky's grave in Leningrad, and took away some Russian earth to replant at Rachmaninoff's grave in New York. He called the Russians "my people" and said, "I've never felt so at home anywhere in my life."

In 1958, Moscow was another planet from Manhattan, little known and less seen. But the slow thawing of the cold war had fostered friendly cultural competition. In 1952, with the support of the State Department and the Ford Foundation, Fleisher competed in the Russian-dominated Queen Elisabeth Competition in Brussels—and won. At the 1955 Queen Elisabeth, Browning was a close second to Russia's Vladimir Ashkenazy. The same year, Gilels and David Oistrakh appeared in the United States for the first time. Silencing these musical exchanges, in 1957, were the headlines of October 5: "SIGHT RED BABY MOON OVER US." "SOVIET LAUNCHES FIRST MOON." "SOVIET FIRES EARTH

SATELLITE INTO SPACE." This was the context in which Moscow, some two months later, invited Americans to participate in the new Tchaikovsky competition. A Russian was thought certain to win, but Cliburn proved to be the American *Sputnik*. Women wept when he played. Students shouted, "First prize!" He was hugged and kissed wherever he went. By the time he gave his final round performance of the Rachmaninoff Third Concerto, his gold medal seemed foreordained. Gilels, the jury chairman, embraced him backstage. Of the other judges, Richter called Cliburn a "genius." The composer Khachaturian said Cliburn's performance was "*better* than Rachmaninoff's; you find a virtuoso like this once or twice in a century." In New York, Cliburn repeated his Rachmaninoff Third at Carnegie Hall with his Moscow conductor, Kiril Kondrashin. RCA's recording of the live performance documents an act of divination. Cliburn surrenders himself to the deepest currents of sadness and nostalgia, surging in the first-movement cadenza to a central climax of dizzying altitude and breadth.

Like Patrick Gilmore's Peace Jubilee, or Toscanini's wartime Beethoven, Cliburn's Tchaikovsky and Rachmaninoff were politically charged. The *Sputnik* challenge was, Americans understood, partly a prestige and propaganda challenge. The *New York Times*'s four-column, page-one headline announced, "U.S. PIANIST, 23, WINS SOVIET CONTEST." *Times* writers worried that America's own piano competitions—of which the Leventritt was chief—were "little publicized," that the American classical music audience was not as passionate and knowledgeable as that glimpsed in Moscow, that the "highest authorities" did not acknowledge the highest culture as in "other countries." Howard Taubman stopped short of espousing government subsidies, calling instead for "the wisdom to recognize and respond" to America's "high competence in performance and creation." In the case of Cliburn, Americans did respond. New York gave him a ticker-tape parade. President Eisenhower received him at the White House. Commercial television showcased him via Edward R. Murrow and Steve Allen (who outmaneuvered Ed Sullivan). RCA signed him to "one of the fattest contracts ever offered a young artist," and topped the LP charts with the first classical recording to sell more than a million copies: Cliburn's version of the Tchaikovsky First Concerto. No less than Toscanini or Horowitz, Cliburn was redrawn as the antithesis of the long-hair snob: a down-home Texan who crooned "Blue Moon," adored big cars, and was once engaged to a "tall, lissome brunette." He was, summarized *Time*, "Horowitz, Liberace, and Presley rolled into one," a classical music folk hero, a cold war Paderewski. But it bears pondering whether Americans responded more to Cliburn's fame than to his music. Even Taubman wrote, "Over and over again the question . . . has been, 'Is this Cliburn really that good?'"

Cliburn was all he seemed in 1958, but times change and so, ideally, do young artists. Intoxicated by his own timeless dream, Cliburn resisted change. The Tchaikovsky concerto remained his signature, which he recycled at a killing pace. Though he acquired fresh repertoire, the range of music in which he excelled stayed narrow and grew stale. Major orchestras stopped engaging him. In 1978, at age forty-three, he retired. Shrewd investments had made him a rich man. Though he resumed performing in 1989, his comeback—playing the same pieces he had quit with eleven years before—was less noticed than an opulent namesake: the Van Cliburn International Piano Competition, held in Fort Worth, Texas, where Cliburn settled in 1985. For four decades, the competition has searched for another Cliburn on which to bestow its generous prize money; a fruitless endeavor. If Horowitz's decadent eccentricity furnished one coda to the heroic Romantic pianists of yore, Cliburn's insatiable yearning and nostalgia yielded another endgame. He actually fetishized the past, saving closets full of old luggage and unworn clothes, having facial creases erased from his photographs, telling visitors, "In *Te*xas, we like to stay *ba*bies." Stuck in an era not his own, he was not emulatable.[24]

■ ■ ■

Glenn Gould was at least Cliburn's peer in eccentricity. He sat at the piano hunched chin to the keys, singing and (when either arm was free) conducting. Other pianists insisted on using certain pianos. Gould traveled with his own archaic wooden *chair*; during orchestral tuttis, he would slouch into it, with his legs crossed and the score in his lap. His low center of gravity and elevated hands forced his fingers to do extra work; even at phenomenal speeds, the passagework was as chiseled as a C major scale played with one thumb. His obsession with clarity dictated slow-motion trills; he could scrutinize every note. His ability to translate precise intention into sound was on a par with Heifetz. No other pianist exercised such control of texture and articulation. The Gould phenomenon was summarized by Szell when he exclaimed, "This nut's a genius."

Gould made his name—instantaneously—with Bach, who never wrote for the piano and so furnished a tabula rasa for interpretation. Gould projected the dense polyphony with incomparable ease and panache. Though no piano could sound less sensuous than his, every line sang, every detail was high-pitched, concentrated, and exact: he played Bach as an ecstatic. Though his basic approach never varied, he was eclectic. His American debut program included the early-seventeenth-century masters Gibbons and Sweelinck, a Bach partita and five inventions, late Beethoven, Berg, and Webern. His recordings included lots of Mozart (whose piano writing he found deplorably homophonic), Beethoven (whose heroic pose he rejected), and Schoenberg (whose dynamics and phrasings he rewrote); he ranged, as well, to Brahms, Grieg, Bizet, Sibelius, Scriabin, Prokofiev, Hindemith, and Krenek. Richard Strauss (whom he considered the "greatest musical figure" of the twentieth century) was a special enthusiasm.

He also left a recording—one of his best—of three Wagner selections. Here, his idiosyncratic clarity of timbre confers a sublime translucence on the *Siegfried Idyll*; more than any conductor, he animates the contrapuntal bustle of the *Die Meistersinger* Prelude; he traverses Siegfried's Rhine Journey as exuberantly as Siegfried himself. Gould's transcriptions are, needless to say, unlike anyone else's. In particular, they are unlike those of Liszt, who knew how to make a piano sound like an orchestra. Gould makes no attempt to sound symphonic. Where the *Meistersinger* polyphony grows densest, he cheerfully overdubs "extra hands"—as Liszt, the virtuoso, would never dream of doing. In short, he does not celebrate the polymorphous possibilities of the piano as a Romantic sound medium. He values the piano for its self-sufficiency: its subservience to his complete command.

Leopold Stokowski also especially excelled in Bach and Wagner, and for the same reason: he could reimagine this music, intended for organ or for opera, in his own sonic image. And Gould revered Stokowski for precisely this achievement. Gould even got Stokowski to record Beethoven's *Emperor* Concerto with him: a thankless assignment. Gould was at all times absolutely self-involved.

The Gould career, no less than Cliburn's, was unique and unrepeatable. He toured for eight years, stirring and delighting, amusing and bemusing North American audiences. He was also, in 1957, the first North American pianist to play in cold war Russia, where his impact was (like Cliburn's) sensational—testimony both to Russian isolation and Russian discernment. Then, in 1964, he retired from the stage. Two years later, he predicted that "the public concert as we know it today" would "no longer exist a century hence," that its functions would have been "entirely taken over by electronic media." He argued that the concert format was not only anachronistic but flawed. It attracted listeners who did not want to listen. It constrained performers' repertoires and overempowered their egos. Recordings, moreover, had in Gould's opinion engendered fresh ways of hearing. No longer was listening an exercise in communal religious devotion, complemented by the cavernous reverberation of cathedral-like spaces. The new penchant was for "analytic clarity, immediacy, and indeed almost tactile proximity." A new kind of artist, ensconced in the studio, could splice together disparate takes and reconstitute balances.

A new kind of listener, ensconced in the living room, could tinker with dials, even combine excerpts from different recordings in pursuit of an "ideal performance."

Gould's McLuhanesque media prophecies—that with the demise of concerts, electronic media would convey the message—made his retirement seem timely. Actually, the timeliness was fortuitous. Gould's aversion to public concerts was partly an aversion to the public. He was a hermit whose personal and musical eccentricities mounted as he receded from the public eye. The new kind of artist, the new kind of listener he endorsed was Gould himself, whose creations included a recording of a Bach fugue edited to alternate between two dissimilar performances.

In addition to recording, Gould continued to write articles and to produce documentaries for radio and television. These extramusical activities furnished further compelling evidence of his high-powered and obdurately self-made intellect. His deepening seclusion facilitated ever more profound exercises in control. He made plans to record the solo part of Beethoven's Second Piano Concerto and, on a separate occasion, its orchestral accompaniment, which he would conduct; the two performances would be combined in the studio. In 1982, three months before succumbing to a heart attack at the age of fifty, he rerecorded the *Siegfried Idyll*, but in Wagner's original chamber version for thirteen players, conducting a freelance group drawn mainly from the Toronto Symphony. Not once do the players sound spontaneous or self-willed.

In their different ways, Gould's overdubbing in the *Meistersinger* Prelude and his manipulation of thirteen instrumentalists in a Toronto studio demonstrated how his obsession with perfection complemented his obsession with the techniques of recorded sound. He epitomized—he espoused—the ways in which the phonograph has infiltrated how we hear and make music. In the studio, as a monitoring agent, recorded sound promotes refinements and hyperrefinements of execution. Toscanini's 1936 *Siegfried Idyll* recording with the New York Philharmonic is surpassingly beautiful. A lyric jet stream binds its parts, and also smooths away Wagner's portraiture of the household at Tribschen: of Cosima's tender lullaby, of the six-month-old Siegfried's drowsiness and slumber. But compared with Toscanini's disembodied Wagner, Gould's performance with orchestra is actually solipsistic.

Serkin transplanted Old World traditions to the New World. Szell attempted to combine those traditions with New World perfectability. Stokowski, Leonard Bernstein, and the Juilliard Quartet all jettisoned tradition to one degree or another. Gould, an independent agent, overthrew tradition as completely as any Martian. Such post–World War I Germanic Bach piano stylists as Edwin Fischer and Wilhelm Kempff were for him as irrelevant as Wanda

Landowska's harpsichord Bach, which predominantly displaced the piano for decades on both sides of the Atlantic. At worst, Gould was the *reductio ad absurdum* of a New World specialty: the perfectionist performer—Toscanini, Szell, Reiner, Heifetz. At best, he was the purest of New World originals.[25]

■ ■ ■

Of the OYAPs, *Time* wrote in 1958, "Some of the Americans are almost sure to step into the shoes of the Backhauses, the Rubinsteins, the Serkins, the Giesekings and Horowitzes."[26] But none did. Cliburn and Gould retired from the stage. Fleisher, Graffman, and Janis were a growing American phalanx, then succumbed to hand problems. The others more quietly faded from view.

In retrospect, what surprises is not the curtailed careers, but the Backhauses, Rubinsteins, and Serkins who continued to tour into old age. Nothing of the kind—steady solo concertizing over a period of decades—occurred before World War I. Liszt, who toured ceaselessly—west to Glasgow and Belfast, north to Copenhagen and Amsterdam, east to Constantinople and St. Petersburg—gave it up at the age of thirty-five. He complained of "great tiredness of life and a ridiculous need for rest." He wished to compose, to conduct, to teach. He was a voracious reader, a searching thinker. Heine testified (and others confirmed), "His intellectual proclivities are quite remarkable; he has a very lively taste for speculation and is less preoccupied with his own artistic interest than with the investigations of the various schools of thought dealing with the great questions of heaven and earth.[27]

Cliburn, in retirement, was once told by an interviewer that his friends "didn't see how Cliburn could be happy unless he returned to the concert stage"; he "roared with laughter" and shouted "*Try me!*" Asked how it felt to play his final concert, in 1978, Cliburn replied, "The one thing I felt when I got off the stage was: I don't have to do this anymore." Fleisher, publicly reflecting on his career as a conductor, pedagogue, and left-handed pianist after his right hand quit, said his finger malady had rescued him from becoming a "concert fool."★ Explaining his decision to leave the stage, Gould once said, "It was never something I wanted to spend my entire life doing. . . . I have pretty well exhausted the [piano] music that interests me."[28] Others let the music exhaust them. (And others, inveterate performers, thrived on a repetitive regimen precluding home, family, or disciples.)

The performance specialists of the preceding generation—a list including the piano icons named by *Time* and also Richter, Gilels, Kempff, Arrau, Hess,

---

★ Late in his career, Fleisher gradually returned, with distinction, to the two-hand repertoire.

Casadesus, Heifetz, Milstein, and countless others—sustained the special glamour of the recital in the twentieth century. They were not Gottschalks, Liszts, Thalbergs, Anton Rubinsteins, Wieniawskis, Ysaÿes, Bülows, or Busonis, all of whom composed or conducted or both. As Toscanini was a new species among conductors, no previous generation of instrumentalists had been so distant from the creative act. And no subsequent generation was as exclusively dedicated to an instrument. Graffman, in 1981, spoke for the OYAPs—and many thousands of pianophiles—in nostalgically recalling a "glorious panoply" of keyboard artists once traveling the breadth of the United States. In 1950–51, Carnegie Hall alone hosted dozens of pianists in recital, including multiple appearances by Horowitz and Serkin, among others; half a century later, the number had shrunk by two-thirds and more.[29] What had happened was that contemporary music had moved to the margins of the concert experience, so that pianists were no longer disposed to compose. But a great many of them retained reasonably direct links—via teachers, via childhood contacts—to the great keyboard composers of yesteryear. This small window of opportunity, yielding the "glorious panoply" of Graffman's childhood, had gently but firmly closed by the turn of the twenty-first century.

The purest exponents of the solo pianist were among the last: Artur Rubinstein and Claudio Arrau, both American-based. Unlike Serkin, Rubinstein and Arrau were not important pedagogues. Unlike Richter, they rarely performed chamber music. Unlike Horowitz, they maintained an uninterrupted itinerary of airports and hotels, rehearsals and concerts, tirelessly visiting and revisiting the musical capitals of the world, performing up to 130 times a season—a rarified and unprecedented twentieth-century calling. Rubinstein, who radiated *joie de vivre*, played in public with undiminished relish for eighty-two years; he gave his final recital and made his last recordings at the age of eighty-nine in 1976. Arrau, whose every concert was a ritual of suffering and redemption he could not suppress, also—strangely enough— sustained a career of eighty-two years; he played in public at the age of eighty-six and last recorded at age eighty-seven. It is safe to predict that no concert pianist or violinist will again pursue a comparable vocation.

CHAPTER 4

Opera for Singers

∎

The remoteness of the Met ▪ *Serving* Tristan *and* Otello ▪
Edward Johnson and the American singer ▪ *Mary Garden and
opera in Chicago* ▪ *Gaetano Merola and opera in San Francisco* ▪
The American culture of performance summarized

The predominance of the orchestra as the principal instrument for American classical music, fulfilling Theodore Thomas's credo, dictated a diminished role for opera. Nineteenth-century New York had been opera mad: opera came in all sizes and shapes and served all kinds of audiences. In twentieth-century Europe, the opera house continued to be the defining musical institution in countless communities, large and small. In the United States after 1930, however, opera did not "show the culture" of any community. Rather, it was centralized in a single megainstitution: the Met.

But the Met was not what it had been. Though as in the past most performances were given in Italian or German, fewer and fewer patrons understood these foreign languages. Though Seidl and Toscanini had once run the house, no conductor enjoyed comparable authority until the coming of James Levine in the 1970s (and Levine would be no Seidl or Toscanini). Though important contemporary opera, by the likes of Debussy or Ravel, Bartók or Janáček, Stravinsky or Shostakovich, Berg, Hindemith, or Weill, was less "grand," more intimate than Wagner or Verdi, the Met stuck with its Valhalla-scaled thirty-six-hundred-seat auditorium. All these factors discouraged the theatrical dimension once cultivated by Seidl, Mahler, and Toscanini. Rather, they favored individual performers, their virtuosity, glamour, and projective force. The Met was about singers.

What the Met was not about bears stressing. In Milan, in the 1920s, Toscanini ruled without interference. He gave *Tristan* in a prophetic staging by Adolphe Appia. He revitalized the Verdi canon, and so revitalized postwar

Italy itself. In Berlin, Klemperer's Kroll Opera headlined Weill, Janáček, Stravinsky, and its "Bolshevik" *Flying Dutchman*. In Dresden, Fritz Busch made a specialty of mounting the latest Richard Strauss. In provincial Münster, Antal Dorati (later music director of four American orchestras) encountered a young ensemble that "rehearsed day and night" and routinely offered repertoire by Stravinsky, Hindemith, Bartók, and Ravel.[1] For certain New York opera goers, the great events of these decades were Stokowski's 1931 *Wozzeck* and Rodzinski's 1935 *Lady Macbeth*, both of which played to wildly enthusiastic audiences at the Met but were (as we have seen) produced and presented by the Philadelphia and Cleveland Orchestras, respectively.

We have heard Henry Krehbiel prophesy in 1908 that opera in America would remain "experimental" until "the vernacular becomes the language of the performances and native talent provides both works and interpreters. The day is far distant, but it will come." That it never did explains, in part, the decline of opera as a genre of living theater, of opera *not* grand as once pursued at Niblo's or Palmo's. Krehbiel also wrote that unless Americans grew accustomed to performing and listening to opera in the language they best understood, American opera would remain "an exotic"—an expensive frill. Rather than spawning a central theatrical form, it would inculcate mere "craving for sensation." Boxes at the Metropolitan Opera House would remain "a coveted asset" only because they were "visible symbols of social distinction." In sum, there would be no such thing as "American opera." And there is not.[2]

The error in Krehbiel's thinking—his assumption that Americans eventually would embrace opera in English—is understandable. He had observed Frenchmen giving *Aïda* and *Lohengrin* in French, Germans giving *Faust* and *Aïda* in German, Italians giving *Faust* and *Lohengrin* in Italian—and in all cases, uncontroversially, as a common practice endorsed by the composers themselves. And Krehbiel had observed a concomitant evolution of French opera, German opera, and Italian opera—of native repertoire informed by native language and style. Compared to their European contemporaries, American singers were eclectics who represented no one school and championed no single canon.

The European practice of giving opera in the vernacular largely survived through the midpoint of the twentieth century. Opera showed the culture of a community. Opera singers were cherished, even idolized, yet remained subsidiary to a larger local enterprise. New York, by comparison, ran a luxury import business: in Krehbiel's vocabulary, an "exotic." The twentieth-century Metropolitan Opera truly was, in a sense, "experimental." By and large, New York now relied on familiar works as a vehicle for celebrity performers.

Departed was the spirit of adventure animating the German seasons of Seidl's day, or Mahler's "new" Mozart and Beethoven, or Toscanini's spare-no-expense *Fanciulla*.

The special remoteness of the Met—from the contemporary arts, from daily Manhattan, even from its audience in the vast horseshoe space—was an ingredient of its special glamour. The void in which it floated, unmoored to present-day time and place, was the heaven of its "stars." We have witnessed in its many manifestations the culture of performance, supplanting the creative act as the locus of American classical music. The great conductors Toscanini, Stokowski, and Koussevitzky, the "world's greatest" orchestras, the greatest pianist, the greatest violinist were the showcase attractions, as were the celebrity soloists featured on its Sunday-afternoon national broadcasts by the otherwise celebrity-less New York Philharmonic. Like American classical music generally, opera in America—at the self-proclaimed world's greatest opera house[3]—became a collection of great names. And yet, as with Toscanini, Stokowski, or Koussevitzky, Horowitz or Heifetz, the greatness of the names was authentic; the outcome, if incomplete, was on its own terms remarkable, a distinctive New World variant.

■ ■ ■

The Met had parted ambivalently with Toscanini in 1915. The company's taut artistic mainspring, he had propelled repertoire, casting, and staging, pressing for maximum results, ensuring a sum greater than its parts. His contract designated him "First Master of Concerts and First Director of Orchestra for the operas, concerts and oratorios which will be executed in the Metropolitan Opera House in New York," in which "The Metropolitan Opera Company reserved to Maestro Toscanini the right of use of all that concerns the performing of the art."[4] That he was impossible to please was both his crowning inspirational tool and his crippling practical defect. He quarreled with singers, with musicians, and with Giulio Gatti-Casazza, who ran the business side of things. Gatti was expected by the boxholders to balance his budget. He had to produce as many as fifty operas for as long as six months at a rate of up to *eight* performances a week. He was burdened with a facility that, however glamorous, was outdated the day it opened. The stage was too shallow and lacked adequate space behind, above, and to the sides. Even the sets for acts two and three of a given opera could not be conveniently stored; and tomorrow's opera had to be carted from a warehouse, to sit on the sidewalk under tarpaulins. Dressing rooms, rehearsal rooms, office space were inadequate.

Absent Toscanini, absent Oscar Hammerstein's Manhattan Opera, Gatti could relax a little. He never again engaged a plenipotentiary music director. Instead, he put himself in charge of the whole show. What sort of man was he? No one knew, or knows today. The Met's first salaried general manager, he had arrived from La Scala with Toscanini in 1908 and would remain for twenty-seven years. Though a ubiquitous presence, ever solemn and courteous, he showed no evidence of speaking or comprehending English. He entrusted many tasks to his assistant and bosom friend Edward Ziegler, a former music critic who was bright and shrewd. Cultivated, well read, Gatti believed that theaters, even opera theaters, were more than museums, but his seeming disconnection from his country of residence was no help in this department.

Gatti did know how to run a theater. His professionalism was evident in his insistence (at least initially) on better stage designs, better costumes, better dancers. His principal conductors, after Toscanini, were Artur Bodanzky, Tullio Serafin, and Ettore Panizza—less illustrious than their predecessors, but much better than most of what came after. Unlike later Met regimes, Gatti's made do with as few as eight conductors at a time, which meant, in effect, that Bodanzky ruled the German wing and Serafin, then (as of 1934) Panizza the Italian. The singers, too, stayed put for months at a time as they never would once they could jet to Europe. The Met remained a company, not a revolving door for traveling artists.

Even the loss of Caruso, who died in 1920, and of Farrar, who retired two years later, even the relative paucity of great Wagner singers to replace Lehmann and Niemann, Fremstad and Jean de Rezske, did not inhibit the superabundance of vocal talent that had ever been the boxholders' first artistic imperative. Newcomers after World War I included two stellar Americans, Rosa Ponselle and Lawrence Tibbett. Feodor Chaliapin returned beginning in 1921 as Boris, Boito's Mefistofele, Massenet's Don Quixote, and Verdi's Philip II. The German repertoire was refreshed by Margarete Matzenauer, Lauritz Melchior, Elisabeth Rethberg, Friedrich Schorr, and the luscious Maria Jeritza. Mainly, the new stars were Italian: Lucrezia Bori, Amelita Galli-Curci, Beniamino Gigli, Giuseppe de Luca, Giovanni Martinelli, Titta Ruffo.

With such an arsenal, Gatti could mount the standard repertoire with casts rightfully legendary in their own time. He also presented the Met's first American opera: *The Pipe of Desire* by Frederick Converse. And under Gatti the Met for the first time mounted world premieres, notably including Puccini's *La fanciulla* and *Il trittico*, plus no fewer than thirteen premieres by Americans—of which, however, only Louis Gruenberg's *The Emperor Jones* and Deems Taylor's *Peter Ibbetson* showed even a trace of staying power. Of first American performances the most notable were *Boris Godunov* (in 1913, under Toscanini), Tchaikovsky's *Pique Dame* (1910, under Mahler), and Strauss's *Der*

Rosenkavalier (1913, under Alfred Hertz), all of which took hold; and of Janáček's *Jenufa* (1924, under Bodanzky), which did not. The distinguished novelties introduced on Gatti's watch included works by Borodin, Dukas, Falla, Granados, Korngold, Montemezzi, Rimsky-Korsakov, and Richard Strauss.

For its time and place, it was less than it might seem. The pace and quality of repertoire renewal slowed markedly with Toscanini's departure. Though sponsorship of American opera was in any case doomed, that Gatti employed Walter Damrosch to judge submissions shows naïveté or a crippling conservatism. In retrospect, the composers the Met needed to encourage were less the ones it commissioned or tested than the ones it did not: Griffes, Loeffler, and Chicago's John Alden Carpenter come to mind. Gershwin was courted but stayed away. By mid-twentieth-century standards, the assemblage of singers was colossal, but this mainly required money, not vision. On the one hand, surviving broadcast performances dating back to 1931 document vocal standards unapproachable half a century later. On the other, one cannot dismiss as nostalgia the testimony of New York's longest-lived expert witness. W. J. Henderson complained in the *New York Sun* of "faded works" performed "over and over again, most of the time with mediocre singers going through their roles like so many robots," of contracts that hired artists for half a season only, producing "vagrant comings and goings" in place of discipline and ensemble. The critic who told the truth about the Metropolitan Opera "was as one decrying in the wilderness." It was intended "for persons in search of relaxation." To which Richard Strauss, commenting on the post-Toscanini Gatti Met, added (in conversation with Deems Taylor) that though he admired the physical productions and organizational efficiency of the house, "they have no dramatic instinct there. Everything is the singing—always the voice." Strauss also thought it inappropriate to stage Mozart's *Così fan tutte* in so large an auditorium, and that it was "a great mistake" not to perform it— or his own *Salome*, for that matter—in English.[5]

In short, Gatti's Met, after Toscanini, was robust or inert, depending on one's point of vision. The artistic machinery hummed in parallel with the financial: through the 1920s, the boxholders' modest subsidies were sufficient for the house to run in the black. More than two-thirds of the seats for the five weekly subscription performances were filled before the season started. As more than one-fifth of the house offered partial or obstructed views, this meant that only a few hundred desirable seats were available for sale on subscription nights.[6] Over time, the anachronism and exclusivity of it all—the boxholders were nearly the same families that had created the Met in 1892— were bound to be tested. The test came in 1929, when Wall Street crashed.

The Met's finances began to dip: in 1929–30, the company posted its first deficit in two decades. In 1930–31, subscriptions sank, tours were lost, costs soared. According to Gatti, in his memoirs, "In three years we lost more than 30 per cent of our subscribers. . . . The wealthy classes . . . formed the bulk of subscribers who cancelled" while "the general public which purchased admission from day to day, continued at about the same level."[7] The very social structure that had created the Met was creaking. Some for whom opera was a frill seemed willing simply to abandon it. Alternative sources of support were needed—swiftly, desperately.

A Committee for Saving the Metropolitan Opera was now formed with the prominent participation of three singers: Lucrezia Bori, Edward Johnson, and Lawrence Tibbett. Fortuitously, a vehicle was at hand. The company had struck a deal with the National Broadcasting Company to air performances nationally in 1931–32 and 1932–33. (Typically, Stokowski had gotten there first: his staging of Stravinsky's *Oedipus Rex* with the Philadelphia Orchestra, presented at the Met on April 21, 1931, was broadcast.)* When Humperdinck's *Hansel and Gretel* went over the airwaves on Christmas Day 1931, the *New York Times* reported on the front page, "Before the first 15 minutes had passed, hundreds of congratulatory messages poured in from all over the country." Two months later, on February 25, Johnson announced the fund drive during an intermission of a broadcast of Massenet's *Manon*. Two weeks after that, NBC gave the Committee a special half hour to appeal for money. The occasion was clearly historic. Paul D. Cravath, a corporate lawyer who in 1931 had become the Metropolitan's president and chairman, announced that opera at the Met could "no longer rely, as heretofore, upon a small group of rich men. We must now rely upon the support not only of the audience at the opera house, but also on the vast radio audience." Bori sang a set of arias and songs, and then—an electrifying moment—spoke directly to her listeners in English (as scripted by Ziegler): "We need your assistance, and if you wish to join the hundreds of radio listeners who have already responded so generously and will communicate with me at the Metropolitan Opera House, you will receive my personal note of appreciation. . . . Are you, my dear radio listeners, going to forsake this national institution, the Metropolitan Opera, in its present crisis, or are you coming to its rescue? I can almost hear you shout: 'To the rescue!' "[8]

Bori kept her word: she acknowledged every contribution, and also every

---

* In 1909–10, performances of *Tosca*, *Cavalleria rusticana*, and *Pagliacci* were transmitted by "wireless telegraphy." See David Hamilton, *The Sound of the Met* (New York, Museum of Broadcasting, 1986), p. 10. The Met first staged *Oedipus Rex* in 1981.

subscription renewal, on the stationery of the Berkshire Hotel, where she lived. During the weeks of the fund drive, she worked tirelessly alongside Cornelius Bliss, who represented the boxholders on the committee, and Eleanor Robson Belmont, a former actress with experience as a Red Cross fund-raiser during World War I. It took only two months to raise the necessary three hundred thousand dollars. One hundred thousand came from radio listeners: more than twice what was raised from boxholders and directors of the Metropolitan Opera Association. In 1933, the broadcasts acquired commercial sponsorship, which would ensure their permanence. As of 1935, the radio audience totaled nine million listeners weekly.[9] The same year, Mrs. Belmont, who had become the first woman member of the board, created the Metropolitan Opera Guild as a link to the outside world in pursuit of "the democratization of opera."

Was the Met becoming democratized? Yes and no. The groundlings had been acknowledged, even solicited. But one look at the boxes of the diamond horseshoe confirmed that the Met was for the mutually admired and admiring. What if mere ticket holders, in the rafters, could not see the entire stage? "Then let them come down," said Gatti. Actually, a more fundamental push toward opera for the people came from higher in the ranks than Mrs. Belmont.

Otto Kahn was once described as "the Lorenzo de Medici of his day . . . with an air of detachment from anything as plebeian as money." *Time* called him "America's foremost patron of the arts." As board chairman, president, and dominant shareholder, Kahn was the financial bulwark of the Metropolitan Opera for more than a decade. Born in Mannheim in 1867, he was many other things as well: a socialite, an aesthete, and the most visible partner of Kuhn, Loeb, and Company, an international banking firm second only to the house of Morgan. He figured in the lives of Caruso (with whom he played cards and shared pasta) and of the sopranos Maria Jeritza and Grace Moore (with both of whom he shared more than food).

Like his banker's politics, Kahn's cultural philanthropies were notably progressive. At a time when classical ballet was little known in America, he sponsored Nijinsky. He helped to subsidize the American tour of the politically controversial Moscow Art Theatre. He backed the pathbreaking Theater Guild and Provincetown Players (whose playwrights included Michael Gold, the Communist editor of *The New Masses*). It was at Kahn's urging that the Provincetown Players introduced Paul Robeson as a singer in 1925. He was Hart Crane's benefactor, and put up ten thousand dollars to help Upton Sinclair pay for Sergei Eisenstein's ill-fated *Que viva México!* He believed that "art is not the plaything of opulence. It is robust and red-blooded, deep-rooted and universal. It is true equality of opportunity." On another occasion he called art "democracy in its very essence. . . . It is far from being appreciated as yet by our wealthy men that art can be as educational as universities, that it is, or can be made, a strong element for civic betterment." As early as 1919, he favored "a Federal Department of Fine Arts, such as exists in many European countries."[10]

How can this picture of debonair enlightenment be reconciled with Kahn's central role at Gatti's Met? It is known that he unsuccessfully pressed for a production of something by Prokofiev, and that it was he who badgered Gatti into mounting Ernst Krenek's "jazz opera" *Jonny spielt auf*—for three performances. It was Kahn, as well, who among Gatti's American premieres commissioned Howard Hanson's *Merry Mount*, and who offered George Gershwin a five-thousand-dollar bonus if the Met could stage *Porgy and Bess* (Gershwin opted for a Broadway run). But notwithstanding his waxed mustache, silver-headed cane, and castled Long Island estate, he was born Jewish: an outsider to Wall Street colleagues who would not consort with artists and who, as Metropolitan Opera boxholders, had denied Kahn's senior partner, Jacob Schiff, a box at the opera. (Kahn, as board chairman, had Gatti's box at his disposal—when he was finally offered a box of his own, the event was called "notable" by the New York press.)

Whatever the degree of Kahn's artistic influence with Gatti and Ziegler, his major initiative was for something grander than a foreign soprano or an American opera: a new, four-thousand-seat opera house with only thirty boxes. He even purchased the site for one, two blocks west of Carnegie Hall. Not only would the new Met be better equipped than the old; its décor would be conspicuously plain and its terms of ownership would make a statement both financial and social. It was Kahn's intention to diminish the power of the share-owning boxholders. But, in a catch-22, he needed their support in order to do so. He flattered, mollified, and cajoled with practiced charm. He also told the press that "the poor brought more zest and enthusiasm to the theater than the rich."[11] Some boxholders thought him a socialist. By the end of 1928, Kahn had put his new opera house property on the market.

Though, like Henry Higginson, Otto Kahn refutes the stereotype of the banker/philanthropist who puts social prestige first and the bottom line before art, he was tellingly ineffectual insofar as progressive opera for the people was what he sought. Aesthetically immovable, socially aloof, the Met did not inch any closer to Oscar Hammerstein's Manhattan Opera (which Kahn had admired) or to such efforts as the New York City Opera to come. Kahn resigned as chairman in 1931 and died three years later. Gatti, financially strapped and otherwise beleaguered, quit a year after that.

The radio broadcasts and Opera Guild had broadened the base of support. Gatti had trimmed the season and slashed fees and salaries (leading Bodanzky to explode in 1933: "I say it was the artists who saved this distinctly great American institution from going to the wall. The bankers and the backers— why, they quit!").[12] But salvation mainly came in another form, a Nordic *deus ex machina* that, paradoxically, would permit things to remain much the same as they had been: in a time warp.

■ ■ ■

The rescue of the Metropolitan Opera is immortalized in one of the best known of all operatic anecdotes. On January 13, 1935, Artur Bodanzky came rushing into Edward Ziegler's office. "My God, Ned!" he exclaimed. "My God, come hear this woman sing!" He did, and so did Gatti. The woman was Kirsten Flagstad and the opera was *Die Walküre*.

Flagstad possessed an instrument as prodigious, in its way, as Heifetz's violin or Horowitz's piano. It was larger than other soprano voices and more lustrous. It was strong and seamless top to bottom. And Flagstad possessed a gift divine for phrasing and legato. Uniquely hers, as well, was a serene purity of diction and pronunciation (other large female voices distorted vowels to enhance resonance). W. J. Henderson wrote:

> The equality of her scale, the excellence of her attack, the suavity and elegance of her vocal line, the perfection of her phrasing, the exquisite beauty of her mezza voce and her head tones, and her flawless management of crescendo and diminuendo were sources of endless delight to connoisseurs of singing. And the really marvelous freshness of her voice excited constant astonishment. The tones had the limpidity and purity of first youth.[13]

At the Met, the beneficiary of this preternatural phenomenon, beginning in 1935–36, was not the departing Gatti but his successor, the Canadian Edward Johnson. Once a tenor with the company, Johnson knew opera and he knew singers. He was also, in the words of the Met's authorized historian, possessed of a "deep regard for social distinction." And Johnson was necessarily mindful of the Depression and its exigencies. No previous Met administrator had so followed the path of least resistance. "There will be no costly experiments with doubtful outcomes," he announced. "Better to produce standard works with great casts than to experiment at great cost."[14] Like Gatti, he relied on Ziegler to run the house day to day.

Johnson's word was good: for the next fifteen years, there would seldom be more than two new productions per season. Deferred maintenance of the facility was further deferred. As Heinrich Conried had once played his Caruso card, Johnson played Flagstad and watched box office receipts climb accordingly. In 1936–37, nearly four of every ten performances were of Wagner, the highest ratio since Seidl's German seasons. For the 1939 World's Fair, the Met contributed a special run of nine consecutive Wagner shows. The house specialty was *Tristan und Isolde*, and Isolde was the role Flagstad sang 73 times, more than twice as often as any other. Her Tristan was Lauritz Melchior, in *his* signature part, which he sang 128 times at the Met.

As Johnson's was the first Met regime to be copiously documented via radio, it is possible to eavesdrop on the Flagstad/Melchior *Tristan* and actually hear what it sounded like, at least over the airwaves. The elemental impact of Flagstad's instrument, of course, is imperfectly conveyed on the broadcast recordings.* The immensity of her portrait registers, but so does a certain temperamental placidity. Lilli Lehmann, Seidl's Brünnhilde and Isolde, had been illustriously imperious, off stage and on. Olive Fremstad, Lehmann's successor at the Met, used to run at full tilt from the farthest backstage wall in order to make a convincing entrance as the desperate and hallucinatory Sieglinde or the frantically possessed Kundry. Flagstad's art was untouched by the demonic. Isolde's rage and erotic languor were not for her. Rather, the serene amplitude of her Isolde achieves a penetrating breadth. Henderson put it this way: "It is true that she does not clothe herself in thunder and lightning, but it is equally true that she plumbs depths of emotion with a moving eloquence which makes her mistress of every audience."[15]

Melchior is a different kind of artist. Vocally, he dwarfs his successors much as Flagstad does hers. If his tenor lacks the transporting timbre of Flagstad's soprano, it is tireless and immense. Like Flagstad, Melchior is a singer of words; more than Flagstad, he is a gifted vocal actor for whom words, clearly pronounced, are a starting point for expressive coloration and inflection. Deftly, spontaneously, he interacts with his Kurwenal and Marke. When, as on February 6, 1943, the Marke is Alexander Kipnis, the Met's *Tristan* is sung drama of Shakespearean density. But Melchior's chemistry with Flagstad is not apparent. A different conductor, a more monumental conception—like Furtwängler's on his famous 1952 *Tristan* recording with Flagstad and Ludwig Suthaus—could effectively meld this Isolde to the opera's larger scheme. But Bodanzky—once an assistant to Mahler in Vienna, later recommended to Toscanini and the Met by Busoni[16]—is a mercurial Wagner conductor whose

---

* A full collection may be auditioned at the Library of the Performing Arts at New York City's Lincoln Center. Some broadcasts are also available via the Metropolitan Opera Guild. A much larger selection may be purchased abroad.

signature trait is a winged intensity; he shuns Teutonic tonnage as surely as Busoni or Toscanini did. And he favors severe cuts (in *Tristan*, 13 percent of the score) that further accelerate and compress the action. James Gibbons Huneker once wrote of him, "No living conductor has the fiery temperament of Bodanzky save Arturo Toscanini." Of his cuts, Bodanzky said (as Seidl might have), "To give an audience too much is criminally mistaken kindness and a real irreverence to the composer." Though he led several unabridged *Ring* cycles in New York, he considered such "reverence" better suited to Bayreuth. When he died in 1939, Bodanzky was succeeded by the twenty-seven-year-old Erich Leinsdorf, who stayed, on and off, for the next forty-five seasons, and for whom the oceanic surrender of the *Tristan* Liebesnacht was as anathema as were Melchior's increasingly lax rhythms. The Met's fabled *Tristan*, in short, was something less than the sum of its parts. One chronicler of the broadcasts summarizes, "The substance of these [interwar *Tristan*] performances is not really the music itself, but how excitingly it can be dealt with, and how much electricity can be generated from it."[17]

Another celebrated achievement of the Met German wing was *Die Meistersinger* with Friedrich Schorr, of whom Henderson wrote in 1924, "We have seen few finer Sachses than Mr. Schorr's. Perhaps, if we had to testify under oath, we should have to confess that we do not remember a more persuasive one since Emil Fischer's great performance in the old days; though Fischer never sang this music, within our recollection, as Mr. Schorr did yesterday.... Some of his mezza-voce and pianissimo singing yesterday was of astonishing delicacy, purity and finesse."

Judging from the broadcast of February 22, 1936, Bodanzky and the Met served Schorr well. The ardent Walther is the Belgian René Maison; however unremembered, he far eclipses most tenors who would assay this taxing role—it demands lyricism, heft, and stamina in equal measure—in subsequent Met decades. Elisabeth Rethberg is a lustrous Eva. Though at least one of Bodanzky's cuts, silencing Sachs's jealously in the workshop scene, cripples the drama, the vibrancy and plasticity of his leadership carry the day. And in *Siegfried*, with Melchior, Schorr, and Flagstad on January 30, 1937, Bodanzky's supercharged style attains a frenzy of exuberance that clinches the ecstatic self-abnegation of Siegfried and the awakened Brünnhilde. Henry Finck, in 1893, called Siegfried "the grandest role for tenors of the future"[18]—an empty prophecy but for Melchior's single prodigious example.

Equally documenting the interwar Met at its finest is the broadcast of February 12, 1938. Giovanni Martinelli began his Metropolitan Opera career under Toscanini in 1913. Over thirty-two seasons, he graduated from Rodolfo and Faust to heavier roles. In 1936, at the age of fifty-one, he attained Otello, which he had studied or discussed with the librettist, Boito; with Victor Maurel, who created Iago; and with Toscanini, who played in the premiere under Verdi's supervision. More than capping Martinelli's career, Otello became his signature legacy. The 1938 broadcast documents a complete portrayal—as lover, as madman, as penitent murderer—each component of which authenticates the impact of the others. So realistic is Martinelli's choked and debilitated projection of grief at the opera's close that his ability actually to sing "Desdemona!" is nothing short of miraculous.

His Iago, Lawrence Tibbett, was the first and most complete in a line of distinguished American Verdi baritones; unlike Leonard Warren, Robert Merrill, Sherrill Milnes, or Cornell MacNeill, Tibbett is a consummate singing actor (he once appeared in *King Lear* on Broadway). Here, his swarthy baritone is prodigious in scale and yet totally pliable. Rethberg's Desdemona is both opulent and strong. No studio recordings of these three famous Verdians convey the high voltage of this live stage performance, not least because (the broadcast's least-anticipated revelation) of the incandescence of the Met's orchestra and its conductor.

By the time James Levine took over in the 1970s, it was a pardonable assumption that singers at the Met had forever suffered indifferent, dull, or inept support. But Seidl, Mahler, and Toscanini would not have tolerated the sorry playing I remember hearing in the 1960s and 1970s. The orchestra Bodanzky is heard conducting in the 1930s broadcasts lacks the glow of a great Wagner band, but the playing is wonderfully firm and fiery. In Verdi, the same group is an Italian powderkeg. And why not? The membership was overwhelmingly Italian, including a few, such as principal oboist Giacomo Del Campo, who had played under Toscanini before World War I.★ With Toscanini's departure, the Met's Italian wing was entrusted to superior leaders: first Tullio Serafin, then Ettore Panizza. The latter (today not even a name), born in Buenos Aires and trained in Milan, from 1921 to 1931 conducted at La Scala, where Toscanini esteemed him (as did Richard Strauss, who arranged for him to conduct *Elektra* in Vienna). His Met years were 1934–43. Given his extensive European career, which also included Covent Garden, it bears emphasis that he considered the Met's "as fine a theater orchestra as I have seen in the world." He was greeted by Martinelli as an old friend and colleague.[19] In the Met's 1938 *Otello*, it is Panizza who stylistically binds the

---

★ A comparison of Met orchestra rosters for 1914–15 and 1934–35 (as found in the Metropolitan Opera Archives) shows that the earlier orchestra was by far more German than Italian. In 1934–35, however, no fewer than fifty-three of eighty-five musicians on the permanent roster had incontestably Italian names: Mario, Luigi, Ettore, Arturo, etc.—further evidence of the plummeting Germanic influence on American classical music after World War I.

polyglot cast. Compared to Toscanini, he favors a broader play of tempo. But the velocity and precision, the taut filaments of tone, the keen timbres, the clipped, attenuated phrasings are all Toscanini trademarks. Like Toscanini, Panizza will bolt suddenly to the end of a scorching musical sentence; like Toscanini's, his musicians are lightning respondents. And Panizza is a master of controlling the show while showcasing his cast; calibrating Martinelli's titanic climaxes and magisterial breadth of phrase, he achieves a unity. Encountering this memento of times past is a humbling experience.

Tibbett may also be heard in Verdi on January 5, 1935, opposite the Met's other great American star of the twenties and thirties. W. J. Henderson, who knew the Met from day one and tirelessly documented its declining vocal standards, made certain exceptions. Flagstad was one. And, following a period of skeptical resistance, he capitulated, too, to Rosa Ponselle: "one of the most voluptuous dramatic soprano voices that present-day operagoers have heard."[20] In *La traviata*, Ponselle's luscious soprano proves (more than in the studio) a galvanizing vehicle for musical theater. Under Panizza (as under Toscanini), the gambling scene is a Dostoyevsky trauma. The Prelude to act four (also a Toscanini specialty), is (like Ponselle's singing as Violetta) finely drawn, boldly elongated, memorably impassioned; a reading of this caliber today would stop the show.

Though on other occasions, as documented by broadcasts and reviews, lack of rehearsal and lesser conductors told, such evidence proves that the post-Toscanini Met, however antiquarian, could rise above its essential identity as a singer's house. By 1940, however, Martinelli and Schorr were weakened by age, and Tibbett by drink. Flagstad was in Norway. Melchior, who begged to sing Canio and Otello, was foolishly told he could not. Ponselle had retired. An abundance of fresh vocal talent materialized, but the institutional momentum continued its long-term retard.

One positive Johnson priority—amid the penny-pinching and belt-tightening—was Americanizing the vocal roster. Events conspired to make this not only possible, but necessary. Lower fees cost him some of his high-priced foreign talent, most notably Beniamino Gigli. The war curtailed transatlantic transportation. And the Met's Depression deficits pressured the house to be less aloof, elitist, and Eurocentric. The incapacity or unwillingness of the boxholder/shareholders to "save the Met" underlined a process of reorganization leading, in 1940, to the shareholders' agreement to sell the Metropolitan Opera House for nearly two million dollars to the nonprofit opera-producing body: the Metropolitan Opera Association. One major player in the transition, the Juilliard Foundation, insisted that the company do more to find and nurture American talent. To this end, a special spring season was attempted—resulting in the discovery of Helen Traubel, a grassroots Wagner soprano of world-class vocal heft and security (and heard to full advantage not with Leinsdorf at the Met, but as partnered in 1940 in three *Wesendonck Lieder* by Leopold Stokowski and the Philadelphia Orchestra: a golden lava flow worthy of Flagstad and Furtwängler). The Metropolitan Opera Auditions of the Air, begun in 1937, uncovered Leonard Warren, Mack Harrell, Eleanor Steber, Robert Merrill, and Regina Resnik. And there were Risë Stevens, Astrid Varnay, Richard Tucker, Jan Peerce, Jerome Hines, Grace Moore, Gladys Swarthout, Richard Crooks, Rose Bampton, Dorothy Kirsten—an endless list of prominent young singers American-born and (for the most part) -trained.

The pertinent lineage extended backward to Ponselle and Tibbett, Louise Homer and Geraldine Farrar, Lillian Nordica and Emma Eames. Never before, however, was the Met so overrun with native talent. And yet Johnson not only abandoned Gatti's futile search for durable American operas, but only sporadically supported opera in English (for a variety of works ranging from the well known—*Falstaff, Fidelio, Hansel and Gretel, The Magic Flute*—to the less familiar—*The Bartered Bride, The Golden Cockerell, The Abduction from the Seraglio, Khovantschina*). Tibbett, a sheriff's son from Bakersfield, California, who discovered music in the local Methodist church, theorized that the "genuine American singer" was characterized by "greater directness and simplicity," "honesty and sincerity of purpose." To the American artist he said, "Be yourself! Stop posing! Appreciate the things that are at your doorstep!" These were not exactly singular New World attributes. And Tibbett was in any event a special case. The American bass Basil Ruysdael, whom Tibbett credited for making him an "honest baritone," gave Tibbett "the best advice I ever had": that "singing is just speaking words to music." He disabused Tibbett of the "sham and strut" of such "high-class" English locutions as "wined" (*wind*), "kees" (*kiss*), "ahn-da" (*and*). Tibbett became a passionate exponent of singing in English. He even offered Schubert Lieder in translation. His recital repertoire included "Shortnin' Bread" and "I Got Plenty o' Nuttin'." His Met triumphs significantly included Louis Gruenberg's *The Emperor Jones*, Howard Hanson's *Merry Mount*, and Deems Taylor's *Peter Ibbetson*—operas whose ephemeral success was due exclusively to Tibbett's communicative flair singing in his native tongue for an appreciative native audience.[21]

In fact, Tibbett notwithstanding, there was no "American school" of vocal performance comparable to the French, Italian, German, or Russian, tangibly grounded in style rather than elusive "simplicity" or "sincerity." That would have required what Krehbiel had said: English as "the language of the performances," and "native talent" furnishing "both works and interpreters." That few "Johnson babies" established major European careers was not just an accident of wartime or limited ambition. For the most part, they sounded denatured in comparison to their finest European counterparts.

There were exceptions, both relative and absolute. Warren possessed an instrument unique in the world, a big, velvety baritone with a clarion high extension a tenor might envy. He had won a Met contract having amassed a repertoire of five arias and "an inkling" of *Rigoletto*. A fastidious perfectionist, he grew slowly but steadily. Midway through the 1959–60 season, he was showing alarming signs of stress. Rehearsing *Simon Boccanegra*, he exploded at Dimitri Mitropoulos, whose slow tempos violated what he had absorbed from revered teachers—including Panizza, with whom he first sang Boccanegra (and other roles new to him) in Buenos Aires in the forties. On March 4, singing Don Carlo in *La forza del destino*, he suddenly pitched forward and died. He was forty-eight years old.

Tucker's lyric tenor, indefatigable and voluminous, was of a caliber in short supply abroad. Like Caruso's and Martinelli's, it gradually darkened, accommodating heavier roles. Like Peerce's, its foundation in cantorial chant yielded a distinctive and flavorful timbre and a style of attack compatible with Italianate abandon. Like Warren, Tucker began "outside" opera and worked his way in.

Steber seemed a singer who could plunge directly into any music—Mozart, Wagner, Verdi, Richard Rodgers—with spontaneous ardor and authority: an artist born, not made. Tibbetts's hackneyed definition of "American" singing, overturning Old World artifice, actually fits her special case. On *The Voice of Firestone* she is the rare opera singer who remains telegenic no matter how closely scrutinized by the camera's eye. Under Johnson, her many and varied assignments included the Marschallin (her first) in *Der Rosenkavalier* for the opening night of 1949–50. But she was disserved by Johnson's successor, Rudolf Bing. Varnay and Resnik, special artists, likewise fell victim to Bing's European bias.

If World War II quarantined foreign singers, it paradoxically furnished foreign conductors: Johnson encountered a buyer's market of eminent refugees. For whatever reason he failed to secure the two most tantalizing candidates: Erich Kleiber and Otto Klemperer, both of whom appreciated twentieth-century works that would have refreshed the Met's parochial repertoire and given its customers something to think about. But Johnson did engage Thomas Beecham, Fritz Busch, George Szell,* and Bruno Walter.

---

* Herbert Witherspoon, poised to succeed Gatti in 1935, had contracted Szell for fourteen weeks. Witherspoon's sudden death propelled Johnson into the top job. Johnson nixed the Szell agreement in favor of the less expensive, less demanding Gennaro Papi, whom Gatti had dropped in 1926. See Martin Mayer, *The Met: One Hundred Years of Grand Opera* (New York, Simon and Schuster, 1983), p. 208.

Among the most acclaimed achievements of the Johnson regime, to which Walter, Busch, Szell, and Steber significantly contributed, was a Mozart revival featuring *The Marriage of Figaro*, which had mainly languished since Mahler's momentous productions; *The Magic Flute*, which had been mounted only once since 1917; *The Abduction from the Seraglio*, which was given for the first time in 1946; and *Don Giovanni*, which furnished an irresistible vehicle for Ezio Pinza, as on the broadcast of March 7, 1942. The starry cast also includes Alexander Kipnis as Leporello, Jarmila Novotna as Donna Elvira, and Bidú Saÿao as Zerlina. And there are three Americans: Charles Kullman as Ottavio, Mack Harrell as Massetto, and Norman Cordon as the Commendatore. Walter is in the pit. On this distinguished occasion, Pinza and Kipnis go for broke: their patter is manic in intensity and velocity. They impel one another toward peak performances: Leporello is here not a comic foil but a formidable goad (his "imitation" of Pinza, under Elvira's balcony, is a wobbly caricature both hilarious and provocative); Pinza is demonic in his seductiveness. Novotna and Saÿao are (as always) distinctive vocal personalities. The Americans are relatively faceless yet hold their own. Walter is a strong motivator, pressing for warmth and drama. At the same time, this is a powerful performance fraying at the edges. There is no binding "Mozart style." The orchestra is untidy. Each new tempo seems a surprise. A polyglot *Magic Flute* the following season, on December 26, 1942, fractures altogether. Only a star turn by Pinza, as Sarastro, retains interest. Orchestra and ensemble, again under Walter, are scrappy. This nonperformance, while by no means representative, is symptomatic of failing leadership at the top.

There was a final infusion of energy when Fritz Reiner appeared in 1949–50 to conduct *Falstaff*, *Figaro*, *Der Rosenkavalier*, and, most famously, *Salome* with Ljuba Welitsch. By then, Bing was already on the premises, readying his stiff broom. Most of the stage settings were twenty to forty years old. Lighting was primitive. Stage direction was all but nonexistent. For the chorus, stock gesticulation was the rule. Solo artists fended for themselves. Notwithstanding the intermittent appearance of a Walter or Reiner, the absence of sustained musical leadership—post-Panizza, post-Bodanzky—was crippling. Though Britten's *Peter Grimes* was given twelves times in 1948 and 1949 (following its 1946 American premiere at Tanglewood), Johnson's Met remained innocent of Berg, Stravinsky, Prokofiev, and Shostakovich. No Janáček was mounted subsequent to Gatti's stab at *Jenufa*. This was the American culture of performance unmediated by contemporary creative input— not even Toscanini's New York Philharmonic or NBC Symphony seemed as fundamentally a museum of venerable foreign artifacts.

And Toscanini himself was, of course, a neighbor to the Johnson Met; his most American years, the period of his residence in Riverdale, coincided with the extinguishing of his Metropolitan Opera legacy as upheld via Panizza, via Martinelli and other older singers, and via old-timers in the pit. True, Erich Leinsdorf—another irony—had been Toscanini's assistant at Salzburg. But Toscanini—a final irony—had recommended to Johnson someone better to take Bodanzky's place: William Steinberg, later the distinguished music director of the Pittsburgh and Boston Symphonies.[22] With the NBC Symphony, Toscanini gave concert performances of *Fidelio, La Traviata, A Masked Ball, Aïda, Otello, Falstaff,* and *La bohème* featuring disappointing casts, phenomenal symphonic support, and a style of leadership that tyrannized all but the fittest survivors of his whiplash tempos. Absent the likes of Martinelli, Tibbett, Ponselle, Schorr, Kipnis, or Pinza, he drew the frame but neglected the picture. Johnson's Met, ultimately, had the singers but not enough of anything else: the picture without the frame.

■ ■ ■

To realize why opera has never really taken root here, why its audience is one-twentieth of what it should be, and why so few American composers have written grand operas, try to imagine the state of the American theatre today if it had faced the conditions under which its sister art has had to struggle. Suppose that, fifty years ago, a group of public-spirited New Yorkers had built a magnificent theatre and installed therein a company of first-rank actors, prepared to give the finest plays written. For fifty years, then, this company has been presenting the works of Moliere, Racine, Rostand, Hauptmann, Sudermann, Schiller, Goldoni, Ibsen, Shakespeare, and other playwrights. None of these plays, however, has been done in English. The French plays have been played in French, the German ones in German, Ibsen in Norwegian, Dostoyevsky and Tchekoff in French or Italian—never English—translations. The company, which at first was entirely European, is now about one-third American. Most of these American actors have received their training in Europe, and know their roles only in foreign tongues; for even Shakespeare, in this imaginary theatre, is played in Italian.

This simplistic yet telling 1937 thought experiment by Deems Taylor was conceived to explain why Americans "have imported opera much as we import caviar and Scotch grouse—as something rare, exotic, and expensive," why opera "means very little in the life of the average American, much less than the symphony orchestra and infinitely less than the theater and the movies." "The average French, Italian, German, or Austrian not only goes to the opera regularly," Taylor continued, "but is even willing to have part of his taxes go toward its support. . . . Has it never struck you as worthy of note that Tony, your barber, who knows and likes all the latest jazz, also knows several opera scores almost by heart?"[23]

More than a generation after Henry Krehbiel complained that opera in American was "an exotic," nothing had changed. Taylor predicted that with the Depression, and hard times for all, opera would have to find a large public or die. His prescription—English-language opera with fresh translations and first-rate native talent—proved as old, and as irrelevant, as Jeannette Thurber's calamitous American Opera Company of 1885. And yet opera in America survived.

The onetime opera madness of pocket-sized opera houses and flourishing frontier outposts was mainly a memory. The Met, however, remained a national company. In its early barnstorming days, it gave as many as 100 tour perform-ances a season; in 1909–10, locked in competition with Oscar Hammerstein, there were 163 performances on the road in sixteen cities.★ Around 1920, the schedule contracted to as few as 33 performances in three cities, and expanded thereafter to as many as 60 performances in ten cities. After World War II, the tour schedule peaked in 1947–48 with 70 performances in seventeen cities, including for the first time Denver, Lincoln, Los Angeles, and Richmond. By the 1950s, a Met national tour might include a troupe of 325, scenery for 16 operas, 400 trunks and 150 musical instruments, all in two special passenger trains with nineteen sleepers, plus a baggage train of twenty-nine cars.[24] Atlanta, a regular stop since 1920, was the operatic outpost with the longest tra-dition and the most famous parties. Dallas, beginning in 1939, vied with Atlanta for lavish hospitality: every member of the company was invited to an annual opening-night gala. Cleveland, with its nine-thousand-seat Public Auditorium, had the largest "opera house," dictating exceptional regional outreach, until Toronto appropriated a twelve-thousand-seat sports arena for *Aïda*, *La bohème*, *Carmen*, and *Rigoletto* in 1952. Met stars also enjoyed a mass audience via radio—the weekly Saturday broadcasts—and even cinema. During the thirties, musical films were a favorite escape. *One Night of Love* (1933), a prototype, made the Met's Grace Moore Hollywood's second biggest draw. She was also voted one of the "ten most beautiful women in the world." Five other Moore pictures followed, powering an international concert and opera career beyond the merits of her bland soprano. Lawrence Tibbett, Lily Pons, Gladys Swarthout, and Risë Stevens also notably starred in the movies.

★ All Met tour statistics count Brooklyn as a "city" distinct from New York.

Meanwhile, Hammerstein-style opera made headway in Chicago, where Hammerstein's footprints were evident. After the 1910 pact that bought him out and banned him, his Manhattan Opera sets and costumes, and many of his artists, wound up in the new Philadelphia-Chicago Grand Opera Company. Along with the Met and Henry Russell's enterprising Boston Opera, it was to comprise a Gatti/Kahn opera cartel ending the cut-throat rivalry that had destroyed Hammerstein and overtaxed the Met. Top singers were peacefully shared. The Philadelphia-Chicago company was even allotted certain New York visits. But opera in Philadelphia failed to take hold, the Boston Opera (as we have seen) died in 1915, and the Chicago component went its own way, led by Hammerstein's ace conductor, Cleofonte Campanini, and his one-of-a-kind diva, Mary Garden.

Though Hammerstein was out of the picture, his maverick spirit lingered. Campanini, a musician of indefatigable diligence and high temper, was possessed by a hatred for the Met. Garden was possessed by something rarer. Born in Scotland, raised in Chicago, introduced and seasoned in France, she applied her modest soprano with fabled nerve. W. J. Henderson called her "the Queen of Parlando." He wrote of her Louise, "She rushes about the scale with extraordinary activity and inaccuracy, scrambles nimbly to the top of the treble clef, slides recklessly down to the bottom again and brings up all standing in a final cadence and key of her own." But he also wrote of Garden that she was "one of the most ingenious women now before the public. She has inexhaustible theatrical resources, a marvelous command of the pictorial lights and shadows of the stage, a profound grasp of the illuminative quality of footlights." She arrived in Chicago, whose operatic affairs she would dominate for the next twenty years, with a French accent, a French maid, a valet, a monocle, and a diamond ring from a Turkish pasha to whom she was supposedly engaged. Her showcase parts in the inaugural season included her greatest creation: Debussy's lethal ingénue, Mélisande. As Massenet's Thaïs, which she played in a pale pink crepe dress that clung to her flesh, she was, wrote Henderson, "a living picture of physical attraction. . . . She has the sinosity of a serpent of old Nile." As Strauss's Salome, she climaxed the Dance of the Seven Veils by bearing aloft the head of John the Baptist, then swiftly kissing it and, sated, falling upon it. This, sung in French, was the Chicago premiere of the most notorious of modern operas. Attacked by police and clergy, it closed after two performances. (Hammerstein, in New York, suggested "toning down" the work by administering a shave and haircut to the severed head.)[25]

A case can be made—and John Diziges, in his *Opera in America*, has made it—that the Chicago Opera surpassed the Met in the 1920s. For one thing, between 1910 and 1929, with a season running from nearly November to late

January, "it became the first large-scale, *national* American opera company by virtue of its lengthy, sustained, geographically wide-ranging tours," logging 216 New York appearances plus 1,009 performances in sixty-two cities as remote as Rochester, Helena, Joplin, Salt Lake, Spokane, and San Diego. Chicago presented some of the Met's top artists, including Nordica, Farrar, Fremstad, and Melba. But, like the Boston Opera, it also inherited some of Hammerstein's biggest stars: in addition to Garden, Luisa Tetrazzini (who happened to be Campanini's sister-in-law) and the Frenchmen Charles Dalmorès and Maurice Renaud. Vanni Marcoux (whom we have encountered scandalizing the locals in Boston opposite Garden's reclining Tosca), Conchita Supervia, and Mariano Stabile were important Chicago singers who never appeared with the Met. Amelita Galli-Curci, Alexander Kipnis, Titta Ruffo, and Tito Schipa were important singers Chicago got to first. Edith Mason was an important American soprano who succeeded Garden as Chicago's enchanting prima donna. Like the Met, Chicago fruitlessly sought the "first great American opera." Mounting in 1911 Victor Herbert's *Natoma* with Garden as an Indian maiden (as also in Philadelphia), the company at least managed to test a new American grand opera by a practiced theater composer. Wolf-Ferrari's *The Jewels of the Madonna* was a 1912 American premiere (with twenty-seven rehearsals) so successful it stayed in the Chicago repertoire for many years. The company's most remarkable world premiere was of a bravely commissioned work by a major composer Kahn tried and failed to present at the Met: Serge Prokofiev. His *Love for Three Oranges*, which he also conducted, was performed on December 30, 1921. The production (in French), costing one hundred thousand dollars, was described in the *New Republic*: "Rose and scarlet, orange and purple, sapphire and gold, backdrops of wild sunset skies, foregrounds of burlesque court furnishings, deserts, mountains, and witches' caverns, all are beautiful beyond reality, and all share the happy overemphasis of the whole production. . . . No stage sets have ever been more beautiful or more daring than these." A third performance, on tour in New York, was pelted by the press. "It was," wrote Prokofiev, "as though a pack of dogs had broken loose and were tearing my trousers to shreds." But, more than any opera first performed by the Met except for *La fanciulla del west* and *Gianni Schicchi*, *The Love for Three Oranges* has endured.[26]

What made it all affordable was the zeal of Harold Fowler McCormick, heir to a farm machinery fortune, and of his wife, *née* Edith Rockefeller, whose father John D. was the richest man in the world. Diziges calls them "the most generous of individual American patrons of opera." It was Harold McCormick who bought out shareholders who were not Chicagoans and made the Chicago Opera independent. The company's first decade sailed

boldly until Campanini's sudden death of pneumonia in 1919. His funeral—
recalling Seidl's in New York twenty-one years before—was a wrenching
public occasion. Lit by candles, framed by masses of flowers and by a
cathedral-like *Parsifal* set, the coffin rested onstage in the vast Auditorium. In
1921, Garden was named Campanini's successor. Invoking Hammerstein, she
vowed to produce "the finest or nothing at all." This was the season of the
Three Oranges (which Campanini had commissioned). It was also the season
that eminent singers were engaged from far away for a single performance,
that others were paid who did not sing at all, that a deficit of one million dollars was greeted by the "Directa" with the comment, "It was news to me. It
may very well have happened, but I didn't know. I do know that we finished
in the way Mr. McCormick wanted us to finish—in a blaze of glory. . . . If it
cost a million dollars, I'm sure it was worth it."[27]

Garden resigned—according to her memoirs, she had agreed to run the
company "for one year only"[28]—but remained. Harold McCormick made up
the deficit, but for the last time. The Chicago Opera became the Chicago
Civic Opera under a new and different Maecenas. Samuel Insull, born in London, came to the United States at the age of twenty-one to work for Thomas
Edison. In Chicago, he amassed a fortune as a utilities magnate. His self-made
style and self-made wealth clashed with the McCormicks and their like. A
populist titan, he has been recalled as "the Babe Ruth, the Jack Dempsey, the
Red Grange of the business world." Insull resolved to run the Civic Opera like
a business, which in his view meant democratizing the support base and cut-
ting back on what did not draw. Garden visited his office to object and there
discovered an enormous painting not of herself but of Adelina Patti. Insull
explained, "Miss Garden, I hate modern opera. I like the old things."

With its new, safer repertoire, the company now embraced the star system
without apology, and Garden remained the one star for whom new and
exotic operas were mounted. The quality of the stagings initially declined but
was rescued with the appointment of a permanent stage manager, Charles
Moor, whose supervision of *Aïda* caused one critic to observe that for the first
time the triumphal scene included no supernumeraries wearing eyeglasses:
"Up to that time many years' attendance upon *Aïda* had firmly convinced me
that opticians drove a thriving trade in ancient Egypt." But the new Chicago
opera was not the popular success the old one had been. Chicagoans seemed
bored by it. Insull, meanwhile, was consumed by a "stupendous dream." As
had the Chicago Orchestra in 1905, the Civic Opera would desert Louis Sullivan's Auditorium for a home of its own. Vowing to "take the high hat out of
grand opera," Insull envisioned a modern and democratic opera house, luxurious but not glamorous. He built a forty-two-story skyscraper symmetrically

flanked by protruding lower towers; it became known as Insull's Throne. The auditorium, with 3,471 seats, hid its thirty-one boxes unobtrusively in the rear; Garden called it a "long black hole," a "convention hall." Its inauguration, with *Aïda* on November 4, 1929, coincided with Wall Street's collapse. The company marched on with its astonishing parade of singers: Garden, Kipnis, Schipa, Vanni-Marcoux, Frieda Leider, Lotte Lehmann, Claudia Muzio. By 1932, Insull could no longer weather the Depression. The Civic Opera abruptly closed. Insull died a broken man in Paris six years later. Chicago would not again acquire an enduring opera company until the 1950s.[29]

■ ■ ■

The relative insignificance of opera in Chicago during the thirties and forties was the interwar norm outside of New York. In Boston, no permanent full-time company ever took the place of Russell's Boston Opera. The Chicago Opera visited from 1917 to 1932; the Met was an annual visitor except between 1912 and 1934. In Philadelphia, a Hammerstein company and the Philadelphia-Chicago Opera, both short-lived, furnished more big-league opera than the city could absorb during the decade before World War I. There was also an extraordinary season, 1934–35, during which the Philadelphia Orchestra, following Rodzinski's lead in Cleveland, presented staged operas as part of its regular subscription series. Fritz Reiner conducted *Falstaff* and *The Marriage of Figaro*, both in English translation, plus *Tristan und Isolde* (uncut), *Die Meistersinger*, and *Der Rosenkavalier*. Alexander Smallens led Gluck's *Iphigénie in Aulide, The Barber of Seville, Carmen, Boris Godunov*, Shostakovich's *Lady Macbeth*, and—a double bill—*Hansel and Gretel* and Stravinsky's *Mavra*. The casts included Lotte Lehmann, Friedrich Schorr, and Elisabeth Schumann. Herbert Graf, obtained to supervise the stagings, installed a revolving stage at the Academy of Music. In *Rosenkavalier*, act three, he used it to remove the intimate final trio to a garden. Carmen was able to seduce Don José in a bedroom rather than the public tavern in which Bizet's second act begins and closes. For *Tristan* Reiner engaged a premier American scenic designer, Donald Oenslager. In his memoirs, Boris Goldovsky—once Reiner's assistant—recollected Oenslager's act-one ship as memorably dramatic, yet eclipsed by the breathtakingly stylized set provided for *Iphigénie* by Broadway's Norman Bel Geddes: "an enormous conic structure with outjutting platforms spiraling up toward an altarlike summit," precisely illuminated by "hundreds of electric lamps and instruments." Of Reiner, Goldovsky recollected the singularity of his cruelty and his mastery.[30] The Philadelphia Orchestra's opera venture, which might have goaded or instructed Gatti's Met, lost over two hundred thousand dollars[31] and was never again attempted. Reiner, marooned at Curtis, aspired to succeed Stokowski; instead, he would continue his spotty post-Pittsburgh career until landing in Chicago in 1953.

The one city outside New York in which an opera company of stature endured was San Francisco. From 1848, when the gold rush created a boom town, it was a city with wealth that needed spending and workers—many of them Italian or German—who needed entertainment. High fees attracted professional musicians, including pianists, conductors, and divas. We have already glimpsed the saloon keeper Tom Maguire, who wore diamonds, built opera houses, and by 1880 went broke. More modest, more permanent, was the Tivoli Opera House, whose resident company specialized in operetta (Offenbach, Gilbert and Sullivan, von Suppé, Johann Strauss) but did not neglect Verdi and even mounted *Fidelio* and *Lohengrin*. In fact, between 1851, when a touring troupe offered *La sonnambula*, and 1906, when the earthquake hit, San Francisco hosted nearly five thousand operatic performances in twenty-six different theaters. (It also had a "Germania Society" offering respectable orchestral performances, with about thirty players, by 1856.)[32]

Today's San Francisco Opera was founded by Gaetano Merola. Born and trained in Naples, he was colorful, democratic, and unpredictable—and so it should come as no surprise that he was once Oscar Hammerstein's choral director, then one of his conductors, both in New York and, in an unsuccessful 1910 venture, in London. He called San Francisco—with its bay, its Mount Tamalpais, its opera-loving Italians—"my other Italy." Shortly after settling there, in 1921, he was invited to a Stanford University football game in Palo Alto. What impressed him was the halftime band. He envisioned an outdoor summer opera season and followed his dream. Two years later, he conducted *Pagliacci*, *Carmen*, and *Faust* at the Stanford stadium. The singers included Giovanni Martinelli in all three works. Thirty thousand attended. Merola lost his shirt but wanted more. Both instinct and personality spurred him to seek the broadest possible backing. The founders of his San Francisco Opera, in 1923, numbered two thousand.

In Chicago, Samuel Insull's new opera house would register the size of Insull's ego. In New York, Otto Kahn's plan for a new opera house was partly a putsch against the Met's boxholders. In San Francisco, the need for a new opera house was simpler: the Civic Auditorium was wholly inadequate. Tellingly, the War Memorial Opera House, opened in 1932, was (and is) municipally owned and maintained. Its décor is reasonably glamorous but not gaudy. Its thirty-two-hundred-seat capacity, though huge by sensible European standards, is smaller than the old or new Met, fostering greater intimacy and a less stratified audience.

With an early fall season of three or four crowded weeks, Merola was able to avail himself of Met singers before they were needed in New York. Casts and repertoire were comparable to the Met. At first, the operas were mainly Italian. In 1935, Merola presented his first *Ring*, with Flagstad, Rethberg, Melchior, and Schorr; Bodanzky conducted. The remaining works were *Aïda* (with Rethberg, Martinelli, Pinza, and Nelson Eddy as Amonasro), *Martha* (Schipa and Helen Jepson), *La Juive* (Rethberg, Martinelli, Pinza), *Werther* (Schipa), *The Barber of Seville* (Schipa, Pinza, Richard Bonelli), *La bohème* (Jepson, Martinelli, Bonelli, Pinza), *Rigoletto* (Schipa, Bonelli, Pinza), and a double bill of *Suor Angelica* and *Le Coq d'Or*. The next season, *Tristan*, *Götterdämmerung*, and *Die Walküre* were led by Fritz Reiner. In 1944 Merola secured a conductor Toscanini had once recommended to Edward Johnson: William Steinberg. More often, top conductors were not a priority, and Merola, who himself often conducted, cared little how the operas looked. His economizing helped the company weather the Depression. By the time he died in 1953, the San Francisco Opera had become a Bay Area fixture—it felt local, not (like the singers) borrowed.

If Merola was no Hammerstein, San Francisco was not New York, and, unlike Chicago, Boston, or Philadelphia, it did not try to be. Its youth, its frontier origins, its remoteness from northeastern arts businessmen (especially in the decades before air travel replaced boats and railroads) all contributed to an indigenous cultural identity. San Franciscans not only voted public funds for an opera house; they also set aside a fraction of their taxes for the San Francisco Symphony. They supported their own ballet. They appreciated West Coast artists and were quickly wary of inferior East Coast goods. Their local loyalties could lose perspective (witness the too long Symphony tenure of Enrique Jordá). But San Francisco pride more than compensated for San Francisco chauvinism.

In 1952 Cecil Smith of *Musical America*, an observer of long experience, assessed the nation's musical health. Pondering San Francisco, he worried about the future of the Symphony in the wake of Pierre Monteux's recent departure. Of the Opera he wrote that Merola "has come to think of his performances too much as showcases for Metropolitan talent, and he puts up more readily than he should with the offhand attitude of stars who drop in by plane for a few days." But Smith nonetheless judged San Francisco "in many ways the model musical city in the country," resistant to pervasive homogenizing tendencies. And he called its audiences the nation's healthiest. "A more spontaneous individualism of taste is evident than in Philadelphia or Chicago. . . . Every San Francisco audience is a general audience, containing within it representatives of all the elements that make New York audiences such separatist affairs. It is a truly democratic audience, because it is not dominated by the social upper crust." By the 1970s, San Francisco's history of feisty musical independence would thrust its Symphony into a national leadership role. And the Opera would ripen impressively, if with less originality, under Merola's formidable successor, Kurt Herbert Adler.[33]

As for the long-deferred dream of a genuine people's opera, absent every symptom of snobbery and privilege, something finally materialized back East. Its catalyst was the Works Progress Administration (WPA), the New Deal's federal jobs program, established in 1935. Federally funded work relief in the arts supported the populist murals of Thomas Hart Benton, the compassionate documentary films of Pare Lorentz (scored by Virgil Thomson), and Orson Welles's crusading Mercury Theater productions (of which *Macbeth*, set in Haiti with a black cast, also used music by Thomson). The mandate of the Federal Music Project was "to give such cultural values to communities that a new interest in music would be engendered and the audience base expanded." The WPA maintained 28 symphony orchestras, including the pathbreaking Illinois Symphony we have encountered in Chicago. All told, its various ensembles offered 225,000 performances for 150 million people until it reverted to state control in 1939. It also supported composers and 250 music-teaching centers.[34]

In the realm of music theater, the WPA's most famous success was illegal. Marc Blitzstein's "play with music," *The Cradle Will Rock*, was an inspired American equivalent of Kurt Weill's *Dreigroschenoper*, treating industrial unrest with the same schematic briskness and bite. Its defiant tone was memorably doubled when the Federal Theater, having commissioned a first production from John Houseman and Orson Welles, was forced by a political firestorm to "postpone" the premiere. The locked-out audience walked or rode twenty-one blocks to another theater, where Blitzstein, alone onstage with piano, began a one-man performance, only to discover that many in the cast were in fact in the house, ready to sing their parts from the front rows. The WPA opera program offered nothing this controversial. Its big hit was a *Swing Mikado* with an African-American cast. Opera in English and opera in concert were also given in abundance.

In the spirit of Federal Project No. 1, New York City's Mayor Fiorello La Guardia, whose father had been an accompanist to Adelina Patti, helped to establish a High School for Music and Art, a Municipal Arts Committee, and a nonprofit corporation with responsibility for a City Center of Music and Drama. In 1944, the City Center's twenty-seven-hundred-seat auditorium—the Mecca Temple on West Fifty-sixth Street—became the home of a New York City Opera. By 1950, the City Opera had been joined by the New York

City Theater (which did not last) and by George Balanchine's New York City Ballet (which illustriously thrived).

Laszlo Halasz, the City Opera's first director, discarded the grand museum model. His singers were young Americans. His repertoire, increasingly adventurous, included *Ariadne auf Naxos, Bluebeard's Castle, Eugene Onegin*, and the Americans Jerome Kern, Gian Carlo Menotti, and William Grant Still. He also managed to mount *Aïda, Die Meistersinger, Der Rosenkavalier*, and *Turandot* on his shallow stage. He moved cautiously into English-language opera, with translations of *The Marriage of Figaro, The Love for Three Oranges*, and Wolf-Ferrari's *The Four Rustics*. As of 1950, the City Opera season totaled ninety-two performances. Its top ticket price was five dollars. The plainness of its auditorium, the bare utility of its lobbies, complemented its mission. In less than a decade, it had eclipsed Edward Johnson's Met in the finish of its stagings and the intellectual distinction of its mandate. Though Halasz was dismissed in a dispute with his board in 1951, his successors, Joseph Rosenstock and (briefly and unhappily) Erich Leinsdorf, oversaw a repertoire boldly incorporating Berg (*Wozzeck* in English), Blitzstein, Copland (*The Tender Land*, a premiere), Frank Martin, Gottfried von Einem, and William Walton.[35] The company would weather further vicissitudes and, as a paradoxical outcome of its growth, a dangerous flirtation with glamour. Its sponsorship of American opera, and opera in English, came too late in the day to make good Krehbiel's prediction of an American school of works and performers, and the Met, in any case, paid no attention. But the City Opera overthrew the culture of performance: as surely as the opera madness of the nineteenth century, it demonstrated that opera in the United States need not be "an exotic."

■ ■ ■

We have now completed the bulk of our survey of the twentieth-century culture of performance: orchestras and conductors, solo instrumentalists, singers and opera houses supremely esteemed by audiences, observers, and participants alike. Olin Downes, in the *New York Times*, was not alone in juxtaposing New World vitality with Old World "decadence" and "decay." Before World War I, Henderson and Krehbiel were already impatient with European ignorance of American institutions of musical performance. Such cultural patriotism was intensified by two ghastly wars on European soil, both of which required American rescue efforts. The boastfulness of American classical music—undeniably one of its striking attributes in the twenties, thirties, and forties—registered, as well, a prolonged condition of cultural adolescence also undeniable.

Not just callow popularizers but experienced musicians supported impressions of American superiority. More than jingoism must have impelled Frederick Stock to tell a Chicago newspaper in 1924 that "opera and symphony" were "maintained on a higher standard" in the United States than in Europe. By 1950, the onetime American preference for music study in Germany or France was ended by Hitler and by a plethora of American-based models and mentors. Gary Graffman, speaking for the Outstanding Young American Pianists, savored a "glorious panoply of performers . . . in residence"; in his 1981 memoirs, he gratefully listed Busch, Elman, Heifetz, Hofmann, Horowitz, Koussevitzky, Kreisler, Landowska, Milstein, Monteux, Ormandy, Piatigorsky, Rachmaninoff, Reiner, Rubinstein, Schnabel, Serkin, Stokowski, Szigeti, Toscanini, and Walter.[36]

Unquestionably, European and Russian wars and revolutions supplied the United States with an astonishing range and caliber of imported talent, an infusion nearly as polyglot as America itself. German, French, and Russian orchestras, with their nationally based repertoires and styles, did not attempt the superb versatility of the orchestras of Boston, New York, and Philadelphia—and Chicago, Cincinnati, Cleveland, Los Angeles, Minneapolis, Pittsburgh, and San Francisco. And European orchestras generally did not cultivate the polish and virtuosity demanded by a Toscanini, Koussevitzky, Stokowski, Reiner, or Szell. No European opera house offered such a cosmopolitan range of artists and works as did the companies of New York and Chicago. No European musical capital as regularly presented such an international roster of virtuosos as did the largest American cities. Furtwängler's secretary Berta Geissmar discovered in 1920s New York "such a galaxy of musical genius and brilliance . . . as I have never seen elsewhere."[37] What is more, by the thirties and forties the majority of the leading conductors, instrumentalists, and singers of New York, Boston, Philadelphia, and Chicago rarely if ever appeared abroad.

The most obvious shortcoming of the culture of performance was its tendency to treat performance as an end in itself. After World War I, classical music in the United States was less nourished than before by the creative act, by a living contemporary repertoire that might have freshened and renewed what otherwise would ultimately become a tired and tiring museum exercise. The absence of a national school bore as directly on the act of performance—on its disembodiment—as on composition. At the Met, a great Italian Don Giovanni could match wits with a great Russian Leporello. But this something gained was also something lost. To hear a gifted Italian ensemble in Verdi's *Falstaff*—as in Toscanini's unsurpassed 1937 Salzburg festival performances, broadcast (and hence recorded) with a frontline La Scala cast—is to

encounter a unity of style as unlikely at the Met as Pinza alongside Kipnis—
or Martinelli with Tibbett, or Tibbett with Ponselle, or Kipnis with Mel-
choir—were unlikely in Milan, Berlin, or Vienna.

Quite possibly no 1940s European house had a Don Giovanni to match
Pinza, an Otello equal to Martinelli, a Tristan or Isolde as vocally resplendent
as Melchior or Flagstad. But the superiority of American-based performing
talent, while truly amazing, could overamaze. Harold Schonberg, who as chief
music critic of the *New York Times* (1960–80) guarded Horowitz's reputation as
the one and only, wrote, "Nobody plays Scriabin better than Mr. Horowitz.
[He possesses] complete affinity with [this] strange, mysterious world." And
Schonberg called Koussevitzky "the most important of all Russian conductors, and still the greatest." But by the 1960s, when Schonberg rendered these
opinions, he should have known better: the lifting of the Iron Curtain had
opened a window on a heretofore concealed Soviet musical world. In Russia,
the dominant Scriabin interpreter had been the composer's son-in-law,
Vladimir Sofronitzki (1902–63). A 1960 Melodiya recording of a Sofronitzki
Scriabin concert documents a musical séance capped by the frenzied trills and
hallucinatory nightlights of the *Black Mass* Sonata. Horowitz was the better
pianist, but never so surrendered his performer's ego in this or any other
music. Sofronitzki did not make it to New York but Evgeny Mravinsky and
his Leningrad Philharmonic did, in 1962. Schonberg's lukewarm reviews were
one reason Mravinsky elected never to return. Those who heard him encountered an incendiary combination of intensity and virtuosity unknown to
American orchestras since the retirement of Toscanini. Mravinsky's was not an
orchestra for all seasons. But its throbbing vibrato and vast dynamic range
revealed suddenly and unforgettably how Tchaikovsky and Shostakovich
sounded in "Russian."[38]

With Busch, Klemperer, Reiner, Schnabel, Serkin, and Walter at hand, and
a lineage including Thomas, Seidl, and Mahler, the American supply of Germanic talent seemed especially ample. But, as with the Russians, the increasing availability of European recordings beginning in the 1960s revealed that
the world's greatest artists were not necessarily Victor-recorded. In particular,
the belated rediscovery of Wilhelm Furtwängler, last heard in New York in
1927, remapped the twentieth-century history of symphonic performance for
two generations of Americans schooled in Toscanini's Beethoven, Brahms, and
Wagner. Furtwängler was a complete Toscanini antipode. Toscanini applied to
all music the coursing melodies, hairtrigger accents, and limpid textures of
Italian opera; in moments of peak arousal, he lashed harder and sped things up.
Furtwängler experienced music as Wagnerian weight and mass; he connected
less with tunes than with their undertow; a Furtwängler climax slows down in

order to give cumulative harmonic tensions space in which to expand and resolve. Toscanini's performance ideal was objective: forthright musical shapes rendered with clarity and precision. Furtwängler's was a blurred communal ecstasy; even his beat was famously vague. The quest for Germanic *Innigkeit* remained his fixed goal even in Verdi or Franck. The absence of lightness and light, humor and irony could seem suffocating. For susceptible listeners, however, no other conductor so attained the cosmic penumbra of Beethoven's Ninth (read as a Bruckner symphony), of the Bruckner slow movements, of the most troubled or exalted pages in Schubert, Schumann, Brahms, or Wagner. Furtwängler's was the tragic or sublime poetry of experience. New World innocence was not for him. He made the criterion of textural fidelity itself seem innocent.

This mystical, roots-in-the-soil Teutonism aligned directly with Wagner. The "vasty deep" of Seidl's New York *Tristan* performances, as accounted by Huneker, belongs to the same legacy. And there are other, disturbing Furtwängler connections: with ecstatic cultural nationalism. Before World War I, the United States had enthusiastically embraced Gericke, Nikisch, Weingartner, Muck. After World War I, Furtwängler seemed "too German": awkward, neurotic, aloof, esoteric. After 1933, he was fatally linked with Hitler. As with Richard Strauss, his antidemocratic, "apolitical" Germanism neither made him a Nazi (neither joined the party) nor predisposed him to leave. Like Strauss, he was slow to understand that he was trapped.

All this forms the backdrop to Furtwängler's abortive American career. When between 1924 and 1927 he was a frequent guest with the New York Philharmonic, and an obvious candidate to succeed Mengelberg, Olin Downes (as we have seen) preferred Toscanini, and so did the men who ran the Philharmonic. In 1936, when at Toscanini's departing suggestion Furtwängler was named the orchestra's principal conductor for the coming season, an anti-Furtwängler committee threatened boycotts and mass cancellations of subscriptions. Furtwängler withdrew by cable. *Time* reported, "NAZI STAYS HOME." In 1948 the Chicago Symphony, searching for a music director, signed Furtwängler to an eight-week commitment. This was in some ways a plausible fit, Chicago's being the most Germanic of American orchestras. But a protest campaign—boycotts of the orchestra were pledged by Horowitz and Rubinstein, among others—forced Furtwängler to rescind. In 1951, Furtwängler was sounded out to conduct the opening of the Metropolitan Opera's 1952–53 season. He was interested but the Met determined that anti-Furtwängler sentiment was still too strong.[39]

Furtwängler's enormous influence remained restricted to Europe. There, the musician who most prominently resembled him was a Swiss pianist:

Edwin Fischer. Fischer's Gothic Bach was untouched by the impact of Wanda Landowska's harpsichord, which had displaced Bach on the piano in the United States. His Mozart performances, fearlessly exploring a wealth and variety of expression, were not about perfection. A 1942 collaboration with Furtwängler in Brahms's B-flat concerto—a live performance preserved on disk—is regal, ruthlessly spontaneous, full of wrong notes. Fischer (who died in 1960) feared flying and never visited North America. Even if he had, it would not have made much difference. He was a nervous and erratic executant. Even compared to Schnabel or Serkin (who disliked him), he stood apart as a cloudy and beclouded artistic personality, old-fashioned or obscure. He barely rates a mention in Schonberg's 1963 survey *The Great Pianists*. His art was not about the act of performance.

If anything like an "American style" materialized in the absence of native repertoire, its basis was the German symphonic classics as rendered by Toscanini: lean, taut, accurate, "objective." Bodanzky (who was to share German repertoire with Toscanini at the Met and was left solely in charge of Wagner with Toscanini's departure), Leinsdorf (who had assisted Toscanini in Salzburg), Rodzinski (who had helped to train the NBC Symphony), Szell (who had admired Toscanini's New York Philharmonic), and Serkin (who made his American concerto debut with Toscanini) all fit this picture. So do the Juilliard String Quartet, initially mentored by Eugene Lehner of the anti-sentimental Kolisch Quartet, and certain of the Outstanding Young American Pianists. Bruno Walter, who does not, became a less "subjective," more straightforward conductor in the United States, far less prone to tempo modification. The same thing happened to Horowitz when he became Toscanini's son-in-law and recorded Brahms and Tchaikovsky with the NBC orchestra. The most original sonic manifestion of the American culture of performance was the Stokowski sound—famous (or infamous) but never influential. Stokowski notwithstanding, the basis of popular appeal was in many instances speed and efficiency: the excitement of the chase, the thrill of perfection.

The influence of recordings is pertinent to this generalization, not because such influence was unique to America, but because it was the more pronounced. In Europe, there were major artists—the pianists Fischer, Kempff, and Alfred Cortot are obvious cases—who failed the polish-and-precision standards of the microphone; they did not play without wrong notes, and their habits of spontaneity precluded splicing in the right ones at the same tempo and dynamic the second (or third, or fourth) time through. In America, there were major artists—Heifetz, Horowitz, and Toscanini, to begin with—who thrived on close scrutiny of precise execution. At Studio 8H, even at Carnegie Hall, RCA Victor's sound engineers adopted a recording acoustic, unknown abroad, so tight and dry that a prickly exactitude of performance, parched of color and natural resonance, became the dominant listening priority. Applied to artists less special, these costly demands produced a narrowed range of interpretive possibilities.

This attempt at a balanced assessment of the American culture of performance is not meant to imply that European music-making was in most ways superior; America had artists and institutions that Europe did not have. But the patriotic wartime view that the United States became the measure of all things classical-musical skewed American musical self-knowledge and self-perception as never before or since.

■ ■ ■

As we have just considered individual American-based performers and institutions of performance from a transatlantic perspective, it remains to similarly assess the chief institutional embodiment of the American culture of performance: the concert orchestra. Great claims were made on its behalf: that, according to Theodore Thomas, it showed the culture of a community; that the Boston Symphony was the first "symphony orchestra pure and simple" whose "only business" was to perform symphonic music; that the Chicago Orchestra offered more paired subscription concerts than any other except in Boston and Leipzig; that, according to Charles Edward Russell in 1927, the symphony orchestra was America's "sign of honor among the nations." The special claims made for the American orchestras of Stokowski, Koussevitzky, Toscanini, Reiner, and Szell are of the same lineage. We must finally inquire, to what degree is the symphonic orchestra in fact a distinctive American achievement?

Taking the Thomas Orchestra as an American bellwether, it may be said to correlate with various private orchestras abroad, whose entrepreneurial conductor/managers offered "popular" concerts at inexpensive prices, and who serviced winter ballrooms and summer public gardens in addition to touring extensively. The orchestras of Joseph Gungl, Louis Jullien, Charles Lamoureux, Philippe Musard, Jules-Étienne Pasdeloup, and Johann Strauss, father and son, were of this kind. Gungl and Jullien also toured as orchestra leaders in the United States; the members of the Germania Orchestra were Gungl alumni. In London, it was Jullien who introduced English audiences to "promenade concerts" for casual listening. Though Thomas found Jullien a "charlatan," he played in Jullien's American orchestra in 1853. Meanwhile, the orchestra of the Leipzig Gewandhaus was Europe's most eminent professional concert ensemble with an ongoing history superseding individual leaders. It was an independent entity including town musicians and freelancers (some of whom also played for the Leipzig opera). It was managed by a lay "directorium." It showed the culture of the community.

In terms of repertoire and program-making, the American experience again parallels developments abroad. In the decades after 1850, "mixed" programs, typically including dances and overtures, evolved into "serious" concerts: shorter programs with fewer but longer works. Commensurately, a canon of masterworks materialized and contemporary music was relegated to a smaller place. In Europe, the Gewandhaus Orchestra performed works by dead composers in the following proportions: 13 percent in 1781–85, 23 percent in 1820–25, 39 percent in 1828–34, 48 percent in 1837–47, 61 percent in 1850–55, 76 percent in 1965–70. The repertoires of Vienna's Gesellschaft der Musikfreunde, London's Philharmonic Society, and Paris's Société des Concerts shifted concurrently. While there exist no comparable analyses of American programs, the same transition was variously reflected in Boston by the formation in 1865 of the Harvard Musical Association's annual concert series, with its sober eschewal of lightweight repertoire as well as "effect pieces of the Liszt, Wagner, Meyerbeer school," and by the Thomas Orchestra's progressive Boston programs of 1870, purer and more "serious" than those offered by Thomas the season before. (The earlier Boston experience of the Germania Orchestra documents a moment—at midcentury—not yet ripe for the exclusive purification of mixed fare.) Wilhelm Gericke, in 1884, led Boston Symphony concerts notably shorter and more earnest than those of his predecessor.*[40]

From other vantage points, however, the American experience stands apart. The Gewandhaus notwithstanding, it was generally the opera house in European cities that showed the culture of the community. The repertoire for opera, while it also underwent canonization, reserved a central place for froth: comic opera and operetta. The symphony halls of America were not only less aristocratic than the opera house with tiers and ornate boxes, but also inherently less intended for amusement. For generations of visiting conductors, from Henschel to Mahler to Toscanini, America signified an opportunity to undertake a menu of weighty symphonies less frequently served at home. We have observed Gericke's amazement at the wealth of orchestral repertoire known to Boston: "You seem to have heard everything already; more, much more, than we ever heard in Vienna!"

Self-evidently, Henry Higginson, who brought Gericke to Boston, was a

* I have earlier documented these successive Boston programming changes by the Germanians, the Harvard Musical Association, Thomas, and Gericke.

unique force, and unique to America; no European patron created anything like the Boston Symphony he owned and operated. Thomas, again, was singular. No European conductor/impresario so mutually embodied the high-minded meliorist and high-minded democrat; no European orchestra served the variety of sermonizing and barnstorming purposes in which the Thomas Orchestra excelled. If the foreign orchestras of Musard or Jullien in some respects resembled the Thomas model, so at home did Patrick Gilmore's touring concert band, which purveyed Beethoven, Wagner, and Verdi as well as marches and polkas, and offered full-time employment to sixty-six expert musicians.* The orchestra Thomas eventually founded in Chicago established a governing triumvirate—conductor, manager, and board—whose reliance on multiple private gifts (rather than government subsidies) would foster civic links to a community of supporters. However these various points of transatlantic resemblance and difference are weighed, that Americans considered the symphony orchestra their special province was a crucial psychological reality, heightening musical purpose and pride.

As a social metaphor, the orchestra has commonly been tagged "bourgeois." In the course of the nineteenth century, it newly served a broad middle-class public[41] in contrast to previous institutions of music associated with church or court. In London, Paris, and Vienna, the promenade concerts of Jullien, Musard, and the Strausses reached out to new populations of listeners. In the egalitarian New World, the democratizing connotations of the orchestra were the more pronounced. Certainly the concert orchestra serves as a central symbol for classical music in the United States. When in the course of the twentieth century individual conductors and instrumentalists

---

* Though they lie slightly outside the scope of this study, bands are not irrelevant to the history of classical music in the United States. In 1889, *Harper's Weekly* estimated that more than ten thousand "military" bands were active in the United States; their renditions of classical works, from Mozart to Wagner, were the first many Americans heard. With Gilmore's death in 1892, John Philip Sousa became the great American bandmaster. Though, like Gilmore, Sousa was an entertainer who proudly eschewed edification (hence his exclusion from the many interwar classical music bibles), his favorite composer was Wagner. His repertoire included excerpts from *Parsifal*. Among his frequent soloists, alongside his own supreme wind virtuosos, was the eminent violinist Maud Powell. The phenomenal popularity of American bands diminished after World War I with the relative disappearance of amusement parks and the marginalization (by jazz) of the dance genres bands had made their own. The bandmaster gave way to the educator. Leading figures in the academic band movement included Albert Austin Harding, a Sousa protégé, at the University of Illinois, and Frederick Fennell, who formed the Eastman Symphonic Wind Ensemble in 1952. The Goldman Band, under Edwin Franko Goldman and his son, Richard Franko Goldman, was an unusually prominent professional band after World War II. For an overview, see Raoul Camus's "Bands" in *The New Grove Dictionary of American Music* (New York, Grove's Dictionaries of Music, 1986).

more defined individual concerts, the orchestra became less paramount than in its dynamic earlier history: a backdrop to the main event. This shift in focus, symptomatic of American classical music growing older but less wise, registered shifting audiences. It is to the new, twentieth-century audience for classical music that we now turn.

PART TWO

Offstage

Participants

■

CHAPTER 5

Serving the
New Audience

■

Babbitt and the new middle classes ▪ *The phonograph and the
decline of* Hausmusik ▪ *Music appreciation* ▪ *Arthur Judson,
Columbia Artists, and Community Concerts* ▪ *Judson and the
New York Philharmonic* ▪ *Who leads taste?*

"Our Ideal Citizen—I picture him first and foremost as being busier
than a bird-dog, not wasting a lot of good time in day-dreaming or
going to sassiety teas or kicking about things that are none of his
business. . . .

"In politics and religion this Sane Citizen is the canniest man on
earth and in the arts he invariably has a natural taste which makes him
pick out the best, every time. In no country in the world will you find
so many reproductions of the Old Masters and of well-known paintings
on parlor walls as in these United States. No country has anything like
our number of phonographs, with not only dance records and comic
but also the best operas, such as Verdi, rendered by the world's highest-
paid singers.

"In other countries, art and literature are left to a lot of shabby bums
living in attics and feeding on booze and spaghetti, but in America the
successful writer or picture-painter is indistinguishable from any other
decent businessman."

Sinclair Lewis's caricature of Middle America—of George F. Babbitt, real
estate salesman, social climber, irrepressible booster and joiner—undeniably
rhymes with the fate of American classical music after World War I. When in
his address to the Zenith Real Estate Board Babbit patriotically sets America

above "the decayed nations of Europe" yet reveres phonographic Verdi, he illustrates the mentality that celebrated America's world's greatest musicians, all of
whom happened to be foreign-born, and orchestras, all of which happened to
specialize in "reproducing Old Masters." His allegiance to the phonograph—
he owns a piano, but only his ten-year-old daughter touches it—documents
the decline of domestic music-making. His discomfort with artists and intellectuals—"longhairs" and "snobs"—parallels the public relations machinery
that synthesized the fun-loving and warm-hearted "other Toscanini."[1]

The psychology of Zenith in Lewis's 1922 novel *Babbitt*, its contorted
ambivalence toward the European parent culture, is as old as America itself.
But Babbitt's bravado and defensiveness, chauvinism and insecurity are especially a product of the surging "consumer society" of the twenties, itself a
product of surging prosperity and world power. A more "scientific" version of
the same web of cultural and material strivings is the 1929 sociological study
Middletown by Helen and Robert Lynd. In Middletown—actually Muncie,
Indiana—"music for adults" had "almost ceased to be a matter of spontaneous, active participation." "The mothers of the present generation of children were brought up in a culture without Victrola and radio when the girl in
the crowd who could play while the others sang or danced was in demand."
"The American citizen's first duty to his country is no longer that of citizen
but that of consumer. Consumption is a new necessity." Among the articles of
prescribed consumption were cultural appliances: the radio, the phonograph.[2]

This picture, too, was overdrawn—the Lynds were no more disinterested
than Lewis was. And yet it fits. The heroic explorations of the Thomas Highway, of Henry Higginson, of Wagnerism at the Met had passed. With change
had come real growth and achievement—American classical music was nothing if not potent and prevalent—but also distortion and digression. The trajectory that had seemed bravely to lead toward an American canon had
yielded instead a curatorial culture of performance. The "gossip of the foyer,"
the "world's largest drum," and "soup for Toscanini" had fostered a climate of
sensation and hype more earnest, sincere, and therefore insidious than any
humbuggery ever countenanced by P. T. Barnum. This was the cultural wind
that chilled Otto Klemperer and Dimitri Mitropoulos, and left Artur
Schnabel feeling "marooned."

Tocqueville, in the 1830s, had observed of Americans, "The humblest artisan casts at times an eager and a furtive glance into the higher regions of the
intellect. People do not read with the same notions or in the same manner as
they do in aristocratic communities, but the circle of readers is increasingly
expanded, till it includes all the people."[3] The new audience for classical music
was different in scope and tone. One component was equidistant from the

rabble enlivening certain mid-nineteenth-century entertainments, and the aristocrats who had calmly absorbed or propagated high culture as an entitlement. Sociologists designate as "the new middle classes" the upwardly mobile white collar workers whose free weekends and evenings, and disposable income, supported 1920s spending habits observed by the Lynds ("a monetary approach to the satisfactions of life"), by John Dewey, and by countless other commentators. The pertinent articles of consumption included cars and refrigerators, movies and concerts. Following Tocqueville, "higher regions of the intellect" were democratized.

The founders of American classical music had included Germanic amateurs and professionals who met as *Singvereine* and Philharmonic societies. A second support system was feminine: the housewife who played the piano, the women's cultural committee, the concert presenter, orchestral manager, or symphonic board member. The Germans were lampooned as whiskered eccentrics, but were tenacious organizers for whom life without music was untenable. The women have been written off as slaves to sentimentality or victims of indolence.[4] A shrewd commentary in the 1875 *New York World* counter proposed:

[The piano] may be looked upon as furniture by dull observers or accepted as a fashion by shallow thinkers, but it is in reality the artificial nervous system, ingeniously made of steel and silver, which civilization in its poetic justice provides for our young women. Here it is, in this parlor with closed doors, that the daughter of our day comes stealthily and pours out the torrent of her emotions through her finger-ends, directs the forces of her youth and romanticism into the obedient metal and lets it say in its own mystic way what she dare not confess or hope in articulate language.[5]

These same musically literate women by century's end became Wagnerites for whom the Liebestod or Brünnhilde's Awakening were explosive libidinal or existential lessons.

Hausmusik—amateur music-making in the home—was a twentieth-century casualty of the radio and the phonograph, of social and demographic change. One substitute was the concert ticket. According to one 1939 survey, the number of American orchestras increased from 17 before World War I to 270; other surveys arrived at even higher totals. In Babbitt's Zenith, the businessman/poet Chum Frink offers advice to the Boosters' Club which conveys that the new audience was newly gendered, that American classical music was increasingly an acceptable domain for men:

"Some of you may feel that it's out of place here to talk on a strictly highbrow and artistic subject, but I want to come out flatfooted and ask you boys to O.K. the proposition of a Symphony Orchestra for Zenith. Now, where a lot of you make your mistake is in assuming that if you don't like classical music and all that junk, you ought to oppose it. . . . [But] culture has become as necessary an adornment and advertisement for a city today as pavements or bank-clearances. It's Culture, in theaters and art-galleries and so on, that brings thousands of visitors to New York every year. . . .

"Pictures and books are fine for those that have the time to study 'em, but they don't shoot out on the road and holler 'this is what little old Zenith can put up in the way of Culture.' That's precisely what a Symphony Orchestra does do. Look at the credit Minneapolis and Cincinnati get. An orchestra with first-class musickers and a swell conductor—and I believe we ought to do the thing up brown and get one of the highest-paid conductors on the market, providing he ain't a Hun—it goes right into Beantown and New York and Washington; it plays at the best theaters to the most cultured and moneyed people; it gives such class-advertising as a town can get in no other way."[6]

In 1930, for the first time since 1870, census data showed that men outnumbered women in "music and music teaching." Piano manufacturing showed a concurrent decline: American piano factories made 364,545 instruments in 1909, 341,652 in 1919, 306,584 in 1925 (during this sixteen-year period the population grew by 22 percent). A 1922 magazine article declared the piano "in danger of becoming as rare now as a brougham, a phaeton or a dogcart for the banished horse." In Middletown, it was a Victrola that the family put in the backseat of its Ford alongside the little girl when setting off to job hunt. Only initially did the Depression hurt the fledgling record industry: RCA Victor's sales increased sixfold between 1933 and 1938, with symphonic releases leading the way. Challenging RCA's Toscanini, Stokowski, and Koussevitzky, Columbia Records signed the New York Philharmonic in 1940. Around the same time, in 1938, eighty-eight percent of all American homes were said to possess one of twenty-five million radios; destitute families valued their radios over refrigerators, furniture, and bedding. Radio's cultural flagships included the New York Philharmonic, Metropolitan Opera, and NBC Symphony on Saturdays, and the *Ford Hour* on Sundays. An average Sunday gave New York City listeners perhaps three additional "light classical" studio concerts and half a dozen additional concerts and recitals; on weekdays the schedule might include more than a dozen live broadcasts of orchestras

(Rochester, Indianapolis, Cleveland, Cincinnati), studio orchestras, and studio recitals.[7]

Broadcasts and recordings spurred one another, and were further refreshed by such technological advances as electrical recording (1925), "high fidelity" (1934), and the long-playing disk (1948). Though musicians feared that live music would suffer in competition, the opposite occurred: never before had classical music enjoyed (or suffered) such powerful (or superficial) tools for promotion and dissemination. One mirror on the outcome—three thousand miles from Carnegie Hall, the Met, and Studio 8H—was Hollywood. The silent screen had already mated *The Thief of Baghdad* and *Birth of a Nation* with *Scheherazade* and *The Ride of the Valkyries*. Many large cinemas maintained symphonic ensembles; at New York's Capitol Theater, the orchestra numbered up to eighty-five musicians, and might give a Sunday-morning Mahler symphony at a dollar a ticket. With the advent of "talkies" in the late twenties, glamorous sound accompaniments became the norm. The most pampered, highest-paid composer was, of course, a European import: Erich Wolfgang Korngold. Meanwhile, a sizable number of films were themselves about divas (*Metropolitan*, 1935), violinists (*Intermezzo*, 1939; *Humoresque*, 1946), pianists (*When Tomorrow Comes*, 1939; *The Great Lie*, 1940; *Dangerous Moonlight*, 1949; *I've Always Loved You*, 1946), and composers (*The Constant Nymph*, 1943; *The Melody Master* with Alan Curtis as Schubert, 1941; *A Song to Remember* with Cornel Wilde as Chopin, 1944; *Song of Love* with Paul Henreid as Schumann, Katharine Hepburn as Clara, and Robert Walker as Brahms, 1947; *Song of Scheherazade* with Jean-Pierre Aumont as Rimsky-Korsakov, 1947). We have already glimpsed Grace Moore and Lawrence Tibbett at the movies. Other famous performers played themselves. In *One Hundred Men and a Girl* (1937), Stokowski rescued unemployed musicians. In *They Shall Have Music* (1939), Jascha Heifetz helped to save a settlement music school. In *Carnegie Hall* (1947), the story of a cleaning woman's son-turned-famous-pianist furnished an excuse for cameo appearances by Heifetz, Jan Peerce, Gregor Piatigorsky, Ezio Pinza, Lily Pons, Fritz Reiner, Artur Rodzinski, Artur Rubinstein, Risë Stevens, Stokowski, and Bruno Walter.

When David Sarnoff's decision to commit forty thousand dollars to Toscanini and untold additional outlays to an NBC Symphony was questioned by some at RCA, *Fortune* magazine in January 1938 scrutinized the investment and reported, "Mr. Sarnoff, in working out the details of his gesture, was not in any music lovers' trance." The Toscanini coup would "make NBC the biggest corporate name in music" (which proved true) and "bring to a climax the long evolution of 'good' music on the air" (a matter of interpretation). According to a *Fortune* poll, 62.5 percent of all Americans liked to listen to classical music on the radio, and 42.7 percent wanted to hear more radio music. As for Toscanini, "Of all the people in the U.S.—Negroes, poor white, farmers, clerks, and millionaires—39.9 percent have heard of the name of Arturo Toscanini; and of those who have heard of him, no less than 71 percent can identify him *as an orchestral conductor.* . . . His name was known to 63.8 percent of the prosperous, and of these 80 percent identified him correctly. In New York City . . . 90.8 percent have heard of him, and 95.7 percent of those know who he is." The Toscanini audience, *Fortune* concluded, is "certainly a mass audience." A comparable sociological study, reported in the April 1939 *Harper's Magazine*, estimated that 21.5 percent of the American public preferred listening to "classical" music and 52.8 percent preferred listening to both "classical" and "popular" music. Of the first group, 31.3 percent were categorized as "prosperous," 24.7 percent as "upper middle class," 20 percent as "lower middle class with regular jobs," 14.8 percent as "poor or unemployed," and 17.2 percent as "Negro." The percentages for the second group were 32.7, 34.8, 20, 26.9, and 32.7. In cities of a hundred thousand or more, 62 percent of all college graduates said they liked to "listen to classical music in the evening."[8]

Though audience ratings disclosed much lower figures for actual radio listeners (as opposed to responses showing preferences), the new popular culture created and supported by electronic media did accord classical music a luxurious berth for a period of decades. According to *Life* magazine in 1939, "As many Americans know that Toscanini conducts an orchestra as know that Joe DiMaggio plays center field."[9] But what else did they know?

■ ■ ■

At issue was what happens to artistic taste when the "circle of readers" expands. If this was an experiment, it was not wholly new. The circle had been large before: for Patrick Gilmore's Jubilees, or Jenny Lind's tours, or Theodore Thomas's Highway. What was different this time were the available means of exposure and tutelage, and the ripeness of the readers already at hand. On the plus side, American classical music had established higher and more uniform standards of presentation. On the negative, the readers were increasingly divorced from the craft of writing: they were not doers.

Music education, clearly, was the task at hand. Many rushed to help, or to help themselves. Amid selfless well-wishing pedagogues and self-serving commercial strategists, Leopold Stokowski, as ever, was tantalizingly different. No one else—no one of consequence—as fervently espoused the music of today and of tomorrow. Few as securely trusted the capacity of the untutored and unprejudiced. And only Stokowski shook hands with Mickey Mouse: he fearlessly befriended popular culture.

In Philadelphia, Stokowski's Young People's Concerts—at which we have glimpsed the guest elephant for *The Carnival of the Animals*—and Youth Concerts—the ones with bouncers to evict unwanted adults—were part of a pedagogical assault that also included exhortations and rebukes from the stage. But Stokowski's best-known, best-loved educational project was his 1940 animated feature with Walt Disney: *Fantasia*. Only Stokowski would have included Stravinsky's *Rite of Spring* on a two-hour cartoon concert for young people. The other repertoire was Bach's D minor Toccata and Fugue, Beethoven's *Pastoral* Symphony, Tchaikovsky's *Nutcracker* Suite, Ponchielli's "Dance of the Hours," Dukas's *Sorceror's Apprentice*, Mussorgsky's *Night on Bald Mountain*, and Schubert's "Ave Maria"—a varied program unified by the conductor's opulent, smooth-skinned sonic signature. Mickey's turn came in the Dukas—otherwise, a faithful rendering of the musical narrative of a mischievously disobedient servant. But the score was trimmed, and other selections were substantially abridged and even restructured.

In fact, the entire film is notably irreverent. The cartoons are funny and clever. The Ponchielli is a sublime send-up of choreographic art, crowned by a dashing *pas de deux* for alligator and hippopotamus: Petipa at the zoo. Inspired, too, is the close of the *Pastoral*, marrying the soaring apotheosis of Beethoven's coda with Helios's chariot of the sun. Earlier in the same work, the grace and majesty of the music (wonderfully conveyed by Stokowski) are mirrored by winged Pegasus on high. Over at Warner Brothers, Rossini was deliciously employed for maniacal bunny chases, but nothing more than fun was afoot. With its detailed invocations of classical ballet and mythology, *Fantasia* was polyvalent: its admixture of innocence and sophistication invited a gamut of responses from a variety of audiences.

The film's narrator was not Stokowski but Deems Taylor, a familiar commentator on radio broadcasts of symphony and opera, but like Stokowski an atypical educator. As a practicing musician—a composer of consequence—Taylor was a musical insider: mystified reverence for composer or performer was not for him. He wore his learning whimsically. In an introduction to a collection of his radio talks he cautioned, "Many a potential music lover is frightened away by the solemnity of music's devotees. They would make more converts if they would rise from their knees."[10] In *Fantasia*, his spoken introductions are informal and laconic. The proceedings slip easily into an impromptu jazz session—the Philadelphia Orchestra longhairs are not to be confused with stuffed shirts. But here, too, the touch is light: not a hortatory word is heard.

Bucking the tide, as well, was Olga Samaroff (who happened to have been
Stokowski's wife from 1911 to 1923). Forced by an arm injury to abandon a
significant piano career, she became a pedagogue for musicians (including
William Kapell) and novices both. For the latter, she established a network of
"layman's music courses," invoking ear training and score reading as aids to
"active listening." In her *Layman's Music Book* (1935), she listed these "points to
be remembered" about "modern tendencies": "There has been modern music
in every age"; "The history of our musical art makes it seem impossible to
assume that any concept of consonance and dissonance is final and unalter-
able"; "A rich musical life should include the greatest things of the past and a
vital interest in modern creative music."[11] Another sophisticated "active listening" advocate was the composer Aaron Copland, whose efforts will be considered in a later chapter. It is arguable that Samaroff and Copland lacked the
common touch. Taylor could seem blasé. Stokowski unquestionably lapsed
into vulgarity. But the instructional style mainly attained silences such
reservations.

Fantasia's melange of high and low forecast the postmodern aesthetics of
the late twentieth century. In 1940, it was a curiosity: philistine to some who
preferred Toscanini rites, ponderous to others who liked their cartoons short
and simple. Though with a 1956 reissue, and 1991 home video sales, *Fantasia*
would more than turn a profit, its initial release failed. For the New York premiere, the Broadway Theater was equipped with ninety speakers to convey
the Philadelphia Orchestra in "Fantasound." Special engagements were
booked coast to coast. But Disney did not recoup his $2.3 million investment
and, to Stokowski's dismay, scuttled plans for a sequel. As for music education,
the mainstream pedagogy of preference was altogether different: loftier in
tone, narrower in content. "Music appreciation" pervaded radio and recordings, and spawned a distinctive literature. If no single individual led the
charge, David Sarnoff was a key player whose personality and tactics illuminate the whole.

Sarnoff, of course, was not a musician. He was a passionate music appreci-
ator. His listening tastes excluded jazz. He enjoyed friendly acquaintance with
Mischa Elman, Jascha Heifetz, Josef Hofmann, John McCormack, Rosa Ponselle. Frederick Lewis Allen, a prime chronicler of the twenties and thirties,
observed "spiritual starvation": "There was the god of business to worship—
but a suspicion lingered that he was made of brass." Driven, self-made, Sarnoff
longed for music, an associate wrote, "in a fogged search." Lordly, autocratic,
he was not in the least humble. "In the presence of artists, though, he became,
if not self-effacing, unpresuming."[12] Like many who lacked firsthand knowledge of how to make it, he mystified music as lofty and ineffable. Lacking a

secure basis of judgment, he deferred to criteria of fame and celebrity. In these respects, he was the new middle classes writ large. However unconsciously, he understood the new audience.

Sarnoff's competitive drive, his insatiable will to win, made him a considered but dogmatic advocate of free enterprise. With his counterpart William Paley at CBS, he battled various public radio proposals—for regulating broadcasting as a public utility, for reserving a percentage of wavelengths for a federal broadcasting chain, for government control at the municipal or state level. The emerging reality was "toll broadcasting," which entrusted programming to advertisers who acted as actual producers. *Amos 'n' Andy*, new in 1928, was radio's first national hit, followed by Rudy Vallee, Eddie Cantor, and other variety-show stars. Radio news steered clear of criticizing public utilities or banks; organized labor was a taboo topic. The proposed Wagner-Hatfield amendment, to set aside one-quarter of all radio frequencies for nonprofit use, was one result of this swift deterioration of early radio ideals. Though this effort failed, the threat of an "American BBC" was a factor in the creation of the *University of Chicago Round Table, America's Town Meeting of the Air*, the *University of the Air, Fables in Verse, Norman Corwin's Words without Music*, and other instructional and cultural offerings.[13]

Toscanini and the NBC Symphony were NBC's jewels in the crown. Late in life, after Toscanini's death, Sarnoff called the Toscanini-NBC alliance his "main object of pride." Specially packaged and presented from Studio 8H, Toscanini's concerts were made to seem as Olympian and unapproachable as Beethoven himself. Unerringly, if unwittingly, they equated great art with great performances of great European masters—with things old, finished, familiar, and foreign. Toscanini was solemnly merchandised as "the world's greatest conductor." When Toscanini was away, Samuel Chotzinoff, in charge of repertoire, kept NBC Symphony broadcasts purged of "modern music." Over at CBS and Mutual Broadcasting, such studio conductors as Bernard Herrmann and Alfred Wallenstein raised a flag for American composers. Herrmann's guests included Bartók, Stravinsky, Milhaud, Villa-Lobos, and Hindemith.[14] The subsidized radio orchestras of Europe championed native contemporary works as a matter of course. One must admire Sarnoff for his visionary Toscanini coup. But the limits of Sarnoff's vision must be borne in mind. Minus Toscanini, he abandoned the NBC Symphony. Minus its validated greatest performer, even validated great music no longer served his purposes.

A somewhat earlier Sarnoff coup again highlights his susceptibility to brand names. In 1928, he obtained Walter Damrosch to create a weekly daytime *NBC Music Appreciation Hour*. Going back to Leopold a half century before, the "Damrosch" imprimatur was venerable and famous. White-haired, old-fashioned, kindly yet formal, Walter began each radio lesson by intoning, "Good morning, my dear children!" His curriculum included the instruments of the orchestra, "the ways in which music becomes expressive," musical forms, and the lives and works of the great composers. He led a studio orchestra in musical examples. Though his repertoire (as with the New York Symphony) was catholic, its crest was the German pantheon, born on high. Presenting Beethoven's Fifth, Damrosch likened the second movement to "a walk in a lovely garden, in which one finds a statue erected to the memory of some national hero." He set its second theme to the words:

> For the hero has come,
> Sound the trumpet and drum!
> He has fought
> The good fight
> He has won!

The *Music Appreciation Hour* was said to reach seven million students in seventy thousand schools, as well as four million adults. As a model embodiment of classical music, Damrosch was august and remote. He spoke with a German accent. Winthrop Sargeant, playing under Damrosch in the New York Symphony, found him "absolutely imperturbable" even on the podium, beating time "like the mechanical pendulum of a grandfather clock," "a great musical symbol rather than a man." When in 1932 Stokowski proposed broadcasting "modernistic" music to schoolchildren so they could "develop a liking for it," Damrosch, the accredited authority, issued a press release "deeply deploring" Stokowski's plan. "Children should not be confused by experiments," he wrote. His radio classroom went off the air in 1942, by which time he was eighty years old and there were practically no concerts left on commercial network stations.

Music appreciation fit into a larger educational project occasioned by expanding literacy and leisure. The twenties produced the Book of the Month Club (1926) and such well-known volumes as H. G. Wells's *Outline of History* (1921) and *Short History of the World* (1922), Hendrik van Loon's The *Story of Mankind* (1921), and Will Durant's *The Story of Philosophy* (1926). This phenomenon was termed by its first chronicler the "day of the popularizers," an "unparalleled cultural happening" characterized by "chirpy ebullience" and "happy energy." Radio was an obvious vehicle for popularized knowledge. The pertinent musical offerings, framing the *Music Appreciation Hour* left and right, ranged from Abram Chasins's ambitious musicians' workshop *Piano*

Pointers to Sigmund Spaeth, who as the "tune detective" traced "I'm Always Chasing Rainbows" to Chopin's Fantaisie-Impromptu and—his most celebrated dissection—"Yes, We Have No Bananas" to the "Hallelujah" chorus, "Bring Back My Bonnie to Me," "Aunt Dinah's Quilting Party," and *The Bohemian Girl.*

Popularized music education also produced libraries of books and recordings. Again, Sarnoff took the lead—via his Radio Corporation of America, which in 1929 absorbed the largest American record manufacturer, the Victor Talking Machine Company. Toscanini, Stokowski, Koussevitzky, Heifetz, and Horowitz were all "RCA Victor" recording artists. And Victor produced innumerable written guides, including *The Victor Book of the Symphony, The Victor Book of Concertos, The Victor Book of the Opera, What We Hear in Music, Music and Romance, Form in Music,* and *Music Appreciation for Children.* A typical Victor touch was the inclusion of "recommended recordings"—always on Victor, of course. Victor books recommended, as well, other Victor books. *The Victor Record Catalogue* was recommended as a reference guide: the "Key to the World's Greatest Storehouse of Music."

The Victor Record Review, a monthly "magazine of musical fact and comment" begun in 1938, recommended not only recordings but upcoming broadcasts of recordings over some sixty stations from Hartford to Hollywood. The curriculum embodied by all these aids favored the symphony among genres, and a short list of Germans, Frenchmen, Italians, and Russians among composers. Contemporary music was not canonized, nor were American composers or American jazz. Instead, the spotlight selected contemporary performers, provided they recorded for RCA. This streamlined merchandising strategy maximized mass appeal. The NBC/RCA musical empire was also an empire of propaganda.

Sarnoff, at the top, was a New World cultural entrepreneur driven to accomplish what governments accomplished in Old World lands. His impact was more complex than Henry Higginson's, more dramatic than Otto Kahn's, more considerable than Samuel Insull's. He oversaw the NBC Symphony and the *Music Appreciation Hour*—and to his enormous credit, a televised, English-language NBC Opera stressing contemporary and American repertoire. The impresario in Sarnoff was authentically grand but susceptible to lapses in taste and judgment; Sarnoff the businessman was truly idealistic but susceptible to self-interest. By post-Sarnoff standards, early radio and TV were cultural oases; public television's *Great Performances,* new in 1973, were puny compared to Sarnoff's blistering Toscanini telecasts of 1948 to 1952. But the institutional structures Sarnoff galvanized for great music were inherently commercial, not aesthetic. With his departure, NBC abandoned highbrow fare and RCA calcified; it was Goddard Lieberson, at Columbia Records, who copiously recorded Stravinsky conducting Stravinsky, Robert Craft's comprehensive survey of Schoenberg's Second Viennese School, and a Modern American Music series.

Sarnoff boasted that NBC presented "every known artist of quality." He initially envisioned hiring the seventy-year-old Toscanini to supervise all "serious music" at NBC. He called the seventy-five-year-old Damrosch "America's leading ambassador of music understanding and music appreciation" and added, "He occupies a position in music that is unique, and justly places him in the ranks of those who have elevated civilization." However naïve, these claims and intentions were not cynical; they expressed the confidence of a true believer—one who ultimately, and fatefully, believed in himself. As Virgil Thomson once memorably (if hyperbolically) remarked in the *New York Herald-Tribune*, "The indiscriminate propagation of culture (from whatever noble motives) can operate easily, if not inevitably, toward the destruction of that culture." In retrospect, the early rejection of public radio was a watershed moment in the history of classical music in the United States. Had it been implemented in the 1930s, an "American BBC" would doubtless have altered the American musical curriculum, with results unknowable both then and now.[15]

■ ■ ■

John Ward (1838–96), who held degrees in law and medicine, kept a diary recording (among other things) his musical activities. He sang (Donizetti, Verdi) and played the piano (Chopin, Wagner in transcription) almost daily. And he attended musicales such as this one from 1865:

> Last evening at Charlie's, Will and I opened the evening with the Overture to the Huguenots (I was very nervous from the effects of a Seidlitz and then of a strong tea). It went well. C got me some wine. Then Mary and Louise M, Lou Nevins and I played the Andante from Schuberth's [*sic*] Symphony on 2 pianos. Went well. J L Lee and I sang the duets from Linda [di Chamounix], Mary acc[ompanied]. Mrs. D. Field sang. Kitty Parker, Amann and I sang "Chi me frena?" very well. Mrs. Arthur and I sang Nabucco, Lou N acc 1st part and Mrs. A the 2nd. The Leupps played Gottschalk's duet without their notes brilliantly. Supper at 10:50. Plenty of strawberries and ice cream, tea and chocolate. Mary and Lou Nevins played Kalkbrünner's [*sic*] Concerto to 2 pianos magnificently after tea. Mrs. A sang twice. She, Kitty P, Amann and I sang Martha quartette.

Mrs. F acc. It began to rain and people left. Mrs. A and I sang Aroldo last. Mary p[layed] Puritani. Mrs. Bemis criticized Leupps, Bellows etc. severely. She stayed all night. M[other] and I home at 12:30.[16]

Ward was exceptional, of course—American men were at all times far less likely than their European counterparts to sing an aria or play second violin in a string quartet. When great numbers of them became classical music lovers, after World War I, *Hausmusik* was in decline. A vignette comparable to John Ward's, seventy-five years later, might show a single individual—an adult male—listening to phonograph recordings. No less than Chum Frink selling the Boosters' Club on a symphony orchestra for Zenith, this is a picture of classical music newly gendered after World War I. Record collectors, like collectors of stamps or baseball cards or automobiles, were and are never women. As women would not, they competed over whose version of Concerto X was better. They argued over which Beethoven symphony was best. Samuel Chotzinoff numbered the Beethoven symphonies "in accordance with the true position of each on the spiritual scale"—1, 2, 4, 5, 3, 7, 8, 6, 9. The champion hairsplitter was B. H. Haggin of the *Brooklyn Daily Eagle* and the *Nation*, a Toscanini diehard considered by many an intellectual. Haggin thought nothing of protesting the inclusion of "such a feeble work" as the Violin Concerto on a Toscanini Beethoven program. *The Victor Book of the Symphony* preached the superiority of phonograph recordings to mere books: "Books preserve in cold type the great thoughts of the ages, priceless even though disembodied, but electrical reproduction actually re-creates the living organism of music, giving it voice and movement and compelling vitality." For Haggin, the phonograph was an indispensable musical instrument. His *Book of the Symphony* (1937) came packaged with a symbol of competence for those who could not read music: a ruler with which to measure the distance from the outer groove of a record; the development section of the first movement of Beethoven's Fifth started at 2 $7/16$ inches as recorded by Koussevitzky and the London Philharmonic. Haggin's most reprinted volume, *Music on Records*, advised (1) readers who "want to know which . . . works are the greatest . . . ; which are enjoyable though of lesser stature; which are of little consequence though by great composers; which to acquire first, which later, which not at all; and (2) readers who want to know which recording of a work offers the best performance, the best-sounding reproduction, which recording to avoid, and in some instances what is offered by different recordings." Even the title of another Haggin book was gendered: *Music for the Man Who Enjoys "Hamlet"*; in praising Toscanini, it deplored "the vehement plastic distortions of Koussevitzky, the sensationalism of Stokowski" and scorned Bruno Walter's version of the *Eroica* Symphony as less "valid" than Toscanini's. This was music appreciation in a pure form.[17]

Its outnumbered opponents included a writer even more acidulous than Haggin: the Frankfurt School tyrant Theodor Adorno, angrily stranded on American shores. Only Adorno could have "theorized" a wholesale condemnation of American listening habits as "infantilized" and "regressive." Keying on Sigmund Spaeth and similar popularizers, Adorno claimed that music appreciation had reduced whole symphonies to a series of memorizable melodies, falsifying as "narratives" or "ballads" the complex dialectics of symphonic thought; innocent of deeper structures, listeners were denied all possibility of subtle intellectual or emotional response. Adorno also excoriated the monaural "radio voice" that clotted orchestral texture, highlighting "neat tunes" and "exciting harmonic stimuli." To this cynical diagnosis one could add, conjecturally, that many lay listeners applied lay criteria of performance—precision, accuracy, energy—peculiarly pertinent to the American favorites Toscanini and Heifetz, Reiner and Szell. Certainly the Toscanini style, bristling with urgency and efficiency, was as "masculine" as the much rehearsed Toscanini persona. And it was a notably simplistic and business-like article of faith of Haggin and other music appreciators that the performer "must produce what the printed score directs that he produce."[18]

Of course, many newcomers to music graduated to score-reading and performance. Others who did not nevertheless experienced Beethoven at least as stirringly and honestly as Adorno did. But the impact of the radio and phonograph remains ponderable. Taken as a whole, the new audience was differently educated. It heard differently. Its predilections with regard to repertoire and performance style were different. And these differences were widely supported. No pre–World War I critic of consequence would have counseled as George Marek did in "How to Listen to Music Over the Radio": "You can enjoy a Beethoven symphony without being able to read notes, without knowing who Beethoven was, when he lived, or what he tried to express." Before becoming a top RCA Victor executive, Marek wrote a column for *Good Housekeeping*. Previously women's magazines had addressed homemakers who played the piano; recommending Toscanini's 1939 version of Beethoven's Fifth, Marek addressed record listeners (who were not only husbands after all) as follows: "You needn't dig or look for 'meaning.' . . . You need only listen. The new Toscanini recording reveals all the blaze of this masterpiece. As has been said so many times, this is not an interpretation, it is the *Symphony* itself." (In fact, the symphony exists in score—every recording is precisely an interpretation, and as such privileges the culture of performance.) The *New York Times*, once a platform for W. J. Henderson, now published music reviews by Olin Downes, who emphasized, "The listener does not have to be a tutored man or a person technically versed in the intricacies of the art of composition to understand perfectly well what the orchestra [is] saying to him." Downes's 1941 lecture "Be Your Own Music Critic" advised the novice to trust his own spontaneous and intuitive wisdom.

These preachings cherished American self-reliance and democratic access to the citadel of art. In celebrating the untutored listener, however, they segregated and mystified the learned practitioner who could read notes and purvey them for a paying audience. A century before, in New York or Vienna, the distinction between "amateur" and "professional" had been blurry at best. Newly professionalized, the performer was also newly rarified. Obviously, rites of classical music worship were long familiar—and Bach and Beethoven retained their high pedestals. In fact, the canon inculcated by Theodore Thomas in the late nineteenth century remained remarkably unchanged: it still started with Bach; it still ended with Richard Strauss and Sibelius. Closed to new acquisitions, it became a body of knowledge to be savored, ranked, and otherwise apprehended while recycled in performance. As there were no living composers deemed worthy of inclusion, living performers took their place, standing shoulder to shoulder with deceased creators. In the case of Toscanini, the culture of performance was actually transcendent. For Haggin, only the "finest, greatest music" was good enough for Toscanini. In the opinion of Lawrence Gilman of the *New York Herald-Tribune*, Toscanini's fame, "probably without equal in the records of music," was "one of the major validations of our period and our race."[19]

This postwar rebeginning for classical music in the United States also rebegan the unraveling of the cultural umbilical cord to Old World Europe. In *The Innocents Abroad* (1869), Mark Twain, a New World man-child, had gawked at and yet debunked German and Italian landmarks of Western civilization. A riper relationship, signified by a Krehbiel, Seidl, or Higginson, was attained by 1900. But the new audience of the 1920s, brandishing the trophy symphonies on high, was again cocky and insecure vis-à-vis the parent culture; no less than John Sullivan Dwight, Haggin was a stern practitioner of snob appeal. A countervailing democratic urge—a defense against subservience—was leveling: the revered living icons of European culture—the great performers—were at the same time cut down to human size by egalitarian American converts. Writing of the "genius act" in 1960, Dwight Macdonald observed, "There is a strange ambivalence. The masses put an absurdly high value on the personal genius, the charisma, of the performers, but they also demand a secret rebate: he must play the game—*their* game—must distort his personality to suit their taste."[20]

The aloof, autocratic Toscanini played hide-and-seek with his granddaugh-

ter and watched children's shows on TV. The high-strung, neurotic Horowitz
enjoyed horror movies on his VCR. When in 1948 Eugene Ormandy and the
Philadelphia Orchestra appeared on the first televised concert, beating
Toscanini and the NBC Symphony by ninety minutes, *Life* magazine
exclaimed, "RIVAL CBS PROGRAM FEATURED A MAESTRO WHO ATE COUGH
DROPS!"—which Ormandy was seen inserting in his mouth midway through
a Rachmaninoff symphony. Six years later, when Toscanini endured a memory lapse during his final concert, *Life* distilled its essence as, "EMOTION MAKES
THE GREAT MAESTRO FALTER." The picture captions read:

> —"Toscanini, bewildered, forgets his place"
> —"His beat faltering under stress of emotion, great
>   Maestro covers his eyes and tries to remember
>   where he is in *Tannhauser* score"
> —"Suddenly lost in his memories, maestro stares off
>   into space"
> —"Leaving the hall, Toscanini avoids the stage door
>   exit to escape a demonstration, his head bowed as
>   he ends already legendary 68-year-career."

The culture gods were reassuringly mortal after all.[21]

If the genius act, a product of mass media and culture, was a twentieth-
century phenomenon, sacralization as practiced by the new interwar audience
was as old as Dwight and Theodore Thomas, Seidl and the American Wagner
cult. Far from rebelling against elitist rites of culture worship, newcomers to
classical music eagerly embraced them. Onetime crusades for American
music, for opera in English, for opera "for the people," for outdoor communal
pageants dissipated: insisting on signatures of greatness, the music appreciators
were worse snobs than had been George Templeton Strong and other upper-
crust Gilded Age connoisseurs. The new middle classes did not riot against
privilege, like the Astor Place mob of 1849; rather, they espoused democratic
access—"Be Your Own Music Critic"—to privileged precincts. They popularized sacralization and spread its effects from great composers to great performers. In the course of the twentieth century, this mass movement to purify
classical music would push it toward hermetic extremes of irrelevance.

■ ■ ■

Music appreciation, the new audience, and the culture of performance were
signature ingredients of American classical music after World War I. Addition-

ally, not all music educators were mere appreciators, not all audiences were new, and there were composers—living ones—as well as performers. The totality, whatever else it seemed, was bigger and more pervasive than before. And more than ever, before or after, the symphony orchestra showed the culture of the community. Orchestras, all told, had more salaried players, more concerts, more tours. As of 1950, symphonic seasons of twenty to thirty weeks were typical in large cities. So, however, were deficits and "save the symphony" campaigns. Especially with the onset of the Depression, which rendered 70 percent of the nation's musicians unemployed,[22] a complex balancing act was required to keep orchestras in business.

The American reliance on private philanthropy had initially transformed local musicians' cooperatives, of which the New York Philharmonic was best known, into large organizations subsidized by civic-spirited individuals, of whom Henry Higginson was the most self-sufficient and publicly prominent. The New York Symphony was supported by Harry Flagler, Cincinnati had the Tafts, Philadelphia the Boks, Chicago Charles Norman Fay, Los Angeles William Andrews Clark, Minneapolis Elbert L. Carpenter, St. Louis Robert S. Brookings. When single benefactors could no longer pay all the bills, committees took their place. Over time, ever more assistance was needed. Joseph Pulitzer's one-million-dollar bequest to the New York Philharmonic in 1911 was a milestone. The Cincinnati Symphony was an early recipient of similarly exceptional gifts. In Chicago, Orchestra Hall yielded an income of rents beginning in 1904. A further phase of stabilization was the principle of the "broad base," enlisting annual contributions, large and small, from myriad individuals and businesses (as we have witnessed at the opera companies in New York, Chicago, and San Francisco). Concomitantly, orchestras established classes and lectures, popular and children's concerts, and women's auxiliary committees with responsibility for fund-raising and promotion.

Different cities invented different strategies of survival.[23] The Minneapolis Symphony bought five million dollars of life insurance in exchange for an auditorium built by the Northwestern National Life Insurance Company. When this arrangement ended in 1930, a cooperative relationship with the University of Minnesota again secured an affordable hall. Public support in various forms—usually, the purchase of special concerts—materialized in Baltimore, Buffalo, Detroit, Indianapolis, Philadelphia, Rochester, San Francisco, and St. Louis. But the first half of the twentieth century also witnessed vicissitudes and failures. The Cincinnati Symphony was disbanded between 1907 and 1909, the Pittsburgh Symphony between 1910 and 1937. The San Francisco Symphony suspended concerts in 1934–35. The Detroit Symphony was inactive in 1942–43 and again from 1949 to 1951. Frequently, it was the musicians who were squeezed when ends were made to meet. Wages for eighty players and more, covering hundreds of rehearsals and concerts, were any orchestra's major expenditure. The precarious budget calculus typically denied these players full-time employment. (As of 1950, the Boston Symphony, with its Pops and Tanglewood seasons, offered the most weeks: forty-seven.) Even in orchestras of consequence, players routinely had second jobs unrelated to their seemingly glamorous stage careers. This formed the backdrop to "labor trouble": a twentieth-century symphonic leitmotif.

The first viable musicians' protection association was formed in New York City in 1863, after which the movement spread rapidly. In 1896 the American Federation of Musicians was created and absorbed most local unions. As far as orchestral players were concerned, the union guarded against incursions by foreigners and unwanted "transfers" by out-of-state musicians. As we have seen, Wilhelm Gericke managed to import Europeans into the Boston Symphony and Theodore Thomas imported New Yorkers to Chicago. The New York local was tougher. In 1893 Walter Damrosch brought Anton Hegner from Denmark to become first cellist of the New York Symphony. Violating an existing "six month rule," Hegner took his seat on stage without accumulating half a year's U.S. residence. The rest of the orchestra thereupon walked out—America's first orchestral strike—leaving the conductor to explain matters to the audience. After some weeks in negotiation, Damrosch was fined and Hegner stayed. Generally, conductors were conceded the right to choose players, but there were exceptions. Pierre Monteux, having earlier endured Boston Symphony labor troubles costing him more than two-dozen members of his orchestra, discovered in San Francisco that he could import "less than half a dozen musicians from the east."[24]

But wages, not hiring practices, were the major union grievance after World War I. During the heady twenties, inflation and immigration restrictions strengthened the bargaining power of American Federation of Musicians locals. An especially flamboyant brand of brinkmanship was practiced in Chicago, where labor war was rife and James Petrillo ruled the union. In 1923, Petrillo demanded a 25 percent increase in minimum salary for members of the Chicago Symphony. The trustees said no. Negotiations broke down after a month. The program book informed subscribers that tickets for the coming season would be sold with the understanding that there might be no concerts. Both sides threatened termination of the orchestra. More than another month passed before the Chicago Symphony became the highest paid American orchestra; the union yielded on demands regarding number of concerts and players. Nine years later, a similar drama was enacted, with both sides crying wolf. This time a pay cut was accepted, but with the number of rehearsal hours reduced. In subsequent decades, memories of paternalistic philanthropists and tyrannical conductors were mainly erased. Musicians grew more militant. They secured longer seasons and higher salaries, and orchestras learned (or did not) how to raise new monies to pay the difference.[25]

Mounting expenses meant mounting pressure on the box office—pressure to program music that would sell. It became one function of the music director to push for new and unfamiliar works as a criterion of artistic integrity. It became one function of the board to serve as a fiscal watchdog, restraining financially irresponsible programming—often without the benefit of musical expertise. It became one function of the chief operating officer—the "manager" or "executive director"—to balance these priorities and keep the peace. This "three-legged stool," with no one in charge, did not simplify matters. Many a foreign maestro was perplexed by the strangeness of it all. Monteux, recalling his San Francisco tenure, wrote:

> It seemed . . . that we were always begging for the orchestra. I feel this manner of supporting and aiding symphony orchestras and art museums absolutely wrong and harmful. I strongly believe we must have a Ministry of fine arts or its equivalent in the United States. These institutions, so necessary to the cultural life of the country, should as in Europe be supported by the government, thus alleviating the burden which falls on a select few. There is something incongruous in begging for beauty. I assure you it is very embarrassing for a fine, talented musician, an artist worthy to play in a first-class orchestra, to meet each year in his peregrinations through his home city such posters as I saw in San Francisco throughout the years—appeals that shamed both reader and musician: Keep Your Symphony from Dying . . . Come to the Aid of Your Orchestra . . . Without your Urgent Aid, No Symphony . . .

Antal Dorati, in 1945 entrusted with a reorganized Dallas Symphony, discovered that the only "really dedicated champion of cultured and cultural life in Dallas" was a local arts critic, John Rosenfield, who "succeeded in mobilizing financial forces powerful enough to set things up. What he could not transmit to his followers was his own genuine, deep interest in and love of the arts, or the strength and the will to continue what had been started. Rich patrons of art, unlike John Rosenfield, often have mixed motives: personal vanity, local patriotism, self-advancement, to name but three." But in Minneapolis, where he succeeded Dimitri Mitropoulos, Dorati encountered an orchestra board "completely unprejudiced, understanding and broad-minded," one "which knew what its job was and what it was not. . . . So the money raisers raised money, the managers managed, the directors directed, the music-makers made music."[26]

Some conductors responded to American conditions with aloof absorption: Toscanini in New York, Fritz Reiner in Chicago could not be bothered with trustees, ticket sales, or fund-raising. Frederick Stock, preceding Reiner, collegially served however he could. George Szell succeeded in his ambition to control everything and everyone—board members, administrators, musicians—in his drive to make the Cleveland Orchestra nonpareil. Klemperer, in Los Angeles, did his best to fit in where he could not.

In the late Gilded Age, when contemporary music was not yet threatening and orchestras did not yet compete with radio and phonograph, the conductor's job was simpler. What Thomas or Seidl, Nikisch or Muck wanted to conduct was more or less what people wanted to hear—at least in New York and Boston. Half a century later, it required a willful missionary act in the face of possible resistance or, worse, indifference to present meaningful new repertoire in substantial doses. Stokowski did it in frequent conflict with audience and trustees; his local record of achievement, his unquestioned authority, and his selected boardroom allies carried the day. Mitropoulos in Minneapolis forged useful bonds of affection. Koussevitzky's famous repertoire excursions were supported by Boston pride; a shared hauteur fortified this arrangement. The volatility of the situation was such that Stokowski was replaced by Eugene Ormandy, of whom it was knowingly said that he was "by temperament a musician who cannot bear not to be popular."[27] Mitropoulos was promoted to New York, and there undone. Koussevitzky was discharged by disaffected trustees and his heir apparent dismissed.

The audience for classical music had become a democratized mass. The conductor was more a team player, whether by choice or necessity. The musicians were attaining relative authority. The orchestra, a nonprofit business, was ever more complicated to run and underwrite. Old and new, commerce and art jostled for attention. Ideally, the situation required a manager of some kind. American laissez-faire precluded creation of a higher power—a government bureaucracy—dispassionately to sort things out. Rather, it favored the machinations of a business elite, of a new class of music businessmen. What materialized was a class of one.

■ ■ ■

Except in the field of opera, the manager is a latecomer to classical music. In the first half of the nineteenth century, Beethoven, Mendelssohn, and

Chopin—all important pianists—had no need of one. Franz Liszt was perhaps the first solo artist to employ a specialist to look after logistics and promotion. This was Gaetano Belloni, who organized for his client the most extensive and lucrative series of concert tours yet undertaken: from Limerick and Lisbon to Constantinople and Elizabethgrad.

Shortly afterward came an American managerial genius: P. T. Barnum. Jenny Lind's legendary 1850 American tour—admired in an earlier chapter—was Barnum's inspiration, not Jenny's, and he publicly (and rightfully) shared her triumph. Barnum's entrepreneurial audacities were distinctly American. And he was not alone. The inimitable impresarios of the day—all previously encountered in this narrative—were Bernard Ullman, Max Maretzek, and the brothers Maurice and Max Strakosch. Ullman's calling was the most varied. It was Ullman who packaged the pianist Henri Herz with "A Thousand Candles"; when Herz and his violinist partner, Frans Coenen, needed help securing an audience in Mexico, Ullman turned a poster of Coenen upside down as if to suggest that he would perform standing on his head—according to Ullman's memoirs, it worked. It was Ullman, too, who masterminded Sigismond Thalberg's "matinees musicales"; to underline their snob appeal, he published an "Important Notice" requiring a "correct address" from every subscriber. The same Ullman subsequently presented opera at the Academy of Music, saw his company go bankrupt, repaired to Europe, and returned to the United States handling Hans von Bülow's 1875–76 piano tour. Ullman's posthumous reputation suffered from such wincing assessments as that of the Chicago critic George P. Upton—"Of all the impresarios I have known, he was the most pretentious, unreliable, and headstrong"—as well as his own pompous pronouncements. He told Herz that music was "the art of attracting to a given auditorium, by secondary devices which often become the principal ones, the greatest possible number of curious people, so that when expenses are tallied against receipts the latter exceed the former by the widest possible margin." He advised Bülow to "take America as it is; the country to make money and nothing else."

But Ullman was more than a businessman or conman; he well illustrates the practical services managers performed for increasingly itinerant artists. When Leopold de Meyer, a pianist of reputation, toured the United States in 1845, his manager/companion was his brother-in-law, G. C. Reitheimer. Only a two-week engagement at New York's Park Theatre had been negotiated beforehand. De Meyer and Reitheimer would travel to a new city, engage a hall, post advertisements, and sell tickets. Ullman, a year later, traveled several days ahead of Herz to book and promote. Herz wound up giving at least ninety-eight performances in forty-two cities, a dozen more than de Meyer managed in twice the time. For Thalberg, Ullman booked at least 340 concerts in seventy-five cities over two seasons—an astonishing feat of planning, based on his accumulated knowledge of train schedules, halls, hotels, and newspapers. It was also the manager's job knowingly to supply nonpaying "dead heads" to fill a hall, and knowingly to bribe susceptible members of the press. Finally, the manager was a talent scout: Ullman went to Europe to induce Thalberg to come to America.[28]

In no department was Ullman more ingenious than enlisting a piano maker, Chickering, to supply instruments for Thalberg's concerts, and again for Bülow's almost twenty years later. This arrangement was practical for the pianist, prestigious for the firm, and profitable for the manager (who admitted to a kickback). Anton Rubinstein's tour of 1872–73, managed by Maurice Grau, was similarly sponsored by Steinway. In this manner, piano manufacturers entered the concert business (as they did the American parlor) as a reckonable force. Bülow returned to the United States in 1888 playing a Knabe. Tchaikovsky, at Carnegie Hall in 1891, first endorsed Knabe, then Steinway. We have observed that Paderewski's Steinway affiliation compelled Theodore Thomas to smuggle a grand piano onto the Chicago fairgrounds in 1893, and that Thomas himself was subsidized by William Steinway.

Though Thomas was his own manager, with the advent of permanent orchestras came a new managerial breed. Henry Higginson hired Charles Ellis, whose managing experience was restricted to one of Higginson's mining concerns, to administer the Boston Symphony in 1885. It was a typically shrewd move: Ellis lasted until 1919, when Higginson retired. He was admired for his patience, integrity, and kindness. He concurrently opened his own agency, with an exclusive roster including Kreisler, Paderewski, and Farrar. For four years he also partnered Walter Damrosch in the Damrosch-Ellis Opera Company. Elsewhere, in the world of opera, managers ranged from Edmund Stanton, nearly invisible behind Anton Seidl at the Met, to Oscar Hammerstein, larger than life at the Manhattan. The leading New York artists' managers around the turn of the century included Henry Wolfsohn, whose bureau Eugene Ysaÿe remembered as "my gang of thieves,"[29] and Loudon Charlton, who from 1910 to 1912 also ran the Philharmonic.

From all these precursors, Arthur Judson stood apart.[30] He was neither a flamboyant artist manqué nor a respectful servant of art. His scope of operation was unique and unprecedented. His model, if he had one, was Ellis, whose power was quiet. More accurately, he resembled a CEO whose word was law. A self-described "salesman of fine music," he was a trained musician who opted for a vast commercial sphere parallel to art and never subservient to it. He did not look like the violinist he once was, but the business scion he became: tall, robust, well fed. His public tone, writing or speaking, was composed and all-knowing: lordly. His competence of judgment was taken on faith. Had he displayed more vulnerability to art, he would have owed the artist, if not deference, the awed admiration a Sarnoff might succumb to. Instead, he at all times appeared to understand things that artists did not.

Judson was born to working-class parents in Dayton, Ohio, in 1881. In 1900 he was already teaching violin at Denison University in Granville, Ohio. By the time he left seven years later, he had become dean of a locally formidable conservatory of music. He expanded, strengthened, and conducted the orchestra and chorus. He became one of the first Americans to perform Richard Strauss's Violin Sonata. He initiated a series of music festivals including the Chicago and Cincinnati Symphonies. But Judson realized he would never become a ranking virtuoso. In New York, he joined the staff of *Musical America*, writing articles and reviews and selling advertisements. The business side of music increasingly interested him. Addressing "The Musician and Publicity" in 1911, he wrote:

> The dry goods merchant has no need of ethics in his profession, provided he gives good value for the money expended, but the musician has a bigger responsibility in that he deals with talent and not materials. Material can be replaced, but talent is a gift and the possessor once misled seldom has a chance to retrace his steps. As a result the musician who is competent has a moral obligation to himself and his profession, to make the most of his powers and opportunities, and advertising is one means of so doing. Viewed from this aspect advertising does not become mere commercialism.[31]

The same year, Judson surveyed "Change in the Musical Management Situation" and prophetically advocated a cooperative network of managers.

One of the benefits of Judson's modest *Musical America* job was the opportunity to travel the country hearing concerts and meeting the people who played, presented, and paid for them. In 1911 he was sent to Cincinnati to review the Symphony and its new conductor, a young man about his own age. He filed no fewer than four stories. He admired the orchestra and found the conductor "magnetic." In an interview, he hailed Leopold Stokowski as "Thinker, Philosopher, and Musician." When Stokowski took over in Philadelphia a year later, Judson was there to call him a "genius." Judson appears to have proposed the meeting with Stokowski in the summer of 1915 that resulted in an invitation to manage the Philadelphia Orchestra. It was during Judson's first season in his new post that Stokowski gave his legendary performances of Mahler's *Symphony of a Thousand*. In his element, Judson supervised planning and promotion. Among other things, he had to find racks for twelve hundred coats. He also needed to transport twelve hundred people to New York on two private trains with eighteen cars. He remarked, "There is as much enthusiasm over this work, it seems to me, as one might expect over a championship baseball series. . . . If I had been told that Philadelphia, New York, or Boston would manifest such enthusiasm over any matter of music or art, as I have witnessed . . . , I would have laughed." But Judson loyally supported Stokowski's repertoire excursions. When Stokowski balked at conducting Schoenberg's Chamber Symphony because he found the music "ridiculous," Judson advised:

> It is unwise possibly, to give this [work] for musical reasons, but perhaps, very wise to give it for business reasons. Why would not it be a good plan to keep it on the program, and for you to announce to the public what you think of the work and tell them that you feel it should be given if only to show them what bad music is and keep them in touch with Schönberg. If you don't give it, you will be criticized for not keeping up with the new musical works of the day; and if you do give it without remark, you will be criticized because it's bad music. So why not tell the public in advance and get some real publicity out of it?

Stokowski did so, with aplomb. One headline read: "RIOT CALL AVERTED AT ORCHESTRA CONCERT."[32]

But relations between conductor and manager grew frostier over time, and not all Stokowski's "modern music" pleased Judson, the board, or the subscribers. Stokowski and Judson tired of one another, and both tired of Philadelphia. The Depression, and the orchestra's financially disastrous (but artistically distinguished) 1934–35 opera series combined to wipe out the reserve fund. Judson resigned in 1935. He had elected long before to concentrate his various music businesses in New York. Starting from scratch in Philadelphia, where like Ellis in Boston he ran a side business, he had become the nation's leading artists' manager. Since 1922 he had concurrently managed the New York Philharmonic. He served as artistic advisor to the Cincinnati Symphony, and manager of New York's summertime Stadium concerts. And he was engrossed in figuring out how to maximize radio exposure—and profits—for classical music.

This last exercise might have fostered "cooperation"—a Judson keyword for all things good in business—with David Sarnoff, who instead chose to support broadcasting, recording, managerial, and symphonic enterprises in competition with Judson's. Both dreamt of radio disseminating distinguished music and culture. In 1926 Judson formed a Judson Radio Corporation to supply music to Sarnoff's NBC national network. When Sarnoff said no, Judson in short order found investors sufficient to create his own national network, a heroic initiative eventually resulting in the Columbia Broadcasting System under the young Philadelphia millionaire William Paley. As the second-largest stockholder, Judson secured an ultimate source of immense personal wealth. He also secured an annual radio market for his clients and for the New York Philharmonic, whose weekly broadcasts were CBS's cultural flagship. To better furnish artists to the Columbia system, Judson in 1930 formed Columbia Concerts Corporation, a spectacular merger of four leading artist-management companies, including the Judson bureau—which itself had absorbed the long prominent Wolfsohn Bureau. As president (with Paley as chairman), Judson now controlled approximately two-thirds of America's most successful concert artists and nearly all its important conductors. In 1939 Paley bought the Columbia Phonograph Company, facilitating enduring contracts with the New York Philharmonic, which Judson managed, and the Philadelphia Orchestra, which he had previously managed. NBC, meanwhile, in 1928 created its own National Broadcasting and Concert Bureau, and in 1929 purchased a recording company, resulting in RCA Victor. As the Federal Trade Commission viewed these conglomerates with a bemused fascination, the two networks parted company with the two management companies in 1941. Columbia Concerts became Columbia Artists Management Incorporated, or CAMI, in 1948.

A still further dimension of Judson's empire was "organized audiences." This was a risk-free concert-presentation strategy begun in the Midwest in the early 1920s. A community would raise money for a concert series, then hire the artists. "Members" would pay an annual fee, and only members could attend the concerts. Judson was influential in establishing Community Concerts Service as an adjunct to Columbia Concerts, and the vast majority of artists so booked were on the Columbia roster. A rival Civic Concerts Service mainly booked National Broadcasting artists. By the 1940s, some two thousand towns were either Community or Civic territory. Every year, a Community or Civic sales representative—"messengers of culture," Judson called them—would appear to inaugurate a membership drive. Only once the drive concluded, and the pot was counted, would the participating artists be chosen. Though no Heifetz or Lily Pons was for sale, a mix of better- and lesser-known performers, governed by fee and availability, was typical.

As of 1930, Community Concerts was headed by Ward French—like Judson, a plainspoken midwesterner who eschewed the arcane. But if Judson was a populist on principle, French was a populist by temperament: a classical music cheerleader who fired his staff with religious zeal. He invoked the Declaration of Independence's "pursuit of happiness" clause on behalf of music and its "usefulness to mankind." The 1931 Columbia Artists Almanac amplified, "This corporation claims that it is able to supply all concert demands, however great or modest, of every club, school, or college, organization or individual entrepreneur. . . . In the task of recovery the solace and inspiration of music will play its accustomed part, and the artists listed in this book, couriers of that lovely muse, are ready and eager to spread the message of cheer and joy to the four corners of this great land."[33] Under French's leadership, Community surpassed Civic. It instilled and sustained the confidence necessary to sell concerts without identifying what music would be played or who would play it. It brought touring recitalists to countless communities that otherwise would not be so served. For the recitalists, it supplied dates that would otherwise not have materialized, and routed them with superb efficiency. For all concerned, it lightened the burden of the Depression.

But there was discontent. "A famous singer, once under our management, was engaged to sing in a rough Pennsylvania mining town," Judson once related. "When she arrived in the early morning a cold rain swept the dreary railroad platform. The enthusiastic Mayor was there with the public and a brass band to greet the prima donna. The tired and worn prima donna, half awake, stepped upon the platform and said, 'Great guns, why does my manager send me to a God-forsaken town like this?'"[34] More than likely the singer's ingratitude had something to do with money. It was a constant complaint among Community artists that after Columbia and Community took their respective cuts, the accompanist was paid, and travel and hotel were added up, two-thirds of the fee was gone. Another perennial grievance was that return engagements on the Community circuit were unlikely after three seasons, at which point many Community artists, lacking exposure in the wider world, were unceremoniously dropped by Columbia. Also, French ruthlessly standardized repertoire: performers felt merchandised. For many, musicians and audiences alike, there was no better option.

In 1950 Judson was ousted in a Columbia putsch in favor of French, but retained his all-important conductors list. He resigned as manager of the New York Philharmonic in 1956. He remained an active artists' manager into his nineties. He died in 1975. A singular player in the culture of performance, he both maximized the participation of the new audience and unerringly spoke the language of the boardroom. He was the man to supply a national Beethoven broadcast or a local piano recitalist. When the Portland (Oregon) Symphony's music director suddenly died in 1925, it was Judson whom the orchestra phoned. He recommended Willem van Hoogstraten; Hoogstraten was hired. It was Judson who recommended Eugene Ormandy to the Minneapolis Symphony, and who recommended Ormandy's successor, Dimitri Mitropoulos, and who recommended Mitropoulos's successor, Antal Dorati, and who recommended Walter Hendl to succeed Dorati in Dallas. It was Judson who wrote Massimo Freccia, music director of the New Orleans Philharmonic, instructing him to engage a certain Hungarian pianist. When Freccia asked to hear the pianist play, Judson did not bother to reply. It was considered dangerous to oppose him.[35]

Otto Klemperer and Eugene Goossens were two conductors who believed that their American careers were aborted by Judson—Klemperer because he crossed Judson in programming a Mahler symphony in New York, Goossens because he decided, a dozen years into his American career, that he no longer needed to pay Judson a commission. Certainly Ormandy's American success—he was conducting in a New York movie theater before obtaining the Minneapolis position in 1931—was Judson-driven. The Minneapolis Symphony was at the time considered a Judson "farm team," a launching pad for greater things. Ormandy moved on to Philadelphia, replacing Stokowski. In Philadelphia, his forty-two-year-regime was as quiescent, musically, as Stokowski's quarter century had been epochal. Next door at Curtis, Fritz Reiner—as difficult as Ormandy was accommodating, as challenging as Ormandy was mild—had coveted the Philadelphia job. Reiner was also a Judson client. Looking back, Ormandy said of Judson, "I owe everything to him."[36]

■ ■ ■

Though the scope of Judson's empire would eventually prove controversial, it initially rhymed with prevalent notions of management efficiency. The early twentieth century was the period during which Toscanini, at the Met, was extolled as a "scientific" conductor and "the man who knows his business." Meanwhile, Otto Kahn engineered the buyout of Oscar Hammerstein's Manhattan Opera. Kahn (as we have seen) attempted an operatic cartel linking New York, Philadelphia, Boston, and Chicago. This was the climate supporting Judson's tireless pursuit of "cooperation" and "concentration." As early as 1911, pondering the future of "musical management," he wrote in *Musical America*:

The large commercial industries, the Trusts, as they are popularly called, were not formed by gradually building up a business from New York, but by the uniting of factories and firms possessing similar interests throughout the country. This meant that the industries were distributed according to the demand (for factories and businesses often spring up haphazard in any locality) and that the dangers of unlimited and ruinous competition were eliminated. A healthy competition based on the value of an article is all right, but a competition having as its main end the elimination of another in the same business means trouble for all concerned.[37]

Because he was at the same time a presenter and an orchestra manager, Judson the artists' manager understood the crippling impact of rising artists' fees. His version of cooperation successfully combined restrained fees and increased earnings. Expanding audiences meant more concert dates. Centralized bookings—via Judson's management consortium, via Community Concerts—meant fewer middlemen, diminished overhead, and more efficient touring. Another advocate of cooperation was the telegraph magnate and musical activist Clarence Mackay, whom we have encountered supporting and departing from Oscar Hammerstein's Manhattan Opera. Mackay was a member of the Metropolitan Opera board from 1903 to 1938. In 1919, he joined the board of New York's New Symphony, a product of (understandable) dissatisfaction with the New York Philharmonic and New York Symphony. The conductor was Artur Bodanzky of the Met. Mackay proposed a bigger name: Willem Mengelberg. In 1920–21, Bodanzky and Mengelberg shared the podium and the New Symphony was renamed the National Symphony. In May 1921, it merged with the New York Philharmonic, with Mackay—a coup—as chairman of the board. Josef Stransky, the incumbent Philharmonic conductor, was out and Mengelberg was in. As Mengelberg was also the conductor of Amsterdam's Concertgebouw Orchestra, the Philharmonic commenced a policy of shared artistic leadership. Mackay added board members who, like himself, were also Metropolitan board members. These embodiments of cooperation—of resources and responsibilities shared or combined—resulted, incidentally or not, in musical leadership superior to Stransky's and directors who were broader based and more enlightened than the guarantors who had bedevilled Mahler and chosen Stransky. Mackay also effectively pushed the orchestra toward enlarging and democratizing its constituency via new educational services and new venues. He even effectively advocated the programming of more American music.

It was Mackay, as well, who in 1922 invited Arthur Judson to manage the Philharmonic. Judson shared Mackay's enthusiasm for cooperative alignment and audience expansion. That he was already manager of the Philadelphia

Orchestra, and of a growing roster of soloists, was not considered problematic. Rather, newspapers in both New York and Philadelphia hailed the appointment as a strategy for "eliminating duplication, conflict, and competition."[38] Judson was obviously regarded as the man to raise the Philharmonic to Stokowski's Philadelphia standard. Instead, Judson's thirty-four-year Philharmonic tenure, far surviving Mackay's death in 1938, proved a disappointment. As it lays bare a central weakness of the Judson method, this is a history that bears close examination.

More than Mengelberg or even Judson, Arturo Toscanini was central to Mackay's Philharmonic plans. And in 1926 the Philharmonic succeeded in luring him back to New York. But Toscanini was not interested in a full-time symphonic post comparable to the norm for Boston (Gericke, Muck, Monteux, Koussevitzky), Chicago (Thomas, Stock), or Philadelphia (Stokowski in the formative years of his regime). We have earlier observed the "cooperative" result: when Toscanini was in town, his magnificent reign of terror held; when he was away, the reign of truancy prevailed. Judson was heard to complain that Toscanini "ruined business," by which he meant that Toscanini's presence was exorbitantly expensive and that in Toscanini's absence the orchestra had no drawing power of its own.

When Toscanini resigned in 1936, Judson, Mackay, and the board were challenged to find a full-time music director, or at least a name to reckon with. The story of Wilhelm Furtwängler's engagement, of the threatened boycotts, and of Furtwängler's withdrawal, has already been told. In retrospect, Furtwängler's New York fate was inescapable: he served Germany at Hitler's pleasure; Hitler's criminal anti-Semitism was already entrenched; more than half the Philharmonic's subscribers were Jewish. For the Philharmonic directors, who had attempted to defend the Furtwängler candidacy, this highly charged, highly publicized false start was both traumatic and pivotal. Fritz Busch, another distinguished Toscanini candidate, was approached but not pressed. Walter Price of the Philharmonic board explained to Toscanini on March 31, 1935:

> Mr. Busch advises that . . . he has European obligations continuing for the whole season and is fixed for several years to come. . . . We feel, until the resentment of the Jewish people subsides against anything apparently German, it is unfair to Mr. Busch to allow him to cancel or change his plans. . . . You see the overhead of [the] orchestra is colossal and with you, our main bower, going, we have got to be very careful, because somebody has got to bear the deficit if there is any, and the Jewish people represent the largest part of our audiences.

In a subsequent letter to board member Charles Triller, Judson offered a list of the "most important conductors in Europe and America with some indication of their availability." He further advised:

> In giving consideration to this list, I think it would be well to bear in mind our recent difficulties and to weigh carefully whether it would be advisable, or even possible, to import either an Aryan German or a Jewish conductor. In case we brought over the former, it is almost absolutely certain that we would run into the same difficulties as with Furtwängler. Should we try the latter, I do not think we will have a public boycott but I do expect that we will alienate the support of an appreciable number of important members of this community. I know that advice is easily given and difficult to accept. I will not feel at all offended if this last opinion of mine is given no consideration. . . .
>
> It is further apparent that there is no single conductor to whom we could wish to offer the whole season. On the other hand, we ought to avoid, if possible, a succession of guest conductors. Under these circumstances, it would seem wise to divide the season as nearly as possible between two conductors, leaving from four to six weeks in the middle of the season in order to try out certain likely candidates for future years.

For 1936–37, Judson proposed Fritz Reiner "for the first 10 or 12 weeks" and Artur Rodzinski for the final eight. He continued:

> I admit that Reiner is not popular from the public standpoint, but I have great faith in his musicianship and conductorial ability. Whether the Board will care to make its decision only on musical grounds and fight it through on that basis is up to them. I must point out that Mr. Reiner is 50% Jewish and Rodzinski is 25% Jewish.

The other names in Judson's letter included that of John Barbirolli.[39]

It was comically typical of Judson to assure recipients of his written advice that he was merely offering a personal opinion, to be accepted or rejected. On this occasion, the Philharmonic board elected to do without Reiner, the unpopular half-Jew, and to assign the season's first ten weeks to Barbirolli, who was neither Jewish nor German. Rodzinski, who was not German and only one-quarter Jewish, was to take the last eight weeks. The intervening guests—the composer/conductors Stravinsky, Enescu, and Chávez—were non-German non-Jews. Made uneasy by the board's incongruously emphatic support for a conductor so young and little known, Judson now undertook to advise Barbirolli on programming, a project that consumed more than four months of detailed correspondence. Barbirolli's half-season the following fall proved so successful that in December he was named permanent conductor. Judson, Barbirolli's American agent, and Judson, the Philharmonic manager, agreed to a three-year contract at thirty, forty, and fifty thousand dollars. A fraction of each season would be otherwise entrusted; not since Stransky's day had the orchestra so dispensed with guest leaders. The appointment was greeted with anger and incredulity by Rodzinski, whose tryout remained pending, and Toscanini, whose counsel was not invited. Weeks later, David Sarnoff asked Toscanini to conduct for NBC with an after-taxes salary of $3,334 *per concert*. Toscanini's acceptance placed the Barbirolli selection in a harsh new light.[40]

Judson and his factotum Bruno Zirato, who handled the Philharmonic's day-to-day administration, were now more than ever thrust into anxious mentoring roles. Under Barbirolli, the Philharmonic could not compete with the Boston, Philadelphia, and NBC orchestras for virtuosity and glamour. On top of that, Barbirolli showed no flair as a program-maker: compared to Stokowski and Koussevitzky—or Mitropoulos in Minneapolis, Klemperer in Los Angeles, or Rodzinski in Cleveland—he failed to impress as a passionate advocate of important new music. Judson and Zirato attempted to help with repertoire suggestions, as did Lawrence Gilman, the Philharmonic's program annotator (who also served as music critic of the *Herald-Tribune*). Meanwhile, Barbirolli was regularly pummeled in the *New York Times* by Olin Downes (who was relieved of his duties as intermission commentator for the Philharmonic broadcasts). In 1940 Barbirolli himself complained to the *New York Sun* that "the public wants to hear nothing but masterpieces." This was the same season Koussevitzky came to Carnegie Hall with two American programs, including four premieres. "Why is it," Judson wrote Zirato, "that every important novelty given in N.Y. is done by Boston, Philadelphia or some other visiting orchestra? I have the feeling, we are asleep: we'd better get up on our toes, musically. . . . Other conductors find new works and new ideas. That's B's job: why doesn't he do it?" Zirato replied, "We have been telling him that it is up to him to make interesting programs and he has failed us. There is nothing that we can do any more, I am afraid."[41]

Barbirolli was eased out in the course of two seasons. In 1941–42 he shared the Philharmonic podium with nine other conductors, in 1942–43 with eight. Finally, in 1943–44, a "music director"—the orchestra's first, so called—was named: the very same Artur Rodzinski who was passed over seven years before. Unlike Barbirolli, Rodzinski was a known quantity with a reputation for whipping orchestras into shape. He was also notoriously mercurial, even unstable. He and his wife considered Judson a power-hungry philistine. They believed he had conspired against Rodzinski with board members of both the Cleveland Orchestra and the New York Philharmonic. They assumed he had engineered Barbirolli's New York appointment because Barbirolli was manipulable. Rodzinski regarded the management fees that were paid regularly to Judson as a form of extortion; "I will not suffer this quietly," he told his wife.[42] In 1940, with his new job at hand, Rodzinski flipped the page. He sought and obtained Judson's support in firing one-seventh of the orchestra, including its concertmaster (five of the fourteen ousted players were subsequently reinstated in a compromise with the musicians' union). It was widely agreed that the Philharmonic sounded tight and clean under Rodzinski's baton and that programming was fresher.

Then, midway through the 1946–47 season, Rodzinski asked to address the board personally. In the course of a harangue lasting more than an hour, he proceeded to denounce Judson as a "dictator" who made musical progress "impossible." He accused Judson of inflicting his own clients on the Philharmonic as soloists, using the orchestra as "a testing ground for unproved performers." The following day, Rodzinski resigned, and announced what Judson and the Philharmonic board already knew: that he would become music director of the Chicago Symphony. He also told the press, "The three pillars of a soundly run orchestra are the board, the manager and the musical director. As the New York Philharmonic is run, these three pillars are not of equal importance, as they must be. The board and musical director revolve around the manager as if they were satellites." Virgil Thomson added in the *Herald-Tribune*, "Arthur Judson is unsuited by the nature and magnitude of his business interests to manage with the necessary self-effacement a major intellectual institution doing business with his other interests."[43]

If Rodzinski imagined Judson's head would roll, he was dreaming. Rodzinski fell out with the Chicago board during his first season; he would never again secure a permanent post. Bruno Walter, who of all the important immigrant conductors was the most estranged from contemporary and American music,[44] was named "Musical Advisor" to the Philharmonic (and let it be known that he had been offered the music directorship ahead of Rodzinski in 1943). But Stokowski and Mitropoulos, not Walter, led most of the concerts for two seasons. In 1949–50, they became coprincipal conductors. In 1950, Mitropoulos was made conductor and entrusted with the familiar challenge of charting an artistic mission for the New York Philharmonic. We have already surveyed the wreckage of his regime. It only remains to inquire what roles Judson and Zirato may have played.

According to Mitropoulos's protégé Paul Strauss, Zirato once upbraided Mitropoulos for programming "excessive" quantities of "modern music" as follows: "You're lucky you have the damned job. We took you instead of Stokowski because we thought you'd be more manageable. Now you be a good boy and take care of yourself." On another occasion Zirato, backstage, berated Mitropoulos for encoring Schoenberg's *A Survivor from Warsaw* following an unexpected ovation. It was doubtless with Judson's blessing that Bruno Walter was prevailed upon to inform Mitropoulos in writing (during the latter's convalescence from his first heart attack) that he would have to "confine . . . future programming to a formula closer to Beethoven, Brahms, and Tchaikovsky" or steps would be taken for his "dismissal."[45]

In the face of such insults, it is necessary to recall what Mitropoulos was doing in New York in the first place. In Boston and Minneapolis, he was Mephisto, Moses, St. Francis. He was what the Philharmonic knew it needed: a star. Judson was not insensitive to New York's simultaneous need for new music—always the businessman, he recognized that a certain portion of the public clamored for it. But he did not bargain for symphonies by Webern and Sessions. Nor could he supply a loyal audience or a proud orchestra, such as Mitropoulos's challenging agenda required and other American cities enjoyed. He was as corporeal and impregnable as Mitropoulos was un- and other-worldly. He lacked the will or the temperament, or both, to buttress a music director who ate at Beefburger Hall, read Kierkegaard, and complained that Americans lacked warmth and craved comfort.

Howard Taubman's terminal diagnosis of the Philharmonic's ills—the 1956 *New York Times* indictment that indelibly fingered Mitropoulos—was a short-term analysis of a long-term problem. His understanding of Judson's complicity was parochial: too many Judson soloists, three Judson violinists playing the Brahms concerto in a single season. Paul Henry Lang, in the *Herald-Tribune*, more aggressively blamed management for lacking initiative and imagination.[46] By the following fall Judson had quietly exited from the Philharmonic offices. Zirato stayed.

■ ■ ■

Arthur Judson was a brilliant music businessman. He ingeniously contributed to the expansion of American classical music after World War I—onto the radio, into the hinterlands.* He knew how to make concerts and concert

---

* According to one tally, by 1952 three times as many concerts were being given annually in the United States and Canada as in all the rest of the world, and the total concert audience in North

artists affordable and attractive to new listeners. At the New York Philharmonic, too, he presided over a period of growth: more subscription concerts, more summer concerts, more tours, more recordings, a regular radio berth. But if the Philharmonic he inherited was a rudderless vessel, a rudderless vessel it remained. During the Judson era, the Philharmonic had up to a dozen "conductors" a season—in addition to "guest conductors," "associate conductors," and "assistant conductors." The longest-tenured music director was Mitropoulos, who logged six consecutive seasons. Prior to Judson, Stransky was music director for twelve seasons. After Judson, Leonard Bernstein stayed for a decade. Of Bernstein's successors, Pierre Boulez lasted six seasons, Zubin Mehta eleven, Kurt Masur thirteen.

What precluded a continuity of musical leadership alongside Judson? According to Rodzinski, Thomson, and countless others, Judson was power-mad, corrupt, commercial. In fact, there is no statistical evidence that he favored CAMI artists for Philharmonic dates. As of 1945, he donated all CAMI commissions from Philharmonic conductors and guest conductors to the orchestra's pension fund,[47] and there is anecdotal evidence of Judson rejecting commissions on Philharmonic soloists as well. The personal wealth he amassed apparently came from CBS stock, not CAMI or New York Philharmonic salaries. The Judson problem was both subtler and more profound. The smoking gun is not money or conflict of interest, but repertoire.

As early as 1911, in *Musical America*, Judson appraised New York audiences and concluded, "Everything in Music—Good, Bad, and Indifferent—is Applauded in New York." He claimed that Brahms's First Piano Concerto, with Harold Bauer and the Philharmonic, was appreciated more for its performance than for the "abstruse" and "forbidding" work itself (which had not yet entered the standard repertoire). In a letter to the editor, Bauer took issue with Judson; writing of the Brahms concerto, he argued, "There is absolutely no opportunity for display of any kind on the part of the virtuoso, consequently, if an effect is produced it must necessarily and obviously be an effect of the music itself and nothing else. The public does not applaud the mere efforts, however sincere and well intentioned, of an artist to make an uninteresting composition effective."[48]

Judson's conservative predisposition as revealed in this exchange—his lack of confidence in an audience's powers of discernment, his emphasis on the difficulties of apprehending what is new or different—would echo throughout his managerial career. In 1931, responding to complaints about Toscanini's

---

America had doubled in twenty years. See Joseph Mussulman, *Dear People . . . Robert Shaw, a Biography* (Bloomington, Indiana University Press, 1979), p. 152.

limited repertoire, he issued this remarkable edict: "There are certain composers like Bruckner and Mahler who have not yet been accepted heartily by
the American public. Certain of their works are played from time to time and
it may be that they will gradually attain their permanent place in the repertory. . . . We can only go as far as the public will go with us." Of Toscanini's
penchant for repeating standard works, Judson said that certain classic compositions should be heard "not only once a season but some of them several
times a season. . . . We Americans are too anxious for the sensational and too
little concerned with the content of the work. I am beginning to sense a
change in the right direction, and I believe within the next few years the
Beethoven Fifth, no matter how badly played, will be welcomed because of
the message it conveys."[49]

By his own lights, Judson did not meddle with program-making. But he
freely offered advice on what the market could bear. In the case of John Barbirolli's first half-season of Philharmonic concerts, he counseled the young
conductor, "My own only inclination is for the recognized masterpieces of
the classic literature. I believe that by far the greater part of the public agrees
with me but, on the other hand, there is a section of our audiences which
desires modern music and which is very insistent and loud with protests when
it does not get it." In his letters to Barbirolli, Judson assessed public taste with
scientific certainty. Liszt's *Faust* Symphony and Walton's Symphony No. 1
were among the works Barbirolli dropped upon learning from Judson that
they would not please. Judson added, in dizzying self-contradiction, "I wonder
whether you wish to end your first concert with Elgar's [*Enigma*] Variations. I
have never found our public very enthusiastic about the 'variations' form,
probably because the continuity of idea is so broken up. To my mind, it would
be much better to end with the Brahms [Fourth] Symphony although,
strangely enough, the last movement of that is also variations." Barbirolli dutifully repositioned the Elgar and ended with the Brahms.[50] When some years
later Judson and Zirato realized Barbirolli was at sea in identifying important
new and American works, they were themselves at a loss: Judson took his cues
from the marketplace; where there was no market, there were no cues. At
Community Concerts, Ward French's repertoire strictures were of the same
kind, only cruder. He insisted on formulaic programs. He forbade certain
works. At one point, he proscribed any composition longer than seventeen
minutes. As with Judson, the audience led taste, not the artist.

This market mentality was previously anathema to classical music.
Theodore Thomas, to be sure, would consider audience taste, but only by way
of identifying a point of departure; his object—in New York, Chicago, or
Peoria—was to take the public to new places. It would never have occurred

to a Seidl, Koussevitzky, or Stokowski to treat audience taste as a given; as artists, their mission was to chart virgin terrain. In fact, Judson's attitude, or French's, demeaned and redefined the performer's role in the larger scheme of things musical. For the most part, music new or unfamiliar was considered not good for business.

The concentration of power achieved by Judson was not fundamentally venal. As likely as not, he was a true believer in bigger audiences and better-fed artists. But his authority crucially exceeded his artistic competence. It was said by some that Judson, in Philadelphia, "made Stokowski." It was also Stokowski who made Judson. The Mahler Eighth that galvanized a city and catapulted its orchestra to prominence was not Judson's idea. In New York, there was no Stokowski to break the artistic stalemate. Even if Barbirolli was not Judson's choice, it was Judson who had the power—and, properly, the obligation—to redirect the board. Instead, he advised against Germans and Jews. Why he counseled that a Jewish conductor would "alienate the support of an appreciable number of important members of this community" remains a mystery. The Philharmonic board was a WASP preserve. But so was Boston's, and Koussevitzky was Jewish. And why was Judson so shy of non-Jewish Germans, such as Erich Kleiber, who had fled Hitler? Like Klemperer, who was both Jewish and German, Kleiber had been a formidable force in musical Berlin. He had guest conducted the Philharmonic in elegant and ingenious programs with notable success. A Klemperer or Kleiber appointment in 1936 would have looked plausible. Both were commanding and demanding; both were associated with important contemporary repertoire.*

That in musical affairs Judson was as meek as he was bold in business is no conundrum: these are different spheres, addressing different needs, populated by different personalities. Writing of Stokowski in 1911, Judson said, "In the last analysis the great man is the man of simplicity. . . . The man who can think of great things with . . . clarity of thought, is the man of true power. . . . I have

---

* In Judson's conductor's memorandum of March 24, 1936 (see p. 424), Kleiber is listed among fifteen conductors who did not "fit" the Philharmonic's plans. Klemperer is offered (with Thomas Beecham, Hamilton Harty, and Eugene Goossens) as an alternative to Fritz Reiner. Klemperer's Mahler and Bruckner performances were praised by the Philharmonic's board president, Marshall Field III. Judson wrote, "I admire many things about Mr. Klemperer from a musical standpoint but I must confess that he is otherwise a difficult man." This was by way of commenting on Klemperer's angry and repeated insistence that Judson had denied him the job given Barbirolli. All relevant correspondence may be found in the New York Philharmonic Archives. See also James Doering, "A Salesman of Fine Music: American Music Manager Arthur Judson, 1900 to 1940" (dissertation, Washington University, 1998), p. 397, and Peter Heyworth, *Otto Klemperer: His Life and Times*, vol. 2 (Cambridge, UK, Cambridge University Press, 1996).

not yet found a truly great man who was complex and abstruse." But this description fits Judson—not Stokowski, Klemperer, Rodzinski, or Mitropoulos. Simple conviction and clarity of thought, never subtlety or complexity, are hallmarks of Judson's letters, articles, and reviews. He doubtless disapproved of Stokowski's dalliance with spiritualism, Klemperer's leftist Weimar politics, Rodzinski's allegiance to the religious Moral Rearmament movement, and Mitropoulos's zeal for St. Francis and Henry Wallace. He urged his artists to avoid political sentiments that might offend status quo business interests.[51]

His own business interest was to increase the American audience for classical music. He did not philosophize about the risks of a lowered common denominator of culture. With his preferred allegiance to the "recognized masterpieces of the classic literature," he subscribed to the agenda of the music appreciators and new listeners, and he appeared to care as little about musical literacy—about teaching how to sing and play—as they did. "Be Your Own Music Critic," preached Olin Downes, disdaining experts and intellectuals much as Judson disdained the abstruse. According to David Sarnoff, "Given a chance, the average man will move slowly, perhaps falteringly, toward a selection of the best."[52] In relation to the popularization of classical music, Judson was both cause and effect.

His legacies were as tangible as he was elusive. Though Walter Damrosch's New York Symphony engaged Mahler, among other eminent visitors, and though Stokowski began stingily sharing his Philadelphia podium in 1918–19, the guest conductor is largely an invention of the New York Philharmonic during Judson's long regime. Also, never before Judson—never in the case of Thomas or Seidl, or of Higginson or Koussevitzky (and Koussevitzky was not a Judson artist)—did the guest soloist loom so large in defining an evening at the symphony. Previously, the orchestra and its own conductor mattered more, the visitors less. The business of music—of sales and marketing— changed accordingly: an appearance by Heifetz or Horowitz became the season's stellar event. As we will see, Judson's successors—who were not simultaneously presenters or orchestra managers—did not restrain artists' fees as he had worked to do. The music business priorities he helped to set in motion would lead to crippling concert costs as well as a crippling surfeit of concerts.

Could the twentieth-century decline of classical music have been cushioned, postponed, or deflected? What if Anton Seidl had lived a normal span of years? The permanent New York orchestra created for him just as he expired in 1898 would likely have matched Boston's and Philadelphia's; the Philharmonic's decades of vicissitudes might never have begun. What if

Toscanini had never materialized in America and Stokowski became the conductor who mattered most? A bold symphonic template, stressing new music and audience education, would have stood higher. What if there had been no Arthur Judson? Here, genuine alternatives were foreclosed: the business forces of concentration and cooperation would still have pressed toward a more standardized, more plentiful concert product favoring what music was already tried-and-true. Some version of the culture of performance was in fact inescapable. Music businessmen and new audiences demanded it. Demographic change and technological invention supported it. And those who most opposed it—America's composers—were increasingly out of touch: our next topic.

CHAPTER 6

Composers on the Sidelines

■

Aaron Copland, modernism, and populism ▪ *Virgil Thomson as critic and composer* ▪ *Roy Harris as the "white hope"* ▪ *Edgard Varèse and the "ultra-moderns"* ▪ *George Gershwin and the jazz threat* ▪ *The four streams of American music*

In the proper scheme of things musical, creators outrank re-creators. But no American classical composer was as famous as Stokowski, or as influential as Arthur Judson, or as famous and influential as Toscanini. George Marek wrote in 1940, "I believe that the United States is the most musical country in the world today. We started from scratch; but we scratched deeply." Marek was no more thinking of composers than was Howard Taubman when he claimed that "even the glowing warmth of the Vienna Philharmonic's pre-Hitler glory did not surpass or match" Koussevitzky's Boston Symphony, Stokowski's Philadelphia Orchestra, or Toscanini's New York Philharmonic."[1] America's composers loomed small.

And they knew it. As their writings and letters attest, they bonded in opposition to orchestras, managers, and radio networks. Their complaints were amplified by immigrant composers for whom the spectacle of the public leading taste was curious and abhorrent. Arnold Schoenberg wrote, "It really is a fact that the public lets its leaders drive it unresisting into their commercial racket and doesn't do a thing to take the leadership out of their hands and force them to do their job on other principles."[2]

Intellectuals were at odds with empowered mass opinion. Walter Lippmann and John Dewey worried about the ignorance and fickleness of the democratic "public." Virgil Thomson, ever the provocateur, called on his fellow composers to arise and seize control. "Only professional solidarity can clear

433

up the obscurantism, take over the musical direction of massive distribution. The doctors have done it. So can we."[3] To the musical public at large, however, the plainspoken voice of reasoned dissent belonged to Aaron Copland, who also happened to be America's best-known classical composer.

Born in Brooklyn in 1900, Copland early studied with Rubin Goldmark, a former Dvořák student. To refine his gift, he did not go to Germany after the fashion of his forebears. The temper of the times dictated France, where he became the first of many Americans to discover in Nadia Boulanger a mentor of genius. Like Dvořák in New York, Boulanger in Fontainebleau believed American music was poised to take off. Like Dvořák, she supported interest in the American vernacular. In fact, ragtime was in vogue in Paris; Stravinsky, Boulanger's lodestar and therefore Copland's, even composed a *Rag-Time* of his own. Through Boulanger, Copland met Koussevitzky, who subsequently led the Copland charge in the United States.

In 1930 Copland produced a bracing wake-up call, a new American sound: the eleven-minute Piano Variations. Its angular rhythms and dissonant tonal shards vibrated with the intensity and nervous energy of Copland's New York. Versus the warm American roots exhumed by Dvořák, and the familiar Germanic models he applied, it was skyscraper music of steel and concrete. No previous American had achieved such concise freshness of style.

This was a sampling of what was meant, in praise or blame, as "modern music." And Copland was a conscious modernist, aligned with writers and painters insistent upon the new. Audiences, especially in America, insisted upon the old. Though composers counseled that Baroque, Classical, and Romantic styles had themselves once been new, that first listeners to Beethoven and Wagner were likewise put off, the modernist impasse was in some ways unprecedented. Never before had composers found themselves addressing a listening public so large and so preponderantly innocent. Never before had composers so believed that music had to jettison its recent past. Even musicians were confounded: performing specialists spurned composing specialists. If orchestras and music businessmen shied away from modern music, their objections were not necessarily commercial or philistine.

Most modernists responded with indifference or consternation. Copland adapted and mediated. The hardships of the Depression—the millions unemployed—were a potent catalyst for sympathetic intervention. The art of the thirties and forties was softened by conscience and compassion. Folk culture, political causes, and national identity were frequent motifs of such painters, photographers, and writers as Ben Shahn, Walker Evans, and Carl Sandburg. Of "the job of the forties" Copland wrote, "The radio and phonograph have given us listeners whose sheer numbers in themselves create a special problem," one whose solution was "to find a musical style which satisfies both us and them." Of "most exciting challenge of our day," he observed:

> The new musical audiences will have to have music that they can comprehend. That is axiomatic. It must therefore be simple and direct. But there is no reason why it should not be a music that exploits all those new devices discovered during the first years of the twentieth century. Above all, it must be fresh in feeling. In no sense must it be capable of being interpreted as a writing down to the level of the public. . . . To write a music that is both simple and direct and is at the same time great music is a goal worthy of the efforts of the best minds in music.[4]

The austerity of Copland's modernist idiom lent itself to a communicative simplicity. He called for a vigorous and unpretentious American style, "plain and bare."

The reorientation Copland espoused is pursued with remarkable subtlety in the three-movement Piano Sonata of 1939–41, in which the distilled and impersonal gestures of the Piano Variations are—a trade-off—made human. The Sonata's scherzo correlates the abstract rhythmic flicker of the faster Variations with snatches of minstrel song and jazz piano. The chordal girders punctuating the Variations in the broader Sonata attain a processional grandeur or tragic knell. The vacant silences and widely spaced chords of the Variations hint at an urban night music; in the Sonata, sweetened dissonances and longer, more yielding lines support a weight of weary sadness. The slow music with which the Sonata ends—gesturing both toward Beethoven's Op. 111 and toward Stravinsky's timeless, frozen codas—is one of Copland's most affecting inspirations. In autobiographical musings, he wrote of the "drab" Brooklyn street on which he "spent the first two years of my life," a place where music "was the last thing anyone would have connected with it"; of "a sense of isolation and of working too much by myself" during his early years of music study. Writing of a colleague, he once identified "subjectivism" as a "Jewish" trait.[5] In the static last page of his Piano Sonata, an essay in quietude, Copland does not seek the religious repose of Beethoven or Stravinsky's subliminal Orthodox ecstasies. Rather, he limns a dignified confession of solitude, of an ageless, Old Testament travail.

Vacancy and loneliness become memorable prairie tropes in the 1938 ballet *Billy the Kid*. Here, Copland's 1930s hunger for a usable American past and his quest for a bigger American musical public (and also the specificity of Lincoln Kirstein's commission for Ballet Caravan) led him to cowboy tunes and to the stage. The ballets *Rodeo*, with its Hoe-Down, and *Appalachian Spring*, with its culminating Shaker hymn, came next, in 1942 and 1944. In the 1930s, Copland was thick with Communists and fellow travelers. He tried his hand at a people's theater piece after the fashion of the *Lehrstücke* (teaching plays) of Hanns Eisler and Kurt Weill: the children's opera *The Second Hurricane*. He also wrote a workers' song: "Into the Streets May 1."

Copland's extensive catalogue of film music also fits this picture of the composer—his sense of utility, his common touch. Of course he wanted nothing to do with the musical styles of Erich Korngold and Max Steiner, their Romantic upholstery and Wagnerian leitmotifs. Scoring a pair of Lewis Milestone films adapting books by John Steinbeck (whom Copland admired), he adroitly applied his spare sonic landscapes to *Of Mice and Men* (1939) and *The Red Pony* (1948). Like Copland's Western ballets, this music influenced the tough and spacious sound worlds of Hollywood Westerns to come. For Sam Wood's film version of Thornton Wilder's *Our Town*, he bent his simplicities of tune and texture toward a homespun warmth. For *The Heiress* (1948), William Wyler's adaptation of Henry James's *Washington Square*, he furnished a scathing and unsentimental score—whose integrity was violated by maudlin interpolations by another hand. Ultimately, Copland was too dissident for Hollywood, both aesthetically and politically. Meanwhile, for the concert stage, he produced wartime patriotic fare as wholesome as the Piano Variations and Piano Sonata had been lean: *Lincoln Portrait*, *Fanfare for the Common Man*, and, incorporating the latter, the tub-thumbing Third Symphony.

The "populist" Copland—especially *Billy the Kid*, *Rodeo*, *Appalachian Spring*, *Lincoln Portrait*, and also *El Salón México* (1936), with its dissection and colorful recombination of dance hall tunes—achieved an enduring popularity among American listeners. The Copland sound—its clean modern lines and tasty colloquial decorations—became an indelible American sound. Meanwhile, Copland supported new American music in ways other than composing it. In France, he had experienced what it felt like when composers rallied together and intellectuals made common cause; he had experienced a world of high culture integral to the culture at large. He wanted something similar for the United States. He quickly emerged as a spokesman for the American composers of his generation. His public persona was equable, affirmative, and civilized, yet capable of firmness. He inspired trust.

Copland reached out to laymen with lectures, broadcasts, articles, and three books: *What to Listen for in Music* (1939), *Our New Music* (1941),* and *Music and Imagination* (1952). The first of these, an intended antidote to music appre-

---

* Revised as *The New Music* in 1968.

ciation, prescribes active and inquisitive listening. There are chapters on
rhythm, melody, harmony, tone, color, and structure. The many musical examples favor twentieth-century non-Germanic repertoire. Attacking sacralizers
who trade on mystification and reputation, Copland is typically plainspoken,
pointedly irreverent: "Composing to a composer is like fulfilling a natural
function. It is like eating or sleeping. It is something that the composer happens to have been born to do; and, because of that, it loses the character of a
special virtue in the composer's eyes." A hortatory chapter on contemporary
music points out that "creative artists, by and large, are a serious lot—their
purpose is not to fool you. This, in turn, presupposes on your part an open
mind, good will, and a certain a priori confidence in what they are up to."
"Modern music" can mean many things. To "bring some order into the
apparent chaos of contemporary composition," Copland divides twenty-eight
composers into "very easy," "quite approachable," "fairly difficult," and "very
tough." In *Our New Music*, he writes:

> There appears to be an unwritten understanding that our musical pub-
> lic is interested in listening only to the best, the greatest, the finest in
> music. Nothing less than an immortal masterwork penned by an
> immortal composer seems to be worth their attention. This assumption
> is fostered by the attitude, almost unconscious by now, of musical con-
> servatories, radio commentators, recording companies; it is reflected in
> advertisements of all kinds mentioning music, in programs of "official"
> concert-giving agencies, in free concerts, and so forth. Being alive seems
> to relegate the composer automatically to the position of an "also ran."[6]

In parallel to his layman's guides were the many Copland writings
addressed to his fellow composers. To foster constructive dialogue, he assessed
his colleagues' work with a sympathetic interest laced with strictures and
rebukes. He equally aspired to bind composers with the world outside. "The
worst feature of the composer's life," he wrote, "is the fact that he does not feel
himself an integral part of the musical community. There is no deep need for
his activities as composer, no passionate concern in each separate work as it is
written. . . . When a composer is played he is usually surrounded by an air of
mild approval; when he is not played no one demands to hear him."[7] As he
urged mistrustful listeners to befriend living composers, Copland (as we have
observed) urged mistrustful composers to befriend listeners. So that composers could make themselves seen and heard, not least among themselves, he
was also a vigorous organizer of concerts, most notably the Copland-Sessions
Concerts of 1928–31 and the Yaddo summer festivals in Sarasota Springs, New

York, of 1932 and 1933. His efforts were amplified by the League of Composers, founded in 1923; under the leadership of Claire Reis, it presented concerts, commissioned new works, and campaigned for composers' rights. When Reis retired in 1948, Copland took her place for two years. The League's superb quarterly, *Modern Music*, was Copland's frequent forum vis-à-vis his peers. Both Reis and Minna Lederman, who edited *Modern Music* for its duration (1924–46), relied on Copland for guidance.

In pursuing this ambitious multiplicity of roles, musical and extramusical, Copland showed exceptional versatility: many a creator is ill-suited to the feats of organization, advocacy, and diplomacy that Copland undertook as a matter of course. It would, however, be idle to argue that he attained the pinnacle of success in any one endeavor. If few European composers enjoyed such broad authority, Copland's limited European reputation puts his achievement in the largest perspective. As a concert composer, he quite obviously does not command the scope and resonance of his sometime-model Stravinsky. As a political composer, he lacks the needling indignation of Kurt Weill. As a heroic patriot, he sounds strained alongside Shostakovich. As a folklorist, his borrowings are thin and synthetic judged by Bartók's. His aesthetic foundation, stressing plainness and economy, was stretched to the limit by the creative tasks he assayed. His American vision, while potent, is not protean; it lacks Ives's mysteries. Copland's educator's voice, too, is limited by the very plainness that conferred credibility; his oratory was ultimately too thin to challenge the masterpiece addicts and Toscanini acolytes.

Roger Sessions (whose modernism was of the diehard variety) once quipped that Copland "was more talented than he realized."[8] Those who most admire Copland insist that the modernist and the populist in Copland were one and the same. For others, the effrontery of the Piano Variations signifies a road not taken. Ever mindful of the isolation of the American artist, Copland resolved to meet the public halfway. Something was lost, something gained. The strains imposed by this trade-off may partly explain why the sense of mission that fired Copland's creativity dissipated after World War II. Beginning in the fifties, he found himself dismissed as a populist has-been by ivory-tower types he had attempted to redirect.

As America's leading composer of classical music, Copland bore a burden both challenging and incongruous. No composer, before or since, as comprehensively worked to foster conditions conducive to an American canon. It may be that this broader effort compromised his own creative potential. But given the magnitude of the American rifts he sensitively understood—between performers and creators, between artists and others—Aaron Copland cannot be blamed for trying.

■ ■ ■

According to Copland's 1941 topography, in *Our New Music*, the other leading American composers of his "come-of-age" generation were Virgil Thomson, Roy Harris, Walter Piston, and Roger Sessions. Of these four, Thomson was the dark horse—an acquired taste—and yet proved the most enduring. Born in 1896 in Kansas City, Missouri, he came from a family of farmers and church-going Baptists; of his midwestern pedigree, he wrote that it was "not of the Sinclair Lewis-Sherwood Anderson-Ernest Hemingway line, all of them worried and preachy, but rather of the more comic-spirited Booth Tarkington-George Ade-Mark Twain connection." He also said, "I considered the creation of an American music by myself and certain contemporaries to be a far worthier aspiration than any effort to construct a wing, a portico, even a single brick that might be fitted on to Europe's historic edifice."[9]

Like Copland, Thomson went to France, studied with Boulanger, and became a Francophile. Like Copland, he returned to the United States both to compose and to write about composers. His differences from Copland are equally defining.

As music critic for the *New York Herald-Tribune* from 1940 to 1954, Thomson enjoyed a regular forum. The culture of performance, the "music appreciation racket," and the music business were constant objects of his scorn and waspish vituperation. His targets included Judson's New York Philharmonic, which (in his inaugural column) he pronounced "not a part of New York's intellectual life." He called Vladimir Horowitz a "master of distortion and exaggeration" and Jascha Heifetz "essentially frivolous." Of Toscanini he wrote, "Almost wholly devoted to the playing of familiar classics, he has at the same time transformed these into an addictive image of twentieth-century America with such unconscious completeness that musicians and laymen all over the world have acclaimed his achievement without, I think, very much bothering to analyze it. They were satisfied that it should be, for the most part, musically acceptable and at all times exciting." Common to all these Thomson edicts was a shrewd insistence on the odd particularity of the performance-specialist species; he once termed Heifetz an "ocelot." Thomson's stylistic brilliance made him compulsively readable—as Copland was not. But his arrogance, compounded by bias and reckless inaccuracy,* reduced him to a formidable gadfly status.[10]

---

* On January 21, 1951, Thomson's *Herald-Tribune* column assailed "concert chains"—"there are only five sonatas by Beethoven that the central office will accept without a row." When this and other generalizations were challenged by the baritone Mack Harrell, Thomson wrote in response, "This is

Thomson the composer was also a gadfly. For Copland, Paris was Boulanger and Stravinsky. For Thomson, the crucial Parisian influence was Dada and its musical priest Erik Satie. Thomson's characterization of Satie's aesthetic illuminates his own: "it has eschewed the impressive, the heroic, the oratorical, everything that is aimed at moving mass audiences." Like Satie, Thomson rejected modernist complexity and also the Germanic "success rhetoric" of "fabricated masterpieces." But his appropriation of Satie was peculiarly American: Satie's style is grave and chaste, Thomson's more consciously cheeky or bizarre. Thomson wrote of Dada, "Such a declaration of independence from commerce, the academies, and all other entangling alliances was congenial to my natural rebelliousness. I loved the climate of it, its high, thin, anti-establishment air. . . . I think all Americans are a little Dada-minded. What else is our freewheeling humor, our nonsense, our pop art?"[11]

And Thomson—like Satie, unlike Copland—was a maverick who kept company with writers and painters, one of whom, in Paris, was Gertrude Stein. In 1927, Thomson requested an opera libretto from Stein. The result, a year later, was *Four Saints in Three Acts*, which has four acts and more than thirty saints and a story both simple and indiscernible. Thomson reasoned that given a text whose meanings were so elusive, if not actually absent, his best option was to set Stein's words (including the stage directions!) clearly, sensibly, fluently, following their speech inflections—and to let the meanings fend for themselves. For music, he assembled fragmentary allusions to the hymns, songs, and marches he had known since childhood (the opera is set in Spain) and set them atop the simplest chords—whose proper use was at times mischievously sidestepped. Saint Ignatius's song "Pigeons on the Grass Alas"—a signature moment—is a kind of children's ditty accompanied by a jaunty minstrel or boogie version of the same tune. The opera's innocent materials are knowingly conjoined.

Opera in America was (as we have seen) everything *Four Saints* was not: grand and foreign. Only in 1934 did Thomson find people willing to mount it—at the Hartford Atheneum in Connecticut. Frederick Ashton and John Houseman directed an all-black cast selected, Thomson said, "purely for beauty of voice, clarity of enunciation, and fine carriage." The scenery, designed by Florine Stettheimer, was entirely of cellophane. A six-week Broadway run followed, then a trip to Chicago. Whatever *Four Saints* was—

---

astounding evidence and can only mean that Mr. Harrell has never worked for the 'community' or 'civic' departments." But Harrell had. Thomson did not care. His writings on the "music business" are full of equally cavalier allegations (see Cecil Smith, *Worlds of Music* [Philadelphia, Lippincott, 1952], pp. 79–81). His critical writings are comparably blithe; he loved to disconcert.

and is—it survives with *Porgy and Bess* (also produced on Broadway, also with an all-black cast, otherwise utterly different) as a distinctive interwar American contribution to the lyric stage. Its appeal lies somewhere in the realm of pseudo-innocence: Thomson's blithe eclecticism, smoothly blending the ordinary and the daft, achieves (for some) a kind of sublimity. Thomson's "trick," Copland wrote in *Our New Music*, was "making his musical emotion entirely serious and entirely unambiguous in its purpose—practically without regard to the thing said. That is what gave the opera its amusement and charm."[12]

In 1947 Thomson similarly set a second Stein libretto, *The Mother of Us All*, with similar success. For a more general audience, his easy melodic gift (rare among his American colleagues) and natural musical speech notably suited five William Blake poems set for baritone and orchestra (1951). And Thomson achieved perhaps his widest appeal as a composer for non-Hollywood cinema, collaborating with Pare Lorentz and Robert Flaherty in the landmark documentaries *The Plow That Broke the Plains* (1936), *The River* (1937), and *Louisiana Story* (1948). In the first two, espousing federal assistance for drought and flood victims, he left social conscience to Lorentz and his superb cameramen, lightening the New Deal rhetoric with pastiche and paradox. His frequent reliance on cowboy tunes prefigured, and doubtless influenced, Copland's more heroic, more populist evocation of the American West. His often ironic application of hymns and dances (including a tango) influenced Copland's initial film score: *The City*, an urban-planning documentary for the 1939 World's Fair in which a traffic jam is set to a refrain heedlessly jaunty. In fact, Thomson preceded Copland and many others in tapping into a wealth of Anglo-Celtic folk song distinct from the late-nineteenth-century compilations of plantation song and Native American chant of which Dvořák was apprised.

Among his fellow composers, Thomson's simplicities were suspect and controversial; he was dismissed as a dilettante. The relative popularity of his concert works was—not inaccurately—linked to his post at the *Herald-Tribune*, which motivated musicians to perform his music. His substantial catalogue includes much that is savorless and bland, even inept. Copland bluntly observed that Thomson "in his relaxed manner . . . sometimes admits such utterly trifling material . . . as to make an entire movement seem like a stale joke."[13]

Doubtless Thomson considered Copland a plodding verbal stylist. But the plainness of speech of Copland the composer was more subtly and meaningfully realized than the plainness of speech of Copland the writer. Even Thomson may have harbored nagging suspicions that it was in fact his prose, with its insouciant guile, easy erudition, and homespun sophistication, that was the more stylistically assured and complex. His musical rejection of high modernism was undeniably prescient. It ingeniously converted into a virtue a necessity also undeniable.

■ ■ ■

If anyone rivaled Copland in the public imagination it was Roy Harris. In 1940, Harris placed first in a national poll of American composers conducted by CBS. Five years previously, he was identified as "the white hope" of American music by *Time* magazine—a tag others repeated.[14]

Music and race remained a potent subtheme of classical music in the United States. We have observed its paramount significance for Dvořák and Krehbiel, and also its different and paramount significance for Boston's Philip Hale, to whom Dvořák was a meddling "negrophile." In fact, before Hitler the notion of racial traits determining or influencing culture and behavior was pervasive throughout the political spectrum. Jews were as likely to surmise Jewish "types" as were non-Jews or anti-Semites. The example of Dvořák and Krehbiel shows that such thinking could be essentially appreciative. Even judgments such as Hale's were grounded not in a paranoid image of what America was not and should not become, but in a positive image of what America was and should be, a moral vision of an elect "Anglo-Saxon" community based in old New England and including the sages Emerson and Thoreau.

After World War I American racial politics intensified. What one central authority has termed the "vague and somewhat benign racial concept of romantic nationalism" among Anglo-Saxonists gave way to racism "as an ideology," stressing heredity and physiology.[15] The pivotal figure was Madison Grant, whose *The Passing of the Great White Race* (1916) achieved a vogue in the twenties. Grant hated Mediterraneans and Jews and claimed that blond "Nordics" exemplified the "white man par excellence." Unlike earlier Anglo-Saxonists who had undertaken a patronizing mission to help newcomers assimilate, he preached racial purity. The new nativism stigmatized a modern world of immigrants and cities.

This was the climate in which a Jewish composer from Brooklyn, championed by a Jewish conductor from Russia, displaced New England composers of a previous era. Copland's enemies muttered about a "League of Jewish Composers." They lumped together degenerate Jews and degenerate blacks, and noted with alarm the Jewish affinity for jazz. Copland sampled jazz in such works as *Music for the Theatre* (1925) and the Piano Concerto (1926). George Gershwin—also Jewish, also from Brooklyn, also without a college pedigree—reveled in it. Those who condemned jazz labeled it "Negro":

hedonistic, animalistic—and also, paradoxically, coldly "mechanistic." Jazz symbolized the social fragmentation and materialism of the metropolis, and a dangerous fascination with the new. As for the Jew, he was a rootless "Oriental" middleman trading on both black sensuality and Yankee uplift; gallingly, Copland and Gershwin spoke for "America."

If Virgil Thomson was, by comparison, a midwesterner of Anglo-Saxon stock, he knew jazz and cast his opera with blacks. And, like Copland, he was gay, as were many of his mutually influential friends and colleagues. Thomson was no white hope. Of Roy Harris, John Tasker Howard—a prominent historian of American music—wrote in 1941, "When he first appeared on the scene, in the late 'twenties, he seemed the answer to all our prayers. Here was a genuine American, born in a log cabin in Oklahoma, like Lincoln, tall, lanky, rawboned, untouched by the artificial refinements of Europe or even the stultifying commercialism of cosmopolitan New York; a prophet from the Southwest who thought in terms of our raciest folk-tunes."[16] Harris was even born on Lincoln's birthday. He grew up in California's San Gabriel Valley. Himself a fledgling farmer, he came to composing late, and though he studied in France with Boulanger, he was a recalcitrant nondisciple. His *Symphony: 1933*, launched by Koussevitzky (as would be five of the first six Harris symphonies), led to commissions from the Boston Symphony, the League of Composers, the Westminster Choir, Columbia Records, Victor Records, CBS, and Elizabeth Sprague Coolidge.

To Harris's supporters, his "America" was the real stuff. Howard wrote, "While racially Harris seems to derive definitely from the Scotch-Irish element of his ancestry, Aaron Copland embodies the Russian-Jewish element transplanted to American soil. Thus we find that while Harris reflects the prairies and vastness of the West, Copland brings us the sophistication of the cosmopolitan cities on the seaboard." Lazare Saminsky, a Russian-born composer who was also music director of New York's Temple Emanu-El, wrote of Harris, "I think he is the most original, the most American of all, inasmuch as the main characteristic of the Anglo-Celtic strain is the source of American music." Harris himself, while neither anti-Semitic nor antiblack, endorsed this line of thinking. "Always is it a lonesome hunger that gnaws within the human heart, forcing us to search for an understandable race-expression," he wrote. America had become "absorbed in material development," yet its "grandeur, dignity, and untold beauty"—an antidote—"waits calmly between the Pacific and the Atlantic while the tide of the Mississippi rises and falls with the seasons." When other composers, notably Copland, likewise claimed the lore and spacious vistas of the West, Harris in 1940 wrote a *Modern Music* article, titled "Folksong—American Big Business," inimitably staking his claim to authenticity:

The thing was getting a little too professional. . . . It's getting to be cut and dried. When the boys ride hell-for-leather because their pardners, the old man or their girls and all the folks are a lookin' on—well that's one thing. That's real cowhide. When they calculate to make it pay for a living—that's a white horse of a different color. . . .

Now that's what folksong is all about. Singing and dancing your heart out for yourself and the people you were born among—whose daily lives you share through the seasons, through thick and thin. From the hearts of our people they have come. . . .[17]

While Harris's populist agenda resonates with Steinbeck, Sandburg, or Copland, it is distinctively scented with nostalgia—for the West as refuge from urban sin and anomie. Unlike Thomson's, more than Copland's, Harris's America conveys moral significance, a virtue in innocence. Crucially, it eschews the influence of jazz.

Koussevitzky's 1934 premiere of *Symphony: 1933* catalyzed all these American interpretations. As with Dvořák, the Boston–New York duality was defining. In Boston, still the city of Anglo-Saxon rectitude, H. T. Parker enthused:

The new symphony is American, first, in a pervading directness, in a recurring and unaffected roughness of speech—an outspoken symphony. . . . In the second place Mr. Harris's symphony is American in the nature of its rhythms, the scope of its melody. . . . They seem to derive, besides, from the West that bred Mr. Harris and in which he works most eagerly—from its air, its life, its impulses, even its gaits.

New York—still the city of immigrants—heard Koussevitzky and the Boston Symphony in the same music a week later. Olin Downes acknowledged, "There are not lacking those who see in [Harris] a present white hope of American music." But Downes found *Symphony: 1933* "an American ineptitude," "fussy," "academic," and "immature."[18]

Harris's Third Symphony—then as now—proved his signature achievement, the main reason why Copland could write of Harris in 1941: "his is the most personal note in American music today," possessing "real sweep and breadth, with power and emotional depth such as only a generously built country could produce." Koussevitzky gave the first performance of the Harris Third in 1939 and also superbly recorded it. The symphony is short: its one movement lasts less than seventeen minutes. The magnificent beginning suggests that the white hope has here, like some musical *deus ex machina*, swooped down from on high to mediate an even exchange between Old World traditions and New World wilderness adventure. A loping, striding cello song probes the surrounding silence. The long lines of this melody, the irregular phrases seamlessly bound, the spacious textures and open fourths and fifths suggest an American plainchant (pun and all). Can this premise, which is also a promise, be kept? Copland cautions, "The composer's greatest weakness has proved . . . an apparent incapacity for shaping a long composition so that the form of the whole is truly logical and inevitable."[19] It is Harris's practice to discard the usual symphonic structures in favor of an "organic" continuity perhaps comparable to Sibelius (also a heroic folklorist); listeners must keep the faith. The Third Symphony's pioneer trek discovers a pastorale: cowboy and honky-tonk snatches wafted above shimmering strings. Then comes a rugged fugue not according to the book. Harris wrestles with a curt, thrusting theme: he thwacks it, turns it upside down, sets it astride galloping strings. All of this is impressively leading somewhere—which turns out, suddenly, to be a grim, fist-shaking close that Copland accurately finds "shocking in its utter conventionality." This failure of technique is also a failure of taste and temperament, of the very qualities of heart and soul that were supposed to make Harris a savior. It is, sadly, an ending as parochial as were the Harris propagandists. Though the Third Symphony deservedly endures, hope for Roy Harris faded fast; he died quietly in 1979.

■ ■ ■

If Thomson and Harris seem self-made composers, the other two on Copland's list—Walter Piston and Roger Sessions—were finished teachers at home on university campuses: in every sense, "academics." Piston's base was Harvard; his students included Elliott Carter, Leonard Bernstein, Arthur Berger, Irving Fine, and Harold Shapero. The Boston Symphony, too, was home. When Piston told Koussevitzky he did not write for orchestra because opportunities for performance were so few, Koussevitzky said, "You write, I play"—and he did. Conventional wisdom holds that Piston is an ingeniously professional composer, but frustratingly reticent. This is wisdom difficult to deny. His graciousness and restraint—Boston traits, reaching back as far as Chadwick—were reinforced by study with Boulanger in France. He mistrusts the Romantics. He favors traditional forms and an abundance of counterpoint. Though he does not sound like Stravinsky, his vigor and rhythmic bite are Stravinskyan. He does not sound like Hindemith, but exemplifies something like Hindemith's artisan integrity. A work such as his Second Symphony (1943), music temperamentally warmed by wartime, can be listened to repeatedly with pleasure because its expressive energies shun vulgarity or cliché.

The first movement pairs a melody on a darkling plain with (unusually for Piston) a smartly syncopated dance-hall tune, deliciously scored; the subtle bindings are both elegant and exhilarating. And yet the symphony remains disappointingly faceless, and it equally lacks Stravinsky's force of impersonality—not to mention the sublimated Russian religion and folklore to be found even in Stravinsky's neoclassical style. Copland wrote, "Piston's music, if considered only from a technical viewpoint, constitutes a challenge to every other American composer. . . . Without men like Piston, without his ease and ability in handling of normal musical materials, we can never have a full-fledged school of composers in this country."[20] But Piston also stands as a caution: that even the most skillful American classical music can easily sound secondhand or denatured. The symphonist in Piston is everything Roy Harris is not.

Roger Sessions was a Princeton and University of California (Berkeley) composer; his students included Milton Babbitt, John Harbison, Leon Kirchner, Peter Maxwell Davies, Conlon Nancarrow, and David Del Tredici. The Boston Symphony did not regularly perform his music, nor did anyone else; he was an outsider, and proud of it. In a 1938 *Modern Music* essay, he argued:

> The American composer, above all, must learn to take a more mature and serious attitude towards his art and abandon the postures which, as we all secretly know, have offered such convenient havens of refuge up to this time. . . . The postures of which I speak are familiar enough—they take the form of feebly conceived artificial and quasi-academic standards, before the fact and beside the point, of the pseudo-provincial dilettantism of the "typically American style," of self-conscious conceptions both of form and content, quite unnecessary to enumerate. Above all American composers will have to abandon resolutely chimerical hopes of success in a world dominated overwhelmingly by "stars," by mechanized popular music and by the box-office standard, and set themselves to discovering what they truly have to say, and to saying it in the manner of the adult artist delivering his message to those who have ears to hear it.[21]

Decoded, this manifesto rejects Harris's technical gaucheries and Copland's "us and them" aspirations. For Sessions, "us" was a fraternity of artists and "them" was beside the point. A historical imperative dictated a musical language densely layered with meaning and, no less than the modernist language of James Joyce, intended for "those with the ears to hear it." If an exclusive audience was the result, it was a matter of considered judgment that this was the modern composer's fate, that the culture of performance—of "stars" and the "box-office standard"—was essentially inimical to contemporary creativity. Schoenberg, whose sense of historical mission was Wagnerian in magnitude, had in 1918 gauged the Zeitgeist and pronounced, "All I know is that [the listener] exists, and insofar as he isn't indispensable for acoustic reasons (since music doesn't sound well in an empty hall), he's only a nuisance." Of America's composers, Sessions was the most outspoken in assent. In retrospect, Schoenberg did not break as radically with past, or with the listener, as he seemed to. And it was also true of Sessions that he retained tradition—of form, of mood, of musical gesture—more than his music at first shock seemed to allow. Like Schoenberg, too, he wrote music difficult to play and even more difficult to play well: its dissonance and density, carelessly rendered, turn everything gray.

Schoenberg was one of many influences Sessions absorbed; he was the rare American of Copland's generation to sound more "German" than "French." But neoclassical Stravinsky was a key early influence. Above all, Sessions—who long lived abroad and maintained close contact with important Europeans; whose most influential teacher, in Cleveland, was the expatriate Swiss composer Ernest Bloch—was untouched by the movement to sound American. He speculated that (as with Boston's composers of the previous century) his long New England lineage freed him from the conscious identity quest undertaken by Copland and others with immigrant parents. He believed, at any rate, that America was too young truly to possess "folk music," and that "the influence of folk music on European music has been vastly exaggerated."[22] Works such as his Violin Concerto (1935) offered American listeners of the time no obvious stylistic guideposts. So relentless is this music in its visceral and intellectual onslaught that the reeling ear is likely to overlook the simplicity of the overall structural design.

The Violin Concerto's performance history is informative. A 1937 premiere was scheduled by Koussevitzky with Albert Spalding, but was canceled when Spalding requested changes Sessions could not accept. Dimitri Mitropoulos gave it in Minneapolis in 1947—the first professional performance—with his remarkable concertmaster Louis Krasner. But Mitropoulos, who considered the Sessions concerto "one of the great achievements in American composition," was unable to program it in New York, allegedly because of Arthur Judson.*

---

* Another conductor with a special relationship to Sessions—another conductor who (as we have seen) was a stranger in America—was Otto Klemperer. Sessions and his wife avidly supported Klemperer's bid to take over the New York Philharmonic after Toscanini. When Klemperer proved intransigent in scheduling Mahler's Second, which Judson opposed, Sessions cabled a friend in Vienna,

But however estranged from the mainstream, Sessions never lacked impassioned advocates. Copland's advocacy was qualified. Aspects of his 1941 assessment, in *Our New Music*, are acutely revealing for both composers: "Sessions [at times] creates without the aid of surface mannerisms a music profoundly his own: music of an ineffable pessimism—resigned, unprotesting, inexpressibly sad, and of a deeply human and nonromantic quality.... [But] sometimes it seems to me that Sessions writes his music for Titans, forgetting that we are, after all, only mortals with a capacity for lending our attention within definite limits."[23]

Half a generation younger than Copland, Thomson, Harris, Piston, and Sessions was William Schuman, who sought guidance from both Copland and Harris and conflated aspects of both their styles. Schuman was also an important educator and administrator at the Juilliard School and Lincoln Center. The former institution, long New York's preeminent school of music, began as the Institute for Musical Art, founded by Walter Damrosch's older brother in 1905. Frank Damrosch, who taught ear training, sight singing, and pedagogy courses, and conducted both chorus and orchestra, personally auditioned every applicant. He supplied inspirational leadership and high standards.[24] His conservative bent, and that of Juilliard generally, mattered over time; opportunities to hire Busoni, Schoenberg, and Boulanger to teach composition were lost. Schuman became the first composer to head the school, in 1945 at the age of thirty-five. His goals included greater emphasis on new music and a broader, less insular curriculum. Subsequently, as president of Lincoln Center for the Performing Arts from 1962 to 1969, he aspired to bind the constituents—Juilliard, the Metropolitan and New York City Operas, the New York Philharmonic, the New York City Ballet—into something greater than the sum of its parts. These were bold but futile intentions. Schuman's most tangible success was the Juilliard String Quartet, which he helped to create in 1948 and which (as we have seen) symbolized a contemporary American approach to repertoire and performance; its impassioned advocacy of Schoenberg, Bartók, and Elliott Carter decisively legitimized important twentieth-century string quartets for discerning American chamber music audiences. Schuman's best-known music projected the same confidence and energy as his public personality.

If among the Americans who came of age after World War I Sessions occupied the far left, with Copland and Harris in the middle, Howard Hanson and Samuel Barber defined the far right. Born in Nebraska of Scandinavian stock,

---

"Please explain to Klemperer utter impossibility of doing anything about programs in New York. Situation controlled by musically ignorant men now intransigent." See Peter Heyworth, *Otto Klemperer: His Life and Times*, vol. 2 (New York, Cambridge University Press, 1996), p. 38.

Hanson was a prominent symphonist. Of his seven works so described, Koussevitzky commissioned and conducted the premiere of No. 2 and invited Hanson to conduct the Boston Symphony in first performances of Nos. 3 and 4. Hanson was also in 1923 named the second director of the Eastman School of Music created by George Eastman (of Eastman Kodak) in Rochester, New York; he was only twenty-eight years old and presided until 1964, when he was sixty-eight. Hanson's many accomplishments at Eastman included an annual festival of American music. Under his baton, the Eastman Philharmonia recorded more than a hundred American works, including landmark LPs of Chadwick, Griffes, Herbert, Ives, Loeffler, and Paine. In the tradition of Thurber and Dvořák, he challenged the culture of performance. No other American conservatory—certainly not Curtis under Hofmann, Zimbalist, or Serkin; certainly not Juilliard, even under Schuman—as significantly championed the American composer. The problem with Hanson was not that he was, as Copland put it, an "archconservative" or, according to Elliott Carter, a "reactionary." Nor did he lack technical mastery. Rather his music was formulaic in sentiment. Absent the demonic, he—like Edward MacDowell, whose two orchestral suites he recorded—could at best simulate Romantic afflatus and heat. His *Romantic* Symphony, the most performed, would barely qualify as a first-rate Hollywood confection. His Eastman agenda, too, was parochial in its pronounced preference for the tamest forms of Americana. There is no polite way to say that it pointed toward a dead end.

Barber, a Pennsylvanian whose aunt was the contralto Louise Homer, achieved a popularity rivaling Copland's; like Copland, he did not have to teach to earn a living. More than Copland, he penetrated the mainstream: Toscanini premiered his *Adagio* for strings and First Essay for Orchestra; Bruno Walter, his Second Essay; Koussevitzky, his Cello Concerto; Vladimir Horowitz, his Piano Sonata; the Metropolitan Opera, his *Vanessa*. His music could be nearly as synthetic as Hanson's: with its fat theme song, tangy harmonies, and discreetly clangorous orchestration, the Barber ballet *Medea* would fit a Goldwyn biblical epic. Barber's Piano Concerto, inspired by Rachmaninoff and Prokofiev, is a luxurious and gustatory entertainment. Like Hanson (but less habitually), Barber could overreach the limits of his temperament and style: works like the Cello Concerto betray a false pursuit of modernist dissonance and intensity. His melodic gift—corollary to a musical sweet tooth—set him above other conservatives. So did his capacity to find and savor his true métier, which happened to be gentle music of the heart, usually sung. The *Adagio*, his gravely tender signature work of 1936, acquired special poignancy as a dirge for the wartime dead. *Knoxville: Summer of 1915* for soprano and orchestra (1947) sets a recollection of small-town childhood by

James Agee. Barber sweetens and distends the prose to produce an undulating lullaby. Italicizing the words "mother" and "sorrow," he evokes a womb both secure and not. Agee's adult existential sadness is not germane to this shadowed exercise in nostalgia, which illustrates both what Barber can and cannot do. A comparison to Benjamin Britten, in some respects the important European he most resembles, is more cruelly illuminating: Britten's stylistic restraint and his idiomatic writing for the voice are core attributes of a body of work remarkable in scope and originality.

Of many another composer of the Copland and post-Copland generation who warrants mention, Paul Creston was a self-made Italian-American who does not fit in any camp. His Symphony No. 2 (1944) remains a fresh experience, unpretentiously strong, unostentatiously different, a sunny American *La valse* in two self-generating movements whose fluidly shifting rhythms and shapes mate with lush harmonics and tunes. Creston wrote six symphonies. David Diamond, whose teachers included Sessions and Boulanger, wrote eleven. Peter Mennin, who succeeded Schuman as president of Juilliard, wrote nine. All told, Copland, Thomson, Harris, Piston, Sessions, Schuman, Hanson, Barber, Creston, Diamond, and Mennin produced seventy-nine symphonies, mainly between 1930 and 1960. When Koussevitzky predicted that "the next Beethoven vill from Colorado come," he was predicting a Great American Symphony. The best of the lot, in the opinion of both Copland and Thomson, was the Harris Third, which was no more an *Eroica* than MacDowell was the Wagner Americans awaited half a century previously. But given the predominance of the Copland-Harris axis (and its influence even on conservatives like Barber), the symphonists under discussion did manage to produce a characteristic symphonic sound. It was muscular in orchestration, optimistic in tone, clean in contour, direct and unsentimental in mood. It was brash, athletic, rhythmically driven, and ingenious in correlation with jazz and the city; hymnic, contemplative, and spacious in correlation with the wide West. These polarities of unbridled energy and panoramic repose somewhat recapitulated Whitman and (though he was not an influence) Ives.

For Koussevitzky and the composers he championed, the postwar creation of an American symphonic template was a central mission. If the outcome, in retrospect, disappoints—if the symphonies produced are more an interesting blip on the wide screen of American musical history—one must ask what kinds of music were being practiced by composers who cued more directly on American popular genres, or whose idiosyncrasies otherwise rejected Eurocentric models. In certain instances their achievement proved more resonant or prescient than the search for an American symphonic master to set within the overseas pantheon.

∎ ∎ ∎

In addition to celebrated immigrant performers—the many famous conductors, singers, and instrumentalists fleeing Russian and Central European political strife—the United States welcomed, however incidentally, the crème de la crème of Europe's twentieth-century composers: Stravinsky, Schoenberg, Bartók, Hindemith. Their presence was by no means ignored, especially if they also happened to play the piano. Stravinsky's much-publicized American debut, in 1925, was as a New York Philharmonic guest conductor. Later the same season, he performed his Piano Concerto with Koussevitzky and the Boston Symphony, with Mengelberg and the Philharmonic, and elsewhere. He also attended the belated Philharmonic premiere of *The Rite of Spring*, under Furtwängler, which filled Carnegie Hall. Bartók's American debut, in 1927, was as piano soloist in his early Rhapsody with the Philharmonic and Mengelberg, who found the First Piano Concerto too difficult to prepare. It was (as earlier noted) with Reiner and the Cincinnati Symphony that Bartók gave the concerto's American premiere the same season. Schoenberg, not a pianist, became a significant teacher in the United States; his pupils at UCLA included Marc Blitzstein, John Cage, and Leon Kirchner. Hindemith, at Yale, taught Lukas Foss and Harold Shapero, and influentially championed Medieval and Renaissance music. Bartók emigrated in 1940 to America, where he fruitlessly sought a position teaching piano. Only around the time of his death did his Violin Concerto, Concerto for Orchestra, and Third Piano Concerto begin notably to penetrate the symphonic repertoire. All four composers were incomparably less central to the nation's musical life than they had been in France, Germany, or Hungary. The music appreciators and great performers had little or no use for them. The leading mainstream critics were more prone to worship Sibelius as a latter-day Beethoven. And America's own composers were busy becoming Americans: for them, the timing of this exceptional creative influx was awkward.

In fact, the influence of America on the actual music of the newcomers was revealingly limited. One can cite important American commissions, the impact of American jazz (which began in the twenties and had nothing to do with emigration), and the inspiration of American democracy (Schoenberg's *Ode to Napoleon* pays tribute to George Washington; Hindemith's *When Lilacs Last in the Door-yard Bloom'd* implicitly memorializes Franklin D. Roosevelt). Stravinsky, Schoenberg, and Hindemith notably set English as a result of living in the United States. Though Stravinsky wielded enormous influence on American composers of "neoclassical" persuasion, this partly emanated from France via Boulanger, not from California via Stravinsky. Especially in the case of Schoenberg, an occasional simplification of style—as in the Suite for Strings or the Theme and Variations for band—may be somewhat attributable to the exigencies of American taste. Virtually unique, in the case of Stravinsky, was the progressive role of Lincoln Kirstein and George Balanchine as indispensable American creative catalysts.

There were also eminent European composers who all but disappeared in the United States. Alexander von Zemlinsky lived in obscurity in Larchmont, New York, neither composing nor conducting, after having been a prominent figure in Vienna through 1938. Ernst von Dohnányi, once a leading European pianist, composer, and pedagogue, became a piano professor in Tallahasee, Florida. At the opposite extreme, at least three immigrants became transformed "American composers" of consequence. Ernest Bloch's music enjoyed an American vogue subsequent to his becoming an American citizen in 1924. Though his stylistic base was more Jewish or neoclassical, he was widely considered an assimilated American. He produced a New World symphony in the form of the epic rhapsody *America*; winner of a 1927 *Musical America* competition, it ambitiously samples Indian chant, "Dixie," and Walt Whitman. More distinguished is his heroic/elegiac Violin Concerto of 1938, whose motto theme is Native American. His American pupils included Roger Sessions. Kurt Weill, upon reaching Manhattan in 1935, successfully abdicated classical music for Broadway; his American adaptation will be considered later in this chapter. But the European composer who most sensationally infiltrated American classical music after World War I was, significantly, a marauding wild man whose paradoxical achievement (rather like Dvořák's three decades before) was to pedigree the New World. In fact, only a European could so persuasively have instructed susceptible American iconoclasts to turn their backs on Europe: to forego Stravinsky and Schoenberg, neoclassicism and twelve-tone theory, the orchestra and the opera house; to thrill to the act of American rebellion. If within the regnant culture of performance, this remained a composers' sideshow, it was both compulsively entertaining and compellingly subversive.

The marauding newcomer, a New Yorker from 1915, was Edgard Varèse. Born in Paris in 1883, he was nearly a generation older than Copland and the other postwar Americans, which made him a potential father figure for those who sought directions more radical than what the Boulangerie supported. An imposing and provocative physical presence, a fount of imposing and provocative pronouncements, he welcomed America as a clean slate on which to inscribe "all discoveries, all adventures, . . . the Unknown." He also called the mainstream American musical organizations "mausoleums, mortuaries of musical reminiscences." Less politely, he privately said of celebrity virtuosos,

"They don't give a [shit] about music, only their 'careers'—their 'interpretations.'" His aversion to American neoclassicism was both visceral and personal; in private correspondence, he denounced Copland and his male friends for crowding out composers "healthy and white." For Copland and company, Europe signified innovation and refinement. For Varèse and his American associates Marcel Duchamp and Francis Picabia, America represented the art of the future.[25]

More than a propagandist, Varèse was an organizer. With the harpist/composer Carlos Salzedo, he founded the International Composers' Guild in 1921. When the Guild folded, he helped to create the Pan American Association of Composers in 1928. These groups presented American premieres of such landmark European repertoire as Schoenberg's *Pierrot Lunaire*, Webern's Five Movements for String Quartet, Berg's Chamber Concerto, and Stravinsky's *Les noces*, *Renard*, and Octet. Their sponsorship of Carl Ruggles, Ives, and Varèse himself was also historic. The equally significant League of Composers split off from the Guild in 1923. It was prominently associated, as Varèse was not, with Copland, Koussevitzky, and neoclassicism. All three composers' organizations worked to promote contemporary music much as Alfred Stieglitz promoted contemporary visual art in pursuit of a cosmopolitan artistic milieu for New York.[26]

Though Leopold Stokowski also conducted for the League, Varèse was the American composer he most performed, and who most benefited from his glamour and panache. (Stokowski even tried, unsuccessfully, to persuade the Curtis Institute to engage Varèse to teach composition.) Stokowski's Composers Guild and Philadelphia Orchestra programs decisively showcased no fewer than four Varèse compositions. Coming first was *Hyperprism*, in 1924. Varèse had led the premiere the year before at a little-noticed Guild concert. Stokowski's performances, with the Philadelphia Orchestra in Philadelphia and New York, were not little-noticed. *Hyperprism* is scored for nine winds and a percussion battery including, notoriously, a siren (a "very good one" from the Philadelphia Fire Department, Stokowski assured the composer). It begins with an onslaught of cymbals, gong, and bass drum, then a stuttering tattoo of repeated notes, fortissimo, for tenor trombone over the slap and rattle of assorted noisemakers, exotic and conventional, all precisely notated. Typical of Varèse is the absence of strings, of tonal harmony, of thematic development. Busoni, with whom Varèse had studied in Berlin, influentially espoused an "absolute music" without boundaries or divisions. Varèse described the "collision and penetration" of "sound masses" activating his designs. The shock of *Hyperprism*—its unmoored forms, its unbridled showmanship, its sheer noise—was liberating or appalling. Many first listeners laughed. Lawrence Gilman, in the *New York Herald-Tribune*, called the music "self-sprung," "lonely, incomparable and unique."[27]

Reviewing *Intégrales*, as performed by Stokowski in 1925, Paul Rosenfeld claimed Varèse for the New World: "he has come into relationship with elements of American life, and found corresponding rhythms within himself set free." *Amériques*, premiered by Stokowski in 1926, was the earliest of Varèse's American works, composed in 1918–21 for a gargantuan orchestra including twenty-seven woodwinds and twenty-nine brass instruments; Varèse considered it the first manifestation of his "own music." Here, the influence of Stravinsky and *The Rite of Spring* is both obvious and clarifying. Stravinsky's violence and primitivism are scented by pagan Russia: the past. If *Amériques* suggests anything extramusical, it is the savage cacophony and polymorphous intensity of contemporary Manhattan. The title refers not to geography but to new worlds of sonic experience, and yet Varèse later said, "When I wrote *Amériques*, I was still under the spell of my first impressions of New York—not only New York seen, but more especially heard . . . the whole wonderful river symphony which moved me more than anything ever had before." In Philadelphia, *Amériques* was vehemently hissed and booed. In New York, it ignited more than five minutes of audience turmoil. Finally, Stokowski and the Philadelphia Orchestra in 1927 introduced *Arcana*, on which occasion Olin Downes, in the *New York Times*, declared Varèse a "hero" and W. J. Henderson, of the old guard, marveled, "Hissing is an honor rarely bestowed upon a composer in this town."[28]

By 1930, Varèse had emerged as a leading figure among the "ultra-modern" composers, whose lineage was directly traceable to Leo Ornstein's *Wild Man's Dance* of 1913, to the Armory Show of 1913, and to other manifestations of defiant experimentation in the decade before World War I.* Alongside Varèse, the ultras included George Antheil, who treated airplane propellers as musical instruments, and Henry Cowell, who pounded the piano with his fists. Carl Ruggles, Dane Rudhyar, Wallingford Riegger, and Ruth Crawford were other members in more or less good standing. Sporadically apprised of the European avant-garde, the creative side of American musical life was still too inchoate to support a rallying cry as considered and magnetic as the manifestos Busoni, Schoenberg, Kandinsky, and *Der blaue Reiter* produced abroad. But certain ultra-modern attributes may be extrapolated. Stokowski notwithstanding, the ultras stood apart from the symphonic establishment, including the Koussevitzky branch admitting Copland; rather, they had their own institutions of performance. They of course offended vestigial genteel ideals of

* See p. 254.

craft and uplift; younger critics, including Gilman and Downes, were viscerally stirred. Their most stalwart advocates, in books and in the *New Republic*, the *Nation*, *Vanity Fair*, and the *Dial*, were Carl Van Vechten, whose estrangement from Eurocentric music ultimately estranged him from American classical music altogether, and Paul Rosenfeld, an insistent modernist whose highbrow sympathies embraced both Copland and Varèse but excluded the likes of Cowell and Gershwin. Both Van Vechten and Rosenfeld appraised the avant-garde in all its forms; Rosenfeld's salon was visited by Ornstein and Varèse, and also e.e. cummings, Hart Crane, and Marianne Moore. A willful individualism ensured that the ultras, though mutually supportive, composed in very different styles. "Emancipation of dissonance" was a common feature, linked to the abdication of tonal harmony by Schoenberg and other Expressionists abroad. Also Expressionist was a pronounced inner intensity whose creative output ranged from primal *Ur-musik* to constructivist rigor. Rosenfeld grouped Ruggles and Rudhyar with Schoenberg and Webern as composers "who find the climate of music only at the pitch of ecstasy."[29] But Ruggles, Rudhyar, and other ultras at the same time crucially resisted a mentored reliance on Europe. Not a single American of the twenties betrays an informed understanding of twelve-tone technique. Every one of these observations suggests kinship with Charles Ives.*

Both the Ives and Schoenberg connections are complexly exemplified in the uncompromising music and curmudgeonly personality of Ruggles. The senior ultra and the longest lived, he was born in Massachusetts in 1876 and died in Vermont in 1971. In New York, beginning in 1917, he was prominently associated with Varèse and Cowell, the Composers' Guild and Pan American Association. Assessing the mainstream, he called Toscanini "a damn swine" and dismissed Juilliard for "teaching good-for-nothing fiddlers and pianists" with "nothing for the composer." He eventually settled on a Vermont farm where he mainly painted. His tiny catalogue comprises fewer than a dozen compositions, fastidiously revised and refined, mostly composed between 1921 and 1947. His cussed individualism and puritanical austerity are New England traits; he may even be considered a regionalist. With Cowell, Crawford, and Crawford's husband Charles Seeger, he would gather to sing folk songs at the Eighth Street loft of Thomas Hart Benton, who himself sought out folk musicians on his rural treks. A leading regionalist painter, Benton was despised by Rosenfeld and other modernists both for his representational style and his reactionary politics. Though also susceptible to xenophobic rants, Ruggles,

---

* And also a potential kinship with Charles Tomlinson Griffes, had Griffes not died in 1920 at age thirty-five; Varèse was a Griffes admirer.

the subject of a 1934 Benton portrait, was anything but a representational styl-ist. Unlike Ives, whom he admired, and who admired him, he quotes no tunes and draws no pictures. But Rosenfeld was not alone in inferring "Portsmouth doorways," "Hawthorne's prose," the "New England country-side," and Mars-den Hartley's "colour" in Ruggles's gnarled sonic canvases.[30]

Ruggles proudly spurned compositional influences. But his free atonality, with its intense chromaticism, stinging dissonance, and concentrated polyphony, intriguingly parallels Schoenberg's Expressionist phase. Though, like Schoenberg, he sometimes employs fixed sets of notes to generate both harmony and melody, he essentially abandons systematized style in pursuit of unmediated personal expression—a limitation that accounts for his small out-put and for Schoenberg's subsequent reliance on twelve-tone rows to channel his creative energies. Like Schoenberg, he was an Expressionist painter of some accomplishment. And Ruggles's teachers, including John Knowles Paine in Boston, were notably Germanic (born Charles Sprague, he even Germanized his first name). Naturally, these resemblances provoked dis-claimers; he once wrote, "There are fine places all through Schoenberg's work. But as a whole his brain runs away with his heart."[31] With Varèse, too, similarities of purpose and affect, as well as Varèse's farsighted promotion of Ruggles's music, impelled interpersonal attraction and repulsion.

The mystic in Ruggles was drawn to such epigraphs as Blake's "Great things are done when men and mountains meet" for *Men and Mountains* (1924), and Whitman's "What are those of the known but to ascend and enter the Unknown?" for *Portals* (1925). His longest and biggest work, lasting less than seventeen minutes, is the exalted orchestral essay *Sun-Treader* (1926–31), which takes its title from a Robert Browning epithet for Shelley. Primal or extraterrestrial, this is music Ives might have eagerly labeled "not for sissies." Its Cyclopean opening motto, which pivotally recurs, transforms piled sonor-ity and pounding timpani into gleaming slabs of pulsating light. Compared to the American Romantics Hanson and Barber, Ruggles is an asensual Roman-tic metaphysician as remote from Hollywood as Pluto is from the sun. Com-pared to the much-performed Third Symphonies of Harris and Copland, *Sun-Treader* is iconically American without succumbing to provincialism: purer in style, more elevated in tone, more original in impact, and yet its meanings are not esoteric. The first performance was in France, in 1931. The Boston Symphony was the first American orchestra to play it—in 1966.

Henry Cowell amassed a catalogue as large and varied as Varèse's or Rug-gles's was small and unified. He was also a promoter and organizer to reckon with. Born in California to "philosophical anarchists," he was subject to com-plete educational freedom, a catalyst for lifelong habits of open ear and mind.

Exploring San Francisco's ethnic neighborhoods, he heard more Chinese, Japanese, and Indian than Western classical music. On midwestern farms he absorbed Irish songs and dances from relatives. He never acquired complete familiarity with the Western classical canon. Rather, his formal training was overseen at the University of California at Berkeley by Charles Seeger, a mentor both inspirational and iconoclastic. A year at Frank Damrosch's Institute of Musical Art in New York was all he could stand; he returned to California. He first made his name as an experimental pianist, pummeling with fists or forearms, leaning over the soundboard to stroke the strings with open hand. At the age of fourteen he had already produced *The Tides of Manaunaun*, in which clusters of rolled notes evoke ocean roars. Among his best-known keyboard miniatures of the twenties, ingeniously exploring new sonorous possibilities, were *The Banshee* (in which strings scraped and plucked produce echoing cries and wailings) and *The Aeolean Harp* (in which swept strings poetically activate silently depressed chords). The tunes and harmonics of these vignettes were as conventional as the vibrating timbres were rare; as inventor/composer, Cowell was a New World naif: Thomas Edison rather than Arnold Schoenberg. "Child-like," "kind," and "trusting" were words used to describe Cowell the man.

The novelty of Cowell's New York debut recital, at Carnegie Hall in 1924, and of a Town Hall recital thirteen days later, made him a national celebrity; of all the ultras, he was by far the likeliest to charm, the easiest to grasp. He annually toured the United States giving lecture-recitals. In 1929 he became the first American composer invited to the Soviet Union, where the state published *Lilt of the Reel* and the fist-flinging *Tiger*. Meanwhile, Cowell intensified his study of non–European music. He wrote a string quartet accompanied by Native American thundersticks. He collaborated in the creation of the electronic Rhythmicon, which played complicated polyrhythms. He explored principles of indeterminacy, leaving choices to the performers. He tested new compositional methodologies linking rhythm and pitch. He was said, by the composer Hugo Weisgall, to be temperamentally incapable of excluding from his music any idea that interested him.

In 1925 Cowell founded a California-based New Music Society. In 1927 he single-handedly launched *New Music*, which published collections of contemporary works on a quarterly basis. Among the composers he chose to support in this fashion were Schoenberg and Webern. But his greater enthusiasm was for the likes of Varèse, Rudhyar, Ruggles, and Ornstein: for an "American" music defined as pioneering, novel, resistant to foreign domination. In later years, he would write, "Transplanted to the United States, the rules of harmony and composition took on a doctrinaire authority that was the more dogmatic for being second hand." His most quoted axiom became, "I want to take in the *whole world* of music." Invaluable was his inspired advocacy of Ives, regularly represented in *New Music*. Ives in turn supported the concerts Cowell organized for the Pan American Association. In 1933 Cowell called Ives "the father of indigenous American art-music"; in 1955, he coauthored, with his wife, *Charles Ives and His Music*. Though his ceaseless explorations led to William Billings and a series of *Hymn and Fuging Tunes*, Cowell stands with Ruggles as an unusually pure example of an American musical identity founded on attitude and personality rather than nationalist musical tags: Ruggles was the stay-at-home Yankee, Cowell the Pacific Rim adventurer. More than anyone else, he united America's least Eurocentric composers in the belief that the future was theirs: a prophecy today more credible than at any moment in Cowell's lifetime.[32]

A fourth ultra-modernist whose reputation endures—indeed, grows—is Ruth Crawford. She encountered Rudhyar and Cowell at the Chicago salon of the theosophist Djane Herz; all three were important influences on her development. In New York beginning in 1929 she studied with Charles Seeger, who also mentored Ruggles and Cowell. A pioneering American musicologist and ethnomusicologist, Seeger had devised a complex system of nontonal "dissonant counterpoint" to which Ruggles and Crawford gravitated. Two years later, Crawford and Seeger married. When Ruth Crawford Seeger traveled to Europe in 1920, Charles advised her to steer clear of European teachers, especially Schoenberg, whose twelve tone method represented an alternative to dissonant counterpoint, and Boulanger, whose neoclassicism represented a threat to ultra-modernism. Crawford obliged; the contemporary Europeans she most admired, she discovered, were Bartók and Berg.[33] Upon returning to New York she produced what became the signature work in her small catalogue: the twelve-minute *String Quartet 1931*. Its striking Andante applies Seeger-style serial organization of pitch, rhythm, and dynamics to achieve pulsations of color—a Schoenbergian *Klangfarbenmelodie* that is equally a harrowing music of the heart.

No sooner had Crawford established her reputation as a brave constructivist than she and Charles witnessed the collapse of the avant-garde during the populist thirties. Koussevitzky, still a hero to Copland and Harris, was seen by more radical composers as the victorious enemy; Stokowski the mystic hedonist, once champion of Varèse, was out of step with the new culture of social responsibility. As "Carl Sands," Seeger now wrote music criticism for the Communist *Daily Worker*; he steered readers away from the "bourgeois music" of Chopin and Schumann, and also from the contemporary "liberal" composer who supported a social system "that gives him a tower and allows him to sit in it."[34] He next moved to Washington, D.C., where in various jobs he became a major force in the belated discovery of an abundant American folk music that Dvořák and Krehbiel had not even glimpsed. Crawford, accordingly, abandoned composition to transcribe, arrange, and edit hundreds of folk songs from field recordings at the Library of Congress. (Her stepson, from Charles's previous marriage, was the folksinger Pete Seeger.)

Copland's populist accommodation—to a patriotic symphonic idiom—was anathema to the ultras. Varèse, Ruggles, and Rudhyar stopped composing. Cowell wound up spending four years in a California prison, convicted of a homosexual transgression. This seeming termination of ultra-modernism was in fact a hibernation. After 1950, the American cultural climate shifted in favor of Schoenberg, Bartók, and the later Stravinsky. Varèse reappeared to compose, prophetically, with tape and electronics. Cowell (who even in jail never stopped writing and making music) emerged as a "world music" guru whose progeny included Lou Harrison and John Cage. As for Crawford, she recommenced composing with a wind quintet in 1952, and died of cancer the following year at the age of fifty-two. Her String Quartet, an acknowledged influence on Elliott Carter, was influentially recorded in 1961, 1973, and 1996.

A posthumous Ruth Crawford revival, coinciding with the turn of the twenty-first century, was partly powered by fascination with her fate as an American woman composer. As with Amy Beach, Crawford's marriage controversially impacted on her creative potential. Charles Seeger was an old-fashioned husband fourteen years her senior (Beach's husband was twenty-five years older). Parenting their children was mostly Ruth's job. Ruth benefited from Charles's instruction and, like Beach, seems willingly to have aligned her dictates with those of her spouse. Her abandonment of her composer's career remains frustratingly swift. More than Beach, she refutes stereotypes of genteel female breeding and musical decorum. Among her contemporaries, Claire Reis and Minna Lederman, tenacious leaders of the League of Composers and *Modern Music*, refute genteel stereotypes of the arts patroness, as do the musical philanthropists Gertrude Vanderbilt Whitney, Alma Morgenthau Wertheim, and Blanche Walton, all backers of the American avant-garde. A sixth patroness, Elizabeth Sprague Coolidge, was more conservative in taste, but her achievement was bold. Knowingly, resourcefully, forcefully, she applied her inheritance to foster chamber music in the United States. She backed string quartets and festivals, and endowed a foundation to build a concert hall in the Library of Congress, which swiftly became a necessary showcase for important musicians and important new music. Either personally, or through the Coolidge Foundation, she commissioned at least 120 compositions, including string quartets by Bartók and Schoenberg, Stravinsky's *Apollo*, and Copland's *Appalachian Spring*.

Coolidge herself played the piano and composed, albeit discreetly. Rather like Beach or Seeger, she seems to have formed a submissive relationship to her spouse; only with his infirmity and death did she find her vocation. The vocation itself, however, was not gender specific. Her contribution to American chamber music bears comparison with that of Serkin. Her successful shepherding of new music into a mainstream arena surpasses what Otto Kahn was able to achieve at the Met.

As late as 1923, Walter Damrosch, echoing Theodore Thomas, could observe, "I do not think there has ever been a country whose musical development has been fostered so almost exclusively by women as America." Most conservatory students remained women and audiences remained mainly female; on the local level, women were, as before, the music teachers, the hostesses, the supporters of the symphony and opera; men—as not in Europe—shunned classical music as "effeminate." This was the world on which Jeannette Thurber, Isabella Stewart Gardner, Laura Langford, Anna Millar, Helen Herron Taft, and Adella Prentiss Hughes made their mark. But music appreciation, recordings, and the new audience (as we have seen) regendered classical music by 1950. As music students and music lovers became men, other doors opened for women. By century's end, women composers were no longer a novelty and female musicologists led the charge to resurrect Beach and Crawford both.[35]

■ ■ ■

If America's composers were a sideshow to classical music's culture of performance, classical music—its great orchestras and great performers—was itself a sideshow to American music at large. With the advent of radio and recordings, the postwar decades produced popular music as we know it, and with it the central achievement of American music in the first half of the twentieth century: jazz. Dvořák and Farwell, Copland and Harris had labored to create a style for art songs, sonatas, and symphonies that sounded schooled in America. To many, the jazz age was a gusty wind that blew aside all such high endeavors. Gilbert Seldes, who with Carl Van Vechten influentially espoused American mass art, called jazz "our characteristic expression," "about the only native music worth listening to in America." In the same vein as Van Vechten's celebrations of Harlem cabaret life, he praised black Americans for articulating "something which underlies a great deal of America—our independence, our carelessness, our frankness, our gaiety."[36]

Dvořák and Copland, tasting "Swing Low" or swing, appropriated the African-American vernacular. In Harlem, Chicago, and New Orleans, the black vernacular had sprung its own genres, beginning with ragtime. In Europe, especially, "jazz" could mean American popular music of all kinds. Europeans enthusiastically embraced it, however understood, as unique, exotic, fascinating, and fresh—"American." An early convert was Darius Milhaud, who in 1924 observed jazz striking "almost like a start of terror, like a sudden awakening, this shattering storm of rhythm, these tone elements never previously combined and now let loose upon us all at once."[37] The queen of England opposed jazz, and so did the pope. Jazz bans were attempted in Italy, in Soviet Russia, even in Montparnasse. When Duke Ellington and Louis Armstrong toured England in 1932 and 1933, their fame preceded them.

The most ardent jazz supporters included Europe's leading composers, who routinely ignored Copland and Harris. Upon visiting New York, they gravitated to Harlem, not Carnegie Hall. Like Dvořák, they endorsed and validated a native music Americans variously took for granted or disowned. Milhaud, who split his time between France and the United States, wrote, "In jazz the North Americans have really found expression in an art form that suits them thoroughly, and their great jazz bands achieve a perfection that places them next to our most famous symphony orchestras." Stravinsky, docking in 1925, was reported by the *New York Times* as "going out at evening to dine and to hear on its native heath the dance music that the Old World has called American jazz." Bartók, arriving two years later, asked about "the latest things in American jazz . . . pretty nearly as soon as he was down the gangplank." Ravel, one year after that, told Olin Downes:

> I think you have too little realization of yourselves and that you still look too far away over the water. An artist should be international in his judgments and esthetic appreciations and incorrigibly national when it comes to the province of creative art. I think you know that I greatly admire and value—more, I think, than many American composers—American jazz. . . . I am waiting to see more Americans appear with the honesty and vision to realize the significance of their popular product, and the technic and imagination to base an original and creative art upon it.[38]

Others abroad speaking up for jazz included Ernest Ansermet, Paul Hindemith, Arthur Honegger, Francis Poulenc, Albert Roussel, Jacques Thibaud, and Kurt Weill. Of innumerable jazz-inspired compositions by non-Americans, Milhaud's *Création du monde*, Ravel's Piano Concerto in G, and Stravinsky's *Ebony* Concerto were among the best and best known.

In America itself, jazz was infinitely debatable. Racist moral discomfort was epitomized by Henry Ford's *Dearborn Independent*, which took note of "the organized eagerness of the Jew to make alliance with the Negro." "Picturesque, romantic, clean" popular songs had been supplanted by "monkey talk, jungle squeals, grunts and squeaks and gasps suggestive of cave love," all of it merchandized by Jews with just the right "cleverness to camouflage the moral filth." Among music educators, Frank Damrosch of the Institute of Musical Art denounced the "outrage on beautiful music" perpetrated by musicians "stealing phrases from the classic composers and vulgarizing them." A typical music appreciation response was a Music Memory Contest in Cleveland aimed to "cultivate a distaste for jazz and other lower forms, and a need for the great compositions." Meanwhile, Nikolai Sokoloff, music director of the Cleveland Orchestra, denounced jazz as "ugly sounds" and forbade his musicians to play it. In Philadelphia, Stokowski predictably acclaimed jazz for its "revivifying effect." Among critics, Henry Krehbiel continued to believe in "elevating" plantation song; he linked jazz with "negro brothels of the South." His younger colleague Olin Downes grew exasperated with European composers for whom jazz epitomized American music; in 1929, he advised the visiting Arthur Honegger, "We do not commend to him American jazz, which too many European musicians have striven to imitate." In the black intellectual community, there were many, like Dvořák's protégé Harry Burleigh, who sided with Krehbiel's view that jazz desecrated a cherished racial inheritance.[39]

If the moral debate over jazz was echoed abroad, American composers responded differently from their European brethren. They did not condemn jazz as unholy, yet regarded it warily or dismissively. Like Stravinsky, like Schoenberg, like Varèse, jazz was cocksure: it threatened to confuse the nascent postwar quest for an American high-cultural identity in music, and not merely for white hopes of the Roy Harris variety. Even Copland, tarred by jazz in the eyes of its opponents, was a notably ambivalent observer of the contagion. Though he invoked jazz in *Music for the Theatre* and the Piano Concerto (and was duly crucified for doing so), he did not rush to Harlem or raise an American flag for Ellington and Armstrong. In his copious writings on American music, he ignored jazz or, having discovered with amazement its high prestige abroad, put it in its place. He testified that rhythm was the "real contribution" of jazz musicians—that polyrhythms were what conferred "whatever rhythmic vitality [jazz] possesses." In a similar vein, Virgil Thomson claimed that "the peculiar character of jazz is a rhythm . . . that provokes jerky motions of the body," stemming from "a certain way of sounding two beats at once." Copland also conceded "the special fascination exerted by the timbre of the jazz band." But "as far as harmony and melody are concerned, it was jazz that did the borrowing." And: "From the composer's viewpoint, jazz had only two expressions: the well-known 'blues' mood, and the wild, abandoned, almost hysterical and grotesque mood so dear to the youth of all ages. These two moods encompassed the whole gamut of jazz emotion. Any serious composer who attempted to work within those two moods sooner or later became aware of their severe limitations." And: "The interest in jazz was temporary, similar to the interest during the same period in the primitive arts and crafts of aboriginal peoples."[40]

Quite apart from the insufficiency of Copland's or Thomson's generalizations regarding the materials of jazz, the parochialism of their critiques is telling. Weill, in Berlin, wrote, "A good jazz musician has complete command of three or four instruments. Above all, he can improvise." Ernst Krenek echoed that jazz "has revived the art of improvisation to an extent unknown by serious musicians since . . . the contrapuntal extemporization of the fifteenth century."[41] Jazz was a music for listening, for dancing, for playing, for living. It undermined the culture of performance, with its separate roles for performer, composer, and audience. It rewrote the very relationship of music and society. Listening to jazz as a stunted art music, Copland was more Eurocentric than his European counterparts: his high-culture pedigree, being newer, mattered more.

Over in the ultras camp, composers like Varèse or Ruggles who disdained popularity could afford to be indifferent. Copland, who campaigned for a music that appealed to "us and them," was compelled to deal with jazz in its most threatening manifestation: that of the composer whose concert works most popularly and completely joined Carnegie Hall to Harlem, and who succeeded in Hollywood and even on Broadway. Not only was George Gershwin a self-made millionaire whose songs were as instantly memorable and treasurable as any by Irving Berlin or Jerome Kern and whose *Rhapsody in Blue* (1924), Piano Concerto in F (1925), and *An American in Paris* (1928) galvanized a broader American public than the concert works of any previous American composer; he was, as well, surrounded by adoring family members and friends, and maddeningly endowed with a supreme ego the more daunting for its immunity to pettiness or jealousy. Alexander Woollcott captured in words what others merely marveled at: "Like you and me, Master Gershwin was profoundly interested in himself, but unlike most of us he had no habit of pretense. He was beyond, and, to my notion, above, posing. He said exactly what he thought, without window dressing it to make an impression, favorable or otherwise. Any salient description of him must begin with this trait."[42]

The admiration Europeans bestowed on jazz was as lavishly bestowed on Gershwin. At ease with folk dance and operetta, comfortably ensconced in ripe national schools of their own, European composers viewed him as an intriguing American cousin. It was not in New York, but in Rome, that a distinguished assemblage of composers—that of the Academy of Santa Cecilia—elected Gershwin an honorary member in 1937. To Ravel, who encountered him in both Paris and New York, Gershwin was a figure of exceptional fascination, to whom he paid exceptional homage in his 1931 Piano Concerto in G. In America, Gershwin was warmly defended against those who would not consider him a "serious composer" by his California friend and tennis partner, Arnold Schoenberg. Charles Martin Loeffler and Carl Engel, likewise European-born, also picked Gershwin as the American who mattered. Loeffler struck up a sustained friendship with Gershwin, to whom he wrote in 1927, "It is needless to say that I have pinned my faith on your delightful genius and on your future. You alone seem to express charm, grace, and invention amongst the composers of our time. When the Anthlands and Coptheils ed tutti quanti will be forgotten . . . you, my dear friend, will be recorded in the Anthologies of coming ages." Upon hearing the Concerto in F, Engel wrote, "You must whisper softly still when you dare suggest that at last America has a music all its own." Otto Klemperer, who in Los Angeles pursued a mostly futile quest for American works he could endorse, remarked in later life that he had not been impressed by the music of Copland, that "the [American] composer who was important was Gershwin."[43] Fritz Reiner (the second conductor to perform the Concerto in F, he positioned it and *Rhapsody in Blue* in between Beethoven's Seventh Symphony and Strauss's *Till Eulenspiegel*)[44] befriended and performed Gershwin. Heifetz transcribed Gershwin's tunes and tried to get him to write a violin concerto. Rachmaninoff, Weill, Percy Grainger, and Leopold Godowski were other émigré Gershwin enthusiasts.

Like that of jazz, Gershwin's appeal to Europe was simple, obvious, and fresh. Like jazz, he poked at the fissures of the American experience: the relation between bloodline Anglos, immigrant Jews, and blacks once imported and sold; between high culture borrowed but pure, and a popular culture born of miscegenation. No less than jazz, Gershwin provoked a cacophony of opinion. By and large, the music appreciators ignored him. Jazzmen and jazz critics were chronically ambivalent. So were classical music critics. So were classical musicians. Walter Damrosch commissioned the Concerto in F and *An American in Paris*; rehearsing the concerto's premiere with Gershwin, Damrosch's New York Symphony, observed from within by the violinist Winthrop Sargeant, "hated Gershwin . . . with an instinctive loathing. . . . [The musicians] pretended to regard Gershwin's music humorously, made funny noises, and played it, in general, with a complete lack of understanding of the American idiom."* Gershwin himself—whose sympathies did not exclude Bach, Mozart, Beethoven, Debussy, Stravinsky, or Richard Strauss—wrote of a "Machine Age America" impacting on notions of "tempo, speed and sound," of a range of American folk music—including southern mountain songs, cowboy songs, spirituals, and most especially jazz—applicable to "the creation of American art music."[45]

For American composers, Gershwin was of course a conundrum; snobbish exclusivity was one instinctive response. *Modern Music* published a series of anti-Gershwin articles in the 1930s. Copland did not list Gershwin in his 1926 *Modern Music* survey of "America's Young Men of Promise"; he omitted Gershwin again in 1936. Though Copland performed Gershwin's music, both as pianist and as conductor, this was mainly after Gershwin died. Decades later Copland reflected, "In many ways Gershwin and I had much in common— both from Brooklyn, we had studied with Rubin Goldmark during the same time and were pianists and composers of music that incorporated indigenous American sounds. But even after Damrosch commissioned Gershwin's Concerto in F for performance in the same season as Koussevitzky premiered my *Music for the Theatre*, Gershwin and I had no contact."[46]

It was Paul Rosenfeld who took the gloves off. Himself a Jew of German extraction, Rosenfeld detected in Gershwin the Russian Jew a "weakness of spirit, possibly as a consequence of the circumstance that the new world attracted the less stable types." Rosenfeld's 1933 *New Republic* essay, "No Chabrier," elaborated:

> Gershwin himself is assuredly a gifted composer of the lower, unpretentious order; yet there is some question whether his vision permits him an association with the artists. He seems to have little feeling for reality. His compositions drowse one in a pink world of received ideas and sentiments. The *Rhapsody in Blue* is circus-music, pre-eminent in the sphere of tinsel and fustian. In daylight, nonetheless, it stands vaporous with its second-hand ideas and ecstasies; its old-fashioned Lisztian ornament and brutal, calculated effects, not so much music, as jazz dolled up. . . . To qualify as a vulgar composer and rank with Chabrier, Albéniz, Glinka, and

---

* Within a dozen years, Gershwin had also performed the Concerto in F with the orchestras of Chicago, Detroit, Los Angeles, New York (the Philharmonic), Philadelphia, Pittsburgh, St. Louis, Seattle, and Washington, D.C. Audiences at these concerts were exceptionally large. The concerto was also toured by the Leo Reisman Orchestra, with Gershwin, and by the Paul Whiteman Orchestra (in an arrangement by Ferde Grofé), with the pianist Roy Bargy. It straddled two musical worlds. I am indebted for this information to Timothy Freeze, author of the unpublished paper "Toward a Reception History of Gershwin's Concerto in F, 1925–1937" (University of Michigan, 2003).

even with Milhaud and Auric at their best, a musician has to "compose" his material, to sustain and evolve and organize it to a degree sufficient to bring its essence, their relationships, their ideas, to expression. And that Gershwin has accomplished to no satisfactory degree, at least not in any of the larger forms he has up to the present time given the public.

The unveiling of Copland's Piano Concerto in 1927 excited from Rosenfeld the proclamation that jazz, as never in the "hash derivative" compositions of Gershwin, had at last "borne music."[47]

Whatever one makes of his highbrow rigidities—a product of the times—Rosenfeld was a very intelligent critic. He acknowledged that there was "no question" of Gershwin's talent, of his "individuality and spontaneity," his "distinctive warmth," his feeling for "complex rhythm" and "luscious, wistful, dissonantly harmonized melodies." And it is true enough that in all of Gershwin's concert works the stitching shows. But this is somehow beside the point. For one thing, Gershwin was learning fast: in *An American in Paris*, four years after *Rhapsody in Blue*, the narrative structure—adventures of a tourist/composer—shrewdly rationalizes the song-medley form, and the culminating song-stew, if thick, cleverly combines many tuneful ingredients. For another, Copland's mediation between concert fare and jazz, in the Piano Concerto Rosenfeld admired, has problems of its own. The tunes are nothing special. The conscious sophistication Rosenfeld endorses—in particular, the shifting meters (an enhancement in such modernist Copland as the *Short Symphony*)—cancels the illusion of spur-of-the-moment inspiration Copland strives to sustain. A crowning irony: though Gershwin's music at all times ignores Copland's (he prefers European examples of advanced harmony), the rocking blues theme of Copland's concerto resembles someone's Second Prelude; Gershwin is the stronger magnet. In any event, seventy-five years after Rosenfeld's critique, the Concerto in F is the piano concerto that endures.[48]

Within the Gershwin camp, there were those who believed that a little suffering would do George's music some good. Gershwin's ambitions outstripped all such urgings: he tackled a full-length opera discarding the high society of his shows. The characters, from the DuBose Heyward novel *Porgy*, would be poor blacks in Charleston, South Carolina. To get to them, Gershwin (who sought out black music and musicians more than any other concert composer of his time)* visited churches, homes, night clubs, and prayer meet-

---

* As a solo pianist whose repertoire included high-powered versions of his own songs, Gershwin intersects with a lineage of black virtuoso pianist/composers beginning with Scott Joplin and including the likes of James P. Johnson and Art Tatum. Composers as early as Louis Moreau

ings in South Carolina. At Folly Island he encountered the exotic "shouting," to the rhythmic beat of feet and hands, of the "Gullah Negroes." Heyward was there: "I shall never forget the night when . . . George started 'shouting' at them. And eventually to their huge delight stole the show from their 'champion' shouter. I think he is probably the only white man in America who could have done it."[49] The famous outcome was the opera for which the Met, through Otto Kahn, bid unsuccessfully, a work whose interpenetration of Broadway and jazz, *Carmen* and *Die Meistersinger* reconnected with the inclusivity of New York's nineteenth-century opera madness, whose story and arias linked both with "negro melodies," turn-of-the-century black musical theater, and black jazz musicians to come, and with Deems Taylor's "Tony the barber," who thrilled to "La donna è mobile" and "Celeste Aïda."

Even more than *Rhapsody in Blue* or the Concerto in F, *Porgy and Bess* is an astounding first try. The style lacks uniformity, the recitatives are stiff, the seams show. But Gershwin, an immigrant's son made good, succeeds triumphantly in traveling the "lonesome road" of the dispossessed and oppressed.* When he hits stride, as in Robbins's funeral with its ceremony of lament and keening widow's song, *Porgy* is—a rarity in American music, because the American experience is so much shorter and more sanguine than centuries of European vicissitude—at once a human and an epic tragedy. If *Rhapsody in Blue* qualifies as iconic Americana for trumping its borrowed European conventions, Gershwin's grand opera grasps greater and more complex New World themes. The organic community of Catfish Row remembers a black Eden: a "Summertime" of rich daddies and easy living. The actual Catfish Row is in part a place of hurricanes and killings. But the real threat, which severs the lovers, is up north: New York. No less than *The Song of Hiawatha*, *Porgy and Bess* is a parable of paradise lost. Longfellow's Indians, a forest community rich in friendship, religion, and ritual, are displaced by the "White Man's Foot." In his *New World* Symphony, in his projected Hiawatha opera, Dvořák—who shunned the city and its habits—likewise conceived an elegiac requiem for past innocence. Gersh-

---

Gottschalk and as recent as William Bolcom have likewise contributed to an enduring American keyboard canon inspired by black American vernacular music. Never mind that Tatum's solos were not written down; posthumously transcribed, they have been brilliantly championed as living American keyboard repertoire by the pianist Steven Mayer.

* Like Dvořák, Gershwin connected with the condition of African-Americans. To Bernard Herrmann, Gershwin said that "'Summertime' sounds Jewish to me . . . the kind of song a cantor might sing." See Steven C. Smith, *Heart at Fire's Center: The Life and Music of Bernard Herrmann* (Berkeley, University of California Press, 1991), p. 41.

win's American parable is in every way darker and less sanitized: the despoiling metropolis is signaled seductively by Sportin' Life and "happy dust," brutally by white policemen who cannot sing. Longfellow projects a beguiling purity of the spirit by evading tragedy. Gershwin's opera projects, via Porgy, an innocence embattled yet unbent.[50]

The 1935 premiere, at the Alvin Theatre, was typically controversial. Olin Downes wrote, "The style is at one moment of opera and another of operetta or sheer Broadway entertainment." Virgil Thomson wrote, "It is crooked folklore and halfway opera, a strong but crippled work." J. Rosamond Johnson, the important African-American singer and songwriter who took the role of the lawyer Frazier, proclaimed Gershwin "the Abraham Lincoln of Negro music." Other blacks denounced *Porgy and Bess* for stereotyping a people and its song. Two years later, Gershwin was dead of a brain tumor at the age of thirty-eight. He had been working on a string quartet. His first biographer, Isaac Goldberg, was not the only member of the Gershwin circle who believed "George had not yet really found himself at the time he died."[51]

Gershwin was of course neither the first nor the last significant composer to attempt to marry Broadway and the Met. In the first decades after *Porgy*, Kurt Weill and Marc Blitzstein were notable candidates to inherit the Gershwin mantle. Weill was already something like the German Gershwin. His *Dreigroschenoper* (1928) and *Die sieben Todsünden* (1933), both in collaboration with Bertolt Brecht, irresistibly mated social protest, popular song, and intellectual savvy; honored distinctions between high and popular culture were not so much tested as smashed. A Jewish refugee, Weill arrived in Manhattan in 1935—the year of *Porgy*—and declared himself an American. The American political distemper of the thirties had for some time been Weill's Weimar distemper. But there were no American opera houses for a composer so committed to serving a broad public, and Broadway was aesthetically remote from the wickedly unsentimental and insidiously parodistic Weimar style he absorbed from Brecht. So Weill selflessly underwent a stylistic remake. This singular surgery was not unsuccessful. His Broadway efforts grew in weight from *Lady in the Dark* (1940) and *One Touch of Venus* (1943) to a pair of quasi-operas: *Street Scene* (1947), a New York tenement drama echoing *Porgy* in its communal detail, and *Lost in the Stars* (1949), after Alan Paton's *Cry, The Beloved Country*. He died a year later, fifty years old, while undertaking an adaptation of *Huckleberry Finn*. It was both a strength and a weakness that Weill molded himself to his surroundings, including his collaborators. Partly because he never found another Brecht, he never consummated his American potential; like every other immigrant composer of note (with the irrelevant exception of Varèse, whose early music perished in a fire), he did his best work at home in Europe.

Blitzstein was Weill's New World offspring. Fired by personal contact in New York with Brecht and Hanns Eisler, he composed the 1937 propaganda opera *The Cradle Will Rock*, whose defiant premiere we have already noted. Less a period piece is *Regina*, Blitzstein's 1949 version of Lillian Hellman's *The Little Foxes*. Set in 1900 in the new industrializing South, the story of the Hubbards is a nightmare of savage greed and materialism in which black servants succor those white masters whose goodness remains salvageable. As with *Porgy and Bess*, both the moral dimension and its American backdrop are compellingly drawn. If Blitzstein lacks Gershwin's human depth and melodic genius, *Regina* surpasses *Porgy* in uniformity of style and ease of construction. Sung speech, masterfully rendered, guides the seamless transitions from aria to recitative to spoken dialogue. Hellman told Blitzstein, "I don't know how you can add anything to the Hubbards that will make them any more unpleasant than they already are."[52] But *Regina* is an adaptation that works: a three-act opera with larger-than-life characters whose musical intersection serves to amplify the theatrical charge. Blitzstein died in 1964 at the age of fifty-nine, having begun a Sacco and Vanzetti opera supported by the Metropolitan Opera and the Ford Foundation. Like Gershwin, like Weill, he promised more than he lived to deliver.

If Weill and Blitzstein were the most notable composers to move from classical training toward popular arts, many others, in addition to Gershwin, headed in the opposite direction. Some were black musicians aspiring, like Dvořák, to apply "negro melodies" to European forms. Harry Burleigh, who as a singer and composer transforming spirituals into something like art songs, was one example.* Scott Joplin, the ragtime king, in 1911 completed a grand opera, *Treemonisha*, and printed the piano-vocal score at his own expense. It died with him, in 1917—to be resurrected fifty-five years later. Among Gershwin's contemporaries, the most prominent black composer was William Grant Still, a model of high/low versatility whose activities included arrangements for W. C. Handy and an *Afro-American* Symphony (1930), first performed by Howard Hanson and the Rochester Philharmonic. Of Gershwin's Broadway colleagues, Jerome Kern broached the musical continuity of operetta and the earnest content of opera in *Show Boat* (1927). Richard Rodgers continued in the same direction in *Oklahoma!* (1943), *Carousel* (1945), and *South Pacific* (1948). (The cheerful *Carousel* Waltz was programmed even by the dour Fritz Reiner.) But, like Irving Berlin and Cole Porter, Kern and Rodgers were

---

* Earlier prominent black concert singers included the "Black Swan," Elizabeth Taylor Greenfield, and the "Black Patti," Sissieretta Jones. Though like Burleigh, Jones was unwelcome on opera stages, her repertoire included some Donizetti, Meyerbeer, and Verdi.

songwriters first and foremost.* No less than jazz, their high achievement—dwarfing in influence the vocal and stage works of their classical music counterparts—falls outside the scope of this book except insofar as they furnish context for high-low interlopers and offer perspective on what classical music was not.

The combination of popular acclaim and critical confusion that greeted his classical output is but one indication that, among composers, Gershwin signified the best hope to challenge the "white" Eurocentricity of American classical music and the masterpiece obsession of its culture of performance. Comet-like, he illuminates the entire American musical landscape, its possibilities and limitations. In the realm of possibilities, Gershwin suggests that something more could be gained than lost by avoiding the European finishing schools other Americans attended in Germany or France. Gershwin had inquired about studying with Boulanger or Ravel—how seriously one cannot tell. But Ravel was deadly serious in saying no; he unforgettably wrote to Boulanger:

> There is a musician here endowed with the most brilliant, most enchanting, and perhaps the most profound talent: George Gershwin.
>
> His world-wide success no longer satisfies him, for he is aiming higher. He knows that he lacks the technical means to achieve his goal. In teaching him those means, one might ruin his talent.
>
> Would you have the courage, which I wouldn't dare have, to undertake this awesome responsibility?†

Would Ives have been "ruined" had he chosen to study in Leipzig or Frankfurt, like Chadwick and MacDowell? Would Melville's originality have been compromised if, like Henry James, he had opted for Paris and London rather than the South Seas? Would Whitman have benefited from European breeding to supplement the schooling he obtained on Civil War battlefields and in

---

* Gian Carlo Menotti is a composer whose Broadway operas, little heard today, were popular in the forties and fifties. A potentially more enduring Broadway opera of the same period—it has better tunes and a lighter touch than such Menotti works as *The Medium* and *The Telephone*—is Frank Loesser's *The Most Happy Fella* (1956), which nonetheless suffers in comparison to its intermittent Italian models; Loesser's nonoperatic *Guys and Dolls* (1950) is a more consummated effort.

† According to her biographer Léonie Rosenstiel, Boulanger told Gershwin, "I can teach you nothing." Rosenstiel comments, "The true significance of this incident has been hotly debated for years. . . . Did Nadia really mean that she could teach Gershwin nothing because he already knew everything? That is how *he* interpreted her comment." See Rosenstiel, *Nadia Boulanger: A Life in Music* (New York, W. W. Norton, 1982), pp. 215–217. (I am indebted to Glenn Watkins for this reference.)

Brooklyn theaters? To the degree that Gershwin and Ives, Melville and Whit-man are all talents unfinished or unpolished, they arguably remain true to "America"—its youth, its sprawling diversity, its cockiness of adventure. "Many American composers, I believe, have been interested in working things out for themselves to a great extent," wrote Ives in his *Memos*. He was of course thinking of himself—but Gershwin, though in constant search of teachers, also fits.[53]

In the realm of limitations, Gershwin's comet sheds light not only on Gershwin's own failings, which he creatively addressed, but also on restric-tions self-imposed on his would-be classical colleagues. They pulled away from Gershwin and jazz. As we have seen, they equally rebuffed Chadwick and his generation as childish; even Ives was damned with faint praise by Copland and Thomson. Copland's 1920s take on Varèse—"limited and some-what sectarian"[54]—well represents their attitude toward the ultra-moderns. This pattern of disparagement—typically reasoned and polite, not mean-spirited or gratuitous—was an unconscious strategy of empowerment. Just as the all-American concert movement of the late Gilded Age had promulgated a tariff against European competition, Copland and Thomson were protec-tionists. It is true that the Composers' Guild sponsored performances of a range of important European contemporary music. It is equally true that, notwithstanding Schoenberg's actual residence in the United States, before World War II scant serious effort was made to figure out how the music of Schoenberg, Webern, and Berg was put together. To have done so any sooner would have constituted a distraction.★

This gain in focus and confidence was quite obviously also a loss. By the standards of Ives and Ruggles, Gershwin and Ellington, the composers on the Copland list are undeniably cramped in range. In particular, they relinquished sensuality. To think of earthy or erotic interwar European music is to think of Ravel, Stravinsky, Berg, Milhaud, Weill. To think of earthy or erotic interwar American music is to think of Gershwin and jazz. The continued protection-ist tendencies of the "new" Americans were as old as the fence John Sullivan Dwight once erected against Patrick Gilmore, as insular as the barriers music

---

★ In the course of a flurry of articles and letters in the *New York Times* on the subject of the impact of immigrant musicians (Jan.–Feb. 1941), Howard Hanson wrote, "We must not solve the problem of providing opportunities for our foreign guests by curtailing the already meager opportunities for the young American. There is some evidence that exactly this situation is occurring." Hanson's protec-tionist instructions were vehemently challenged, in the *Times*, by Roger Sessions. See David Joseph-son, "The Exile of European Music: Documentation of Upheaval and Immigration in the *New York Times*," in Reinhold Brinkmann and Christoph Wolff (eds.), *Driven into Paradise: The Musical Migration from Nazi Germany to the United States* (Berkeley, University of California Press, 1999), pp. 112–120.

appreciation raised in favor of exclusively "great music" and the "world's greatest musician." In Europe, the parent culture earlier appreciated Ellington and Armstrong at something like their full worth, and did not elevate Toscanini or any other conductor above the station of a Richard Strauss or Prokofiev.

That American classical music closed ranks against Gershwin, that its performers and composers largely failed to find common cause, that it maintained an exaggerated pedigree for high art were symptoms of borrowed origins, of a lingering immaturity.

■ ■ ■

Any assessment of American composers should beware the music appreciators' masterpiece syndrome, which insisted that only great music was good enough for a great conductor. During the interwar search for the Great American Symphony, the thrill of the chase should have furnished excitement enough. But it remains pertinent to inquire, in retrospect, what the chase produced.

Copland, in 1926, announced, "The day of the neglected American composer is over." Fifteen years later, sounding a bit less robust, he wrote, "A nation may be said to have come of age, musically speaking, only when it begins to produce composers—original composers. . . . I have the fond illusion —even though I do not pretend to be an absolutely disinterested onlooker— that it is not merely wishful thinking to prognosticate the emergence of important [American] composers. . . . There may not be maturity in our musical America as yet, but there should be plenty of fun in watching us grow." A year after that a less partial observer, the London-born Eugene Goossens, could despair:

> During the past nineteen years I have guest-conducted every [major] orchestra—save one—in the [United States]; not once, but many times. On these occasions I have observed audience-reaction very closely, particularly at certain times when the resident conductor happened to be in charge. I have—regrettably be it noted—watched the vague atmosphere of suspicion and mistrust creep over sections of the audience when the performance of an unknown piece of contemporary music has started. . . . In the past 10 years I have watched an audience at Carnegie Hall superciliously condescending to sit through a good American piece whilst deliberately refusing to be carried away by its virtues, and completely intolerant of its intricacies.

. . . There is far too much of the "I-know-what-I-like, and I-like-what-I-know" attitude among our audiences today. It displays itself in a thinly veiled indifference to everything new and unfamiliar—especially American.[55]

Copland himself, writing in 1967, found his 1941 prediction that "future American composers will build" on the music of Roy Harris "downright naïve. . . . As it turned out, the young men . . . show no signs of wishing to build on the work of the older American-born composers, the generation of the '20s and '30s." Program statistics show that native music increased as a percentage of the American symphonic repertoire from 2 percent before World War I to 10 percent during the war, then subsided to 7 or 8 percent until World War II. Of 280 American composers played on subscription programs by the ten oldest major American orchestras between 1925 and 1950, only 18—including the foreign-born Ernest Bloch and Charles Martin Loeffler—were played by as many as nine orchestras, accounting for 45 percent of all American music for the twenty-five-year period. John H. Mueller, who tabulated these figures, concluded that "most of the quota of American composers is consumed in purely token performances of local or regional interest."[56]

That the American composer "came of age" in the twenties and thirties is an article of conventional wisdom that deserves to be rethought or retired—though American orchestras continue to pay it knee-jerk allegiance. Would that for every ten performances of *Appalachian Spring* or the Barber Violin Concerto there might be a single hearing of Chadwick's *Jubilee*, or a few outings of *An American in Paris* (on something other than a pops program), or a suitably ceremonious airing of Ives's Second Symphony or Ruggles's *Sun-Treader*.

In fact, by 1950 American composers had produced at least four distinct streams of music, all of which achieved substantial results and none of which reached fruition. There were the "come of age" composers Copland endorsed. There were the ultra-moderns. There were the interlopers who, with Gershwin, moved in and out of popular culture. And there was a variegated pre-1920 bunch, including Gottschalk, Chadwick, Griffes, and Ives. It would be idle to attempt to rank the four streams. In some respects, they were closer together than their jealous adherents dared to suppose. In the long view, Gershwin and Copland were bedfellows of a kind. Paul Rosenfeld in a 1939 paean called Harris's music "wider than Copland's, comprehensive of tragedy and eloquent of it in mournful accents and melodies. . . . the limitless feeling of the plains, the fierce impulses and frustrations of the American migrations, the long patience of the poor, often seem to sound in it"[57]—all of which strikingly applies to Dvořák's American style, with its long lines and open chords, its melancholy spaciousness and nostalgia for preindustrial roots in the soil. For that matter, Harris's chief propagandists included his sometime-teacher Arthur Farwell, who consciously "took up Dvořák's challenge." Copland found inspiration from Boulanger in France; even so, that he studied in New York with Rubin Goldmark, whose studies with Dvořák impelled him toward a conscious nationalism, cannot be irrelevant.

In 1965 Elliott Carter lamented "the tendency for each generation in America to wipe away the memory of the previous one, and the general neglect of our own recent past, which we treat as a curiosity useful for young scholars in exercising their research techniques—so characteristic of American treatment of the work of its important artists."[58] Carter was pondering the late "discovery" of the ultra-moderns, but his plaint applies to all four streams of American classical music, each of which so little interacted with any other. It points to a pervasive fragmentation, to an absence of lineage and continuity complicated by a late start and a heterogeneous population, by two world wars and the confusing influx of powerful refugees. But this same fragmentation may be read as a protean variety: of composers who imitated Europe or rejected it; who preferred German music or French; who viewed the popular arts as a threat or as a point of departure. To a surprising degree—surprising because American institutions of performance have understood so little— American composers have partaken in the diversity of American music as a whole. It is, in the aggregate, a defining attribute.

CHAPTER 7

Leonard Bernstein
and the Classical Music
Crisis

■

*Leonard Bernstein succeeds and fails ▪ Orchestras succeed
and fail ▪ Rudolf Bing at the Met ▪ Regional opera ▪
The Three Tenors and midcult ▪ Elliott Carter and the
stranding of the American composer*

If as of 1950 the culture of performance reigned undiminished, a challenger now appeared who flaunted the combined aspirations of George Gershwin, Aaron Copland, and Serge Koussevitzky. He was no Gershwin, yet composed one of the outstanding mid-century Broadway musicals, in which elements of opera powerfully intermingled. He was no Copland, but produced enduring concert works infectiously infused with the American vernacular. To his eternal chagrin, it was Koussevitzky, the re-creator, whose podium glamour, educational mission, and passion for advocacy Leonard Bernstein completely reembodied. That Bernstein failed to achieve more—a failure often examined and lamented, not least by Bernstein himself—was typically blamed on overweening ambition. But both the triple attempt and its predominant failure flowed logically from the fractured diversity of Bernstein's inheritance as a musical American: fundamentally, it reflected the tensions and contradictions of a musical high culture borrowed and homegrown in unequal measure. There were not firm shoulders to stand on—or, rather, the shoulders were various and misaligned. No other career so registers and illuminates the twentieth-century fate of classical music in the United States.

Born in Lawrence, Massachusetts, in 1918 to Russian Jewish immigrants—and so, generationally, a son to his American heroes—Bernstein was ten when the family acquired an upright piano and fourteen when he first heard an orchestra. His teachers at Harvard included Walter Piston; it was then, as well, that he met Dimitri Mitropoulos and played the piano for a production of *The Cradle Will Rock*; both Mitropoulos and Marc Blitzstein were formative, if incompatible, influences. His conducting teachers, also incompatible, were Fritz Reiner at Curtis and Koussevitzky at Tanglewood. In 1942 he became Koussevitzky's assistant. A year later, replacing Bruno Walter on short notice, he scored a triumph conducting the New York Philharmonic. Prominent conducting engagements in America, Europe, and Israel ensued. Meanwhile, he composed. His concert works included a Biblical *Jeremiah* Symphony (1942) and a second symphony (*The Age of Anxiety*, 1949) spiked with jazz. Having previously joined Betty Comden and Adolph Green at Greenwich Village's Village Vanguard, and arranged popular songs as Lenny Amber, he also scored the Broadway hits *On the Town* (1944) and *Wonderful Town* (1954) as well as *Candide* (1956), which though not a hit contained the ingredients of a world-class operetta.

After Koussevitzky's death in 1951, Bernstein became head of the orchestra and conducting departments at Tanglewood. His ardent pedagogical genius invaded the public arena in 1954: the year he first appeared on *Omnibus*, then American television's premier cultural showcase. For his debut studio telecast, "Beethoven's Fifth Symphony," he stood on a large reproduction of page one of Beethoven's score and admired its famous four-note motto underfoot; a more perfect unconscious metaphor for his American cockiness could hardly be invented. The most personal of his early TV investigations were of American musical theater. "The American Musical Comedy" (1956) begins:

> The glittering world of musical theater is an enormous field that includes everything from your nephew's high school pageant to *Götterdämmerung*. And somehow in that great mass of song and dance and drama lies something called the American musical comedy—a magic phrase. . . . We anticipate a new musical comedy of Rodgers and Hammerstein or of Frank Loesser with the same excitement and partisan feeling as Milan used to await a new Puccini opera, or Vienna the latest Brahms symphony. We hear on all sides that America has given the world a new form—unique, vital, inimitable.[1]

Carried away by his sincere hyperbole, Bernstein pokes fun at Europe. In a musical show, he explains, dialogue would impart that "chicken is up three cents a pound." In opera, where everything is sung, this becomes a recitative— and Bernstein sings, à la Mozart, "Susanna, I have something terrible to tell you. I've just been talking to the butcher, and he tells me that the price of chicken has gone up three cents a pound! Please don't be too depressed, dear."

There follows a pocket history of the American musical, a polemic of New World promise and achievement in the course of which he compares the similarly plotted first-act finales of *The Mikado* and Gershwin's *Of Thee I Sing*, switching back and forth, to argue an equivalent technical mastery. This conditions Bernstein's culminating hyperclaims—that "for the last fifteen years we have been enjoying the greatest period our musical theater has ever known," that "a new form has been born," that:

> we are in a historical position now similar to that of the popular musical theater in Germany just before Mozart came along. In 1750, the big attraction was what they called the *Singspiel*, which was the *Annie Get Your Gun* of its day, star comic and all. This popular form took the leap to a work of art through the genius of Mozart. After all, the *Magic Flute* is a *Singspiel*; only it's by Mozart. We are in the same position; all we need is for our Mozart to come along.... And this event can happen any second. It's almost as though it is our moment in history, as if there is a historical necessity that gives us such a wealth of creative talent at this precise time.

A mere second later, the following August, *West Side Story*—Bernstein's crowning compositional achievement, marrying high and low—opened on Broadway.

One year after that, in 1958, Bernstein—in parallel with the fifties' emergence of the Outstanding Young American Pianists and Juilliard String Quartet—became the first American-born music director of the New York Philharmonic. He could not bring Broadway to Carnegie Hall, yet triumphantly maintained his public educational mission. His nationally televised New York Philharmonic Young People's Concerts were unlike anything previously attempted in the democratization of classical music—like Copland's books, but far more resourcefully and invitingly, they crafted an antidote to music appreciation. Their subtext was a relentless self-inquiry asking, again and again, "What is American music?" Bernstein's answer, on a 1958 Young People's Concert so titled, is even more sanguine than Copland's or Thomson's. George Chadwick and company represented "the kindergarten period of American music," Edward MacDowell was "grade school," Dvořák's *New World* Symphony was a wrong turn, not really "American."* Then—a different, less parochial tack than Copland or Thomson—jazz "changed everything . . . at last

---

* Supporting this scenario, Bernstein in 1966 made the preposterous claim that there was nothing inherently "American" about Dvořák's Largo, that "with Chinese words it could sound Chinese." See Bernstein's *The Infinite Variety of Music* (New York, Simon and Schuster, 1966), p. 160.

there was something like an American folk music that belonged to *all* Americans." Even serious composers couldn't keep jazz out of their ears. Bernstein here illustrates with bits of Copland's *Music for the Theatre* and Gershwin's *Rhapsody in Blue*—and also, by way of demonstrating America's transatlantic reach, of Stravinsky's *Rag-Time*. But Copland and Gershwin remained in "high school": they "were still being American on purpose." By way of exemplifying the "many-sidedness" of "mature" American contemporary concert music, Bernstein samples Schuman's *American Festival* Overture, Harris's Third Symphony, Copland's *Billy the Kid*, Thomson's *The Mother of Us All*, and—illustrating a "sentimentality . . . that comes out of our popular songs, a sort of crooning pleasure"—a tune from Randall Thompson's Second Symphony. In sum, "We've taken it all in: French, Dutch, German, Scotch, Scandinavian, Italian, and all the rest, and learned it from one another, borrowed it, stolen it, cooked it all up in a melting pot. So what our composers are finally nourished on is a folk music that is probably the richest in the world, and all of it is American."

Other Young People's Concerts cite Simon and Garfunkel and the Beatles. Less than a generation after Walter Damrosch's *Music Appreciation Hour* went off the air, Bernstein on TV cheerfully constructs unholy anticanons. He explicates sequential progression with examples from Mozart, Gershwin, and Elvis Presley. Exploring "What Is Orchestration?," he tests the sound of a trumpet in a flute solo by Debussy and has a viola play a Gershwin clarinet riff. He dismantles European masterpieces to see how they work, or irreverently juxtaposes them with popular tunes he adores. His admiration for "All Shook Up," which he bellows, and "Eleanor Rigby," which he croons, is not even ironic. The urgency of his need to place himself as an American classical musician, to mediate between Old World and New, reinforces the energy of his delivery. One can disagree with how he answers this need—following Copland and Koussevitzky, he far undervalues what came before 1920—or complain that he succumbs to a naïve enthusiasm for his own enthusiasm. But his communicative passion is irresistible: in the heat of engagement, what he says matters—and mattered to his young people, even when his ideas sailed over their heads—because we feel sure it matters to him.

All this suggests why Bernstein never seems a patronizing or sanctimonious teacher. It also suggests the degree to which his style is self-referential—and that this is a strength. The music appreciators were sensitive to how America looked through European eyes. Bernstein, who cannot be embarrassed, directly and familiarly engages composers from other countries. For him, the United States is the place to be: young, versatile, breathless with possibility, suddenly the measure of all things musical.

Bernstein's public self-explorations peaked with his advocacy of Gustav

Mahler, whose music he featured in Philharmonic concerts for eight consecutive weeks in 1959–60 and in a 1960 Young People's Concert titled "Who Is Gustav Mahler?" Mahler's uniqueness, Bernstein argues, is his ability to "recapture the pure emotions of childhood," oscillating between extremes of happiness and gloom. Mahler is at the same time Romantic and modern. He is both conductor and composer. He is rooted, yet marginal. Torn between East and West, he is Jewish, he is Austrian, he absorbs Slavic and Chinese influences. He is an exuberant and depressive man-child, a twentieth-century American eclectic.

Though Bernstein's detractors tirelessly pointed out that Mengelberg, Klemperer, Walter, Mitropoulos, and Mahler himself had previously championed Mahler with the New York Philharmonic, it was Bernstein's personal urgency and messianic tenacity that turned the tide. Mahler had predicted that his time would come. As Bernstein astutely insisted, Mahler's combination of yearning nostalgia and tortured foreboding suited the late twentieth century. A second vital Bernstein cause was Charles Ives. Far more than such pioneering Ives champions as Henry Cowell, John Kirkpatrick, or Nicolas Slonimsky, Bernstein in his quest for American self-identity brought Ives center stage. It was he who conducted the first New York Philharmonic performance of Ives, the 1951 premiere of the Second Symphony; he who first recorded the same protean work, who took Ives on tour to Europe, who eagerly shared with his young people *The Circus Band* and *The Unanswered Question.*

In 1962, Bernstein's great expectations for Mahler and Ives, for the Philharmonic, for his own American mission attained a spectacular new venue. A plan hatched by John D. Rockefeller III and other New York corporate and financial executives had created Lincoln Center for the Performing Arts, a cultural complex of unprecedented size and scope. The constituents included the New York Philharmonic, the Metropolitan Opera, the New York City Ballet, the City Opera, and the Juilliard School, as well as a resident theater, a library/museum, and an outdoor amphitheater. An early critic of the plan, the writer Martin Mayer, shrewdly noted the absence of artists "at the moments of major decision." Mayer also observed an "astonishing blend of ignorance and optimism" in the financial projections, and could not discern a "built-in aesthetic purpose." Though William Schuman, who left Juilliard to become Lincoln Center's president, envisioned a "dynamic and constructive" synergy favoring American and contemporary arts, no such plan was set in place.[2]

For the Philharmonic, Lincoln Center represented an opportunity to build a home of its own, which Carnegie Hall, a private corporation, was not. And Carnegie, observed the chairman of the Philharmonic board, was "architecturally undistinguished" and "acoustically not one of the great halls." The orchestra's new twenty-six-hundred-seat Philharmonic Hall was inaugurated on September 23, 1962. Bernstein chose for the occasion a work commissioned from Aaron Copland, Vaughan Williams's *Serenade to Music*, and movements from Beethoven's *Missa solemnis* and Mahler's Eighth Symphony. Backstage during intermission, he asked Jacqueline Kennedy about the acoustics. The First Lady enigmatically replied, "I never saw anything like it." Other reactions were not enigmatic. Bernstein's orchestra had been assigned to a Lincoln Center hall in which the musicians could not adequately hear one another, and the sound from the stage was clotted and dull. As for synergies, the Lincoln Center constituents chose to keep a wary distance from one another; though Bernstein was signed to conduct *Falstaff* across the plaza at the Met, he would in later years return only for *Cavalleria rusticana* in 1970 and *Carmen* in 1972.

The move to Lincoln Center was unhappy in other ways. The Philharmonic under Bernstein had already acquired a keener sense of mission than it had sustained at any time during the long regime of the departed Arthur Judson. But never under Bernstein was it the great orchestra it had been under Toscanini; it also suffered in comparison with what Szell and Reiner—conductors as autocratic as Bernstein was congenial—had created in the hinterlands. Nor had Bernstein consolidated a reputation as a major symphonic interpreter. What was worst, his compositional output had diminished in quantity and importance. In 1964–65 Bernstein took a year's sabbatical and composed "a lot of music, twelve-tone music and avant-garde music of various kinds," only to discard it. Writing in the *New York Times* in 1965, he mulled "the ancient cliché that the certainty of one's knowledge decreases in proportion to thought and experience," pondered "the present crisis in composition," asked if tonality were forever dead, and worried that orchestras would "become museums of the past." A 1967 television interview in conjunction with the Philharmonic's 125th birthday revealed a spent and disillusioned musician; he had recently announced that he would relinquish his music directorship as of 1969.[3]

Koussevitzky's predictions notwithstanding, neither Bernstein nor anyone else produced the Great American Symphony. Gershwin's Broadway, too, had not proved the predicted boulevard to greatness. American popular music—not only jazz, but 1960s and 1970s rock, which Bernstein loved for its vitality and inventiveness—had in his opinion also lost its way. A new popular culture, with which he could not identify, erased the high-culture berths once reserved for classical music on commercial television. Outside music, the demise of the Kennedy White House, in which he had been a frequent guest, tarnished his dreams for America. His famous 1970 fund-raising party for the Black Panther defense fund, savagely ridiculed by Tom Wolfe as "radical chic," again caught him out of step. On *Omnibus*, in his Young People's Concerts, Bernstein had excitedly chronicled the growing up of American classical music and musical theater. "All we need is our Mozart to come along." It could "happen any second." It never did.

Bernstein's final television classroom reveals changes wrought in a decade in Bernstein's America. In six Norton lectures delivered at Harvard in 1973 and televised three years later, Bernstein asks, "Whither music in our time?" A second component of the lectures is an exercise in "musico-linguistics," applying Chomskyan language theory to the phonology, syntax, and semantics of symphonies. Never before or after did Bernstein appear so uncomfortable on screen. He struggles visibly toward his accustomed aplomb, scratching his ear, mussing his hair, pinching his nose. He strains for intellectual credibility as an original thinker. The terminology of structural linguistics spreads a scholarly patina. And Chomsky's belief in a universal and innate linguistic grammar leads in a direction Bernstein wants to go—toward a universal and innate musical grammar grounded in tonality, whose gravitational pull he considers irreplaceable.

As the lectures progress, Bernstein in fact jettisons Chomsky; the less he strives for originality, the more authentic he becomes. In the fifth lecture, "The Twentieth Century Crisis," Bernstein is most in his element and farthest from Harvard. The emblematic twentieth-century composer, he proposes, is Mahler, whose attempts to relinquish tonality are reluctant and incomplete and whose longing for past practice is overt and tragic. Mahler's Ninth Symphony, his "last will and testament," shows "that ours is the century of death, and Mahler is its musical prophet." That is the "real reason" his music suffered posthumous neglect—it was "telling something too dreadful to hear." The Ninth Symphony embodies three kinds of death—Mahler's own, which he knew was imminent; the death of tonality, "which for him meant the death of music itself"; and "the death of society, of our Faustian culture." And yet his music, like all great art, paradoxically reanimates us. While Bernstein concludes by prophesying a more wholesome musical future, a "new eclecticism" grounded in tonality, his once-boyish optimism now seems freighted with Old World gravitas and gloom. Even without the strained appeal to Chomsky, the sanguine rhetoric of the final lecture is strained. We know at a glance that the twentieth-century crisis is also Bernstein's crisis, with an American history of its own.[4]

Bernstein's disillusionment might have signaled the derailment of his career. Instead, his career was rerouted in the only possible direction: Europe.

In particular, Vienna, the city of Beethoven and Mahler, exerted an ineluctable pull. In Vienna he led *Falstaff, Der Rosenkavalier, Fidelio*, and his own *A Quiet Place*. The Vienna Philharmonic supplanted the New York Philharmonic as the orchestra with which he most often toured and recorded. On television, he now turned up purveying symphonies by Mozart, Beethoven, Brahms, and Mahler—the same Great Performances routine associated with Herbert von Karajan. Jetting between Vienna, London, Tel Aviv, Rome, New York, he trailed a cornucopia of CDs, cassettes, and souvenir books. The more ubiquitous he became, the more elusive became the American Lenny of yesteryear. He increasingly acquired a reputation for eccentricity.

The retrenchment to Great Performer worked for Bernstein because he happened to retrench into a great conductor. Perhaps the cradling traditions of the Vienna Philharmonic and its Musikverein taught and inspired him as the New York Philharmonic and Lincoln Center could not. Perhaps he had needed to grow older, or to concentrate his talents more narrowly. In any event, his later recordings thrive on a Furtwänglerian mastery of long-range tension and release. The streak of American vulgarity that taints Bernstein's own music—which in Gershwin's popular style is checked by irony, and in Copland's by a chaste classicism—is rarely apparent in his readings of other composers. In combination with new interpretive largesse, his American rhythmic élan and unbridled, heart-on-sleeve emotionalism—his Jewish/American emotional chutzpah—produces Brahms, Tchaikovsky, and Mahler performances different from anyone else's. Like Stokowski, like Glenn Gould, Bernstein the conductor was ultimately a New World original.

He continued to mentor young musicians in Fontainebleau, Sapporo, Schleswig-Holstein, and Tanglewood. But he stopped teaching laymen and their offspring. He last appeared at a Lincoln Center children's event on March 14, 1984, the sixtieth anniversary celebration of the New York Philharmonic's Young People's Concerts. He conducted but, incongruously, did not speak. A member of the Philharmonic's staff confided afterward that since Bernstein was "crazy," he could not be trusted to address an audience of children.[5] Another bizarre Bernstein event was a performance of Mahler's *Resurrection* Symphony at Avery Fisher Hall in April 1987, a sublime concert confused by its denouement. Lauren Bacall stepped to a microphone to present Bernstein with the "Albert Schweitzer Music Award." The popping flashbulbs of this rude ceremony epitomized the artist upstaged by his own celebrity.

The teachings of Leonard Bernstein chart a process of disengagement from the America that shaped him, and in which he had placed great confidence. They help to explain why the memorial concerts held in New York in the wake of Bernstein's death seemed so charged with the bewilderment of personal loss. Most of the mourners could not have known Bernstein the man. What they sensed, however subliminally, were the damaged hopes of this most American of classical musicians.

■ ■ ■

Bernstein no more stabilized the New York Philharmonic than Toscanini had: it remained an orchestra without a sustained identity. His one-of-a-kind Young People's Concerts, his advocacy of Ives and America departed with him. Even the Philharmonic's Mahler tradition lacked a life of its own; the spotless Pierre Boulez, coming after the sweaty Bernstein, lived Mahler as differently as Mitropoulos did from Walter or Mengelberg. Boulez and his successor, Zubin Mehta, enjoyed at best a fitful success with the players, and Mehta's thirteen-year tenure—incongruously, the longest in the Philharmonic's twentieth-century history—failed to generate anything like the sense of mission driven by the repertoire excursions and experimental formats of Bernstein and Boulez. Kurt Masur, who lasted from 1991 to 2002, imposed or inspired a degree of discipline unknown at the Philharmonic for decades, but was not the cultural leader in New York that he had been in Leipzig.

In fact, both in spite and because of the "cultural explosion" of the American performing arts after World War II, the second half of the twentieth century was not a happy time for orchestras. The unhappiness began with the musicians themselves, grown tired of slave drivers and slave wages. According to 1960 census data, musicians and music teachers were paid an average of $4,757 a year, compared with a median of $6,778 for all professions and $4,750 for all experienced male labor over fourteen years of age. Salesmen and funeral directors were paid more. Orchestra musicians were barely employed in the summer months. In the 1950s, even a member of the New York Philharmonic might earn $6,000—a plumber's wages. A spirit of militancy swept the field. Between 1954 and 1970 seventeen strikes, totaling 439 days, afflicted ten orchestras, including four against the Philadelphia Orchestra alone.[6]

Meanwhile, in 1966, the Ford Foundation initiated an $80.2 million infusion for orchestras. The orchestras, in turn, had to raise twice that amount in matching funds. In combination with pressure from the ranks, the new money steeply increased the number of concerts. In 1960, full-time, twelve-month employment was unknown. By 1970–71, six orchestras had agreed to fifty-two-week contracts, and another five had contracts of forty-five weeks or more. This new frequency of performance was not audience-driven. It may be safely assumed that neither Beethoven nor Brahms, in music-obsessed Vienna, remotely envisioned a diet of three and four symphonic performances per orchestra per week—or up to 171 (the New York Philharmonic in 2000–2001) and 159 (the Boston Symphony the same season) each year.

Many who played in American orchestras now attained a respectable living wage for the first time. Whether they knew or admitted it, the victory was Pyrrhic. Scrambling to manufacture new "services" promised by new agreements, orchestras created new concerts that could not adequately be planned, prepared, sold, or assimilated. Many were underrehearsed summer programs, children's programs, or pops programs, or exhausting "run-outs" to high school auditoriums. Boredom and resentment were rife. In a much-publicized 1979 address to his charges as director of the Berkshire Music Center at Tanglewood, Gunther Schuller warned of the "apathy, cynicism, and hatred of new music" they would encounter as professionals. Reflecting on his own performing career—he became principal horn at the Metropolitan Opera at the age of nineteen before emerging as an important composer and educator—Schuller said:

> As I travel around the country guest-conducting various orchestras, it is often former students, who once had that shine in their countenance when they heard or made music, who long since have lost that spiritual identification with music.... Or consider the spectacle of musicians getting up from their chairs and walking off the stage in the middle of a phrase—even in the middle of a note—because the clock has struck 4:30 or 5:00. How dare we interrupt music in such a brutal fashion? It is an insult to our calling, an indignity that we visit on the work of master for whose sake we went into music in the first place, and whose genius may be greater than all the talents in such an orchestra put together.[7]

Between 1960 and 2000, the New York Philharmonic's budget grew from $2 million to $34 million, the Boston Symphony's from $2 million to $55 million. In combination with precipitously rising costs, excess concerts dictated a new orchestral function: marketing. The intensified audience search, itself expensive, mandated focus groups, radiothons, computerized mailings, and telemarketing departments—a dense scaffold of merchandising activity behind which many an orchestra plotted to standardize its product. Burdened with an expanding gap between income and expenses, orchestras found themselves thick in the business of fund-raising; the Boston Symphony's development staff grew from seventeen to twenty-nine in the final decade of the twentieth century. Gone were the days of *Luxushunden*, as observed by Furtwängler, maintained by a handful of philanthropists. The likes of Higginson, Fay, Flagler, and Mackay gave way to foundations and corporations, to a multiplicity of modest private donations, to—at long last—a range of mainly modest government subsidies.

Not only because the need was more obviously urgent, but because the available staff was deeper and more expert, many an orchestra demonstrated greater creativity competing for gifts than putting on concerts. Even the dullest among them, for which a gala occasion meant another Beethoven's Ninth, worked furiously to invent new ways of giving. They crafted special strategies of acknowledgment for banks and tobacco companies shopping for prestige. They convinced charitable foundations of their quest for audience "diversity." For better or worse, artistic policy and institutional priorities were shifted by the money search. The federal government got into the act with the creation in 1965 of the National Endowment of the Arts—whose annual grants to orchestras proved neither crucial nor insignificant. Some states and localities far surpassed Washington as arts donors; in New York City, frantic politicking preceded the generous seasonal allotment to and by the Department of Cultural Affairs.

Exigent union demands, marketing demands, and fund-raising demands were of course the tail wagging the dog. As for the dog itself, it could be difficult to discern. Artur Nikisch, hired by Henry Higginson's Boston Symphony, would arrive from Germany every October by boat, conduct his one hundred concerts, and depart for home in April. A century later, music directors, jetting from continent to continent, typically kept two or more jobs; their commitment to a Boston Symphony or New York Philharmonic might total as few as nine weeks per season. For many an American orchestra, cranking out programs week after relentless week, the music director was less an ally than an obstruction, difficult to contact and slow to make decisions; scheduling an actual meeting of any length could become a formidable logistical challenge. Like executive directors, marketing directors, and development directors, music directors frequently switched jobs. Conductor searches were a chronic motif of symphonic life; at the turn of the twenty-first century, the Boston Symphony, the Cleveland Orchestra, the New York Philharmonic, and the Philadelphia Orchestra (among others) were simultaneously hunting for a new music director.

The resulting sellers' market was one reason (though not the only one, as we will shortly discover) why conductors grew exorbitantly expensive—and this notwithstanding ever lengthier periods of absence. What was worse, many in the orchestra field credibly complained of a paucity or absence of "great conductors." The paucity or absence of great contemporary music was unquestionably pertinent. Of the century's two seminal conductors, Toscanini (as we have earlier observed) was a product of Verdi and Italian opera: everything he touched, not excluding Beethoven or Debussy, was shaped by tensile cantabile lines. Furtwängler was a product of Wagner; he read the Ninth Symphonies of Beethoven and Schubert as massively as he did Bruckner's Ninth. The advantage of such national schools was twofold. Ingrained traditions channeled and intensified countless aspects of performance. And the traditions, though old, were also new: Verdi, Brahms, and Bruckner died after Toscanini and Furtwängler were born; their late operas and symphonies were still settling, still in need of initial inquiry and advocacy. Half a century later, with no comparable contemporary repertoire at hand, conductors were expected to be generalists. Some degree of versatility—of generalized "fidelity"—was gained. But if compared to Toscanini or Furtwängler a new chameleon species—aligned with chameleon orchestras—could exercise comparable command of Beethoven and Verdi both, deeper stylistic distinctions were blurred and interpretations once divergent were standardized. When Seidl first conducted *Lohengrin* in New York, when Nikisch first led Beethoven's Fifth in Boston, it was plausibly reported that these works, while hardly unfamiliar, sounded completely different than in previous local performances. One hundred years later, travel and recordings had canceled this possibility; only a rare genius or eccentric—a Carlos Kleiber or Sergiu Celibidache—could evade a binding mainstream experience. Recordings also made a fetish of perfection. Unmediated interaction with the music of one's own time and place had given way to self-conscious grapplings with internalized performance norms.

During the final quarter of the twentieth century, orchestras in cities large and small played with better ensemble, better intonation, and fewer wrong notes than in decades past. Dozens of conductors worthily applied their talents. The orchestras of Cleveland and Chicago remained objects of intense civic pride. Christoph von Dohnányi accustomed his Cleveland audience to a variety of European modernists; he and his players also excelled in Varèse. And Dohnányi maintained the Cleveland Orchestra's high reputation without imposing himself as blatantly as his predecessors George Szell and Lorin Maazel. Georg Solti's competitive drive to make the Chicago Symphony "first in the world" proved contagious. At New York's Carnegie Hall (a louder, more reverberant space than Orchestra Hall in Chicago), the muscularity and sheer volume of the Chicago sound bested all comers. A 1971 international tour—remarkably, the orchestra's first—world-certified its amazing solidity and intensity in high Romantic repertoire. Solti also gamely tackled a considerable quantity of American music, not excluding Ives, Ruggles, Sessions, and Carter. A deficit in mystery and nuance was addressed between 1969 and 1972, when Carlo Maria Giulini was the principal guest conductor. Solti's successor, Daniel Barenboim, worked for more variety of sonority and style. Though he resided abroad and gave Chicago no more than thirteen subscription weeks per season, Barenboim also made a cause of the Chicago Civic Symphony, the training orchestra that feeds the Chicago Symphony 16 percent of its members.

David Zinman, of the Baltimore Symphony, a rare adherent to something like Bernstein's example, subverted rituals of deference at nationally broadcast Saturday-morning Casual Concerts that found him crooning "Full Moon and Empty Arms" by way of illustrating that Rachmaninoff's tunes "could be popular songs." A Casual Concerts contest solicited lyrics "to any Rachmaninoff tune"; the winning entry was performed. At Casual Concerts featuring Elgar's First Symphony or Mahler's Sixth, the Zinman immersion experience, including writings by the composers and a Tom Lehrer song, was both irreverent and inspirational. In San Francisco Edo de Waart—a native of Holland, home to an unusually vigorous contemporary music culture—teamed with Executive Director Peter Pastreich, Artistic Advisor Michael Steinberg, and composer-in-residence John Adams to create the most sophisticated artistic brain trust of any American orchestra of the 1970s and '80s. De Waart's subscription programs registered his commitment to the important European modernists. And in championing Adams, he made a cause of the most important new native symphonic composer. The 1981 premiere of Adams's *Harmonium* was experienced by the pianist/conductor Jeffrey Kahane as "the first time in my life I ever heard an audience moved to shouts, cheers, and an extended standing ovation for a major new work. It felt like a watershed moment."[8] Adams himself presided over a New and Unusual Music series that equally showcased European masters (Louis Andriessen, Pierre Boulez, György Ligeti) and an assortment of significant Americans ranging from John Cage, Steve Reich, and Terry Riley to Leon Kirchner and Elliott Carter. With the exception of Bernstein, no living American composer had previously exercised such meaningful authority, or attained such local popularity, in association with an orchestra. If nothing comparably fresh enlivened the tenures of Seiji Ozawa in Boston (1973–2002) or Riccardo Muti (1980–1992) and Wolfgang Sawallisch (1993–2003) in Philadelphia, all three worked to mold a more versatile instrument than what Koussevitzky and Munch, Stokowski and Ormandy had bequeathed. And there are orchestras, like Newark's New Jersey Symphony, that have pumped new life into discarded downtowns; and even orchestras, like California's Pacific Symphony with its cutting-edge annual American Composers Festival, that attempt to lead taste.

But it would be idle to deny the frequent blandness of interpretations "tastefully" distinguishing (as Toscanini or Furtwängler failed even to attempt) the weight and timbre of Beethoven's style from Wagner's, Tchaikovsky's, or Debussy's, or the numbing familiarity and predictability of symphonic concerts, generally, by century's end. And it would be naïve to deny the greater freshness of the entire enterprise before 1950. The repertoire quests of Stokowski and Koussevitzky; the educational mission pursued by Koussevitzky at Tanglewood; audience education as practiced by Stokowski; Mitropoulos's ideal of community service and leadership in Minneapolis; the radically distinctive sounds cultivated in Philadelphia and Minneapolis by Stokowski and Mitropoulos; the galvanizing impact of Toscanini; the urgency of Beethoven during World War II; the consolidation and refinement of Cleveland's orchestra under Rodzinski and Szell, and of Cincinnati's and Pittsburgh's under Reiner—all these are benchmarks without subsequent parallel.

Further back, before 1900, Thomas and Seidl newly instilled classical music itself. Or consider Higginson's Boston Symphony concerts. No such orchestra could be heard elsewhere in the United States, not least in one's living room via radio or recordings. Vital new repertoire—Brahms, Dvořák, Wagner—was regularly introduced and absorbed. Local composers were regularly programmed and proudly received. More than any other Boston institution (including its Red Sox), the orchestra "showed the culture of the community." By the year 2000, no American orchestra could remotely bestir such an automatic sense of occasion.

■ ■ ■

If laws of supply and demand were mocked by the surfeit of symphonic concerts in the decades after World War II, the number of recitals plummeted with logical finality: the surfeit was of artists. The *Musical America* annual directory, also known in the business as "the world's greatest collection of people who don't work," continued to list more than one thousand pianists, violinists, and cellists. But the number of paying dates was proportionately miniscule. In 1999 Columbia Artists sold what was left of Community Concerts. Columbia Artists' big-name draws were ever fewer and further between.

An average Carnegie Hall season of the 1920s might list recitals by (among many others) Backhaus, Casals, Cortot, Flesch, Gieseking, Hofmann, Hubermann, Landowska, Horowitz, Szigeti, and Thibaud. Every one of these justly eminent artists was also touring, appearing as a matter of course with hinterlands orchestras in Cincinnati, St. Louis, or Pittsburgh. Six decades later, the director of concerts and artists for Steinway and Sons tabulated the frequency with which pianists were engaged and found "that half or more than half the annual opportunities to be employed by North American orchestras, major and minor, went to 10 pianists, who were getting, on average, 15 concerto jobs each—which of course could mean many more than 15 performances. And there were somewhere between 125 and 150 getting one or two opportunities each. So you had 10 pianists getting virtually all the repeat business."

As great a problem was that solo artists, some of them tyros in their twenties and thirties, began to cost more than they took in at the box office. As with conductors, their fees spiraled into hyperinflation. As with conductors, they did not command the singularity of artistry or sense of occasion once exemplified by a Nikisch or Toscanini, Rachmaninoff or Casals. And yet even Heifetz's startling, top-of-the-market $3,500, circa 1950, was at least ten times less than Itzhak Perlman's fee a few decades later.

What drove artists' fees so high? While those who book soloists typically enjoyed friendly relations with individual artists' managers, the big agencies—CAMI and ICM—increasingly became objects of scorn. A "superstar" instrumentalist could vitally bolster an orchestra's entire subscription offering. But the superfee of up to $80,000 per concert violated fiscal prudence. And it was not discommensurate with the fees and salaries orchestras had grown accustomed to paying conductors. If these fees and salaries in turn had a first cause, some believed that it was Ronald Wilford.

Arthur Judson's "conflicts of interest" sensitized him to others' needs. He claimed to keep a lid on fees, and it seems that he did. Wilford, Judson's successor at CAMI as of 1961, is an operator legendary for his charm and business wizardry. Unlike Judson, he has never run an orchestra. His governing priority appears to be maximizing the careers and earnings of his clients. In a rare interview, he told the *New York Times* in 1971, "My client is the artist—not the Philharmonic, not the Metropolitan Opera, not any one else, and I am absolutely ruthless if it comes to telling an orchestra to go to hell if I feel something is unfair to an artist of mine. I really don't care, because if I have an artist they want, they will have to book him." Even more than Judson, Wilford specializes in conductors; like Judson, he represents the vast majority of those that matter. According to the British classical music gadfly Norman Lebrecht, "From the time [Wilford] became president of CAMI, the price of conductors went soaring." Lebrecht also writes, "Between 1960 and 1990, the nightly fee for a top conductor increased twelvefold [in the United States], while industrial earnings merely quadrupled. Put another way: in 1910, a top conductor earned ten times as much for a concert as a factory worker took home in a week. In 1990, he was paid fifty times as much." Tracking music director salaries (not to be confused with total earnings) as of 1990, Lebrecht lists Riccardo Muti at more than $400,000 with the Philadelphia Orchestra and Kurt

Masur and Daniel Barenboim at more than $700,000 with the New York Philharmonic and Chicago Symphony, respectively.[9]

As for soloists, by Lebrecht's reckoning, as of 1995–96 Perlman was taking in over $5 million a year, and at least ten conductors and conductor/instrumentalists annually earned $1 million or more. In some orchestras, the musicians' salaries were no more than twice what a guest soloist might be paid for several days' work. And these disparities coincided with the death throes or teetering survival of orchestras in cities the size of Toronto, New Orleans, and Denver. In 1992, the American Symphony Orchestra League reported that orchestra costs had risen eightfold since 1971, with more than half the increase ascribable to "artistic costs"—in part, money paid to conductors and soloists.[10]

Wilford dismisses Lebrecht's scenario as crass fiction. But his own analysis of classical music's ills paradoxically parallels that of Lebrecht in his book *Who Killed Classical Music?* For both of them, classical music is a poorly run business. Lebrecht fingers rapacious artists and music-businessmen. Wilford fingers poorly run orchestras and presenting institutions, which (through an overreliance on subscriptions) do not properly market individual events and will not take risks on fledgling careers, as CAMI once did when it was in the presenting business and could rent Carnegie Hall. He blames the big orchestras for capitulating to unreasonable musicians' salaries and work rules. Surveying the demise of Community Concerts, he sees a paucity of leisured women to service the grassroots organizations that once corralled audiences and raised money. He says, "The audience is there"—but is not nurtured and served as people like Judson were once able to nurture and serve it.[11] Whatever the truth of this analysis, it ignores the many sociocultural changes that have marginalized classical music. Wilford prides himself in his low profile and clearheaded practicality, in the Judson mold, and it is Judson's vanished world of music and culture that he seems to inhabit.

If Wilford embodies something like Judson's style and purview, another species of artists' manager is today extinct. Judson's most conspicuous rival was the flamboyant immigrant impresario Sol Hurok. Hurok's roster included Marian Anderson, Maria Callas, Arthur Rubinstein, and Andrés Segovia. But his specialty was Russians: Mischa Elman, Nathan Milstein, Ana Pavlova, and Gregor Piatigorsky, whom he found in America; David Oistrakh, Mstislav Rostropovich, the Bolshoi Ballet, and the Moiseyev Dance Company, all borrowed from the Soviet Union. His artists were inherited by Sheldon Gold, who opened a classical music division within Hollywood's ICM. Of the Hurok clients who became ICM clients, the violinist Isaac Stern was a force unto himself. One of the most-told tales of the Leventritt Competition was how Stern, in 1967, patiently talked his fellow jurors into changing their minds so that nineteen-year-old Pinchas Zukerman, whose studies and early career he had guided, could share the award with Kyung-Wha Chung. Stern also helped to father the careers of Emanuel Ax, Yefim Bronfman, Perlman, Yo-Yo Ma, Shlomo Mintz, and Gil Shaham. Other causes with which he was passionately associated included Israel, the NEA, and Carnegie Hall, which he heroically rescued from the wrecking ball in 1960. As president of the Carnegie Hall Corporation, he oversaw the evolution of a powerful new presenting organization in competition with Lincoln Center. Like Serkin at Marlboro, he influentially supported the post–World War II "chamber music boom." As a soloist, he premiered concertos by William Schuman, George Rochberg, and Krzysztof Penderecki, as well as Bernstein's Serenade. Though others in his elite entourage submitted to routinized classical music agendas or struggled visibly to find means of artistic renewal, all were major instrumentalists and most were major (and expensive) draws. Born in the Ukraine in 1920, raised and schooled in San Francisco, of the same age as Bernstein and the OYAPs, Stern forged the most sustained, most international, and most meaningful career in music of any American instrumentalist of his generation. A surrogate artists' manager in the Hurok mold, Stern—who died in 2001— has no present-day successors.

■ ■ ■

As of 1950, opera in the United States was stagnating: the Met's Edward Johnson had just presided over the most static decades in the house's history; once-vital companies in Boston and Chicago had folded. Fifty years later, the Met was adding important repertoire, and adventurous companies had sprung up in unlikely places; it was orchestras that seemed moribund, and recitals that were dying.

Johnson's successor, Rudolf Bing, was a Viennese who had served as general manager of Britain's Glyndebourne Opera and artistic director of the Edinburgh Festival. He spent the 1949–50 season observing the operations of Johnson's house and not liking what he saw and heard. He went into action with *Don Carlo*, a late Verdi masterpiece that had not been performed in New York since 1922, in a new production by the Shakespeare specialist Margaret Webster. Bing's early Met seasons also featured new stagings of *Aïda*, also by Webster, of *Carmen* by Tyrone Guthrie, of *Faust* by Peter Brook, of *Die Fledermaus* by Broadway's Garson Kanin, of *Così fan tutte* by Alfred Lunt, and of *La Périchole* by Cyril Richard (who also starred as the Viceroy)—of which the last three were given in English translation. Bing's designers included Eugene

Berman. A momentary controversy was the return, in *Fidelio*, of Kirsten Flagstad, whom Johnson had not asked back due to scurrilous rumors about her loyalties in wartime Norway (her husband was tried as a Nazi collaborator). At the same time, Bing saw fit to release Lauritz Melchior, who was said not to attend rehearsals (Bing was known not to like Wagner).

All this demonstrated a capacity for conspicuous leadership. Bing would not tolerate dilapidated productions dating back to World War I. He would not throw operas on stage without any molding of the action. He freshened the repertoire with company premieres of *Nabucco* and *Wozzeck* and the American premiere of Stravinsky's *The Rake's Progress*. He decisively undertook the first Metropolitan appearance by a black singer—Marian Anderson, age fifty-two, in *La forza del destino*—an initiative, scandalously overdue, paving the way for Leontyne Price, Martina Arroyo, Grace Bumbry, and Shirley Verrett, all black, all brought to the Met by Bing. To the singers he inherited, including the ever-popular Americans Robert Merrill, Risë Stevens, Richard Tucker, and Leonard Warren, he added the soon indispensable Carlo Bergonzi, Franco Corelli, Nicolai Gedda, George London, Birgit Nilsson, Leonie Rysanek, Cesare Siepi, Joan Sutherland, Renata Tebaldi, and Jon Vickers.

In 1966 Bing's Met moved to a new Lincoln Center home with production facilities, on stage and off, as sophisticated as the old Met's were antiquated. There was no acoustical debacle, as at Philharmonic Hall. But the new auditorium lacked glamour—it looked cheap but was not—and its great size would prove problematic. Bing remained five more seasons, during which it became apparent that having caught up with what should have been done before, he had little new to offer. And times were changing in ways that demanded institutional change. Like the music directors of America's orchestras, singers who once stayed put were quite suddenly appearing on different continents in the course of a week. And, like the conductors, they seemed a shallower crop than yesteryear's. Even more obviously than in the concert hall, the erosion of national styles eroded tools of interpretation—in opera, conducive to vocal finesse and dramatic impersonation. Also, the really big voices seemed to be disappearing. Tannhäuser, Tristan, Siegfried, Wotan, and Sachs were already not well supplied at Bing's Met.

The activity of shopping for singers became more taxing, and questions were raised about Bing's competence in this department. Many prominent newcomers had first sung in the United States in Chicago, Dallas, or San Francisco. Even the vast majority of the important North Americans Bing brought to New York had already made reputations elsewhere. A nonmusician who disdained engaging a music director, Bing was not a discoverer of voices.

Even less was he a discoverer of operas. Adapting to a new status quo, European companies began absorbing twentieth-century repertoire that stressed sophisticated theatrical values and made heroic voices unnecessary. Notwithstanding Bing's upgrade of the way operas looked, the Met remained a "singer's house," fundamentally invested in vocal glamour. In fact, Bing squandered the great singing actors of the day: Maria Callas, whom he dismissed for breaching a letter of agreement, and Hans Hotter, who quickly quit when Bing relegated him to secondary roles. He clung to Puccini while houses elsewhere mounted Bartók, Busoni, Debussy, Janáček, Prokofiev, Ravel, Schoenberg, Shostakovich, and Tippett; of Britten, Bing offered only *Peter Grimes*. In twenty-two seasons, he offered three world premieres—*Vanessa* and *Antony and Cleopatra*, both by Barber, and David Martin Levy's *Mourning Becomes Elektra*.

Finally, and crucially, there were Bing's conductors. The big names—Bernstein, Böhm, Kempe, Reiner, Solti—came and went. Long forgotten were the times when house conductors of the stature of Bodanzky and Panizza would ensure excellence in the pit. For starved New York Wagnerites, to hear top-level orchestral playing in *Tristan* or *Die Meistersinger* meant going to Europe or listening to recordings. The exception that proved the rule was Herbert von Karajan, who appeared in 1967, 1968, and 1969 to lead *Die Walküre* and *Das Rheingold*, and overnight transformed the orchestra into a world-class ensemble whose manicured attacks and subtly gauged dynamics copied Karajan's Berlin Philharmonic. Equally revealing was the audience for *Das Rheingold*, so little prepared for an opera so fundamentally theatrical that it gabbled noisily during the interludes between scenes; Karajan turned and stared to no avail. That he withdrew from *Siegfried* and *Götterdämmerung* spared him exposure to the Met chorus.

In a 1965 radio interview, Bing claimed that there were "quite a few distinguished conductors today" and that "the Met has most of them." He then cited Böhm, Thomas Schippers, Francesco Molinari-Pradelli, Fausto Cleva, Georges Pretre, Silvio Varviso, and Joseph Rosenstock as a list "not to be ashamed of."[12] This shameful exhibition of hubris was not atypical. Bing's virtues were undercut, and his shortcomings exacerbated, by a prickly personality. He all too obviously projected the purported cultural superiority of Europe, reinforcing a snobbery and aloofness long associated with the Met and intellectually limiting for opera in America generally. If he enjoyed considerable success persuading his singers of the Met's importance, he was not necessarily close to the members of the board (like his predecessors Heinrich Conried and Maurice Grau, Bing was Jewish), and he regularly offended unionized labor, from musicians to stagehands. By the time a bitter strike postponed the opening of the 1969–70 season by more than three months, it was time for Bing to leave. In fact, in complete contrast to its Lincoln Center neighbors, the New York Philharmonic (under Bernstein) and New York City Ballet (under Balanchine), the Met had again receded into a time warp. And its gaudy and gargantuan auditorium, a posthumous embodiment of Romantic grandiosity, threatened to keep it there. The audience capacity (3,824 plus standees, versus 3,600 in the old Met, 2,800 in Milan, 2,276 in Vienna, 2,174 in Covent Garden, 1,925 in Bayreuth) was already a relic from another New York time, when sellouts were common and nonsubscribers were turned away. The new house was too big for the singers the Met now had and, because it promoted performance styles inimical to conversational intimacy and gestural subtlety, far too big for the operas it now needed. To imagine spoken drama screamed at 4,000 spectators is to glean the difficulty of conveying Berg, Janáček, or Britten in such a space. But, inevitably, even the Met would have to try.

■ ■ ■

Others tried first, and succeeded. The surprise development in the culture of performance during the second half of the twentieth century was not symphonic. Opera audiences grew and grew younger. Meanwhile, on stage, the repertoire diversified and a place was made for operas new, American, or both.

The demise of touring was the first cause. In the decades before World War I, troupes of all sizes continued to travel, from the Metropolitan (which gave out-of-town performances in a dozen cities and more) and the Chicago Opera (which in 1913 toured to the West Coast and back) to Henry Savage's Grand Opera Company (which successfully purveyed opera in English). Even after the Depression decimated operatic activity outside New York, the Met toured vigorously, and so did Fortune Gallo's San Carlo Opera Company. Speight Jenkins, later general director of the Seattle Opera, remembers the annual three-day stop in Dallas, with singers like Warren and Tucker, Zinka Milanov and Eleanor Steber, as a childhood epiphany, and he was not the only one. The San Carlo company, also based in New York, typically toured to Toronto, Detroit, Chicago, Milwaukee, Minneapolis, and Kansas City, then more quickly through the South and up the Pacific Coast to Vancouver, then back to St. Louis. During the 1930s, the top ticket cost $1.50. The company, mostly foreign, included an American prima donna: Coe Glade.

The San Carlo Opera folded in 1950. The Met gave its last national tour in 1986. Transportation and production costs had grown prohibitively. As significant for the Met was the unwillingness of its frontline singers to perform with the company outside New York. The loyal ensemble of Americans—of Steber and Stevens, Tucker and Peerce, Warren and Merrill—was history. European houses beckoned with higher fees. Transatlantic transportation was quick and easy. As the Met's presence had planted operatic seeds, the Met's absence now made room for local growth. Opera companies sprang up in Tulsa, Memphis, Kansas City. In the quarter-century beginning in 1962, the number of companies with budgets over $100,000 increased from 27 to 154 and audiences for those companies increased from 4.5 million to 13 million.[13] Not only symphony orchestras but also opera companies were quite suddenly understood to "show the culture of the community."

A second catalyst, on the heels of new grassroots growth, was the advent of projected surtitles: for the first time since the days when many in the United States spoke German or Italian, American audiences could understand every word of operas sung in foreign tongues. The Canadian Opera Company used them first: for *Elektra* in January 21, 1983. The New York City Opera implemented surtitles comprehensively in 1984–85. Other companies followed suit. Not everyone was delighted. Surtitles effectively killed the opera-in-English movement—a sporadic innovation for more than a century, as we have seen. They ensured that Americans for the most part would, as before, sing in languages other than their own—and that the great singing actors for the most part would, as before, not be American-trained. But this loss in immediacy, crippling singer and audience both, was a trade-off. Even in tuneful arias by Mozart, Verdi, and Puccini, the opportunity to hear and comprehend international casts singing the words the composers set was informative. In Wagner, it was transformative. In a newfound modern repertoire including Janáček, Berg, Bartók, and Prokofiev, it was indispensable.

Artur Bodanzky, at the Met, had drastically trimmed *Die Walküre* and *Parsifal* in deference to an audience otherwise tortured by the monologues of Wotan and Gurnemanz. Deems Taylor had likened opera in America to a world-class foreign-language theater "imported like caviar" and inimical to "the average American." Henry Krehbiel had written that opera would remain "experimental" in the United States until "the vernacular becomes the language of the performances and native talent provides both works and interpreters." Surtitled opera was not quite the same as vernacular opera and had not quite the same effect. Even so, Americans for the first time in almost a hundred years attended new operas as willingly as new plays or films. It was late in the day to cultivate an American canon linked to *Porgy and Bess*, *Four Saints in Three Acts*, and *Regina*. Carlisle Floyd, with *Susannah* and *Of Mice and Men*, produced two works old-fashioned but durable; many other composers failed. Other successes, by Philip Glass and John Adams (subjects of a coming chapter), significantly ignored Gershwin, Thomson, Blitzstein, and Floyd. Even so, proliferating opportunities to hear new American operas, even bad ones, were a sign of health.

For decades opera in America had contracted to a single ideal of "grand opera." Revealed as sung theater, it actually underwent a change of genre at the close of the twentieth century. As in the nineteenth century, opera again meant many things: it was massive or intimate, posed or acted, exotic or familiar, glamorous or prestigious, old or very new. And its most influential purveyors were not aristocrats but mavericks, of whom the least aristocratic was Boston's Sarah Caldwell. She was a protégé of Boris Goldovsky, an important popularizer of opera as theater and opera in English. Alone among American producers of opera, she was also influenced by Germany's Walter Felsenstein, whom many in Europe regarded with Bayreuth's Wieland Wagner as the most insightful operatic stage director after World War II. As creator, administrator, artistic director, stage director, and principal conductor of the Opera Company of Boston beginning in 1958, Caldwell did everything but sing. Her personal eccentricities, which helped to propel her onto the cover of *Time* magazine, included sleeping in the theater and ignoring her girth. It was merely predictable that her company lacked a home; old movie houses made do. She equally embodied an intellectual boldness and sophistication rarely associated with opera in America. Her repertoire included major works by Bartók, Berg, Luigi Nono, Prokofiev, Schoenberg, Sessions, Stravinsky, and Weill. She gave the first American performances of *Boris Godunov* and *Don Carlo* in something like their original versions. She revived important operas by Bellini, Berlioz, Glinka, Rameau, Rimsky-Korsakov, and Rossini. Though hers was not a singers' house, she was able to attract the services of Boris Christoff, Regine Crespin, George London, Beverly Sills, Joan Sutherland, and Renata Tebaldi. Don Quichotte, in Massenet's opera, was in Caldwell's production caught up and hurled about in the blades of a great windmill. Rosina, the *The Barber of Seville*, shattered a champagne glass with a high note. Berlioz's Benvenuto Cellini, a triumphant Jon Vickers interpretation not seen elsewhere, smashed a smoking mold to reveal a gleaming statue of Perseus.[14]

Caldwell's company lacked stability and disappeared without a trace. She had no progeny, yet proved decisively that the Met was not a pinnacle but an option. Among her contemporaries, John Crosby founded the Santa Fe Opera in 1956 and proceeded to showcase twentieth-century composers— Stravinsky, Hans Werner Henze, and the later Richard Strauss were house specialties—in a spectacular outdoor theater seating 1,150. David Gockley, who took over the Houston Grand Opera in 1972, has assiduously pursued his vision of a supple American canon ranging from Scott Joplin (*Treemonisha*, a historic 1975 production by Frank Corsaro), John Philip Sousa (his 1895 operetta *El Capitan*), and Gershwin (a much-admired *Porgy and Bess* that toured and was recorded) to Blitzstein, Floyd, and Stephen Sondheim. It was Houston that premiered Bernstein's *A Quiet Place* and Adams's *Nixon in China*. And Gockley also capitalized on Christoph Eschenbach's potent tenure as music director of the Houston Symphony: for Houston Grand Opera, Eschenbach led ten operas by Mozart, Richard Strauss, and Wagner.

In Seattle, Glynn Ross audaciously resolved to mount Wagner's *Ring of the Nibelung* every summer in both German and English, beginning in 1975. Speight Jenkins, who took over the Seattle Opera in 1983, is an equally zealous Wagnerite (the office closes for Wagner's birthday) who insisted on world-class musical and production values. This meant relinquishing Ross's annual *Ring* in favor of more-varied summer repertoire keying on fresh productions of *Lohengrin*, the *Ring*, *Tristan*, *Die Meistersinger*, and *Parsifal*. Seattle's 1986 *Ring*, directed by François Rochaix and designed by Robert Israel, remains the only North American version with the intellectual panache of Patrice Chéreau's landmark Bayreuth *Ring* of 1976. Seattle's 2001 *Ring*, directed by Stephen Wadsworth, was hyperrealistic yet psychologically astute. Both productions were cast not according to glamorous past exposure but actual competence shrewdly assessed; both were complemented by first-rate Wagner lectures and (an amenity unknown at Lincoln Center or Carnegie Hall) a serious bookstore. The one *Ring* secured and the other consolidated Seattle's status as the leading North American Wagner house.

If Jenkins's regular season is overshadowed by his summer Wagner festivals, it nonetheless registers a confident independence of judgment and taste. The Opera Theater of St. Louis, with a thrust stage and only 954 seats, can afford to be more adventurous. Under Richard Gaddes, a Santa Fe Opera alumnus (who in 2000 returned to New Mexico to succeed John Crosby), it keyed on such intimate works as *Così fan tutte* (directed by Jonathan Miller in his American operatic debut), Britten's *Albert Herring*, Delius's *Fennimore and Gerda* (toured to the Edinburgh Festival), and Gluck's *Orfeo ed Euridice* (with sets and costumes by Louise Nevelson). Like Caldwell, Crosby, and Jenkins, Gaddes overthrew "regional opera" as practiced elsewhere: generic productions, standard works, eleventh-hour fittings and rehearsals for imported principal singers.

Meanwhile, more traditional grand opera was pursued in San Francisco and, after a post–World War I hiatus, in Chicago. In the latter city, the Chicago Lyric Opera, born in 1954 as the Lyric Theatre, was the creation of Carol Fox, Lawrence Kelly, and Nicola Rescigno. Kelly and Rescigno split away in 1955 to create the Dallas Civic Opera. Both companies showcased Maria Callas: a triumphant launching pad. Fox's essential affinities were Italian. Her successor in 1981, Ardis Krainik, pushed the repertoire into twentieth-century Europe and America, presenting Kurt Weill and Philip Glass years before the Met and commissioning new works at a steady pace. Her boldest strokes included the American premiere of Luciano Berio's *Un re in ascolto* and an *enfant terrible* production of *Tannhäuser*, by Peter Sellars, in which the hero was an errant televangelist and Venus worked out of a Las Vegas hotel. Thanks in part to the company's state-of-the-art subscription campaigns, these works played to sold-out or nearly sold-out houses.

The San Francisco Opera was ruled from 1953 to 1981 by Kurt Adler. Like Gaetano Merola, Adler was an impresario who also conducted (if much less frequently); like Merola's, his personality imprinted the company. Adler's San Francisco Opera was a great deal more sophisticated than Merola's had been. By 1972, the season had doubled from five to ten weeks. The emphasis on celebrity voices remained, but the repertoire broadened dramatically to include Berg, Berlioz, Britten, Janáček, Poulenc, and Shostakovich. Adler's formidable achievements were locally overrated (I remember a *Siegfried* that sounded like it was being sight-read in the pit). But he was a presence; he knew singers; he made the company important without creating (as Caldwell and Gockley did) a distinctive template. This reform awaited the advent of Pamela Rosenberg in 2002. An American schooled in the contemporary operatic culture of Germany, she arrived with a full-time dramaturg and a couple of startling productions from Munich and Stuttgart. Repertoire was her guiding priority. Her inaugural season began with the American stage premiere of Messiaen's *Saint Francis of Assisi*. (Her tenure will end in 2006.) Meanwhile, in southern California, Plácido Domingo's fast-growing Los Angeles Opera likewise plunged into a new world of bold directors and unusual repertoire.

All this operatic ferment—in Boston, Houston, Seattle, St. Louis, Chicago, San Francisco, Los Angeles—oddly excluded New York, where the City Opera had charted an original course after World War II. But the company lost its way after being seduced to Lincoln Center in 1966, a move for which no one was subsequently willing to take credit. Certainly the move was fought and denounced by Rudolf Bing, who believed Lincoln Center was no place for New York's second company. And yet, initially, the second company outdistanced the first. Its casts included Plácido Domingo, Beverly Sills, and Norman Treigle. Its house director, Frank Corsaro, imaginatively achieved integrated musical theater. Its house conductor, Julius Rudel, electrified the orchestra and, as general director from 1957, added operas by Britten, Falla, Poulenc, Prokofiev, and Stravinsky as well as three spring seasons of American works by Bernstein, Blitzstein, Floyd, Gian Carlo Menotti, Douglas Moore,

Weill, and Hugo Weisgall, among others. For its debut at Lincoln Center's New York State Theater, the company presented the American premiere of Alberto Ginastera's *Don Rodrigo* with Domingo in the title role; beating the odds against contemporary nontonal music, it scored a popular and critical success for its intense theatricality. Treigle's City Opera career peaked in 1969 as Boito's Mefistofele. In an opera indelibly associated with Chaliapin, and not seen in New York since Chaliapin's time, he was the complete singing actor, athletically dominating the stage in a skintight costume accentuating his cadaverous physique. Sills's signature vehicle in the early 1970s came in a rare revival of Donizetti's "Tudor Trilogy": *Roberto Devereux*, *Maria Stuarda*, and *Anna Bolena*.

These City Opera highlights made the company a worthy State Theater companion to George Balanchine's New York City Ballet. But the State Theater was no place for opera. Balanchine had obtained a stage acoustic that muffled his dancers' footfalls—as it muffled the human voice. And the pit acoustic was impossibly thin. As crippling were the new house's rental and operating costs, which far exceeded expenses in the company's former City Center home. Lincoln Center dictated high ticket prices and a more conservative repertoire. Meanwhile, Domingo and Treigle left the company—the former to glory at the Met, the latter to Europe and an early death in 1975. In 1979 Sills replaced Rudel as the City Opera's general director, in which capacity she proved an expert fund-raiser and cheerleader while the company languished artistically. Christopher Keene, who took over in 1989, refueled the repertoire with important New York stage premieres of Schoenberg's *Moses und Aron*, Busoni's *Doktor Faust*, and Bernd Alois Zimmermann's *Die Soldaten*. Keene's successor, Paul Kellogg, if less intellectually ambitious, brought fresh voices and stagings and a winning enthusiasm for Britten and Janáček.

Both Keene (who privately compared the State Theater acoustic to a "car radio") and Kellogg sought to escape Lincoln Center. Vaguely envisioned as an intellectual hub, it more embodied art as commerce. What the Union Square of Dvořák and Seidl had been, what Joseph Papp created at his Public Theater in lower Manhattan, what Harvey Lichtenstein created at the Brooklyn Academy of Music—an alternative house of culture invigorated by contemporary feeling and thought—was what the City Opera needed and deserved. As of the turn of the twenty-first century, it was still looking.[15]

■ ■ ■

Back at the Met, there was catching up to do. Entrenched resistance to change was there both habitual and practical. The relentless schedule—thirty-two weeks, more than two hundred performances—dwarfed Chicago's, San Francisco's, or Los Angeles's. And only Chicago, of the important American houses, had as large an auditorium in which to attempt the theatrical intimacy newer operas and production styles demanded.

To succeed Rudolf Bing, the board in 1970 appointed Goeren Gentele, intendant of the Swedish Royal Opera: an exciting choice. Gentele was as approachable as Bing was aloof. As important, he was an established innovator whose signature achievements included productions previously unthinkable at the Met: an arresting *Masked Ball* in which the king was homosexual; the premiere of Karl-Birger Blomdahl's "space" opera *Aniara*, which had more than a hundred Stockholm performances; acclaimed productions of Busoni and Janáček, which he himself directed; and a *Rake's Progress* directed by Ingmar Bergman. He also had an exceptional knack for reaching out to students and young people. For the Met, he appointed a world-class music director: Rafael Kubelik. And he surprised the board by announcing a "Mini-Met" for works unsuited to a 3,824-seat theater. Eighteen days into his term, he was killed in an automobile accident.

The Met now blundered through seasons of painful disarray. Emerging from the wreckage was James Levine, whom Kubelik (who soon quit) had named principal conductor. Levine became music director in 1975, artistic director in 1986. Born in 1943, he was young, eager, and disciplined. He moved decisively to remold the orchestra and chorus into proudly energized ensembles. The 1974 addition of John Dexter, a distinguished British director, as head of production gave the company a complementary push toward more creative stagings. The post-Bing debacle also resulted in a modernized administrative apparatus, including the first Met marketing department and vastly enhanced fund-raising capacity.

The musical landmarks of the new regime were such overdue additions to the Met repertoire as Berg's *Lulu*, importantly conducted and staged by Levine and Dexter. But Kurt Weill's *The Rise and Fall of the City of Mahagonny*, a brave attempt, irredeemably jarred with the scale and trappings of the auditorium. And Dexter proved inept rethinking Verdi. With his departure in 1981 theatrical values relapsed toward literalism—in American classical music a frequent symptom of insecurity. Bankrolled by Sybil Harrington, after whom the auditorium was renamed in 1987, Franco Zeffirelli spent millions on opulent sets and costumes that duly received the attention they craved. Otto Schenk and Gunther Schneider-Siemssen furnished a series of sanitized Wagner productions closer to Walt Disney than contemporary Bayreuth. A third house director, Jean-Pierre Ponnelle, was erratic: with his *Flying Dutchman* of

1979, whose one stage picture resembled a high school auditorium at Halloween, the Met's visual aesthetic hit bottom.

Resisting deconstructionist "director's opera" as practiced in Europe (where masterworks remained less sacrosanct), the Met risked neither the inanities of revisionism gone awry nor the bracing intellectual energies of a Patrice Chéreau or Harry Kupfer. Dexter-less, it retreated toward what it had traditionally been: a singers' house. The roster now included North American singing actors of high accomplishment, including Teresa Stratas, Frederica von Stade, and (later) Thomas Hampson, Lorraine Hunt Lieberson, and Dawn Upshaw, as well as such stellar homegrown vocal phenomena as Marilyn Horne, Jessye Norman, and (later) Samuel Ramey, Renée Fleming, and Deborah Voigt.

What finally plunged the Metropolitan Opera into a new world was a technological brainstorm. Levine had resisted surtitles as an involuntary intrusion on the experience of stage and singers. In 1995, a decade after audiences elsewhere were apprised of the meaning of sung words, "Met Titles" were unveiled. A tiny screen was installed on the back of every chair. It furnished a running translation in English. It could be turned on or off. And it was so engineered as to be invisible to nonusers alongside. Suddenly, Levine's push for repertoire reform acquired new plausibility. Vital twentieth-century operas by Britten, Busoni, Janáček, Prokofiev, Schoenberg, Shostakovich, and Richard Strauss—all Met premieres—gripped and held. New American operas were tested. With the ascent of Joseph Volpe as general manager, the company achieved an unsurpassed international reputation for efficiency of administration and production. And a flurry of new stage directors yielded some remarkable results. A rethinking of Tchaikovsky's *Eugene Onegin* by Robert Carson, awash with autumn leaves, was both achingly Romantic and schematically acute; it invited a controlled exercise in integrated musical theater that at the same time inspired the singers to live and breathe.

And yet the most memorably integrated stagings at the Met during the Levine era were furnished by two visiting Russian companies: the Bolshoi and the Kirov. The visits had their ups and downs, but when the performers hit stride, as in *Onegin*, *Pique Dame*, or *Khovantschina*, the rightness of it all was startling. The timbre of the voices, even of the orchestra (the Bolshoi's plaintive vibrato, the Kirov's darkly majestic tones) were specific to Tchaikovsky and Mussorgsky. The individual artists were of the highest international caliber, yet subordinate to the ensemble and to the works themselves. Equally illuminating were *Pique Dame* and *Boris Godunov* as presented (in Russian) by the Met in 1995 and 1997 under Valery Gergiev, the Kirov's demonic master intelligence. Plácido Domingo as Hermann, Samuel Ramey as Boris, in exogenous star turns, were eclipsed by memories of their obscure Russian predecessors. The sum total was a generic opera product more glamorous than gripping. Gergiev's input was neutralized.

The Russian time machine long maintained by Soviet cultural borders enabled New Yorkers to catch a glimpse of nationalized opera from the epoch that produced Tchaikovsky and Mussorgsky, Verdi and Wagner. But even Moscow and St. Petersburg will eventually find it impossible to support traditional repertoire in traditional performance. What will take its place? At today's Metropolitan Opera the answer remains ambiguous. Gergiev's Kirov is a company weighted by its institutional history, of which Gergiev himself is a keen and inquisitive student. His articulated mission includes restoring neglected or disused native repertoire (as Toscanini once did at La Scala) and commemorating such peak past achievements as the world premiere of *La forza del destino* (in St. Petersburg in 1862). His 140-year-old Mariinsky Theater, with its intimate dimensions and pastel décor, is itself redolent of past glories. The Met, by comparison, shows no interest in its own distinguished history, which mainly transpired in another, more inspiring space.* Levine some time ago completed his catch-up projects: upgrading the orchestra, updating the repertoire. Unlike Gergiev (or Bernstein, Koussevitzky, Stokowski, Toscanini, Mahler, or Seidl), he is not a public personality and does not embody a highly delineated institutional vision.

In the late 1980s, Levine conceived a Mini-Met in collaboration with Peter Sellars. "If it ever became clear to me that such a small house will be an impossibility, I will just have to leave the Met," he said. "I would see the future here as just more of the same." At the turn of twenty-first century, Levine and the Met seem comfortable in their anachronistic Lincoln Center home.[16]

■ ■ ■

The most original Met artist during the Bing and Levine years was the Canadian tenor Jon Vickers. In an era when other singers worked to recapture the fleeting essence of styles Italian, French, German, or Russian, Vickers eschewed every pretext of stylistic authenticity; like the great singers of the Met's Golden Age and before, he was always the same. For Fernando De Lucia in the 1920s, performing "Nun sei bedankt, mein lieber Schwann" as "Mercé,

---

* When Richard Tucker begged for a revival of Halévy's *La Juive* so he could cap his Met career, as Caruso ended his, as the Jewish goldsmith Eleazar, Bing rejected a rare opportunity both to honor institutional memory and to serve a loyal and popular artist.

mercé, cigno gentil," Lohengrin was quite simply an Italian role, as enthrallingly and sinuously lyric as Puccini's Rodolfo. As a Canadian, Vickers had no such recourse: like the comparable New World originals Stokowski, Gould, and the later Bernstein, he was *sui generis*, one of a kind. None of his signature roles—not Beethoven's Florestan, sung in German; not Berlioz's Enée, sung in French; not Leoncavallo's Canio, sung in Italian; not Tchaikovsky's Hermann, sung in English—sounded idiomatic as he sang it. In fact, closer contact with a Giovanni Martinelli or Peter Pears could only have diluted his Otello or Peter Grimes—not because he was the greater artist, but because his artistry was whole, and wholly iconoclastic.

One foundation for Vickers's singular vocal personality is obvious: unlike most other North Americans of his generation, he had extensive experience singing—in oratorio, in opera in translation at Covent Garden—in his mother tongue. He could not otherwise have become a peerless singer of words. This was not merely a function of diction and coloration, but of veracity: the words Vickers sang sounded lived, not learned. When he cried, "Amfortas, die Wunde!," Parsifal's sudden illumination registered as an actual epiphany.

A specialist in outcasts—Tristan and Siegmund were also among his roles—he was himself an operatic pariah who disdained publicists and interviews. In this, and much else, Vickers's opposite number was another tenor: Luciano Pavarotti. Pavarotti was in fact (as everyone knows) the Met's signature artist and the closest thing to a national operatic icon. He came by his fame honestly: Italy continued to mass-produce tenors, but Pavarotti was the purest and most enduring version of the lyric variety once embodied by a Gigli or di Stefano. He, however, had greater ambitions: to become a latter-day Caruso, equivalent in repertoire, personal appeal, and fame. *Pavarotti: My Own Story* (1981) summarized: "Pavarotti projects a niceness and a lack of guile that people sense right away." Tracking Pavarotti, *People* discovered "opera's newest sex symbol" serving spaghetti and hobnobbing with movie stars. He was featured in the first "Live from the Met" telecast, the first telecast of a solo recital from the Met stage, and "Luciano Pavarotti at Madison Square Garden," fulsomely publicized by public television as "perhaps [Madison Square Garden's] finest hour." Following Caruso, he had pursued the stentorian glamour roles: Manrico, Radames, Calaf. Caruso's tenor expanded into a *spinto*; Pavarotti's merely grew thicker and more coarse. Other aspects of the Caruso analogy were equally dubious. Caruso was truly gregarious, democratic, and public. At the Met, Pavarotti was accustomed to secreting himself in his dressing room with a secretary, a nutritionist, and at least two press agents. When Caruso sang Puccini or "Over There!," he was as fresh and contemporary as Pavarotti grew stale, recycling worn goods.[17]

A third Metropolitan Opera tenor, Plácido Domingo, is a marvel of late-twentieth-century versatility. Born in Spain, raised in Mexico, he sings 120 roles, many of them rarities. In midcareer, he added Wagner. He learned Tchaikovsky in Russian. He also took up conducting and became artistic director of both the Los Angeles and Washington Operas. Domingo in Italian opera is not as authentic as Pavarotti, nor is he the searing vocal actor Vickers was. But he is a model of musical taste and intelligence, and the resilience of his honeyed instrument is a marvel. He enjoyed a reputation for collegiality until he went to war with Pavarotti with a television special and Madison Square Garden show of his own. Then—a twist of fate—a fourth famous tenor, José Carreras, contracted leukemia. When Carreras returned to singing after a bone-marrow transplant and radiation therapy, he proposed a benefit concert for his José Carreras Leukemia Foundation at the 1990 Italian World Cup. The result—"The Three Tenors"—eclipsed anything Pavarotti or Domingo had previously concocted to draw attention to themselves, and also earned all three tenors hefty fees via Decca, which made audio and video recordings of the event. The next Three Tenors event was auctioned by Pavarotti's outdoor-events specialist for many times what the first had cost. On CD, *Three Tenors II* outsold the next biggest classical release nine to one. Three Tenors tours followed. According to Norman Lebrecht, the annual earnings of each tenor as of 1995–96 were ten million dollars or more.[18]

What Theodore Thomas's itinerant orchestra had been in the Gilded Age, what the *New World* Symphony had been in the 1890s, what Toscanini's Beethoven Fifth had been in the 1940s, the Three Tenors now became: the dominant symbol of American classical music. On public TV, the tenors brandished a friendly vulgarity as remote from the first Toscanini telecasts, from Bernstein's *Omnibus* specials and Young People's Concerts as Carson and Letterman were remote from such early commercial television icons as Alistair Cooke and Edward R. Murrow—an odyssey so rapid and momentous that it must be retraced, however concisely.

The adventurous network radio orchestras conducted by Bernard Herrmann, Alfred Wallenstein, and (briefly) Leopold Stokowski, committed to new and American repertoire, were doomed by a 1940 Supreme Court ruling approving the playing of phonograph recordings without compensation to the performers; classical music was eventually ghettoized on non-network FM stations. The disbanding of Herrmann's CBS Symphony in 1951, the termination of the NBC Symphony in 1954 and of the *Bell Telephone Hour* in 1968 were landmarks in the ghettoization of televised classical music on the Public Broadcasting System. PBS's *Great Performances*, inaugurated in 1973, offered nothing like the NBC Opera, with its adventurous repertoire of operas in English, some commissioned or premiered. As it is more a purchaser of programming than a producer, and as it relies on ratings to attract support from corporations and its own affiliated stations, and as its cultural programming too often failed to take a discernible aesthetic or intellectual initiative, PBS typically favored mainstream performer packages: the Three Tenors, Bernstein conducts Beethoven, even (incredibly) adoring "documentaries" on Karajan and Horowitz produced by a CAMI subsidiary. In 1984, summarizing "25 years of achievement" with clips from *Great Performances* and *Live from the Met*, PBS culled two gala hours of which ninety seconds featured music by American composers. This was a far cry from public broadcasting as practiced in European nations.

Record companies, meanwhile, fastened on "crossover" as the marketing strategy of choice. Pavarotti recorded "O Holy Night" and "Mamma"; Domingo's "Perhaps Love," with John Denver, was a best seller. When the LP was new, suitable importance was attached to recording music unavailable on 78s. As late as the 1970s, Goddard Lieberson of Columbia Records set aside certain profits to document little-heard Stravinsky, Schoenberg, and Webern. But it proved more profitable to record music thrice-familiar—freshened with a new conductor or high-fidelity breakthrough. Prophetic was W. J. Henderson, who in 1934 observed, "Critical comment . . . is almost entirely directed to the 'readings' of mighty magicians of the conductor's wand. . . . Can [the public] ever again be trained to love music for its own sake and not because of the marvels wrought upon it by supermen?"; and also Theodor Adorno, who in 1945 wrote of radio listeners, "The less the listener has to choose, the more is he made to believe that he has a choice."[19] As of 2000, literally countless versions of Beethoven's Fifth were available on CD. In short, as with Arthur Judson, the audience—coddled yet mistrusted—was eventually permitted to lead taste. The early visionaries of American classical music, the early visionaries of commercial broadcasting, were in the absence of government subsidies supplanted by the marketplace.

Also symptomatic of TV times was *Fantasia 2000*, Disney's sequel to the most celebrated of all classical music movies. In place of Stokowski and the Philadelphia Orchestra, James Levine leads the Chicago Symphony. As Stokowski is more iconic than any present-day popularizer of classical music, there is also, by way of compensation, a gaggle of celebrity hosts, including Steve Martin, Bette Midler, and Itzhak Perlman. Judged by *Fantasia*, *Fantasia 2000* is about brevity. It lasts seventy minutes, compared to *Fantasia*'s majestic two hours. Its longest segment is twelve minutes. Its closing credits are longer than two of the nine episodes: Beethoven's Fifth (reduced to fewer than four minutes of the opening movement) and the finale of Saint-Saëns's *Carnival of*

506 "Great Performances": Decline and Fall

the Animals. Roy Disney, in an interview, allowed, "There's no getting away from the fact that MTV has affected us all and that audiences are a little bit more impatient than they used to be." He had intended to include the *Nutcracker* Suite from 1940, but "when we spliced it in, we discovered that everything suddenly slowed down."[20] Revisiting the *Nutcracker* makes the problem understandable. Its fourteen minutes are nonnarrative: a patient and poetic exploration of how forms—hovering fairies, darting fishes, floating flowers, dancing mushrooms, leaping radishes—follow music, the arabesques and piquancies of which are subtly corporealized. The difference between this treatment and *Fantasia 2000* is the difference between reading a book and answering questions posed by an "interactive" CD-ROM. Alongside *Fantasia*'s send-up of classical ballet, and its thunder-throwing Zeus and Pegasus on high, the dancing flamingos of *Fantasia 2000* are a vaudeville team. The diminished cultural vocabulary diminishes the music thus accompanied.

Or consider, as a successor to Bernstein's 1960 CBS Young People's Concert "Who Is Gustav Mahler?," the *Great Composers* segment "Gustav Mahler," telecast on PBS in 1999. In place of Bernstein's Carnegie Hall, there are cities and mountains, houses and "composing huts" Mahler knew and used, and enacted re-creations of incidents from his life. In place of a single commentator and a sustained point of view, there are no fewer than sixteen talking heads—sources of dozens of sound bites of less than a minute each. In place of Bernstein and his musicians, a piano quartet, a couple of singers, and the BBC Symphony Orchestra produce tiny music bites rarely exceeding thirty seconds, unless a sound bite is overlaid. Bernstein, who never talks while music is being played, introduces his young people to the Abschied from Mahler's *Das Lied von der Erde* with a four-minute exegesis culminating in a personal interpretation: that the Abschied is, among other things, Mahler's necessary but intensely nostalgic farewell to German Romanticism. He then conducts the final five minutes of this painful leave-taking. In public TV's "Mahler," forty-five seconds of the Abschied yields a twenty-five-second sound bite, then twenty-five seconds of music embellished by a danced interpretation and images of trees and flowers. While these enhancements are less banal than the rainy window pane superimposed on *Kindertotenlieder*, they fracture music better admired as hypnotically inviolable. Then come two more sound bites totaling forty-five seconds, another ten seconds of music, and we are done with *Das Lied von der Erde*.

All six Great Composers in the PBS series are subject to the same formulaic restrictions, a strategy to ward off boredom and placate short attention spans. Nervous cameras compete for novelty of perspective. There are close-ups of fingers, fingernails, and fingerboards, of vibrating hands and strings.

One shot, from the floor, shows a bloated elbow connecting, at a great height, with a tiny fiddle. Even conceding that PBS lacks the financial resources that David Sarnoff and William Paley commanded before commercial television was relieved of responsibility for cultural programming through the advent of public TV, even appreciating the need to satisfy a gamut of affiliated public television stations and to compete with popular commercial fare, it remains questionable whether such programming is desirable. One version of the usual rationale, from Pavarotti, argues, "You reach a lot of people. Let's say, the people are scared of serious music. . . . Then little by little they begin to go to the opera . . . and then they begin to love classical music."[21] Three Tenors and "Gustav Mahler" define classical music in terms of foreign celebrity. They inculcate a type of listening that does not really suit symphonies and operas. The only certainty, as any CAMI manager will confirm, is that performers who appear frequently on television are more lucrative to book than performers who do not.

In an influential 1960 essay,[22] the culture critic Dwight Macdonald coined a term for what classical music has too much become. "Midcult" is the hybridization of mass culture and high culture beginning after World War I. It is mass culture propping high culture on a pedestal. It exhibits "the essential qualities of masscult [but] decently covers them with a figleaf." It "pretends to respect the standards of high culture while in fact it waters them down and vulgarizes them." It insidiously purports to raise mass culture while corrupting high culture. Macdonald's examples include John Steinbeck, Rodgers and Hammerstein, *Our Town*, and *The Old Man and the Sea*. The Toscanini cult and the music appreciation bibles also exemplify midcult. So do the Three Tenors, *Great Composers* on PBS, *Amadeus*, and most concerts defined by warhorses and celebrities. Humor, irony, and self-awareness are antidotes to midcult.★ P. T. Barnum, hawking the likes of Tom Thumb and Jenny Lind, proclaiming "the bigger the humbug, the more people like it," is mass culture. NBC hawking "the world's greatest conductor" is midcult. So are defensive populist sermons, like Pavarotti's, that "classical music is not something to be scared of." Though midcult's argument that it paves the way to high culture is not always specious, it remains a dilution, often a trivialization.

Midcult "threatens to corrupt both its parents," writes Macdonald; it may become "stabilized as the norm of our culture." Forty years later, there is no

★ In *Dialectic of Enlightenment* (New York, Herder and Herder, 1972, p. 158), Max Horkheimer and Theodor Adorno muse that an American strain of "Mark Twain absurdity" might correct misguided culture because of the "effort it demands from the intelligence to neutralize its burdens. . . . The culture industry is corrupt not because it is a sinful Babylon, but because it is a cathedral dedicated to elevated pleasure."

such danger: like classical music, midcult is marginalized in the culture at large. *Time* and *Newsweek* years ago jettisoned their classical music correspondents. Classical music is fast disappearing from FM radio. The big classical record labels are all but gone. Americans of the 1930s, 60 percent of whom said they liked to listen to classical music,[23] knew who Toscanini was; for most people today, Leonard Bernstein is not even a memory. Van Cliburn, in 1958, played Tchaikovsky on commercial television. The Funeral Music from *Götterdämmerung*, played at Anton Seidl's funeral in 1898, was as heroic and tragic as had been Seidl's achievement and his early death. At today's Forest Lawn Memorial Park, the same dirge accompanies an automated unveiling of "the largest religious painting in the world," representing the Crucifixion on a canvas as wide as a twenty-story building is tall. At the same famous Glendale, California, cemetery, the Prelude to *Lohengrin* and the Largo from the *New World* Symphony lend gravity to the "Last Supper Window," and Mozart and Saint-Saëns serenade the crypts.

■ ■ ■

As classical music lost its way, the search for renewal not only looked forward but backward: a pre-Classical repertoire omitted from the music appreciation canon and largely inaccessible to orchestras was newly championed by the "early music" movement.

As late as 1853, John Sullivan Dwight could discover, upon hearing a performance of a three-piano concerto, that Bach was not merely "dry and learned."[24] In New York, Frank Damrosch's Musical Art Society, founded in 1894, pioneered in exploring the Baroque and Renaissance polyphonists. Theodore Thomas led gargantuan Bach and Handel performances.* An early American landmark in the Baroque revival was the U.S. premiere of Bach's B minor Mass, undertaken in 1900 by John Frederick Wolle in Bethlehem, Pennsylvania. The Bethlehem Bach Festival became a unique New World institution. The chorus included workers from the local steel mill and students from the local university; Wolle invited the audience to join in Bach's

---

* But we should not assume that Thomas and his contemporaries were altogether heedless of earlier performance styles. Henry Krehbiel, ever the scholar, admired Thomas's rendering of Bach's figured bass in his orchestral transcription of movements from a sonata for violin and keyboard. But when Walter Damrosch gave Handel's *Messiah* with a reinforced wind complement in the name of authenticity, Krehbiel took him to task for basing this exercise on Mozart's edition rather than Handel's own. His scholarly exegesis of "a few facts touching old orchestras" is typically formidable. See Krehbiel, *Review of the New York Musical Season, 1888–89* (New York, Novello, Ewer and Co., 1888–89), pp. 67, 47.

chorales, which many knew by heart. Beginning in the 1920s, Wanda Landowska convinced Americans, as she had Europeans, that Bach's keyboard works belonged on the harpsichord, not the piano. Later in the twentieth century, the operas of Monteverdi, Purcell, and Handel were dramatically reinvigorated.

The principal instigator of pre-Baroque early music, as in Europe, was Arnold Dolmetsch, whose instruments (some of which he made himself) included the viola d'amore, virginal, and clavichord; his residence in Cambridge, from 1902 to 1909, helped to make Boston America's first city for early music. Dolmetsch's American heirs were largely immigrant academics, and it was largely on university campuses that Medieval and Renaissance music was rescued, edited, published, and performed. Especially influential was the Collegium Musicum at Yale, where Hindemith (who played the viola d'amore, gamba, and recorders) was a driving force. Medieval and Renaissance music reached a larger public via Noah Greenberg's ensemble New York Pro Musica, whose *pièce de résistance*, introduced in 1958, was *The Play of Daniel*.

What most propelled early music into the classical music mainstream, however, was the "historical performance" movement of the late twentieth century. Previously, the ideal of replicating the way music sounded to its actual composers had been of scant interest to many who played or researched pre-Classical repertoire. But with the dissipation of national schools as a basis for interpretation, and increasing emphasis on stylistic versatility, the issue of "authenticity" in performance assumed unprecedented importance, not least in the academy. Fifty years before, Stravinsky, Toscanini, and Klemperer, variously embodying neoclassicism, *Werktreue, neue Sachlichkeit*, and other antidotes to Romanticism, had led the charge against subjective "interpretation" —and left performers with a blank slate other than the score at hand and a desire to honor it. Now, a new template, supplanting once-instinctive "tradition," was generated by scholarly research into old times and instruments.

A fresh basis for stylistic coherence was suggested by light-framed fortepianos, which rendered the music of Mozart, Beethoven, and Schubert with a crispness of articulation and transparency of texture that the nine-foot Steinway sacrificed to power and adaptability. New habits thus acquired were not without influence on orchestras. But the attendant claims to authenticity were frequently overstated or naïve. Even establishing definitive readings of French Baroque *notes inégales* or Beethoven's trills proved an impossibility. Landowska, who famously quipped, "You play Bach your way, I play him his way," also said, "The idea of objectivity is utopian. . . . Can an interpreter restrict himself to remaining in the shadow of the author? What a commonplace! What a joke!" Hindemith wrote, "Our spirit of life is not identical with that of our ancestors, and therefore their music, even if restored with utter technical perfection, can never have to us precisely the same meaning it had for them. We cannot tear down the barricade that separates the present world from things and deeds past." Nietzsche observed, "The really historical performance would talk to ghosts."[25]

Crucially, the post-Baroque historical performance movement failed to discover fresh repertoire; rather, it became a fresh branch of the culture of performance. Nor did it produce an instrumentalist or conductor to set beside a Landowska or Gould—or, for that matter, a Bernstein or Vickers. The performers of Stravinky's generation who indelibly espoused objectivity were themselves indelible musical personalities drawing upon the potent *Zeitgeist* of interwar Paris or Berlin, which is to say that their stylistic anchor was contemporary culture. To think of a comparably anchored late-twentieth-century instrumentalist is to think of the Russian-trained Gidon Kremer, raised where new music still mattered: his Bach and Schubert are emanations of a singular style grounded in the intensities of Shostakovich and Schnittke. In short, the historical performance movement must be partly understood as a surrogate for new music. Not the performer but the composer, as in Bernstein's Norton lectures, is the inescapable crux of the question, "Whither music?"

There was no American Shostakovich or Schnittke, beacon lights to two generations of Soviet conductors, singers, and instrumentalists. Representative of the aroused estrangement of the American composer from the American performer was Milton Babbitt, who in a 1958 magazine article,[26] notoriously titled (by an editor) "Who Cares If You Listen?," calmly argued that contemporary music had necessarily passed beyond the powers of comprehension of "the normally well educated man," and Ralph Shapey, who in 1969 proclaimed an angry ban on the performance of his music. Babbitt, based at Princeton University, and Shapey, based at the University of Chicago, were important creative voices—the former a mad hatter eagerly and comprehensively stripping serialism of Wagnerian rhetoric and Viennese angst, the latter an Abstract Expressionist whose twin métiers were exaltation and biblical despair. For Shapey, Babbitt, and other postwar Americans, the Copland experiment in befriending the new audience was dead. Decrying the humiliation of their ally Mitropoulos, they were as alienated by Bernstein's New York Philharmonic as by the orchestras of Boston, Philadelphia, Chicago, and Cleveland; Bing's Metropolitan Opera was not mentionable. Ignoring Koussevitzky's misguided progeny, they turned for inspiration and instruction to the eclipsed ultra-moderns and Europe's Second Viennese School. For the first time, American composers took a close look at the nontonal music of Schoenberg (residing in the United States since 1933), Berg, and Webern in order to figure out exactly how it was put together. Concurrently, Edgard Varèse, ever the avant-gardist, broke a long silence with two pioneering excursions: *Déserts* (1954), combining winds, percussion, and electronic inter-polations, and *Poeme électronique*, served over four hundred loudspeakers at the 1958 Brussels World Exposition. A stream of performances, recordings, and honors sealed Varèse's second coming. But Stokowski, once Varèse's indispensable conduit to the musical public, was no longer a force. Rather, new music acquired a culture of its own based in academia, where the composers and even the pertinent performers taught.

Of the composers who first emerged after 1950, Elliott Carter, born in 1908, was among the oldest, but his capacity for sustained growth was unique. Both Carter's music and reviews of music (the latter diminishing in frequency as the former increased) exceptionally articulated the challenges—compositional and sociological—confronting the American composer. Assessing native roots and circumstances, he was both empathetic and dismissive—one of countless antinomies texturing a creative personality also formidably conversant with poetry, mathematics, and philosophy. "Chaos and geometry," he observed in one 1965 essay, were twin tendencies of certain early-twentieth-century musicians and painters possessed of an "inner vision and disdain for the 'material' world"—the first tendency being elemental, the second constructivist. Glancing at his own forebears, he acknowledged Ruth Crawford Seeger's "geometric systems," which had influenced his own techniques of organization. In the "chaos" category he named, among others, Charles Ives, who half-mentored him between 1924 and 1932. Carter's essay closed with this passage from Ives: "There may be an analogy—and on first sight there seems to be—between the state and power of artistic perceptions and the law of perpetual change, that ever-flowing stream, partly biological, partly cosmic, ever going on in ourselves, in nature, in all life. . . . Perhaps this is why conformity in art (a conformity which we seem naturally to look for) appears so unrealizable, if not impossible."[27] The protean energies of Ives, layering multiple streams of changing experience, were also Carter's energies. But he faulted Ives's lack of geometry. The quest for a living, growing "inner vision" wielded with discipline, unfettered yet coherent, was Carter's quest.

Carter's origins, and also his direction of development, may be gleaned from the powerful Piano Sonata of 1946. It clearly owes a debt to the Piano Sonata completed five years previously by Copland, whose teacher, Boulanger, also taught Carter and encouraged certain Stravinskyan ideals of discipline. Carter's sonata shares with Copland's both its lean declamatory rhetoric and its bursts of fleet, nervous dance figments in turn inspired by jazz. But, more than Copland at age forty-one, Carter at thirty-eight betrays an incipient inner vision that jettisons traditional European notions of form, rhythm, and harmony; the music grows through an accretion of impetus and ideas. Also, more than Copland, he shows off both the pianist and the piano. The First String Quartet, five years later, is the ripe starting point for Carter's future music. The four instruments interact—or do not—as powerful and powerfully distinct personalities. A tremendous energy source, physical and cerebral, propels their forty minutes of activity. The organizing influences of the high modernist masters Stravinsky and Schoenberg are absorbed, not borrowed. Central to Carter is "metric modulation," a notational device that permits the precise calibration of minute tempo change: the listener experiences an Ivesian "spontaneity"; the composer retains command. As the Carter scholar David Schiff has pertinently observed, Carter is one of the few composers who has been able to draw on both Ives and Boulanger, on American experimentalists seeking transcendence and European high modernists in search of an autonomous, nonreferential language. To another writer, Wilfrid Mellers, the streaking velocities and teeming densities of Carter's musical ontology suggest a passage from Wallace Stevens:

> And out of what one sees and hears and out
> Of what one feels, who could have thought to make
> So many selves, so many sensuous worlds,
> As if the air, the midday air, was swarming
> With the metaphysical changes that occur
> Merely in living as and where we live.[28]

Carter's rejection of the formulaic, including serialism, dictated a search for new and newer challenges and solutions. Carter's self-definition is an American trait. Pondering his situation, he asked how Americans such as himself could discover or commit to "an order of values" in the absence of "a unified culture such as France." He questioned the point of "learning to achieve the order and control which until now were thought to be so fundamental to the art" when "the composer cannot always count on the listening ability of even a small part of his audience, or when this small part, if it exists, has no influence over the majority of listeners on whom most of the qualities and skills of even the accepted works of the standard repertory make little impression." In 1962, observing Europe, he took note of the "almost nihilistic defiance" of younger composers intent on breaking decisively with the past—a movement, variously opting for mathematical determinacy and carefree indeterminacy, whose prophets (unnamed by Carter) included the American John Cage. In the United States, Carter reasoned, the musical high culture remained so fragile and diffuse that there was not enough to rebel against. Also, whatever the exasperation or pessimism of the American composer under siege, there was too much unfinished business. "It is by carrying on the European tradition and by following the methods of some of its experiments in the different context of his own experience that our composer affirms his identity and the identity of American music." He concluded, "In any case, the random development of music here, without the imposition of authoritarian and customary attitudes and tastes, will be the prime factor in molding our own music into something of its own, with a freshness, we hope, drawn from these very circumstances."[29]

Carter was fortunate to enjoy a coterie of dedicated performers, at least four of whom, comprising the Juilliard String Quartet, were part of the classical music mainstream. But he was at all times an outsider to the world of orchestras and opera companies, and his pronounced success in Europe, with audiences more attuned to his advanced language, could only have made him feel lonelier in America. No less than Shapey or Babbitt, he lacked common ground with the central institutions of performance. In fact, the majority of composers of consequence followed the modernist thread toward more rarified idioms and audiences. Even Bernstein, who considered Mahler the emblematic twentieth-century composer and tonality the only innate musical language, in 1983 arduously completed an abortive opera, *A Quiet Place*, gnarled with dissonance.*

For Carter, modernist complexity was a necessity deeply reasoned and felt; he understandably regretted the initial populist orientation of his First Symphony and *Holiday* Overture.[30] Even Copland, whose populism succeeded, arguably never surpassed his modernist Piano Variations. And there were Americans, native-born or transplanted, authentically close in spirit to the European modernist masters. Stefan Wolpe—born in Berlin in 1902, an American from 1938—was such a composer, whose influences included the Second Viennese School, Abstract Expressionism, and American jazz. Of

---

* A safer refuge for tonality was Hollywood, whose composers included Bernard Herrmann, collaborator with Orson Welles on *Citizen Kane* (1941) and with Alfred Hitchcock on such films as *Vertigo* (1958) and *Psycho* (1960). The recognition scene in *Vertigo* is eight minutes of cinema without dialogue or sound effects. Herrmann compared his art to musical melodrama (i.e., spoken text plus music). In a 1973 address, he maintained, "In the present day certain works by Carl Orff might be considered melodram[a], while a great part of Berg's *Wozzeck* is really melodram[a] rather than opera. [Debussy's] *Pelléas* . . . is practically spoken drama with music." In truth, Hermann was a formidable musical dramatist; few American classical composers achieved as much writing for the stage. See Steven C. Smith, *A Heart at Fire's Center: The Life and Music of Bernard Herrmann* (Berkeley, University of California Press, 1991), p. 359.

Schoenberg's UCLA pupils, Leon Kirchner, born in Brooklyn in 1919, was like Schoenberg equally a modernist and an instinctive Romantic. In an impassioned 1956 "credo," he dissociated himself from colleagues "dominated by the fear of self-expression" in favor of "the superficial security of current style and fad."

Though Kirchner's music was not simple, he did not succumb to Schoenberg's twelve-tone method. Others of his generation, as aesthetically and temperamentally remote from Schoenberg as Kirchner was not, became serialists.★ Relatively few were well served by a system questionable on its own terms and conditioned by exigencies of fin de siècle Viennese disillusionment and disintegration. Sustained by a lifeline to the universities, shunning tonality as history's detritus, lacking a constituency beyond themselves, they produced an undistinguished species of hermetic art. Holdouts like Harold Shapero, whose Symphony for Classical Orchestra (1947) impressively amalgamates Stravinsky with Beethoven, simply stopped composing. Oft-cited conventional wisdom held that great music was frequently unpopular in its own time. But most American music of the sixties and seventies was irremediably unpopular. George Rochberg and David Del Tredici were among the first prominent serialists to defect to a robust tonality. By century's end, even Carter and Kirchner were writing in a friendlier style.

Whether individual nontonal styles suited individual American composers, the mainstream culture of performance grew the more stranded and anemic in the decades after 1950.

■ ■ ■

Early in the twenty-first century, economic recession and the terrorist attacks of September 11, 2001, produced formidable deficits in the American symphonic community. Endowments shrank. Gifts from individuals, corporations, and foundations plummeted. A spokesman for the American Symphony Orchestra League commented, "It really is 'the economy, stupid'. . . . I don't want to say, don't worry, this will correct itself . . . [but] orchestras have proved surprisingly resilient."[31] But in New York, while attendance slumped at Lincoln Center and Carnegie Hall, the ever-adventurous Brooklyn Academy of Music experienced record ticket sales in 2002–2003. Surveying widespread artistic retrenchment among other performing arts presenters, BAM Execu-

---

★ In most "serial" music, an ordered series of notes is a basic component of a given composition (yet may be transformed by many voluntary operations). "Twelve-tone" serial music utilizes a series ordering the twelve chromatic pitches.

tive Producer Joseph Melillo commented that the field was "not adapting well" to economic hard times.[32] Also, notwithstanding assurances to the contrary, the patriotic surge of 2002 lacked any galvanizing classical musical anthem: Beethoven's Fifth, America's victory symphony of World War II, no longer spoke to the community; no native repertory had materialized to take its place.

An unusually subtle optimistic analyst of "The Economic Health of American Symphony Orchestras in the 1990s and Beyond" was Douglas Dempster of the University of Texas College of Fine Arts. Writing in late 2002, Dempster argued that orchestras in the long run would continue to sustain rapid growth in terms of offerings, budgets, and audiences.

> Most important, orchestras have managed to keep the income gap, as a percentage of total revenue, from growing over the last 10 years. In fact, the industry has gained some ground, improving the ratio of earned to unearned income by better than 10 percent over the period. There are several reasons for this, but one of the clearest and most significant has been the ability to pass along highly inflationary costs to the audience through greatly increased ticket prices. The performing arts, like education and health care, have grown not through greater productivity, but through greater perceived value. In each case, consumers have proved a willingness and the wherewithal to spend a larger and larger portion of their incomes on these "stagnant services."
>
> [T]he key is to understand how these organizations control the perceived value of their service in order to keep pace with highly inflationary costs so as to sustain growth in earned income, as well as in private and public subsidies.[33]

Commenting privately on symphonic salesmanship and "perceived value," Dempster amplified:

> The symphony orchestra is not dying in the U.S. It's thriving, but thriving in the fashion of any mass-marketed product: like McDonald's hamburgers, its very success—economic and not artistic success—is built on uniformity (all look exactly alike), reliability (the bathrooms are always clean and the fries always salty), and the marketed perception that this is an acceptable and even wholesome pastime.[34]

Dempster concluded that there was no evidence that orchestras, like the single-choreographer dance companies of the 1990s, would be decimated by harsher economic times. Nor did he foresee a looming "paradigm shift." But a paradigm shift has to some degree already occurred. The further back one looks, the less artistic "uniformity" is observable among orchestras distinct in sound, repertoire, mission, and schedule. The current one-size-fits-all full-time template, encouraged by Ford Foundation subsidies, is discouragingly remote from the different orchestral worlds once inhabited by Thomas and Higginson, by Stokowski's Philadelphia Orchestra, Mitropoulos's Minneapolis Symphony, and Koussevitzky's Boston Symphony.

A favorite defense of classical music at the turn of the twenty-first century is a culling of statistics arguing that the average age of listeners has not increased. This blinkered obsession with the market, an act of denial in itself a symptom of decline, ignores that classical music is a composed music and can only fully flourish when buttressed by important living composers. Copland's search for a music that satisfies "both us and them" was ultimately a search that failed; after Prokofiev's death in 1953, and Stravinsky's defection to serialism a few years later, and Hindemith's fading presence in the same decade, only two composers—Dmitri Shostakovich and Benjamin Britten, both resident abroad—could be considered central embodiments of a grand Western line-age at the same time attuned to a comparably grand audience. With the death of Shostakovich in 1975 and of Britten in 1976, classical music for the first time had to endure without the presence of a major mainstream contempo-rary practitioner.

Taken as a whole, American classical music describes a simple trajectory, rising to a height at the close of the nineteenth century and receding after World War I. In the decades of ascendancy, the quest for an American canon was its defining virtue, whether or not the reigning Germanic model prof-fered true hope for an indigenous American style. The decades of decline were at first highly interesting: a new culture of performance was crowned by amazing feats of virtuosity and probity, and textured, as well, by an exciting if subsidiary pursuit of the Great American Symphony. After 1950, the absence of a native canon was a defect no longer disguised or minimized by spectacu-lar borrowed goods. By century's end, intellectuals had deserted classical music; compared to the theater, cinema, or dance, it was the American per-forming art most divorced from contemporary creativity, most susceptible to midcult decadence.

Though the wedge between composer and performer had been thrust home by impersonal historical forces—European classical music underwent the same general crisis—three individuals embodied the schism and aggra-vated its severity. Arturo Toscanini, through his artistic genius and excessive self-regard, excited unprecedented allegiance to the performer's art as an end in itself. Arthur Judson, through his business genius and excessive self-satisfaction, standardized concert production in the interest of operational efficiency. David Sarnoff, through his entrepreneurial genius and excessive self-reliance, masterminded classical music's infiltration of radio, recordings, and TV, yet misjudged the need to legislate public responsibility for a time when Sarnoffs and Paleys were no longer in control of things. The ultimate result, in each case, was a failure—by artists and businessmen alike—to lead taste. The same could be said of the composers—including Aaron Copland, who tried hardest to stem the tide of complacency.

In short, the marketplace took command. Driven by ticket sales, by strategems for fund-raising and public relations, for seducing but not challenging the laissez-faire listener, classical music blundered toward a stalemate—or a crossroads.

Postlude:
Post-Classical Music

■

Minimalism and postmodernism ■ *American*
mavericks ■ *BAM and the need for change* ■
Classical music in the year 2000

On November 21, 1976, the Metropolitan Opera House at Lincoln Center was—a rare event—the site of an American premiere. The new work was *Einstein on the Beach* by Philip Glass. Its operatic magnitude was sealed by its five-hour length, its sung text, and the continuity of its musical fabric. But the "libretto" consisted of numbers and *solfège* syllables, and nothing resembling a story intruded upon the glacial grandeur of Glass's pulsating scales and arpeggios, or of Robert Wilson's surreal stage pictures. During one twenty-minute sequence, a horizontal slab of light tilted vertically and arose, an event so artfully integrated with music that its ascent was hypnotic. Elsewhere, the exhilaration of streaking roulades of tone mated, but precisely, with the whipping physicality of furiously disciplined bodies. The performers, who were not trained as vocalists, sang, acted, and danced in equal measure. The orchestra, in the pit, was the Philip Glass Ensemble: on this occasion, two electronic organs (one of them played by the composer), three woodwinds, a female voice, and a solo violin, all highly amplified.

According to a scenario, the slab of light was a "bed" and the ricocheting bodies manned a "spaceship." Albert Einstein's feats as a scientist, humanist, and amateur violinist were obviously at play, but to what end? Wilson later remarked:

> Ours is the easiest of all operas. You don't have to think about the story, because there isn't any. You don't have to listen to the words, because they don't mean anything. I'm not giving you puzzles to solve, only pictures to hear. You go to our opera like you go to a museum. You appreciate the color of the apple, the line of the dress, the glow of the light. You go to the park, you look at the scenery which contains people

moving about and sounds changing. Watch clouds passing. Look at the music. Listen to the pictures.[1]

This gargantuan spectacle was the product of a musical aesthetic, born in America, called "minimalism"—a reductionist antidote to modernist complexity, born in Europe. Musical structure was created through repetition. The steady pulse, simple harmonies, and electronic instruments of American popular music were potent influences, as were such non-Western genres as Indonesian gamelan and Indian raga. The result was a music of stasis, quicscently hovering or racing in place. Glass—who consciously charted a radical break with serialist composers of "crazy creepy music"; who studied with Ravi Shankar, traveled in Morocco and India, and practiced Tibetan Buddhism—called it "intentionless" music, in contradistinction to tension-and-release Western trajectories.[2]

Einstein on the Beach was introduced in Europe, where it quickly acquired a following. The Met performance—a rental, rather than a Met production—was sold out; so was an impromptu second performance a week later. The audiences were young but varied. Glass connected with world music, with rock, with intellectuals for whom classical music was passé. He also incited hostility and defensiveness among upholders of midcult banality and high cultural sophistication. Krehbiel, Gershwin, Blitzstein, and Bernstein in their different ways had anticipated a distinctive American musical theater transcending melodrama or Broadway. But, by the standards of Mozart, Wagner, Verdi, or Mussorgsky, *Porgy and Bess*, *Regina*, and *West Side Story* did not add up to much. Perhaps what was needed was a radically maverick New World genre, as different from Old World models as Charles Ives's symphonies or Jackson Pollack's drips.

Glass attained both a radical departure and a popular success. What came next? For Glass personally, it was the "Einstein debt," exceeding $100,000; he returned to driving a cab. To his rescue came the City of Rotterdam, which put up $20,000 to commission a new work—a "*real* opera"—for the Netherlands Opera. The result was *Satyagraha* (1979), with more conventional vocal and instrumental forces, in which the achievements of Mahatma Gandhi were represented by a series of semistatic musical-dramatic tableaux. As with *Einstein*, the work's limitations—setting Sanskrit, Glass did not attempt to deal with a comprehensible language, nor did he attempt to narrate the complex eventfulness of real life—were a sublime strength. But the closer Glass approached sung narrative, the more confining his simplicities became: an opera in English about Columbus for the Met, *The Voyage* (1992), was less refreshed than impoverished.

Glass has since proved fitfully resourceful in discovering new ends for old means. He is a gifted collaborator with dancers and filmmakers. His abstract music, moving beyond intentionless equipoise, includes a forty-minute Second Symphony whose spacious layout remains an empty trough (would that its admirers knew Bruckner). More successful is his moody Violin Concerto: a single fiddler running a minimalist obstacle course is exciting in ways a keyboard or orchestra is not. Glass's connectedness with a mass of listeners is something new in American concert music since Bernstein's *Candide* Overture and *West Side Story* Dances. As significant, he is a player: not since Bernstein has so popular a concert composer been so popular a performer. And he is not alone.

Steve Reich was born in New York in 1936, a year before Glass was born in Baltimore. Both wound up at Juilliard. Both rejected nontonal music; unfashionably, emphatically, prophetically, they recognized the point of no return toward which compositional complexity was speeding. They considered jazz and rock unalterably part of their musical world. As minimalists, they learned from non-Western styles.* They wrote music that was played in galleries and museums. They formed their own ensembles, in which they themselves performed and with which they regularly toured Europe as well as the United States. For Reich, the big move uptown took place in 1978—a Carnegie Hall concert, two years after *Einstein* at the Met; everyone was there.

But Reich's detailed simplicity did not court popularity. And the only stage picture he permitted was Steve Reich and Musicians, attired in black, making music with mallets and drums. If Glass mounted a kind of rock show, Reich's medium was the percussion ensemble. His compositional ingredients, technical and aesthetic, included cool jazz, the polyrhythms of West African drumming, and a tape-recording phenomenon, called "phasing," combining kinetic repetition with gradual desynchronization. *Music for 18 Musicians* (1976) is quintessential Reich. The instruments are xylophones, marimbas, pianos, and maracas, plus a violin, a cello, a clarinet, a bass clarinet, and four female vocalists who blend wordlessly with the rest. The duration is sixty-seven minutes and forty-two seconds. The ticking pulse and static harmony are "minimal." But this is also music of change: an intricate sound fabric in steady motion, a kaleidoscope of shimmering, subtly shifting tints and timbres, a transmutation of mobile sound-shapes. The listening options are wonderfully discrete. To

* Reich's own list of influences: European music from 1200 to 1750, Balinese and West African music, American jazz from 1950 to 1965, Stravinsky, Bartók, Webern, traditional Hebrew cantillation. He also writes, "It seems that the wall between serious and popular music was erected primarily by Schoenberg and his followers." Paul Hiller (ed.), *Steve Reich: Writings on Music 1965–2000* (New York, Oxford University Press, 2000), pp. 95, 168.

switch metaphors: you can stare at the clockface in a beatific stupor; you can scrutinize the internal mechanism and study its elegance of design. There are also two musical layers: a periodicity of soundwaves, breaking and receding; a pulsating backdrop, strobe-lighting the whole. The affect is rigorously impersonal but also wholesomely or therapeutically communal: a palpitating eighteen-member organism that even swings.

No less than Glass, Reich has been challenged to stretch a language whose simplicity is its pure pedigree. Like Glass, he is an intellectual, not an innocent. His recent music is informed by social conscience, a product of renewed Jewish roots. In *Different Trains* (1988), he freshly applies his early fascination with tape loops, and with the rhythms and inflections of human speech, in remembrance of the Holocaust. The musical materials, which double as dramatic texts, include snatches of words: "from Chicago to New York," "one of the fastest trains," "1939," "1941"; and then, "the Germans walked in," "lots of cattle wagons there"; and then, alluding to either trains or human beings, "But today they're all gone." The formal rigor of the piece, for string quartet and tape, safeguards its authenticity; whatever pathos it conveys demands the listener's initiative.

If Reich's charmed moment is past, it will not prove ephemeral. *Music for 18 Instruments* is among the best of all American concert works. Who, among Reich's contemporaries (in the United States or abroad), has produced a style more original or recognizable? Whither music? asked Leonard Bernstein. Of Reich's answer, John Adams has remarked, "For him, pulsation and tonality were not just cultural artifacts. They were the lifeblood of the musical experience, natural laws. It was his triumph to find a way to embrace those fundamental principles and still create a music that felt genuine and new."[3] Adams himself is with Glass and Reich the third minimalist to invade the classical music mainstream. Born in New England in 1947, he is as polyglot as Glass and Reich are not. His father was a jazz saxophonist. His grandfather owned a dance hall. At Harvard, he was initiated into the mysteries of serial composition while simultaneously immersing himself in the sixties' counterculture. In 1971, he drove his Volkswagen cross country to the Bay Area, where he heard Steve Reich and Musicians and the Philip Glass Ensemble, and became a minimalist. And yet he retained a passion for Romantic and modernist music. Esteemed or disparaged as a "Romantic minimalist," he emerged a twenty-first-century eclectic, deeply schooled in a gamut of musical possibilities. "To be a modern composer," he believes, "you have to be able to move with promiscuous ease."[4]

Adams's *Nixon in China* (1987) may be the most important American opera produced in the aftermath of *Einstein* and *Satyagraha*, a feat of musical synthesis that manages to build on Glass's shock therapy without corrupting its aesthetic freshness. Richard Nixon's 1972 mission to Beijing proved a shrewd topic. Proposed by the director Peter Sellars, already an electrifying influence on stagings of Handel and Mozart, and developed by Sellars, Adams, and the librettist Alice Goodman, the story is not a satire or political tract, but a contemporary myth for contemporary audiences. However fortuitously, its message of East meets West resonates with the postmodern moment. And the materials of minimalism inherently suit both the tale and its telling. As Glass had demonstrated, the impersonality of minimalism—the inhuman stamina of patterned repetition—generates an aura of ritual dignity; it readily evokes the mythic. At the same time, the chugging and stuttering musical particles, especially when subjected, as by Adams, to Stravinskyan shifts of meter and accent, tremble with energy. In *Nixon*, minimalism seals the necessary sense of occasion in both its personal and impersonal dimensions. The events of the opera are made properly momentous; Dick and Pat tremble or flutter with nervous excitement; Mao, Zhou En-lai, and Madame Mao are coldly or serenely commanding.

If Adams's musical vocabulary seems precariously limited for a full-length narrative opera, he proceeds to fortify his minimalism with stylistic asides: for the Nixons to dance to, the crooning saxophones and slick strings of Glenn Miller; for the "unknown soldier" invoked by Nixon, a military trumpet; for the succoring of an oppressed peasant, enacted in a dance pageant, a Romantic apotheosis borrowed from Wagner and Richard Strauss; for a wedding allusion, a church organ wobbly with sentimental vibrato. Adams does not quote "Moonlight Serenade," or "Taps," or *Thus Spake Zarathustra*, or "Here Comes the Bride"; his distillation of these mixed ingredients, each "minimalized," is crucially deft. The result, rather than pastiche, is a feat of ironic absorption paralleling Stravinksy's osmotic neoclassical appropriations of older styles.

Adams has since composed prolifically in the classical music genres. He has also played with tape, like Reich, and with electronics, like Glass. Like Glass's, his abstract music can suffer from a paucity of information. As a remedy, his stylistic versatility is both an aesthetic risk and a pragmatic strength. In *Naïve and Sentimental Music* (1999), his longest symphonic work to date, Adams's capacity to spin a forty-five-minute musical daydream is a tour de force of technique at the service of spontaneous inspiration. The result helps to define the inheritance of American classical music. Adam's "naïveté"—his breezy acquisitiveness; the loopy "slang" of the recurrent opening tune—documents American eclecticism and informality. The spacious layout of the second movement evokes open horizons as surely as Dvořák's Largo or Copland's prairie style. The racing ostinatos of the finale, rising to a high plateau of tolling brass, limn a psychedelic landscape of the mind equally registering (for at least one listener) Sibelius's Fifth and the West Coast counterculture Adams absorbed and fed on. No less than Reich and Glass, he has fashioned a durable, individual style of his own. And, like Reich and Glass, he is his own best and most visible advocate, as a busy conductor of his own and others' music. He is sufficiently free of Old World influence that even those who look askance at him cannot look down. Like Reich and Glass, he confronts at every turn the twentieth century's Eurocentric culture of performance.

■ ■ ■

The minimalists represented something old and something new. The something old was non-Western and primitive. The something new was Western and technological: tapes and amplifiers used in composition and performance; airplanes and CDs that helped to collect, in one intelligence, the once far-flung musics of the world. In both respects, old and new, composers like Glass, Reich, and (to a lesser degree) Adams fall outside the evolutionary straight line leading from Bach to Schoenberg, Bartók, and Stravinsky. Their freedom of movement, mixing high and low, East and West, also violates the traditional Western continuum.

And yet their lineage as American classical musicians bears pondering. In a 1962 affirmation that was equally a prediction, Elliott Carter (as we have seen) wrote, "It is by carrying on the European tradition and by following the methods of some of its experiments . . . that our composer affirms his identity and the identity of American music." But Carter was plainly wrong. If four streams of American classical music may be identified through 1950—the pre–World War I Germanics, the Boulangerie, the ultra-moderns, the interlopers—Carter and other high modernists comprised a fifth, post-1950 strain, "carrying on the European tradition." Postmodern eclectics, a sixth strain, reject high modernism. They also connect to the ultras' quest for Eastern illumination, and to Gershwin and other interlopers for whom pop was a necessary ingredient of any American music. If they possess a father figure, it is certainly more the renegade Cowell than the one-time patriarch Copland.

A subset of postmodernism, minimalism is maverick and experimental, like Heinrich, Fry, or Ives. In the more recent past, the Canadian Colin McPhee, who lived for seven years on Bali, and Lou Harrison, an eloquently ecumenical apostle of Asian musics who rises, as in his Piano Concerto, to majestic heights of originality, significantly influenced the postmodern absorption of once-exotic strains. Harry Partch created an impressive exotic style of his own, using quasi-Polynesian instruments of his elaborate invention and a scale of forty-three tones. The *enfant terrible* phase of early minimalism—of Glass, Reich, and Adams before moving "uptown"—overlaps with composers, on the outer fringe of classical music, who asked "What is music?" The hovering sound "clouds," lasting up to six hours, of La Monte Young's *Well-Tuned Piano* fit this description, as does Terry Riley's *In C*, whose single page of repeating "modules" can take several hours to exhaust. Morton Feldman was an elder statesman whose compositions hovered delicately on the threshold of immobility. But the guru of all such composer/philosophers was of course John Cage.

Born in Los Angeles in 1912, Cage studied at UCLA with Schoenberg and there learned what sort of composer he did not wish to become. Schoenberg's twelve-tone system had spawned (however accidentally) music controlled in every parameter by an ordered series of events. Cage's antidote was to "compose" a kind of music that happened by itself. As with other West Coast composers—Cowell, Harrison, Partch all come to mind—his Pacific Rim affinity for Eastern thought predisposed him to suppress the ego as a catalyst to creativity or enlightenment. He reasoned that any sound, in and of itself, constituted "music." And so did silence, because—as he discovered in a soundproof anechoic chamber—silence, too, produced sound: of his nervous system and of his coursing blood. His most notorious creation, *4′33″* (1952), instructs the performer to play nothing: a situation actually more conducive to acute aural awareness than most Beethoven or Brahms performances. Six years later, Cage defined an "experimental action" as "one the outcome of which is unforeseen." His own subsequent experiments included composing by tossing coins or consulting the Chinese *I Ching*. Cage wrote of fashioning "a way of waking up to the very life we're living, which is so excellent once one gets one's mind and one's desire out of its way and lets it act of its own accord"—an ideal affirmed by Cage's own charmed persona. The experience of taking part in a Cage composition such as *Theater Piece* is freshly to experience oneself and one another.[5]

Cage's embodiment of art as therapeutic ritual, rejecting personal will and passion, ignoring Wagnerian catharsis, applies to Glass and Reich, to Young, Feldman, Harrison, and Partch. But the postmodernists also include composers far from Cagean. Conlon Nancarrow was, like Partch, an outcast by choice who disdained existing musical means. He was equally a precisionist driven to devise rhythms of maximum complexity. Born in Texarkana in 1912, he dabbled with jazz and classical trumpet, and had lessons with Sessions and Piston, before joining the Abraham Lincoln Brigade and fighting in Spain. Back in New York, he fell in with Copland and Carter. Like Cage, he wrote articles for *Modern Music* dismissing the nationalism of new works flaunting jazz clichés. He settled in Mexico and isolated himself from compositional influences. In Cowell's *New Musical Resources* he read about complex rhythms only a mechanical piano could reproduce. He bought such a piano and the machinery to make music for it. Among the conceits comprising his *Piano Player Study* No. 3c, otherwise notable for its Gershwin lilt, is a seven-note repeated rhythm in combination with a repeating six-note descent. Study No. 5 consists of thirteen distinct motifs gradually piled atop one another: a musical train-wreck engineered with maniacal exactitude, its madcap climax inescapably blanketed by a cartoonish density of activity. Study No. 6 is a languorous cowboy tune in dialogue with versions of itself. In No. 7 the reprises of the catchy main tune are fantastically barnacled with new additions. The exhilarating naughtiness of this music, capped by a fractious coda, is both intellectual and visceral.

Other New World eclectics are comprehensive, even encyclopedic. Lukas Foss, born in Berlin in 1922, was a neoclassicist, a serialist, a minimalist, and an improvisatory wild man. Especially in his own music and that of Bach, he was also one of the exceptional American pianists of his generation. As a conductor, his readings of Mozart, Beethoven, and Tchaikovsky, lean and electric, surpassed those of glitzier maestros. William Bolcom, born in Seattle in 1938, was a prime mover in the ragtime revival of the 1970s. Performing as a pianist with his wife, the singer Joan Morris, he pioneered in excavating the history of American popular song. As a solo pianist, he recorded the music of Gershwin and Milhaud. He composes rags and cabaret songs, symphonies and operas. His *summa*, embodying his personal philosophy and incomparable stylistic range, is the *Songs of Innocence and of Experience*, after William Blake, whose two hours-plus culminate with an infectious reggae setting of "A Divine Image." (Reggae, he explains, "is apocalyptic stuff with a happy beat, a curious dichotomy. It perfectly captures Blake's non-tragic acceptance of that which we are.")[6]

Taking stock of this list of Americans, circa 2000, at least three generalizations may be extrapolated. As postmodernists, they swing high and low, East and West, or both. Nearly every one of these composers was or is also a notable and notably visible performer. Taken as a group, they challenge the schism between composer and audience: Cage enjoins listeners to take part as doers; the minimalists engender communal experience; Bolcom deploys the familiar. The culture of performance, which coexisted with a Babbitt, Kirchner, or Carter by simply ignoring them, is here directly confronted. Atomized twentieth-century classical music, with its celebrity conductors and equally remote composers, is potentially restored to some degree of wholeness.

A fourth generalization: never have so many major American composers been so divorced from European practice. But then Europe is today divorcing from its own past. The transatlantic direction of influence is shifting.

■ ■ ■

For Europe, the first half of the twentieth century was a time of political and cultural upheaval. Schoenberg, Webern, and Berg, the destroyers of tonality, were ensnared by a nihilism ripping apart fin de siècle Vienna. The Great War devastated confidence in culture as a civilizing force. Neoclassicism, as practiced by Stravinsky in France, was one expression of postwar neutrality, a search for order counteracting Romantic subjectivity. Among Schoenberg and his followers, the 1920s quest for objectivity took the form of a systematic pursuit of posttonal dissonance. The *neue Sachlichkeit* of Hindemith and Weill was a less esoteric response to the crisis of Romanticism. With Hitler, music as a vehicle for Romantic high art underwent a hideous reprise. Modernism, *neue Sachlichkeit*, and other signatures of Weimar culture were erased as "decadent"; Beethoven, Bruckner, and Wagner were enlisted to amplify the Nazi cause. Stalin, too, understood the uses of music for public uplift; like Hitler, he propagated cultural policies eradicating modernism in favor of symphonies and operas politically understood. In the short run, the impact of World War II on music was literal and visceral: a tragedy of civilization is the topic of Schoenberg's *A Survivor from Warsaw*, of Shostakovich's Seventh Symphony, of Strauss's *Metamorphosen*. In the long run, the poisoning of Romantic uplift had the more enduring impact. Modernism redoubled. Contemporary music was abstract music for a limited audience. Music of mass catharsis was in abeyance.

The United States did not participate in fin de siècle decadence, and neither world war touched American soil. But Schoenberg, Stravinsky, Hindemith, and Weill all came to America with their political and aesthetic traumas in tow. One reason so much American music of the twentieth century seems a pale copy of European music is that in the United States the European styles had no necessary cause. In the decades after World War II, however, cultural conditions in the United States and Europe converged.

Beginning in Russia with Shostakovich, moral music staged a comeback. The Shostakovich legacy includes such religious minimalists as Arvo Pärt, Giya Kancheli, and Henryk Górecki, all born in the 1930s. A new music of meditation or ecstasy encompassed Europeans as varied as Olivier Messiaen, Sofia Gubaidulina, and John Tavener. From another European vantage point, in 1889 Debussy and Ravel encountered the music of Indonesia at the Paris

World's Fair. A Javanese gamelan orchestra performed Eastern music such as they had never heard—not romantically sultry and mysterious, but bright, clean, precise, joyful. Composers everywhere were shopping for post-Romantic, post-Wagnerian possibilities. What Hungarian folk music offered Bartók, Indonesian music offered impressionistically inclined French composers. The late works of Debussy and Ravel proved transitional: they led to more ethnographically minded scholar/composers, and to a dispersion of Western classical music, no longer headquartered in Germany.

In fact, never before have American composers been as influential, as well known, or as personally visible abroad as in the past quarter century. The religious minimalists of Europe are cohorts or progeny of Glass and Reich. Holland's Louis Andriessen impressively mixes American bebop and minimalism with Stravinsky. For the many post–World War II Europeans who needed a radical break, and for whom indeterminacy was a crucial catalyst, no countryman could have managed a tonic iconoclasm as effortless or thorough as Cage's or Feldman's. Among such high modernists as Pierre Boulez and György Ligeti, the Americans Carter and Nancarrow enjoyed an international prestige never accorded members of the 1920s Boulangerie. And it was Colin McPhee, not Debussy or Messiaen, who impelled Benjamin Britten toward gamelan and toward his own *Death in Venice*.

Not so long ago, Russia and Eastern Europe were guarded by an Iron Curtain and China was Martian. Today's composers e-mail Beijing and Novosibersk from San Francisco and Jakarta. For ethnomusicologists, Western music's broad interface with the rest of music is the most important and characteristic development of the last quarter century—a development in which Americans took the lead. As I write these words, among the most exciting midgeneration composers in the United States are Chinese-Americans forging a synthesis between Asian folk traditions and Western modernism. The ethnomusicologist Marc Perlman remarks that "musical borders can be crossed, but the value of crossing them depends on the degree to which you respect them."[7] Some hybrids are exploitative or slapdash; music such as Zhou Long's *Poems from T'ang* is neither. Of growing significance, too, are Native American composers similarly engaged—a fresh chapter in the ongoing saga of race relations, of music "red" and "black" as a perceived taint or enrichment, in American classical music.

A century after MacDowell was hailed as the great American composer, six decades after the Harris Third seemed the Great American Symphony, American classical composers are no longer entangled in the psychology of adolescence—adoring or mistrusting Old World parents, ambivalently eyeing the surrounding popular culture. The new borrowers of classical music—Japan,

Korea, China—look as much to the United States as to Germany, France, or Russia.

■ ■ ■

If only this new American ripeness could penetrate the American bastions of performance. Too many orchestras and opera companies seem not to notice or to care. Funding for unusual business is scarce. Audiences, spoon-fed brand-name European masterworks, continue to set taste. Only in the United States could an indigenous musical landmark as formidable as Bolcom's *Songs of Innocence and of Experience* wait two decades for a recording. Only four professional American orchestras have even performed it. The premiere, under Dennis Russell Davies, took place in Stuttgart, whose state-subsidized opera footed the bill for the expanded orchestra, three choruses, and nine vocal soloists. Similar tales could be told of European partiality to works by Carter and Glass that are less affordable in the United States. In any European land, a symphonic achievement of the magnitude of John Adams's *Naïve and Sentimental Music* would be broadcast, recorded, and widely played. In the United States, as of 2004, only Adams, Alan Gilbert, David Robertson, Esa-Pekka Salonen, and David Zinman had conducted it; as Adams enjoys a charmed relationship with Nonesuch Records, a recording appeared in 2002 to help do the work of derelict American music directors (mostly foreign-born) who feel no obligation toward important American music.

If the music of Adams, Glass, and Reich has an American home, it is the Brooklyn Academy of Music. The creator of that home was not a music director but a self-made impresario: Harvey Lichtenstein. When Lichtenstein arrived at BAM as executive director in 1967, it was a moribund fifty-seven-year-old facility in a moribund neighborhood. But the main auditorium was an opera house, with two thousand seats, more plausibly scaled than the Met or New York State Theater at Lincoln Center, and there were two smaller performance spaces as well. Lichtenstein reasoned that if BAM were to again become the vibrant institution it had been when Brooklyn was vibrant, he would have to draw patrons from Manhattan, which would require offering what Manhattan did not. As with Oscar Hammerstein, this David-and-Goliath act proved that one man can make a great difference in determining what opportunities are offered gifted performing artists and their actual and potential audiences. (Would that PBS had found such a person to oversee its classical music programming.) Lichtenstein's first seasons included the decades' overdue New York premiere of Berg's *Lulu*, as conducted and directed by Sarah Caldwell; the first major New York season ever afforded

Merce Cunningham, the maverick choreographer long associated with John Cage; the return from European exile of the Living Theatre of Julian Beck and Judith Malina; and Robert Wilson's state-of-the-art epic *The Life and Times of Sigmund Freud*. Over the course of a mercurial thirty-year tenure, Lichtenstein proceeded to forge sustained relationships with the theater directors Peter Brook and Ingmar Bergman, with the Royal Shakespeare Company, and with a variety of important younger choreographers including two, Mark Morris and Jiri Kylian, clairvoyantly sensitized to classical music.

As a former dancer, Lichtenstein was not only attuned to the important new dance companies; he assumed the importance of new work in the performing arts generally. As BAM was not the place for classical ballet, neither was it any longer intended for classical music as elsewhere understood. Lichtenstein offered *Einstein on the Beach*, *Nixon in China*, the Philip Glass Ensemble, Steve Reich and Musicians. He impetuously installed Lukas Foss as music director of the resident Brooklyn Philharmonic. He heedlessly dismantled a resident chamber music series (stranding its subscribers). And in 1989 he began presenting, as BAM Opera, exceptional productions of unusual repertoire. William Christie's Les Arts Florissants regularly visited from France with stagings of French Baroque works no longer considered stageworthy. The seamless musical-dramatic integration of Christie's revelatory Rameau and Lully, paralleling the high polish sublimely attained by such Lichtenstein favorites as Bergman, Wilson, Morris, and Kylian, embodied an ideal unknown to Manhattan's two repertoire opera houses. And Lichtenstein found other such productions: Verdi directed by Peter Stein; Schoenberg and Bartók directed by Robert Lepage.

The BAM formula—including tenacious fund-raising, driven by Lichtenstein and his development genius Karen Hopkins, and tenacious salesmanship, driven by Lichtenstein and a series of harassed and overworked marketing directors—triumphed in New York; by 1987, even Lincoln Center had cloned a version of BAM's Next Wave Festival. And it triumphed nationally: in place of touring pianists, string quartets, and orchestras with their dwindling audiences, the eclectic postmodern entertainments pedigreed by BAM began turning up everywhere.

"Presenters" like Lichtenstein—importers of finished goods, not "producers" of first-time concert and stage events—broke away from traditional high culture, including classical music, in ways orchestras and opera companies did or could not. In the case of presenters on university campuses, there was a dawning awareness that universities and their affiliates could take on some of the cultural initiatives, including the commissioning of new work, once shouldered by an American patronage class, and still substantially supported by governments abroad. Leon Botstein, as president of Bard College and music director of the American Symphony, was a leading force in pushing for a more intellectually adventurous, less ghettoized classical music experience.

Meanwhile, individual classical musicians reinvented themselves as postmodern artists. The most astonishing case is Gidon Kremer, a peerless advocate of Schubert and Shostakovich, of Pärt and Gubaidulina, of the Argentine tango guru Astor Piazzolla. As of 2000, Kremer had his own Austrian summer festival and his own crack ensemble of young Baltic musicians; he rarely performed with orchestra. The closest thing to an American Kremer is the cellist Yo-Yo Ma, also a supreme instrumentalist, who has similarly restricted his concerto engagements in favor of projects like The Silk Road, a collaboration with Asian composers and folk musicians. The Kronos Quartet, formed in California in 1973, has dedicated its energies to postmodern repertoire and won an avid following.

More traditional instrumentalists, hard-pressed to keep up with so much change, increasingly reject twentieth-century specialization. As such important composers as Adams, Boulez, and Salonen have returned to the pre-twentieth-century composer/performer norm, a plethora of major pianists and violinists—think of Daniel Barenboim, Christoph Eschenbach, Pinchas Zukerman, Itzhak Perlman, Mikhael Pletnyev—have launched podium careers big and small. The single-purpose performance specialists—Heifetz, Horowitz, Rubinstein—are demonstrably a dying breed: an ephemeral twentieth-century phenomenon. So, too, is a subset: the specialist "interpreter" who diligently aspires toward worshipful fidelity to old fashions and styles. Anton Rubinstein's Beethoven specialties included his own thundering version of the *Egmont* Overture as well as Op. 111. Theodore Thomas's Schumann specialties included *Träumerei* with whispering strings, as well as the four symphonies. Twenty-first-century performers need to loosen up.

If the simplest accommodation to the twenty-first century is enjoyed by presenters, and individual performers are acquiring a new versatility, the toughest act to change is that of full-time opera companies and orchestras with resident musicians, fixed costs, and weighty traditions. Compared to a dance or theater troupe, an orchestra, whether on a concert stage or in an opera pit, cannot be the measure of all things: its distinctive configuration of strings, winds, brass, and percussion chiefly suits a repertoire beginning with Mozart and Haydn and ending with Romantic cathedrals of sound or modernist pagan rites. The American orchestra that has most aggressively challenged the traditional template may be the orchestra at BAM. Under Lukas Foss, Dennis Russell Davies, and Robert Spano, the Brooklyn Philharmonic has featured—not as sideshows, but as main events—Adams, Glass, and Reich;

McPhee and Harrison; Nancarrow, Bolcom, and (naturally) Foss. Of contemporary Europeans, it early recognized the significance of Górecki, Kancheli, Gubaidulina, and Andriessen. It has also pioneered in presenting concert works in tandem with piquant folk or vernacular sources: flamenco artists with Gerhard and Falla; gamelan orchestras with Debussy and McPhee; Russian folk ceremonies with Stravinsky; Hungarian gypsy and peasant dances with Brahms, Bartók, and Ligeti. This considered interpenetration of musical worlds, which has since proved popular and compelling on other symphonic stages, more than hints at new and necessary opportunities to supersede classical music.* But the Philharmonic's crippled infrastructure and a fractious relationship with BAM curtailed further experiments.

The most conspicuously adventurous of the fifty-two-week orchestras have come not from the old guard in Boston, New York, Philadelphia, Chicago, and Cleveland, but from the West Coast. Building on the Edo de Waart/John Adams years, and the Bay Area's established subcultural tendencies, the San Francisco Symphony in 1995 hired an irredeemably American music director as susceptible to popular culture as his mentor Leonard Bernstein. Michael Tilson Thomas bonded with San Francisco. And he shows Bernstein's gift for translating an acute awareness of America's quest for a musical identity of its own into an absorbing institutional quest. Thomas made his statement with a seventeen-day "American Mavericks" Festival in June 2000. The featured composers included Ives, Varèse, Antheil, Ruggles, Seeger, and Cowell; Babbitt and Nancarrow; Cage, Feldman, Foss, and Harrison; Riley, Reich, and Adams—and also Aaron Copland and Duke Ellington. The result was less a thesis than a revised and updated musical topography: a museum of modern and contemporary art in place of the "ageless" symphonic edifices elsewhere perpetuated.

Meanwhile, in Los Angeles, an activist orchestra manager, Ernest Fleischmann, insisted on shaking up his own Los Angeles Philharmonic. When he could not persuade Simon Rattle to become his music director, Fleischmann

---

* The author was the principal architect of this programming experiment, of which Linda Sanders wrote in *Civilization* (May 1998), "The Brooklyn approach essentially redefines the symphony orchestra from purveyor of the canon to community center for music and musical knowledge," and Alex Ross wrote in the *New Yorker* (November 1997) that the Brooklyn Philharmonic "more or less went off the grid of American orchestral culture." An audience survey showed that 88 percent of the orchestra's subscribers valued "the fact that the BPO is a different kind of concert-going experience," that 79 percent believed it "should play challenging music, especially 20th century pieces and music I haven't heard before," and only 38 percent wanted "more big name soloists and guest conductors." For more, see "Post-Classical Music in Brooklyn" in Joseph Horowitz, *The Post-Classical Predicament: Essays on Music and Society* (Boston, Northeastern University Press, 1995).

in 1989 took a knowing gamble on thirty-one-year-old Esa-Pekka Salonen. Salonen comes from Finland, where generous government subsidies have brought sophisticated contemporary music into the classical music mainstream. Accordingly, Salonen is not a performance specialist but a composer/conductor with a passion for such European modernists as Stravinsky, Bartók, Schoenberg, Ligeti, and Lutoslawski. "I think it would be healthier if every performer had some aspect of authoring, and vice versa," he has said. "This . . . works so much better in pop and rock, where these limits between creating and performing are so much more flexible and fluid." In the same interview, Salonen related going to Paris to hear the French National Orchestra perform one of his compositions: "French radio had booked me and my wife into a little bed and breakfast kind of place, close to the radio building. I started complaining loudly to my wife, 'Look at this dump. How could any human being exist in this kind of place? It's just awful.' And she looked at me and said, 'Look. You are being treated as a composer, don't forget.' That was a very good lesson, because I was the same guy who, when conducting, was staying at five-star hotels in Paris. It's crazy, ridiculous, but that's how it is."[8] Salonen has made the Los Angeles orchestra his own, guiding it to a pinnacle of sleek un-Romantic virtuosity. He is too creative a musician to pose as a re-creative generalist. If American music is generally not for him, he has made his home in Los Angeles; his concerted explorations of Schoenberg and Stravinsky paid special attention to their Los Angeles connection; his Los Angeles recordings, in addition to Adams's *Naïve and Sentimental Music,* include important Latin American repertoire by Silvestre Revueltas and a program of excerpts from *Psycho, Vertigo,* and five other classic Hollywood scores by Bernard Herrmann. His orchestra's Walt Disney Concert Hall, new in 2003, is itself a creative achievement. As designed by Frank Gehry, it so positions the musicians that the surrounding audience becomes part of the main event. Rather than occupying a raised platform from which it speaks on high, the Philharmonic is communally experienced by listeners themselves situated at a height. Gehry's playful architecture contributes to a casual, extroverted space that negates the impulse to worship. The very opposite of a church, Disney Hall is today as timely as was Henry Higginson's Symphony Hall a century ago.

Not that musicians in Higginson's day were as deified as in Toscanini times. In the early years of the Bayreuth Festival, Richard Wagner would receive visitors at his home every Monday and Thursday night at 8:30. Anyone could walk in the door. One who did, in 1882, was the future conductor Felix Weingartner, then nineteen years old. "There was a heterogeneous collection of people present," Weingartner later recalled.

The venerable figure of Franz Liszt caught the eye at once. . . . Wagner hurried to meet Liszt, threw his arms about his neck and poured out a spate of excited affectionate words. This touching scene, which I witnessed by a mere chance, was only a prelude. Immediately afterwards Wagner entered the reception room and greeted his guests. . . .

Wagner shook hands with us all amicably and asked us whether we had seen any of the performances. He seemed to notice that I was agitated, for he suddenly laid his hand on my chest and called out, "your heart is palpitating!" When I was silent in surprise and confusion, he said in an unadulterated Saxon dialect: "Well, well, for a young man such as you are, the Flower Maidens are the principal attraction in *Parsifal*, but they mustn't make you lose your heart." Then he shook hands with us again. We were already at the door when his voice rang out again: "But don't lose your heart." I turned around. There stood Wagner, alone in the middle of the room. Smilingly he waved his hand to me.[9]

Could a Toscanini or Karajan be imagined receiving visitors twice a week at the Salzburg Festival? They were far too Olympian. And yet these performance specialists must be considered midgets alongside a Wagner or Liszt. Would that service to a major living composer were applied as a criterion of sanity to our loftiest present-day maestros. As Seidl once served Wagner, as Koussevitzky served Copland or Stokowski served Varèse, Tilson Thomas has known and served Copland and Ruggles; in Los Angeles, Salonen has received György Ligeti and Witold Lutoslawski as honored guests. At least as typical is the "major" music director who remains a stranger except to himself, whose aloofness is reinforced by his podium and whose glamour, as in Hollywood, is pedigreed by his income.

That Sir Simon Rattle is the most sought after of today's younger conductors is a positive and revealing sign. In Birmingham, he was a veritable Theodore Thomas, both remaking the orchestra and repositioning it in the civic consciousness until it rivaled soccer and rugby as a focus of communal attention. As music director of the Berlin Philharmonic since 2002, he has lent his full authority and participation to a vanguard initiative designed to embrace a younger and broader public via such contemporary composers as Ligeti and György Kurtág. Twenty-first-century orchestras are challenged to reinvent a mission transcending the act of performance. To date, the education programs they administer tend to be satellite enterprises of no intellectual distinction. But some orchestras may yet become what many art museums are: centers for education and the humanities, equally linked to public school classrooms and cutting-edge scholarship. It is no longer enough to serve as great vehicles for great music.

■ ■ ■

If Simon Rattle suggests a role model for twenty-first-century conductors, John Adams suggests a role model for twenty-first-century composers. As in Rattle's case, this is partly a function of breadth. In his capacities as conductor and artistic advisor, Adams embodies a reconnection of composers to institutions of performance: a return to the pre–twentieth-century norm. Ideally, some of the excess prestige accorded performers may prove transferable to composers, not least in the eyes of performing musicians themselves. In fact, orchestra members are influential as never before. As fifty-two-week employees, they are a more constant presence than any conductor. No longer can trustees retain a manifestly incompetent music director, like Enrique Jordá in San Francisco, or choose a new music director without support from the players, as occurred when Lorin Maazel was named George Szell's successor in Cleveland in 1972. Musicians attend board meetings, serve on committees, superintend their own outreach activities in schools, nursing homes, and community centers. In some cases, they are already empowered to help choose repertoire and soloists. In others, music directorships will evolve into leadership teams including administrators, members of the orchestra, and a composer or two. Like the dictators Toscanini, Reiner, and Szell, the days of peonage are gone for good.

Some orchestra musicians welcome a deeper institutional involvement, others resist it. In any event, too many are unready. When in 2001 the members of the New York Philharmonic lobbied for Riccardo Muti and, after Muti said no, lobbied successfully for Maazel, they seem not to have realized that orchestras do more than rehearse and perform, that Muti had insufficient time to remold a drifting institution and Maazel insufficient interest. This blinkered perspective, which drives many an orchestra administrator to ask, "Why am I doing this?," is endemic because the culture of performance is strongest where it can do the most harm: at music schools and conservatories. For many gifted young instrumentalists, music school is a type of job training: they want to know how to play the notes and how to win an audition. This parochial agenda is reinforced by teachers of piano and violin who with their time demands and vested interests hold hostage more nuanced institutional priorities. And yet never before have external conditions—the challenged professional world of music and music-making, the insufficiency of instrumental training in America's schools—so demanded a variegated post-classical curriculum including jazz, improvisation, and ethnomusicology, as well as music education and audience development as likely components of most careers. Defending a narrow mandate, the director of a leading American conservatory says, "If it's not broken, don't fix it." Those with heads not in sand or clouds lack the vision or the will to attempt substantial change.*

Gunther Schuller's revolutionary tenure at the helm of Boston's New England Conservatory, from 1967 to 1977, is the exception that proves the rule. As Leopold Stokowski once galvanized the Curtis Institute in support of the Philadelphia Orchestra's American premiere performances of *Wozzeck*, Schuller mounted *Wozzeck*, a consuming institutional adventure, at the New England Conservatory, and presented Schoenberg's gargantuan *Gurrelieder* in the same semester. Sharing his discovery of Scott Joplin, whom he helped to rescue from obscurity, he created a Ragtime Ensemble that toured the United States, Europe, and Russia and made a best-selling recording. Culling Boston's own musical past, he revived John Knowles Paine's Mass of 1865. He created the first full-fledged jazz department of any American music school, and with it a Duke Ellington Orchestra, which performed his own transcriptions of Ellington classics years before Wynton Marsalis; he also fielded a swing band, a Paul Whiteman Orchestra, and a country fiddle band. He invented an early music department and mounted Monteverdi's *Orfeo* with a seventeenth-century orchestra including theorbos, sackbuts, and recorders. He hired seventeen composers to rebalance the faculty in pursuit of graduating "complete musicians." Schuller is unique: he importantly composes and conducts, researches and writes. Updating the spadework of Thurber and Dvořák, he equally espouses classical music and jazz; he compasses a broader swath of American music than any other musician of his generation. At the New England Conservatory, he was less an educator than a zealous creator whose initiatives spilled into pedagogy and whose pedagogical achievements reshaped the musical life of a city.

At the Eastman School, Howard Hanson and his second successor, Robert Freeman, set priorities less favoring a factory for virtuosos and would-be

---

* In no music school or conservatory is much attention paid to the institutional history of classical music or to the history of music in performance—that is, to the preponderant subject matter of the present book. Young musicians need to know about the history of the orchestra and of individual orchestras, of opera and of opera houses, of conducting and of conductors. These are topics that lead, early on, to essential questions otherwise overlooked: What are the purposes of a concert? What are a performer's obligations to an audience? What is the role of music in society? Too often, the musicians most indifferent or hostile to undertaking new roles are not the veterans, but young instrumentalists proud of their ignorance. It is not enough to teach music history as a history of composers and compositions.

virtuosos than at other schools of comparable renown. Freeman, whose pedagogical priorities include intellectual development and community service, properly decries the fragmentation of American classical music into "islands" of activity. Public television embraced as *Great Performances* a Lincoln Center island rather than elsewhere seeking opera and concerts fresher than the Met's Verdi or the New York Philharmonic's Beethoven. What Schuller's New England Conservatory was to education, Robert Hurwitz's Nonesuch and Klaus Heymann's Naxos have been to recordings. While the "major" labels complained or assumed that only brand names would sell, Hurwitz and Heymann showed that names new and unfamiliar, delivered stylishly or inexpensively, could find an audience.

A decades-old contemporary music island, with its own venerable gurus, remains largely invisible from the distant land mass of mainstream symphony and opera. The academic island, too, is needlessly remote. It would be illuminating to compare the percentage of American historians studying American history (reasonably high) with the number of American musicologists studying American music (disappointingly low); as with American classical music generally, the European canon continues to loom larger than it should. At the annual meeting of the American Musicological Society (an organization indebted to twentieth-century German immigrants), only 93 of 624 papers from 1998 to 2001 dealt with topics in American music.[10] For every Michael Beckerman, David Schiff, Richard Taruskin, or Robert Winter, scrutinizing the vagaries and celebrating the triumphs of the American musical experience, challenging the public with writings and lectures, hundreds of musical scholars live island lives. No writer on music since Henry Krehbiel has so seamlessly ranged from daily criticism to ceaseless scholarship, or played so active a role in the musical life of a city: influentially befriending Seidl and Dvořák, researching music and race, annotating the Philharmonic concerts, proselytizing for Wagner in person and in print. Krehbiel, Seidl, and Dvořák—all of whom taught when they were not writing, conducting, or composing—were not island dwellers. And New York City music, by any later standard, was a unity a century ago. Today's fractured cultural environment is not the place for ivory towers. When in the 1980s the *New York Times* stopped making its critics write in the third person, this was a terminally embattled posture of lordly objectivity: there was no cultural consensus to gird it. Logically, this concession—*Times* critics can now write "I"—dictates a more engaged critical presence. In composition, too, the postmodern future holds out the prospect of productive intercourse between previously separated musical worlds.

Music as a mirror of society has at various moments seemed a useful metaphor or misguided cliché. (The reader will recall earlier discussions of the orchestra or opera house as embodiments of a new monied elite, or as instruments of social control.) Be that as it may, at the turn of the twenty-first century, the troubled status of classical music in the United States suggests a metaphor for geopolitical disarray. Certainly the twentieth-century American trends explored in this book—toward a culture of performance, sidelining the composer, supporting commodification—have crossed over to classical music in Europe. Insofar as this is so, the mutant American model of a performer-based musical high culture has become the dominant model, in parallel with American dominance as a political superpower and superpurveyor of fast-food mass culture. And, as at the White House, American classical music is crippled by a crisis in leadership. As Joe Klein writes in his biography of Bill Clinton:

> Marketing has been the most insidious force in the shrinking of public life. The ubiquitous pollsters and advertising consultants who dominated late-twentieth-century politics were thuddingly pragmatic. They asked people what they wanted. The answers were always predictable: better schools, better health care, safer streets—and lower taxes. And so, the politicians themselves became thuddingly pragmatic. They became followers, not leaders—the most slavish, craven sort of followers, trailing desperately after the whims and wisps of public opinion as discerned by their pollsters and media consultants. Their messages tended to congeal in the safest, most conservative precincts of the political middle, without any of the spontaneous brilliance and stray eccentricities and unplanned moments of courage that sparkle when a true leader is at work.[11]

The indulged and uninquisitive American electorate thus engendered is paralleled by American classical music audiences that, as countless musicians will privately testify, ask for little and give little back. A tangible acuity of knowing attention still to be found in Berlin or Budapest—a spur to performer and listener alike—is no longer much encountered in New York. Every American orchestra and opera house of size has, or hopes to obtain, its own marketing guru, whose business it is to devise strategies—invariably impinging on repertoire—to sell more tickets. They may succeed—but does music benefit?

What does "classical music" mean today? If the term is to retain anything like its old aplomb, it must refer to a moment now past and to its attendant prestige and influence. What comes next in these post-classical times? We will find out. Certainly we will not abandon Bach and Beethoven. Bruckner's symphonies will continue to furnish cathedral experiences in the concert hall. But this tradition, on its own, can only diminish. Renewal, if renewal there will be, will likely come from the outside—from a postmodernism freed from the pantheon and its backward pull. The possible convergence of old ways and new will greatly depend on composers and other persons determined to lead taste.

What the composers may contribute remains an open question. The art historian Arthur Danto has declared the "end of art," a "post-historical moment" marking an end to a "great master narrative" of six centuries. "There can now be no historically mandated form of art," he writes.[12] In music, the recidivism of a Richard Strauss, defying the modernist imperative to innovate, proclaimed that music can take any style: a premise echoed in the United States by the repentant tonalists Rochberg and Del Tredici, and by the "new Romantics" Stephen Albert and John Corigliano. Posthistoricism equally expounds that anything can be art—or music: a premise proclaimed by Cage. If the master narrative is indeed over (and music typically lags behind the visual arts in aesthetic fashion), are Glass, Reich, and Adams a post-pantheon phenomenon? A new chapter in the narrative? A footnote merely? How influentially might they challenge the culture of performance bequeathed by the twentieth century?

Equally unknowable, equally crucial is the coming contribution of the tastemakers—the people who run orchestras and opera companies, write about them, broadcast and record them. Traditionally, America's high-cultural currents have benefited from the shaping initiatives of individuals of vision, or have submitted to the vicissitudes of the market. Practical dreamers—Theodore Thomas, Henry Higginson, Jeannette Thurber, Anton Seidl, Oscar Hammerstein in the vibrant early decades of American classical music; Leopold Stokowski, Serge Koussevitzky, and the young Leonard Bernstein in the conflicted middle years—once mapped a distinctive New World. In a later phase, classical music more became a business whose commercial challenges and opportunities swallowed up the entrepreneurial visionaries who were artists first and businessmen second. Sarah Caldwell and Harvey Lichtenstein loom smaller than their illustrious predecessors. For David Gockley, bucking the tide in Houston becomes increasingly Herculean: the relative costs, versus mass-produced entertainments, continue to mount; the indispensable funders, absent government monies, grow less generous and more conservative; urban demographics strand and shrink the available audience. "The faster I go," he says, "the behinder I get";[13] as elsewhere, there is too much classical-music "product" for the present-day classical music market. And, behind the scenes, there is far too little music-making in home and school.

This account of classical music in the United States began with John Sullivan Dwight, whose worshipful promulgation of dead European composers defined "classical music" in contradistinction to popular culture generally and—in the case of the Peace Jubilee of 1869, with its anvil-pounding firemen—Patrick Gilmore specifically. Gilmore's eclecticism—mixing high and low, New Worlds and Old—blithely embodied what classical music was not. Today, closing the circle, it is Dwight who signifies the past and Gilmore who suggests the future. No more than Patrick Gilmore are Reich or Glass, Adams or Kremer "classical musicians." Rather, they are eclectics for whom neither Europe nor the concert hall represents the measure of all things musical. Unquestionably, they point toward a post-classical music of the future. But there is no predicting the topography of this new terrain, or its crucial impact on the residual classical music landscape it will diminish or synergistically refresh.

NOTES

APOLOGIA (*pp. xiii–xix*)

1. Alexis de Tocqueville, *Democracy in America* (1835; repr., New York, A. A. Knopf, 1945), vol. 2, book 1, chapter 9, pp. 40–41.
2. *New York Times*, Mar. 7, 1991.

BOOK ONE "Queen of the Arts": Birth and Growth

INTRODUCTION: A TALE OF TWO CITIES (1893) (*pp. 5–11*)

1. *New York Herald*, Dec. 16, 1993.
2. *New York Herald*, May 21, 1893. *New York Tribune*, Dec. 15, 1893.
3. Composers quoted in Adrienne Fried Block, "Dvořák, Beach, and American Music," in Richard Crawford, R. Allen Lott, and Carol J. Oja (eds.), *A Celebration of American Music: Words and Music in Honor of H. Wiley Hitchcock* (Ann Arbor, Mich., University of Michigan Press, 1990). pp. 258–261.
4. Hale in *Boston Journal*, undated clipping in Boston Symphony Orchestra Archives, and *Musical Courier*, Jan. 4, 1894. Apthorp in *Boston Transcript*, Jan. 1, 1894.
5. Boston Symphony Orchestra program, Dec. 23 and 24, 1910.
6. *Boston News*, undated clipping in Brown Collection, Boston Public Library (the performance was Nov. 28, 1892). Hale ("homesick") in Boston Symphony Orchestra program, Dec. 23 and 24, 1910. Hale in *Boston Journal*, undated clipping in Boston Symphony Orchestra Archives (the performance was in Jan. 1893). Krehbiel cited in Michael Beckerman (ed.), *Dvořák and His World* (Princeton, Princeton University Press, 1993), p. 166.
7. Karl Baedeker (ed.), *The United States: Handbook for Travellers* (Leipzig, 1893), p. 23. Ira Rosenwaite, *Population History of New York City* (Syracuse, Syracuse University Press, 1972). Boston statistics from U.S. Census of 1890, the number of Irish determined by country of birth plus country of birth of mother.
8. Bülow in *Chicago Times*, Feb. 6, 1876. Chadwick and Parker quoted in Richard Crawford, *America's Musical Life: A History* (New York, W. W. Norton, 2001), p. 354.

PART ONE: BOSTON AND THE CULT OF BEETHOVEN
CHAPTER 1: JOHN SULLIVAN DWIGHT, THEODORE THOMAS, AND THE SLAYING OF THE MONSTER CONCERTS (*pp. 15–42*)

1. This account draws upon *Dwight's Journal of Music*, June 19, July 3, and July 17, 1869, and Patrick Gilmore, *History of the National Peace Jubilee and Great Musical Festival* (Boston, published by the author, 1871).
2. *New York Tribune*, June 28, 1869. *New York Sun*, June 23, 1869.

3. According to Henry C. Watson in *The Musical Review and Choral Advocate*, Dec. 1853, as cited in Vera Brodsky Lawrence (ed.), *Strong on Music: The New York Music Scene in the Days of George Templeton Strong, 1836–1875*, vol. 2: *Reverberations 1850–1856* (Chicago, University of Chicago Press, 1995), p. 363.

4. Gilmore, *History of the National Peace Jubilee*, pp. 53–57.

5. Ibid., p. 418.

6. Dwight quotes from Michael Broyles, *Music of the Highest Class: Elitism and Populism in Antebellum Boston* (New Haven, Yale University Press, 1992), pp. 244–257, and Lawrence Levine, *Highbrow/Lowbrow: The Emergence of Cultural Hierarchy in America* (Cambridge, Mass., Harvard University Press, 1988), p. 121.

7. This account draws upon *Dwight's Journal of Music*, June 29, July 13, July 27, and Aug. 10, 1872.

8. H. Earle Johnson, *Hallelujah, Amen! The Story of the Handel and Haydn Society of Boston* (Boston, B. Humphries, 1965), pp. 34, 39.

9. Quoted in John Swan, *Music in Boston: Readings from the First Three Centuries* (Boston, Trustees of the Public Library of the City of Boston, 1977), p. 81. See also, in the same volume, readings by Lowell Mason, J. S. Dwight, and W. F. Apthorp.

10. Nancy Newman, "Good Music for a Free People: The Germania Musical Society and Transatlantic Musical Culture of the Mid-Nineteenth Century" (dissertation, Brown University, 2002). See especially pp. 59–61, 353–354, 370.

11. Quoted in Swan, *Music in Boston*, p. 76.

12. *Dwight's Journal of Music*, Oct. 6, 1869; Oct. 8, Oct. 22, Nov. 5, 1870. On Dresel, see especially David Urrows, "Apollo in Athens: Otto Dresel and Boston 1850–90," in *American Music*, Winter 1994. On early Boston orchestras, see also H. Earle Johnson, *Symphony Hall* (Boston, Little, Brown, 1950) and John Sullivan Dwight, "Music in Boston," in Justin Winsor (ed.), *The Memorial History of Boston*, vol. 4 (Boston, J. R. Osgood and Company, 1883).

13. Charles Edward Russell, *The American Orchestra and Theodore Thomas* (Garden City, N.Y., Doubleday, Page and Company, 1927), pp. 2–3.

14. Ezra Schabas, *Theodore Thomas: America's Conductor and Builder of Orchestras, 1835–1905* (Urbana, University of Illinois Press, 1981), p. 9.

15. Theodore Thomas, *Theodore Thomas, A Musical Autobiography*, edited by George Upton (1905; repr. New York, Da Capo Press, 1964), pp. 3, 127.

16. Rubinstein and Lehmann quoted in Joseph Horowitz, *Wagner Nights: An American History* (Berkeley, University of California Press, 1994), pp. 53–54.

17. Upton quote in Thomas, *Musical Autobiography*, p. 215. Aldrich quote in Joseph Horowitz, *Understanding Toscanini: How He Became an American Culture God and Helped Create a New Audience for Old Music* (New York, A. A. Knopf, 1987). p. 30. Thomas quotes in Schabas, *Theodore Thomas*, p. 229, and Philip Hart, *Orpheus in the New World: The Symphony Orchestra as an American Cultural Institution* (New York, W. W. Norton, 1973), p. 38.

18. All quotes from Horowitz, *Wagner Nights*, pp. 53–72.

19. Thomas, *Musical Autobiography*, p. 51.

20. Dwight quotes from Winsor, *Memorial History of Boston*, vol. 4, p. 446. Arthur Foote, "A Bostonian Remembers," *Musical Quarterly*, vol. 23 (1937), p. 42. Apthorp quoted in Swan, *Music in Boston*, pp. 77–78. Strauss quoted in *Dwight's Journal of Music*, July 27, 1872.

21. William Apthorp, "John Sullivan Dwight," in William Apthorp, *Musicians and Music-Lovers, and Other Essays* (New York, C. Scribner's Sons, 1894).

22. Thomas Ryan, *Recollections of an Old Musician* (Boston, E. P. Dutton, 1899), p. 120.

23. Dwight quoted in Swan, *Music in Boston*, pp. 62, 65.

24. Thomas quotes from Thomas, *Musical Autobiography*, pp. 335, 336, 341. Van Wyck Brooks, "America's Coming of Age," in *Three Essays on America* (New York, E. P. Dutton, 1934).

CHAPTER 2: HENRY HIGGINSON AND THE
BIRTH OF THE BOSTON SYMPHONY ORCHESTRA (*pp. 43–69*)

1. Quotes from M. A. D. Howe, *The Boston Symphony Orchestra 1881–1931* (Boston, Houghton Mifflin, 1931), pp. 16–20. The account of Henry Higginson also draws heavily on Philip Hart, *Orpheus in the New World: The Symphony Orchestra as an American Cultural Institution* (New York, W. W. Norton, 1973); Bliss Perry, *The Life and Letters of Henry Lee Higginson* (Boston, Atlantic Monthly, 1921); and clippings in the Boston Symphony Orchestra Archives.
2. *Dwight's Journal of Music*, Apr. 9, 1881.
3. *Boston Transcript*, Sept. 9, 1881.
4. Unidentified clipping, Boston Symphony Orchestra Archives. The account of Henschel's tenure is mainly based on newspaper articles and reviews to be found in these archives.
5. *Traveller* and Elson quoted in Howe, *Boston Symphony Orchestra 1881–1931*, p. 43.
6. Brahms quoted in George Henschel, *Musings and Memories of a Musician* (London, Macmillan, 1918), p. 274. Henschel description from an unidentified clipping, Boston Symphony Orchestra Archives. Eggschel announcement in *Boston Home Journal*, undated clipping (Oct. 1881), Boston Symphony Orchestra Archives.
7. Letter quoted in Howe, *Boston Symphony Orchestra 1881–1931*, p. 39. Newspaper quotes from unidentified clippings, Boston Symphony Orchestra Archives.
8. Higginson and *Advertiser* quoted in Howe, *Boston Symphony Orchestra 1881–1931*, pp. 28, 41.
9. Henschel, *Musings and Memories of a Musician*, p. 282.
10. Rose Fay Thomas, *Memoirs of Theodore Thomas* (New York, Moffat, Yard, 1911), p. 214.
11. Collected in the Boston Symphony Orchestra Archives. See especially Apr. and Oct. 1884 (e.g., *Evening Transcript*, Oct. 11).
12. Gericke quoted in Howe, *Boston Symphony Orchestra 1881–1931*, p. 67.
13. *Boston Evening Transcript*, Oct. 20, 1884. *Boston Gazette*, Oct. 20, 1884.
14. Gericke quoted in Howe, *Boston Symphony Orchestra 1881–1931*, p. 64. Disciplined musicians in Ellen Knight, *Charles Martin Loeffler: A Life Apart in American Music* (Urbana, University of Illinois Press, 1993), p. 75. Gericke wrote in Howe, p. 65. Franko quoted in Knight, p. 57. The press quoted in Howe, p. 72.
15. *Boston Transcript*, Oct. 11, 1884. Elson quoted in Howe, *Boston Symphony Orchestra 1881–1931*, p. 73.
16. Elson and Gericke quoted in Howe, *Boston Symphony Orchestra 1881–1931*, pp. 69, 73.
17. Quoted in ibid., p. 17.
18. *Boston Globe* and *Boston Evening Transcripts* quoted in Steven Ledbetter, *One Hundred Years of the Boston Pops* (Boston, Boston Symphony, 1985), pp. 4, 7.
19. Gericke quoted in Howe, *Boston Symphony Orchestra 1881–1931*, p. 66.
20. Gericke quoted in Howe, *Boston Symphony Orchestra 1881–1931*, p. 65. Higginson quoted in Perry, *Life and Letters of Henry Lee Higginson*, pp. 307, 308.
21. Richard Wagner, *On Conducting* (New York, Dover, 1987), pp. 30–31, 34–35, 37.
22. Henry Finck (ed.), *Anton Seidl: A Memorial by His Friends* (New York, C. Scribner's Sons, 1899), pp. 114–116.
23. Tchaikovsky and Clara Schumann quoted in Julius H. Block, *Mortals and Immortals* (distributed by Yale University library, 1965), pp. 54–55.
24. Henderson and Paine quotes from unidentified clippings, Oct. 1889, Boston Symphony Orchestra Archives.
25. All quotes from clippings, mostly undated, Boston Symphony Orchestra Archives.
26. Apthorp on *Tannhäuser* from *Boston Evening Transcript*, undated clipping (Dec. 1889), Boston Symphony Orchestra Archives. Hale cavils from *Boston Home Journal*, Feb. 1, 1890.

27. Clippings, Apr. 29 to May 6, 1893, Boston Symphony Orchestra Archives. Higginson private correspondence, Boston Symphony Orchestra Archives.

28. Higginson private correspondence in Boston Symphony Orchestra Archives; see especially Apr. 25, 1893.

29. *New York Tribune*, Dec. 18, 1889.

30. Krehbiel in *New York Tribune*, Oct. 12, 1889. Florsheim in *Musical Courier*, Mar. 19, 1890.

31. Letter to Higginson in Perry, *Life and Letters of Henry Lee Higginson*, pp. 317–318. Higginson quoted in Howe, *Boston Symphony Orchestra 1881–1931*, p. 87.

32. On Hale, see Jean Ann Boyd, "Philip Hale, American Music Critic: Boston 1885–1933" (dissertation, University of Texas, Austin, 1985).

33. *Boston Home Journal*, Apr. 26, 1890.

34. On Bach, Quaintance Eaton, *The Boston Opera Company* (New York, Appleton-Century, 1965), p. 110. Quotes of gaffes and on Brahms from *Boston Home Journal*, Oct. 19, 1889, and Boyd, "Philip Hale," pp. 98, 61.

35. For an overview of Hale's views of Debussy and other composers, see Boyd, "Philip Hale." Hale's putdowns from Boston Symphony Orchestra program note for the *New World* Symphony, Dec. 23–24, 1910. Quote on Grieg from *Boston Home Journal*, Feb. 1, 1890.

36. *Musical Courier*, Jan. 4, 1894.

37. Clippings (many unidentified) collected in Brown Collection, Boston Public Library (music division). Hale in *Boston Home Journal*, Dec. 22, 1896.

38. Clippings, Brown Collection, Boston Public Library.

39. Cited in Michael Beckerman (ed.), *Dvořák and His World* (Princeton, Princeton University Press, 1993), p. 166.

40. Hale on Foster, etc., in John Swan, *Music in Boston: Readings from the First Three Centuries* (Boston, Trustees of the Public Library of the City of Boston, 1977), pp. 92–93. Hale on Chadwick in Boyd, "Philip Hale."

CHAPTER 3: BUILDING A HALL, CHOOSING A CONDUCTOR (*pp. 70–93*)

1. Higginson quoted in Steven Ledbetter, "Higginson and Chadwick: Non-Brahmins in Boston," *American Music*, vol. 19, no. 1 (Spring 2001), pp. 51–58.

2. Higginson quoted in M. A. D. Howe, *The Boston Symphony Orchestra 1881–1931* (Boston, Houghton Mifflin, 1931), p. 8.

3. Higginson quoted in Bliss Perry, *The Life and Letters of Henry Lee Higginson* (Boston, Atlantic Monthly, 1921), p. 124.

4. Ibid., pp. 142, 179.

5. Higginson quoted in *Symphony Hall: The First One Hundred Years* (Boston, Boston Symphony Orchestra, 2000), p. 13. One million dollars cited in Perry, *Life and Letters of Henry Lee Higginson*, p. 294.

6. Higginson quoted in Perry, *Life and Letters of Henry Lee Higginson*, pp. 392, 315.

7. *Symphony Hall*, p. 30.

8. Higginson quoted in Richard P. Stebbins, *The Making of Symphony Hall Boston* (Boston, Boston Symphony Orchestra, 2000), pp. 16, 21, 130–131.

9. McKim and *Musical Courier* quoted in ibid., pp. 85–93.

10. Higginson quoted in ibid., p. 103.

11. Strauss quoted in Tim Ashley, *Richard Strauss* (London, Phaidon, 1999), p. 82.

12. Higginson private correspondence from Henry Lee Higginson Collection, Baker Library, Harvard Business School. (Copies can also be found in Boston Symphony Orchestra Archives.) Letter to George Chadwick, Apr. 4, 1906. The pertinent correspondence extends to June 4, 1906.

13. Quotes from clippings (mostly unidentified), Boston Symphony Orchestra Archives. Muck quoted in Feb. 1907.

14. Parker quoted in John Swan, *Music in Boston: Readings from the First Three Centuries* (Boston, Trustees of the Public Library of the City of Boston, 1977), p. 96.

15. Ibid., pp. 96–97.

16. Unattributed album note, *The First Recordings of the Boston Symphony*, BSO Classics 171002 (1995).

17. *New York Sun*, Nov. 9, 1906.

18. Gilman and Whiting quoted in Quaintance Eaton, *The Boston Opera Company* (New York, Appleton-Century, 1965), pp. 41–42.

19. Parker, Hale and St. John Brenon quoted in ibid., pp. 41, 44.

20. Fitzgerald quoted in ibid., p. 200.

21. Hale quoted in Jean Ann Boyd, "Philip Hale, American Music Critic: Boston 1885–1933" (dissertation, University of Texas, Austin, 1985), p. 168.

22. Higginson quotes from Perry, *Life and Letters of Henry Lee Higginson*, pp. 480, 482.

23. Ibid., pp. 486–487.

24. Muck's letter quoted in Philip Hart, *Orpheus in the New World: The Symphony Orchestra as an American Cultural Institution* (New York, W. W. Norton, 1973), p. 66.

25. Higginson quoted in Perry, *Life and Letters of Henry Lee Higginson*, pp. 491, 500. Taft and Roosevelt quoted on p. 505.

26. Villard quoted in Rochelle Gurstein, *The Repeal of Reticence: A History of America's Cultural and Legal Struggles Over Free Speech, Obscenity, Sexual Liberation, and Modern Art* (New York, Hill and Wang, 1996), p. 19.

27. Norton quoted in ibid., pp. 22–28.

28. Emerson quoted in Joseph Mussulman, *Music in the Cultured Generation: A Social History of Music in America, 1870–1900* (Evanston, Ill., Northwestern University Press, 1971) pp. 25, 32.

29. Martin Green, *The Problem of Boston: Some Readings in Cultural History* (London, Longmans, 1966), pp. 45–46.

30. D. Maggio and Hamm quoted in Joseph Horowitz, *Wagner Nights: An American History* (Berkeley, University of California Press, 1994), p. 375.

31. Green, *Problem of Boston*, pp. 110–111. Lawrence Levine, *Highbrow/Lowbrow: The Emergence of Cultural Hierarchy in America* (Cambridge, Mass., Harvard University Press, 1988), pp. 123–128.

32. Green, *Problem of Boston*, p. 130.

33. Ibid., pp. 139, 141.

34. Higginson private correspondence (Dec. 7, 1884) from Henry Lee Higginson Collection, Baker Library, Harvard Business School.

35. Higginson quoted in Howe, *Boston Symphony Orchestra 1881–1931*, p. 87.

36. Steven Ledbetter, "Higginson and Chadwick, pp. 56, 58. Bliss, *Life and Letters of Henry Lee Higginson*, pp. 329, 535.

CHAPTER 4: COMPOSERS AND THE BRAHMIN CONFINEMENT (*pp. 94–117*)

1. Martin Green, *The Problem of Boston: Some Readings in Cultural History* (London, Longmans, 1966), p. 192.

2. Ibid., pp. 40, 42, 75.

3. Ibid., pp. 91–92, 99.

4. Ibid., pp. 24, 45–46.

5. Ibid., p. 115.

6. Ibid., p. 175.

7. Billings quoted by H. Wiley Hitchcock, *Music in the United States: A Historical Introduction* (Engle-

wood Cliffs, N.J., Prentice-Hall, 1974), p. 10. Paine quoted by Peter Eliot Stone in album note for Paine's Mass in D, New World Records 80262-3 (1978).

8. Nicholas Temperley, *The Lost Chord: Essays on Victorian Music* (Bloomington, Indiana University Press, 1989), p. 144. Dwight's umbrella in Steven Ledbetter, album note for Paine's Second Symphony, New World Records 350-2 (1987). Chadwick quoted by Ledbetter, album note for Paine's First Symphony, New World Records 374-2 (1989).

9. Arthur Foote, "A Bostonian Remembers," *Musical Quarterly*, vol. 23 (1937), p. 41.

10. Arthur Foote, *Arthur Foote, 1853–1937: An Autobiography* (Norwood, Mass., Plimpton Press, 1946), p. 62.

11. Quoted in Hitchcock, *Music in the United States*, p. 138.

12. Joseph Horowitz, *Conversations with Arrau* (New York, A. A. Knopf, 1982), p. 91.

13. Hale quoted in Adrienne Fried Block, *Amy Beach: The Life and Work of an American Composer, 1867–1944* (New York, Oxford University Press, 1998), p. 31.

14. Dwight quoted by Michael Broyles, *Music of the Highest Class: Elitism and Populism in Antebellum Boston* (New Haven, Yale University Press, 1992), p. 234. Chadwick quoted by Block, *Amy Beach*, p. 103.

15. Block, *Amy Beach*, p. 243.

16. Ibid., p. 99.

17. Ibid., pp. 132, 137, 139.

18. Ibid., pp. 135, 176.

19. Ibid., p. 248.

20. Chadwick quoted in Hon-Lun Yang, "Nationality versus Universality: The Identity of George W. Chadwick's Symphonic Poems," *American Music*, vol. 21, no. 1 (Spring 2003), p. 38.

21. I am indebted to Steven Ledbetter for sharing excerpts from Chadwick's untitled, unpublished family memoir (in possession of the composer's grandson Theodore Chadwick).

22. Victor Fell Yellin, *Chadwick: Yankee Composer* (Washington, D.C., Smithsonian Institution Press, 1990), p. 3.

23. Apthorp and Parker quoted in ibid., pp. 94, 116; Yellin quoted from p. 115.

24. Howells and Mencken quoted in Rochelle Gurstein, *The Repeal of Reticence: A History of America's Cultural and Legal Struggles Over Free Speech, Obscenity, Sexual Liberation and Modern Art* (New York, Hill and Wang, 1996), pp. 118, 133.

25. Joseph Mussulman, *Music in the Cultured Generation: A Social History of Music in America 1870–1900* (Evanston, Ill., Northwestern University Press, 1971), p. 54.

26. Yellin, *Chadwick*, pp. 59, 24.

27. H. L. Mencken, "Theodore Dreiser," reprinted in H. L. Mencken, *The American Scene, A Reader*, edited by Huntington Cairns (New York, A. A. Knopf, 1965).

28. Chadwick's untitled memoirs, courtesy of Steven Ledbetter.

29. Adams quoted in Green, *Problem of Boston*, pp. 149–150.

30. Henry James, *The Bostonians* (1886; repr. New York, Penguin Books, 1984), pp. 45, 67, 70, 164–165, 376.

31. Mary Blanchard, *Oscar Wilde's America: Counter culture in the Gilded Age* (New Haven, Yale University Press, 1998), p. 169.

32. The best account of Gardner and music is Ralph Locke, "Living with Music: Isabella Stewart Gardner," in Ralph Locke and Cyrilla Barr (eds.), *Cultivating Music in America: Women Patrons and Activists since 1860* (Berkeley, University of California Press, 1997). "One recent historian" is Douglass Shand-Tucci, *The Art of Scandal: The Life and Times of Isabella Stewart Gardner* (New York, Harper-Collins, 1997). For Leblanc, see Quaintance Eaton, *The Boston Opera Company* (New York, Appleton-Century, 1965), pp. 140–141.

33. "Recent scholarship" is Ellen Knight, *Charles Martin Loeffler: A Life Apart in American Music* (Urbana, University of Illinois Press, 1993). On German music, see Knight, p. 136.

34. Ibid., pp. 53, 244.

35. Loeffler letter quoted in Shand-Tucci, *The Art of Scandal.*

36. Loeffler quoted in Knight, *Charles Martin Loeffler*, pp. 97, 99, 129, 130, 232.

37. Ibid., pp. 69, 106.

38. Ibid., pp. 150, 230.

39. Henderson quoted in ibid., p. 251.

40. Quotes from ibid., pp. 216, 107.

41. Green, *Problem of Boston*, pp. 147, 119, 107.

PART TWO: NEW YORK AND BEYOND

CHAPTER 5: ANTON SEIDL AND THE SACRALIZATION OF OPERA (*pp. 121–147*)

1. John Dizikes, *Opera in America: A Cultural History* (New Haven, Yale University Press, 1993), p. 63.

2. James quoted in Joseph Horowitz, *Understanding Toscanini: How He Became an American Culture-God and Helped Create a New Audience for Old Music* (New York, A. A. Knopf, 1987), pp. 73–74. Whitman in Dizikes, *Opera in America*, pp. 65, 283. Strong in Joseph Horowitz, *Wagner Nights: An American History* (Berkeley, University of California Press, 1994), p. 73.

3. Dizikes, *Opera in America*, p. 6.

4. Ibid., p. 84.

5. Ibid., p. 30.

6. "Viator," in *Dwight's Journal of Music*, Feb. 29, 1868, quoted in Irving Sablosky (ed.), *What They Heard: Music in America, 1852–1881—From the Pages of Dwight's Journal of Music* (Baton Rouge, Louisiana State University Press, 1986), p. 159.

7. See especially Katherine Preston, *Opera on the Road: Traveling Opera Troupes in the United States, 1825–60* (Urbana, University of Illinois Press, 1993).

8. Edwin M. Good, "William Steinway and Music in New York 1861–1871," in Michael Saffle (ed.), *Music and Culture in America, 1861–1918* (New York, Garland, 1998), pp. 12–14.

9. Lawrence Levine, *Highbrow/Lowbrow: The Emergence of Cultural Hierarchy in America* (Cambridge, Mass., Harvard University Press, 1988), p. 87.

10. Ibid., p. 88.

11. Whitman quoted in Dizikes, *Opera in America*, p. 158. On Lind, see Horowitz, *Understanding Toscanini*, pp. 19–22.

12. Strong quoted in Levine, *Highbrow/Lowbrow*, p. 85.

13. Vera Brodsky Lawrence (ed.), *Strong on Music: The New York Music Scene in the Days of George Templeton Strong, 1836–1875*, vol. 3: *Repercussions 1857–1862* (Chicago, University of Chicago Press, 1999) p. 118.

14. Ibid., pp. 406–412.

15. Max Maretzek, *Crotchets and Quavers, or Revelations of an Opera Manager in America* (New York, S. French, 1855), p. 15.

16. Theodore Thomas, *Theodore Thomas, A Musical Autobiography*, edited by George Upton (1905; repr. New York, Da Capo Press, 1964), pp. 24, 28, 33, 45.

17. Levine, *Highbrow/Lowbrow.*

18. Maretzek and Huneker quoted in Maretzek, *Crotchets and Quavers*, p. 20, and Horowitz, *Understanding Toscanini*, p. 33.

19. Quotes from Dizikes, *Opera in America*, pp. 19, 153.

20. Karen Ahlquist, *Democracy at the Opera: Music, Theater, and Culture in New York City, 1815–60* (Urbana, University of Illinois Press, 1997).

21. Dizikes, *Opera in America*, pp. 172–173.

22. Katherine Preston, "Between the Cracks: The Performance of English-Language Opera in Late

Nineteenth-Century America," *American Music*, vol. 21, no. 3 (Fall 2003), pp. 349–374. Peter G. Davis, *The American Opera Singer: The Lives and Adventures of America's Great Singers in Opera and Concert, from 1825 to the Present* (New York, Doubleday, 1997).

23. On the National Opera, see Joseph Horowitz, *The Post-Classical Predicament: Essays on Music and Society* (Boston, Northeastern University Press, 1995), pp. 168–170. *New York Times* quoted by Ezra Schabas, *Theodore Thomas: America's Conductor and Builder of Orchestras, 1835–1905* (Urbana, University of Illinois Press, 1989), p. 160.

24. Wagner quoted in Stewart Spencer and Barry Millington (eds.), *Selected Letters of Richard Wagner* (London, J. M. Dent, 1987), p. 452.

25. Henry Krehbiel, *Chapters of Opera* (New York, H. Holt and Co., 1908), pp. 170–172.

26. Ibid., p. 171.

27. Lilli Lehmann, *My Path Through Life* (New York, G. P. Putnam's Sons, 1914), p. 366. "Information Bureau," *Musical Courier*, June 22, 1922.

28. Quotes from Horowitz, *Wagner Nights*, pp. 91–92.

29. Ibid., pp. 106–124.

30. Ibid., pp. 138–156, 181–198, 118, 212.

31. Wharton in Diziges, *Opera in America*, p. 189. Dimensions of opera house in Martin Mayer, *The Met: One Hundred Years of Grand Opera* (New York, Simon and Schuster, 1983), p. 36.

32. John Frederick Cone, *First Rival of the Metropolitan Opera* (New York, Columbia University Press, 1983), pp. 21–22.

33. Diziges, *Opera in America*, p. 218. Horowitz, *Wagner Nights*, p. 76.

34. All quotes from Horowitz, *Wagner Nights*, especially pp. 133, 96, 128.

35. Quotes from H. Earle Johnson, *First Performances in America to 1900: Works with Orchestra* (Detroit, Published for the College Music Society by Information Coordinators, 1979), p. 376.

36. Adams and Homer quoted in Diziges, *Opera in America*, p 243.

37. Quotes from Horowitz, *Wagner Nights*, p. 147.

38. Diziges, *Opera in America*, p. 243.

39. Fischer and Seidl quoted in Krehbiel, *Chapters of Opera*, p. 207.

40. Horowitz, *Wagner Nights*, p. 142.

41. See Horowitz, *Wagner Nights*, ch. 12 ("Proto-feminism"). Also T. J. Jackson Lears, *No Place of Grace: Antimodernism and the Transformation of American Culture, 1880–1920* (New York, Pantheon Books, 1981).

42. Cather quoted in Horowitz, *Wagner Nights*, pp. 214, 219, 342.

43. Helen Horowitz, " 'Nous Autres'—Reading, Passion, and the Creation of M. Carey Thomas," *Journal of American History*, June 1992.

44. Ahlquist, *Democracy at the Opera House*, p. 108.

45. Hone quoted and observed by Krehbiel, *Chapters of Opera*, pp. 21, 44.

46. Schott quoted in *New York Times*, Feb. 20, 1885.

47. Oscar Sonneck, *Miscellaneous Studies in the History of Music* (New York, Macmillan, 1921; repr. New York, Da Capo Press, 1968), pp. 91–92.

Chapter 6: Symphonic Rivalry and Growth (*pp. 148–178*)

1. Ureli Corelli Hill, *Diary and Notes from European Trip, 1835–1837* [manuscript], pp. 41, 108, 130, 146, 154, concert program Mar. 5, 1837. New York Philharmonic Archives. I am indebted to the Philharmonic's archivist, Barbara Haws, for obtaining Hill's diary and for clarifying certain details about its contents.

2. Prospectus quote from Howard Shanet, *Philharmonic: A History of New York's Orchestra* (New York, Doubleday, 1975), p. 85.

3. Henry Krehbiel, *The Philharmonic Society of New York: A Memorial* (New York, Novello, Ewer and Co., 1892), reprinted in *Early Histories of the New York Philharmonic* (New York, Da Capo Press, 1979), p. 60.

4. Theodore Thomas, *Theodore Thomas, A Musical Autobiography*, edited by George Upton (1905; repr. New York, Da Capo Press, 1964), p. 36. Violinist quote from George Martin, *The Damrosch Dynasty: America's First Family of Music* (Boston, Houghton Mifflin, 1983), p. 50.

5. Quotes from Mary Sue Morrow, "Somewhere between Beer and Wagner: The Cultural and Musical Impact of German Männerchöre in New York and New Orleans," in Michael Saffle (ed.), *Music and Culture in America, 1861–1918* (New York, Garland, 1998), especially pp. 84–85. Also see, in the same volume, Suzanne G. Snyder, "The Indianapolis Männerchor; Contributions to a New Musicality in Midwestern Life."

6. Finck and Thomas quotes from Joseph Horowitz, *Wagner Nights: An American History* (Berkeley, University of California Press, 1994), p. 159.

7. Damrosch quote from Martin, *Damrosch Dynasty*, p. 56.

8. Tchaikovsky quote from Elkhonon Yoffe, *Tchaikovsky in America: The Composer's Visit in 1891* (New York, Oxford University Press, 1986), p. 58.

9. Tchaikovsky quotes from ibid., p. 169.

10. Tchaikovsy, *Morning Journal*, and *Tribune* quotes from ibid., p. 88.

11. Critics and Carnegie quotes from Richard Schickel, *The World of Carnegie Hall* (New York, Messner, 1960), p. 25.

12. Tchaikovsky diary quote from Yoffe, *Tchaikovsky in America*, p. 111.

13. Martin, *Damrosch Dynasty*, pp. 120, 196. Carnegie uses from Gino Francesconi of the Carnegie Hall Archives.

14. *Herald* quote from Schickel, *World of Carnegie Hall*, p. 46.

15. Horowitz, *Wagner Nights*, ch. 10.

16. Finck, Lehmann, and *Daily Eagle* quotes from ibid, p. 191.

17. I am grateful to Maurice Edwards for sharing with me his unpublished history of the Brooklyn Philharmonic.

18. Steven Bauer, "Music, Morals, and Social Management: Mendelssohn in Post-Civil War America," *American Music*, vol. 19, no. 1 (Spring 2001). *Daily Eagle* quoted in Horowitz, *Wagner Nights*, p. 194.

19. Repertoire and Seidl's quote from Horowitz, *Wagner Nights*, pp. 205, 211.

20. Henry Finck, *My Adventures in the Golden Age of Music* (New York, Funk and Wagnalls, 1926; repr. New York, Da Capo Press, 1971), p. 255.

21. Damrosch quote from Horowitz, *Wagner Nights*, p. 178.

22. According to Robert Tuggle of the Metropolitan Opera Archives.

23. *Staats-Zeitung* quoted in Horowitz, *Wagner Nights*, p. 35. Hermann Mosenthal (ed.), *Geschichte des verein Deutcher Liederkranz in New York* (New York, F. A. Ringler, 1897), a copy of which can be found at the Music Library of Columbia University.

24. Finck quotes from Horowitz, *Wagner Nights*, pp. 247–248.

25. Finck and *Staats-Zeitung* quotes from ibid., pp. 11–17.

26. The account of the beginnings of the Chicago Orchestra is principally based on Philip Hart, *Orpheus in the New World: The Symphony Orchestra as an American Cultural Institution* (New York, W. W. Norton, 1973); Helen Horowitz, *Culture & the City: Cultural Philanthropy in Chicago from the 1880's to 1917* (Lexington, University of Kentucky Press, 1976); Ellis A. Johnson, "The Chicago Symphony Orchestra 1891–1924" (dissertation, University of Chicago, 1955); John H. Mueller, *The American Symphony Orchestra: A Social History of Musical Taste* (Bloomington, Indiana University Press, 1951); Philo A. Otis, *The Chicago Symphony Orchestra: Its Organization, Growth and Development, 1891–1924* (Chicago, Clayton F. Summy, 1925); Ezra Schabas, *Theodore Thomas: America's*

Conductor and Builder of Orchestras, 1835–1905 (Urbana, University of Illinois Press, 1989); and Theodore Thomas, *Theodore Thomas: A Musical Autobiography*, edited by George Upton (1905; repr. New York, Da Capo Press, 1964).

27. Horowitz, *Culture and the City*.

28. Fay and Thomas quotes from Johnson, "Chicago Symphony Orchestra 1891–1924," p. 44.

29. Schabas, *Theodore Thomas*, p. 191.

30. Johnson, "Chicago Symphony Orchestra 1891–1924," p. 53. Mathews quoted in Schabas, *Theodore Thomas*, p. 189.

31. Higginbotham quote from Schabas, *Theodore Thomas*, p. 209.

32. Healy quote from Johnson, "Chicago Symphony Orchestra 1891–1924," p. 73.

33. *Record Herald*, Higginbotham, and Thomas quotes from Schabas, *Theodore Thomas*, p. 208.

34. Thomas quoted in Johnson, "Chicago Symphony Orchestra 1891–1924," p. 87. Rose Fay quoted in Schabas, *Theodore Thomas*, p. 210.

35. Thomas quote from Horowitz, *Wagner Nights*, p. 71.

36. *New York Times*, Hale, New York, and *New York Press* quotes from Schabas, *Theodore Thomas*, pp. 223–225.

37. Max Maretzek, *Crochets and Quavers, or Revelations of an Opera Manager in America* (New York, S. French, 1855), p. 318.

38. Thomas quote from Joseph Horowitz, *Understanding Toscanini: How He Became an American Culture-God and Helped Create a New Audience for Old Music* (New York, A. A. Knopf, 1987), p. 73.

39. Rose Thomas quotes from Horowitz, *Wagner Nights*, p. 70, and Schabas, *Theodore Thomas*, p. 190.

40. Carl Smith, *Urban Disorder and the Shape of Belief: The Great Chicago Fire, The Haymarket Bomb, and the Model Town of Pullman* (Chicago, University of Chicago Press, 1995), p. 114. Peck quoted in John Diziges, *Opera in America: A Cultural History* (New Haven, Yale University Press, 1993), p. 251.

41. Peck quote and words from cantata from Mark Clague, "Chicago Counterpoint: The Auditorium Theater Building and the Civic Imagination" (dissertation, University of Chicago, 2002). See especially p. 124.

42. *InterOcean* quote from ibid., p. 377.

43. Fay quote from Horowitz, *Culture and the City*, p. 111.

44. Thomas and *Chicago Evening Post* quotes from Horowitz, *Wagner Nights*, pp. 70–71. Armstrong quote from unidentified obituaries, the Chicago Symphony Orchestra Archives.

45. Thomas quote from Johnson, "Chicago Symphony Orchestra 1891–1924," p. 112.

46. *Staats Zeitung* quote from ibid., p. 82.

47. See, e.g., E. Douglas Bomberger, *"A Tidal Wave of Encouragement": American Composers' Concerts in the Gilded Age* (Westport, Conn., Praeger, 2002).

48. Schabas, *Theodore Thomas*, p. 249.

49. Unidentified obituaries from the Chicago Symphony Orchestra Archives. Trustees statement in Otis, *Chicago Symphony Orchestra*, p. 158.

50. Schabas, *Theodore Thomas*, p. 253. Times and *Musical* Courier quoted in Horowitz, *Wagner Nights*, p. 72.

51. Fay quote from Johnson, "Chicago Symphony Orchestra 1891–1924," p. 452.

CHAPTER 7: LEOPOLD STOKOWSKI, GUSTAV MAHLER, ARTURO TOSCANINI, AND THE GOSSIP OF THE FOYER (*pp. 179–210*)

1. My principal Stokowski sources are Abram Chasins, *Leopold Stokowski: A Profile* (New York, Hawthorn Books, 1979), and Oliver Daniel, *Stokowski: A Counterpoint of View* (New York, Dodd, Mead and Co., 1982).

2. Farwell review from Daniel, *Stokowski*, p. 70.

3. Letter from ibid., p. 90.

4. On Seidl and Nikisch, see the private correspondence of George Templeton Strong and Edward MacDowell, Music Division, Library of Congress.

5. Stokowski and Schwar quotes from Chasins, *Leopold Stokowski*, pp. 70–71.

6. Judson, Lacier, Rensselaer quotes in Daniel, *Stokowski*, pp. 121, 158. Stokowski on Mahler in John H. Mueller, *The American Symphony Orchestra: A Social History of Musical Taste* (Bloomington, Indiana University Press, 1951), p. 128.

7. Henderson review from Daniel, *Stokowski*, p. 161.

8. Mueller, *American Symphony Orchestra*, p. 129.

9. Quote from Joseph Horowitz, *Understanding Toscanini: How He Became an American Culture-God and Helped Create a New Audience for Old Music* (New York, A. A. Knopf, 1987), p. 38.

10. Bruno Walter, *Gustav Mahler* (New York, Vienna House, 1973), p. 83.

11. For reviews of Mahler in New York, see Zoltan Roman, *Gustav Mahler's American Years, 1907–1911: A Documentary History* (Stuyvesant, N. Y., Pendagron Press, 1989). For more on Mrs. Sheldon, including "excellent" strings, see Marion R. Casey, "Mary Sheldon: A Woman of Substance," *Mahler in New York*, a companion booklet to the New York Philharmonic CD set *The Mahler Broadcasts* (1998).

12. Martin Mayer, *The Met: One Hundred Years of Grand Opera* (New York, Simon and Schuster, 1983), p. 108. For Krehbiel on Chaliapin and *Marriage of Figaro*, see Roman, *Gustav Mahler's American Years, 1907–1911*, p. 104.

13. *Musical America*, November 5, 1910. Krehbiel in *New York Tribune*, Nov. 7, 1910. Henderson in *New York Sun*, Nov. 6, 1910.

14. Krehbiel in *New York Tribune*, Nov. 11, 1909, and Nov. 23, 1910. Henderson in *New York Sun*, Jan. 16, 1910.

15. From Krehbiel's Mahler obituary, *New York Tribune*, May 21, 1911.

16. *New York Sun*, Mar. 22, 1908.

17. Roman, *Gustav Mahler's American Years, 1907–1911*, p. 93.

18. Mahler quote from Horowitz, *Understanding Toscanini*, pp. 48–56, 69–77.

19. New York Philharmonic Archives.

20. Alma Mahler, *Gustav Mahler: Memories and Letters* (London, J. Murray, 1946), p. 158. Alma quoted in article in *Musical America*, May 13, 1911, p. 1.

21. *New York Tribune*, May 21, 1911.

22. *Musical America*, May 20, 1911, p. 20.

23. Henry Krehbiel, *Chapters of Opera* (New York, A. Holt and Co., 1908), pp. 286, 343–357.

24. On Krehbiel and Wagner, see Joseph Horowitz, *Wagner Nights: An American History* (Berkeley, University of California Press, 1994), especially ch. 6.

25. Carl Van Vechten, *In the Garret* (New York, Alfred A. Knopf, 1920), p. 244. Huneker quoted in Vincent Sheean, *Oscar Hammerstein I: The Life and Exploits of an Impresario* (New York, Simon and Schuster, 1956), p. 79. Hammerstein quoted in John Diziges, *Opera in America: A Cultural History* (New Haven, Yale University Press, 1993), p. 325.

26. Ronald Davis, *Opera in Chicago* (New York, Appleton-Century, 1966), p. 79.

27. Krehbiel, *Chapters of Opera*, pp. 366–367. Melba quoted in Sheean, *Oscar Hammerstein I*, p. 17.

28. Krehbiel, Henderson, and Conried's biographer quotes from Horowitz, *Understanding Toscanini*, pp. 39, 38, 40.

29. Krehbiel quote from ibid., p. 53.

30. Hammerstein, *Times* obituary, and Van Vechten quotes from Sheean, *Oscar Hammerstein I*, pp. 345–346.

31. Puccini and Henderson quoted in Diziges, *Opera in America*, pp. 337–344. Henry Krehbiel, *More Chapters of Opera: Being Historical and Critical Observations . . . from 1908–1918* (New York, Henry Holt, 1919), p. 211.

32. Herbert quoted in Stanley Jackson, *Caruso* (New York, W. H. Allen, 1972), p. 228. Caruso quoted in Mayer, *Met*, p. 115.
33. Krehbiel quoted in Mayer, *Met*, p. 116.
34. Henderson quote from Diziges, *Opera in America*, p. 404. See also Peter G. Davis, *The American Opera Singer: The Lives and Adventures of America's Great Singers in Opera and Concerts, from 1825 to Present* (New York, Doubleday, 1997), pp. 246–263.
35. Henry James, *The Ambassadors* (Greenwich, Conn., Fawcett Publications, 1960), p. 69. Alexis de Tocqueville, *Democracy in America* (New York, A.A. Knopf, 1945), vol. 2, book 1, ch. 1, p. 4. Chicago paper and *Musical Courier* quotes in Horowitz, *Understanding Toscanini*, pp. 319, 65.
36. Smith quoted in Horowitz, *Understanding Toscanini*, pp. 63–64.
37. Slezak and Krehbiel quoted in ibid., pp. 62, 60.

Chapter 8: Antonín Dvořák and Charles Ives in Search of America (*pp. 211–241*)

1. Vera Brodsky Lawrence (ed.), *Strong on Music: The New York Music Scene in the Days of George Templeton Strong, 1836–1875* vol. 3: *Repercussions 1857–1862* (Chicago, University of Chicago Press, 1999), p. 400.
2. Fry quoted in Mark N. Grant, *Maestros of the Pen: A History of Classical Music Criticism in America* (Boston, Northeastern University Press, 1998), pp. 166–168.
3. Fry, *Tribune*, Burkhardt, Willis, and Bristow quoted in Lawrence (ed.), *Strong on Music*, vol. 2: *Reverberations 1850–1856* (Chicago, University of Chicago Press, 1995), pp. 375–378, 480–483.
4. Howard Shanet, *Philharmonic: A History of New York's Orchestra* (New York, Doubleday, 1975), p. 117.
5. *Musical World* and Fry quoted in Lawrence, *Strong on Music*, vol. 2, pp. 629, 401. Gottschalk quoted in Gilbert Chase, *America's Music* (Urbana, University of Illinois Press, 1987), p. 286.
6. Louis Moreau Gottschalk, *Notes of a Pianist* (New York, A. A. Knopf, 1964; repr. New York, Da Capo Press, 1979), p. 160.
7. Ibid., pp. 63, 127. Lawrence, *Strong on Music*, vol. 3, pp. 479, 476. S. Frederick Starr, *Bamboula! The Life and Times of Louis Moreau Gottschalk* (New York, Oxford University Press, 1995), p. 165.
8. Committee, Hughes, and Gilman quotes from Chase, *America's Music*, pp. 344–347.
9. *New York Tribune*, Mar. 6, 1889.
10. Correspondence of Strong and MacDowell, Music Division, Library of Congress. Chadwick quoted in Steven Ledbetter, "A House of Dreams Untold: The Story of the MacDowell Colony," *Historical New Hampshire*, Spring/Summer 1996.
11. Correspondence of Strong and MacDowell, Music Division, Library of Congress.
12. Ledbetter, "House of Dreams Untold."
13. Nicholas Tawa, *The Coming of Age of American Art Music: New England's Classical Romanticists* (New York, Greenwood Press, 1991), p. 141.
14. Henderson and Krehbiel quoted in William C. Loring Jr., *An American Romantic-Realist Abroad: Templeton Strong and His Music* (Lanham, Md., Scarecrow Press, 1996), pp. 177–178.
15. Wilfrid Mellers, *Music in a New Found Land: Themes and Developments in the History of American Music* (London, Barrie and Rockliff, 1964), p. 27. MacDowell quoted in Tawa, *Coming of Age of American Art Music*, p. 133, and Lawrence Gilman, *Edward MacDowell: A Study* (1909; repr. New York, Da Capo Press, 1969), p. 84.
16. Strong quote from Lawrence, *Strong on Music*, vol. 3, p. 400.
17. Krehbiel quoted in E. Douglas Bomberger, *"A Tidal Wave of Encouragement: American Composers' Concerts in the Gilded Age* (Westport, Conn., Praeger, 2002), p. 65. Dvořák quoted in John Tibbetts (ed.), *Dvořák in America* (Portland, Ore., Amadeus Press, 1993), p. 390.

18. Dvořák quoted in Tibbetts, *Dvořák in America*, pp. 355, 360.

19. Louis Menand, *The Metaphysical Club* (New York, Farrar, Straus and Giroux, 2001), pp. 111, 391.

20. Thomas quoted in "World's Fair Music," *The Etude*, Aug. 1892 (courtesy Adrienne Fried Block). *Chicago Tribune* in Robert Rydell, *All the World's a Fair: Visions of Empire at American International Expositions, 1876–1916* (Chicago, University of Chicago Press, 1984), ch. 2. Dwight quoted in Starr, *Bamboula*, p. 166.

21. James Gibbons Huneker, *Steeplejack* (New York, Scribner's, 1920), vol. 2, p. 68. Henry Krehbiel, *Afro-American Folksongs: A Study in Racial and National Music* (New York, G. Schirmer, 1914), pp. 64–65, vii.

22. Agassiz quoted in Menand, *Metaphysical Club*, p. 105.

23. Antonín Dvořák, "Music in America," *Harper's Magazine*, Feb. 1895 and letter Sept. 15, 1893—both much reprinted (e.g., Tibbetts, *Dvořák in America*, pp. 378, 399).

24. Tibbetts, *Dvořák in America*, p. 71. Willa Cather, *The Song of the Lark* (Boston, Houghton Mifflin, 1915; repr. New York, Signet, 1991), pt. 2, ch. 5, p. 174. Henderson in *New York Times*, Dec. 17, 1893.

25. Henry Wadsworth Longfellow, *The Song of Hiawatha* (Boston, Ticknor and Fields, 1855), ch. 11. The fullest analysis of Hiawatha and Dvořák is to be found in Michael Beckerman, *New Worlds of Dvořák: Searching in America for the Composer's Inner Life* (New York, W. W. Norton, 2003).

26. A point stressed in the Dvořák writings of Michael Beckerman.

27. E. Douglas Bomberger, "American Students in Germany, 1850–1900," "Swapping Lies and Exchanging Bedfellows: The Code Against Music Study in Germany," papers read at conferences of the American Musicological Society (Chicago, Nov. 6, 1991) and Sonneck Society (Kansas City, Feb. 2, 1998), respectively.

28. Farwell quoted in Tibbetts, *Dvořák in America*, p. 163.

29. Griffes quoted in H. Wiley Hitchcock, *Music in the United States: A Historical Introduction* (Englewood Cliffs, N.J., Prentice-Hall, 1974), p. 147. Loeffler in Ellen Knight, *Charles Martin Loeffler: A Life Apart in American Music* (Urbana, University of Illinois Press, 1993), p. 206. Griffes on Loeffler, in E. M. Maisel, *Charles T. Griffes; the Life of an American Composer* (New York, A. A. Knopf, 1943; repr. New York, Da Capo Press, 1972), p. 161.

30. There is a splendid recording of the MacLeod songs by Phyllis Bryn-Julson with Seiji Ozawa conducting the Boston Symphony (New World Records NW 273-2).

31. *Musical America*, Mar. 9, 1918.

32. Whitman quoted in David Reynolds, *Walt Whitman's America: A Cultural Biography* (New York, Knopf, 1995), pp. 178–179.

33. Ralph Waldo Emerson, *The American Scholar* (New York, American Book, 1893). Thoreau cited in Frank Rossiter, *Charles Ives and His America* (New York, Liveright, 1975), p. 91.

34. Quotes from Vivian Perlis (ed.), *Charles Ives Remembered: An Oral History* (New Haven, Yale University Press, 1974), p. 53.

35. Henry David Thoreau, "Sounds," in *Walden* (1854).

36. Ives quotes from Charles Ives, *Essays Before a Sonata*, reprinted in Charles Ives, *Three Classics in the Aesthetic of Music* (New York, Dover Publications, 1962).

37. J. Peter Burkholder, *All Made of Tunes: Charles Ives and the Uses of Musical Borrowing* (New Haven, Yale University Press, 1995), p. 424.

38. Ives quoted in MacDonald Smith Moore, *Yankee Blues: Musical Culture and American Identity* (Bloomington, Indiana University Press, 1985), p. 55.

39. Ibid.

40. Dvořák, "Music in America."

41. Martin Green, *The Problem of Boston: Some Readings in Cultural History* (London, Longmans, 1966), pp. 166–167.

42. Perlis, *Charles Ives Remembered*, p. 152.

CODA: MUSIC IN THE GILDED AGE (*pp. 242–262*)

1. Vera Brodsky Lawrence (ed.), *Strong on Music: The New York Music Scene in the Days of George Templeton Strong, 1836–1875*, vol. 3: *Repercussions 1857–1862* (Chicago, University of Chicago Press, 1999), p. 247.

2. Lewis Mumford, *The Brown Decades: A Study in the Arts in America, 1865–1895* (New York, Harcourt, Brace and Company, 1931), pp. 3–4.

3. Some examples: Charles Hamm, "United States of America," in Jim Samson (ed.), *The Late Romantic Era: From the Mid-19th Century to World War I* (Englewood Cliffs, N.J., Prentice-Hall, 1991); Robert Rydell, *All the World's a Fair: Visions of Empire at American International Expositions, 1876–1916* (Chicago, University of Chicago Press, 1984); Carl Smith, *Urban Disorder and the Shape of Belief: The Great Chicago Fire, The Haymarket Bomb, and the Model Town of Pullman* (Chicago, University of Chicago Press, 1995); Richard Schickel, *The World of Carnegie Hall* (New York, Messner, 1960); M. H. Dunlop, *Gilded City: Scandal and Sensation in Turn-of-the-Century New York* (New York, W. Morrow, 2000); and Helen Horowitz, *Culture & the City: Cultural Philanthropy in Chicago from the 1880s to 1917* (Lexington, University of Kentucky Press, 1976), pp. 16, 17, 20.

4. Alan Trachtenberg, *The Incorporation of America—Culture and Society in the Gilded Age* (New York, Hill and Wang, 1982), ch. 5.

5. Paul DiMaggio, "Cultural Entrepreneurship in 19th Century Boston," parts 1 and 2, in *Media, Culture, and Society* (New York, Academic Press, 1982), vol. 4.

6. Leading historian is Smith, *Urban Disorder and the Shape of Belief*, p. 31. Quote about benefactors in Helen Horowitz, *Culture & the City*, p. 6.

7. Huneker, Howells, *Musical Courier*, DiMaggio quoted in Joseph Horowitz, *Wagner Nights: An American History* (Berkeley, University of California Press, 1992), pp. 329, 323, 324.

8. Neilson, Huneker quoted in ibid., pp. 133–134.

9. Thomas quoted in Yoshinobu Hakutani (ed.), *Art Music and Literature, 1897–1902 / Theodore Dreiser* (Urbana, University of Illinois Press, 2001), p. 140.

10. Thomas Kessner, *Capital City: New York City and the Men Behind America's Rise to Economic Dominance, 1860–1900* (New York, Simon and Schuster, 2003), especially pp. 238–239, 24, 29, xvii. Adams quoted on p. 332.

11. Lawrence Levine, *Highbrow/Lowbrow: The Emergence of Cultural Hierarchy in America* (Cambridge, Mass., Harvard University Press, 1988), pp. 101–102.

12. Embedded in a Brahmin community and cultural capitalists in Paul DiMaggio, "Cultural Entrepreneurship in 19th Century Boston," p. 35. A set of cultural institutions and programmatic ideas in Sven Beckert, *The Monied Metropolis: New York City and the Consolidation of the American Bourgeoisie, 1850–1896* (Cambridge, Cambridge University Press, 2001), ch. 8. See also Ronald Story, *Harvard and the Boston Upper Class: The Forging of an Aristocracy, 1800–1870* (Middletown, Conn., Wesleyan University Press, 1980), ch. 9.

13. Hammerstein quoted in Vincent Sheean, *Oscar Hammerstein I: The Life and Exploits of an Impresario* (New York, Simon and Schuster, 1956), pp. 252–253.

14. Quotes from Smith, *Urban Disorder and the Shape of Belief*, pp. 199, 206.

15. Bourne quoted in Henry F. May, *The End of American Innocence: A Study of the First Years of Our Own Time, 1912–1917* (New York, Knopf, 1959), p. 297.

16. Ibid., p. 346.

17. Henry Krehbiel, *Chapters of Opera* (New York, A. Holt and Co., 1908), pp. 345–346.

18. Hale quotes in Jean Ann Boyd, "Philip Hale, American Music Critic: Boston, 1889–1933," (dissertation, University of Texas, 1985), pp. 189, 192. Henderson quotes in Barbara Mueser, "The Criticism of New Music in New York 1919–1929," (dissertation, City University of New York, 1975),

and Paul M. Shurtz, "William James Henderson: His Views on the New York Musical World, 1887–1937" (dissertation, University of Colorado at Boulder, 1980), p. 58.

19. Krehbiel, *Chapters of Opera*, pp. 343–357. Henry Krehbiel, *More Chapters of Opera* (New York, Henry Holt, 1919), pp. 122–123.

20. Mariana Van Rensselaer, *Harper's Magazine*, Mar. 1883. W. S. B. Matthews (ed.), *A Hundred Years of Music in America* (Chicago, G. L. Howe, 1889), p. 79.

21. Arthur Farwell, *"Wanderjahre of a Revolutionist" and Other Essays on American Music*, edited by Thomas Stoner (Rochester, N.Y., University of Rochester Press, 1995), p. 29.

22. Evelyn D. Culbertson, *He Heard America Singing: Arthur Farwell, Composer and Crusading Music Educator* (Metuchen, N.J., Scarecrow Press, 1992), p. 382.

23. Farwell, *"Wanderjahre of a Revolutionist,"* pp. 96, 134, 135.

24. David Bispham, *A Quaker Singer's Recollections* (New York, Macmillan, 1920), p. 355.

25. Farwell, *"Wanderjahre of a Revolutionist,"* p. 157.

26. Ibid., pp. 12, 146, 147, 148, 185, 98.

27. Farwell, *"Wanderjahre of a Revolutionist,"* pp. 123, 47. Arthur Farwell, "America's Gain from a Bayreuth Romance: The Mystery of Anton Seidl," *Musical Quarterly*, Oct. 1944.

28. Jackson Lears, "In Defense of Nostalgia," *Lingua Franca*, (Dec./Jan. 1998), pp. 59–66.

29. Krehbiel, *Chapters of Opera*, p. 167.

BOOK TWO "Great Performances": Decline and Fall

The epigraph to Book Two is from Aaron Copland, *The New Music, 1900–1960* (New York, W. W. Norton, 1968), p. 99.

INTRODUCTION: THE GREAT SCHISM (1914) *(pp. 265–270)*

1. Henry F. May, *The End of American Innocence: A Study of the First Years of Our Own Time, 1912–1917* (New York, Knopf, 1959), p. 388.

2. James R. Mock and Cedric Lawson, *Words That Won the War: The Story of the Committee on Public Information, 1917–1919* (Princeton, Princeton University Press, 1939), p. 64.

3. *New Republic* in May, *The End of Innocence*, p. 361. Henry James in Paul Fussell, *The Great War and Modern Memory* (New York, Oxford University Press, 1975), p. 8.

4. Rochelle Gurstein, *The Repeal of Reticence: A History of America's Cultural and Legal Struggles over Free Speech, Obscenity Sexual Liberation and Modern Art* (New York, Hill and Wang, 1996).

5. Boston Symphony in Barbara L. Tischler, *An American Music: The Search for an American Musical Identity* (New York, Oxford University Press, 1986), New York Philharmonic in Howard Shanet, *Philharmonic: A History of New York's Orchestra* (New York, Doubleday, 1975), p. 227.

6. Jay quoted in Irving Lowens, "L'affaire Muck," *Musicology*, vol. 1, no. 3 (Fall 1965), p. 3.

7. Glenn Watkins, *Proof through the Night: Music and the Great War* (Berkeley, University of California Press, 2003), p. 304.

8. Boston Symphony in Andrea Olmstead, *Juilliard: A History* (Urbana, University of Illinois Press, 1999), p. 52. Stransky in Joseph Horowitz, *Wagner Nights: An American History* (Berkeley, University of California Press, 1994), p. 298. Gadski in Watkins, *Proof through the Night*, p. 309. Kreisler in Tischler, *American Music*, p. 88.

9. Tischler, *American Music*, p. 85. John H. Mueller, *The American Symphony Orchestra: A Social History of Musical Taste* (Bloomington, Indiana University Press, 1951), p. 259.

10. *Musical America* in Tischer, *American Music*, p. 83. Mueller, *American Symphony Orchestra*, p. 259.

11. Virgil Thomson, *American Music since 1910* (New York, Holt, Rinehart and Winston, 1971), pp. 1–2.

Leonard Bernstein, "What Makes Music American" (Feb. 1, 1958) in Jack Gottlieb (ed.), *Leonard Bernstein's Young People's Concerts* (New York, Anchor Books, 1992). Hugo Leichtentritt, *Serge Koussevitzky, the Boston Symphony Orchestra and the New American Music* (Cambridge, Mass., Harvard University Press, 1946), p. 10.

12. Charles Edward Russell, *The American Orchestra and Theodore Thomas* (Garden City, N.Y., Doubleday, Page and Co., 1927), Preface.

PART ONE: THE CULTURE OF PERFORMANCE
CHAPTER 1: THE BIG THREE (*pp. 273–304*)

1. Winthrop Sargeant, *Geniuses, Goddesses, and People* (New York, E. P. Dutton, 1949), pp. 67, 79, 84, 96, 106.
2. Downes quoted from Joseph Horowitz, *Understanding Toscanini: How He Became an American Culture-God and Helped Create a New Audience for Old Music* (New York, A. A. Knopf, 1987), pp. 101, 98.
3. Gilman in Horowitz, *Understanding Toscanini*, p. 113. George Szell, "Toscanini in the History of Orchestral Performance," *Saturday Review*, Mar. 25, 1967. Harvey Sachs, *Toscanini* (London, Wiedenfeld and Nicholson, 1978), p. 198.
4. For more on Toscanini and performance, see Horowitz, *Understanding Toscanini*, especially pp. 321–372.
5. Igor Stravinsky, *Stravinsky: An Autobiography* (New York, Simon and Schuster, 1936), pp. 203–205. Howard Shanet, *Philharmonic: A History of New York's Orchestra* (New York, Doubleday, 1975), pp. 270–275.
6. Horowitz, *Understanding Toscanini*, p. 133.
7. Henderson in *New York Sun*, Oct. 11, 1930. Gilman and Downes in Horowitz, *Understanding Toscanini*, p. 121.
8. Gilman and Furtwängler quoted in Horowitz, *Understanding Toscanini*, pp. 132, 142, 147.
9. All quotes from ibid., p. 163.
10. *New York Times*, Apr. 16, 1938 (dateline), May 8, 1938.
11. *Life*, NBC release, and scripted announcement quoted in Horowitz, *Understanding Toscanini*, pp. 256, 164, 165.
12. Barbirolli quoted in Michael Kennedy, *Barbirolli, Conductor Laureate* (London, MacGibbon and Kee, 1971), p. 136. Virgil Thomson (including Harris quote) in *New York Herald-Tribune*, Oct. 28, 1946.
13. Sarnoff announcement quoted in Horowitz, *Understanding Toscanini*, photo insert and p. 271.
14. *Time*, Apr. 26, 1948.
15. On the Toscanini tour, see Horowitz, *Understanding Toscanini*, pp. 278–282.
16. Gavazzeni quote from Sachs, *Toscanini*, p. 173.
17. William Trotter, *Priest of Music: The Life of Dimitri Mitropoulos* (Portland, Ore., Amadeus Press, 1995), p. 81 Joseph Szigeti, *With Strings Attached: Reminiscences and Reflections by Joseph Szigeti* (New York, A. A. Knopf, 1947), p. 245.
18. Leopold Stokowski, *Music for All of Us* (New York, Simon and Schuster, 1943), pp. 196. Abram Chasins, *Leopold Stokowski: A Profile* (New York, Hawthorn Books, 1979), p. 78.
19. Chasins, *Leopold Stokowski*, p. 81.
20. Ibid., p. 104.
21. Charles O'Connell, *The Other Side of the Record* (New York, A. A. Knopf, 1947), p. 281.
22. Chasins, *Leopold Stokowski*, p. 81.
23. Stokowski, *Music for All of Us*, pp. 309, 190–191.
24. Stokowski quoted in Oliver Daniel, *Stokowski: A Counterpoint of View* (New York, Dodd, Mead, and Co., 1982), p. 224.

25. Stokowski quoted in ibid, p. 325. Chasins, *Leopold Stokowski*, p. 98.

26. *Time*, Nov. 18, 1940.

27. Stokowski quoted in Horowitz, *Understanding Toscanini*, pp. 173–177.

28. Doris G. Monteux, *It's All in the Music* (New York, Farrar, Straus and Givoux, 1965), p. 108.

29. *Boston Traveler*, Mar. 5, 1920.

30. On Koussevitzky, M. A. D. Howe, *The Boston Symphony Orchestra 1881–1931* (Boston, Houghton Mifflin, 1931); Hugo Leichtentritt, *Serge Koussevitzky, the Boston Symphony Orchestra and the New American Music* (Cambridge, Mass., Harvard University Press, 1946); Moses Smith, *Koussevitzky* (New York, Allen Towre and Heath, 1947); and clippings in Boston Symphony Archives.

31. Harry Ellis Dickson, *"Gentlemen, More Dolce Please,"*; *An Irreverent Memoir of Thirty Years in the Boston Symphony Orchestra* (Boston, Beacon Press, 1969), pp. 46, 47, 44.

32. Ibid., p. 49.

33. See Philip Hart, *Orpheus in the New World: The Symphony Orchestra as an American Cultural Institution* (New York, W. W. Norton, 1973) and Dickson, *"Gentlemen, More Dolce Please,"* pp. 96–97.

34. Dickson, *"Gentlemen, More Dolce Please,"* p. 42. Bernstein quote in Herbert Kupferberg, *Tanglewood* (New York, McGraw-Hill, 1976), p. 136. *Thomson in New York Herald-Tribune*, Nov. 16, 1944.

35. The performance is currently available on Naxos CD 8.110105 (2000).

36. Aaron Copland, "Serge Koussevitzky and the American Composer," *Musical Quarterly*, vol. 30 (1944), p. 258.

37. "Koussevitzky" clippings, Music Research Division, New York Public Library for the Performing Arts.

38. Hans W. Heinsheimer, *Best Regards to Aïda; The Defeats and Victories of a Music Man on Two Continents* (New York, A. A. Knopf, 1968), p. 198.

39. Koussevitzky quoted in Dickson, *"Gentlemen, More Dolce Please,"* p. 97.

40. Copland, "Serge Koussevitzky and the American Composer," p. 258.

41. *Time*, July 22, 1946. Kupferberg, *Tanglewood*.

42. Leichtentritt, *Serge Koussevitzky*, pp. 171–191.

43. Smith, *Koussevitzky*. John H. Mueller, *The American Symphony Orchestra: A Social History of Musical Taste* (Bloomington, Indiana University Press, 1951), p. 95.

44. Koussevitzky quote in Kupferberg, *Tanglewood*, p. 126. Lukas Foss, "Koussevitzky—A Reminiscence," album note for *A Treasury of Immortal Performances: Serge Koussevitzky*, RCA Victor VCM 6174 (1966).

CHAPTER 2: MORE CONDUCTORS (*pp. 305–327*)

1. For example, *Baker's Biographical Dictionary of Musicians*, 6th ed. (New York, Schirmer Books, 1978), and H. Wiley Hitchcock and Stanley Sadie (eds.), *The New Grove Dictionary of American Music* (New York, Grove's Dictionaries of Music, 1986).

2. *New York Herald-Tribune*, Nov. 21, 1940 (cited in Dena Epstein, "Frederick Stock and American Music," *American Music*, vol. 10, no. 1 [Spring 1992]).

3. *A Tribute to Frederick Stock*, a two-CD set produced by the Chicago Symphony, CSO-CD93-2 (1992).

4. Philo Otis, *The Chicago Symphony Orchestra: Its Organization, Growth and Development, 1891–1924* (Chicago, Clayton F. Summy, 1925), pp. 269, 258. Ellis Johnson, "The Chicago Symphony Orchestra 1891–1942" (dissertation, University of Chicago, 1955), pp. 371–375.

5. *Chicago InterOcean*, Apr. 20, 1913 (cited in Johnson, "Chicago Symphony Orchestra 1891–1942," p. 221). Stock in Johnson, p. 291. *Chicago Daily News*, Feb. 28, 1936 (in Johnson, p. 383).

6. Johnson, "Chicago Symphony Orchestra 1891–1941," p. 399. *Time*, Nov. 2, 1942 (in Johnson, p. 430).

7. Philip Hart, *Fritz Reiner: A Biography* (Evanston, Ill., Northwestern University Press, 1994), pp. 31–32.

8. These Reiner broadcasts are available on "Reiner Era" CD sets sold by the Chicago Symphony.

9. Lang quote and other information from Hart, *Fritz Reiner*, pp. 186, 188.

10. A useful general Cleveland reference is Adella Prentiss Hughes, *Music Is My Life* (Cleveland, World Publishing, 1947). Donald Rosenberg, *The Cleveland Orchestra Story: Second to None* (Cleveland, Gray and Co., 2000), p. 81. Erich Leinsdorf, *Cadenza: A Musical Career* (Boston, Houghton Mifflin, 1976), p. 118.

11. Rodzinski and Downs; quotes from Rosenberg, *Cleveland Orchestra Story*, p. 159.

12. Quotes from ibid., pp. 279, 267, 268, 336.

13. Kurt Loebel in conversation with the author, 2002. Prokofiev recording: *The Cleveland Orchestra Seventy-fifth Anniversary Compact Disc Edition*, TCO93-75 (1993).

14. Steinberg quoted in Rosenberg, *Cleveland Orchestra Story*, p. 335. Szell quotes from Paul Henry Lang, "'A Mixture of Instrument and Intellect'—George Szell on Conducting," *High Fidelity*, Jan. 1965. "Lower his pants" from author's interview with Kurt Loebel, 2002.

15. Peter Heyworth, *Otto Klemperer: His Life and Times*, vol. 1: *1885–1933* (New York: Cambridge University Press, 1983), p. 75.

16. Ibid., pp. 283, 349. Beethoven quote in Martin Anderson (ed.), *Klemperer on Music: Shavings from a Musician's Workbench* (London, Toccata Press, 1986), p. 102.

17. Klemperer quoted in Heyworth, *Otto Klemperer, His Life and Times*, vol. 2 (New York, Cambridge University Press, 1996), p. 47.

18. Ibid., p. 28.

19. Los Angeles critic and Dr. Kelly in ibid., p. 94. Henderson in *New York Sun*, Nov. 3, 1934.

20. A valuable biography is William Trotter, *Priest of Music: The Life of Dimitri Mitropoulos* (Portland, Ore., Amadeus Press, 1995).

21. Mitropoulos quoted in ibid., p. 147.

22. Ibid., p. 143.

23. Ibid., p. 126.

24. *Time* quoted in ibid., p. 119.

25. Mitropoulos quotes from ibid., pp. 248, 252.

26. *Dimitri Mitropoulos, Katy Katsoyanis: A Correspondence, 1930–1960* (New York, Martin Dale, 1973).

27. Downes quoted in Trotter, *Priest of Music*, p. 315.

28. Ibid., pp. 380, 292.

29. Babbitt, Mitropoulos quotes from ibid., p. 325.

30. *Times* quote from ibid., p. 411.

31. Klemperer quoted in Anderson, *Klemperer on Conducting*, p. 209. Trotter, *Priest of Music*, p. 57.

32. Klemperer quoted in Heyworth, *Otto Klemperer*, vol. 2, p. 47. Mahler quoted in Kurt Blaukopf (ed.), *Mahler—A Documentary Study* (New York, Oxford University Press, 1976), p. 262. Mitropoulos quoted in Trotter, *Priest of Music*, pp. 177, 130.

33. One musician, Frankenstein, and Szell quotes from David Schneider, *The San Francisco Symphony: Music, Maestros, and Musicians* (Novato, Calif., Presidio Press, 1983), pp. 41, 126, 127.

34. Antal Dorati, *Notes of Seven Decades* (Detroit, Wayne State University Press, 1981), p. 197.

CHAPTER 3: THE WORLD'S GREATEST SOLOISTS (*pp. 328–357*)

1. Richard Capell, *Schubert's Songs* (London, E. Benn, 1928), p. 250.

2. *New York Sun*, Feb. 17, 1930.

3. A. and K. Swan, "Rachmaninoff—Personal Reminiscences," *Musical Quarterly*, vol. 30 (1944), p. 185.

4. Hallé quoted in Alan Walker, *Franz Liszt, vol. 1: The Virtuoso Years 1811–47* (New York, Knopf, 1983), pp. 180–181.

5. Liszt quoted in Walker, *Franz Liszt*, p. 174.

6. Lewis Mumford, *The Golden Day; A Study in American Literature and Culture* (Boston, Beacon Press, 1957), p. 20. Schumann quoted in Robert Schumann, *On Music and Musicians*, edited by Konrad Wolff, transl. by Paul Rosenfeld (New York, Pantheon, 1946), p. 81. Hanslick quoted in John H. Mueller, *The American Symphony Orchestra: A Social History of Musical Taste* (Bloomington, Indiana University Press, 1951), p. 22.

7. R. Allen Lott, *From Paris to Peoria: How European Piano Virtuosos Brought Classical Music to the American Heartland* (New York, Oxford University Press, 2003), p. 44.

8. Quotes from Vera Brodsky Lawrence (ed.), *Strong on Music: The New York Music Scene in the Days of George Templeton Strong, 1836–1875*, vol. 3: *Repercussions 1857–1862* (Chicago, University of Chicago Press, 1999), p. 23.

9. Rubinstein in Ezra Schabas, *Theodore Thomas: America's Conductor and Builder of Orchestras, 1835–1905* (Urbana, University of Illinois Press, 1989), p. 52. Bagby in Arthur Loesser, *Men, Women, and Pianos: A Social History* (New York, Simon and Schuster, 1954), pp. 516–518. Huneker in David Dubal, *The Art of the Piano: Its Performers, Literature, and Recordings* (New York, Summit Books, 1989), p. 220.

10. Lott, *From Paris to Peoria*, p. 281.

11. Ibid., especially pp. 36, 89, 131, 133.

12. Henderson in *New York Times*, Nov. 30, 1887.

13. *New York Times* quote from Maja Trochimczyk, "Paderewski, *Chant d'amour*, and the Aestheticism of the Gilded Age," read at the annual conference of the Society for American Music, Feb. 28, 2003, Tempe, Ariz.

14. Henderson in *New York Times*, Nov. 17, 1895.

15. Rachmaninoff quoted in Dubal, *Art of the Piano*, p. 221.

16. Charles O'Connell, *The Other Side of the Record* (New York, A. A. Knopf, 1947), p. 107. *RCA Record Review* cited in Joseph Horowitz, *Understanding Toscanini: How He Became an American Culture-God and Helped Create a New Audience for Old Music* (New York, A. A. Knopf, 1987), photo insert.

17. H. R. Axelrod, *Heifetz* (Neptune City, N.J., Paganiniana Publications, 1976), p. 553. RCA contracts in David Schoenbaum, "Jascha Heifetz at 100," *New York Times* (Arts & Leisure), Dec. 12, 2001. Concealed bar in O'Connell, *Other Side of the Record*, p. 214.

18. Boris Schwarz, *Great Masters of the Violin* (New York, Simon and Schuster, 1983), pp. 386–392.

19. For sources of quotes, and a longer version of this section on Horowitz, see Joseph Horowitz, "Letter from New York: The Transformations of Vladimir Horowitz," *Musical Quarterly*, vol. 74, no. 4 (Fall 1990).

20. Artur Schnabel, *My Life and Music* (London, Longmans, 1961), pp. 88, 117. Horowitz, *Understanding Toscanini*, p. 262.

21. Joseph Horowitz, *The Ivory Trade: Music and the Business of Music at the Van Cliburn International Piano Competition* (New York, Summit Books, 1990), pp. 70–77.

22. *Time*, May 19, 1958. See Horowitz, *Ivory Trade*. On the OYAPS, Gary Graffman, *I Really Should Be Practicing* (Garden City, N.Y., Doubleday, 1981).

23. Graffman, *I Really Should Be Practicing*, p. 150.

24. Horowitz, *Ivory Trade*, especially pp. 19–38.

25. On Gould, see Joseph Horowitz, *The Post-Classical Predicament: Essays on Music and Society* (Boston, Northeastern University Press, 1995), pp. 134–138. Gould on the new listener and Richard Strauss in Tim Page (ed.), *The Glenn Gould Reader* (New York, A. A. Knopf, 1984), pp. 84–91, 331–352.

26. *Time*, May 19, 1958.

27. Liszt and Heine quoted in Charles Suttoni (translator and annotator), Franz Liszt, *An Artist's Journey: lettres d'un bachelier ès musique* (Chicago, University of Chicago Press, 1989), pp. 4–38.

28. Cliburn, Fleisher, and Gould in Joseph Horowitz, *The Ivory Trade: Piano Competitions and the Business of Music* (Boston, Northeastern University Press, 1991), pp. 321, 273, 259.

29. According to Gino Francesconi (Archivist, Carnegie Hall).

CHAPTER 4: OPERA FOR SINGERS (*pp. 358–391*)

1. Antal Dorati, *Notes of Seven Decades* (Detroit, Wayne State University Press, 1981), p. 116.

2. Henry Krehbiel, *Chapters of Opera* (New York, H. Holt and Co., 1908), pp. 44, 207–208.

3. John Diziges, *Opera in America: A Cultural History* (New Haven, Yale University Press, 1993), p. 424.

4. Martin Mayer, *The Met: One Hundred Years of Grand Opera* (New York, Simon and Schuster, 1983), p. 133.

5. Henderson in Diziges, *Opera in America*, p. 424. Strauss in Deems Taylor, *Of Men and Music* (New York, Simon and Schuster, 1937), p. 55.

6. Mayer, *Met*, p. 168.

7. Giulio Gatti-Casazza, *Memories of the Opera* (New York, C. Scribner's Sons, 1941), pp. 118–119, 313.

8. *New York Times*, Cravath, and Bori quoted in Mayer, *Met*, p. 179.

9. David Hamilton, *The Sound of the Met* (New York, Museum of Broadcasting, 1986), p. 15.

10. John Kobler, *Otto the Magnificent: The Life of Otto Kahn* (New York, Scribner, 1988), pp. 64, 101. "Federal department" in Theresa Collins, *Otto Kahn: Art, Money and Modern Time* (Chapel Hill, University of North Carolina Press, 2002), p. 129.

11. Diziges, *Opera in America*, p. 429.

12. Bodanzky quoted in ibid., p. 436.

13. *New York Sun*, Dec. 12, 1935.

14. "Authorized historian" is Mayer, *Met*, p. 205. Johnson quoted in Paul Jackson, *Saturday Afternoons at the Old Met: The Metropolitan Opera Broadcasts, 1931–1950* (Portland, Ore., Amadeus Press, 1992), p. 98.

15. *New York Sun*, Mar. 23, 1935.

16. Harvey Sachs (ed.), *The Letters of Arturo Toscanini* (New York, Alfred A. Knopf, 2002), p. 380.

17. Bodanzky and Huneker quoted in *Opera News*, Jan. 15, 1972, p. 29. The chronicler is David Hamilton, "*Tristan* in the '30s," *Musical Newsletter* (Fall 1976/Spring 1977).

18. Henderson in *New York Sun*, Feb. 24, 1924. Henry Finck, *Wagner and His Works* (New York, C. Scribner's Sons, 1893; rep. New Yorker, Greenwood Press, 1968), vol. 2, p. 349.

19. On Panizza, see *Opera News*, Feb. 29, 1974, and clippings, Music Research Division, New York City Public Library of the Performing Arts at Lincoln Center.

20. Peter G. Davis, *The American Opera Singer: The Lives and Adventures of America's Great Singers in Opera and Concert, from 1825 to Present* (New York, Doubleday, 1997), p. 265.

21. Tibbett quoted in ibid., pp. 303–321.

22. Sachs (ed.), *Letters of Arturo Toscanini*, p. 380.

23. Taylor, *Of Men and Music*, pp. 203–209.

24. Quaintance Eaton, *Opera Caravan: Adventures of the Metropolitan on Tour, 1883–1956* (New York, Da Capo Press, 1978), p. xiv.

25. Henderson in H. P. Schurtz, "W. J. Henderson: His Views on the New York Musical World 1887–1937" (dissertation, University of Colorado, Boulder, 1980), pp. 128–130. Hammerstein in Ronald Davis, *Opera in Chicago* (New York, Appleton-Century, 1966), p. 90.

26. Diziges, *Opera in America*, pp. 413–421. *New Republic* cited in Michael Pisani, "A Kapustnik in the

American Opera House: Modernism and Prokofiev's *Love of Three Oranges*, *Musical Quarterly*, vol. 81, no. 4 (Winter 1997).

27. "Directa" quoted in Diziges, *Opera in America*, pp. 414, 416.

28. Mary Garden and Louis Biancolli, *Mary Garden's Story* (New York, Simon and Schuster, 1951), p. 171.

29. Eyeglasses in Davis, *Opera in Chicago*, p. 160. On Insull, see Diziges, *Opera in America*, pp. 416–421.

30. Boris Goldovsky, *My Road to Opera: The Recollections of Boris Goldovsky* (Boston, Houghton Mifflin, 1979), pp. 190–222.

31. Philadelphia Orchestra Archives (thanks to archivist JoAnne Barry).

32. *Dwight's Journal of Music*, May 3, 1856, cited in Irving Sablosky (ed.), *What They Heard: Music in America, 1852–1881—From the Pages of Dwight's Journal of Music* (Baton Rouge, Louisiana State University Press, 1986), p. 172.

33. Cecil Smith, *Worlds of Music* (Philadelphia, Lippincott, 1952), p. 159. On San Francisco Opera, see Diziges, *Opera in America*, and Arthur Bloomfield, *50 Years of the San Francisco Opera* (San Francisco, San Francisco Book Co. 1972).

34. Joseph Horowitz, *Understanding Toscanini: How He Became an American Culture-God and Helped Create a New Audience for Old Music* (New York, A. A. Knopf, 1987), p. 200.

35. Martin Sokol, *The New York City Opera: An American Adventure* (New York, Macmillan, 1981).

36. Stock quoted in Ellis Johnson, "The Chicago Symphony Orchestra 1891–1941" (dissertation, University of Chicago, 1955), p. 289. Gary Graffman, *I Really Should Be Practicing* (Garden City, N.Y., Doubleday, 1982), p. 52.

37. Geissma quoted in Horowitz, *Understanding Toscanini*, pp. 94–95.

38. Harold Schonberg, *The Great Conductors* (New York, Simon and Schuster, 1967), p. 302, and quoted in Joseph Horowitz, "The Transformation of Vladimir Horowitz" *Musical Quarterly*, vol. 74, no. 4 (Fall 1990). Mravinsky elected, from the author's interview with the violinist Lazar Gosman (once a member of Mravinsky's orchestra).

39. Horowitz, *Understanding Toscanini*.

40. On private orchestras, Gungl, Jullien, and the Germanians, see Nancy Newman, "Good Music for a Free People: The Germania Musical Society and Transatlantic Musical Culture of the Mid-Nineteenth Century" (dissertation, Brown University, 2002), and Adam Carse, *The Life of Jullien* (Cambridge, UK, Cambridge University Press, 1951). For European repertoire statistics and shifting program templates, see William Weber, "Mass Culture and the Reshaping of European Musical Taste, 1770–1870," *International Review of the Aesthetics and Sociology of Music*, vol. 8 (1977), pp. 5–21, and Weber, "Consequences of Canon: The Institutionalization of Enmity between Contemporary and Classical Music," *Common Knowledge*, vol. 9, no. 3 (Winter 2003). I am also indebted to Nancy Newman, William Weber, and Jonathan Spitzer for sharing with me their knowledge of the history of the concert orchestra.

41. See various writings by William Weber, including "The Muddle of the Middle Classes," *19th Century Music*, vol. 3 (1979), pp. 175–185, and *Music and the Middle Classes: The Social Structure of Concert Life in London, Paris, and Vienna between 1830 and 1848* (London, Croom Helm, 1975).

PART TWO: OFFSTAGE PARTICIPANTS
CHAPTER 5: SERVING THE NEW AUDIENCE (*pp. 395–432*)

1. Sinclair Lewis, *Babbitt*, pp. 78, 161, 151, 150 (Signet paperback edition, n.d.).

2. Helen and Robert Lynd, *Middletown, A Study in Contemporary American Culture* (New York, Harcourt, Brace, 1929), pp. 201–248.

3. Alexis de Tocqueville, *Democracy in America*, vol. 2 (New York, Knopf, 1945), pp. 40–41 (chapter 9).

4. Ann Douglas, *The Feminization of American Culture* (New York, Knopf, 1977).

5. R. Allen Lott, *From Paris to Peoria: How European Piano Virtuosos Brought Classical Music to the American Heartland* (New York, Oxford University Press, 2003), p. 262.

6. Joseph Horowitz, *Understanding Toscanini: How He Became an American Culture-God and Helped Create a New Audience for Old Music* (New York, A. A. Knopf, 1987), pp. 200, 199. Lewis, *Babbitt*, p. 249.

7. Men outnumbering women, see Judith Tick, "Charles Ives and Gender Ideology," in Ruth Solie (ed.), *Musicology and Difference: Gender and Sexuality in Music Scholarship* (Berkeley, University of California Press, 1993), p. 93. Horowitz, *Understanding Toscanini*, pp. 401, 190, 198, 151, 198.

8. *Fortune* and *Harper's* quotes and numbers from Horowitz, *Understanding Toscanini*, pp. 154, 198.

9. Christopher Bruhn, "Taking the Private Public: Amateur Music-making and the Musical Audience in 1860s New York, "*American Music*, vol. 21, no. 3 (Fall 2003), p. 268.

10. Deems Taylor, *Of Men and Music* (New York, Simon and Schuster, 1937), p. xviii.

11. Samaroff quotes from Horowitz, *Understanding Toscanini*, p. 52.

12. Frederick Lewis Allen, *Only Yesterday* (New York, Harper and Row, 1964), p. 195. George Marek, *Toscanini* (New York, Atheneum, 1975), pp. 220–221.

13. Eugene Leach, "Snookered 50 Years Ago," *Current* (Jan.–Mar. 1983).

14. Eugene Lyons, *David Sarnoff* (New York, Harper and Row, 1966), p. 195. Steven C. Smith, *A Heart at Fire's Center: The Life and Music of Bernard Herrmann* (Berkeley, University of California Press, 1991), p. 102. Horowitz, *Understanding Toscanini*, pp. 270–306.

15. All quotes from Horowitz, *Understanding Toscanini*, pp. 204, 314, 203.

16. *Life*, Nov. 27, 1939.

17. Quotes from Horowitz, *Understanding Toscanini*, pp. 132, 209–211, 220.

18. For more on Adorno, see Horowitz, *Understanding Toscanini*, pp. 229–243. Haggin quoted on p. 220.

19. Marek, Downes, Haggin, and Gilman quotes from ibid., pp. 213, 143.

20. Dwight Macdonald, "Masscult and Midcult," reprinted in Macdonald, *Against the American Grain* (New York, Da Capo Press, 1983). See p. 10.

21. *Life* quotes from Horowitz, *Understanding Toscanini*, pp. 272, 303.

22. Richard Crawford, *America's Musical Life: A History* (New York, W. W. Norton, 2001), p. 590.

23. Two useful sources: John H. Mueller, *The American Symphony Orchestra: A Social History of Musical Taste* (Bloomington, Indiana University Press, 1951), and Cecil Smith, *Worlds of Music* (Philadelphia, Lippincott, 1952).

24. Doris G. Monteux, *It's All in the Music* (New York, Farrar, Straus and Giroux, 1965), p. 185.

25. On Petrillo, see especially Mueller, *The American Symphony Orchestra*.

26. Monteux, *It's All in the Music*, p. 189. Antal Dorati, *Notes of Seven Decades* (Detroit, Wayne State University Press, 1981), pp. 199, 225.

27. Smith, *Worlds of Music*, p. 149.

28. R. Allen Lott, "Bernard Ullman—Nineteenth-Century American Impresario," in R. Allen Lott, Richard Crawford, and Carol J. Oja (eds.), *A Celebration of American Music: Words and Music in Honor of H. Wiley Hitchcock* (Ann Arbor, Mich., University of Michigan Press, 1990). "Correct address" in Vera Brodsky Lawrence (ed.), *Strong on Music: The New York Music Scene in the Days of George Templeton Strong, 1836–1875*, vol. 3: *Repercussions 1857–1862* (Chicago, University of Chicago Press, 1999), p. 22.

29. Norman Lebrecht, *Who Killed Classical Music?: Maestros, Managers, and Corporate Politics* (Secaucus, N.J., Carol Publishing Group, 1997), p. 68.

30. On Judson, see James Doering, "A Salesman of Fine Music: American Music Manager Arthur Judson, 1900 to 1940" (dissertation, Washington University, 1998); Lebrecht, *Who Killed Classical Music?*; Smith, *Worlds of Music*; and Philip Hart, *Orpheus in the New World: The Symphony Orchestra as an American Cultural Institution* (New York, W. W. Norton, 1973).

31. Judson quoted in Doering, "A Salesman of Fine Music," p. 95.

32. Ibid., pp. 146–151.

33. Almanac quote from Lebrecht, *Who Killed Classical Music?*, p. 108.

34. Judd quote from ibid., p. 109.

35. Hart, *Orpheus in the New World*, p. 88. Lebrecht, *Who Killed Classical Music?*, p. 101.

36. Ormandy quote from Hart, *Orpheus in the New World*, p. 87.

37. Judson quote from Doering, "A Salesman of Fine Music," p. 96.

38. Ibid., pp. 204, 221.

39. Correspondence from New York Philharmonic Archives. (Triller letter dated Mar. 24, 1936.)

40. Horowitz, *Understanding Toscanini*, pp. 443–445.

41. Barbirolli, Judson, Zirato quotes from Doering, "A Salesman of Fine Music," pp. 438, 441–442.

42. Halina Rodzinski, *Our Two Lives* (New York, Scribner, 1976), pp. 152, 162, 179.

43. New York Philharmonic board minutes, Feb. 3, 1947, New York Philharmonic Archives. *Herald-Tribune* quotes from Lebrecht, *Who Killed Classical Music?*, p. 122.

44. As evidenced by Walter's repertoire in the United States, and confirmed by, e.g., Gunther Schuller, in conversation with the author. (Schuller played horn in New York City under Walter, Mitropoulos, Rodzinski, Busch, Reiner, Szell, etc.)

45. Quotes from William Trotter, *Priest of Music: The Life of Dimitri Mitropoulos* (Portland, Ore., Amadeus Press, 1995), pp. 295, 339.

46. Howard Shanet, *Philharmonic: A History of New York's Orchestra* (Garden City, N.Y., Doubleday, 1975), p. 324.

47. Doering, "A Salesman of Fine Music," p. 73.

48. Judson, Bauer quotes from ibid., p. 116.

49. Judson quotes from Horowitz, *Understanding Toscanini*, p. 127.

50. Ibid., p. 443.

51. Judson quoted in Doering, "A Salesman of Fine Music," p. 127. Avoid politics, see Philip Hart, *Fritz Reiner: A Biography* (Evanston, Ill., Northwestern University Press, 1994), p. 58.

52. Sarnoff quoted in Horowitz, *Understanding Toscanini*, p. 227.

CHAPTER 6: COMPOSERS ON THE SIDELINES (*pp. 433–474*)

1. George Marek in *Good Housekeeping*, Oct. 1990. Howard Taubman, *Music on My Beat, An Intimate Volume of Shop Talk* (New York, Simon and Schuster, 1943), pp. 228, 115.

2. Schoenberg quote from Erwin Stein (ed.), *Letters of Arnold Schoenberg* (New York, St. Martin's Press, 1964), p. 270.

3. Virgil Thomson, *The State of Music* (New York, W. Morrow and Co., 1939), p. 154.

4. Aaron Copland, "From the '20s to the '40s and Beyond," *Modern Music*, Jan./Feb. 1943, p. 82. Copland, *Our New Music; Leading Composers in Europe and America* (New York, McGraw-Hill Book, 1941), p. 233.

5. Aaron Copland, *The New Music, 1900–1960* (New York, W. W. Norton, 1968), pp. 151, 153, 60.

6. Aaron Copland, *What to Listen for in Music* (New York, McGraw-Hill Book, 1939), p. 16. Copland, *New Music*, p. 99.

7. Aaron Copland, *Music and Imagination* (Cambridge, Mass., Harvard University Press, 1952), p. 110.

8. Sessions quoted in Howard Pollack, *Aaron Copland: The Life and Work of an Uncommon Man* (New York, Henry Holt, 1999), p. 169.

9. Virgil Thomson, *Virgil Thomson* (New York, A. A. Knopf, 1966), pp. 417, 117.

10. *New York Herald-Tribune*, Oct. 11, 1940 (New York Philharmonic), Mar. 7, 1942 (Horowitz), Oct. 31, 1940 (Heifetz), May 17, 1942 (Toscanini). A useful collection of Thomson's reviews can be found in John Rockwell (ed.), *A Virgil Thomson Reader* (New York, E. P. Dutton, 1984).

11. Thomson, *Virgil Thomson*, pp. 64, 58.

12. Thomson quoted in John Diziges, *Opera in America: A Cultural History* (New Haven, Yale University Press, 1993), p. 455. Aaron Copland, *Our New Music* (New York, McGraw-Hill, 1941), p. 193.

13. Copland, *The New Music*, p. 137.

14. Beth Levy, "The White Hope of American Music: Or, How Roy Harris Became Western," *American Music*, vol. 19, no. 2 (Summer 2001). MacDonald Smith Moore, *Yankee Blues: Musical Culture and American Identity* (Bloomington, Indiana University Press, 1985), pp. 161–168.

15. John Higham, *Strangers in the Land: Patterns of American Nativism, 1860–1925* (New Brunswick, N.J., Rutgers University Press, 1955), pp. 131–133.

16. Howard quoted in Moore, *Yankee Blues*, p. 16.

17. Ibid., pp. 163, 166. Levy, "White Hope of American Music," p. 156.

18. Parker and Downes quoted in Levy, "White Hope of American Music," p. 149.

19. Copland, *The New Music*, pp. 119, 121.

20. Ibid., p. 131.

21. Roger Sessions, "Vienna—*Vale, Ave*," *Modern Music*, vol. 15, no. 4 (May/June 1938), p. 207.

22. Schoenberg quote from Stein, *Letters of Arnold Schoenberg*, p. 54. Andrea Olmstead (ed.), *Conversations with Roger Sessions* (Boston, Northeastern University Press, 1987), p. 217.

23. Mitropoulos quoted in Michael Steinberg, *The Concerto: A Listener's Guide* (New York, Oxford University Press, 1998), p. 431. Copland, *Our New Music*, p. 128.

24. Andrea Olmstead, *Juilliard: A History* (Urbana, University of Illinois Press, 1999), p. 26.

25. Judith Tick, "Charles Ives and Gender Ideology," in Ruth Solie (ed.), *Musicology and Difference: Gender and Sexuality in Music Scholarship* (Berkeley, University of California Press, 1993), p. 104. On celebrity virtuosos, see Carol A. Oja, *Making Music Modern: New York in the 1920s* (New York, Oxford University Press, 2000), p. 126.

26. Oja, *Making Music Modern*, p. 184.

27. Varèse at Curtis and fire department in Oliver Daniel, *Stokowski: A Counterpoint of View* (New York, Dodd, Mead, and Co., 1982), pp. 228, 226. Gilman in Oja, *Making Music Modern*, p. 35.

28. Oja, *Making Music Modern*, pp. 40–41. Varèse quoted in Daniel, *Leopold Stokowski*, p. 225.

29. Elise and Kurt Stone, *The Writings of Elliott Carter* (Bloomington, Indiana University Press, 1977), pp. 234, 236. Rosenfeld quoted in Oja, *Making Music Modern*, p. 121.

30. "Swine" in Tick, "Charles Ives and Gender Ideology," p. 104. Rosenfeld in Oja, *Making Music Modern*, p. 309.

31. Ruggles quoted in Oja, *Making Music Modern*, p. 114.

32. Michael Hicks, *Henry Cowell: Bohemian* (Urbana, University of Illinois Press, 2002), especially pp. 116–119. Henry and Sidney Cowell, *Charles Ives and His Music* (New York, Oxford University Press, 1955), p. 8.

33. Judith Tick, *Ruth Crawford Seeger: A Composer's Search for American Music* (New York, Oxford University Press, 1997), p. 142.

34. Joseph Horowitz, *Understanding Toscanini: How He Became an American Culture-God and Helped Create a New Audience for Old Music* (New York, A. A. Knopf, 1987), p. 267.

35. Ralph Locke and Cyrilla Barr (eds.), *Cultivating Music in America: Women Patrons and Activists since 1860* (Berkeley, University of California Press, 1997). Cyrilla Barr, *Elizabeth Sprague Coolidge: American Patron of Music* (New York, Schirmer Books, 1998). Walter Damrosch, *My Musical Life* (New York, C. Scribner's Sons, 1923), p. 323. "120 compositions" —Cyrilla Barr, in conversation with the author (2004).

36. Lawrence Levine, "Jazz and American Culture," *Journal of American Folklore*, Jan./Mar. 1989.

37. Milhaud in Moore, *Yankee Blues*, p. 116.

38. Ibid., p. 116. Stravinsky, Bartók, Ravel in Oja, *Making Music Modern*, pp. 295–296.

39. *Dearborn Independent* quote from Moore, *Yankee Blues*, pp. 143, 100, 85. Damrosch quote in Levine,

"Jazz and American Culture," p. 13. Sokoloff in Donald Rosenberg, The Cleveland Orchestra Story: "Second to None" (Cleveland, Gray & Co., 2000), p. 73. Downes in Oja, *Making Music Modern*, p. 196.

40. Moore, *Yankee Blues*, p. 141. Copland on polyrhythms in *What to Listen for in Music*, p. 36. Rockwell, *Virgil Thomson Reader*, pp. 16–17. Copland, *The New Music*, pp. 67, 63, 71.

41. Weill and Krenek quotes from Levine, "Jazz and American Culture," p. 16.

42. Woollcott quote from Edward Jablonski, *Gershwin Remembered* (Portland, Ore., Amadeus Press, 1992), p. 44.

43. Rome in Merle Armitage (ed.), *George Gershwin* (New York, Longmans, Green and Co., 1938). Loeffler in Ellen Knight, *Charles Martin Loeffler: A Life Apart in American Music* (Urbana, University of Illinois Press, 1993), pp. 236–237. Engel in Oja, *Making Music Modern*, p. 319. Klemperer in Peter Heyworth (ed.), *Conversations with Klemperer* (London, Gollancz, 1973), p. 99.

44. Timothy Freeze, "Toward a Reception History of Gershwin's Concerto in F, 1925–1937" (unpublished, University of Michigan, 2003).

45. Winthrop Sargeant, *Geniuses, Goddesses, and People* (New York, Dutton, 1949), p. 109. Gershwin in Armitage, *George Gershwin*, p. 225.

46. Copland quoted in Pollack, *Aaron Copland*, p. 163, and David Schiff, *Gershwin, Rhapsody in Blue* (Cambridge, Cambridge University Press, 1997), p. 83.

47. Paul Rosenfeld, *Discoveries of a Music Critic* (New York, Harcourt, Brace and Co., 1936), p. 269. *New Republic* quote in Jablonski, *Gershwin Remembered*, p. 116. Oja, *Making Music Modern*, p. 355.

48. Rosenfeld in Jablonski, *Gershwin Remembered*, p. 116. Second Prelude cited in Oja, *Making Music Modern*, p. 351.

49. More than any other composer, according to Charles Hamm, in Wayne Schneider (ed.), *The Gershwin Style: New Looks at the Music of George Gershwin* (New York, Oxford University Press, 1999), p. 7. Heyward in Jablonski, *Gershwin Remembered*, p. 99.

50. Wilfrid Mellers, *Music in a New Found Land: Themes and Development in the History of American Music* (London, Barrie and Rockliff, 1964), pp. 392–413.

51. Downes and Thomson in Dizikes, *Opera in America*, p. 461. Johnson in Jablonski, *Gershwin Remembered*, p. 106. Goldberg in Armitage, *George Gershwin*, p. 165.

52. Hellman quoted in Eric A. Gordon, *Mark the Music: The Life and Work of Marc Blitzstein* (New York, St. Martin's Press, 1989), p. 288.

53. Ravel quoted in Schiff, *Rhapsody in Blue*, p. 74. Ives quoted in David Nicholls, *American Experimental Music, 1890–1940* (Cambridge, Cambridge University Press, 1990), p. 1.

54. Copland, *The New Music*, p. 184.

55. Oja, *Making Music Modern*, p. 241. Copland, *The New Music*, pp. 99–101. Goossens in Horowitz, *Understanding Toscanini*, p. 264.

56. John H. Mueller, *The American Symphony Orchestra: A Social History of Musical Taste* (Bloomington: Indiana University Press, 1951), p. 276.

57. Rosenfeld quoted in Moore, *Yankee Blues*, p. 163.

58. Stone, *Writings of Elliott Carter*, p. 214.

CHAPTER 7: LEONARD BERNSTEIN AND THE CLASSICAL MUSIC CRISIS (*pp. 475–517*)

1. All of Bernstein's television programs may be viewed at the Museum of Television and Radio, New York City. The Young People's Concerts are available as home videos. Unreliable scripts were published as Jack Gottlieb (ed.), *Leonard Bernstein's Young People's Concerts* (New York, Anchor Books, 1992).

2. Martin Mayer, "New York's Monument to the Muses," *Horizon*, vol. 4, no. 6 (July 1962).

3. Chairman quoted in Mayer, "New York's Monument to the Muses," p. 6. Mrs. Kennedy quoted in Humphrey Burton, *Bernstein* (New York, Doubleday, 1994), p. 331. Bernstein TV interview from New York Philharmonic Archives.

4. Tom Wolfe, "Radical Chic: That Party at Lennie's," *New York*, June 8, 1970. Mozart quote in "The American Musical Theater," a televised Young People's Concert, October 7, 1956. Leonard Bernstein, *The Unanswered Question: Six Talks at Harvard* (Cambridge, Mass., Harvard University Press, 1976). Also available on video cassette.

5. Indiscreet conversation with the author (1984).

6. Philip Hart, *Orpheus in the New World: The Symphony Orchestra as an American Cultural Institution* (New York, W. W. Norton, 1973), p. 110. William Trotter, *Priest of Music: The Life of Dimitri Mitropoulos* (Portland, Ore., Amadeus Press, 1995), p. 381.

7. Gunther Schuller, *Musings: The Musical Worlds of Gunther Schuller* (New York, Oxford University Press, 1986), pp. 184–193.

8. Interview with the author, 2002.

9. Norman Lebrecht, *Who Killed Classical Music?: Maestros, Managers, and Corporate Politics* (Secaucus, N.J., Carol Publishing Group, 1997), p. 173. Norman Lebrecht, *The Maestro Myth: Great Conductors in Pursuit of Power* (Secaucus, N.J., Carol Publishing Group, 1991), pp. 324, 320.

10. Lebrecht, *Who Killed Classical Music?*, pp. 421, 175.

11. Interview with the author, 2003.

12. Bing quote from Paul Jackson, *Saturday Afternoons at the Old Met: The Metropolitan Opera Broadcasts, 1931–1950* (Portland, Ore., Amadeus Press, 1992), p. 542.

13. John Dizikes, *Opera in America: A Cultural History* (New Haven, Yale University Press, 1993), p. 510.

14. "Sarah Caldwell" and "Boston Opera" clippings, Music Research Division, New York Public Library of the Performing Arts at Lincoln Center.

15. Author's interviews with David Gockley, Speight Jenkins, Christopher Keene ("car radio"), Paul Kellogg, with assistance from press officers at various opera companies.

16. Levine quoted by Peter G. Davis in *New York Magazine*, Apr. 29, 1987, cited in Johanna Fiedler, *Molto agitato: The Mayhem behind the Music at the Metropolitan Opera* (New York, Nan A. Talese/Doubleday, 2001), p. 232. Her book is a useful resource on recent Met history. I was also assisted by the Met press officers and archivists.

17. Joseph Horowitz, *Understanding Toscanini: How He Became an American Culture-God and Helped Create a New Audience for Old Music* (New York, A. A. Knopf, 1987), pp. 406–407, 425–429. Fiedler, *Molto agitato*, p. 243. William Wright, *Pavarotti: My Own Story* (New York, Doubleday, 1981), p. 127.

18. Lebrecht, *Who Killed Classical Music?*, p. 319.

19. Henderson and Adorno in Horowitz, *Understanding Toscanini*, pp. 403, 416.

20. Disney quote from Joseph Horowitz, "A 'Fantasia' for the MTV Generation," *New York Times* (Arts & Leisure), Jan. 1, 2000.

21. Pavarotti quote from Horowitz, *Understanding Toscanini*, p. 426.

22. Dwight Macdonald, "Masscult and Midcult," reprinted in Macdonald, *Against the American Grain* (New York, Da Capo Press, 1983).

23. Pavarotti quote and 60 percent in Horowitz, *Understanding Toscanini*, pp. 426, 154.

24. Harry Haskell, *The Early Music Revival: A History* (New York, Thames and Hudson, 1988), p. 95.

25. Quotes from ibid., pp. 178–179.

26. Milton Babbitt, "Who Cares If You Listen?," *High Fidelity*, Feb. 1958.

27. Kurt and Elise Stone (eds.), *The Writings of Elliott Carter* (Bloomington, Indiana University Press, 1977), pp. 230–241.

28. David Schiff, *The Music of Elliott Carter* (New York, Da Capo Press, 1983), p. 17. Wilfrid Mellers, *Music in a New Found Land: Themes and Developments in the History of American Music* (London, Barrie and Rockliff, 1964), p. 102.

29. Stone, *Writings of Elliott Carter*, pp. 193, 216–218.

30. Michael Steinberg, *The Concerto: A Listener's Guide* (New York, Oxford University Press, 1998), p. 157.

31. Jack MacAuliffe, ASOL vice-president and chief of operations, *Los Angeles Times*, Oct. 29, 2002.

32. Interview with the author, Apr. 2003.

33. Douglas Dempster, "The Economic Health of American Symphony Orchestras in the 1990s and Beyond," *Harmony*, Oct. 2002.

34. In correspondence with the author, Dec. 2002.

POSTLUDE: POST-CLASSICAL MUSIC (*pp. 518–539*)

1. Wilson quote from K. Robert Schwarz, *Minimalists* (London, Phaidon, 1996), p. 135.

2. Glass quote from ibid., p. 115.

3. Adams in notes for Steve Reich, *Works 1965–95*, Nonesuch Records 79451-2 (1997).

4. Adams quote from Schwarz, *Minimalists*, p. 170.

5. Cage quotes from John Cage, *Silence: Lectures and Writings* (Middletown, Com., Wesleyan University Press, 1961), pp. 13–17, and Wilfrid Mellars, *Music in a New Found Land: Themes and Developments in the History of American Music* (London, Barrie and Rockliff, 1964), p. 192.

6. Interview with author (2003).

7. Interview with author (1996).

8. Jesse Rosen and Esa-Pekka Salonen, "Holistic Approach," *Symphony*, vol. 54, no. 2 (Mar./Apr. 2003), p. 19.

9. Robert Hartford (ed.), *Bayreuth, the Early Years: An Account of the Early Decades of the Wagner Festival as Seen by the Celebrated Visitors & Participants* (Cambridge, Cambridge University Press, 1980), pp. 133–134.

10. I am indebted to Elaine Sisman for this information.

11. Joe Klein, *The Natural: The Misunderstood Presidency of Bill Clinton* (New York, Doubleday, 2002), p. 211.

12. Arthur Danto, *After the End of Art: Contemporary Art and the Pale of History* (Princeton, Princeton University Press, 1997), ch. 2.

13. Interview with author (2001).

CREDITS

Philharmonic Archives; Aaron Copland, Virgil Thomson, Nadia Boulanger, and Walter Piston: New York Philharmonic Archives; George Gershwin and Walter Damrosch: New York Philharmonic Archives; Jascha Heifetz poster: Courtesy Thomson/RCA; Vladimir Horowitz in crowd: Carnegie Hall Archives; Horowitz on television: Carnegie Hall Archives; Rudolf Serkin and Busch brothers: Frederick Plaut, MSS 52, the Frederick and Rose Plaut Archives in the Irving S. Gilmore Music Library of Yale University; Serkin at piano: Pete Checchia; Glenn Gould and Bernstein: New York Philharmonic Archives; Van Cliburn: New York Philharmonic Archives; Bernstein and *Carmen*: New York Philharmonic Archives; Bernstein onstage: New York Philharmonic Archives; The Three Tenors: Reuters/Corbis; Disney Hall: Los Angeles Philharmonic Orchestra Archives.

INDEX

About the Author

■

Joseph Horowitz was born in New York City in 1948. He was a music critic for the *New York Times* from 1977 to 1980. His previous books are *Conversations with Arrau* (1982, winner of an ASCAP/Deems Taylor Award), *Understanding Toscanini: How He Became an American Culture-God and Helped Create a New Audience for Old Music* (1987), *The Ivory Trade: Music and the Business of Music at the Van Cliburn International Piano Competition* (1990), *Wagner Nights: An American History* (1994, winner of the Irving Lowens Award of the Society of American Music), *The Post-Classical Predicament: Essays on Music and Society* (1995), and (for young readers) *Dvořák in America: In Search of the New World* (2003). From 1992 to 1997 he served as artistic advisor and then executive director of the Brooklyn Philharmonic Orchestra, resident orchestra of the Brooklyn Academy of Music, and there pioneered in juxtaposing orchestral repertoire with folk and vernacular sources, engaging gamelan orchestras, flamenco dancers and singers, and Russian and Hungarian folk artists; the orchestra won the American Symphony Orchestra League's 1996 Morton Gould Award for innovative programming. He has subsequently served as an artistic advisor to many American orchestras, most regularly the New Jersey Symphony and the Pacific Symphony. He has also cofounded, with the conductor Angel Gil-Ordóñez, the Post-Classical Ensemble, a chamber orchestra in Washington, D.C. All told, he has participated in the creation of more than three-dozen interdisciplinary music festivals. He has taught at the Eastman School, the Institute for Studies in American Music at Brooklyn College, the New England Conservatory, the Manhattan School of Music, and Mannes College. He regularly contributes articles and reviews to the Sunday *New York Times,* the *Los Angeles Times* Book Review, and the *Times Literary Supplement* (UK); other publications for which he has written include *American Music, The American Scholar, The New Grove Dictionary of Music and Musicians, The New Grove Dictionary of Opera, The Musical Quarterly, The New York Review of*

Books, and *Nineteenth Century Music.* He is the author of "Classical Music" for both the *Oxford Encyclopedia of American History* and the *Encyclopedia of New York State.* His next book will be *Cultural Exchange,* a study of immigrants in the arts and twentieth-century America. He lives in New York City with his wife, Agnes, and children Bernie and Maggie.